CW00922272

Medieval Bruges

Bruges was undoubtedly one of the most important cities in medieval Europe. Bringing together specialists from both archaeology and history, this 'total' history presents an integrated view of the city's history from its very beginnings, tracing its astonishing expansion through to its subsequent decline in the sixteenth century. The authors' analysis of its commercial growth, industrial production, socio-political changes and cultural creativity is grounded in an understanding of the city's structure, its landscape and its built environment. More than just a biography of a city, this book places Bruges within a wider network of urban and rural development and its history in a comparative framework, thereby offering new insights into the nature of a metropolis.

Andrew Brown is Associate Professor at Massey University in New Zealand and a historian of late medieval religion and society. His books include *Civic Ceremony and Religion in Medieval Bruges, c.1300–1520* (Cambridge, 2010).

Jan Dumolyn is a senior lecturer at Ghent University and historian of the political, social and cultural history of the medieval county of Flanders. He has published widely on late medieval popular politics.

Medieval Bruges, c. 850–1550

Edited by

ANDREW BROWN
Massey University

JAN DUMOLYN
Ghent University

CAMBRIDGE
UNIVERSITY PRESS

University Printing House, Cambridge CB2 8BS, United Kingdom

One Liberty Plaza, 20th Floor, New York, NY 10006, USA

477 Williamstown Road, Port Melbourne, VIC 3207, Australia

314–321, 3rd Floor, Plot 3, Splendor Forum, Jasola District Centre, New Delhi – 110025, India

79 Anson Road, #06-04/06, Singapore 079906

Cambridge University Press is part of the University of Cambridge.

It furthers the University's mission by disseminating knowledge in the pursuit of education, learning and research at the highest international levels of excellence.

www.cambridge.org
Information on this title: www.cambridge.org/9781108419659
DOI: 10.1017/9781108303842

First published 2018
3rd printing 2019

Printed in the United Kingdom by TJ International Ltd. Padstow Cornwall

A catalogue record for this publication is available from the British Library.

Library of Congress Cataloging-in-Publication Data
Names: Brown, Andrew, 1964– editor. | Dumolyn, Jan, editor.
Title: Medieval Bruges, c. 850–1550 / edited by Andrew Brown, Massey University; Jan Dumolyn, Ghent University.
Description: Cambridge; New York, NY: Cambridge University Press, 2018. | Includes bibliographical references and index.
Identifiers: LCCN 2017045622 | ISBN 9781108419659 (hardback)
Subjects: LCSH: Bruges (Belgium) – History. | Cities and towns, Medieval – Belgium – Bruges.
Classification: LCC DH811.B8 M43 2018 | DDC 949.3/12201–dc23
LC record available at https://lccn.loc.gov/2017045622

ISBN 978-1-108-41965-9 Hardback

In memoriam

Yann Hollevoet

Contents

Maps

Figures

Tables

Contributors

Marc Boone is full professor of medieval history at Ghent University, Department of History, Henri Pirenne Institute for Medieval Studies, and a member of the Royal Flemish Academy of Belgium for Sciences and Arts.

Andrew Brown is associate professor in medieval history at the School of Humanities, Massey University, New Zealand.

Frederik Buylaert is senior lecturer in medieval history at Ghent University, Department of History, Henri Pirenne Institute for Medieval Studies.

Hendrik Callewier is chief archivist at the State Archives in Bruges and research fellow and guest lecturer at KV Leuven.

Georges Declercq is full professor of medieval history at the University of Brussels (Vrije Universiteit Brussel), Department of History.

Wim De Clercq is senior lecturer in Historical Archaeology at Ghent University, Department of Archaeology, Henri Pirenne Institute for Medieval Studies.

Heidi Deneweth is a postdoctoral fellow of the Research Foundation Flanders (FWO) and member of the research team HOST (Historical Research into Urban Transformation Processes) at Vrije Universiteit Brussel.

Luc Devliegher is an architectural historian. He is a member of the Royal Flemish Academy of Belgium for Science and the Arts.

Jan Dumolyn is senior lecturer in medieval history at Ghent University, Department of History, Henri Pirenne Institute for Medieval Studies.

Guy Dupont is archivist and curator of image collections at Ghent City Archives.

Nele Gabriëls is Field Manager of Digitisation at the KU Leuven Libraries and Independent Researcher in Historical Musicology. At the time of writing, she was a postdoctoral researcher at KU Leuven, Department of Musicology, Alamire Foundation.

Jelle Haemers is senior lecturer at the Department of Medieval History at the University of Leuven (KU Leuven).

Bieke Hillewaert is Senior Archaeologist at Raakvlak (Heritage and Archaeological Service of Bruges), and connected to the Department of Archaeology at Ghent University.

Yann Hollevoet (1962–2012) was Assistant to the Director at the Flemish Heritage Institute.

Bart Lambert is a postdoctoral research associate in the Department of History and the Centre for Medieval Studies at the University of York.

Maximiliaan P. J. Martens is full professor in art history, late medieval and early modern period, at Ghent University, Department of Art History, Musicology and Theatre Studies, Henri Pirenne Institute for Medieval Studies, and a member of the Royal Flemish Academy of Belgium for Sciences and Arts.

Brigitte Meijns is senior lecturer in medieval history and head of the Department of History at KU Leuven.

James M. Murray is full professor of history at Western Michigan University, Kalamazoo, Michigan.

Johan Oosterman is full professor in medieval and early modern Dutch literature at Radboud University Nijmegen, Department of Dutch Language and Culture, Institute of Historical, Literary and Cultural Studies.

Jeroen Puttevils is lecturer in medieval history, at the University of Antwerp, Department of History and Centre for Urban History.

Andy Ramandt is a PhD student in medieval history at Ghent University, Department of History, Henri Pirenne Institute for Medieval Studies.

Marc Ryckaert is an independent scholar specializing in the history and historical geography of Bruges.

Peter Stabel is full professor of the social and economic history of the Middle Ages at the University of Antwerp, Department of History, Centre for Urban History.

Ludo Vandamme is curator of manuscripts and early printed books at Bruges Public Library.

Foreword

MARC BOONE

When in the 1970s I began to investigate the social history of Flemish cities during the (late) Middle Ages, focusing mainly on my native city of Ghent, the city of Bruges inevitably entered the frame. Within the exceptionally urbanized county of Flanders, Ghent and Bruges (as well as Ypres) dominated the late medieval urban landscape in such a way that no history of any one of these cities could afford to overlook what happened in the other two. I therefore had to have some grasp of the history of late medieval Bruges on many an occasion. Strange and remarkable as it may seem, somebody looking for a global overview of the history of Bruges still had to reach for a publication dating from 1910, *Bruges, histoire et souvenirs*, written by a local erudite canon Adolphe Duclos (1841–1925), which was a goldmine of details.[1] Duclos was of course a man of his age, and that age was particularly propitious for the study of urban history. The golden period of the fin de siècle and the start of the twentieth century was characterized by a general boom in the economy and culture, a process in which cities appeared to be the harbours of modernity. Urban history therefore became a highly successful field of study for which German and French historians had paved the way. In Belgium the historian Henri Pirenne (1862–1935), who taught from 1886 at the University of Ghent, had embarked upon an intellectual journey that would reveal to the outside world the historical significance of the cities of the former Low Countries.[2] Pirenne set the tone of research for many generations of historians to come. Almost all the authors of this book belong to the tradition he set in motion in Ghent or came into contact with his successors.

Although Duclos' work was therefore embedded in a broad intellectual interest that was gaining ground in the years of its publication, it was inspired

1 On Duclos, see J. Dumolyn, 'Een strijdbare Vlaamse kanunnik over de Brugse Metten', in *Uit de korf van de Emulatie: Baanbrekende historische bijdragen gepubliceerd in 175 jaar Handelingen van het Genootschap voor Geschiedenis te Brugge* (Bruges, 2014), pp. 35–9.

2 The medievalist Pirenne obtained his doctorate in history at the university of Liège under the direction of Godefroid Kurth. All of his writings on urban history have been collected in a posthumous publication: H. Pirenne, *Les villes et les institutions urbaines*, 2 vols. (Paris and Brussels, 1939). On Pirenne see: S. Keymeulen and J. Tollebeek, *Henri Pirenne, Historian: A Life in Pictures* (Leuven, 2011).

more by local interests than by a specific research agenda. Nevertheless, his book proved to be a great success: it was reprinted in 1913, became much sought after, and therefore ranked high in bibliophile fairs. A reprint by the Westvlaamse Gidsenkring (association of tourist guides of Western Flanders) was put on the market in 1976 and sold out in no time. In 1972 another guide organization had already published a new overview on the history of Bruges, under the direction of several Bruges-based academics, the best known being the Ghent professor Egide Strubbe (1897–1970). One had to wait until 1982, however, for the emeritus professor at the Catholic University of Louvain, Jan Arthur van Houtte (1913–2002), to publish his magnum opus *De geschiedenis van Brugge* (The history of Bruges). On the frontispiece of the book he enthusiastically cites a sixteenth-century humanist and professor in Louvain, Adrianus Barlandus: 'Pulchrae sunt Ganda, Antverpia, Bruxellae, Lovanium, Mechlinia, sed nihil ad Brugas!" Twelve out of the eighteen chapters of his book deal with the medieval history of Bruges, not only because Van Houtte himself was a medievalist by training, but as he stated in his introduction, after the Middle Ages Bruges never played the same pivotal role in the political, economic, and cultural history of Europe as it had during that period. Van Houtte originated from Bruges and in his long and prolific career published prolifically on the history of his native town. Despite the fact that Van Houtte's monograph was generally welcomed as a much needed aggiornamento of Duclos', it was never translated into another language and its content therefore remained confined to a relatively restricted group of readers able to read Dutch.

It was mainly so-called 'coffee-table books' on the (art) history of Bruges that were published after then, with two notable exceptions. First, Marc Ryckaert's seminal *Historische stedenatlas van België: Brugge* (Historical Atlas of Belgium: Bruges) was published in 1991 in a series of historical atlases edited by the financial bank institution, the Belgian state bank 'Crédit communal – Gemeentekrediet' (which for more than a century had acted as a Maecenas for local history, until it was swallowed up by a French group in 1996 to continue its existence as Dexia and finally disappear in 2011, in the aftermath of the financial crisis).[3] Ryckaert's book, however, still stands as a most original contribution, looking at the history of his native city from the angle of spatial history and the history of urban development, long before these topics became fashionable. The same author, together with the city's

[3] On the role of this bank and the development of urban history in Belgium in general, see C. Billen and M. Boone, 'L'histoire urbaine en Belgique: construire l'après-Pirenne entre tradition et rénovation', in *Città & Storia*, 5/1 (2010), 3–22.

archivist André Vandewalle, coordinated a general overview, *Brugge: De geschiedenis van een Europese stad* (Bruges, the history of a European city) which was published in 1999, simultaneously in Dutch and French versions. The publication was evidently part of the preparation for the year 2002, when Bruges adopted with pride the title of Cultural Capital of Europe. In addition, though, the book wanted to bring to the fore the historiography of the city since Van Houtte's publication seventeen years before. It also reflected the fact that writing a comprehensive history of a city was no longer conceived as being the work of a single author, but one that had to rely on several specialists of different periods and approaches (historians, art historians, archaeologists, and the like). The five principal authors – all of them members of the city's historical and cultural institutions – therefore received the support of twenty-four specialists who wrote limited contributions on very specific topics or highlights of the history of Bruges.

The following book, edited by Andrew Brown and Jan Dumolyn, has to be seen with this prehistory in mind, for only in such a perspective does it become clear how much it was needed and how valuable it will prove to be.

First of all, it is written in English, today's global language of communication in science, an extremely laudable effort since it will allow a much broader field of interested readers to participate in the historical knowledge concerning one of Europe's leading commercial metropolises. Second, although it does not aim at a general public in the first instance – and thanks to the abundant references to existing literature and for some topics directly to unedited sources, its state-of-the-art research will be of primary interest to fellow historians – it will nevertheless also appeal to a wider audience, interested in medieval and/or urban history, and indeed to the general public, whose serious desire to be well informed in the best way possible has to be acknowledged. Third and foremost, it brings together a team of authors who have clearly reflected on the larger topics they were invited to write about. The chapter on art and culture, for instance, stands out in this respect as it assembles insights and visions that transcend the traditional boundaries between literary history, art history, musicology, and the like. But the other chapters do so as well. Particularly innovative are the many recent insights that (urban) archaeology has yielded over the last decades and which are bound to offer, as the first two chapters illustrate, new insights into how the city came about, and into urban space in general. Space, following in the footsteps of Henri Lefebvre and the historiographic realization of his writings, is an important aspect of urban history, and as a topic it is very well served in this book. Paradoxically, the chapters on economic history may seem less innovative, or at least less exciting to read, because of recent and decades-long efforts to focus on the economic role of Bruges as a centre of commerce. Yet the deconstructive reading here allows the traditional image of Bruges as a unique commercial centre (a true 'image d'Épinal' in itself) to be replaced by a much more realistic view of a city that throughout the medieval period also remained an important centre of industrial (textile) production. This, combined with an emphasis on the development of an early service economy, is of great value. There are more surprising insights, some of which deserve particular mention: the role of the communal movement in medieval Flanders; the attention given to ecological history through the lens of water management, an issue of perennial concern in the Low Countries; and the view on the gradual decline of Bruges in the first half of the sixteenth century. A much quoted principle in economics, indeed, states that what goes up, must come down. For all its uniqueness, medieval Bruges was no exception to this.

Marc Boone
Honorary president of the European Association of Urban Historians and Member of the Royal Academy of Science and Arts of Belgium

Acknowledgements

The book began life as an idea in 2008, when we met up in Edinburgh; but it was never conceived as a project we could undertake alone. Collaboration between us has required the support of many institutions, our own universities, Ghent and Massey, as well as others. In 2008 Jan was a visiting fellow at the University of Glasgow on the invitation of Graeme Small and supported by a grant from the Caledonian Research Foundation; we were able to meet for a longer period of collaboration in New Zealand in 2014, thanks to a visiting fellowship supported by the School of Humanities and Massey University Research Fund. We are also very grateful for the collaboration of so many colleagues who have become co-authors of chapters in this book: without their commitment and time the book could not have been written.

The help of graduate and postgraduate students in correcting footnotes, inserting the bibliography, and drawing up maps and the index has also been invaluable: our thanks go to Ward Leloup, Alexander Linsingh, Wout Saelens and Joppe Vermeyen. We are grateful too for the professional cartographic assistance provided by Hans Blomme, historical cartographer of Ghent University Department of History, and by Dr Jan Trachet of the Department of Archaeology.

Apart from Ghent University Library, the research for this book essentially took place in Bruges institutions. Bruges has a very fine tradition of local history, which has formed a strong basis for work on this book, not all of which can be directly acknowledged here. We have benefited greatly from the Public Library and the many archives of the city, including the State archives. We thank all staff members of those institutions, and particularly the entire staff of the Bruges City Archives where we have spent months and months in total. Much thanks is owed to Dr Noël Geirnaert, Dr André Vandewalle, Jan D'hondt, Isabelle Debie, Bram Vanaelst, Willy Timmerman, Pieter Kerckhove, Véronique De Schepper, Peter Bultinck, Jan Anseeuw, Peter Goetghebeur and Eddy Costenoble for creating the efficient, generous, and also very pleasant work environment for which the Bruges City Archives have an international reputation.

The book is dedicated to the memory of Yann Hollevoet (1962–2012), archaeologist of early medieval Flanders and co-author of this work.

Abbreviations

ADN	Archives départementales du Nord, Lille
AGR	Archives Générales du Royaume/Algemeen Rijksarchief, Brussels (General State Archives)
BAB	Bischoppelijk archief, Bruges (Episcopal Archives, Bruges)
BO	*Brugs Ommeland*
BTFG	*Belgisch Tijdschrift voor Filologie en Geschiedenis*
GVS, *Cartulaire*	L. Gilliodts-Van Severen (ed.), *Cartulaire de l'ancienne estaple de Bruges*, 3 vols. (Bruges, 1904–6)
GVS, *Coutume*	L. Gilliodts-Van Severen (ed.), *Coutume de la ville de Bruges* (Brussels, 1874–5).
GVS, *Inventaire*	L. Gilliodts-Van Severen, *Inventaire des archives de la ville de Bruges*, 7 vols. (Bruges, 1871–85)
HGG	*Handelingen van het Genootschap voor Geschiedenis*
HKZM	*Handelingen van de Koninklijke Zuidnederlandse Maatschappij voor Taal- en Letterkunde en Geschiedenis*
HMG	*Handelingen der Maatschappij voor Geschiedenis en Oudheidkunde te Gent*
JMH	*Journal of Medieval History*
OBB	Openbare Bibliotheek, Brugge (Public Library of Bruges)
OCMW	Openbaar Centrum voor Maatschappelijk Welzijn
RAB	Rijksarchief, Brugge (State Archives of Bruges)
RN	*Revue du Nord*
SAB	Stadsarchief, Brugge (City Archives of Bruges)
TG	*Tijdschrift voor Geschiedenis*

Introduction

ANDREW BROWN AND JAN DUMOLYN

A new history of medieval Bruges needs little justification.[1] From the twelfth century, such was the expansion of its commerce and industry that the city became one of the most important in Europe, serving as a gateway for international trade, and as the home of a large-scale export-oriented cloth industry. By the end of the Middle Ages, Bruges had become a 'creative environment' with a flourishing luxury industry, one of Europe's foremost production centres of leatherworks, furs, illuminated manuscripts, tapestries, goldsmiths' work, early printing, and famously of paintings now considered part of a 'Flemish Renaissance'. Bruges had become a metropolis: a major city, a central hub of industry, commerce, and culture, with regional and international significance.

While considerable research has been conducted in recent years on various aspects of Bruges, no full synthesis of the city's history, in all its aspects, has ever been written, as Marc Boone emphasizes. The authors of this book, though, have aimed to produce more than a synthesis. Bruges has been treated from wider theoretical and comparative perspectives. New approaches to urban history have offered alternative views on the medieval city,[2] and an up-to-date history of Bruges has a contribution to make to the study of other towns. Urban history can also offer a 'totalizing' view onto the past: the city may be seen as 'a total phenomenon where the economic, the social, the political, the cultural, the technical and the imaginary are condensed'.[3] The city is both an object and a frame of analysis. By taking a 'total history' approach to one town, and by integrating the specialist research from a range of scholarly fields, a deeper understanding may be reached of the connections between many different aspects of urban life and of society as a whole.

1 Cf. G. Brucker, *Renaissance Florence* (New York, 1969), p. vii: 'A book on Renaissance Florence does not require an elaborate justification.'

2 For overviews, see for instance, globally: P. Clark (ed.), *The Oxford Handbook of Cities in World History* (Oxford, 2013); for Europe: P. Clark, *European Cities and Towns, 400–2000* (Oxford, 2009); for the Netherlands: W. Blockmans, *Metropolen aan de Noordzee: de geschiedenis van Nederland, 1100–1560* (Amsterdam, 2010).

3 P. Boucheron and D. Menjot, *Histoire de l'Europe urbaine*, vol. II: *La ville médiévale* (Paris, 2003), p. 8.

The book follows a broadly chronological pattern, starting with the early settlement that became Bruges, based on the latest findings of archaeological research (Chapter 1). It charts Bruges' expansion up to the end of the thirteenth century when the city was struck by economic and political crises (Chapters 2–5); and then turns to the city's 'golden age' (Chapters 6–8), ending with its decline in the sixteenth century (Chapter 10). But the trajectory traced does not follow the classic logic of 'origins, growth, maturity and decay'. From its beginnings to its final decline, Bruges was shaped by wider patterns of urban, rural and European development; and its eventual loss of importance was comparatively a shift from exceptionality to normalcy, from a city unusually positioned and structured in its 'golden age' to profit from circumstances, but which could not ultimately adapt when circumstances changed.

The city is 'a system within systems of cities'.[4] Medieval urban historiography has come to situate towns within wider urban networks and in relation to their hinterlands, emphasizing their 'central-place functions', be they market, industrial, political or judicial.[5] The astonishing economic growth and cultural efflorescence of medieval Bruges has to be placed within the urban networks of northwestern Europe and within a complex set of relations between town and countryside. James M. Murray has called Bruges 'the cradle of capitalism'.[6] Indeed, according to the classic theories of Marx, Weber, Pirenne, Park, Simmel, Benjamin and others, the city is a locus for change, progress, market development, democracy, social and political struggle and polarization, cultural innovation, bourgeois ideology, workers' class consciousness, secularization, individualism and modernity in general.[7] Whether, or rather in what ways, this was the case for Bruges is also an underlying theme of this book. Comparisons are made between Bruges and medieval cities of comparable importance such as Venice, Genoa, Florence, Paris, London, Ghent, Cologne and Lübeck. The implicitly comparative approach adopted in most chapters, whether on demographic, social, political or cultural themes, is drawn out in the final Conclusion.

The city has also been defined as a 'distinctive space of lived and living interaction'.[8] Concepts of social space, as outlined in the works of Henri

[4] The expression was coined by the geographer Brian Berry, quoted in W. Prevenier, J.-P. Sosson, and M. Boone, 'Le réseau urbain en Flandre (XIIIe – XIXe siècle): composantes et dynamique', in *Le réseau urbain en Belgique dans une perspective historique (1350–1850): une approche statistique et dynamique* (Brussels, 1992), p. 157.

[5] On the historiography of this, see Conclusion below.

[6] J. M. Murray, *Bruges, Cradle of Capitalism, 1280–1390* (Cambridge, 2005).

[7] Cf. Clarke, *European Cities and Towns*.

[8] H. Lefebvre, *La production de l'espace* (Paris, 1974).

Lefebvre and others,[9] have partly guided the structure of this book and informed many of its chapters' themes: how the city's markets and 'central-place' functions (Chapters 3, 6) and its power relations (Chapters 4, 7) developed within the changing cityscape; how religious practices (Chapter 8) emerged in and related to the urban environment; how text, sound and visual art (Chapter 9) were shaped by – and also shaped – the particular morphology of the city.

The history of Bruges is thus grounded on an understanding of the landscape and its built environment. The proximity and influence of the sea, and the liminal space that, according to the signs of early settlement, the locality occupied between coastal and inland Flanders, provide the keys to Bruges' initial development; and indeed the hydrography of the city and its access to the sea remained of prime importance to its inhabitants throughout the medieval period. Chapter 1 considers Bruges' origins, and revisits controversy on the rise and definition of towns, so much associated with the work of Henri Pirenne. It offers a more nuanced approach to the importance of *castrum* and *suburbium* as key nuclei in urban development. The early character of Bruges in the ninth century as a military and even spiritual stronghold of the counts of Flanders, and as a 'proto-urban' centre with portuary functions, was also determined by the early development of another nucleus of settlement that may well have served as an agrarian market, linked to the castle economy and the wider region. Economic take-off in the eleventh century has also to be set in a wider perspective of population growth and rural development, particularly cloth production. Chapter 2 examines the spatial evidence in landscape and building for the phenomenal expansion of Bruges' capacity in the twelfth and thirteenth centuries to produce textiles and other artisanal goods, to serve as a market for regional and international commerce, and to meet new social and spiritual needs that accompanied unprecedented immigration into the city. By the end of the thirteenth century, an entirely different urban environment had been created, in which the earlier nuclei of settlement had been subsumed into a more complex and diversified pattern of buildings, habitation and functionality. The city reached its greatest areal extent at the end

[9] See for example: P. Arnade, M. C. Howell and W. Simons, 'Fertile Spaces: The Productivity of Urban Space in Northern Europe', *Journal of Interdisciplinary History*, 32 (2002), 515–48; C. Goodson, A. E. Lester and C. Symes (eds.), *Cities, Texts and Social Networks, 400–1500: Experiences and Perceptions of Medieval Urban Space* (Farnham, 2010); M. Boone and M. C. Howell (eds.), *The Power of Space in Late Medieval and Early Modern Europe: The Cities of Italy, Northern France and the Low Countries* (Turnhout, 2013); M. Cohen and F. Madeline (eds.), *Space in the Medieval West: Places, Territories, and Imagined Geographies* (Farnham, 2014).

of the thirteenth century, but even in the later Middle Ages, as Chapter 5 shows, the urban landscape was continually reshaped, to become at one level more socially diversified still, but at another, increasingly consolidated into a more coherent unit. The new city walls built after 1297 to contain the sprawling population came to encompass a space that was no longer the sum of its initial nuclei, nor one divided, as it had been in the thirteenth century, between older centre, newer suburbs and lordly enclaves, but one more clearly managed, judicially, administratively and ecologically, as a single whole.

Spatial developments were the result of interactions between environment and various agencies. The economic, demographic and social changes that moulded city space are examined in two chapters. Chapter 3 places the period of urban expansion from 1100 to c.1300 within its rural, demographic and political context, to explain how it was possible for the city to develop its industrial and commercial capacity. Agricultural development in the region was underpinned but was also altered by the rapid urban expansion, particularly in cloth production. Bruges grew from a regional trading centre into an international business centre, as Flemish trade shifted from an 'active' to a 'passive' phase. In many ways, the staggering growth of Bruges in the later Middle Ages as a centre of luxury production, banking and international commerce (Chapter 6) would seem to be a natural progression from these earlier signs of expansion. Yet this ignores the massive structural conversion of the local economy that was required in the process, particularly the shift away from cloth production towards clothing and luxury industries that began to occur in the early fourteenth century, in a period of recession and demographic reversal. The same conversion also accounts for the structural weaknesses behind Bruges' phenomenal success in the fifteenth century. The glamour of high living was built on fragile ground: trade, demand and consumption of added-value commodities, were ultimately vulnerable to market forces beyond the metropolis' control.

The agents effecting and affected by these changes in the urban landscape and society become more visible in the documentary record from 1100 onwards. Behind urban expansion were the counts of Flanders protecting and profiting from 'market peace'; ecclesiastical bodies; noble elites and merchant-entrepreneurs, and other elite groups like the hostellers who began to service the influx of foreign merchants. Yet of particular importance was the appearance of the 'commune' that became the urban authority over the expanding territory of markets and collective properties. How and when this communal agency arose, and who held sway over it, are the questions asked in Chapter 4. By the thirteenth century, for all its ideals of community, the commune was in effect dominated by the class rule of great merchants; but not without tensions. Growing polarization is apparent between elite merchant groups and the proletarianized labour force behind industrial growth. Social division was tempered by the appearance of middling groups and craft organizations by the late thirteenth century, but these groups had also begun to claim a place within communal politics. In the context of crisis in the textile industry, tensions spilled over into outright revolt by the 1280s and into the 'revolution' of 1302. The changes that resulted were to determine the logic of Bruges' turbulent politics for the next two centuries. As Chapter 7 shows, guild power assumed a new ascendancy after 1302, as did the corporate ideals that guildsmen claimed to represent – even though guilds and corporatism were constantly challenged by a commercial elite who also populated the civic magistracy; and by the rise of comital and state power, driven after 1384 by the Valois dukes of Burgundy and after 1477 by their Habsburg successors. These broad outlines of change need refining though. The categories historians use to describe these social groups (such as 'classes', 'elites', 'patricians', 'middling guildsmen'), need further scrutiny in order to understand social mobility and political office-holding. So too does the influence of networks created by faction, family ties, commerce or work. The importance of other social groups, and the role of women in the economy, also demand attention for a fuller picture of urban society to emerge.

The urban landscape, society and politics shaped cultural practices and values; but these practices and values also framed perceptions of the urban environment. Late medieval religion in Bruges (Chapter 8) reflects the city's social complexity, competition and wealth; and it could serve the interests of powerful lay people. Bruges' annual Holy Blood procession, beginning in the early fourteenth century, in which so many guilds, magistrates and clergy participated, expressed communal ideals and defined city space as sacred by its itinerary around the new walls. But the relationship between religion, society and authority was complex. The Holy Blood procession emerged in a period of divisive turmoil within the city; religious institutions and currents of spirituality could corrode social aspirations and secular power. 'Civic religion' may not be the most useful term to describe the city's religious practices, especially as the clerical presence within Bruges remained strong. Religion was also part of wider cultural practices: were these distinctively urban or peculiar to Bruges? Chapter 9 examines the texts, images and sounds produced in the city. The conditions that favoured the production of art, music and literature were the result of supply and demand: artisanal skill, the networks and markets within and beyond the city; but also the diverse needs of a wide range of patrons. Courtly, noble, merchant and municipal investment in cultural capital served power or particular social and political needs; but some texts – even those produced by rhetoricians in the pay of city magistrates – reveal frictions in urban society, while other cultural activity sought more subversive ends. The complex interplay in Bruges between local patriotism and cosmopolitanism, 'civic' and 'court' culture, opulence and social tensions, together shaped a vibrant and distinctive cultural environment.

The final Chapter 10 takes up the many threads of Bruges' spatial, economic, social, political and cultural history in order to explain its dwindling fortunes in the sixteenth century. How was it that an international metropolis could be reduced to a town that was, according to one ageing citizen in 1590, little more than a 'retail shop'? Was it the result of structural flaws, hydrographical and economic, or of changing circumstances? The city's decline – or rather the process by which an exceptional city became a more normal one – has to be viewed from a European context of profound change; just as the city's longer history should also be set ultimately (see the Conclusion) within a broader comparative framework.

1 Origins and Early History

JAN DUMOLYN, GEORGES DECLERCQ, BRIGITTE MEIJNS, BIEKE HILLEWAERT, YANN HOLLEVOET(†), MARC RYCKAERT AND WIM DE CLERCQ

By the 1040s Bruges was widely celebrated, according to the *Encomium Emmae reginae*, 'as much for the number of merchants resorting there, as for the abundance of all things that men desire'.[1] Yet its fame was of recent origin. The toponym 'Bruges' appears first in the ninth century, and the beginnings of the settlement that acquired the name are obscure. How it emerged from obscurity is the subject of this chapter. The task is difficult because it requires assessment of archaeological investigations that are still incomplete; and because these need to be contextualized both in relation to the available written sources, and in relation to a wider context of urban and regional development. Debate on the rise and definition of medieval 'towns', begun by Henri Pirenne more than a century ago, is ongoing. Analysis of Bruges' development contributes to this debate for, as we shall see, the growing functionality of the settlement in the ninth century as a military stronghold of the counts, as a producer and market for local and inter-regional exchange, and as a religious centre are all characteristics that are considered significant in the rise of towns from the ninth to the eleventh century. Yet reasons for the emergence of 'Bruges' have to be sought within the landscape.

The Coastal Plain of Flanders

The origins and early development of the settlement must be primarily understood in relation to its position close to the sea. Of crucial importance was its location at the edge of two different landscapes: the higher Pleistocene sandy soils of inner Flanders and the lower Holocene wetlands of the coastal plain. The edge of the sandy region was subject to the continuing and sometimes overpowering presence of the sea: coastal Flanders rises only 2–5 metres above sea level, and until the central Middle Ages, it was strongly influenced by tidal dynamics, and was protected only fitfully from the water by a line of barrier dunes and later by dykes. The name

[1] A. Campbell (ed.), *Encomium Emmae reginae* (London, 1949), pp. 46–50.

Vlaanderen (Flanders) is derived from the Germanic root *flauma*, meaning 'inundated region'.[2] But the maritime location also presented settlers there with opportunities. It was largely isolated from most of inner Flanders by forests, and like parts of eastern England and Frisia, was oriented towards other 'coastal societies' bordering the North Sea. By the seventh or eighth century at the latest, people in coastal Flanders lived in equilibrium with the natural resources at their disposal, and exchanged both luxury and bulk goods (fish, wool, woollen garments and salt), acting as intermediaries between hinterlands and other maritime areas.[3] This liminal though strategic location on the fringes of two totally different landscapes would generate an urban development unlike any other in the Low Countries.

This location was made more strategic because of the lines of access to it over land and water. The shoreline's proximity was a major element in the eventual growth of Bruges because natural waterways guaranteed more or less navigable connections between the settlement and the sea, before human interference began to arrest the natural evolution of the landscape. The coastal region was cut through by tidal inlets, the course of which slowly changed, and through which ships might approach Bruges from the sea. Important parts of the plain, however, remained mud flats, marshlands and to a lesser extent moorlands used occasionally for transhumance, pasturing livestock or for extracting peat. From the ninth and tenth centuries at the latest, the entire Flemish plain became suitable for stable settlement, as a result of land reclamation, drainage, and natural desiccation. Some parts of it would remain affected by the sea for longer, especially the region just to the northeast of Bruges, which was hit by storm surges in at least 838, 1014 and 1042 (according to surviving written sources).[4] The area of

[2] J. Dhondt and M. Gysseling, 'Vlaanderen, oorspronkelijke ligging en etymologie', in *Album Prof. dr. Frank Baur* (Antwerp, 1948), pp. 192–220.

[3] Y. Hollevoet, 'De nederzetting die later Brugge zal worden genoemd', in B. Hillewaert, Y. Hollevoet and M. Ryckaert (eds.), *Op het raakvlak van twee landschappen: De vroegste geschiedenis van Brugge* (Bruges, 2011), pp. 103–13; D. Tys, 'The Medieval Embankment of Coastal Flanders in Context', in E. Thoen et al. (eds.), *Landscapes or Seascapes? The History of the Coastal Environment in the North Sea Area Reconsidered* (Turnhout, 2013), pp. 199–239; D. Tys, 'La formation du littoral flamand et l'intervention humaine', in L. Verslype (ed.), *Villes et campagnes en Neustrie: Sociétés, économies, territoires, Christianisation* (Montagnac, 2007), pp. 211–19; D. Tys, 'The Scheldt Estuary as a Framework for Early Medieval Settlement Development', in A. Willemsen and H. Kik (eds.), *Dorestad in an International Framework: New Research on Centres of Trade and Coinage in Carolingian Times* (Turnhout, 2010), pp. 169–75.

[4] M. K. E. Gottschalk, *Stormvloeden en rivieroverstromingen in Nederland*, 3 vols. (Assen, 1971), vol. I, pp. 17–30, 43–5, 47–9; L. Denys and C. Baeteman, 'Holocene Evolution of Relative Sea-Level and Local Mean High Water Spring Tides in Belgium: A First Assessment', *Marine Geology*, 124 (1995), 1–19; C. Baeteman and P.-Y. Declercq, 'A Synthesis of Early and Middle Holocene Coastal Changes in the Western Belgian Lowlands', *Belgeo*, 2 (2002), 77–107;

Bruges was also the forming-up point for a series of small rivers draining rain water from inland Flanders towards the coastal plain and the sea. The most important of these was the river Reie (the *Roya* in the oldest Latin sources) which entered the city through what is now the *Minnewater*, an artificial lake made in the thirteenth century. Some of these small waterways would be canalized during medieval times to become the network now known as the Bruges *reien*, a hydrography that so typifies the city today. These streamlets with their changing seasonal flow rates carried the diluvial water from the region south and east of the city towards the sea. The most important ones were the Waardammebeek/Rivierbeek (which can be considered the upper part of the Reie), the Zuidleie, the Hertsbergebeek and the Kerkebeek, all unnavigable brooks that could not connect Bruges to regions further inland.[5]

As early as Roman times the locality where Bruges would develop had been directly connected to the North Sea through a navigable gully which also formed the lower course of the Reie. It merged with the sea somewhere between the present towns of Blankenberge and Zeebrugge. Another tideway or system of gullies called the Sincfal (known later, though greatly changed, as the *Zwin*) was directed towards the northeast and merged near Cadzand. The Sincfal, mentioned in the *Lex Frisionum*, formed a natural border between early medieval Frisia and the core region of the Merovingian Frankish kingdom. From about AD 300, it developed into a veritable sea-bosom. Later on, the waterway connecting the regions of Bruges and Blankenberge had silted up as sedimentation began to dominate over erosion. Its navigation was probably difficult or even no longer possible. From the ninth century, and particularly from the tenth, another connection to the sea was sought out. At some point, a canal was dug through the sandy ridge of Koolkerke towards one of the waterways belonging to the Sincfal system.[6]

C. Baeteman, 'De laat holocene evolutie van de Belgische Kustvlakte: Sedimentatieprocessen versus zeespiegelschommelingen en Duinkerke transgressies', in A. M. J. de Kraker and G. Borger (eds.), *Veen-vis-zout: Landschappelijke dynamiek in de zuidwestelijke delta van de Lage Landen* (Amsterdam, 2007), pp. 1–18; C. Baeteman, 'History of Research and State of the Art of the Holocene Depositionary History of the Belgian Coastal Plain', in Thoen et al. (ed.), *Landscapes or Seascapes*, pp. 11–29.

5 M. Ryckaert, *Historische stedenatlas van België*, vol. II: *Brugge* (Brussels, 1991), pp. 31–2; F. Mostaert, 'De Reie te Brugge gedurende de Romeinse periode', in H. Thoen (ed.), *De Romeinen langs de Vlaamse Kust* (Brussels, 1987), pp. 30–2.

6 H. A. Heidinga, *Frisia in the First Millennium: An Outline* (Utrecht, 1997), p. 14; W. Wintein, 'Historische geografie van de Zwinstreek: Een stand van zaken', *Bijdragen tot de Geschiedenis van West-Zeeuws-Vlaanderen*, 30 (2002), 9–54.

Thus, the settlement that became known as *Brugjo* or *Bryggja* (*Brucghe* or *Brugghe* in Middle Dutch and *Brugge* in contemporary Dutch) formed at a location strongly oriented towards the sea, and linked to it by the Reie. But, as we shall see, the settlement also developed at a point where the river intersected with a minor road system of Roman or even earlier origin, between the Roman *castella* of Oudenburg and Aardenburg.[7] This road ran along a sandy ridge (still detectable today) bordering the coastal plain in the south and rising five metres above it. The ridge would later run as an axis through the urban landscape of Bruges from the present Blacksmiths' Gate (*Smedenpoort*) towards the present Burg Square; and alongside this ridge stretching out from west to east, depressions with brooks and creeks would allow water to run off and a catchment basin to form to the south of the city. It was on this ridge also that the the oldest parish church of St Saviour and – most significantly for the future rise of the city – the Carolingian stronghold would be constructed. But when was 'Bruges' first settled?[8]

The Oldest Traces of Settlement

Few archaeological traces of prehistorical occupation in Bruges have been uncovered so far. Recent excavations, field surveys and aerial photography have produced significant new results but have also made clear how little we yet know. Leaving aside the scattered traces of human presence dating to the mid Paleolithic, the first indications of habitation appear during the Neolithicum (5000–2000 BC). In situ settlement traces showed up in the form of a neolithic farmhouse at Waardamme south of Bruges. In this period the encroachment of the coastal line and the gradual wetting of the littoral plain became more important. During the Bronze Age (2000–800 BC), the coastal area mostly developed into moorland, blocked off from the sea by a large coastal barrier. Aerial photography has revealed many circular cropmark features, several being on the sandy ridge in the neighbourhood of Bruges: most are the remains of ditches surrounding Bronze Age burial mounds. Iron Age remains have been attested at sites in and around Bruges.

[7] Aardenburg lost its importance as a Roman fortress during the third century, while Oudenburg remained an important *castellum* in the defence system against Germanic invaders until the fourth century: J. A. Trimpe Burger, *Romeins Aardenburg* (Aardenburg, 1992); H. Thoen and S. Vanhoutte, 'De Romeinse wegen in het Vlaamse kustgebied: Leiden alle wegen naar Oudenburg?', in J. L. Meulemeester (ed.), *Alle wegen leiden naar… Romeinse wegen in Vlaanderen* (Oudenburg, 2004), pp. 50–6.

[8] A. Verhulst, *The Rise of Cities in North-Western Europe* (Cambridge, 1999), p. 90.

A little to the north of the city centre, at a site now known as Fort Lapin, traces of an Iron Age salt makers' settlement (about 500–300 BC) have been uncovered. Salt was won there from seawater brought by a tidal inlet.[9]

Shortly before the first century AD the Bruges region was made accessible by sea for the first time, when littoral erosion began and gullies broke through the coastal barrier. In the same period the region also yields evidence of contact with a wider world. The region was part of the area of the Gaulish tribe of the Menapii, conquered by Julius Caesar after battles in 59, 57 and 53 BC, with Cassel (the so-called *castellum Menapiorum*) being the capital of this *civitas Menapiorum*.[10] However, the first indications of Roman influence on everyday life in the region of Bruges are only attested a century later. An important feature was the construction of a road on the sandy ridge bordering the coastal plain, presumably on an earlier line of transfer. The track ran more or less parallel to the coast and was joined by other roads connecting the coastal region with the hinterland. The most important Roman axis was the so-called *Steenstraat* (Stone Street), a *diverticulum* from the Cassel–Tournai road, linking the region of Bruges with the southwestern part of the *civitas* and its capital. To the west of what would later be Bruges, this road connected with the *Zandstraat* (Sand Street) which ran parallel to the coast, connecting the fortress of Oudenburg to the west of Bruges with Aardenburg to the east.[11] The scattered Roman finds in the present city centre of Bruges, often encountered on and around the sandy ridge and along the *Zandstraat*, are still hard to interpet. They are perhaps part of a continuous, dense and diverse archive of Roman traces

9 H. Thoen, *De Belgische kustvlakte in de Romeinse tijd* (Brussels, 1978), pp. 53–5; and for what follows, see the recent archaeological and landscape historical synthesis on early medieval Bruges: Hillewaert et al. (eds.), *Op het raakvlak.*

10 S. J. De Laet, 'Les limites des cités des Ménapiens et des Morins', *Helinium*, 1 (1961), 20–34; W. De Clercq and R. van Dierendonck, 'Extrema Galliarum: Noordwest-Vlaanderen en Zeeland in het Imperium Romanum', *VOBOV-Info*, 64 (2009), 34–75; W. De Clercq, 'Lokale gemeenschappen in het Imperium Romanum: Transformaties in de rurale bewoningsstructuur en de materiële cultuur in de landschappen van het noordelijk deel van de civitas Menapiorum (Provincie Gallia-Belgica, ca. 100 v. Chr. – 400 n. Chr.)', unpublished PhD thesis, Ghent University (2009), pp. 17–19.

11 J. Mertens, *Les routes romaines de la Belgique* (Brussels, 1957); J. Mertens and L. Van Impe, *Het laat-Romeinse grafveld van Oudenburg* (Brussels, 1971); Thoen, *Kustvlakte*, pp. 72–6; E. M. Wightmann, *Gallia Belgica* (London, 1985), pp. 208–9; Thoen and Vanhoutte, 'De Romeinse wegen'; S. Vanhoutte, 'Het Romeinse castellum van Oudenburg (prov. West-Vlaanderen) herontdekt: de archeologische campagne van augustus 2001 tot april 2005 ter hoogte van de zuidwesthoek. Interim-rapport', *Relicta: Archeologie, Monumenten- en Landschapsonderzoek in Vlaanderen*, 3 (2007), 199–236; S. Vanhoutte, 'The Saxon Shore Fort at Oudenburg (Belgium): New Excavation Results', in A. Morillo et al. (eds.), *Limes XX. XXth International Congress of Roman Frontier Studies*, vol. III (Madrid, 2009), pp. 1386–94.

dating from the first to the third century, stretching out over the whole of the sand ridge and bordering the coastal plain. Indeed during the Roman period the sandy northern part of Flanders and especially the Bruges region had already been intensively reclaimed and inhabited.[12] Recent excavations in Bruges' surroundings have revealed the presence of many sites: agrarian settlements built in a form typical of native tradition, and some cemeteries. A concentration of farms from this period can be found along the road bordering the coastal plain, not far from the later medieval city centre. At the Fort Lapin site, the remains were found (in the late nineteenth century) of at least one wreck of a seagoing vessel, which were probably reused to construct a pier at the bank of an active gully.[13] The large quantities also found there of 'samian-ware' pottery, from the first half of the third century, point to the integration of the site with a harbour, within the networks of trade and exchange running along the coast. The presence of the Roman army near Bruges in the second century indicates that Roman roads must still have been intact at that time. This contrasts with the inland region where occupation had already declined from the late second century onwards.[14]

The coastal plain itself seems to have been more densely occupied than previously supposed.[15] Recent excavations have revealed intensive Roman reclamation of the plain. Parts of this area were withdrawn from tidal influence by embankments, while other parts, though still affected by the tides, were populated more permanently on natural sandy elevations surmounting the tidal muds, or on artificial platforms.[16] As in other areas along the Flemish coast, fishing, pasturing of cattle and small livestock (most notably sheep husbandry), peat extraction and the production of salt were undoubtedly important economic activities in the area north of present-day Bruges. During the late nineteenth-century building of the Zeebrugge Docks (the

[12] Hollevoet, 'De nederzetting'; W. De Clercq, 'Roman Rural Settlements in Flanders: Perspectives on a 'Non-Villa' Landscape in Extrema Galliarum', in N. Roymans and T. Derks (eds.), *Villa Landscapes in the Roman North: Economy, Culture and Lifestyles* (Amsterdam, 2011), pp. 235–58.

[13] E. Jonckheere, *L'origine de la Côte de Flandre et le Bateau de Bruges* (Bruges, 1903); P. Marsden, 'A Boat of the Roman Period Found in Bruges, Belgium, in 1899, and Related Types', *International Journal of Nautical Archaeology and Underwater Exploration*, 5 (1976), 23–55; K. Vlierman, 'Een nieuwe blik op de boot van Brugge', in Hillewaert et al. (eds.), *Op het raakvlak*, pp. 49–50.

[14] De Clercq, *Lokale gemeenschappen*, pp. 491–5.

[15] A. Ervynck et al., 'Human occupation because of Regression or the Cause of a Regression? A Critical Review of the Interaction between Geological Events and Human Occupation in the Belgian Coastal Plain during the First Millennium AD', *Probleme der Küstenforschung im südlichen Nordseegebiet*, 26 (1999), 97–121.

[16] De Clercq, *Lokale gemeenschappen*, pp. 202–17; De Clercq, 'Roman Rural Settlements'.

new port of Bruges), an impressive wooden installation was found which may well have been intended to allow the natural evaporation of salt water, comparable to the *marais salants* in the Guérande region of France.[17] The Fort Lapin site and other sites north of Bruges have yielded ample evidence of salt making dating to the Roman period.[18] Given that salt production was controlled by the Roman state, and given the proximity of the Roman army from at least AD 170 when a first line of coastal defence was erected, the region of Bruges must have assumed some importance in Roman times.[19] The presence of a large tidal inlet heading from the coastal barrier to the Fort Lapin harbour also shows that the location was situated strategically for trade and military control.[20]

After 270, the situation in the region changed profoundly. The existing line of coastal fortresses bordering the sandy region of inner Flanders was reinforced.[21] Germanic seaborne invasions have traditionally been posited to explain the need for such defences, which is why these are called the *litus Saxonicum*. But recent studies offer another explanation: these fortresses probably belonged to the Gallic Empire of Postumus, a usurper who separated Gaul from the Roman empire (260–9) and had to build defences against Rome itself. While the existence of a *castellum* close to Bruges, and similar to the ones in Aardenburg and Oudenburg, has been thought likely, no proof of it has yet come to light.[22] Late Roman finds (276–410) are scarce and, in general, the situation of the Bruges area during the late Roman and Merovingian times remains unclear. From 276 onwards only the *castellum* of Oudenburg remained occupied. This fortress may be identified as the *Portus Epatiacus* mentioned in the *Notitia Dignitatum*, an early

[17] Thoen, *Kustvlakte*, pp. 90–2.

[18] H. Thoen, 'L'activité des sauniers dans la plaine maritime flamande de l'âge du fer à l'époque romaine: Le sel des Morins et Ménapiens', in A. Lottin, J.-C. Hocquet and S. Lebecq (eds.), *Les hommes et la mer dans l'Europe du Nord-Ouest de l'Antiquité à nos jours* (Lille, 1986), pp. 23–46; Y. Hollevoet, 'Archeologisch noodonderzoek in de Zeebrugse achterhaven: De Romeinse vondsten', *Westvlaamse Archaeologica*, 5 (1989), 33–48; De Clercq and Van Dierendonck, 'Extrema Galliarum'.

[19] W. Dhaeze, 'The Military Occupation along the Coasts of Gallia Belgica and Germania Inferior, from ca. AD 170 to 275', in Morillo et al. (eds.), *Limes*, pp. 1231–43.

[20] Thoen, *Kustvlakte*, pp. 103–5.

[21] J. Mertens, 'Oudenburg et le Litus Saxonicum en Belgique', *Helinium*, 2 (1962), 51–62; W. Dhaeze, 'Een schakel in de 2de-eeuwse kustverdediging: Het castellum te Aardenburg', in Hillewaert et al. (eds.), *Op het raakvlak*, pp. 55–6; Dhaeze, 'Military Occupation'; Vanhoutte, 'Het Romeinse castellum'.

[22] Y. Hollevoet, 'Een Romeinse versterking in Brugge?', in Hillewaert et al. (eds.), *Op het raakvlak*, pp. 72–5; coins from the time of Postumus were found in Western Flanders: see P. van Gansbeke, 'Les trésors monétaires d'époque romaine en Belgique', *Revue Belge de Numismatique*, 101 (1955), 5–44.

fourth-century list of Roman offices and army units, and it probably formed the heart of the early Frankish *Pagus Flandrensis* (see below).[23]

For the Merovingian period, there are hardly any traces of habitation in Bruges itself, although evidence is accumulating for the existence of early medieval settlements near the present city's location at the edge of the sandy region, again lining the old Roman road, which suggests the road was still in use as a line of transfer. Material culture and house-building traditions indicate a strong connection between the Bruges region and the Anglo-Saxon world.[24] However, nothing confirms significant local continuities from the Roman past within the territory later occupied by the city. In the meantime, from late Roman times, coastal erosion had entered a more dynamic phase, partly as a result of neglect in water management and probably also of intensive peat extraction. Gradually, almost the entire coastal plain fell back under the influence of tidal activity. During the period 550–750 a new balance between sedimentation and erosion was reached. The larger part of the coastal plain now became a more stable landscape of mud flats and marshlands and by 1000 the eastern coastal plain was largely sedimented. Most gullies had been weakened or had silted up with sandy deposits which developed into ridges; as a consequence of soil settling, these eventually surmounted the surrounding former mud flats.[25]

At a political and administrative level, the locality of Bruges lay within the Frankish empire, but how it fitted into the organization of the empire's *pagi* (districts) is unclear. Presumably, it found itself at the frontier of the *pagus Flandrensis* with Oudenburg as a military and administrative centre, and the *pagus Rodanensis* with Aardenburg as its capital (see Map 1). However, it is uncertain whether the *pagi* that existed by Carolingian times were already there under Merovingian rule, or if so, whether they functioned in the same way. The Frankish *pagus* 'Flanders', the wooded sandy ridge with adjacent marshlands between the River IJzer and present Bruges, presumably had Oudenburg as its initial centre.[26] This was probably the place called the *municipium Flandrense* in the *Vita Eligii* (dating from the first quarter of the eighth century but with an older core dated around 673–5). Until recently, this *municipium* was assumed to be Bruges itself.[27] Thus, the earliest region taking the name of 'Flanders' was inhabited by the

23 Mertens and Van Impe, *Het laat-Romeinse grafveld*, p. 36.

24 H. Hamerow, Y. Hollevoet and A. Vince, 'Migration Period Settlements and "Anglo-Saxon" Pottery from Flanders', *Medieval Archaeology*, 38 (1994), 1–18; Hollevoet, 'De nederzetting'.

25 Baeteman, 'History of Research'.

26 Hollevoet, 'De nederzetting'.

27 A. Verhulst, 'An Aspect of the Question of Continuity between Antiquity and Middle Ages: The Origin of the Flemish Cities between the North Sea and the Scheldt', *JMH*, 3 (1977),

Flandrenses, literally 'the people of the flooded areas' (who in later ecclesiastical sources would acquire a dubious reputation for brutality).[28] In the west the *pagus Flandrensis* was bordered by the *pagus Iseritius* and in the east by the *pagus Rodanensis*. To the south there was the *pagus Mempiscus*. It is tempting to suppose that, perhaps during the eight century, a settlement at 'Bruges' came about as a primitive market at the border of these three *pagi*, since it was well connected to their centres by the surviving older road system.[29] However, this remains hypothetical because the first solid indications of a settlement of some size at Bruges only date from the mid ninth century.

Although archaeological research may yet change our view, at present it indicates that before the ninth century there was little activity at the location of Bruges itself, and at most there existed only modest pre-urban habitation. It seems that Bruges only developed into an incipient agglomeration around the middle of the ninth century, or at the earliest from about 800. But describing and explaining this development is difficult. To begin with, terminology is tricky. In the historiography on early medieval towns, terms such as 'pre-urban core', 'pre-urban nucleus', 'proto-urban settlement' or 'proto-town' have often been used for this stage of embryonic growth, though they have also as often been contested.[30] Historians and archaeologists have further distinguished between 'trading settlements', 'stronghold settlements' and 'market settlements', and during recent decades discussion of the *wics*, *emporia* and so-called 'ports of trade' has generated rapidly changing frameworks of interpretation inspired by increasing archaeological knowledge and by anthropological theory.[31] As we will show, Bruges

192; Ryckaert, *Historische stedenatlas*, p. 41; C. Mériaux, 'Du nouveau sur la Vie de saint Eloi', *Mélanges de science religieuse*, 67 (2010), 71–85.

28 Dhondt and Gysseling, 'Vlaanderen'; R. Doehaerd, 'Flandrenses dans la Passio Karoli de Galbert de Bruges (1127)', *BTFG*, 71 (1993), 841–9.

29 Y. Hollevoet, 'De Vroege Middeleeuwen in Noordwestelijk Vlaanderen: Het ruimere historische kader', in Hillewaert et al. (eds.), *Op het raakvlak*, p. 97; G. Declercq, 'Vlaanderen en de Vlaanderengouw in de vroege middeleeuwen', *Vlaanderen: Tweemaandelijks Tijdschrift voor Kunst en Letteren*, 44 (1995), 10–17; and see for the general debate C. Wickham, *Framing the Early Middle Ages: Europe and the Mediterranean 400–800* (Oxford, 2005), pp. 591–3, 681–8; and R. Hodges, *Dark Age Economics: A New Audit* (London, 2012).

30 The use of the term 'proto' has been contested: see F. Verhaeghe, C. Loveluck and J. Story, 'Urban Developments in the Age of Charlemagne', in J. Story (ed.), *Charlemagne: Empire and Society* (Manchester, 2005), p. 261; but we feel that this classification may still be useful to indicate a phase in a processual economic development.

31 H. Clarke and A. Simms, 'Towards a Comparative History of Urban Origins', in H. Clarke and A. Simms (eds.), *The Comparative History of Urban Origins in Non-Roman Europe: Ireland, Wales, Denmark, Germany, Poland and Russia from the 9th to the 13th Century* (Oxford, 1985), pp. 669–714 (at 672, 678, 681, 686).

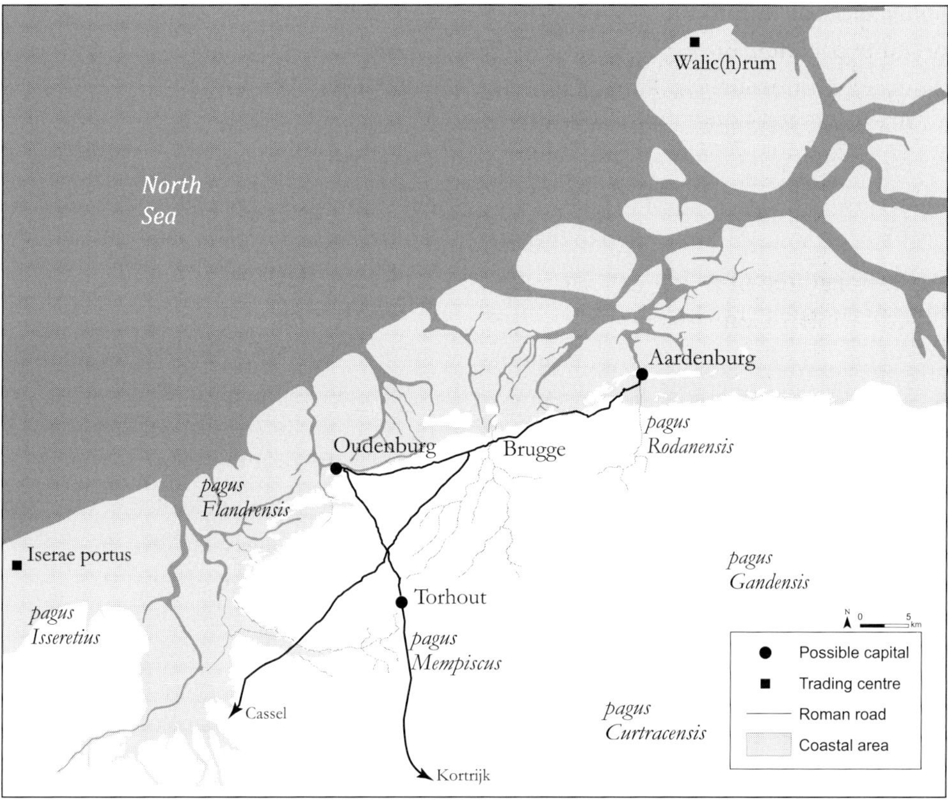

Map 1 Coastal Flanders with *pagi*

combined characteristics of several of these 'ideal types' used in explanations for the rise of early medieval towns in northwestern Europe.

As to explaining the rise of medieval 'towns', particularly those of non-Roman origins, debate has been lively ever since its initiation by Henri Pirenne. His shadow still looms large over the historiography of medieval Flanders. Pirenne, inspired by the German historian Rietschel, established a bipolar model to explain the emergence of the early medieval town, viewing it as a *suburbium* that developed next to a *castrum*. His model also attributed much importance to the role of trade and 'wandering' merchants.[32] The tendency in recent decades, however, has been to emphasize the manorial economy in the growth of towns and to diminish the

[32] S. Rietschel, *Markt und Stadt in ihrem rechtlichen Verhältnis: Ein Beitrag zur Geschichte der Deutschen Stadtverfassung* (Leipzig, 1897); Pirenne, *Les villes*. For an overview of the earliest historiographical debates on the rise of cities, see C. Stephenson, *Borough and Town: A Study of Urban Origins in England* (Cambridge, MA, 1933), pp. 3–21, and E. Ennen, *Frühgeschichte der Europäischen Stadt* (Bonn, 1953).

significance of merchant activity.[33] For Bruges, as we shall see, the situation was quite complex. But the main factor in its rise seems to have been the presence of a Carolingian stronghold, most likely dating from the reign of Charles the Bald (840–77) and possibly erected against the raids of the Normans.[34]

The Emergence of a Comital Stronghold (Ninth–Tenth Centuries)

In the Low Countries, urban development generally started later along the Flemish coast than it did in the Meuse or Scheldt valleys. Compared to Roman towns like Tournai, Saint-Omer, Arras and Tongeren, Bruges was a relative latecomer.[35] While its development before the ninth century is obscure, thereafter its growth is clearer, and more obviously linked with the rise of the early counts of Flanders. Baldwin, the first count of the *pagus Flandrensis* mentioned in the historical records, apparently already operated quite autonomously from his Frankish overlord. Perhaps he took up Bruges as the location for his residence partly because its navigable access to the sea was improving, in contrast to that of the older centre of Oudenburg, which seems to have silted up. Baldwin controlled the royal stronghold in Bruges and, over the following centuries, much of the territorial expansion made by the early counts would be organized from there. During the central Middle Ages, the town would become a political and economic centre of a new territorial entity, the powerful county of Flanders.[36]

Floods such as one in 838 had made Bruges more accessible from the sea, and this would soon come to the attention of the Normans. Perhaps it was around then that a first stronghold was erected as part of the Carolingian coastal defences. Indeed the toponym of Bruges was mentioned for the first

[33] The major reference point is Verhulst, *Rise of Cities*; and his collected articles in A. Verhulst, *Rural and Urban Aspects of Early Medieval Northwest Europe* (Aldershot, 1992); and see also R. Hodges, *Towns and Trade in the Age of Charlemagne* (London, 2000).

[34] At the end of the ninth century, more *castella* were erected with this goal; see H. Van Werveke, *"Burgus": Versterking of nederzetting?* (Brussels, 1965); and J. De Meulemeester and A. Lehouck, 'L'archéologie des zones littorales à la période carolingienne', in S. Lebecq, B. Bethouart and L. Verslype (eds.), *Quentovic: Environnement, archéologie, histoire* (Lille, 2010), pp. 39–55.

[35] See in general Verhulst, *Rise of Cities*.

[36] J. Dhondt, 'Het ontstaan van het vorstendom Vlaanderen', *BTFG*, 21 (1942), 533–72.

time in 851, in a written source showing it to be a place safe enough to serve as a refuge for the clerics of St Bavo abbey, the major monastic house at Ghent. In the *Breviarium de thesauro sancti Bavonis, quod invenerunt fratres remansisse post Nordmannicam infestationem*, an inventory of church treasure belonging to this house, compiled after it had been looted by the Vikings, a golden cross is mentioned as having been lost in Bruges, where it had apparently been hidden ('crux illa aurea, que Bruggis fuit ad servandum missa nec postea reversa'). The inventory can be dated to a period between 851 and 864; and it might be connected with an ordinance of Charles the Bald dated April 853, that sent out royal messengers (*missi*) to inventorize all monastic treasures.[37] The oldest archaeological traces of a Carolingian stronghold on the Square known as the Burg (a toponym meaning 'fortification') confirm its ninth-century origins, although a connection with Norman invasions cannot be materially established. There is no doubt, however, that in the year 850 the *pagi Mempiscus* and *Flandrensis* were raided. Excavations at the Burg Square in the 1980s revealed traces of a ditch and at least one earthen wall. Dating these structures, however, remains problematic. Only a *terminus ante quem* can be established dating all these features before 950, but it seems likely that fortification works in the shape of a curved ditch and bank protecting the *castrum* site at Bruges originated around the mid ninth century.[38]

The 860s were crucial for the future of Bruges. In 862, a certain Baldwin, a Frankish magnate from Laon, kidnapped Judith, daughter to King Charles the Bald and twice widowed (from the Wessex King Aethelwulf and from the latter's stepson Aethelbald). After Charles the Bald's furious reaction, Baldwin allied himself to the pope and to Rorik, the Viking warlord of nearby Frisia.[39] In 863, however, Baldwin was reconciled with Charles and received several *honores* including the *pagus Flandrensis*, the *pagus* of Waas, and possibly the *pagi* of Aardenburg, Ghent, *Mempiscus* and Thérouanne. Baldwin probably became the lay abbot of St Peter's abbey of Ghent and

[37] B. Bischoff, *Mittelalterliche Schatzverzeichnisse* (Munich, 1967), pp. 38–9; G. Declercq, 'Brugge als toevluchtsoord tijdens de Noormanneninval van 851', *BO*, 28 (1988), 131–9; A. Boretius and V. Krause (eds.), *Capitularia Regum Francorum* (Hanover, 1897), p. 267; G. Declercq, 'Bruggas, Bruciam, Brutgis: De oudste eigentijdse vermeldingen van Brugge', in Hillewaert et al. (eds.), *Op het raakvlak*, pp. 129–36 (at 129).

[38] B. Hillewaert, 'De Brugse Burg', in Hillewaert et al. (eds.), *Op het raakvlak*, pp. 119–22; Verhaeghe et al., 'Urban Developments', p. 274; H. De Witte, 'Dendrochronological and Radiocarbon Data and the Development and Chronology of the "Burg" of Bruges', *Medieval and Modern Matters*, 2 (2011), 77–88.

[39] J. L. Nelson, *Charles the Bald* (London, 1992), p. 203; S. Joye, 'Le rapt de Judith par Baudouin de Flandre (862): Un *clinamen* sociologique?', in F. Bougard, L. Feller and R. Le Jan (eds.), *Les élites au Haut Moyen Âge: crises et renouvellements* (Turnhout, 2006), pp. 361–79.

of the *cella* of Torhout, a monastic house where missionaries were trained. Baldwin I died in 879 and was succeeded by his son Baldwin II, who can be considered the first de facto independent count of Flanders and who married Alfred the Great's daughter Aelfthryth, demonstrating the early and intensive connections between Flanders and England. Baldwin I had been a *comes* in the original sense of the term (meaning a Carolingian regional official), but by the end of the ninth century, as West Francia became more decentralized, the second count of Flanders was occupying an office that had become hereditary. The original *pagus* around Oudenburg began to lend its name to the larger territory of the count. Thus, in 888 the whole of 'Flanders' in its broader sense belonged to Baldwin II and by 918 his power stretched as far as the Canche and the hills of Artois. He had also become the lay abbot of two further major monastic houses, St Bertin in Saint-Omer and St Vaast in Arras.[40] As with other Frankish great men, the power of the counts derived from their retinue, their landed property (notably their extensive domain in the coastal plain) and their marriage strategies, but also from their role in trade networks and control over artisanal production.[41] Over the following centuries, Bruges would become a central locus for the counts' accumulation of power.

The effect of Viking raids on Bruges' development was also significant. The first Norman invaders had appeared before the coast of the Carolingian empire at the beginning of the ninth century. As a response to this threat, Charlemagne had orchestrated the building of a defence system with *praesidia* or garrisons along the coast.[42] A raid in 820 was unsuccessful but eventually the Viking incursions became more dangerous, and the attack on Flanders in 850 was followed by another in 864, again repelled by the Flemings. A large Viking fleet descended *in Flandris* and met the fierce resistance of the *pagenses*, the local population, perhaps under the leadership of Count Baldwin. Between 879 and 883, however, another Norman attack had disastrous consequences and the whole area was looted. Inland Flanders suffered more than the coast from this campaign. During this time, Bruges appears to have been the centre or rather

40 Dhondt, 'Het ontstaan'; Declercq, 'Vlaanderen'.

41 F. Theuws, 'Exchange, Religion, Identity and Central Places in the Early Middle Ages', *Archaeological Dialogues*, 10 (2004), 121–38 (at 123); on the historiographic discussion on trade or gift exchange during the early Middle Ages, see Hodges, *Dark Age Economics*, pp. 31–4.

42 G. Declercq, 'Oorsprong en vroegste ontwikkeling van de burcht van Brugge (9de –12de eeuw)', in H. De Witte (ed.), *De Brugse Burg: Van grafelijke versterking tot moderne stadskern* (Bruges, 1991), pp. 15–45; and in general see S. Coupland, 'The Carolingian Army and the Struggle against the Vikings', *Viator*, 35 (2004), 49–70.

the refuge from which Count Baldwin II operated. During the summer of 883, from their winter camp in Condé on the upper Scheldt River, an army of Normans penetrated the coastal areas. They attacked the *Flamingos* and destroyed everything they could find. It has been concluded from this that Baldwin II was powerless to react, that he left Bruges to the invaders – no traces of fire or war have been encountered in the Burg – and retreated with his retainers to the region's forests and swamps. The impact of Norman invasions in Frankish territory became less important after 887, although in 890 and 891 the Flemish coast was attacked again. Then, in 892, a conflict broke out between Baldwin II and King Odo of West Francia. The *Annales Vedastini*, written by a monk of the fortified abbey of St Vaast in Arras, mentions that the count hid in Bruges ('in Bruciam' or 'Bruociam') and that the king's men failed to take it, which suggests that Bruges had not been weakened as a stronghold, or that Baldwin had recently improved it.[43]

The counts of Flanders, and their fortress at Bruges, emerged from the period of Viking assaults in a strengthened position. Arnulf I (918–65), was the first in a series of powerful and expansionist counts who often operated from Bruges. He further increased the territory and influence of Flanders. He was called a *marchio* or *marchysus* (margrave) in the sources, a title recognized by the West Frankish kings, boosting his status as a powerful warlord in a frontier zone of the kingdom. Probably around the middle of the century, Arnulf had the Bruges stronghold extended with a square plan. The count's Carolingian genealogy – he was, after all, the great grandson of Charles the Bald – likely inspired him to build, alongside the fortress his ancestors had erected in the Burg, the church of St Donatian as a smaller copy (about two thirds the size) of the royal Palatine chapels in Aachen and Compiègne, partly using stones from the ruins of Oudenburg castellum. Arnulf also probably founded a chapter of secular canons there after 950.[44] Bruges was now one of the major comital residences of Flanders and thus required spiritual protection. From the *cella* of Torhout, Baldwin I had already brought the relics of St Donatian, a fourth-century bishop of Reims.

43 F.-L. Ganshof, 'Les origines du comté de Flandre: À propos d'un ouvrage récent', *BTFG*, 16 (1937), 367–85 (at 372); A. D'Haenens, *Les invasions normandes en Belgique au IXe siècle* (Leuven, 1967), pp. 98, 158–9; B. de Simson (ed.), *Annales Xantenses et Annales Vedastini, Monumenta Germaniae Historica. Scriptores 7: scriptores rerum Germanicarum in usum scholarum* (Hanover, 1909), pp. 71–2.

44 P. Grierson, 'The Translation of the Relics of St. Donatian to Bruges', *Revue Bénédictine*, 49 (1937), 170–90; A. C. F. Koch, 'Het graafschap Vlaanderen van de 9de eeuw tot 1070', in *Algemene Geschiedenis der Nederlanden*, vol. I (Haarlem, 1981), pp. 354–83 (at 357–60); L. Devliegher, 'De voorromaanse, romaanse en gotische Sint-Donaaskerk: Evolutie en

Count Arnulf further stimulated the veneration of these relics by building a collegiate church that followed a royal model.[45] By this he also demonstrated his political ambitions in Western Europe. That he chose Bruges as a power base may indicate a desire to construct a maritime principality,[46] but it also reflects the importance gained by the young settlement in only one century.

Succeeding counts continued to renovate its fortifications, and Bruges' function as a centre of government steadily rose during the tenth century. The importance of the castle to the local economy cannot be underestimated. The presence of *milites*, servants and clerics in and around the castle and St Donatian's church must have increased demand for wine, salt, weaponry, leather, textiles and luxury products, while the relics would also have attracted pilgrims to the feast of the saint. As examples in other early medieval towns have shown, such pilgrim traffic would have stimulated gift-giving through which the counts and the church oiled relations with clients and allies, and these activities were perhaps combined with commerce.[47] By the end of the tenth century, the *Vorburg* around the castle may already have been surrounded by water on all sides. In the middle, most probably, stood the church of St Walburga, perhaps the predecessor of St Donatian's (see further Chapter 2) and also the church, as we shall see, of a possible trade settlement. Street names next to the castle refer to the shoemakers using Spanish leather (the *cordouaniers* or cordwainers) and weapon makers, and suggest the early presence of specialized artisans working within the castle economy.[48]

Bruges continued to function as a safe haven for the dynamic Flemish counts who in the century that followed expanded their territory towards the south and east. The nearby *fisci* (royal demesnes) of Weinebrugge, Snellegem and Maldegem, as well as a demesne in Aartrijke that had belonged to the bishop of Noyon-Tournai, had been appropriated by the

invloeden', in De Witte (ed.), *De Brugse Burg*, pp. 118–36 (at 118–25); Declercq, 'Oorsprong'; G. Declercq, 'Wanneer ontstond het Sint-Donaaskapittel te Brugge?', *HGG*, 122 (1985), 145–57; B. Meijns, *Aken of Jeruzalem? Het ontstaan en de hervorming van de kanonikale instellingen in Vlaanderen tot circa 1155*, 2 vols. (Leuven, 2000), vol. I, pp. 303–25. See also Chapter 2.

45 Declercq, 'Bruggas', p. 134.

46 J.-F. Nieus, 'Montreuil et l'expansion du comté de Flandre au Xe siècle', in Lebecq et al. (eds.), *Quentovic*, pp. 493–505 (at 496).

47 Cf. Frans Theuws' remarks for early medieval Maastricht in Theuws, 'Exchange, Religion, Identity', p. 126.

48 H. Van Werveke, 'De oudste burchten aan de Vlaamse en de Zeeuwse kust', *Mededelingen van de Koninklijke Vlaamse Academie voor Wetenschappen, Letteren en Schone Kunsten van België. Klasse der Letteren*, 27 (1965), 16; Verhulst, *Rise of Cities*, pp. 88–90; A. Verhulst, 'Die gräfliche Burgenverfassung in Flandern im Hochmittelalter', in H. Patze (ed.), *Die Burgen im deutschen*

Baldwins and now served as nearby sources of income, transferring rural surpluses to the comital residence.[49] The contribution of the Flemish agricultural economy to urban growth needs to be stressed: the level of income from surrounding demesnes must also have benefited the development of what might indeed be called a 'proto-urban settlement' adjoining the military and religious infrastructure that surrounded the count's stronghold at Bruges. Certainly butchers, bakers, brewers, millers, fishermen, carpenters, masons, tailors, shoemakers, weavers, fullers, shearers, dyers, tanners, blacksmiths, sword makers, gold- and silversmiths, shipmen, carters and other trades had to be present to service the basic needs of the elites inhabiting the castle and the chapter of St Donatian, thus supporting a typical 'castle economy'.[50] During this time, most if not all of the artisans and merchants connected to the Bruges fortress were probably of servile status, though no source explicitly tells us so. We do know, for instance, that inhabitants of abbey or castle demesnes had to perform transport labour duties with their carts.[51]

Also apparent by this period is a wider network of exchange within which the castle and settlement of Bruges operated. This is exemplified by the *Refuge* site in Sint-Andries, not so far from the Bruges centre, where a settlement existed from the Carolingian period, comprising at least one farm. Excavations there have revealed that unlike its Merovingian predecessors, the farm was contained inside a rectangular ditch, and its main buildings were built centrally inside the compound. These were three-aisled timber structures, surrounded by smaller outbuildings such as granaries and haystacks, and with wells nearby. The ditch enclosing the farm, as well as the so-called *Roedenbergen* (haystacks), hint at cattle and small livestock breeding.[52] The material culture of late Merovingian or Carolingian

Sprachraum: Ihre rechts- und verfassungsgeschichtliche Bedeutung (Sigmaringen, 1976), pp. 266–82. On the *Vorburg* and St Walburga, see Declercq, 'Oorsprong', pp. 37–8.

49 G. Berings, 'Het oude land aan de rand van het vroegmiddeleeuws overstromingsgebied van de Noordzee: Landname en grondbezit tijdens de Middeleeuwen', *HMG*, 39 (1985), 37–84.

50 On Carolingian craft production, see R. Doehaerd, *Le haut Moyen Âge occidental: Économies et sociétés* (Paris, 1975), pp. 205–11, 238–43. A systematic analysis of the growing amount of archaeological evidence for artisanal activities during this period is still lacking: see J. Henning, 'Early European Towns: The Development of the Economy in the Frankish Realm between Dynamism and Deceleration, AD 500–1100', in J. Henning (ed.), *Post-Roman Towns, Trade and Settlement in Europe and Byzantium*, 2 vols. (Berlin and New York, 2007), vol. I, p. 6.

51 Doehaerd, *Le haut Moyen Âge*, p. 215.

52 Y. Hollevoet and B. Hillewaert, 'Het archeologisch onderzoek achter de voormalige vrouwengevangenis *Refuge* te Sint-Andries/Brugge', *Archeologie in Vlaanderen*, 6 (1997/1998), 197–207.

farms in northern Flanders, as at Sint-Andries, testifies to a wider system of exchange that allowed local communities at least an indirect access to commodities of inter-regional provenance, as was the case for Carolingian farms further inland. Although much of the material culture retrieved seems to be of local or regional origin, some items such as stone, glass and high-quality pottery were acquired from further afield. Millstones were imported from the volcanic Eifel region, while some pottery vessels of the early Carolingian period originated in the Rhineland or the Eifel region, or were imported from the Meuse valley. Fragments of the Rhenish so-called *Badorf-amphorae*, found at several sites, for instance in the village of Roksem but also on the Burg Square in Bruges, probably served as containers for wine. And high-quality 'black and grey wares', probably from the Meuse valley, were found at several sites in the Bruges area and deeper inland in Flanders and beyond.[53] These farms clearly had some access to a wider network of commodities in the Carolingian era. The Bruges fortress may already have played a crucial role in providing such access, acting as a centre for the redistribution of goods.

Remarkable surface finds of metal jewellery, coins and ornaments belonging to Carolingian times, discovered to the northeast of Bruges at Koolkerke and Mikhem, point to the presence of other settlements of an elitist character, probably populated by groups of middlemen, traders or nobility close to the count, who had access to wider networks of exchange. Material culture suggests that the inhabitants of these settlements exchanged imported commodities for local products such as cloth. Flemish cloth production, which would become the main economic stimulus for the region, must have been important by the Carolingian period. Cloths were already being traded from the seventh century by 'Frisians' (a term often denoting merchants in the North Sea area in general, rather than any specific ethnicity); and although not all scholars agree, many of the 'Frisian cloths' (*pallia fresonica*) mentioned in the sources may have been Flemish. At any rate, during the ninth century the territory referred to as Frisia still bordered the region of Bruges, and as well as modern-day Frisia, it could also include the Scheldt estuary and the Flemish coastal plain.[54] Whether the region around Bruges

[53] See the work of R. Hodges, *The Hamwih Pottery: The Local and Imported Wares from 30 Years' Excavations at Middle Saxon Southampton and their European Context* (London, 1981); Wickham, *Framing*, pp. 801–2; P. Demolon and F. Verhaeghe, 'La céramique du Vème au Xème siècle dans le Nord de la France et la Flandre belge: état de la question', in D. Piton (ed.), *La céramique du Vème au Xème siècle dans l'Europe du Nord-Ouest* (Berck-sur-Mer, 1993), pp. 385–407.

[54] Doehaerd, *Le Haut Moyen Âge*, pp. 233–4; H. Pirenne, 'Draps de Frise ou draps de Flandre? Un petit problème d'histoire économique à l'époque carolingienne', *Vierteljahrschrift für*

played a role in such early cloth production is unknown, but it may be surmised from the presence of extensive sheep farms active in the coastal plain and from mention in some sources.

The cumulative evidence for economic activity strongly suggests that by the end of the tenth century Bruges had grown into a more economically diversified settlement. Certainly, the locality was no longer merely a military stronghold. During this 'Iron' century (for which written sources are notoriously scarce), a *suburbium* inhabited by artisans and traders developed alongside the fortified zone. In the case of Bruges, the term *burgus* was used to refer to the earliest urban agglomeration or to the city as a whole, much as the term 'borough' or 'bourg' was used in other towns. By the twelfth century, this developing settlement must have been what some written sources called the *suburbium*; and given that these sources sometimes refer to the *Burg* as the *urbs*, it is reasonable to assume that Bruges had by then acquired a more pronounced 'urban' character.[55] Thus, the Bruges stronghold played a significant role within the local economy; but, as we shall see, there is also evidence for the town's development as a centre of wider commercial activity.

A Commercial Settlement from Carolingian Times?

At the beginning of the tenth century, in the kingdom of *Francia*, towns still functioned primarily as military settlements. However, commercial agglomerations referred to as *wic* in place names or *portus* in written sources had been developing from the eighth century, and some from even earlier. In the North Sea area, perhaps from the seventh century (though scarcity of evidence makes their status then almost mythic), trading centres referred to as *emporia* in Latin sources and *wic* in Germanic toponyms, like Hamwic, Lundenwic, Quentovic, Haithabu, Birka, Dorestad and Domburg, were the main ports for commerce within the region and beyond, and were often situated at the frontiers of kingdoms. An earlier generation of historians characterized them as centres where wandering merchants and other

Sozial- und Wirtschaftsgeschichte, 7 (1909), 308–16; D. Jellema, 'Frisian Trade in the Dark Ages', *Speculum*, 30 (1955), 15–36 (at 32); even if S. Lebecq, in *Marchands et navigateurs frisons du haut Moyen Âge*, 2 vols. (Lille, 1983), vol. I, p. 132, maintains that the *pallia fresonica* were purely 'Frisian', there is evidence for production of *cottae* (woollen jackets) for the Ghent abbey of Saint Bavo in this part of 'Frisia' in A. Verhulst, 'Das Besitzverzeichnis der Genter Sankt-Bavo-Abtei von ca. 800 (Clm 6333)', *Frühmittelalterliche Studien*, 5 (1971), 193–234 (at 225).

55 Van Werveke, "*Burgus*", pp. 49–53.

travellers took rest, where resident merchants lived, where agricultural surpluses were sold by lords and small peasants and, most of all, as centres to which luxury goods were imported, and where princely and ecclesiastical institutions were provided with services and goods. More recently, scholars have viewed them more as markets situated at the periphery of a civilization that was heir to the Roman world; ones offering access to less commercially developed hinterlands, where Anglo-Saxon, Scandinavian and Frisian traders met with the Frankish population.[56]

The debate is ongoing, and can only be advanced with fresh archaeological insights. The place of Bruges within this regional network of commerce is hard to assess, but its significance may have increased after Dorestad, the main commercial settlement of the Low Countries, declined from the 830s and was subjected to Viking raids between 834 and 863.[57] Not far from the Bruges region, the *wic* of Domburg (referred to in the sources as *Walichrum* or *villa Walachrium*) on the isle of Walcheren in Zeeland, which had developed from the sixth century onwards, also declined after the ninth century. Perhaps a trading settlement at Bruges was thus able to fill the vacuum left by the disappearance of Walichrum. At the very least the Carolingian *castellum* of Bruges, more or less accessible from the sea, could have served as one regional distribution point for goods imported through maritime trade.[58] Conclusive evidence for this hypothesis, however, is still lacking, and arguably the reasoning is teleological, a projection back from later evidence for the city's commercial hegemony. Perhaps the finds in Mikhem, a hamlet (since disappeared) southwest of the village of Oostkerke and a

[56] A. Chédeville, J. Le Goff and J. Rossiaud, *Histoire de la France urbaine*, vol. II: *La ville médiévale, des Carolingiens à la Renaissance*, 2nd edn (Paris, 1998), pp. 35, 50; J. Dhondt, *Le Haut Moyen Âge, VIIIe – XIe siècles* (Paris, 1976), pp. 279–81; R. van Uytven, 'Les origines des villes dans les anciens Pays-Bas, jusque vers 1300', in G. Despy (ed.), *La fortune historiographique des thèses d'Henri Pirenne* (Brussels, 1986), p. 21; K. Polanyi, 'Ports of Trade in Early Societies', *Journal of Economic History*, 23 (1963), 30–45; K. G. Hirth, 'Inter-Regional Trade and the Formation of Prehistoric Gateway Communities', *American Antiquity*, 43 (1978), 25–45; and recent states of the art in S. Lebecq, 'The New *Wiks* or *Emporia* and the Development of a Maritime Economy in the Northern Seas (7th–9th Centuries)', in S. Gelichi and R. Hodges (eds.), *From One Sea to Another: Trading Places in the European and Mediterranean Early Middle Ages* (Turnhout, 2009), pp. 11–21; and in Wickham, *Framing*, pp. 683–8.

[57] See a recent update on the research on Dorestad in Willemsen and Kik (eds.), *Dorestad*.

[58] A. Verhulst, 'The Origins of Towns in the Low Countries and the Pirenne Thesis', *Past and Present*, 122 (1989), 3–35 (at 20–1); Lebecq, *Marchands*, vol. I, pp. 142–4; S. Lebecq, 'L'*emporium* proto-médiéval de Walcheren-Domburg: une mise en perspective', in J.-M. Duvosquel and E. Thoen (eds.), *Peasants and Townsmen in Medieval Europe. Studia in honorem Adriaan Verhulst* (Ghent, 1995), pp. 73–89; Tys, 'Scheldt Estuary', p. 172.

few miles from Bruges, as well as in Koolkerke, suggest commercial activity linking these places to early Bruges and to the wider North Sea area.[59]

It is tempting to consider Mikhem and Koolkerke as part of the earliest 'port system' of the Bruges area, and to resist treating Bruges itself as a settlement similar to earlier North Sea *emporia*. After all, with its stronghold, its elite inhabitants, and above all its religious community and saintly relics, Bruges resembled places like Tiel, Deventer or even Maastricht more than it did places like Dorestad or Domburg.[60] Even so, the wider commercial connections of the area surrounding Bruges cannot be dismissed. Archaeological finds from Frankish times are rare, but as we have seen, excavations in settlements between Bruges and Oudenburg show imports with various provenances. These commodities could only have reached the region by sea, for instance through Domburg, where coins from Bruges have been unearthed.[61] 'Frisian', 'Anglo-Saxon' and Scandinavian merchants – it is often unclear what the sources mean by these ethnic terms – must have transported these to the Bruges region.[62] In this context we must again emphasize the evidence that links the region with the Anglo-Saxon world: the presence of Anglo-Saxon *sceattas* (silver coins) in Koolkerke and Roksem as well as material culture (hair pins, brooches, pottery); and the Merovingian house-building tradition resembling Anglo-Saxon forms, which is evident in the coastal region of Flanders, but absent from inland areas.[63]

Thus, it is plausible to argue that the rising importance of Bruges as a military and political stronghold was given commercial impetus after the disappearance of *emporia* such as Dorestad and Walichrum.[64] Despite short-term destruction, the Norman invasions did not have a profoundly negative impact on economic development in Flanders. The effect of Viking raids was to open up commerce in the North Sea and to drive the location of commercial centres in the region further inland. These in turn were stimulated by elite demands for luxury products and by the regional market functions that these same places also developed under the protection of a local strongman. During the

59 In the terminology of Hodges, *Towns and Trade*, this might have been a 'type A Emporium', an ephemeral periodic market on a coast or riverbank; see also Verhaeghe et al., 'Urban Developments', p. 268.

60 F. Theuws, *De sleutel van Sint-Servatius: Uitwisseling, religie, identiteit en centrale plaatsen in de Vroege Middeleeuwen* (Amsterdam, 2003), pp. 15–16.

61 A. Verhulst, 'Roman Cities, Emporia and New Towns (Sixth–Ninth Centuries)', in I. L. Hansen and C. Wickham (eds.), *The Long Eighth Century* (Leiden, 2000), p. 116.

62 Hollevoet, 'De nederzetting'.

63 Hamerow et al., 'Migration Period Settlements'.

64 Lebecq, 'L'*emporium*', p. 86.

Carolingian period, the demand for luxury products among princes, noblemen and clergy played a major role in the revival of commerce in luxury items.[65] As a centre of military power Bruges seems to have concentrated such demand and provided a platform for the redistribution of goods.

Also relevant here is the fact that the name of Bruges, after its first appearance in a written source in 851 or slightly later, is again mentioned on two or perhaps three Carolingian types of coin from the second half of the ninth century. These coins are of the 'GDR-type', and were minted from 864 onwards, first in the name of Charles the Bald, and later in that of Charles the Simple. On the front side they carry the monogram of the name *Karolus* with the legend GRATIA DEI REX around it; on the back a cross is depicted, surrounded with a legend naming the place where they had been coined. These coins were minted not by the kings whose names they carried but by the counts of Flanders in their place. They have been found in several hoards from the late ninth century, for instance in Glisy (near Amiens) and in Cuerdale (England).[66] In the tenth century, the counts of Flanders continued to mint coins of this type in Bruges as a so-called *type immobilisé*, which is datable to 930–60 or later. Bruges coins of this type were found in hoards dating to the late tenth and early eleventh centuries in Scandinavia and the Baltic region.[67] The presence of a mint in the comital stronghold shows the importance of Bruges as a centre of government, but the diffusion of these coins also suggests that Bruges was playing a role in maritime trade, especially from the reign of Count Arnulf I. Further archaeological finds may substantiate this hypothesis. In fact the discovery in 1993, as yet unpublished, of a hoard at Grisebjerggård in Denmark, datable to shortly after 942/3, may point in this direction: it apparently contains nine (or possibly thirteen) Bruges coins, out of a total of 1,200 Danish, Anglo-Saxon, continental and Islamic coins.[68]

65 Verhulst, 'Origins of Towns', p. 8; and in general see A. Verhulst, *The Carolingian Economy* (Cambridge, 2002), and R. Hodges and D. Whitehouse, *Mohammed, Charlemagne and the Origins of Europe: Archaeology and the Pirenne Thesis* (Ithaca, NY, 1983).

66 H. Frère, *Le denier carolingien spécialement en Belgique* (Louvain-la-Neuve, 1977), pp. 49–51; H. Frère, 'Le denier carolingien', *Revue Belge de Numismatique*, 126 (1980), 113–15; Declercq, 'Bruggas', pp. 129–30.

67 G. Albrecht, *Das Münzwesen im Niederlothringischen und Friesischen Raum: vom 10. bis zum beginnenden 12. Jahrhundert* (Hamburg, 1959), p. 52; D. M. Metcalf, 'Coinage and the Rise of the Flemish Towns', in N. J. Mayhew (ed.), *Coinage in the Low Countries (880–1500)* (Oxford, 1979), p. 5.

68 J. C. Moesgaard, 'Le monnayage d'Arras, Bruges et Tournai dans les années 920 et 930', in C. Lorren (ed.), *La Gaule, le monde insulaire et l'Europe du Nord au haut Moyen Âge* (Saint-Germain-en-Laye, 2013), pp. 349–53.

So had Bruges now become a merchant settlement by the late Carolingian period? A number of additional elements need considering. An intriguing issue is that the name Bruges itself may be of Scandinavian origin. Toponymists have suggested that the contemporary place name *Brugge* is derived from the Old Norse word *bryggja* meaning 'pier' or 'landing point', or more recently, from a reconstructed Germanic root *brugjo,* with roughly the same meaning, or more specifically 'corduroy road'.[69] The first toponymic hypothesis might point to a very early Nordic presence in the town, perhaps even to commercial contacts with Scandinavia before Bruges was first mentioned in 851. However, toponymic evidence is seldom conclusive in itself and if the *brugjo* hypothesis is correct, no necessary Scandinavian connection is implied.[70] Still, another argument in favour of the trade settlement hypothesis is the fact that until the mid eleventh century, Bruges was in all likelihood easily accessible from the sea. The part of the Reie River now known as the Lange Rei had long functioned as the entry to the military zone. The depression along the current Spiegelrei canal was a logical terminus for trade, as the configuration of the territory offered ships the possibility of anchorage. It is tempting to see this quarter as the oldest port of the city, receiving the name of 'the landing point' or 'the quay' from visiting merchants, a name that would ultimately be used to designate the whole city.[71]

The Nordic connection is further suggested by two other pieces of evidence. One is the list of inhabitants of the demesne of Snellegem near Bruges, which according to one scholar showed a remarkable number of names of Scandinavian origin. This specific onomastic argument, however, is also far from solid.[72] A second, more significant piece of evidence for

69 Compare with the eleventh-century port zone of Bergen in Norway which is still called Bryggen or 'the quay'.

70 M. Gysseling, 'Etymologie van Brugge', *Handelingen van de Koninklijke Commissie voor Toponymie en Dialectologie*, 18 (1944), 69–79; M. Gysseling, 'Een nieuwe etymologie van Brugge', *Naamkunde*, 3 (1971), 1–4; M. Gysseling, 'Inleiding tot de oude toponymie van West-Vlaanderen', *De Leiegouw*, 25 (1983), 39–58; F. Debrabandere, 'Brugse plaatsnamen', *Brugge die Scone*, 26 (2005), 46; F. Debrabandere, 'Brugge', in F. Debrabandere. et al. (eds.), *De Vlaamse gemeentenamen. Verklarend woordenboek* (Brussels, 2010), p. 55; Tys, 'Scheldt Estuary', similarly suggests that ninth-century Antwerp developed as a 'port, town and crafts centre under influence of Scandinavian traders' though, in this case as well, further archaeological confirmation would be needed to prove this.

71 A. C. F. Koch, 'Brugge's topografische ontwikkeling tot in de 12e eeuw', *HGG*, 99 (1962), 5–67 (at 42), who located a merchant settlement more to the south, around the Boomgaardstraat and the Ridderstraat; M. Ryckaert and B. Hillewaert, 'De vroegste topografische ontwikkeling van het middeleeuwse Brugge, van de 9de tot het begin van de 12de eeuw', in Hillewaert et al. (eds.), *Op het raakvlak*, pp. 148–9.

72 A. C. F. Koch, 'Vikingen in Vlaanderen? Een 10de-eeuwse lijst met persoonsnamen uit Snellegem (bij Brugge)', *Naamkunde*, 16 (1984), 183–200; and the critique by A. Quak,

a connection with the Viking world is the presence, from 834 in Torhout (15 kilometres from Bruges), of a school that trained men to evangelize in Scandinavia. According to the *Vita Anskarii*, Louis the Pious had granted this *cella* of Torhout to St Anskar, bishop of Hamburg in 834. Danish boys were sent there to be trained as missionaries. Charles the Bald later appropriated this monastic house, and from royal hands it slipped into those of the counts of Flanders.[73] The same text seems to tell us that as early as 840 Charles the Bald helped install in Torhout a certain Raginarius, who has been identified as the Danish warlord 'Ragnar'. However, this vassal later fell from royal grace, and his Viking origins are conjecture.[74] Tenuous though these Scandinavian connections are, cumulatively they have supported further hypotheses: Van Houtte has suggested, somewhat boldly, that in the ninth century Bruges was already involved in Varengian trade through Russia with the Byzantine empire and Persia, importing spices, silk and other luxury goods and exporting cloth. Again, the proximity of the missionary centre in Torhout could be an indication of this.[75] The hypothesis of links with Varengian trade, however, remains speculative; but the *Vita Anskarii* does suggest that Torhout formed a point in a network of exchange that involved Scandinavia. The thirty-five episodes of travel mentioned in the *Vita,* involving merchants, pirates and *emporia*, and encompassing Reims, Dorestad, Hedeby, Cologne and Birka, to name but a few, conjure up a picture that the archaeologist Sindbaek has called 'the small world of the Vikings'. Bruges was within walking distance of Torhout, and could have served as its access to the sea. In other words, the region of Bruges, if not Bruges itself, appears to have constituted an area that not only formed a part of the Anglo-Saxon world but also connected Viking with Carolingian Europe.[76]

The earliest solid evidence for the city functioning as a commercial centre is provided by some sources dating from the first half of the tenth century.

'Wikinger in Flandern?', in L. Peterson and S. Strandberg (eds.), *Studia Onomastica: Festskrift till Thorsten Anderssohn den 23 Februari 1989* (Stockholm, 1989), pp. 297–302.

[73] Grierson, 'Translation', 182; A. Dierkens, 'Saint Anschaire, l'abbaye de Torhout et les missions carolingiennes en Scandinavie. Un dossier à réouvrir', in M. Sot (ed.), *Haut Moyen-Âge. Culture, éducation et société* (Paris, 1990), pp. 301–13.

[74] Nelson, *Charles the Bald*, p. 151, identified him with the Ragnar who captured Paris in 845 but S. Coupland, 'From Poachers to Gamekeepers: Scandinavian Warlords and Carolingian Kings', *Early Medieval Europe*, 7 (1998), 85–114 (at 107–8), showed that this is unlikely and suggested that Raginarius might simply have been Frankish.

[75] J. A. Van Houtte, 'De opkomst van een grote middeleeuwse markt: Brugge', *Academiae Analecta*, 47 (1985), 1–15 (at 5).

[76] S.M. Sindbaek, 'The Small World of the Vikings: Networks in Early Medieval Communication and Exchange', *Norwegian Archaeological Review*, 40 (2007), 59–74.

In these Bruges is called a *vicus* and *portus* – terms which in this region without doubt refer to a settlement with at least some 'urban' or 'commercial' characteristics.[77] A list of tenants owing yearly rents to the monastic community in the *Liber traditionum antiquus* of St Peter's abbey at Ghent was composed in the first half of the century. Among these tenants there is a certain Ubilin, who with his three sisters 'in Brutgis uico manet'. Apart from counts Baldwin I and II, this makes Ubilin the first resident of Bruges known by name. The use of the term *vicus* in this list to describe Bruges is significant, because almost all the other place names are refered to as mere *villae*, agrarian settlements. The only other *vicus* mentioned is Antwerp, which had a portuary function in that period.[78] And between 941 and 946, most likely in 944 or 945, Count Arnulf wrote a letter to Archbishop Hugues of Reims, his brother-in-law, to ask for a *vita* of St Donatian, whose relics had been translated from Torhout to Bruges by Baldwin I. In this text, Bruges is called a *portus* ('ad Brudgias portum'). This does not necessarily mean that Bruges had been a *portus* in Baldwin's time, but the use of the term does show it was an urban settlement of considerable importance by the mid tenth century.[79] These sources suggest that the reign of Arnulf I (918–65) was decisive in the development of Bruges from a mere 'castle economy' into a proper urban settlement. Moreover, an account of the translation of the relics of Sts Wandregisilus and Ansbertus to St Peter's abbey in Ghent by a group of monks accompanied by Count Arnulf and his entourage – written in the early twelfth century, but based on a lost text from around 950 – further indicates the settlement's growing significance. It describes the miraculous healing of archdean Bernaclius in Bruges ('Bruzzias') as a remarkable event 'as much because of the fame of this place as of the dignity of this person'. It also alludes to the land routes by which Bruges was linked to a wider world: Bernaclius seems to have lived near a church, possibly St Saviour's, on the *Steenstraat*, along which the monks had come with the relics from Boulogne.[80]

[77] Declercq, 'Bruggas', pp. 131, 134; Verhulst, *Rise of Cities*, p. 64: this might have specifically referred to the Oudeburg.

[78] A. C. F. Koch, 'De Ouderdom van de Stad Brugge', *HGG*, 86 (1949), 145–50 (at 146); Declercq, 'Bruggas', p. 131; G. Declercq and A. Verhulst, 'Villa et mansus dans le Liber Traditionum du Xe siècle de l'abbaye Saint-Pierre-au-Mont-Blandin à Gand', *BTFG*, 81 (2003), 1016–17.

[79] V. Lambert (ed.), *De oorkonden van het Sint-Donatiaanskapittel te Brugge (9de eeuw – 1300)* (Brussels, 2008), pp. 4–5 (the letter of Arnulf I) and pp. 5–6 (the reply by Archbishop Hugues), both dated '925–931 or 941–946'. Grierson, 'Translation', 173–4, declared this letter to be a late eleventh-century forgery, but F. Dolbeau, 'Un sermon inédit de Rathier pour la fête de Saint Donatien', *Analecta Bollandiana*, 98 (1980), 335–53) and Dierkens ('Saint Anschaire', 309–13) have convincingly argued for a tenth-century dating.

[80] N. Huyghebaert (ed.), *Une translation de reliques à Gand en 944: Le Sermo de Adventu Sanctorum Wandregisili, Ansberti et Vulframni in Blandinium* (Brussels, 1978), pp. 45–9.

The survival of certain toponyms within the town hints tantalisingly at the early commercial function of Bruges. The place names *Wic* and *Koetelwic* both occurred in the quarter of the Spiegelrei, which was the logical site, functionally and geographically, for a port connecting with the castle and its immediate surroundings. These microtoponyms are first recorded in the thirteenth century (few sources for such place names survive before this date), but they clearly have older origins.[81] The term *wic* needs cautious handling though. As we have seen, the classic type of North Sea *wic* or '-wich town' had not necessarily been a permanent market settlement although it had been a place where travelling merchants could trade and where commodities could be stored. It had comprised a population of non-basic producers engaged in locally based industries[82] – which is not quite the type of settlement formed around a military stronghold that describes Bruges in the ninth and tenth centuries. Not every toponym that includes the root *wic* derives its name from a type of trading settlement comparable, for instance, to Dorestad; and nor does it belong to a definite period. The meaning of the Bruges *wic* is a matter of speculation: the toponym may have derived from the Germanic word for 'inlet' or 'bay', or from the Latin *vicus* (as Bruges was termed during the tenth century). In any case, the term *vicus* does not necessarily refer to a *wic* type of settlement: it can mean any kind of agglomeration, though it often refers to a settlement close to a *castrum*.[83] However, when *vicus* is used in conjunction with *portus* to describe a settlement, in sources from the same period, it is more than likely that some commercial activity was present there.

Thus, even if we still lack conclusive archaeological proof, written sources suggest that Bruges was developing a mercantile function from the middle of the tenth century. Perhaps the development of the Koetelwic/Wic quarter only took place between 1000 and 1200; perhaps before that time, other places between Bruges and the North Sea such as Mikhem, Koolkerke or others yet unidentified, functioned as original maritime landing points for

81 W. Vogel, 'Wik-Orte und Wikinger: Eine Studie zu den Anfängen des germanischen Städtewesens', *Hansische Geschichtsblätter*, 60 (1935), 5–48; J. De Smet, 'De Brugse WIIC-namen', *HGG*, 85 (1948), 112–17; L. Schütte, *Wik: Eine Siedlungsbezeichnung in historischen und sprachlichen Bezügen* (Cologne and Vienna, 1976); T. De Meester and B. Schotte, 'De Koetelwijkpoort en de Houtbrekersdam aan de Spiegelrei', *BO*, 42 (2002), 195–219.

82 D. Nicholas, *The Growth of the Medieval City: From Late Antiquity to the Early Fourteenth Century* (London and New York, 1997), p. 58.

83 G. Köbler, '"Civitas" und "Vicus", "Burg", "Stat", "Dorf" und "Wik"', in H. Jankuhn, W. Schlesinger and H. Steuer (eds.), *Vor- und Frühformen der europäische Stadt im Mittelalter* (Göttingen, 1973), pp. 61–76; H. Clarke and B. Ambrosiani, *Towns in the Viking Age* (London and Leicester, 1991), pp. 15–20.

the castle of Bruges. There is at the very least strong evidence at a *regional* level for functional continuity in trade and connections with Anglo-Saxon, Frisian, Scandinavian and Baltic areas, even if not necessarily at a *local* level in the place called *Brugjo* or *Brygghia* itself, though the alleged Scandinavian roots of the toponym suggest this possibility. Certainly, changes visible in the region's landscape hint at efforts to stimulate trade. During the ninth and tenth centuries the counts or the people of Bruges, or probably both in cooperation, were seeking to create better connections between the Reie and the gullies of the Sincfal: their efforts included digging a canal (later called the 'Oude Zwin', the Old Zwin) through the sand ridge of Koolkerke towards a gully near Mikhem.[84] But some texts also suggest that Bruges by this time was readily accessible by land. In 1011 a west Frisian woman from the region of Heiloo, now in north Holland, was sent to the church of St Donatian to be miraculously healed. The story informs us that she had come by a 'publica via' to the 'castrum Brugga'. The woman had not heard of this place, but hagiographic sources of the eleventh century do testify to the growing fame of Bruges: from there St Donatian performed miracles in a region of maritime Flanders that was still largely barren and violent.[85]

Other, chiefly political, changes also contributed to the growth of Bruges. During the second half of the tenth century, comital power had weakened again under the young Count Arnulf II. The coastal plain on which Bruges lay, where the comital demesne was centered and where counts still exerted power, now truly became the centre of Flanders.[86] Possibly as a result of storm surges in 1014 and 1042, Bruges also became more accessible by water for flat-bottomed ships.[87] Strong comital power was gradually restored during the reigns of Baldwin IV (988–1035) and Baldwin V (1035–67). In Bruges the latter ordered renovations of the *castrum* and extended the fortress with a square wall (again recycling stones from the Roman ruins at Oudenburg).[88] From Baldwin V's rule dates the first written

[84] B. Hillewaert, *Oostkerke-bij-Brugge*, Archeologische Inventaris Vlaanderen 2 (Ghent, 1984), 444–5; B. Hillewaert, 'Verdwenen bewoning te Michem', in *Liber Amicorum René De Keyser* (Oostkerke, 1982), pp. 109–22; B. Hillewaert et al., 'De ontginning van het landschap', in Hillewaert et al. (eds.), *Op het raakvlak*, pp. 115–17 (at 116).

[85] B. Meijns, 'Hoe een heilige verdienstelijk werd: Het beeld van Sint-Donatianus van Brugge in de elfde-eeuwse mirakelverhalen', in R. Bauer et al. (eds.), *In de voetsporen van Jacob van Maerlant: Liber amicorum Raf De Keyser. Verzameling opstellen over middeleeuwse geschiedenis en geschiedenisdidactiek* (Leuven, 2002), pp. 114–39.

[86] J. Dunbabin, *France in the Making, 843–1180* (London, 1985), pp. 72–4 and Nieus, 'Montreuil', p. 499.

[87] A. Verhulst, 'Les origines et l'histoire ancienne de la ville de Bruges', *Le Moyen Âge*, 66 (1960), 37–63 (at 57–8); Gottschalk, *Stormvloeden*, vol. I, pp. 43–5.

[88] Declercq, 'Oorsprong', pp. 25–7.

source to provide clear information on Bruges' commercial function: the *Encomium Emmae reginae* (*c.*1040–2), written by a Flemish monk in honour of the English Queen Emma, widow to Kings Aethelred and Canute. While on the run, Emma was received by the count and countess in Bruges and stayed 'in oppido'. Bruges, the *Encomium* says (as quoted above), was widely known for the abundance there of merchants and goods ('Hoc castellum Flandrensibus colonis incolitur, quod tum frequentia negotiatorum tum affluentia omnium quae prima mortales ducunt famosissimum habetur'). The place where Emma's ships moored, the *Encomium* also says, was not far away from the fortress ('haud longe a castello Bruggensis'):[89] this was almost certainly the Koetelwic or Wic near the Spiegelrei, some 300 metres from the Burg.

Numismatic evidence also indicates Bruges' increased importance for trade. While ninth- and tenth-century Bruges coins have rarely been found, eleventh-century ones issued by Baldwin IV or V have been encountered in ones or twos in some twenty hoards in the Baltic area (Gotland, the east coast of Sweden, Poland and Letland) and on the west coast of Russia.[90] Thus, the oldest merchant settlement of the Bruges castle may have been situated in what Bruges historians have commonly called the *Groot Vierkant* (Great Square) to the northwest of the Burg, a quarter situated at a higher elevation next to the Reie and along the Hoogstraat. A chapel devoted to St Walburga may have stood there. Its date of foundation is unclear, and it only appears first in thirteenth-century sources; but St Walburga was a popular patron saint among merchants during the first half of the tenth century.[91] This quarter was situated between the Wic and the castle, so the possible presence of this chapel may support the hypothesis that an early port of trade existed in Bruges.

Thus, by the middle of the eleventh century, as the *Encomium* suggests, Bruges must have developed a commercial function of some importance in this region of Europe. Quite when this function first began to develop remains uncertain. Perhaps too, its permanence was not as yet secure: Bruges may have suffered a decrease in maritime trade during the second half of the eleventh century, as the connection to the sea temporarily became more

[89] Campbell (ed.), *Encomium*, pp. 46–50; R. Häpke, *Brügges Entwicklung zum mittelalterlichen Weltmarkt* (Berlin, 1908), p. 17; trans. M. Letts in *Bruges and its Past* (London, 1926), p. 2; and D. Nicholas, *Medieval Flanders* (London, 1992), p. 36.

[90] N. Bauer, 'Die Russischen Funde abendländischer Münzen des 11. und 12. Jahrhundert', *Zeitschrift für Numismatik*, 39 (1929), 1–187 (at 62, 181); Metcalf, 'Coinage', pp. 8–9; Albrecht, *Das Münzwesen*, vol. I, pp. 52–3 and vol. II, table 5 and map 9.

[91] Koch, 'Brugge's topografische ontwikkeling', 38–48.

difficult.[92] Nevertheless, its increasing importance as a domanial and government centre is shown by its continuing ability to attract trade overland. It was also developing as a significant religious centre, its prestigious relics and institutions attracting visitors bringing alms and other gifts. In 1058 'a great crowd of clergy and people' left the Bruges *castellum* to meet a procession carrying the relics of St Lewinna across the coastal plain. Crowds form part of a hagiographic topos, but it is possibly telling that when the procession arrived in other towns and villages, no mention is made of any abundance of people living in them.[93] From the mid eleventh century onwards Bruges would continue to grow in size and importance.

The Suburbium of the Oudeburg

By the beginning of the twelfth century, the port at the Spiegelrei would have found itself in a somewhat peripheral location within the expanding agglomeration. The part of town in which it lay was encircled by waterways, and formed part of the Great Square around the original *castrum*. The waterways now known as the Groene Rei and the Sint-Annarei were segments of the natural course of the Reie, while the Spiegelrei and the Kraanrei had been turned into canals, a process assisted by natural depressions in the landscape. The Kraanrei might have been dug to bring maritime transport closer to what had by then become the heart of the city, the square now known as the Markt. Or it might have been constructed for military reasons, closing off the Burg with ditches as an advanced line of defence.[94] If so, the *castellum* mentioned in the *Encomium Emmae reginae* may have been referring to the entire area of the Great Square, encircled by waterways, in other words to the *burgus* and its *Vorburg*. This kind of geographical layout fits with a model of economic growth that stresses the importance of a castle economy thriving around a major residence of strong Flemish counts like Arnulf I and Baldwin V – an economy interacting with the increase in overseas trade in luxury goods that followed from changes to commercial

[92] Verhulst, 'Les origines', 48.

[93] *Acta sanctorum, Julii*, vol. V (Paris and Rome, 1867), p. 625.

[94] G. De Poerck, 'Enceintes castrales et urbaines à Bruges', in *Premier congrès international de géographie historique*, 3 vols. (Brussels, 1931), vol. II, p. 82; F.-L. Ganshof, 'Iets over Brugge gedurende de preconstitutioneele periode van haar geschiedenis', *Nederlandsche Historiebladen*, 1 (1939), 281–303 (at 284–5); J. Dhondt, 'De vroege topografie van Brugge', *HMG*, 11 (1957), 5–13 (at 9–10); E. I. Strubbe, 'Van de eerste naar de tweede omwalling van Brugge', *HGG*, 100 (1963), 271–300 (at 271–2). On the 'Great Square' as 'Vorburg': Declercq, 'Oorsprong', pp. 37–8.

dynamics in the North Sea after the Viking Age. The growing agricultural surpluses from the large comital demesnes arriving at early urban centres such as Bruges further stimulated both regional and inter-regional trade.[95] As outlined above, the *fisci* of Snellegem (mentioned in 941), Weinebrugge (mentioned in 962) and Maldegem (mentioned shortly before 941) probably belonged to the counts in the late ninth century. Thereafter, the Flemish comital dynasty usurped many demesnes from abbeys and other ecclesiastical institutions in the region, including pastoral land for sheep, vital to cloth production.[96] Moreover, under the impulse of important abbeys from inland Flanders, such as St Peter's and St Bavo's in Ghent, and of the count himself, the royal demesnes at the edge of the coastal plain, and marshlands on the plain, were now being used as *terrae ad oves*, meadow land for sheep.[97] Thus, Bruges probably became a centre that concentrated and redistributed agricultural products, which itself stimulated general urban economic growth.

At first sight, then, the development of Bruges appears to fit the bipolar model of urban morphogenesis. A topographic dualism between *castrum* and *suburbium* – between the fortress and the agglomeration of merchants and artisans – is apparent. Besides the military, administrative and clerical *castrum*, *castellum* or *burgus*, there was the *portus* or *vicus* of the Wic (assuming the name existed before the thirteenth century). However, there was also a third nucleus, referred to in the sources as a *suburbium*, named the Vetus Burgus or the Oudeburg. A charter of 1089 mentions a 'castellum forinsecum', though it remains unclear if this denotes the Great Square area or the Oudeburg.[98] The presence of this third nucleus provides a strong argument for replacing the bipolar model of growth with a tripolar one.

This locality called the Oudeburg had long functioned as an agrarian market and settlement for an artisanal economy. Probably at the end of the ninth century, the first two parish churches of the city had been erected near the Oudeburg, respectively dedicated to St Saviour and Our Lady. In the eleventh century some chapels were already in place next to St Donatian's (see Chapter 2). The area that formed the Oudeburg quarter was enclosed

95 A. Verhulst, 'La ville et son émergence en Flandre', in P. Demolon and H. Galinié (eds.), *Archéologie des villes dans le Nord-Ouest de l'Europe (VIIe – XIIIe siècle)* (Douai, 1994), pp. 41–6.

96 Declercq, 'Vlaanderen', 13.

97 Verhulst, 'Das Bezitsverzeichnis'; D. Tys, 'Domeinvorming in de 'wildernis' en de ontwikkeling van vorstelijke macht. Het voorbeeld van het bezit van de graven van Vlaanderen in het IJzerestuarium tussen 900 en 1200', *Jaarboek voor Middeleeuwse Geschiedenis*, 7 (2004), 31–83.

98 On these terms, see Van Werveke, "*Burgus*"; C. Wyffels, '"Voetnoot" bij urbs, suburbium en vetus urbs', *Archief- en Bibliotheekwezen van België*, 42 (1971), 289–93.

by the current Steenstraat, the street now called Oude Burg, the Wollestraat and the Simon Stevinplein. The Oudeburg suburb thus directly adjoined the Burg itself, though it is unclear if it was fortified. There is archaeological evidence in this area of several stone houses, dating to the twelfth century, and this is only a partial indication of settlement since houses constructed of wood in Bruges (that is, the great majority) have left no trace. The name Oudeburg should be translated as 'the old borough' and must have been a settlement of artisans and merchants.[99] As a result of digging the Kraanrei ditch around the fortified zone, the central sandy ridge of Bruges was cut through, and the stronghold became more isolated from the western part of town between the Market and the Zand. Town-plan analysis also shows that the Oudeburg quarter, and notably the current Simon Stevinplein, was in all likelihood the first central market square, around which Bruges radio-concentrically developed.[100]

Thus, it seems that the city's economic centre of gravity shifted from the Wic towards the Oudeburg; and this probably occurred when Bruges' access to the sea once again became more difficult during the later eleventh century.[101] During the same period Flemish overland trade was stimulated by new roads and by the economic development of inner Flanders along the axis that ran through Bruges, Torhout, Ieper, Mesen, Lille and Aire. Economic growth had also been stimulated by the counts, notably Baldwin V, who constructed or renovated a belt of castles in these places and encouraged in some of them the foundation and development of collegiate churches.[102] The Bruges Steenstraat – on the sandy ridge that had been the traditional route for overland commerce and, as we have seen, a route of Roman or even earlier origin – was part of this axis; and it passed through the Oudeburg settlement, where, at the square now called the Simon Stevinplein, it joined the roads from Ghent and Kortrijk: this confluence of routes likely stimulated the market function of the Oudeburg. It was there that the parish church of St Saviour and to the south the parish church of Our Lady were established, testifying to concentrations of people in this area. Under Count Robert the Frisian (r.1071–93) the Flemish system of annual fairs also gradually started to function, to which Bruges seems to

[99] Van Werveke, *"Burgus"*, pp. 49–53; M. Ryckaert, 'De Oudeburg te Brugge', in *Album Albert Schouteet* (Bruges, 1973), pp. 155–68; Ryckaert, *Historische stedenatlas*, p. 49.

[100] Ryckaert, *Historische stedenatlas*, pp. 48–9, 64; Ryckaert and Hillewaert, 'De vroegste', p. 151.

[101] Verhulst, 'Les origines', 48–9.

[102] J. Dhondt, 'Développement urbain et initiative comtale en Flandre au XIe siècle', *RN*, 30 (1948), 133–56 (at 152–6); G. Declercq, 'Le comte Baudouin V de Flandre et les origines urbaines de Lille', *BTFG*, 89 (2011), 227–38.

have been connected, although there is no evidence of a fair in the town itself (and one would only be established in 1200).[103]

So was the 'Old Borough' older than the Koetelwic? Or did the two nuclei develop at the same time in the shadow of the fortress, the first being oriented to overland agricultural commerce and the second to maritime trade? Only new archaeological data will allow decisive answers. We can only conclude that for Bruges, as for many other medieval towns, different nuclei played roles of varying importance in stimulating urban growth before the twelfth century. Before Bruges became a centre for international trade in the thirteenth century, however, the primary importance of the Oudeburg as the most thriving area of the city is undeniable. Town-plan analysis demonstrates that this settlement grew spontaneously but intensively, in all likelihood from the tenth century. Sources from later periods show that meat was traded on the Simon Stevinplein, in the 'Meat House' of the butchers, and the cattle market took place at the Zand Square (the Sands), showing an orientation of this part of town to local and regional trade which may well have begun much earlier. The international business community, however, would continue to be localized in the Great Square and along the Kraanrei and the Spiegelrei, where the portuary zone of Bruges would eventually develop to its fullest extent.[104]

In the meantime, by 1100 at the latest, the new market (called the Forum in 1127–8) was shifted from the Simon Stevinplein to the current Markt, on a swampy terrain which was gradually drained (and which had originally functioned as a fishmarket). The new market square found itself in the middle of the Wik/Great Square merchant zone, the castle and clerical zone of the Burg, and the Oudeburg quarter. This indicates that by 1100, these different proto-urban quarters had been united into a single urban territory and the new market square had become the centre where regional and international commerce drew together. It was there, probably during the final decades of the twelfth century, that a merchant hall (first mentioned in 1208) would also be constructed, where cloth and other commodities were traded.[105]

[103] M. Yamada, 'Le mouvement de foires en Flandre avant 1200', in J.-M. Duvosquel and A. Dierkens (eds.), *Villes et campagnes au Moyen Âge: Mélanges Georges Despy* (Liège, 1991), pp. 773–89; J. A. Van Houtte, *De geschiedenis van Brugge* (Tielt, 1982), p. 85.

[104] M. Ryckaert, 'Les origines et l'histoire ancienne de Bruges: L'état de la question et quelques données nouvelles', in Duvosquel and Thoen (eds.), *Peasants and Townsmen*, pp. 117–34.

[105] A. Duclos, *Bruges: Histoire et souvenirs* (Bruges, 1910), pp. 449–52; Ryckaert, *Historische stedenatlas*, pp. 160–1.

Economic Take-off in the Eleventh Century

This unification of the urban territory by the early twelfth century also matches the general historiographical picture of decisive urban growth in Flanders and the southern Low Countries during the eleventh century. Indeed, the urban development of Bruges is better understood when set within this wider context. In the Low Countries and Northern France under Carolingian rule, the principal urban centres had been Huy, Dinant, Namur and Maastricht on the Meuse River; Ghent, Tournai and Valenciennes on the Scheldt; Quentovic at the estuary of the Canche; and Dorestad in the Rhine delta. These places formed the oldest network of urban settlements that, apart from Tournai and Maastricht, lacked bishops and hence were not called *civitates*. After Dorestad and other *emporia* had lost their function, new centres such as Tiel and Deventer became the main ports of the Low Countries. During this period, aside from its military importance, the economic function of Bruges was probably still a modest one (notwithstanding hypotheses for the presence of a maritime port). As argued, Count Arnulf's reign had an impact on the growth of the proto-urban cores of Bruges, as the town was already called a *vicus* and a *portus* in the mid tenth century. The real take-off of the city, however, was in the eleventh century, as shown by the enthusiastic description of it in the *Encomium Emmae reginae* around 1041–2. If by the year 1000 Bruges was already active as a centre with military, judicial, ecclesiastical, demesne and market functions, it thenceforward became part of a general acceleration in urban development taking place throughout the southern Low Countries. In the eleventh century, a number of proto-urban centres such as Ypres, Valenciennes, Saint-Omer, Douai and Lille, for which no Roman past can be traced, rose to become major towns. But older episcopal *civitates* like Arras, Cambrai and Tournai also began to enjoy a new prosperity.[106]

Henri Pirenne explained urban growth between the ninth and the eleventh centuries with reference to the contiguity of fortress and merchant agglomeration, to the primary role of commerce and artisanal production in town formation, and to the notion that wandering merchants were attracted to new centres of growth. It was not long before scholars such as Des Marez, Lyna and Despy, in a dialogue with similar historiographical debates in Germany and elsewhere, criticized this thesis and instead

[106] Verhulst, *Rise of Cities*, passim; S. Lebecq, 'Pour une histoire parallèle de Quentovic et Dorestad', in Duvosquel and Dierkens (eds.), *Villes et campagnes*, pp. 415–28; S. Coupland, 'Trading Places: Quentovic and Dorestad Reassessed', *Early Medieval Europe*, 11 (2002), 209–32.

emphasized an internal dynamic in which towns developed from castle or abbey domains in the context of a general economic upheaval, from the ninth century, characterized by commercial recovery and demographic growth.[107] As Pirennian orthodoxy prevailed in Belgian historiography until the 1980s, the views of these critics were marginal, but following the work of scholars like Verhulst and Devroey and historiographical debates on other European regions, they are now generally accepted.[108] Although primary sources shed little light on Flemish economic growth before the end of the twelfth century, it is clear enough that growth was directly related to a rise in agricultural productivity, to regional specialization and inter-regional exchange as well as to social developments.[109] In other words, urban and commercial growth would have been impossible without rural development and an increase in population: these created surpluses which could be transformed into a more broad-based economic development.[110]

According to Verhulst, until the tenth century wealth had been concentrated in the hands of the aristocracy and the church at the expense of the unfree and half-free peasants. Between the end of the seventh and the first quarter of the ninth centuries, this had led to a greater circulation of luxury goods in *emporia* like Dorestad and Quentovic. After their downfall during the later ninth century, new trading places came into existence, though these were not yet fully 'towns'. Merchants traded in the service of the king, or of bishops and abbeys, but in all likelihood for their own profit too. As the ties between the peasants and the demesnes loosened and population increased, immigrants from the countryside settled in proto-urban agglomerations and became permanently engaged in artisanal production.[111] In the case of Bruges and its hinterland, it seems that the

107 Van Uytven, 'Les origines', pp. 16, 22; G. Des Marez, 'De la phase préconstitutionnelle dans la formation des villes belges', in G. Des Marez, *Études inédites publiées par un groupe de ses anciens élèves* (Brussels, 1936), pp. 47–68; J. Lyna, 'Aperçu historique sur les origines urbaines dans le comté de Looz et subsidiairement dans la vallée de la Meuse', *Bulletin de l'Institut Archéologique Liégeois*, 55 (1931), 5–103; G. Despy, 'Villes et campagnes aux IXe et Xe siècles: L'exemple du pays mosan', *RN*, 50 (1968), 145–68.

108 J.-P. Devroey and Ch. Zoller, 'Villes, campagnes, croissance agraire dans le pays mosan avant l'An Mil, vingt ans après', in Duvosquel and Dierkens (eds.), *Villes et campagnes*, pp. 223–60.

109 R. Doehaerd, *L'expansion économique belge au Moyen Âge* (Brussels, 1940); A. Verhulst, 'The Alleged Poverty of the Flemish Rural Economy as Reflected in the Oldest Account of the Comital Domain known as "Gros Brief" (A.D. 1187)', in E. Aerts et al. (eds.), *Studia Historica Oeconomica: Liber amicorum Herman Van der Wee* (Leuven, 1993), pp. 369–82; D. Nicholas, 'Of Poverty and Primacy: Demand, Liquidity and the Flemish Economic Miracle, 1050–1200', *American Historical Review*, 96 (1991), 17–41.

110 D. J. Keene, 'Towns and the Growth of Trade', in D. Luscombe and J. Riley-Smith (eds.), *The New Cambridge Medieval History*, vol. IV (Cambridge, 2004), p. 53.

111 Verhulst, *Rise of Cities*, pp. 153–5.

combination of a more productive rural economy – stimulated by the accelerating embankment of the coastal plain, probably by peasants of free status or with few servile duties, and by a rising demand for fuel, notably peat, and for foodstuffs – and of a market for luxury products ultimately led to the strong economic growth that characterized the period between about 1050 and 1270. Around the mid twelfth century, as we shall see in Chapter 3, a whole range of goods was already being imported to Bruges by merchants from Cologne.[112]

Even more important than the role of international trade is the fact that, from the beginning of the eleventh century, inter-regional commercial circulation in Flanders had also steadily increased. New towns and markets took shape, and this process would continue throughout the twelfth century. Perhaps from the end of the eleventh century and certainly from the beginning of the twelfth, trade overland increased, passing the cities of Brabant to make an important connection with Cologne.[113] Moreover, shortly before 1100, the Flemish textile industry changed profoundly as weaving became a predominantly male and urban activity and the horizontal loom was adopted. The expansion of the Flemish textile industry, which increasingly produced for foreign markets, also contributed to the economic rise of the region.[114] The creation of an annual fair in Bruges in 1200 showed that by then the town had become a hub linking the landed markets to the sea, with Flemish textiles being the main export product. And the favourable political situation should not be underestimated in the process: an almost uninterrupted series of strong Flemish counts beginning with Baldwin IV (r.988–1035) played an important role by providing merchants with an increasingly secure environment for commerce. Baldwin IV had managed to restore strong central power in Flanders. During his reign and that of his son Baldwin V, the Peace and Truce of God movement gained momentum in Flanders, which stimulated conditions conducive to trade.[115]

Erik Thoen has convincingly argued that elite demand for luxury products played the key role in stimulating both trade and artisanal production

[112] A. Verhulst, T. de Hemptinne and L. De Mey, 'Un tarif de tonlieu inconnu, institué par le comte de Flandre Thierry d'Alsace pour le port de Littersuerua, précurseur du port de Damme', *Handelingen van de Koninklijke Commissie voor Geschiedenis*, 164 (1998), 143–72; and J. De Groote, 'Het toltarief van Letterswerve', *Rond de Poldertorens*, 42 (2000), 18–28.

[113] P. Bonenfant, 'L'origine des villes brabançonnes et la route de Bruges à Cologne', *BTFG*, 31 (1953), 399–447; Van Houtte, 'De opkomst', 7.

[114] Yamada, 'Le mouvement'.

[115] H. Platelle, 'La violence et ses remèdes en Flandre au XIe siècle', *Sacris Erudiri*, 20 (1971), 101–73.

in Flanders.[116] David Nicholas has also emphasized the importance of this demand factor for what he has called the 'Flemish economic miracle', though he attributes less significance than Thoen to the simultaneous development of Flemish agriculture.[117] The agents of seigniorial power who lived close to castles in the early urban agglomerations usually included *milites*, *monetarii*, goldsmiths, publicans, demesne receivers, people who farmed windmills, and collectors of tithes, rents and other levies. The presence in Bruges of a large fortification, and the fact that by the tenth century the town had become one of the main centres of comital administration, and where demesne revenues were concentrated, undoubtedly contributed to the local demand for wine, salt, metalry and luxury items (perhaps originally imported by 'Frisians', 'Saxons' and Scandinavians, later on also by merchants from Cologne).[118] These castle elites also engaged in commercial activities; but most of all, it was their purchasing power, and that of the clerics serving the main churches, that must have provided a crucial stimulus to the urban economy.[119]

The purchasing power of the elites was undoubtedly based partly on the growing production in their domains. The count's own revenues, drawn mostly from his demesne land, were similarly growing, and these were in turn partly redistributed to comital retainers. As we have seen, Bruges was situated in the midst of large *fisci*. To the north and east there were the wastelands of the coastal area, the marshlands (*schorren*) and moorlands (*moeren*) and the dunes.[120] A significant part of the comital domain was concentrated in the coastal plain of Flanders. Even before the year 1000, stockbreeding had been important in the Flemish coastal area. Sheep and cows were being reared in large numbers to produce meat, dairy and wool to sell at agricultural markets. From the mid eleventh century, the revenues from the count's sheep farms on salt marshes, the *terrae ad oves* in the coastal area, strongly increased, and the production of peat in comital *mori* or moorlands also turned a profit.[121] A lot of peat was produced on the

[116] E. Thoen, 'The Count, the Countryside and the Economic Development of the Towns in Flanders from the Eleventh to the Thirteenth Century: Some Provisional Remarks and Hypotheses', in Aerts et al. (eds.), *Studia Historica Oeconomica*, pp. 260–2.

[117] Nicholas, 'Of Poverty'.

[118] Rhineland merchants are certainly present in the Zwin estuary by 1150: see Verhulst et al., 'Un tarif'.

[119] Compare with C. Wickham, 'Rethinking the Structure of the Early Medieval Economy', in J. R. Davis and M. McCormick (eds.), *The Long Morning of Medieval Europe: New Directions in Early Medieval Studies* (Aldershot, 2008), pp. 19–32.

[120] Thoen, 'The Count', p. 261; L. Voet, 'De graven van Vlaanderen en hun domein', *Wetenschappelijke Tijdingen*, 7 (1942), cols. 25–31.

[121] Tys, 'Domeinvorming'.

marshlands and moorlands of the coastal area and on inland terrains with older peat found underground. The peat was used in industrial activities such as cloth-dying, brickworks, beer production and salt making. It was also used as household fuel, so the growth of the urban population further triggered demand for it.[122] Moreover, Flemish agriculture was very dynamic by medieval standards. The three-field rotation system seems to have been present earlier than in other regions, and horses were used by peasants at an early stage instead of the far less productive oxen.[123]

Apart from agriculture, the coastal population was intensively engaged in herring fishing, and probably also in trade and piracy. Flemish exports might have included salt, fish and dairy products but certainly wool and cloth. As we have seen, whether 'Frisian cloths' of the Carolingian period were mostly or partly Flemish is open to debate, but by the end of the eleventh century Flemish cloth was widely known as an export product and the county had established a reputation for high-quality cloth.[124] Adding to this mechanism of economic growth, the importance of the Bruges fortress, with its storehouses and cellars (*lardaria*, *spiccaria*, *vaccaria*), was augmented by the political reorganization of the county in the eleventh century – which will be discussed shortly. From that period onwards the Oudeburg quarter of Bruges seems to have functioned as an important regional market for these products.[125] Near the fortress, whether in the Oudeburg or next to the comital residence and the ecclesiastical complex of St Donatian's in the Great Square, arms, textiles and leather products were also manufactured. The surpluses of these industries were partly consumed by the castle residents themselves, but they could also be sold elsewhere, further stimulating the early Bruges economy.[126]

At the same time, the export of Flemish luxury cloth and the import of English wool became increasingly important. A London toll tariff, usually dated to about 1000 and attributed to King Aethelred II, but perhaps dating from the reign of Cnut (1016–35), also records the customs governing the arrival of foreign merchants in port. Men from Ponthieu, Normandy, France and some Meuse cities in Lotharingia are listed, but also mentioned

[122] Verhulst, 'Alleged Poverty', p. 380; Tys, 'Medieval Embankment', p. 208.

[123] Thoen, 'The Count', pp. 264–72.

[124] Verhulst, 'Origins of Towns', p. 33.

[125] Verhulst, *Rise of Cities*, p. 78.

[126] Compare with A. Verhulst, 'Grundherrschaftliche Aspekte bei der Entstehung der Städte Flanderus', in Verhulst and Y. Morimoto (eds.), *Économie rurale et économie urbaine au Moyen Âge* (Ghent and Fukuoka, 1994), pp. 157–64; and E. Thoen, 'Le démarrage économique de la Flandre au Moyen Âge: Le rôle de la campagne et des structures politiques (XIe–XIIIe siècles)', in Verhulst and Morimoto (eds.), *Économie rurale*, pp. 165–84.

are the 'Flemish': among these were probably merchants from Bruges.[127] Flemish–English trade grew during the eleventh and twelfth centuries and Bruges was a participating port.[128] Bruges was familiar to the inhabitants of England. The Anglo-Saxon Chronicle shows how Anglo-Saxon and Anglo-Danish exiles, between 1037 and 1052, regularly took refuge at the court of Baldwin V in Bruges, using the town as a base to plot armed returns to England or as a staging post between England and Denmark. Gunhilde, daughter of Godwin, earl of Wessex, and sister of King Harold, died in Bruges in 1087 where she had fled after the Battle of Hastings: her name appears on a memorial inscription on a small sheet of lead, found in the cloister of St Donatian's. She had also donated an important relic to this church, the cloak of the Holy Bridget. The canons celebrated her obit thereafter.[129]

In short, a picture emerges of Bruges as a settlement steadily growing from the ninth century to become, in the eleventh, a fully fledged 'city' that not only served as a military, administrative and religious centre, but also, by the standards of this period, played a major role in overseas commerce, artisanal industry and the regional distribution of goods. This picture has had to be constructed from a variety of fragmented sources; but in the early twelfth century we suddenly have available to us a source that reveals topography and urban life in startling detail: the chronicle of Galbert of Bruges.[130]

Social Groups and Political Power

Galbert's chronicle was written in the immediate aftermath of the murder of Count Charles the Good who ruled Flanders between 1119 and 1127;

[127] Van Houtte, 'De opkomst', 10; F. Liebermann (ed.), *Die Gesetze der Angelsachsen*, 3 vols. (Halle, 1903), vol. I, pp. 32–237; N. Middleton, 'Early Medieval Port Customs, Tolls and Control on Foreign Trade', *Early Medieval Europe*, 13 (2005), 313–58.

[128] Häpke, *Brügges Entwicklung*, pp. 48–9.

[129] P. Grierson, 'The Relations between England and Flanders before the Norman Conquest', *Transactions of the Royal Historical Society*, 4th series, 23 (1947), 71–112; F. Barlow, *Edward the Confessor* (London, 1970), pp. 47–8, 80, 91, 100–1, 114, 120, 122; F. Barlow, *The Godwins: The Rise and Fall of a Noble Dynasty* (Harlow, 2002), p. 120; W. C. Robinson, 'Une fille de Godwin', *Annales de la Société d'Émulation de Bruges*, 53 (1903), 31–48; and see in general the recent work by E. Oksanen, *Flanders and the Anglo-Norman World, 1066–1216* (Cambridge, 2012), esp. pp. 148–53.

[130] J. Rider (ed.), *Galbertus Brugensis: De multro, traditione, et occisione gloriosi Karoli comitis Flandriarum* (Turnhout, 1994); M. Ryckaert and J. M. Murray, 'Bruges in 1127', in J. Rider (ed.), *The Murder, Betrayal, and Slaughter of the Glorious Charles, Count of Flanders*, by Galbert of Bruges (New Haven, CT, 2013), pp. lvii–lxxv. On biographical data for Galbert, see J. Rider, *God's Scribe: The Historiographical Art of Galbert of Bruges* (Washington, DC, 2001).

and in describing the calamitous events of 1127–8, it sheds unprecedented light on the social and political structure of the town in Galbert's day, if not before. Bruges' population then may be guessed at around 5,000 (as a maximum figure, given its surface area of 70 hectares, and comparison with other Flemish towns);[131] but without Galbert's account we can tell little about its social composition. Galbert distinguishes between the *castrenses* living in the *castrum* and the burghers (*burgenses, cives, suburbani, vicini*) inhabiting the *suburbium*, but his narrative does not present them as living in separate worlds. Neither were Galbert's city-dwellers as separated from the surrounding countryside as they would be in later centuries. High medieval towns were often surrounded by gardens and meadows, and the first artisans who worked and lived in Bruges were probably still partly engaged in agricultural activities.[132] Social divisions among the city-dwellers already existed but were not yet as clear-cut as they would later become. Galbert writes about a knight who fought in the service of the city, perhaps a mercenary, and he also talks of working men such as 'artifices et operaios' or 'carpentariis'. He mentions a burgher who was related to a nobleman, another burgher who was the brother-in-law of a knight, and another knight who adopted the child of a shoemaker. Lineage formation was perhaps a priority only for the higher nobility, and in this nascent urban society social structures were still relatively fluid and dynamic. The group Galbert calls the 'sapientiores', 'meliores' or 'civibus seniores et prudentiores', certainly ruled in the city, but they do not yet fully resemble a so-called 'oligarchic' or 'patrician class', which came to dominate the city in the thirteenth century.[133]

The most powerful elites in Bruges during the eleventh century, however, were still the great men in the service of the count. Baldwin V (r.1035–67) subdivided the territory of Flanders into 'castellanies' (*castellatura* or *castellania* in Latin, *kasselrijen* in Dutch, *châtellenies* in French) with a *castrum* as a centre and under the authority of a castellan.[134] The castellany of

[131] Nicholas, 'Of Poverty', p. 18.

[132] Chédeville et al., *La ville médiévale*, pp. 99–102.

[133] Rider (ed.), *Galbertus Brugensis*, pp. 137, 146; A. Derville, *Les villes de Flandre et d'Artois (900–1500)* (Lille, 2002), p. 91.

[134] A. C. F. Koch, 'Die flandrischen Burggrafschaften: Wesenszüge und Entstehung', *Zeitschrift der Savigny-Stiftung für Rechtsgeschichte. Germanistische Abteilung*, 76 (1959), 153–72, thought that castellanies originated at the end of the tenth century, while J. Dhondt, 'Note sur les châtelains de Flandre', in *Études historiques dédiées à la mémoire de Roger Rodière* (Arras, 1947), pp. 43–51, considered them introduced by Baldwin V. As several castellanies and castellans are mentioned for the first time during the reign of Baldwin V, there is good reason to follow Dhondt. The arguments advanced by Koch are less convincing.

Bruges, first mentioned in 1066, was created from the *Pagus Flandrensis*, the *Pagus Rodanensis* and the northern part of the *Pagus Mempiscus*. It had its own 'bench' of aldermen, the *scabini Brugenses*, first recorded in 1094, who were nominated for life by the count and who assembled in the *aula comitis* at the Burg, or sometimes in other places, such as the house of Isaac, the count's chamberlain, in 1115.[135] Thus, by the mid eleventh century, the strongest man in Bruges in the absence of the count was the castellan (*castellanus*, *vicecomes*, *burggraaf*, *châtelain*). He commanded the *milites* of the castle and could mobilize soldiers in the whole region. He was responsible for the fortifications but he did not hold the comital castle in fief, being responsible only for its *custodia*. He could impose a corvée on the inhabitants of the castellany of Bruges called the *balfart*, to maintain its walls and ditches (a relic from servile times which in the rural castellany would be abolished only in the thirteenth century).[136] The castellan was also the main judicial and police officer, holding a part of the count's rights of high justice or *comitatus* and accordingly competent to deal with all types of crime. He presided over the aldermen of the castellany, the *scabini terrae*, and he commanded lower officers who also had jurisdiction in Bruges, such as the *amman* (*praeco*) and the *schout* (*scultetus*) or sheriff. Most Flemish castellans were descended from families who had been 'noble' before the year 1000, and who comprised the Carolingian and post-Carolingian upper class, while the *milites* of the castle were 'warriors' rather than men who in the twelfth century would become known as 'knights'.[137]

The origin of the office of castellan in Bruges is obscure. A certain Robert, mentioned in a charter of 1046, is often cited as its first holder. However, as this document is a forgery, his existence is dubious; and according to Galbert's chronicle, a man named Boldranus, whose wife was called Dedda or Duva, appears to have been castellan around 1050. Later, this Boldran was rumoured to have been murdered by his vassal Erembald who then married

[135] F.-L. Ganshof, *Recherches sur les tribunaux de châtellenie en Flandre avant le milieu du XIIIe siècle* (Antwerp, 1932), pp. 10, 15–17, 75; F.-L. Ganshof, 'Anmerkungen zu einer flandrischen Schenkungsurkunde des frühen 12. Jahrhunderts', in H. Beumann (ed.), *Historische Forschungen für Walter Schlesinger* (Cologne and Vienna, 1974), pp. 215–25; E. Warlop, 'De vorming van de grote schepenbank van het Brugse Vrije (11de – 13de eeuw)', *Standen en Landen*, 44 (1968), 1–28 (at 1–5). On Flemish institutions during the early and central Middle Ages in general, see F.-L. Ganshof, 'La Flandre', in F. Lot and R. Fawtier (eds.), *Histoire des institutions françaises au Moyen Âge*, 3 vols. (Paris, 1957), vol. I, pp. 343–426.

[136] C. Verlinden, 'Le balfart, corvée-redevance pour l'entretien des fortifications en Flandre au Moyen Âge', *Revue d'Histoire du Droit*, 12 (1933), 107–36.

[137] E. Warlop, *The Flemish Nobility before 1300*, 2 vols. (Kortrijk, 1975–6), vol. I, pp. 135–54.

his widow.[138] One Erembald is mentioned as castellan in a forged charter of 1067, but the list of witnesses seems reliable and was possibly copied from a genuine document.[139] Erembald only regularly figures as castellan of Bruges in sources from the years 1084–9, and in the *Vita Arnulphi*, a saint's life by Abbot Hariulf of Oudenburg, he is called a *pretor* in 1084, clearly a literary term for his office. In that year, the castellan and some *prudentes viri*, probably the aldermen of the castellany, were ordered by Count Robert to organize an inquiry into the high number of murders and private wars in the Bruges region ('Brugensis coloniae vel aliorum locorum') – which meant both in the city and in the surrounding region, as comital jurisdiction in the urban territory had not yet been separated from jurisdiction in the rural castellany.[140] Galbert's story suggests that this Erembald had effectively become castellan of Bruges around the mid eleventh century. He had supposedly been of unfree origin and had entered into the service of the castellan Boldran. Boldran probably disappeared during a comital expedition on the Scheldt River which can be dated to 1055: the story of his murder was probably inspired by rumours that Erembald had been his wife's lover; and Erembald did marry his widow.[141] Erembald was probably also involved in the successful coup that Count Robert the Frisian organized against his sister-in-law Countess Richilde of Hainaut and her son Count Arnulf III. In 1071 Bruges, Ghent and Ypres may have sent men to support Robert against Richilde.[142] As Robert landed on the coast north of Bruges, Erembald must have played some role in this affair and this might have strengthened his position as the local strongman in Bruges, unconditionally loyal to the count and his policies.

Erembald remained castellan until 1089, but in 1087 his son and successor Robert was already acting as castellan for his father. After Robert's death, probably in 1109, he was succeeded by his son Walter (1110–1115) who was in his turn succeeded by his uncle Haket (also a son of Erembald and thus a brother of Robert). In 1091 another son of Erembald, Bertulf, became provost of St Donatian's and chancellor of Flanders. Thus the Erembald clan,

[138] G. Blancquaert, 'L'expédition contre Anvers en 1055 et les premiers châtelains de Bruges', *Annales de la Société Royale d'Archéologie de Bruxelles*, 46 (1942–3), 167–71.

[139] These first mentions of the Bruges castellans can be found in Warlop, *Flemish Nobility*, vol. I, pp. 113–17 and 411–14 (though the charters of 1046 and 1067 should be used with caution).

[140] Ganshof, *Recherches*, p. 62; O. Holder-Egger (ed.), 'Ex Vita Arnulfi Episcopi Suessionensis Auct. Hariulfo Abbate Aldenburgensi', in *Monumenta Germaniae Historia. Scriptores* (Hanover, 1888), vol. XVI^2, p. 890 (written shortly before 1120).

[141] Warlop, *Flemish Nobility*, vol. I, pp. 113–14.

[142] C. Verlinden, *Robert Ier le Frison, comte de Flandre: Étude d'histoire politique* (Antwerp, 1935), pp. 64–5.

strong men but from servile origin, clearly enjoyed comital favour under three successive counts (Robert the Frisian, Robert II and Baldwin VII). Combining military power with spiritual authority, this family effectively ruled Bruges in the absence of the count in the decades before and after 1100.[143] Fortune turned against them, however, when Charles the Good, son of the king of Denmark, became count in 1119. An ambitious count, Charles tried to clip their power and use their unfree origins against them. As a member of the Erembald clan responsible for the murder of Count Charles the Good, Haket had to flee from Bruges in 1127 and was replaced by Gervase, lord of Praet, a powerful Bruges nobleman. Between 1130 and 1133, after Gervase's dismissal, Haket apparently returned to power; yet from 1134 the office of castellan would belong to the powerful French noble family of the lords of Nesle and Soissons: Raoul, Cono and Jean from this family successively received the office from the new Alsace dynasty. During the later twelfth century, however, the castellan's powers and competences would be weakened, and undermined by a new non-hereditary comital officer of justice, the bailiff; and in 1224 Countess Joanna finally bought the office back from the Nesle family and merged it with comital authority.[144]

The fortunes of the castellans of Bruges shaped but did not ultimately change the fortunes of the town. The influence of the counts was more significant. Bruges had long been one of the main comital residences, and remained so during the eleventh century when Baldwin V promoted Bruges as one of his main towns. It is interesting in this respect that the Anglo-Saxon Chronicle sometimes calls him 'Baldwin of Bruges'.[145] Two members of the comital family died in the castle: Countess Adela in 960 and Count Baldwin VI in 1070. It was also in Bruges that Count Baldwin made his brother Robert the Frisian solemnly swear to respect the succession rights of Baldwin's son Arnulf III. Robert later usurped power, but he also seems to have used Bruges as his administrative centre.[146] His son and successor Robert II made St Donatian's chapter the centre for his Flemish finances and demesne administration. Then, on 31 October 1089, Count Robert II appointed the provost of St Donatian's as his chancellor and financial receiver ('susceptor et exactor') for the whole county and head of all *notarii*,

[143] Ryder (ed.), *Galbertus*, p. 96.

[144] Warlop, *Flemish Nobility*, vol. I, pp. 185–208, 457–72.

[145] Van Houtte, 'De opkomst', 7; Barlow, *Edward the Confessor*, pp. 97–9.

[146] G. Declercq, 'Entre mémoire dynastique et représentation politique: Les sépultures des comtes et comtesses de Flandre (879–1128)', in M. Margue (ed.), *Sépultures, mort et représentation du pouvoir au Moyen Âge/Tod, Grabmal und Herrschaftsrepräsentation im Mittelalter* (Luxemburg, 2006), pp. 321–72 (at 328, 362); Verlinden, *Robert*, p. 147.

capellani and *clerici* of his court. All local receivers were accountable to the chancellor of Flanders, and his *notarii* oversaw the accounts of the domain drawn up by the comital receivers.[147]

The *Vita Arnulphi* describes the castle as a 'palatium', a centre of comital administration where the *pretor* (the castellan) and the 'prudentes viri' (most likely the aldermen of the castellany) were summoned by the count.[148] These powerful men, warriors and comital officials also appear a generation later in Galbert's narrative: it is they, not the early merchant class, who appear to be the most powerful elite of the city. The notary Fromold for instance lived in a substantial residence; he wore the golden ring of a knight and had his own servants and clients. Most other officials such as *villici*, *majores*, *sculteti*, *ammans* and *praecones* probably enjoyed less conspicuous but still opulent lifestyles.[149] Besides Galbert's chronicle, we can also use the first preserved account of the comital domain, dating from 1187, to shed light retrospectively on these castle elites. The *custodes* at Bruges were comital servants who, from the end of the eleventh century at the latest, had to protect the offices and the storage places of the demesne revenues. One 'Lambertus notarius', a comital administrative official, was the receiver of the *Brevia de Roya*, that is, of all revenues from the region of the Reie River. The so-called *rationicatores* or 'accountable receivers' were in charge of collecting the demesne revenues. The *milites* of Bruges also appear in this source, being given a quantity of beer. And there are carpenters and other craftsmen at work. References to imported luxury products such as pepper also afford a glimpse into the luxurious lifestyles of the castle elites.[150]

The earliest charters of the counts, or of ecclesiastical institutions such as St Donatian's, indicate the presence of other individuals besides comital officials. Bruges was by no means simply a service station for the counts and their men. As in charters of other towns of the Low Countries, the names of burghers appear alongside those of canons from collegiate churches.

[147] B. Lyon and A. Verhulst, *Medieval Finance: A Comparison of Financial Institutions in Northwestern Europe* (Bruges, 1967), pp. 12–13; A. Verhulst and T. de Hemptinne, 'Le chancelier de Flandre sous les comtes de la maison d'Alsace (1128–1191)', *Handelingen van de Koninklijke Commissie voor Geschiedenis*, 141 (1975), 267–311. According to recent research by Jean-François Nieuss, the 1089 charter is a pseudo-original, however, and this passage is probably an interpolation.

[148] Holder-Egger (ed.), 'Ex Vita Arnulfi', p. 890.

[149] H. Nowé, *Les baillis comtaux de Flandre, des origines à la fin du XIVe siècle* (Brussels, 1929), p. 32; Lyon and Verhulst, *Medieval Finance*, pp. 13–15.

[150] A. Verhulst and M. Gysseling (eds.), *Le compte général de 1187 connu sous le nom de "Gros Brief" et les institutions financières du comté de Flandre au XIIe siècle* (Brussels, 1962), pp. 102, 110, 118, 128, 176.

In a witness list of a comital charter drawn up in Bruges in 1113, the last three people mentioned are 'Disdir Gildebrida', 'Folcardus frater ejus' and 'Sigaardus'. These were probably Bruges burghers and merchants. As the epithet following his name shows, Disdir may well have been a 'guild brother'. This is the only reference to indicate the existence of a merchant guild in Bruges before the thirteenth century, but by the eleventh century such guilds have been attested in other towns of the region, for instance in Tiel, Saint-Omer and Valenciennes, so the name 'Disdir Gildebrida' suggests that one also existed in Bruges.[151]

The possible presence of a merchant organization in Bruges once again raises the question about the origins of early merchants. We can only speculate whether for instance they were descended from serfs who had originally traded in the service of their masters (the count or other important lords), or whether some of them were descended, as Pirenne classically argued, from 'wandering merchants'. Pirenne's thesis may seem fanciful now, but it drew some support from the *Encomium*, which called the inhabitants of Bruges 'coloni', perhaps 'settlers' who had only recently arrived. Hariulf's early twelfth-century Life of St Arnulf also calls Bruges a *colonia*.[152] Even if a *colonus*, according to the standard dictionaries of medieval Latin, means a 'city-dweller', a 'manumitted serf' or even a 'landholder', in classical Latin it also meant 'settler'. Given that these sources were written during a period of demographic and economic growth in Flanders, it is tempting to argue that they both, independently, intended the term 'colonus' to mean 'free urban immigrant'. So perhaps Pirenne's conjectures, though based on the vague social terminology of literary sources, were not unfounded. After all, during this period of strong growth, Bruges must have attracted many new settlers seeking to engage in commercial and artisanal activities.

Was this early merchant elite supported more on regional than on long-distance trade? Was it in a fluctuating state of constant renewal or did it depend on established family connections? Was it dynamic or static? What relationship existed between the castle knights and other men of free or unfree origin? None of these questions is easy to answer, and until archaeological excavations yield new evidence, hypotheses can only be constructed by the tentative projection of later evidence back onto earlier periods. At any rate, the possession of land must have played an important part in the formation of the earliest urban elites: most cities in the southern Low

[151] Ganshof, 'Iets over Brugge', 301; F. Vercauteren, *Actes des comtes de Flandre, 1071–1128* (Brussels, 1938), no. 61.

[152] Holder-Egger (ed.), 'Ex Vita Arnulfi', p. 890.

Countries emerged from a manorial background. The earliest urban elites would have acquired land from the urban or manorial lord who could give out this land in free hereditary tenure for modest sums of money. But this process does not in itself explain why these elites extended their control over the urban landscape. Lordship was still strong in the twelfth century: in 1127 the comital rents on urban land were acquitted but many ecclesiastical rents remained and lords still had interests in urban territory. Yet by the thirteenth century, urban elites in Bruges had become properly differentiated, socially and legally, from other town-dwellers and were able to co-opt friends and relatives into offices, control tax collection, lease out urban lands, mills, fisheries, and exact payments for the use of urban scales.[153] It is safe to suppose, therefore, that the development of this control followed from the fruits of commerce: as Flemish economic activity accelerated after about 1050, wealth generated from the commercial, industrial and service sectors must have increased more rapidly than rents from landownership, although (as the next chapter will show) land rents in the city also went up in value. As we shall see (in Chapter 4), it is in the same period of economic growth, by 1100, that we can also date the beginnings of an urban 'commune'.

Thus, the location of what became Bruges proved to be a propitious one: set just inland, but with access points to the sea meeting a land route that dated back to the Roman period, it came to serve, even before the tenth century, as a centre of comital power, and played some role in a network of commercial exchange that reached beyond the surrounding region. Pirenne's original bipolar model, which gave particular importance to the *castrum* and *suburbium* in the growth of early medieval towns, does apply to Bruges (as does the significance Pirenne attributed to merchants), but is not sufficient to explain the expansion of the town from the ninth century onwards. A third main nucleus developing within the town points to the importance of the agrarian market and agricultural commerce, though this too was linked to the castle economy, the demesnes of the counts, and demands from the castle elites. Evidence from the eleventh century begins to show the various elements in this process in sharper detail: the continuing importance of the comital presence, the wider role of local and foreign trade, artisanal production, the stimulus of demand for luxury products that came from the needs of elites, landowners and merchants, who also emerge in sharper relief, and whose ambitions Galbert of Bruges purports

153 B. Van Bavel, *Manors and Markets: Economy and Society in the Low Countries, 500–1600* (Oxford, 2010), p. 117.

to record. By 1100, the three principal nuclei that had constituted the town had also become more obviously integrated into a single urban unit, and possibly, as we shall see, into an urban 'commune'. But although in the centuries that followed, Bruges would retain many of the forms and functions that it had already developed, it would also greatly expand some, create others, and would drastically alter its size and social topography in ways that often made unity difficult.

2 | The Urban Landscape I: c.1100–c.1275

JAN DUMOLYN, MARC RYCKAERT, BRIGITTE MEIJNS, HEIDI DENEWETH AND LUC DEVLIEGHER

The original growth of the early town had been conditioned by its military character but also by its favourable market location; and in the eleventh century, if not before, its commercial role already interacted with its developing political and religious functions. Between the mid twelfth century and the end of the thirteenth, however, the spatial dynamics of Bruges would be influenced by far stronger economic and demographic growth. The development of markets for local, regional and international trade stimulated specialization and further division of artisanal labour. This in turn required a sophisticated and efficient organization of production and commerce which soon overshadowed the original military, political and religious character of the city, and in ways that were typical for so many high medieval towns. Intensive economic growth, notably of a booming textile industry, attracted migrants to Bruges from all over the county of Flanders and beyond. This continuous immigration eventually caused the town to burst out of the straitjacket imposed by its first set of ramparts constructed in 1127.

The development of the urban landscape of Bruges is the primary focus of this chapter. The city witnessed a steady extension of its inhabited surface and a marked development of its architectural form largely as a result of this economic and demographic growth (see Map 2).[1] In this key period of the city's history, urban space developed in a state of constant interaction with processes of production, reproduction and circulation. Though the main focus here will be on 'material urban space', that is, on the physical landscape and the built environment, the city's morphology cannot be considered simply as a backdrop to historical events. The spatiality of medieval Bruges must not be conceived either as an inert location in which the city-dwellers lived their lives or even merely as an arena in which social and property relations were actively contested. According to Henri Lefebvre,[2] space is a productive force of society rather than simply a receptacle in

[1] The development of population, industry and commerce will be more fully explained in Chapter 3.

[2] Lefebvre, *La production de l'espace.*

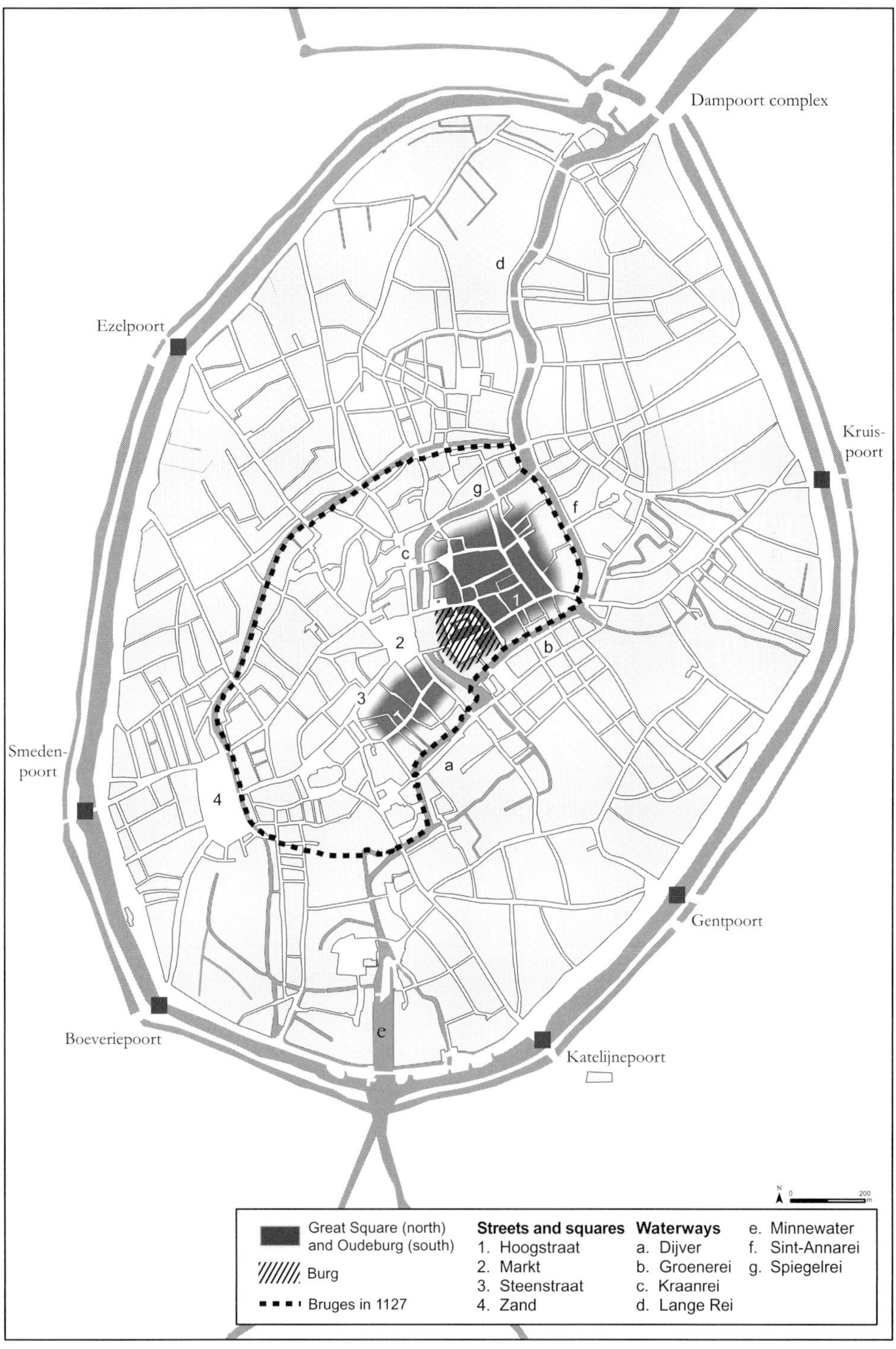

Map 2 Bruges with (1) Great Square, Burg, and (2) city ramparts, gates and waterways

which social actions take place. Urban space is as much about social and political relations, ideological representation and symbolic power as it is about economics and demography.[3] In order to grasp fully how the urban tissue of Bruges was created by the agency of various social groups and institutions, each with their own socio-economic, political and symbolic agendas,[4] we need a prior understanding of the landscape relief, soil and hydrography. The material setting of the city interacted with changes on the macro and meso levels, such as town–countryside relations, demographic growth, socio-economic diversification and functional specialization of certain quarters, as well as with the judicial and political subdivisions of the urban landscape. But it was also shaped on a micro level in relation to changes in housing, public buildings and infrastructure.

Urban historians have long been aware that no medieval town, least of all a developing commercial centre, can be considered in isolation from its surroundings. Bruges had numerous 'central place' functions providing goods and services, not only as a market but also as a centre offering judicial, administrative, devotional, cultural, charitable and medical services to its rural hinterland and the smaller towns within the region.[5] From the thirteenth century onwards at the latest, these functions of production and distribution that were directed towards the surrounding zone interacted more and more with the developing role of the city in international commerce. Thus, to understand its internal morphological development, Bruges must be studied as a node in the medieval urban network. Its morphogenesis has to be explained in relation to its agricultural hinterland, to the Flemish economic and transport system, to the Zwin Estuary and its portuary system (the outports of Damme, Hoeke, Monnikerede, Mude and Sluis) which formed its connection to the sea from the mid twelfth century,[6] but also to a wider European industrial and commercial network within which it became one of the main markets and a major centre of artisanal production.

Expanding from possibly 5,000 inhabitants at the beginning of the twelfth century to probably well over 50,000 at the end of the thirteenth, Bruges became a very large city by medieval standards. Situated in the

[3] On Lefebvre's influence on the study of urban space, see Introduction, above.

[4] Political developments will be dealt with in Chapter 4.

[5] W. Christaller, *Die zentralen Orte in Süddeutschland: Eine Untersuchung über die Gesetzmässigkeit ihrer Anzahl, Verteilung und Grösse* (Darmstadt, 1933).

[6] B. Fossion, 'Bruges et les petites villes du Zwin: À propos des "réseaux urbains" ', in *Le réseau urbain*, pp. 327–39; W. Leloup and B. Vannieuwenhuyze, 'Damme en Sluis: De oorsprong en primitieve stadsontwikkeling van twee middeleeuwse Zwinstadjes', *HGG*, 150 (2013), 13–56, and references quoted there. On the relationship of Bruges to the North sea generally: V. Vermeersch (ed.), *Bruges and the Sea: From Bryggia to Zeebrugge* (Antwerp, 1982).

county of Flanders, it was also part of one of the densest urban networks of Europe, rivalled only by Lombardy and Tuscany. Around 1470, 36 per cent of Flemish people lived in a town, but even before 1300 (though quantitative evidence for this period is lacking) it seems that the size and population levels of cities like Ghent, Bruges or Ypres had already peaked. Medieval Flanders had truly become a society dominated by urban life and culture, for no country-dweller was ever more than 20 kilometres away from a town of at least a couple of thousand inhabitants.[7] There were up to twenty-seven dependent towns, which by the fourteenth century owed Bruges *hoofdvaart* or *chef de sens*, meaning that their aldermen's verdicts could be reformed by those of the capital city. They were all situated between 10 and 25 kilometres from Bruges. Apart from the Zwin towns, the most important of these were Aardenburg, Oostburg, IJzendijke, Torhout, Oudenburg, Gistel, Diksmuide, Eeklo, Kaprijke, Ostend, Poperinge and Blankenberge. Thus the internal landscape of Bruges should be examined as a 'system within a system of cities'.[8] And as will be explained further, it was also the principal gateway for the export of industrial commodities produced in the Low Countries.

A Snapshot of the City in the Twelfth Century

Galbert of Bruges put pen to parchment to explain the tumultuous events of 1127–8, but in doing so he provided a record of the town that is unusually rich in topographic details. It allows us to see that the different nuclei from which the city originated had now become more integrated. The Carolingian *burgus* remained a major military and administrative centre, and was immediately adjacent to an area for the elites in the so-called Great Square quarter. The Oudeburg artisan suburb had developed into the city's core. Galbert's Bruges appears as a place that had become one of the main towns of Flanders, and whose inhabitants were capable of voicing a clear sense of local and political identity, while embracing a wider world of foreign merchants.[9]

7 P. Stabel, *Dwarfs among Giants: The Flemish Urban Network in the Late Middle Ages* (Leuven, 1997); P. Stabel, 'Urbanization and its Consequences: Spatial Developments in Late Medieval Flanders', in P. Moraw (ed.), *Raumerfassung und Raumbewusstsein im späteren Mittelalter* (Stuttgart, 2002), pp. 179–202; W. Blockmans, 'Urban Space in the Low Countries, 13th–16th Centuries', in A. Grohmann (ed.), *Spazio urbano e organizzazione economica nell'Europa medievale* (Naples, 1994), pp. 163–75; Prevenier et al., 'Le réseau urbain en Flandre', pp. 157–200.

8 GVS, *Coutume*, vol. I, p. 286; Prevenier et al., 'Le réseau urbain', p. 157 (quoting Brian Berry).

9 Ryckaert and Murray, 'Bruges in 1127'.

The material layout of the city in this period is hard to reconstruct. The oldest pre-Romanesque remains date from the tenth century and can be found at the Burg. Excavations in 1987–9 cleared three parts of the eastern wall of the fortification but a complete turret, the so-called 'culina' (kitchen), was unwisely demolished in 1963. This tower is depicted on the 1562 map by Marcus Gerards.[10] Galbert's chronicle, however, to some extent compensates for the scarcity of archaeological data for the tenth and eleventh centuries. Apart from the fortification complex (see below), the chronicle shows that the city's churches were the most imposing markers in the urban landscape: the comital church of St Donatian, the two parish churches of St Saviour and Our Lady, and two important chapels near the fortress and the Market Square, St Peter's and St Christopher's. These churches were significant as places of worship and as central points for socio-geographic groupings, but they also reveal other aspects of the earliest spatial developments of the city. In this period ecclesiastical institutions are comparatively far better documented than city governments; and their diffusion is itself an indicator of early demographic changes.

However, the spatial development of early medieval Bruges was not initially shaped by ecclesiastical institutions as was the case in other Flemish cities. Ghent, Arras and Saint-Omer grew up in the shadow of important monastic communities, but none had been founded in Bruges.[11] The earliest monastic community close to Bruges was the *cella* of Torhout, and during Merovingian and Carolingian times, more distant abbeys such as Saint-Amand-les-Eaux (of Elnone) and St Bertin (of Saint-Omer) received landed donations in the vicinity of Bruges, from princes and nobles.[12] Monks and canons did erect places of worship near the town: the canons of the cathedral chapter of St Martin's of Utrecht, more than 200 kilometres from Bruges, probably set up the dependent church of St Martin's at Sijsele, 7 kilometres east of Bruges.[13] The bishop of Noyon-Tournai, in whose

[10] For details on this excavation, see De Witte (ed.), *De Brugse Burg*.

[11] For the early history of Ghent, see H. Van Werveke, *Kritische Studiën betreffende de oudste geschiedenis van de stad Gent* (Antwerp, 1933); and A. Verhulst, 'Neue Ansichten über die Entstehung der flämischen Städte am Beispiel von Gent und Antwerpen', in Verhulst (ed.), *Anfänge des Städtewesens an Schelde, Maas und Rhein bis zum Jahre 1000* (Cologne, 1996), pp. 283–97. On Saint-Omer: A. Derville, 'Les humbles débuts', in Derville (ed.), *Histoire de Saint-Omer* (Lille, 1981), pp. 11–28. For Arras: P. Bougard, Y-M. Hilaire and A. Nolibos, *Histoire d'Arras* (Lille, 1988), pp. 11–34.

[12] Berings, 'Het oude land', 42–8.

[13] B. Meijns, 'Een "valse start" en een omstreden erfenis uit het verleden: De bewogen ontstaansgeschiedenis van het kapittel (1091-einde 12de eeuw)', in H. De Smaele, E. Flour, V. Heyndrickx et al. (eds.), *De Onze-Lieve-Vrouwekerk te Brugge: Kunst & Geschiedenis* (Bruges, 1997), pp. 19–50 (20–8, 36–8).

bishopric the region of Bruges lay, also possessed demesnes and churches close to the town, for instance in the villages of Jabbeke and Varsenare, along the Roman Zandstraat between Oudenburg and Aardenburg, as well as in Leffinge and Vlissegem on the coastal plain.[14] In Bruges, however, not a single major monastic institution influenced the morphogenesis of the city until the mid twelfth century.

As we have seen, the oldest religious community in Bruges, and one which would continue to influence the city's character, was the collegiate chapter of secular canons of St Donatian next to the comital castle. Although a basilica devoted to this saint is only mentioned in 944, a tenth-century tradition ascribes its foundation to Baldwin I (*c.*863–79).[15] The first count of Flanders apparently organized the *translatio* of the saint's relics from Torhout to Bruges and constructed a chapel dedicated to both St Donatian and the Virgin Mary (according to a later falsified charter), in order to legitimize his authority, to seek spiritual protection for himself and his retainers, and to obtain revenues from pilgrims' offerings and gifts from powerful men.[16] It remains unclear where this first chapel stood. Perhaps it was none other than the church of St Walburga, only mentioned in later sources, within the Great Square,[17] or else the chapel of Our Lady situated in the *castrum* itself (comparable to chapels in the late ninth-century comital castles at Bergues and Veurne).[18] Whether the basilica mentioned in 944 was actually the impressive octagonal chapel apparent in the archaeological record (discussed below) is uncertain, even if this chapel was constructed under Arnulf I (918–65). It was probably the same count who created a community of twelve canons in St Donatian's, since he was more certainly responsible for similar foundations in Douai. These clerics were required to perform commemorative services for the comital family, and to maintain

[14] Berings, 'Het oude land', 57–61. On the papal bull of 988, see E. Van Mingroot, 'Duizend jaar geleden: De bul van paus Johannes XV voor bisschop Liudolf van Noyon-Doornik (maart 988)', in M. Denduyver et al. (eds.), *Gestella 988: Duizend jaar Gistel. Bijdragen tot de geschiedenis, archeologie en genealogie van Gistel* (Gistel, 1988), pp. 10–72.

[15] Huyghebaert (ed.), *Une translation de reliques*, pp. 46–9; Meijns, 'Hoe een heilige verdienstelijk werd', pp. 115–17; Meijns, *Aken of Jeruzalem*, vol. I, pp. 303–25.

[16] For contemporary English examples, see B. Meijns, 'The Policy on Relic Translations of Baldwin II of Flanders (879–918), Edward of Wessex (899–924), and Æthelflaed of Mercia (d. 924): A Key to Anglo-Flemish Relations?', in D. Rollason, C. Leyser and H. Williams (eds.), *England and the Continent in the Tenth Century: Studies in Honour of Wilhelm Levison (1876–1947)* (Turnhout, 2010), pp. 473–92.

[17] G. Declercq, 'Oorsprong en vroegste ontwikkeling', pp. 32–9; S. J. Fockema-Andreae, 'Sint Walburg en haar wegen', *Tijdschrift van het Koninklijk Nederlandsch Aardrijkskundig Genootschap*, 71 (1954), 182–5.

[18] Meijns, *Aken of Jeruzalem*, vol. I, pp. 326–41.

the cult of the patron saint of the fortification complex of Bruges.[19] The twelve canons received regular gifts (churches, tithes and land) from Arnulf and his successors, spread over more than forty villages in Flanders.[20] As of 1089, these possessions of the provost and of the canons formed two seigniories (the Proosse and the Kanunnikse), parts of which, forming twelve enclaves, would remain within the urban territory of Bruges as separate jurisdictions and would only be legally attached to the city after the French Revolution.[21] The canons also possessed St Michael's church in the *fisc* of Weinebrugge and its possibly dependent chapel of the Holy Cross in the demesne of Gera, both in the immediate surroundings of Bruges.[22]

The impressive architecture of St Donatian's, as the principal secular church of the county of Flanders, was meant to match the prestige of the counts and the clerics themselves. It had an octagonal central space, connected by semicircular openings with a sixteen-sided gallery, surmounted by an upper gallery. At its east side stood a small rectangular choir and at its west a heavy tower that split higher up into two sharper and smaller turrets. The high nucleus was covered with a vault of pottery and tiles which replaced, so Galbert tells us, an earlier wooden roof that had burned down. The church was part of a complex of chapter buildings to the north (cloister with a graveyard, refectory and dormitory above) and to the west (the provost's house, and canons' convent with three wings, containing a chapter school, a refectory and a dormitory). In the cellars under the convent and the residences of count and provost, stocks of food from the demesnes were conserved. In 1089 St Donatian's also became the parish church of the territory of the *castrum*, in the middle of an area which would retain its distinctive character throughout the medieval period and beyond.[23]

19 B. Hillewaert, Y. Hollevoet, M. Ryckaert et al., 'Wat de archeologie vertelt over de Brugse binnenstad', in Hillewaert et al. (eds.), *Op het raakvlak*, pp. 118–26 (at 118–22); Declercq, 'Oorsprong en vroegste ontwikkeling', pp. 22–7; Declercq, 'Bruggas, Bruciam, Brutgis', pp. 132–4; Meijns, *Aken of Jeruzalem*, vol. I, pp. 362–8.

20 Lambert (ed.), *De oorkonden*, pp. 12–15; Rider, *God's Scribe*, pp. 16–28 and references quoted there; B. Janssens de Bisthoven, 'Het kapittel van Sint-Donatiaan te Brugge', in J.-L. Meulemeester (ed.), *Sint-Donaas en de voormalige Brugse katedraal* (Bruges, 1978), pp. 51–60.

21 Ryckaert, *Historische stedenatlas*, pp. 82–3.

22 Lambert (ed.), *De oorkonden*, pp. 14–17. The dependency of the Holy Cross chapel on St Michael's church can be deduced from the order in which they are mentioned in this charter.

23 Duclos, *Bruges*, p. 277; Meijns, 'Een "valse start"', pp. 19–28; L. Devliegher, 'Het koor van de Romaanse Sint-Donaaskerk te Brugge', in Meulemeester (ed.), *Sint-Donaas*, pp. 32–42; L. Devliegher, 'Galbert en de topografie van Brugge', in R. C. Van Caenegem, A. Demyttenaere and L. Devliegher (eds.), *De moord op Karel de Goede*, trans. A. Demyttenaere (Antwerp, 1978), pp. 254–64; and L. Devliegher, 'Brugge in het dagboek van Galbert' in Van Caenegem et al., *De moord op Karel de Goede*, pp. 91–106.

The canons possessed several chapels within the expanding agglomeration of Bruges. St Basil's chapel in the Burg is first attested between 1134 and 1157, and from the thirteenth century it would house the relic of the Holy Blood. St Christopher's chapel at the north side of the Market Square is first attested in 1089. Interestingly, like St Walburga's, it also had a patronym referring to a saint known to protect travellers, and one rare in Flanders. St Peter's chapel, just north of the Burg, was first mentioned in 1127 and belonged to the count. The chapel of St Walburga, first mentioned in 1214 but as we have seen probably much older, was close by. Finally, close by and within the Great Square, lay St John's chapel, first mentioned in 1305 but again probably much older. Even if the age, original form and functions of these dependent chapels remain unclear, it is striking that they were all concentrated in an area to the north of the castle and along the Market Square. Presumably, at least some of them served as places of worship for the early Wic settlement of merchants and artisans located there. Better known is the architectural history of the (still surviving) comital chapel of St Basil. It became a double chapel, the elegant mid-twelfth-century Romanesque lower chapel now being the only church of that style and period in Bruges: this is a small three-aisled vaulted chapel; its choir is fairly deep, with a semicircular apse; the side aisles are closed at the east side; a side entrance in the southern wall has a sculptured semicircular tympanum representing 'the baptism of the Holy Basil'. The upper chapel was later replaced by the gothic chapel of the Holy Blood and would become a symbolic place of worship more for the city than for the count (see below).[24]

The origins of the two main parish churches in Bruges, outside the area of the *castrum* and the Great Square, are also uncertain. St Saviour's, next to the Oudeburg suburb, is first mentioned in 988, but it possibly dates to the late ninth century, as St Saviour's was a cult that became popular during the Carolingian period.[25] Its beginnings were likely connected with the demographic growth of this nucleus of Bruges from the mid tenth century

[24] T. de Hemptinne, A. Verhulst and L. De Mey (eds.), *De oorkonden der graven van Vlaanderen (Juli 1128 – September 1191), II. Uitgave*, vol. I: *Regering van Diederik van de Elzas (Juli 1128 – 17 Januari 1168)* (Brussels, 1988), pp. 258–9; Ryckaert, *Historische stedenatlas*, pp. 83, 206–7, 216–17; D. Farmer, *Oxford Dictionary of Saints* (Oxford and New York, 1997), pp. 100–2; A. Duclos, 'Sint-Janskerke te Brugge', *Rond den Heerd*, 25 (1894), 233–42; J. Colens, 'L'église Saint-Jean à Bruges: Les tombes polychromées', *HGG*, 41 (1891), 309–12; F. De Smidt [Broeder Firmin], *De romaansche kerkelijke bouwkunst in West-Vlaanderen* (Ghent, 1940), pp. 39–57; J. Squilbeck, 'Un baptème du Christ à la basilique Saint-Basile de Bruges', *Bulletin de la Commission Royale des Monuments et des Sites*, 15 (1964), 207–25.

[25] A. Angenendt, 'In honore Salvatoris: Vom Sinn und Unsinn der Patrozinienkunde', *Revue d'histoire ecclésiastique*, 97 (2002), 431–46, 791–823; Van Mingroot, 'Duizend jaar geleden'.

at the latest. The second original parish church, Our Lady's, is first mentioned in a charter dated 1075, which claims the church had existed for almost two centuries. It is also situated close to the Oudeburg and along the access roads bringing in visitors from the directions of Ghent and Kortrijk. In the ninth century, it had probably been a dependent chapel of the church of Sijsele, and its patronage belonged to the chapter of the faraway Utrecht cathedral.[26] Only from the high Middle Ages onwards, however, did parish boundaries gradually become demarcated, as a result of the introduction of tithes, the need to protect tithal income supporting priests, and the increased importance placed by the church, especially from the twelfth century, on the sacraments in the lives of the laity. Particular chapels may have served from the beginning as focal points of community and worship for early neighbourhoods, but local attachments to them were doubtless strengthened over time: if both parish churches already existed during Bruges' development as a *vicus* or *portus* from the tenth century onwards, the increase in population from then on and an increasingly legalistic approach adopted by churchmen to the sacraments and to church properties such as cemeteries would have further stimulated the effort to define and demarcate parochial territories within the town.[27]

Almost nothing, however, is known about the appearance of the earliest (perhaps ninth-century) churches of St Saviour and Our Lady, or even about their appearance in the eleventh and twelfth centuries, when their parish populations were rapidly growing. In the choir of Our Lady's a wall of local sandstone is possibly all that remains of the foundations of the eastern wall of a Romanesque church. But the location of St Saviour's and Our Lady's – the one lying on the sandy ridge along the Roman Zandstraat, the route between the Roman *castella* Oudenburg and Aardenburg, and the other next to a bend of the Reie at the edge of its flood area, and linked

[26] M. Ryckaert, 'Van ruraal hulpkerkje tot stadskerk: Stichting en oudste geschiedenis van de parochie', in De Smaele et al. (eds.), *Onze-Lieve-Vrouwekerk*, pp. 9–17; B. Meijns, 'Een "valse start"', pp. 21–8. The traditional view, that the Reie was the border of two extensive 'mother parishes', Snellegem and Sijsele, from which respectively St Saviour's and Our Lady's were split off – see E. I. Strubbe, 'De parochies te Brugge vóór de XIIe eeuw', in *Album Michiel English* (Bruges, 1952), pp. 355–80 – can no longer be maintained. See B. Meijns, 'De oorsprong van de Brugse parochies: Een complex vraagstuk', in Hillewaert et al. (eds.), *Op het Raakvlak*, pp. 136–40; B. Meijns, 'Het ontstaan van de Brugse parochies tijdens de vroege middeleeuwen: Nieuwe inzichten bij een oud vraagstuk', *HGG*, 152 (2015), 3–82 (at 61–8); and from the archaeological point of view, Ryckaert and Hillewaert, 'De vroegste topografische ontwikkeling', pp. 140–6.

[27] D. Iogna-Prat, 'Churches in the Landscape', in T. F. X. Noble and J. M. H. Smith (eds.), *The Cambridge History of Christianity*, vol. III: *Early Medieval Christianities, c. 600 – c.1100* (Cambridge, 2008), pp. 363–80; M. Carnier, 'De middeleeuwse parochie in het graafschap Vlaanderen tijdens de volle middeleeuwen: Een overzicht', *HGG*, 136 (1999), 3–31.

to the roads coming from the east and the south – suggests a growing concentration of people in the Oudeburg settlement, surely artisans and merchants, and confirms Bruges' central-place function for its hinterland (particularly as during this period churches were mostly built in the vicinity of markets).[28] However, the inhabitants of the Great Square – who were probably mostly *milites*, officials of the count and clerics, including the Wic at the Spiegelrei where the presence of merchants may be supposed as well – also found themselves on the same sandy ridge, further along the road to Aardenburg. Perhaps St Saviour's originally served as their parish church too, assuming they did not worship in the chapels (named above) that were closer by. St Saviour's might also have been the parish church for the Burg inhabitants, before St Donatian's became so.[29]

As explained in Chapter 1, the oldest market of Bruges, in all likelihood with a regional and agricultural function, was probably situated at the current Simon Stevinplein. Town-plan analysis strongly suggests that this was the centre from which the city expanded radio-concentrically during the eleventh and twelfth centuries. This square lay close to the two main parish churches at the junction of the Steenstraat, itself a part of the Zandstraat, and the road coming from Ghent. Up until the end of the eleventh century, Our Lady's church was in an area forming part of the demesne and later seigniory of Sijsele, but by 1127 it had been integrated into the urban territory. Our Lady's may therefore have been established originally for the inhabitants of this part of the lordship of Sijsele, attracted to the growing trade settlement of the Oudeburg and settling nearby along the junction of the roads coming from Ghent, Kortrijk and Lille. There may also be a connection between the parish of Our Lady and the River Reie, as all new land reclaimed along its banks became part of its territory.[30] In 1091, two clerics petitioned for the installation of a chapter of twelve canons at Our Lady's – which testifies to the church's increasing importance. One of these clerics was a certain Bertulf, maybe the same member of the Erembald clan who became provost of St Donatian's. In Our Lady's, a chapter comprising a provost and eight canons was eventually founded in 1101; and it was to

[28] F. Mostaert, 'De geologische en geomorfologische gesteldheid van de Brugse binnenstad', in H. De Witte (ed.), *Brugge onder-zocht: Tien jaar stadsarcheologisch onderzoek, 1977–1987* (Bruges, 1988), pp. 43–51; Ryckaert and Hillewaert, 'De vroegste topografische ontwikkeling', pp. 147–9; L. Devliegher, 'De bouwgeschiedenis van de kerk', in De Smaele et al. (eds.), *De Onze-Lieve-Vrouwekerk*, pp. 99–108; R. E. Künzel, *Middeleeuwse groepsculturen in de Nederlanden: Historisch-antropologische studies* (Amsterdam, 1996), p. 70.

[29] On the sandy ridge not yet interrupted by the digging of the Kraanrei, see Ryckaert and Hillewaert, 'De vroegste topografische ontwikkeling', p. 146.

[30] Meijns, 'Een "valse start"', pp. 21–5; A. C. F. Koch, 'Brugge's topografische ontwikkeling', p. 37.

maintain close relations with St Donatian's. Two of the canons – three from 1186 – also functioned as parish priests.[31]

Although, unusually for towns in Flanders, no institutions of regular clergy were created inside Bruges before the twelfth century and none outside had land or influence within, some new priories were founded nearby: one in 1100 in St Andrew's church in Bethferkerka or Straten, a dependency of the Benedictine abbey of Affligem (in Brabant), and another between 1106 and 1113 in St Trudo's church in Odegem (in what is now the neighbourhood of Steenbrugge outside Bruges).[32] More importantly, in 1130, some *servi Dei* under the leadership of a monk named Folcrammus established themselves near a church devoted to Our Lady, St Bartholomew and St Willibrord, at a site called Eeckhout, a depression to the south of the Burg which then served as a fish pool for the count.[33] This little church appears to have been built by a hermit called Everelmus who died there in 1060 and who subsequently became an object of veneration.[34] This hybrid religious community, of a kind typical in this period of religious revival and desire for the *vita apostolica*, joined the order of regular canons of Arrouaise (northern France) in 1146. The women who had belonged to this initial community were later installed in the priory of Odegem and this became an independent abbey in 1248, joining the order of St Victor.[35] Nevertheless, even if the Eekhout abbey at the edge of twelfth-century Bruges possessed its own clearly demarcated space, donated by the count, it would not be until the thirteenth century, with the arrival of the mendicant orders in Bruges, that institutions of regular clergy would make any significant imprint on the urban landscape.

During the twelfth century, the military and residential features in Bruges' topography continued to play a vital role in the town's morphogenesis. Galbert's chronicle does not provide sufficient detail from which to draw an accurate plan of the Burg, but it can be supplemented by archaeological

[31] Meijns, 'Een "valse start"', pp. 34–5; M. Vandermaesen, *Inventaris van het Oud Archief der Kerkfabriek van O.-L.-V. te Brugge* (Brussels, 1984), pp. 5–6.

[32] N. Huyghebaert, 'Abbaye de Saint-André-lez-Bruges', in *Monasticon Belge III: Province de Flandre occidentale*, 4 vols. (Liège, 1960), vol. I, pp. 93–7; N. Huyghebaert, 'Origines et rapports des deux monastères brugeois de Saint-Barthélemy de l'Eeckhout et de Saint-Trond', *Augustiniana*, 19 (1969), 257–90.

[33] De Hemptinne et al. (eds.), *De oorkonden*, pp. 36–7; Ryckaert, *Historische stedenatlas*, pp. 185–7; C. D'Hooghe, 'De evolutie van de Eekhoutstraat en Garenmarkt', *BO*, 43 (2003), 194–209.

[34] N. Geirnaert, 'Vroege religiegeschiedenis en plaatsnaamkunde: Vage sporen van de vroegste Brugse geschiedenis', *HGG*, 148 (2011), 45–54.

[35] Meijns, *Aken of Jeruzalem*, vol. II, pp. 677–9, 848; K. Van Wonterghem, 'L'abbaye Saint-Trond à Odeghem, à Bruges et à Male', in *Monasticon Belge*, vol. IV, pp. 1027–65; Ryckaert, *Historische stedenatlas*, pp. 202–3.

and architectural investigations. The chronicle often mentions the *castrum*, because Count Charles the Good was murdered in the Burg and his assassins were besieged in the castle where they had fled.[36] The fortress area had a surface of about 1.7 hectares and was completely walled.[37] On two sides of it, there were waterways, the Groene Reie to the south and the man-made or canalized Kraanrei to the west. Bridges connected it to the rest of the city. Following a building programme begun by Arnulf I, the Burg was divided into two zones, separated from each other by a road (*platea*) running west to east, part of the old Roman road that had been so crucial for the origins of the Burg and city. Before Arnulf's reign, the Burg had been limited mainly to the area south of the road, but in order to encompass the chapter house of St Donatian, it had been extended: an earlier ditch was filled up and the site heightened. Galbert calls the central square, between the southern 'comital' and the northern 'clerical' parts of the fortified area, the 'curtis castri' or the 'curtis comitis'; and he describes the castle's heavy walls, with an inner gallery, and the gates of the fortified area which the besieged had blocked with stones and earth.[38]

The fortification complex must have presented a reassuring aspect to those merchants going to nearby markets, or to clerics and pilgrims coming to the churches of Bruges. The sandstone wall around the castle is described as 'altior et fortior'. At the southwest corner of the *castrum* stood the count's house, a stone residence accessible from the Burg square by a staircase, and possibly built by Arnulf or Baldwin V; it was mentioned in a charter of 1088 as the 'lapidea domus comitis'. It had a lower floor with a basement, an upper floor, a tower ('turris camerae'), and at least one gallery ('lobium') on a vaulted substructure connecting the comital residence to St Donatian's church. Galbert also mentions separate parts of the 'domus comitis' such as the 'aula' and the 'camera comitis'. Later texts call the building the 'Steen' (stone house). From the later twelfth century it seems to have

36 Devliegher, 'Galbert en de topografie'; Dhondt, 'De vroege topografie van Brugge' (though note that Dhondt's hypothesis on the fortification ditches is no longer accepted).

37 H. De Witte, 'De opgraving 1987–1989 op de Brugse Burg: De site Burghotel', in De Witte. (ed.), *De Brugse Burg*, p. 109. See in general on the Reie, M. Lingier, M. Ryckaert, B. Beernaert et al., *De Brugse Reien, aders van de stad* (Tielt, 2005); L. Devliegher, 'Enkele nota's over de burcht en de oudste stadsomwalling van Brugge', *HGG*, 134 (1997), 5–24 (at 19–24).

38 Devliegher, 'Galbert en de topografie'; Devliegher, 'Brugge in het dagboek van Galbert'; L. Devliegher, 'De voorromaanse Sint-Donaaskerk en de Romaanse westelijke kloostervleugel (opgravingen 1955 en later)', in De Witte (ed.), *De Brugse Burg*, pp. 46–92; Devliegher, 'De voorromaanse, romaanse en gotische Sint-Donaaskerk'; Devliegher, 'Enkele nota's'; Declercq, 'Oorsprong en vroegste ontwikkeling'; De Witte, 'De opgraving'. For the most recent insights, see Ryckaert and Hillewaert, 'De vroegste topografische ontwikkeling' and Ryckaert and Murray, 'Bruges in 1127'.

been abandoned as the count's residence but it would continue to serve as a comital prison and, from the end of the thirteenth century, as the city's own prison. Probably from the end of the twelfth century, the comital family had moved into what was presumably a more comfortable wooden house on the east side of the Burg called the *Love*.[39] Though hard to pinpoint, there were also other wooden buildings around the Burg square, such as the houses of some nobles (mentioned by Galbert) and kitchens.[40]

Galbert includes little description of the city proper, outside the Burg, which he usually calls the 'suburbium': market functions are none of his concern; and artisans are rarely of interest. He is silent about the appearance of chapels (St Christopher's and St Peter's), churches (St Saviour's and Our Lady's), and private residences he mentions only in passing. Some iconographic sources and (thus far) limited archaeological research give some idea of their shape. Most of the smaller houses would have been made from wood and lime or clay with straw roofs, but some larger houses belonging to the comital officials and *milites*, perhaps also to an early merchant elite, were made of sandstone, limestone and tuff. They stood apart from each other within large plots. For instance, Galbert talks of the house of a chamberlain named Isaac which was 'quite sturdy' ('fortem satis') and which stood on a parcel of land accessible only by a bridge. Large stone houses were situated in the Great Square area between the Burg area and the port zone of the Wic.[41]

Archaeological surveys confirm that the oldest documented domains in Bruges were large plots of at least 1,000 square metres separated by ditches. These large 'patrician' or perhaps 'noble' demesnes dating to the twelfth and thirteenth centuries often had their own walls, ditches or moats, and contained one or more main buildings and several annexes for kitchens, stables or staff. It is impossible to link these sites to specific social groups but they clearly had an elite character. A domain of more than 1,200 square metres at the Vlamingstraat, for instance, has revealed traces of such habitation dating to the tenth century. In the twelfth or thirteenth century this plot was subdivided and additional buildings were constructed.[42] Within the Great Square other similar domains, mostly between 1,500 and 2,000

[39] Declercq, 'Oorsprong en vroegste ontwikkeling', pp. 19, 27.

[40] De Witte, 'De opgraving', pp. 107–8.

[41] Hillewaert et al., 'Wat de archeologie vertelt'; H. Deneweth, 'Huizen en mensen: Wonen, verbouwen, investeren en lenen in drie Brugse wijken van de late middeleeuwen tot de negentiende eeuw', unpublished PhD thesis, Vrije Universiteit Brussel (2008), p. 244.

[42] D. Van Eenhooge, 'A 12th-Century Patrician Domain in Bruges', in G. De Boe and F. Verhaeghe (eds.), *Urbanism in Medieval Europe: Papers of the 'Medieval Europe Brugge 1997' Conference* (Zellik, 1997), pp. 291–5; Hillewaert et al., 'Wat de archeologie vertelt', pp. 123–4.

square metres, have been identified. A large parcel at the north side of *Sint-Jansstraat* and adjacent to the castle was an estate held from the count. Merovingian and Carolingian remains (between the fifth and ninth centuries) have been attested there but there is no sign of the wooden structures probably erected at that site. Traces from a house built around 1200 in local sandstone and limestone and a thirteenth-century brick house show phases of occupation. Later, the open space within this domain would be further parcelled out. By the first quarter of the fifteenth century, it was to contain ten houses, and by the end of the century at least twelve.[43] These old nuclear domains originally had buildings at their centre with open spaces around them. Thus it appears that the elite houses of the high medieval city did not yet stand next to each other along streets but were distributed throughout the city. From the twelfth and thirteenth centuries onwards, new buildings were erected at the sides of streets and the previously square parcels split up into smaller plots. Gradually additional dwellings were constructed at the backsides of the parcels, and corner parcels were divided to build several small houses along the side streets. This development was not atypical in northern Europe: similar patterns have been detected for instance in Lübeck.[44]

Galbert does not mention streets but he does write about two areas which are still the main city squares today: the Forum or Market Square (the present Markt) and the Harenae or Sands (the present Zand). The Market occupied a larger area than its counterpart today. A bridge over the Kraanrei canal linked it to the castle; St Christopher's chapel stood in its middle and part of it was still an undrained swamp.[45] The Sands was a large open square just to the west of the twelfth-century city ('apud Harenas in exitu suburbii'), its name referring to the sandy soil on which it lay. By the twelfth century it was one of the main political centres of the early sworn commune of the city. As Galbert testifies more than once, when the king or the count addressed the people of Bruges or when political meetings of the

43 D. Van Eenhooge, 'Twee 13[de]-eeuwse domeinen in de Sint-Jansstraat te Brugge', *BO*, 42 (2002), 139–62; D. Van Eenhooge, 'Middeleeuwse Brugse huizen: bouwhistorisch onderzoek in de huizen In Sint-Jacobs en Den Ancker', *Monumenten en Landschappen*, 21 (2002), 44–63; B. Beernaert and B. Schotte, *Het huis Coppieters 't Wallant Sint-Jansstraat 13: Unedited report of Levend Archief* (Bruges, 2001); B. Beernaert and B. Schotte, *Het huis Oudt Inghelandt of de Roo Schildt Sint-Jansstraat 15: Unpublished report of Levend Archief* (Bruges, 2001); J. D'hondt et al. *"In Sint-Jacobs", Twijnstraat 13 en 15 te Brugge: Unpublished report of Levend Archief* (Bruges, 1999).

44 R. Hammel-Kiesow, 'Property Patterns, Buildings and the Social Structure of Urban Society: Some Reflections on Ghent, Lübeck and Novgorod', in F.-E. Eliassen and G. A. Ersland (eds.), *Power, Profit and Urban Land: Landownership in Medieval and Early Modern Northern European Towns* (Aldershot, 1996), pp. 39–60.

45 Ryckaert and Hillewaert, 'De vroegste topografische ontwikkeling', p. 147.

burghers or of the knights and aldermen from the region were organized, and when justice was administered, this usually happened 'apud Harenas'.[46] Again, this demonstrates one of the central-place functions that the city had developed by this time: the Zand was an easily accessible location for the representatives of the rural elites when they conducted legal and political business in the centre of the castellany.

Major Structural Changes to the Urban Landscape

For the period after 1127, sources gradually provide more information about the actors involved in shaping the urban landscape: the count, the 'commune' as the political organization of the burghers (to which we shall return in Chapter 4), and the clerical and lay elites. In the aftermath of Charles the Good's murder, the people of Bruges made their first city fortifications, and their commune obtained new privileges from William Clito, who had been appointed as Charles' successor. One privilege was that the land within these city ramparts would be made free from rents due to the count. This is the first clear reference in a written source to the city's judicial separation from the surrounding castellany and (aside from the count's and St Donatian's) to private ownership within its territory. This urban territory in 1127 occupied an area of about 70 hectares in which the older nuclei, the Burg, the Oudeburg and the Wic, with the new Forum in the middle, were fully integrated and protected by new ramparts. Galbert writes that on 3 March 1127, the day after Count Charles was killed, the burghers started constructing these first fortifications at the orders of the Erembalds. These ramparts were probably little more than a moat with a wooden palisade surrounded by ditches and with basic gates. The job was apparently finished within three days, and used up all the wood available to the commune. Such a construction, so hastily put together, was presumably not one that would merit a place among the finest of medieval city walls, but it did extend for more than 3 kilometres.[47] It included the existing waterways, and wooden gates were constructed on the bridges. To the south and east, the course of the River Reie formed a natural line of defence. The theory that the north side consisted of a ditch running along the street now called the Lane is doubtful but there is as yet no alternative to it. The moats and ditches mostly ran through areas that had already been built upon. Galbert mentions that

46 Ryckaert and Murray, 'Bruges in 1127', p. lxiv.

47 Strubbe, 'Van de eerste', pp. 273–6.

in May 1128, further 'new ditches' were dug, connecting with the Reie near the current Carmers Bridge. The entire urban territory was now defended by water. The rest of the defensive ditch system was provided by the expanded complex of so-called 'inner canals' (*binnenreien*): the Goudenhandrei, the Augustijnenrei, the Speelmansrei and finally the Poortgracht or Smedenrei along the Zand. Other waterways outside the defensive system were probably filled up at this time.[48]

During the next decades, these 'first city ramparts' of Bruges were further fortified with seven stone gates, with walls (encompassing at least part of the city) and with semicircular defence towers. Part of one of these is preserved near the Pottenmakersstraat. The six or seven gates included the Oude Molenpoort (Old Mill Gate) at the end of the Hoogstraat, the Mariapoort (Mary Gate) near Our Lady's church, the Zuidzandpoort and the Noordzandpoort (at the south and north sides of the Sands) connecting the city centre to the communal field of the Zand, the Ezelpoort (Donkey Gate) or Sint-Jacobspoort (St James' Gate) at the end of the Sint-Jacobsstraat, the Vlamingpoort (*Vlaming* referring to the marshy area nearby) and finally the Coetelwijkpoort at the Spiegelrei, next to the Koningstraat. This latter gate might have been part of an earlier fortification of the Great Square and should be associated with the portuary zone of the Wic or Coetelwic. Perhaps it was through this gate that Queen Emma entered the Bruges *castellum* around 1040.[49] The fortifications built in 1127–8 may have reinforced the communal ethos among the inhabitants and a sense of difference between inhabitants within the walled area, and those who lived in the surrounding countryside, between *cives* or *suburbani* (as Galbert calls them) who were 'insiders' and people who were 'outsiders' – a sense of difference that would persist, despite the later growth of new suburbs just outside these gates and moats.

During the same period, the urban landscape continued to be vitally shaped by changes made to the city's hydrography. Some changes probably resulted from initiatives of the count and the early communal government; but the extent of these initiatives is hard to gauge. A still inconclusive debate has focused on the waterway systems to ascertain which parts were 'natural' and which were man-made. Natural processes played a part, given the lie of the land; water has always been crucial in structuring the city's morphology.

48 Ibid., pp. 274–7; Ryckaert, *Historische stedenatlas*, pp. 60–4; J. De Smet, 'De oude hydrografie der stad Brugge', *HGG*, 86 (1949), 9–10; E. Vandevyvere, *Watervoorziening te Brugge van de 13de tot de 20ste eeuw* (Bruges, 1983), p. 36.

49 Ryckaert, *Historische stedenatlas*, pp. 61–4; De Meester and Schotte, 'De Koetelwijkpoort'; L. Devliegher, 'Van Oudenburg naar Aardenburg via Brugge', *Biekorf*, 111 (2011), 413–18.

But human intervention evidently took place long before the period when written sources inform us directly about it: brooks and creeks were certainly narrowed, rectified or closed, and new canals were created. Research on the city centre is incomplete, but some conclusions can be drawn. South of the Eekhout abbey, there was a small waterway, the Eekhoutrei, that split off from the Reie and was connected to the Pandreitje. Both of these were canalized. Past the Rozenhoedkaai, the Reie subsequently splits off into two arms, also both canalized; one being the man-made Kraanrei (currently arched over), with the Spiegelrei as its extension; the other being the Groene Rei and the Sint-Annarei. These two arms embraced the Great Square district.[50] Further on, the Spiegelrei and the Sint-Annarei join again into a single riverbed (the Lange Rei), which may well flow mostly in its original bed. At the north of the city, though, there is an artificial bend, constructed during the late twelfth century, when a connection towards Bruges' new outport Damme was dug to link the Reie to the Zwin.[51] The inner city also had a number of other natural waterways such as the Vuldersreitje, the Boterbeek and the Lane, which have now mostly disappeared. Apart from the Kraanrei there are other artificial branches of the Reie, forming an arch from the Zand at the edge of the twelfth-century town towards the Lange Rei: the Speelmansrei, Augustijnenrei, and Goudenhandrei.[52]

Knowledge of the town's hydrography is an important starting point for research on economic activity. In every pre-industrial city the presence of water significantly determined the placing of trades such as those of the tanners, fullers, brewers, potters and dyers. Their locations are revealed by archaeology, and by toponymic evidence from the thirteenth century.[53] Proximity to water also allowed freshwater fishing, important for the

[50] Duclos, *Bruges*, pp. 11–13; De Poerck, 'Enceintes'; De Smet, 'De oude hydrografie'; M. Ryckaert, 'Brugse havens in de middeleeuwen', *HGG*, 109 (1972), 5–27; M. Coornaert, 'Over de hydrografie van Brugge', in *Album Albert Schouteet*, pp. 23–35; F. Mostaert, 'De Reie'; Mostaert, 'De geologische en geomorfologische gesteldheid', p. 51; Ryckaert, *Historische stedenatlas*, pp. 28–41.

[51] Koch, 'Brugge's topografische ontwikkeling', 13–14; Ryckaert, *Historische stedenatlas*, p. 32.

[52] On the subsequent discussions and reinterpretations of the hydrography of Bruges, informed by new podological research, see Ryckaert and Hillewaert, 'De vroegste topografische ontwikkeling'.

[53] On the dyers in Bruges and their neighbourhood, see H. Deneweth and Y. Kemel, 'Van de Mane tot Sint Anthuenis: Een stuk Verversdijk in geuren en kleuren', *BO*, 42 (2002), 219–42; H. Deneweth and Y. Kemel, 'Een verdwenen middeleeuwse wijk tussen Koningstraat, Boomgaardstraat en Verversdijk', *BO*, 40 (2000), 143–68. On the tanners, see K. D'Hooghe, 'Een belangrijke vestiging van leerlooiers in Brugge tussen 1300 en 1480: De gegevens uit de geschreven bronnen', *Jaarboek, Stad Brugge Stedelijke Musea* (1989–90), 124–38; B. Hillewaert and A. Ervynck, 'Leerlooierskuipen langs de Eekhoutstraat', *Jaarboek, Stad Brugge Stedelijke Musea* (1989–90), 109–23.

city-dwellers' diet; although waterways also served as sewers. In the thirteenth century, the city owned the fishing rights in the Reie, having bought them from the lords of Assebroek. These waterways had thus become communal waters for all inhabitants to use – although in later periods they were farmed out to rich burghers, while some remained in private hands. The hospital of St John's, for instance, had its own fishing ponds outside the city.[54] Moreover, management of urban water and landscape became increasingly crucial matters for the expanding commune of Bruges. Very probably in the early thirteenth century, ingenious locks were constructed at the point where the brooks feeding the Reie entered the urban territory, the so-called *Minnewater* (possibly a natural broadening of the river in a deep-seated area, artificially enlarged). These locks were intended to control the river's flow rate, to regulate the water supply from the brooks flowing from inland Flanders, and to improve conditions for inland navigation. The city accounts of 1281–2 mention repair work on this *ingenium*. By then, it was necessary to prevent flooding at times of heavy rain because the surrounding lower areas of the city had become inhabited. Even today, the water level is higher there than it is in the rest of the city.[55]

Significant also for the city's topographical development were human interventions in the landscape relief. Two depressions were clearly filled in: one to the north of the Market Square and the Burg, and another between the Spiegelrei and the Goudenhandrei. The first one still existed in the early twelfth century, for Galbert mentions a puddle or swamp ('paludes, cloacarium in medio fori') into which dead bodies were pitched.[56] During the twelfth and thirteenth centuries, this area was filled up and heightened to allow houses to be built upon it.[57] The second depression was also levelled, and in the early thirteenth century the area was heightened and made ready for construction. During the course of the century, a series of large freestanding stone houses was built there. These were mainly the residences of merchants with adjoining storage places – which testifies to the flourishing

[54] J. A. Mertens, 'Zoetwatervisvangst in de omgeving van Brugge in de late middeleeuwen', *Biekorf*, 81 (1981), 215–19.

[55] Deneweth, 'Huizen', p. 420. The Minnewater's name may be derived from *minne*, meaning 'water spirit', a toponym of Germanic origin. Even if the oldest name of the lake is the 'Brede water' ('large water'), the *Minnebrug* bridge, mentioned earlier than the *Minnewater*, may have caused this colourful name-change in popular usage, see F. Debrabandere, 'De plaatsnaam Minnewater', *BO*, 34 (1994), 5–12; M. Gysseling, *Gents vroegste Geschiedenis in de Spiegel van zijn plaatsnamen* (Ghent, 1954), p. 88; L. Devliegher, 'De waternaam Minnewater', *Biekorf*, 103 (2003), 12–15.

[56] Rider (ed.), *Galbertus Brugensis*, pp. 71, 91.

[57] E. Van Besien, 'Archeologisch rapport 2009', *BO*, 49 (2009), 251–2.

maritime trade that resulted from a new connection made with the Zwin (see below). During the thirteenth and fourteenth centuries, the Spiegelrei, and later also the Lange Rei, were called the Houtbrekersdam (Wood Merchants' Quay), being the main area for an important trade in timber imported from Scandinavia, the Baltic and the Rhineland.[58] Finally, areas alongside the Reie (for example, between Oude Burg and the Dijver and between the Verversdijk and the Sint-Annarei), were also filled in to allow house-building in the thirteenth century.[59]

The Construction of New Monumental Churches

As in other medieval cities, demographic and economic change in Bruges can also be traced through the history of its ecclesiastical buildings. The most monumental of these were often built and rebuilt over one or more centuries, attracting capital not only from ecclesiastical revenues and from the city government but also from local lay donors. As Robert Lopez argued, such construction work became one of the principal stimulants of urban economies during this period.[60] In the late twelfth century, the original church of St Donatian was rebuilt completely: according to the *Annales Egmundenses*, a devastating fire swept through the Burg in 1184: 'castrum Bruggis cum aecclesia beati Donatiani et quibusdam aliis aecclesiis et domo comitis totum pene concrematur'.[61] The church was eventually demolished and the Burg's entire layout was probably altered. The previous church was replaced by a grander building that befitted the elevated status of what had become Flanders' most important ecclesiastical institution. First the choir was constructed, allowing temporary use of the former damaged church. The extensive choir had an ambulatory on which three rectangular chapels were constructed. The four-storey interior elevation consisted of alternated piers and columns, a gallery, a triforium and fanlights. Above the crossing

[58] Mostaert, 'De geologische en geomorfologische gesteldheid', p. 49; Van Eenhooge, '12th-Century Patrician Domain'; Ryckaert, *Historische stedenatlas*, pp. 66–71; J.-P. Sosson, 'Pour une approche économique et sociale du bâtiment: L'exemple des travaux publics à Bruges aux XIVe et XVe siècles', *Bulletin de la Commission Royale des Monuments et des Sites*, 2 (1972), 102–12; De Meester and Schotte, 'De Koetelwijkpoort'.

[59] Ryckaert and Hillewaert, 'De vroegste topografische ontwikkeling', pp. 146–7.

[60] R. Lopez, *The Commercial Revolution of the Middle Ages, 950–1350* (Cambridge, 1971); L. Devliegher, *De Sint-Salvatorskathedraal te Brugge: Geschiedenis en architectuur*. Kunstpatrimonium van West-Vlaanderen 7 (Tielt, 1981), p. 18.

[61] G. H. Pertz (ed.), 'Annales Egmundani', *Monumenta Germaniae Historica: Scriptores* (Hanover, 1859), vol. XVI, p. 469; de Hemptinne et al. (eds.), *De oorkonden der graven van Vlaanderen*, pp. 282–4.

stood a central tower (known only in its later gothic form). The southern transept façade, demarcated by two quadrilateral staircase turrets, had a large entrance porch, two rows of windows, an exterior gallery and niches. Little is known about the Romanesque three-naved lower church, since it was replaced during the fourteenth century by a gothic nave with two moulds. In this state the church would dominate the Burg square until its demolition after 1799.[62]

The rebuilding of St Donatian's in a grander style testifies to economic and demographic change, and must have stimulated the building and service sectors. It indicates investment by the elites, and it displayed the wealth and status of the rich burghers in a period of rapid demographic growth. Other projects did so too. Construction began on a new monumental western tower for St Saviour's church, work that lasted almost a century. The stylistic evolution from late Romanesque (with a western entrance) to early gothic (the upper floor with lights, filled up with bricks after a fire in 1358) and the development of building techniques show up in the materials. During the first phase, natural stone (sandstone and tuff) were used, thereafter alternately tuff and bricks, materials that were increasingly used during the thirteenth century, and ultimately bricks and stone from Tournai. The form of this Romanesque church is unknown: after the tower was finished around 1275, the church was almost completely replaced. A new main choir and two side choirs were constructed in a classic French gothic style. By the end of the century the choir and part of the nave had been finished.[63] Our Lady's church was reconstructed. In the second quarter of the thirteenth century an early gothic three-aisled nave was erected in the 'Scheldt Gothic' style, typified by the use of limestone from Tournai. The threefold elevation of the middle nave consisted of pillars on which pointed arches rested (to be replaced during the fourteenth century), a triforium with round arches on small pillars, and three-lights with an external gallery. At the western front wall two stepped towers were erected. Construction continued in this style at the new choir, beyond the reduced transept, but during the third quarter of the thirteenth century a choir with an ambulatory and five radial chapels was built in a more classic gothic style, using bricks and white limestone. The elevation has columns and piers below, a triforium and upper windows without wall-passage. Flying buttresses support the pressure of the vaults. Next to the northern transept arm a profiled pointed arch was built towards a tower that was apparently being planned. Following work on the choir, the

[62] Devliegher, 'De voorromaanse, romaanse en gotische Sint-Donaaskerk'.
[63] Ibid.

new brick tower was moved some metres to the north, probably in anticipation of further enlargements to the building.[64] By the end of the thirteenth century, these large churches dominated the Bruges urban landscape, making the city's skyline and importance visible from afar.

Charitable Institutions, New Parishes and the Arrival of the Mendicant Orders

The rebuilding of older churches was not the only indication of Bruges' expansion and social diversification. From the later twelfth century and especially in the thirteenth, the number of charitable institutions increased, several new parish churches appeared, and mendicant houses were settled in the suburban neighbourhoods around the 1127 walls. Although these were the product of reforming movements within the Church and of changing spiritual needs among lay people (see Chapter 8), they were also a response to social pressures. Increasing mobility and the loosening of family ties, typical of urban living, helped prompt a thorough overhaul of the city's religious and charitable infrastructure. Social inequalities in the booming city, and the health and environmental problems associated with the population's increasing density, not least the danger of contamination, created an urgent demand for pastoral, charitable and medical care. Although laymen controlled most of the charitable institutions, religious and semi-religious institutions also provided for these social and spiritual needs. Under these pressures, Bruges became a haven for religious life in many forms, including the new communal ways of living for lay people. The locations of these new institutions indicate the areas where the town was expanding. The oldest charitable institutions were St John's hospital (by 1188), the Lepers' House (mentioned in 1227) and the House of the Holy Spirit (mentioned in 1231): they catered respectively for the ill and homeless, lepers and poor workers whose numbers were presumably growing. It is important to note that these institutions were under the control of the city government, not of churchmen; and in them even the mendicant orders were to play only a supporting role.[65]

[64] L. Devliegher, 'De opkomst van de kerkelijke gotische bouwkunst in West-Vlaanderen gedurende de dertiende eeuw', *Bulletin de la Commission Royale des Monuments et des Sites*, 5 (1954), 179–344, and 7 (1956), 7–121 (at 188–201); Devliegher, 'De bouwgeschiedenis van de kerk'.

[65] The fundamental study on Bruges' charitable institutions is G. Maréchal, *De sociale en politieke gebondenheid van het Brugse hospitaalwezen in de Middeleeuwen* (Kortrijk, 1978).

St John's hospital – across from Our Lady's, next to the Mary Gate of the first city wall, and just inside the 1127 urban territory where the roads from Ghent and Kortrijk entered the town and therefore easily accessible for visitors – was first mentioned in 1188 (the date of its first rule). It was probably founded in the middle or the third quarter of the twelfth century. The chapter of Our Lady's had likely been involved in the foundation, but from the beginning, the government of the hospital was firmly in the hands of guardians who were recruited from, and appointed by, the merchant elite and who were supervised by the town government. It cared for the sick, pilgrims, drifters and homeless, but many of its residents also belonged to the elite groups for whom St John's functioned as an old people's home.[66] A major city landmark (and it still occupies a relatively large area of the city), it was also one of the more important hospitals of medieval Europe. Its impressive architecture (much of it still standing) indicates the heavy investments made by the urban elites in charitable purposes. Its construction also reveals changing social needs. The original building that lay along the street was probably two-naved and made from sandstone and tuff; on the inside it was 32 metres long and 13 metres wide. In the early thirteenth century it proved necessary to expand the building. A brick hall measuring a similar width was erected at right angles to the first building. This hall was later re-roofed, probably around 1234–40 or perhaps later. In the middle, a row of Tournai pillars supports the ceiling. The façade, made of brick with some layers of tuff at its base, has an oculus and semicircular windows at the level of the ceiling. As the new Romanesque brick wing was constructed against the older sandstone building, there would have been a connection between them at ground-floor level, and an eastern façade would probably have been unnecessary.

About the same time as the central hall was built, a small brick tower was erected against the eastern wall of the oldest hospital wards. Around 1270, another hall was built against the northern side of the central hall. To connect both halls, the existing northern wall was knocked through, and two pillars of Tournai stone were added to support the pointed arches. Around 1289–92 another hall was added at the south side: it may indicate both the increasing social difficulties in the city, and the need felt by the ruling merchant class, who ran the hospital, to demonstrate its concern for charity. In the middle of the lower and upper floors, a row of heavy poles supports the

[66] Ryckaert, *Historische stedenatlas*, pp. 220–1; G. Maréchal, 'Het Sint-Janshospitaal in de eerste eeuwen van zijn bestaan', in *Sint-Janshospitaal Brugge 1188–1976* [exh. cat.] (Bruges, 1976), pp. 41–75.

main beams. The southern wall of the middle hall was knocked through on the ground level, as on the north side, to give access to the new hall. At the western façade daylight penetrates the upper floor through five stone cross-windows which, if original, are probably the oldest of their kind in Bruges. At the attic, the roof has a temporary closing wall some metres away from the eastern façade. This suggests that the oldest building was then still standing, and that the street façades were only constructed at that time. Work at the sick-bays was completed by the building of a magnificent entrance, known as the portal of Our Lady. In the two pointed niches, the original sculpture has been largely preserved, giving some idea of the sculpture work decorating major thirteenth-century buildings. The right tympanum carries a picture of Mary on her deathbed, surrounded by the Apostles with Christ in the middle carrying the souls of the deceased on his left arm. Above, there is the coronation of Mary by her Son. On the left tympanum angels appear next to Mary's dead body, on the point of carrying her to heaven. Above there is the Deesis with Christ between the two advocates Mary and John the Baptist. On both sides an angel holds a censer.[67]

Later charitable institutions created in the thirteenth century were also managed by lay governors who were appointed and financially supervised by the urban government.[68] The St Magdalen lepers' house in St Baaf's parish outside the city is first attested in 1227 and it was governed as a corporate institution by the lepers themselves, who usually belonged to the upper social layers of the city. The House of the Holy Spirit was the oldest institution in Bruges dealing strictly with poor relief. First recorded in 1231, it might have been considerably older. Close to St Saviour's church in the Goezeputstraat, it was presumably created to support poor textile workers – a nearby toponym refers to fullers – and other artisans of the Oudeburg settlement. In 1276, when the demographic expansion of Bruges was peaking, the Hospital of Our Lady of the Potterie, a name referring to the activities of potters there, was created at the end of the Lange Rei. This site was part of the linear development at that time of the northern part of the city along the Reie in the direction of Damme. The main thirteenth-century building still exists – certainly the roofing is original – but it has undergone drastic reconstructions. The Potterie hospital was probably the successor of an older one (about which nothing is known): this earlier charitable institution lay between the Gotje and the Oliebaan, just outside

[67] Devliegher, 'De opkomst', pp. 33–43; J. P. Esther, 'Monumentenbeschrijving en bouwgeschiedenis', in *Sint-Janshospitaal Brugge*, pp. 258–337.

[68] Maréchal, *Gebondenheid*, pp. 42–8.

the first walls and close to the Wic. Also situated at the edge of the expanding urban landscape, at the other end at the Boeveriestraat, was St Julian's hospital. Its origins are also obscure. In 1290, a house for 'fallen women' of an ephemeral and obscure order called the Filles de Dieu was created. In 1305 this institution fused with the charitable guild of St Julian, forming the new refuge for poor travellers dedicated to St Julian. After 1300, when the expansion of the urban territory came to a halt, both the Potterie and St Julian's would find themselves included just inside the second ramparts, built between 1297 and 1300.[69]

The second quarter of the thirteenth century also witnessed a strong extension of pastoral care for the growing population. New places of worship were erected and older chapels gained full parochial rights. The chapels of St Walburga and St James, former dependencies of St Saviour's, became full parish churches in 1239.[70] And in 1241, Our Lady's church erected an auxiliary church dedicated to St Giles in the seigniory of the Praetse, close to the Vlaming gate of the first wall, for the growing population of that suburb which was also a site for textile workers. St Giles' obtained full parochial rights before 1258. At the end of the thirteenth century the simple chapel was replaced by a three-naved cruciform church. In its central nave (four bays long), Tournai pillars support brick pier arches. Above this, the upper lights are made up of two rows of ten small windows. Parochial provision was also extended beyond the main concentrations of urban settlement. In 1270, along the road to Kortrijk, the chapter of Our Lady had a new parish church constructed, dedicated to St Catherine. Other semi-rural parishes had already come into existence to the city's northwest at Sint-Pieters-op-de-Dijk (between 1198 and 1220), and to the southwest the church of Sint-Baafs was built (shortly before 1216).[71] These churches would eventually find themselves outside the main urban area when the second ring of fortifications was built (1297–1300).

Growing pastoral needs were also met by the new mendicant orders. The spread of the friars throughout Christendom was rapid in the thirteenth century, but few towns outside Italy acquired so many mendicant foundations as Bruges. Their success in Bruges was partly the result of a complex combination of supply and demand during a period of rapid socio-economic

[69] Ryckaert, *Historische stedenatlas*, pp. 220, 223–6.

[70] M. Ryckaert, 'De oorsprong van de Brugse parochies', in J. Rau and M. Ryckaert (eds.), *De Brugse parochies*, vol. I: *Het leven in Sint-Anna, H. Familie, H. Magdalena* (Bruges, 1987), pp. 9–12; Ryckaert, *Historische stedenatlas*, pp. 83–9, 211, 216.

[71] Ryckaert, 'De oorsprong', p. 11; Devliegher, 'De opkomst', p. 27–8.

change.[72] The first mendicant houses were founded (as in many towns) in areas where new pastoral demands were thought most urgent and least well met by existing parochial provision: just outside the first ramparts, where there was still space for building, where land prices were lower, and also where poorer and potentially unruly neighbourhoods of workers were being established. The pastoral work of the friars was supported by commercial elites, for social and devotional reasons, whose prosperity provided the means for mendicant expansion. Clerics who were already active in urban land reclamation and investments facilitated the establishment of mendicant houses. Foreign merchants, whose presence was beginning to make Bruges a distinctive city, also played a role in this expansion of religious networks.[73] Thus, somewhere between 1227 and 1233 the first Franciscan convent was founded by the wealthy merchant and burgomaster Hendrik Ram in an area, north of the first ramparts, that had not yet become part of St Giles' parish: this was where Hendrik Ram had previously drained land, to supply the rising demand for building plots. In 1246 the city provided communal land in the Braamberg quarters, adjoining the Burg square, again just outside the 1127 ramparts, to allow the building of a new and grander convent.[74] There, the Franciscans would be surrounded by leather and textile workers.

The Dominicans founded their convent in Bruges in 1234 in the seigniory of Sijsele right outside the 'Old Mill Bridge'. The Carmelites settled in the seigniory of the Voormezeelse (in 1264 or 1265) close to the Reie; the Augustinian hermits were placed in 1286 next to St Nicholas' chapel, founded ten years earlier in the seigniory of the Praetse, and partially overlapping St Giles' parish. Two smaller branches of mendicants, the Friars of the Sack and the Eksterbroeders (Pied Friars, or Friars of Our Lady) arrived some time before 1274, and their convent still existed in 1312. The dominance of the mendicants drew other religious groups towards them. In 1258, a community of women that had recently formed around a female hermit in St Baaf's parish outside Bruges, joined the Clarisses; and in 1286–8 some sisters of the Potterie hospital joined the female branch of the Dominicans.

72 See W. Simons, *Bedelordekloosters in het graafschap Vlaanderen: Chronologie en topografie van de bedelordenverspreiding vóór 1350* (Bruges, 1987); and W. Simons, *Stad en apostolaat: De vestiging van de bedelorden in het graafschap Vlaanderen (ca. 1225 – ca. 1350)* (Brussels, 1987).

73 J. Dumolyn, 'Economic Development, Social Space and Political Power in Bruges, c. 1127 – 1302', in H. Skoda, P. Lantschner and R. Shaw (eds.), *Contact and Exchange in Later Medieval Europe: Essays in Honour of Malcolm Vale* (Woodbridge, 2012), pp. 33–58; Strubbe, 'Van de eerste'.

74 Simons, *Bedelordekloosters*, pp. 45–74.

The Clarisses soon moved to the northwestern part of Bruges and in 1292 the Dominican nuns set up a convent in the nearby village of Assebroek.[75] Thus the particular combination of prosperity, demographic growth but also social problems such as poverty and crime explains why so many mendicant houses were founded in Bruges. Ghent, for instance, boasted more inhabitants but probably fewer wealthy benefactors.[76]

The spread of mendicant houses was not simply the product of social need: the influx of other monasteries and semi-conventual institutions such as beguinages and the house of the Bogarden, the male equivalent of the beguines, exemplifies a strong need for varied forms of religiosity and lay devotion, for women as well as men. They also formed enclosed or semi-enclosed spaces within the urban landscape in which a life was followed in the footsteps of Christ, and work was practised somewhat differently from elsewhere. But most of these forms required material means to take shape and survive. A group of 'mulieres religiosae', who around 1242 settled without institutional attachments on a terrain called *Wijngaard* (the Vineyard)' outside the first ramparts, obtained parish rights for their community. The gothic three-naved church of what became the main beguinage of Bruges, dedicated in 1245, now has a baroque furnishing; and the houses around its square date from later periods. Yet its distinctive spatial character as a 'city of ladies' within Bruges, under the legal protection of comital power, still marks out the urban landscape, as do other beguinages in many towns of the southern Low Countries.[77]

The Connection to the Sea and the Portuary Infrastructure

Besides the rapid expansion of a wide range of religious buildings, further evidence of growing prosperity is the investment made in the portuary infrastructure of the city. A mooring point, where boats could bring merchandise into the city, would have been crucial to the city's economy. While a Bruges port, probably the Wic, had appeared in the *Encomium Emmae reginae*, some ninety years earlier, Galbert does not mention any

[75] Ryckaert, *Historische stedenatlas*, pp. 183, 200.

[76] Apart from some parts of the Dominican convent, few traces of mendicant buildings now survive. S. Gilté, A. Vanwalleghem and S. Van Aerschot-Van Haeverbeeck (eds.), *Bouwen door de eeuwen heen: Inventaris van het cultuurbezit in België. Architectuur, deel 18nb, stad Brugge, middeleeuwse stadsuitbreiding noord* (Turnhout, 2004), pp. 476–80.

[77] W. Simons, *Cities of Ladies: Beguine Communities in the Medieval Low Countries, 1200–1565* (Philadelphia, 2003), p. 36; Ryckaert, *Historische stedenatlas*, pp. 71, 182, 205.

such location, perhaps because it was not germane to his story; but this may also suggest that Bruges' direct link to the sea was at this time in doubt. Although archaeological research has as yet not provided a clear chronology of Bruges' changing connection to the sea, it seems that the city's maritime trade was encountering difficulties: natural dune formation combined with dyking in the coastal plain had caused tidal creeks to silt up.[78] Only the Sincfal system of creeks and ditches near the present coastal towns of Knokke and Cadzand, remained open. The Oude Zwin, a partly canalized waterway connected to the Sincfal near the village of Westkapelle, possibly remained Bruges' only serious connection to the sea. Research remains to be done on these early connections: it is still uncertain as to when the Oude Zwin canal itself was dug out (which may have happened in the eleventh century).[79]

Yet it is clear that Bruges was suddenly made more accessible from the sea as a result of twelfth-century storm surges, most notably one in October 1134, which enlarged the Sincfal, flooding great swathes of land. Around then, an important waterway was formed towards Bruges, the well-known estuary of the Zwin, probably as an existing waterway, the Budanvliet, had now become deeper and navigable up to the place where the later outport of Damme would be built. As will be explored in the following chapter, these developments opened a new phase in the history of Bruges. The Zwin would develop into a commercial axis for Flanders and Europe in general, attracting merchants from the Baltic to Venice. The first outport of Bruges to appear in the sources – if Mikhem and Koolkerke are discounted – was Letterswerve, a small settlement of fishermen and merchants, situated in or near the later town of Damme (though its exact location is uncertain). A toll tariff from Letterswerve, dated between 1159 and 1163, shows that merchants from Cologne were already visiting the place and were importing a wide range of commodities and primary materials. During the later twelfth century, the Bruges commune, supported by Count Philip of Alsace, secured its maritime commercial supply route by digging a canal up to Letterswerve, whose name was soon changed to Damme: meaning 'barrage' or 'dam', it referred to the barrage that was constructed there by the city.[80]

[78] Mostaert, 'De geologische en geomorfologische gesteldheid', pp. 49–50; Ryckaert, *Historische stedenatlas*, pp. 39–40.

[79] Wintein, 'Historische geografie van de Zwinstreek'; and most recently, J. Trachet et al., 'Turning Back the Tide: The Zwin Debate in Perspective: A Historiographical Review of the Medieval Port System Northeast of Bruges', *RN*, 97 (2015), 305–21.

[80] Verhulst et al., 'Un tarif de tonlieu inconnu'; M. Ryckaert, 'Damme: Van bruisende havenstad tot schone slaapster', in W. Blockmans and H. Pleij (eds.), *Plaatsen van Herinnering: Nederland van prehistorie tot Beeldenstorm* (Amsterdam, 2007), pp. 131–43.

The counts of Flanders and the city would continue to cooperate in maintaining Bruges' maritime connections for their mutual profit. In 1180, Damme obtained from Count Philip of Alsace an urban privilege of its own, though its lock and quays remained the property of the city of Bruges. As the lock was too small to let seagoing vessels pass through, their merchandise was off-loaded onto barges to continue their journey to the Bruges port via the canal connecting to the Reie. Damme itself was not free from problems of silting; and as it became more difficult to sail ships even as far as Damme, but also in order to diversify the existing portuary infrastructure, new smaller ports were created along the Zwin. Mude (Sint-Anna-ter-Muiden) was first mentioned in the sources in 1213 and received a city charter in 1242. The now-vanished port of Monnikerede is first attested in 1226 and became a town in 1242. Hoeke appears around 1250, receiving charters between 1255 and 1274, and in 1290 so did Lamminsvliet or Sluis, closest to the sea. Over sixty ships could moor in Sluis; and at its peak the population there reached perhaps 10,000, making it a city of some importance in its own right. The port would eventually be protected by two fortresses. Damme counted probably about 2,000 people, while Hoeke, Monnikerede and Sint-Anna-ter-Muiden would have had no fewer than 200 to 500 inhabitants each. All the outports possessed mooring infrastructure, and cellars and storehouses to store goods. For the next three centuries, as judicial and economic overlord of these smaller towns, Bruges would jealously guard its privileges, forbidding other goods to be sold there apart from those itemized in the staple rights that the outports obtained (such as timber in Hoeke, dry fish in Monnikerede or wine and herring in Damme). The history of these outports needs more research before their precise appearance and functions can be determined. The entire portuary zone in the Zwin estuary should be considered part of the 'Bruges metropolitan area', a topic deserving a book of its own.[81]

The Urban Land Market and the Development of Artisanal and Popular Quarters

During the phase of economic growth between c.1140 and 1280, urban land itself became a major means of capital formation for investing elites.

[81] Leloup and Vannieuwenhuyze, 'Damme en Sluis'; A. De Smet, 'L'origine des ports du Zwin: Damme, Mude, Monikerede, Hoeke et Sluis', in *Études d'histoire dédiées à la mémoire de Henri Pirenne* (Brussels, 1937), pp. 125–41; L. Devliegher, *Damme* (Tielt, 1971).

The market mechanisms that influenced supply of and demand for land in this period can be inferred from evidence such as the creation of land taxes and the measures taken to prevent abuses. Land taxes probably date from the earliest phase of the city's development and were raised to compensate the owners of land upon which a house was built. The land of the *suburbium* had originally belonged to the count, who levied a demesne tax on it, until this was abolished in 1127 by the privilege obtained by the Bruges commune from Count William. However, as they parcelled out their land in smaller plots, the owners of large domains in Bruges subsequently demanded new and lucrative rents from the inhabitants of these plots.[82] Thus, from then on Bruges had two groups of house owners: those who held their land in full allodial ownership and whose demesne tax had been acquitted, and those who continued to pay a heritable land rent – which could be adapted to inflation and market fluctuations. The elite landowners could therefore profit from their rent income for the purposes of commercial investment, while the lower classes remained continually vulnerable to repossession.[83]

Extensive portions of urban land passed into the hands of ecclesiastical and charitable institutions, but much also into those of noblemen and rich burghers. Large parcels were subdivided and would later become a resource for land speculation: steeply rising prices stoked by escalating demand for land in the city made such speculation profitable business for merchants who sought less risky investments than those to be made in international commerce. As in other major medieval cities, population growth forced the inhabitants of Bruges to build on all available terrain. Between 1170 and 1183, for instance, a strip of land between the Hoogstraat and the Groenerei, on which construction had previously been banned for security reasons as it was situated next to the castle, was parcelled out by the chapter of St Donatian's. The newly laid streets, the Peerdenstraat, Meestraat and Hertsbergestraat, were narrow and the plots were small, probably housing people from lower social groups.[84] They form a still visible example of a planned neighbourhood, the profitable venture of a clerical body acting as a contractor.

Other major urban landowners, whether clerics, nobles or burghers, doubtless acted within the same economic logic, and took advantage of the rising price of land. In the side streets between the Oude Burg street and the Reie, in the thirteenth century, owners divided their own plots in order to

[82] G. Des Marez, *Étude sur la propriété foncière dans les villes du Moyen Âge et spécialement en Flandre* (Ghent, 1898), pp. 7–8, 17.

[83] Van Houtte, *De geschiedenis van Brugge*, p. 49.

[84] Strubbe, 'Van de eerste', 278–9; Ryckaert, *Historische stedenatlas*, pp. 68–9.

offer cheap housing, uniformly built, for servants and workers, thus creating a mix of social groups in these quarters.[85] Such speculative initiatives are usually undocumented, but some of them can still be read from the current town plan. The narrow parallel streets north of the Smedenstraat, for example, are clearly the result of another planned allocation that created as many parcels as possible within the available area. Streets bearing the names of private individuals may also originate from similar operations, for instance the *Jan Boninstraat* outside the first ramparts, its name referring to the Bonin family who formed one of the top Bruges merchant and hosteller lineages in the later medieval period. Further speculative subdivisions are visible in the plot structure of other areas of the city, where small one-room houses (*cameren*) built by their owners on parcelled-out land were clearly rented out, perhaps as in nineteenth-century industrial cities, to poor wage-earners who worked in the service of their landlord.

Other transformations of the urban landscape were effected as a result of initiatives taken by the city government. Some of them were undertaken to expand commercial capabilities. The zone to the north of the Spiegelrei, a muddy depression next to the Wic, was made construction-ready after 1200. Archaeological research has revealed that this quarter was heightened by more than a metre and large stone houses were built there: these undoubtedly belonged to merchants and hostellers who lodged foreign merchants, and they indicate a continuing expansion of the city's commercial district towards the north.[86] Thus, during the thirteenth century, the area denoted by the toponym Wic seems to have broadened out from its original location at the Spiegelrei along the Reie to encompass the seigniory of the Praetse.[87] As a result of Bruges' increasing international market function, merchants from all over Europe started settling in a now enlarged commercial area; and particularly from the end of the thirteenth century, groups of foreign merchants and the hostellers who housed them began to cluster around the Spiegelrei and the Kraanrei (see Chapters 3 and 6).

Further changes to the urban landscape were made to develop industrial potential. Bruges' artisanal industry was evidently growing. As we have seen, the original Oudeburg settlement formed the nodal point for a radio-concentric street plan development within the 1127 territory and later morphological developments outside of it, caused by the parcelling

[85] B. Beernaert and B. Schotte, *De Halleux: Het huis De Halleux, Oude Burg 21* (Bruges, 2001).

[86] H. De Witte, 'Archeologisch Jaarrapport 1985–1986', *Jaarboek, Stad Brugge Stedelijke Musea* (1985–6), 108; M. Ryckaert, 'De inbreng van de stadsarcheologie bij het onderzoek naar het ontstaan en de vroegste geschiedenis van Brugge', in De Witte (ed.), *Brugge onder-zocht*, p. 56.

[87] De Smet, 'De Brugse WIIC-namen', pp. 112–17.

out of larger plots, as in the case of the Braamberg or Gistelhof quarter, or by linear growth along the Lange Rei and the main streets leading towards the gates. The suburbs thus housed the expanding artisanal sectors, firstly the textile industry. During the thirteenth century, and perhaps earlier, industrial zones were systematically created there, organized and expanded on the initiative of the city government and merchant-entrepreneurs. They were situated away from the main centres of habitation as many artisanal activities, especially fulling and shearing, required space, while others, like pottery works and dyeing, presented fire hazards. Thus, shortly before 1246, the city government purchased a site to the southeast of the Burg, called the Braamberg, and brought it under urban jurisdiction. The draughtboard-like street pattern of this quarter housing the leather industries, into which it was emplotted, betrays a planned origin.[88] Between the Eekhoutstraat and the Pandreitje, a water course canalized by the Eekhout abbey, thirteenth-century patricians and aldermen such as Gervase Tobbin systematically bought up the land, drained it and parcelled it out to the tanners (who would later establish their guildhouse close by).[89]

As might be expected, the immigrant workers newly arrived in the city settled in these lowlier zones outside the city centre, near the approach roads towards the gates or next to the commercially expanding port area along the Reie. Although some of this settlement was planned, certain popular and industrial quarters developed more spontaneously. A district for the textile industry emerged in the lordship of the Praetse that lay next to the twelfth-century city; and, as we have seen, it was there that St Giles' parish would be formed and, not coincidentally, the first Franciscan house built. The street pattern of this suburban textile industry zone around the Freren Ackere, presumably dating from the later twelfth or early thirteenth century, still retains its anomalous morphology within the urban landscape. Excavations have shown that during the twelfth century there were potters at the Spinolarei, and that during the thirteenth century they were concentrated at the east bank of the Reie, in the seigniory of the Voormezeelse to the north of what would become the new urban area within the second walls of 1297–1300 – explaining the toponym Potterierei and the eponymous hospital.[90]

88 Ryckaert, *Historische stedenatlas*, p. 71.

89 Deneweth, 'Huizen', pp. 182–5; D'Hooghe, 'De evolutie'; Hillewaert and Ervynck, 'Leerlooierskuipen'; D'Hooghe, 'Een belangrijke vestiging'.

90 M. Jacobs and F. Verhaeghe, 'Laat-middeleeuws pottenbakkersafval op de Potterierei', *BO*, 20 (1980), 79–95; H. De Witte, 'Potterierei-Sint-Leocollege', *Jaarboek, Stad Brugge Stedelijke Musea* (1982), 149–54; H. De Witte, 'Potterierei 40', *Jaarboek, Stad Brugge Stedelijke Musea* (1982), 155–68.

Another industrial quarter attested by the archaeological record is the 'Dyers' Quay' (Verversdijk), a river bank east of the Great Square. This was drained, embanked and heightened during the thirteenth century to make it ready for an industry that was both polluting and, with its ovens, open to the risk of fires. Many dyers lived as well as worked there, and the urban wardens responsible for monitoring the quality of dyed products also operated from the same spot.[91] As a retrospective reading of fourteenth-century documents, sixteenth-century maps and toponyms reveals, other suburban zones concentrated on textile production – such as the so-called *raamlanden* or 'tenter fields' with their frames for drying and stretching cloth (for instance Ter Hoye southeast of the Langestraat, and Cattevoorde west of the Ezelstraat).[92] Further from the oldest centre, other more sparsely populated and less densely built areas had semi-rural and horticultural functions, such as the communal fields for the grazing of livestock of the Boeverie. Parts of this large unbuilt area to the southwest also had industrial functions, since in 1285 tenter frames were installed there.[93]

Access to fresh water was of paramount importance for households and industries alike. It had a double function: providing clean water and draining waste. In the southern (upstream) part of the city, St John's hospital, Eeckhout abbey and the convents of the Dominicans and the Colettines had their own pipes tapping directly from the Reie. The water was sufficiently clean to be used in fish ponds, and also for washing, cooking and even brewing. The relocation of dyers and tanners downstream in the southeastern and eastern part of the city (as described above) was prompted by ecological considerations familiar to medieval and early modern cities.[94] The prevailing western winds would blow away from the city centre the stench of urine and other fixers, and even more important, possible sparks from furnaces and ovens. The pottery works also posed a fire hazard, which was one reason why the potters were concentrated along the Potterierei north of the city centre, only to be moved further outside the city once the second rampart had been constructed. River water had other uses: both tanners

[91] J. Vandevelde and J. Vansteenkiste, 'Verversdijk 12: Houtconstructie', *Raakvlak Nieuwsbrief*, 10 May 2005; Deneweth and Kemel, 'Een verdwenen middeleeuwse wijk'; Deneweth and Kemel, 'Van de Mane tot Sint Anthuenis'.

[92] More systematic research into these industrial areas, clearly visible on the oldest maps of Bruges, is necessary.

[93] Duclos, *Bruges*, pp. 30, 507–8.

[94] B. Ayers, 'The Infrastructure of Norwich from the 12th to the 17th centuries', in M. Gläser (ed.), *Lübecker Kolloquium zur Stadtarchäologie im Hanseraum*, vol. IV: *Die Infrastruktur* (Lübeck, 2004), p. 33; C. Spence, *London in the 1690s: A Social Atlas* (London, 2002), p. 28; P. Poulussen, *Van burenlast tot milieuhinder: Het stedelijk leefmilieu, 1500–1800* (Kapellen, 1987).

and dyers used it to clean and prepare skins, wool and cloth, and water pipes were constructed to conduct the water from the Reie into reservoirs in their back gardens. Well levers along the Verversdijk are still visible on Marcus Gerards' sixteenth-century map, and water pipes were uncovered during excavations along the Verversdijk. Such use of water brought its own problems though: wastewater from these industrial activities flowed back into the river and made it unfit for consumption. Once the residential areas overlapped with these industrial zones, the problem of water supply and waste management became urgent.[95]

Also fundamental to the urban economy was the presence of ovens and stews (*stoven*). These could be industrial furnaces, for instance for the dyeing and brewing industries, but a 'stove' could also be a bathhouse (a number of which were places of prostitution).[96] The presence of different mills in the city should also be noted, although hard to locate for this period. The first water mill, outside the 'Old Mill Bridge', is mentioned by Galbert in 1128. By the end of the Middle Ages, there were between twenty-five and thirty windmills placed on the city ramparts. Various types existed: grain, fulling and bark mills.[97] In general, the dangers inherent in industrial production within the city and its suburbs soon became clear to the authorities. Large and destructive fires, whether caused by banal private accidents or as a result of artisanal production, are regularly documented. One of the first recorded was the fire of 1184 mentioned above which destroyed the Burg, St Donatian's and other buildings around it. Most of these major city fires, however, quickly destroyed the quarters of the less wealthy, where thatched roofs on wooden and clay houses were more likely to cluster. These would prove to be perennial problems. Straw roofs were discouraged by a communal ordinance dated before 1232, but they would still be present two centuries later.[98]

Thus, between c.1140, when Bruges' second commercial expansion began, and the late thirteenth century, when it was faced with an economic and political crisis (as we shall see), the city expanded its population levels, economic strength, areal extent and the number of its buildings – and at a rate never previously experienced nor subsequently matched in the city's history. The city's 'functions of centrality' also increased in number and

95 H. Deneweth 'De wippen van de Verversdijk', *Biekorf*, 105 (2005), 236–9.

96 On prostitution, see Chapter 6.

97 On mills, see L. Devliegher, 'Brugge de stad van Breydel en De Conink', in R. C. Van Caenegem (ed.), *1302: Feiten en mythen van de guldensporenslag* (Antwerp, 2002), p. 143; Ryckaert, *Historische stedenatlas*, pp. 187–8.

98 W. P. Dezutter and M. Ryckaert, 'Brandgevaar en bouwvoorschriften in de middeleeuwen: Een vroeg Vlaams voorbeeld: Aardenburg 1232', in *Archief uitgegeven door het Koninklijk Zeeuwsch Genootschap der Wetenschappen* (Middelburg, 1976), pp. 14–38.

importance.[99] Between the ninth and the early twelfth century the town had developed around the comital fortress, and had primarily functioned to serve the military, ecclesiastical, administrative and demesne needs of the fortress complex, although some luxury and agricultural trade had also helped it grow. Between c.1140 and c.1280, however, the shape of the urban landscape would be determined to a much greater extent by other central-place functions of rapidly increasing importance: textile and other artisanal industries that provided export products and profits that could be used for importing; the markets and infrastructure for international commerce itself; and new clerical and charitable institutions such as mendicant houses, hospitals, leper colonies and almshouses. The presence of merchant-entrepreneurs and a 'patrician' elite, who benefited most from commercial expansion, was made manifest in both secular and ecclesiastical buildings; but at the same time, the developing infrastructures within and outside the city's expanding territory, to cope with rapidly changing needs, point to the growing significance of communal agency in determining the shape of the urban landscape. As we shall see in Chapter 5, efforts by the city government to increase its authority over urban space became even more marked from 1275, though amid rising social and political tensions, and as the following chapter will show, in a context of industrial and commercial upheaval.

[99] See the views developed in G. Sjoberg, *The Pre-Industrial City: Past and Present* (Clencoe, 1960); and P. M. Hohenberg and L. Hollen Lees, *The Making of Urban Europe, 1000–1950* (Cambridge, MA, 1985).

3 | Production, Markets and Socio-economic Structures I: c.1100–c.1320

PETER STABEL, JEROEN PUTTEVILS AND JAN DUMOLYN

Admiration from outsiders for the commercial wealth of Bruges began early and lasted long. The anonymous monk of Saint-Omer had already praised Bruges c.1040 for 'the number of its merchants and the abundance of valuable goods.'[1] William the Breton who lauded the French King Philip Augustus and his campaigns in Flanders in his Latin epic poem *Philippide*, would have seen an even greater variety of commodities when he witnessed the looting of Bruges' outport Damme by French soldiers in 1213.[2] Indeed, a list compiled sometime during the thirteenth century reveals an impressive range of imports from the Christian and Islamic worlds arriving in Bruges.[3] Other signs of urban strength were also admired. In the early fourteenth century, Dante Alighieri compared the Flemish defence system against the sea with the shored-up banks of the River of Blood in Hell: 'the Flemings, between Wissant and Bruges, fearing the flood which advanced in their direction … raised a dyke so the sea would flee.'[4] Dante also praised the fierce Flemish towns in general, writing with the benefit of hindsight that they would soon stand up to the occupying forces of the French crown.[5]

Thus, by the turn of the fourteenth century, the economic power of the great Flemish cities, Bruges but also Ghent, Ypres, Lille and Douai, had attracted attention from all over Europe. Land reclamation and control over the elements, agricultural improvements, a thriving cloth industry and, in the case of Bruges, a growing central role as a hub in North Sea trade, had brought about the Flemish 'economic miracle', and a prolonged period of demographic, industrial and commercial growth. This reached an initial

1 Ryckaert, *Historische stedenatlas*, p. 47; Campbell (ed.), *Encomium Emmae reginae*, p. 46.

2 H. F. Delaborde (ed.), *Œuvres de Rigord et de Guillaume Le Breton, historiens de Philippe-Auguste*, 2 vols. (Paris, 1882–5), vol. II, pp. 263–4; GVS, *Cartulaire*, vol. I, p. 28.

3 GVS, *Cartulaire*, vol. I, pp. 19–21.

4 'Quali Fiamminghi tra Guizzante e Bruggia, temendo 'l fiotto che 'nver' lor s'avventa, fanno lo schermo perché 'l mar si fuggia' (Dante Alighieri, *Inferno*, Canto XV). Wissant and Bruges were at the outer ends of the Flemish dyke system. Dante may have heard about this from a merchant returning from Bruges: even in his years of exile he is unlikely to have visited the city.

5 'Ma se Doagio, Lilla, Guanto e Brugia potesser, tosto ne saria vendetta; e io la cheggio a lui che tutto giuggia' (Dante Alighieri, *Purgatorio*, Canto XX).

peak around 1270 and would later continue, after a series of crises had led to economic conversion, specialization and diversification in commerce and the artisanal industry. From the final decades of the thirteenth century onwards, Bruges had become an exceptional city, to be ranked alongside other great European commercial centres such as Venice, Genoa, Florence, Barcelona or London. But it was not commerce alone that provided the backbone of the city's economy. Like other urban centres in the Low Countries during the high medieval period, Bruges had also become a real industrial city. The foundations for Bruges' economic vitality were indeed laid not in the later Middle Ages, when the city's international fame would rise higher still, but during the period 1150–1320. Frustratingly, sources for this key period of Bruges' economic boom from the mid twelfth century onwards are scarce. For commercial change we have to rely mostly on external sources and evidence for the activity of Bruges' merchants abroad. For the development of the artisanal industries during the thirteenth century, we have to fall back on indirect and retrospective deductions, and on hypothesis. It is only from the 1280s onwards that archival sources become more plentiful.

As elsewhere in the Low Countries – Ghent, Douai, Saint-Omer, Arras and Ypres in Flanders and Artois, Leuven, Brussels and Mechelen in Brabant, Leyden in Holland, and many of the smaller Flemish, Holland and Brabantine towns – it was textile manufacture that provided Bruges with an industrial foundation and turned it into a society geared towards the exploitation of labour and the accumulation of wealth. Intrinsically linked to its commercial expansion, the city also became a laboratory of industrial organization, which at a later stage would result in the expansion of highly skilled, luxury-oriented industries. This period of economic 'take-off' brought about a massive accumulation of wealth for the commercial elites, and an opportunity for upward social mobility among the artisan middling groups. But it also led to sharp social polarization and a desire among the working classes for political emancipation and participation. Thus the city became a social battleground, spearheaded by the emerging urban middle classes of guild-organized craftsmen and retailers, who tried to carve out a new position in society alongside the wealthy and privileged. Tensions increased in the late thirteenth century, when the first major signs of contraction also appeared. The Anglo-Flemish conflict of 1270–4 hit cloth manufacture and commerce in Bruges hard. This would lead to social and political upheaval between 1280 and 1302 (to be treated in Chapter 4), and finally to a stronger role for the craft guilds in town government and its economic policies. The fourteenth century would also be momentous for Bruges and Flanders in general. Strong demographic growth came to an end; the European-wide 'great famine' of 1315–17 struck Bruges severely. Succeeding decades would impose an urgent need on the textile industry to change course, as Chapter 6 will show. This chapter examines the commercial and industrial nature of Bruges, from its expansion in the twelfth and thirteenth centuries to the early fourteenth century when checks to economic growth became apparent.

Agricultural Development and Urban Expansion

We have seen how a combination of environmental change, human intervention in the landscape, and princely power led to the emergence of a pastoral economy dominated by sheep-raising in the region around Bruges. Growing flocks led to more demand for pasturage, for which land recently reclaimed from the sea was ideally suited: this fuelled the developing Flemish textile industry with the necessary wool, until around 1100, when inland production no longer sufficed and the vital raw material had to be imported from England and Scotland.[6] The building and maintenance of dykes, ditches, sluices, and sea walls needed to turn marsh and tidal flats into pasture and arable land required investment and social organization.[7] The rise of Bruges was also stimulated by agricultural development in the surrounding area, where the counts of Flanders were instrumental in creating landed estates through embanking and draining tidal channels. The process of land acquisition began before 900, and at first, the initiative for reclaiming land mostly came from local peasant communities, intent it seems on providing pasturage for sheep (the so-called *marisci* or salt mud flats that served as sheep meadows and *bercaria* or specialized sheep farms) and also for cows, if the land had already been desalted and developed into grassland meadows.[8] Circular dykes were constructed by the counts to protect land from seasonal floods; later systematic and interlocking dyking and drainage projects protected more pasturage, with the addition of sluices, canals and culverts that constituted a fully fledged water management

[6] A. Verhulst, 'La laine indigène dans les anciens Pays-Bas entre le XIIe et le XVIIe siècle: mise en oeuvre industrielle, production et commerce', *Revue historique*, 247 (1972), 281–327; J. H. A. Munro, 'Medieval Woollens: Textiles, Textile Technology, and Industrial Organisation, c. 800 – 1500', in D. Jenkins (ed.), *The Cambridge History of Western Textiles*, 2 vols. (Cambridge, 2003), vol. I, pp. 181–227.

[7] A. Verhulst, *Landschap en landbouw in middeleeuws Vlaanderen* (Brussels, 1995), p. 19.

[8] Tys, 'Domeinvorming', 53; Van Bavel, *Manors and Markets*, pp. 40–1.

system.[9] Reclaimed and reclaimable land was also given to the prominent Ghent abbeys of St Peter and St Bavo. In the second quarter of the twelfth century the word *polder* appears in the sources, probably derived from the Old Germanic *polla* and meaning 'a height raised from the sea'. Typical for the regions of Flanders, Zeeland and Holland, polders were plots of up to a few dozen hectares, locked from the salt or saline water by 'offensive' dykes and drained by a system of ditches during low tide, a technique acquired and refined in preceding centuries. The initiatives in the coastal plain of the great abbeys and of the new monastic orders, the Premonstratensians and Cistercians dating from the twelfth century, were never as significant, however, as the projects of the counts of Flanders and the actions of the local peasantry.[10] During the last quarter of the twelfth century, new polders in the region of Bruges were organized, which had become necessary since the flood of 1134 had created the Zwin estuary. Shortly after 1180 the flooded land east of Damme was also empoldered, and up until the second quarter of the thirteenth century more and more plots were made ready for cultivation by private entrepreneurs, usually comital officials and members of the Bruges merchant elites. The last major polders near Bruges were created between the later thirteenth and early fourteenth centuries, for instance the Poorterspolder (Burghers' Polder), the result of a joint venture among several Bruges patricians.[11]

Urban growth in Flanders also began to make a strong environmental impact. By the late twelfth century, the count and major landowners expressed concern at the diminishing forest resources in Flanders. The oldest preserved comital account, of 1187, already shows the importance of peat exploitation in the Bruges area. The speed of peat extraction and deforestation in Flanders, including the region around Bruges and neighbouring Aardenburg, testifies to the strong pace of urbanization: city-dwellers needed construction materials and fuel for housing and artisanal activities such as brewing, metalwork and dyeing. During the thirteenth century, we have evidence for large-scale peat exploitation by abbeys, hospitals, princely servants, noblemen and wealthy burghers: like land reclamation, this must have been a profitable investment opportunity. The demographic surplus in the countryside likely provided a workforce for cutting peat.

[9] T. Soens, *De spade in de dijk? Waterbeheer en rurale samenleving in de Vlaamse kustvlakte (1280–1580)* (Ghent, 2009), pp. 17–57.

[10] A. Verhulst, *Précis d'histoire rurale de la Belgique* (Brussels, 1990), pp. 47–57; Verhulst, *Landschap*, pp. 44–5. Recent scholarship has concluded the Cistercian abbeys' role in reclamation was less significant than once thought: Van Bavel, *Manors and Markets*, pp. 42–3.

[11] Verhulst, *Landschap*, pp. 54–9.

By the thirteenth century most Flemish forests were degraded as a result of clearances and grazing. Prices for peat marshes reached their zenith at the century's end, matching the demographic growth of the urban population.[12] From the end of the twelfth century onwards, sources also mention the systematic cultivation in the Flemish coastal plain of madder – used as a red dye in the Flemish textile industry. And besides the extension of land for arable farming and animal husbandry, there were signs of systematic improvement of agricultural productivity: better ploughs were pulled by horses and the traditional three-field crop rotation system was replaced by an agricultural regime in which leguminous vegetables were sown on fallow land to increase soil fertility.[13] Progressive Flemish agriculture stimulated urban growth in Bruges and in other cities, and was in its turn strongly stimulated by urban demand. The rural economy also became more monetized. Rents were increasingly paid in money instead of in kind and the important wool sales and peat ventures must have strengthened this process. This agricultural expansion, intensification and commercialization turned coastal Flanders into one of the most densely urbanized regions of the county. Small markets developed in towns (such as Torhout, Veurne and Oudenburg), some of which were able to attract cloth manufacture (most prominently Aardenburg and Diksmuide).[14] The process of commercialization, attested also in England in the same period, was in this region swiftly followed by important investment in textile manufacture.[15]

[12] Verhulst, *Landschap*, pp. 77–82, 100–1; T. Soens and E. Thoen, 'Mais où sont les tourbières d'antan? Géographie, chronologie et stratégies économiques du tourbage en Flandre (XIIe–XVIe siècles)', in J. M. Derex and F. Gregoire (eds.), *Histoire économique et sociale de la tourbe et des tourbières. Deuxième colloque international du groupe d'histoire des zones humides, Laon, 18–20 octobre 2007* (Cordemais, 2008), pp. 45–60; I. Jongepier, T. Soens, E. Thoen et al. 'The Brown Gold: A Reappraisal of Medieval Peat Marshes in Northern Flanders (Belgium)', *Water History*, 3 (2011), 73–93.

[13] Verhulst, *Précis*, pp. 64–72; Verhulst, *Landschap*, pp. 92–3.

[14] On the monetization of the Flemish rural economy, see Verhulst, *Précis*, pp. 76–86. The urbanization process is discussed in P. Stabel, 'Composition et recompositions des réseaux urbains des Pays-Bas au bas Moyen Âge', in E. Crouzet-Pavan and E. Lecuppre-Desjardin (eds.), *Villes de Flandre et d'Italie: Relectures d'une comparaison traditionnelle* (Turnhout, 2007), pp. 29–64.

[15] For the process of commercialization, particularly well studied for England, see R. H. Britnell, *The Commercialisation of English Society, 1000–1500* (Cambridge, 1993); and J. C. Davis, *Medieval Market Morality: Life, Law and Ethics in the English Marketplace, 1200–1500* (Cambridge, 2014). The early textile expansion in smaller towns is discussed in P. Stabel, 'Dmeeste, oirboirlixste ende proffitelixste let ende neringhe: Een kwantitatieve benadering van de lakenproductie in het laatmiddeleeuwse en vroegmoderne Vlaanderen', *HMG*, 51 (1997), 113–53; J. H. A. Munro, 'Industrial Transformations in the North-West European Textile Trades, c.1290–c.1340: Economic Progress or Economic Crisis?', in B. M. S. Campbell (ed.), *Before the Black Death: Studies in the 'Crisis' of the Early Fourteenth Century* (Manchester,

Security and Market Peace

Urban development was not just sustained by changes in rural society, vital though these were; also crucial was a measure of political stability and security for townspeople to pursue their artisanal and commercial activities. It is unlikely that a true urban commune with a degree of legal and political autonomy had developed before 1100 (as we will see in the next chapter), yet fragmentary evidence and contemporary developments in other towns in the region do indicate an economic and political community in the making. In Bruges as elsewhere, comital power seems to have supported urban interests, since the rise of market towns directly benefited the Flemish count's coffers. An ambitious prince like Baldwin V (r.1035–67) had good reason to establish Bruges as a centre with market functions since he had invested in his estate there. He also took measures throughout Flanders to strengthen his administrative and military apparatus and to stimulate the development of commerce.[16]

In 1058 a crowd of people and clergy left the Bruges *castellum* to greet the relics of St Lewinna (see Chapter 1). Perhaps Bruges had begun to attract more merchants, and pilgrims to its churches, following Baldwin V's renovation of his castle in the mid eleventh century, which must have made the town safer as a meeting place. Yet despite the attempts by counts to stimulate trade and urban development, notably by imposing a stronger system of justice, Flemish society remained violent, especially in coastal Flanders. The 1084 inquiry of the castellan of Bruges into crimes and murders in the region testifies to the common interest felt by clergy and count – and probably also by the early urban communities – in improving overall security. Other eleventh- and twelfth-century sources, admittedly written often with propagandistic intent, present the counts as keepers of the peace. Their effort to subjugate unruly lords and warriors was one with which the early urban communities could make common cause: their economies depended on the rule of law which was threatened by feuding lords who harassed abbeys and merchants alike. The desire to uphold the peace and curtail private vengeance may well have prompted town-dwellers collectively to swear oaths of peace.[17] A movement towards greater urban and market security

1991), pp. 110–48; and P. Chorley, 'The Cloth Exports of Flanders and Northern France during the Thirteenth Century: A Luxury Trade?', *Economic History Review*, 40 (1987), 349–79.

[16] Declercq, 'Le comte Baudouin V'.

[17] R. C. Van Caenegem, *Geschiedenis van het strafrecht in Vlaanderen van de XIe tot de XIVe eeuw* (Brussels, 1954), pp. 10–15; J. B. Ross (trans.), *The Murder of Charles the Good, Count of Flanders, by Galbert of Bruges* (New York, 1960), pp. 9–12.

was thus the outcome, and this must have reduced transaction costs for trade and manufacture.

The surviving sources suggest that the comital 'market peace' already operated in the town of Geraardsbergen in the eastern part of Flanders in 1067/70, but also in the nearby small town of Torhout in 1084, part of the cycle of fairs in Flanders. By the end of the eleventh century this was almost certainly also the case in the larger town of Bruges.[18] Comital influence on the early development of urban markets is apparent in other ways. Even if markets in Flemish towns seem to have been organized without the systematic intervention of the counts, they were usually situated close to castles whose garrisons could provide protection.[19] Changes in the management of comital income also affected the local economy and this was significant for the transfer of rural surpluses to Bruges. Since the rise of the county of Flanders, the count's landed property had been concentrated in the coastal plain, particularly in the original *pagus Flandrensis* around Oudenburg and Bruges. As we saw, during the later eleventh century, this 'old demesne' of the counts, including fixed and regular rent income derived from it, was reorganized in *briefs* or *brevia*, each with a receiver who centralized the revenues from each castellany of the county. The oldest surviving comital account, the 'Gros Brief' from 1187, shows that in the twelfth century Bruges accounted for no fewer than six such offices. It was the most important demesnal centre of the count. Apart from the *spiccarium* and the *lardarium* (receiving respectively revenues from wheat and oats, and from cows, pigs, chickens or eggs), there were also offices centralizing money rents from the *bercariae* (the count's sheep farms) and income from peat, which were typical features of the coastal plain.[20] It was this concentration of income in Bruges that led the count to install the provost of St Donatian's as his general receiver and chancellor, making him the head of all comital officials (*notarii*) and clerics. The chronicler Galbert of Bruges was one of these *notarii*, and probably a cleric (possibly a canon) of St Donatian's.

[18] R. C. Van Caenegem, *Geschiedenis van het strafprocesrecht in Vlaanderen van de XIe tot de XIVe eeuw* (Brussels, 1956), p. 4; Holder-Egger (ed.), 'Ex Vita Arnulfi', pp. 877–99 (written immediately before 1120).

[19] Verhulst, *Rise of Cities*, p. 152.

[20] Verhulst and Gysseling (eds.), *Le compte général de 1187*, pp. 149–53, 170–3, 175–8; G. Declercq, 'De kustvlakte en de ontwikkeling van het graafschap Vlaanderen', in J.-L. Meulemeester (ed.), *Met zicht op zee* (Tielt, 2000), pp. 20–3; A. Verhulst, 'Sheep-Breeding and Wool Production in Pre-Thirteenth-Century Flanders and their Contribution to the Rise of Ypres, Ghent and Bruges as Centres of the Textile Industry', in M. Dewilde, A. Ervynck and A. Wielemans (eds.), *Ypres and the Medieval Cloth Industry in Flanders* (Zellik, 1998), pp. 33–40.

Despite this role, economic affairs, as for the great majority of medieval chroniclers, were for him of little concern.[21]

Economic Growth and Social Diversification

Even if facts, let alone quantitative data, about the urban development of Bruges are difficult to trace, it is possible to identify the interplay of factors that accelerated economic growth. Foremost among these, was the increasing demand for artisanal goods and services from the counts, their household members and armies, the regional nobility and clergy, and also wealthy merchants who aspired to more ostentatious lifestyles. The purchasing power of these elite groups was fuelled by rising transfers of surplus extraction from the countryside. Debate surrounds the nature of this accumulation. David Nicholas argued controversially that agriculture in eleventh-century Flanders – a 'poor and dangerous no-man's land' – was incapable of generating the surplus necessary for urbanization; instead, institutional arrangements and the specific industrial and commercial dynamics of urbanization were responsible for growth, as the county became increasingly dependent upon trade to supply its growing urban population.[22] To refute these arguments, Adriaan Verhulst pointed to the dynamic nature of rural developments, especially in coastal Flanders, which was able to produce not just oats but also wheat, meat and dairy products (and the wool needed by the rising urban textile industries); and questioned evidence for any regional trade networks at this early stage.[23] It does seem that rising agricultural productivity cannot be discounted as a cause of urban economic growth, but that its interplay with manufacture and regional trade in both foodstuffs and industrial commodities was crucial; while capital also flowed into Bruges as profits increased from international trade, especially from growing cloth exports. In this period Bruges also became the leading commercial city in Flanders (see below), and Bruges merchants were active in commerce with England, France and Germany, and particularly at the growing international fairs in Champagne. But also essential for industrial expansion was the creation of a more flexible labour market. This was provided especially by immigration of peasants from the

[21] On Galbert's connection with St Donatian's, see: G. Declercq, 'Galbert van Brugge en de verraderlijke moord op Karel de Goede: Beschouwingen over tekst en auteur naar aanleiding van een nieuwe uitgave', *HMG*, 49 (1995), 71–117.

[22] Nicholas, 'Of Poverty'.

[23] Verhulst, 'Alleged Poverty', pp. 369–82.

countryside, whose ties to the land had been loosened by the weakening of servile bonds (all relics of which were abolished by the mid thirteenth century). Many of them were perhaps descendants of free colonists (*coloni*) on reclaimed land. Their situation in the countryside was also becoming more precarious in the thirteenth century because of overpopulation, cultivation of marginal lands and falling agricultural returns.[24]

In the meantime urban land became more valuable and could be used as a source of capital for urban investors and merchants. As we saw, the increasing tempo of urban growth from Galbert's time to the revolt of 1302 unleashed a building boom. The investments in real estate by the canons of St Donatian's are symptomatic of this development. They laid out a new urban quarter on land granted them by Count Thierry of Alsace in 1155–7. The grant stipulated that it should remain undeveloped, but the opportunity proved too tempting to pass up. By 1180, the chapter had made a deal with a comital officer absolving it from the non-development clause in return for two-thirds of the profit. As a result, care was taken to divide up and build on the land to ensure that a large number of residents could be concentrated into a relatively small space.[25] The buildings constructed were typically rows of 'rooms' (*cameren*) with a single storey and sleeping lofts built in the rafters. They were intended to house immigrants from the countryside: during this period the many new cloth workers and their families must have come from the city surrounds. And, as we have seen, they usually settled in the poorer quarters outside the first city ramparts.[26] The canons' investments are only one example of probably many speculative ventures that turned the territory around the old centre of Bruges into industrial suburbs. In turn the old centre was becoming more residential, inhabited by the commercial elites and wealthier craftsmen. By 1302, many of these urban elites and settled middle classes owned extensive properties in the suburbs. In a growing city, speculative investment in real estate was an important source of wealth.[27]

As a result, social inequalities and tensions sharpened between what some thirteenth-century sources call 'the poor' and 'the rich'. However, sources allowing study of the lower social groups are patchy before the

[24] A. Verhulst, 'On the Preconditions for the Transition from Rural to Urban Industrial Activities (9th–11th Centuries)', in B. Blondé, E. Vanhaute and M. Galand (eds.), *Labour and Labour Markets between Town and Countryside, Middle Ages – Nineteenth Century* (Turnhout, 2001), pp. 33–42.

[25] Strubbe, 'Van de eerste'; Ryckaert, *Historische stedenatlas*, pp. 68–9 and n. 119.

[26] T. Boogaart, *An Ethnogeography of Medieval Bruges: Evolution of a Communal Milieu* (Madison,WI, 2000), pp. 162–5.

[27] Murray, *Bruges*, p. 51 (n. 121 and literature there).

1280s.[28] The first craftsmen must have been descended either from the servile craftsmen connected to the comital demesne and the Bruges castle or from immigrants settling in Bruges to practise their trade. It appears that in the twelfth-century commune, all these typically 'urban' manufacturing and commercial groups gradually formed a kind of community with a common identity. In 1127, Galbert of Bruges considered the 'burghers' – he uses the terms 'burgenses', 'cives' and 'vicini' – to be a social category that needed no further explanation. In his narrative the people of Bruges often show common interests, whether they are clerics of St Donatian's, *milites* of the castle, or common townsmen of the *suburbium*. Distinctions among the burghers were perhaps not yet as clear cut at this point as they would become later on. Although social tensions doubtless existed, all inhabitants of Bruges wanted peace and security, control over urban land, personal freedom and a common management of urban space to create prosperous conditions for trade and craftsmanship. It was probably from the later twelfth century, in the wake of rapid growth, that a more diversified social structure began to develop, creating the conditions for political struggle that would come to characterize the city. During the thirteenth century, two main social groups appear to have emerged, though they may well have been internally divided even before 1300. One group might be described as 'the popular classes': usually they were led politically by independent craftsmen engaged in petty commodity production, but they also encompassed wage labourers (many active in textile manufacture) and the poor. A second group comprised the commercial elites who also monopolized political office in the city. As the original communal institutions withered during the thirteenth century (see Chapter 4), judicial and administrative powers passed into the hands of aldermen appointed by the count. The communal ideal still mattered to both groups, but it also began to serve narrower purposes, gradually becoming voiced most stridently when used to justify popular opposition to oligarchy.

Although the precise mechanisms that brought about the guilds in Bruges remain uncertain due to a lack of sources, it is clear that the decisive period for their development was the thirteenth century. By then they combined economic, social, military and also religious functions (as some craft guilds had devotional brotherhoods attached to them). In 1252, statutes are first mentioned for the drapery sector (which organized entrepreneurs, rather than craftsmen) but their texts, or rather fragments of them, only survive

[28] W. Prevenier, 'La bourgeoisie en Flandre au XIIIe siècle', *Revue de l'Université de Bruxelles*, 4 (1978), 407–28.

from 1260 onwards. At first the wardens, called *dekens* (deans) and *vinders* (finders), were not chosen by the artisans themselves but were appointed by the city government. Although before 1302 craft guilds had no autonomy, artisans were sometimes consulted by the urban magistracy on technical and economic matters. Textile workers participated in meetings in which salaries were discussed but they lacked any power of decision-making. Usually their dean was a merchant-entrepreneur rather than a craftsman, a practice that would be contested during the revolutionary protests of 1280–1 when the Bruges commoners first demanded the right to participate in urban legislation. By the end of the thirteenth century some twelve craft guilds paid excises to the city, including those of the textile and leather industries, the bakers, butchers, carpenters and blacksmiths. Unfortunately almost all guild statutes and regulations before the fourteenth century have been lost. But particular guilds producing for the local markets or active in the retail sector were fully organized by the end of the thirteenth century. And guild members participated in the inspection of both production and marketing. Between 1280 and 1302 the economic and political influence of guilds and their potential for subversive action steadily increased, a danger realized by the urban authorities who were wary of artisan meetings and collections for mutual aid that could be used as strike funds or for the purchase of arms.[29]

Demographic Development

During the thirteenth century, population levels rose considerably. In part this was a result of a dramatic rise in the number of 'urban poor': pressures on agricultural land drove migrants to town, where they joined the ranks of a low-paid and unskilled workforce in a proto-capitalist textile industry. Calculating the extent of this immigration and rise in numbers is not easy. More is known about checks to the population than about its growth. The city had faced poverty and periods of high mortality before the thirteenth-century textile boom. Like the rest of Flanders, Bruges had suffered from a major famine in 1124–6 because of successive hard winters and rainy

[29] C. Wyffels and J. De Smet (eds.), *De rekeningen van de stad Brugge 1280–1319: Eerste deel 1280–1319* (Brussels, 1965), pp. 686–97; Van Houtte, *De geschiedenis van Brugge*, p. 85; G. Espinas and H. Pirenne (eds.), *Recueil de documents relatifs à l'histoire de l'industrie drapière en Flandre*, 4 vols. (Brussels, 1906), vol. I, pp. 532–60, and passim; C. Wyffels, *De oorsprong der ambachten in Vlaanderen en Brabant* (Brussels, 1951), pp. 48, 52, 61–2, 66–9, 86, 91–7, 127–30.

summers: Galbert describes how hundreds of paupers in Bruges received alms. Another chronicle describes high grain prices in the city in 1151; other famines occurred in 1196–8. The most severe of these, though, came in 1315–17. A general European famine struck Flanders after bad harvests in 1315–16 followed heavy rains.[30] Grain became ten to twenty-four times more expensive than in normal years. The worst food crisis ever to hit the city occurred, and though the authorities were surprised by its scale, they quickly took measures, engaging foreign merchants to import bread grains. Death tolls were astonishingly high. Three successive years of grain shortage directly cost the lives of up to 10 per cent of the city's (poorer and migrant) population, and the middle classes must have suffered as well. The city government's attempts to mitigate the crisis were of little avail. Every week 100 to 150 corpses were collected from the streets (according to the city accounts). The total number of victims rose to about 2,000. Economic and social hardship had undermined the resilience of the city's population. Moreover, Flemish cities were dependent upon grain imports, particularly from northern France, and when imports fell and prices soared, hunger became difficult to avoid. Because the 'great famine' happened when the Malthusian tension between population and supply was at its peak, it was much worse than any previous ones caused by cyclical disasters in agricultural production. The famine of 1315–17 was the worst of its kind, though there were other peaks in mortality, for instance in 1302 and in 1328, as a result of hunger and civil war.[31]

The effects of urban mortality in this period can thus be partly grasped, but as we have no data on birth, marriage or migration, nor any useful fiscal documents covering the whole population, no precision is possible about its growth during the twelfth and thirteenth centuries. The first more or less reliable data survive only from the 1330s: how the 'great hunger' affected the urban population long-term is unclear. But it is beyond doubt that urban growth ceased and population decline began. Walter Prevenier estimated the population of Bruges in 1338–40, depending upon household

30 H. Van Werveke, 'La famine de l'an 1316 en Flandre et dans les régions voisines', *RN*, 41 (1959), 5–14; and more recently S. Geens, 'De grote hongersnood in het graafschap Vlaanderen (1315–1317). De invloed van grondbezit op de regionale resistentie', unpublished MA thesis, University of Antwerp (Antwerp, 2014).

31 Murray, *Bruges*, pp. 99–106; P. Grierson (ed.), *Les annales de Saint-Pierre de Gand et de Saint-Amand* (Brussels, 1937), p. 112; H. Van Werveke, 'De middeleeuwse hongersnood', *Mededelingen van de Koninlijke Vlaamse Aacademie voor Wetenschappen, Letteren en Schone Kunsten van België* 29 (1967), 3–22; H. Van Werveke, 'Bronnenmateriaal uit de Brugse stadsrekeningen betreffende de hongersnood van 1316', *Handelingen van de Koninklijke Commissie voor Geschiedenis*, 125 (1960), 431–510.

size, to be between 36,500 and 46,000 (preferring the latter figure).[32] There is, however, something amiss with this number. The data are based on the draft lists of the city militia. They contain the number of militiamen that the fifty-three craft guilds and the merchant class had to deliver to the urban authorities. Although Prevenier added into his figures another 4,000 or so inhabitants (brokers, town officials and civil servants, clergy, foreigners, etc. who were not involved in the militia), we think that even his 'optimistic' figure should be treated as a strict minimum.[33] It is unclear what percentage of the Bruges adult male population was then integrated into the corporate framework of guilds, but 4,000 seems a very low estimate. Relatively high poverty and, more importantly, a large number of unskilled workers who were not within the craft guild system and who were unable to exercise their 'citizens' right' of trading – which would make them members of the *poorterij* (see Chapter 4) – was a feature of every premodern town, and Bruges cannot have been much different. In some cities more than half of the population would fit into these categories. As Bruges in the mid fourteenth century was already moving towards an economy of skill in which guilds played a crucial role, the proportion of non-guild and non-mercantile groups would have been somewhat lower, but if only a quarter of the population were involved in craft guild organization, commerce and retail, Bruges' total population must then have been at least 57,000, and therefore considerably higher in the late thirteenth century during the final stages of growth. It is safe to estimate the population of thirteenth-century Bruges, before the 'great hunger', to be around 60,000. This figure was a high point that would never be matched again – as would be the case for other large medieval cities, particularly later in the wake of the Black Death.

Textiles and Urbanization, 1150–1300

The burgeoning population of the later twelfth and thirteenth centuries found several sources of employment (for instance the leather and metal

[32] W. Prevenier, 'Bevolkingscijfers en professionele structuren der bevolking van Gent en Brugge in de XIVe eeuw', in *Album Charles Verlinden* (Ghent, 1975), pp. 269–303; W. Prevenier, 'La démographie des villes du comté de Flandre aux XIVe et XVe siècles: État de la question: Essai d'interprétation,' *RN*, 65 (1983), 255–75; J. Dumolyn, 'Population et structures professionnelles à Bruges aux XIVe et XVe siècles,' *RN*, 81 (1999), 43–64. The data had earlier been analysed by J. De Smet, 'L'effectif des milices brugeoises et la population de la ville en 1340', *BTFG*, 12 (1933), 631–6; and J. F. Verbruggen, *Het gemeenteleger van Brugge van 1338 tot 1340 en de namen van de weerbare mannen* (Brussels, 1962).

[33] Prevenier, 'Bevolkingscijfers,' pp. 281–4.

industries and a growing service economy and food sector, on which little is known); but a significant percentage of it was employed in the cloth industry. This had become the jewel in the crown of the Flemish economy, although proportionally fewer townspeople in Bruges were probably employed in the textile industry than those in the quintessentially textile cities of Ghent, Douai or Ypres. The proximity of raw materials (wool from sheep in the coastal salt marshes) and a supply of cheap labour turned the cities of Flanders into hotspots of industrial activity and into the sweatshops of northern Europe. The relative ease with which merchants could access European markets and the strategic location of the Low Countries on the main European trade routes ensured a constant supply of raw materials, and facilitated export. Bruges entrepreneurs, although traditionally seen as less associated with this industrial development than their counterparts in cities such as Douai, Ghent, Ypres, Arras, Saint-Omer, Mechelen, Leuven and Brussels, nonetheless took part in this process of massive industrialization. Furthermore, Bruges' commercial preponderance in the region ensured that its merchants kept in touch with their main European outlets through the Champagne fairs. They took a leading role in the Flemish 'Hanse of the Seventeen Cities', the merchant guild coordinating Flemish trade at the fairs, and they assured supply of what gradually became the essential staple of refined English wool by developing trading networks in England. Around 1250, at the height of the industry, Bruges was, so to speak, a truly industrial city.[34]

The Flemish cloth industry had long roots. By Galbert's time, wool imports had already joined domestically produced stocks to supply the looms of Flemish towns. Like sheep rearing, cloth production even of the highly desired *pallia Fresonica* (Frisian cloth) had been a rural pursuit in the ninth and tenth centuries. Although the origins of this cloth are debated (as seen in Chapter 1), it is safe to assume that coastal Flanders formed part of the cloth production zone known as 'greater Frisia'. This was a peasant household-based industry, and its remains are revealed in excavations of dozens of sunken-floor buildings. There, under conditions of high

[34] The bibliography on the Flemish textile industry is extensive. The classic studies on the early Flemish textile industries concern mostly manufacture in the French-speaking parts of Flanders and Artois, amongst them H. Laurent, *Un grand commerce d'exportation au Moyen Âge: La draperie des Pays Bas en France et dans les pays mediterranéens, XIIe-XVe siècle* (Paris, 1935); and G. Espinas, *La draperie dans la Flandre française au Moyen Âge* (Paris, 1923). For introductions to the most important industrial centres in the Dutch-speaking parts of Flanders: Espinas and Pirenne (eds.), *Recueil*. More recent approaches include Munro, 'Medieval Woollens: Textiles'; and R. Holbach, *Frühformen von Verlag und Grossbetrieb in der gewerblichen Produktion (13.–16. Jahrhundert)* (Stuttgart, 1994).

humidity and low temperatures, numerous peasant women laboured at what was probably a side occupation. Monasteries and local lords may have helped organize this production, but the surplus must have ended up in the markets of places like Bruges alongside wool and other agrarian commodities.[35] Commercial exchange centred in Bruges might never have developed had it not been for the tradition of cloth manufacture in Flanders and the wider region.

Thus strong urban growth, the security of the count's castles, flourishing local and developing long-distance markets, together formed the preconditions for the first 'industrial revolution' in European history – the urban-based mass production of woollen textiles.[36] Like their urban competitors in the southern Low Countries, Bruges merchants and cloth entrepreneurs (organized in the 'draperie', a guild-like structure of merchants and entrepreneurs controlled by the city authorities, who were themselves often members of the city's mercantile elites) were able to manage and distribute production across increasingly specialized crafts whose practitioners came to reside chiefly in the city. In the twelfth and early thirteenth centuries, craft associations were not yet present in cloth manufacture. The textile workshops and the division of labour were still controlled by commercial capital.[37] By the thirteenth century, up to fifty specialist occupations contributed to the production of a Flemish woollen fabric. They could count on a varied supply of wool from Flemish and later English sheep above all, and on cheaper locally produced and more expensive imported dyestuffs. Rural labour was probably integrated in the production chain to produce large quantities of cleaned wool and spun thread, yet many townswomen were also involved in manufacturing yarn and cleaning woven fabrics. Complex systems of division of (relatively cheap) labour; ready access to investment and credit in cities that had grown from regional servicing centres into hubs of manufacture and trade; the introduction of new technologies: all these developments required flexible labour markets while generating important gains in productivity, and together they created the conditions for industrial growth. In particular the use of the broad loom, requiring several craftsmen

35 Van Bavel, *Manors and Markets*, pp. 153–5.

36 Munro, 'Medieval Woollens: Textiles'.

37 H. Van Werveke, 'De koopman-ondernemer en de ondernemer in de Vlaamsche lakennijverheid van de late middeleeuwen', *Mededeelingen van de Koninklijke Academie voor Wetenschappen, Letteren en Schoone Kunsten van België, Klasse der Letteren*, 8 (1946), 5–26; Holbach, *Frühformen*; and J. H. A. Munro, 'Industrial Entrepreneurship in the Late Medieval Low Countries: Urban Draperies, Fullers and the Art of Survival', in P. Klep and E. Van Cauwenberghe (eds.), *Entrepreneurship and the Transformation of the Economy (10th –20th Centuries): Essays in Honour of Herman van der Wee* (Leuven, 1994), pp. 377–88.

to coordinate their labour, proved crucial in shaping a huge urban industry that outstripped its rural rivals, which were not able at this stage to achieve such complex ways of organizing manufacture.[38]

Little is known of the early cloth industry in Bruges (since most of the early documents were destroyed in the Belfry fire of 1280). The first surviving governing statutes for the industry date only from 1277 and they reveal production chiefly of cheaper and middle-range quality cloth, from semi-worsted to so-called greased woollens. Some of these fabrics required less expensive wool and manufacturing methods, but many were processed by Bruges fullers, dyers and shearers, resulting in far higher quality woollens than the ones manufactured rurally. Rather than the wide range of woollens, from very expensive scarlets to worsteds, manufactured by cloth entrepreneurs in Ghent, Ypres and Douai, Bruges drapers seem, however, to have preferred producing (semi-)worsteds known as 'says from Gistel' (*Ghistelsaaien*), named after a nearby small town.[39] They were made from coarser wool brought from the Flemish countryside or from England, Scotland and Ireland. These lighter types of cloth constituted the bulk of Flemish cloth exports towards the Mediterranean in the thirteenth century.[40]

By the 1280s, however, the market for woollens was changing dramatically. The changes revealed the structural weakness of Bruges cloth manufacture in the face of new cost structures and competitive pressures.[41] On the one hand, the price of English wool rose sharply from the 1270s. The kings of England started to increase export duties.[42] Bruges entrepreneurs

38 The manufacturing process of medieval woollen cloth is discussed in J. H. A. Munro, 'Textile Technology', in J. R. Strayer et al. (eds.), *Dictionary of the Middle Ages*, 13 vols. (New York, 1988), vol. XI, pp. 693–715; and in W. Endrei, 'Manufacturing a Piece of Woollen Cloth in Medieval Flanders: How Many Work Hours?', in E. Aerts and J. H. A. Munro (eds.), *Textiles of the Low Countries in European Economic History* (Leuven, 1990), pp. 14–23.

39 Espinas and Pirenne (eds.), *Recueil*, vol. I, p. 343ff.

40 Chorley, 'Cloth Exports'; H. C. Krüger, 'The Genoese Exportation of Northern Cloths to Mediterranean Ports, Twelfth Century', *BTFG*, 65 (1987), 722–50.

41 Munro, 'Industrial Transformations'; J. H. A. Munro, 'The Origins of the English "New Draperies": The Resurrection of an Old Flemish Industry, 1270 – 1570', in N. B. Harte (ed.), *The New Draperies in the Low Countries and England, 1300–1800* (Oxford and New York, 1997), pp. 35–127; J. H. A. Munro, 'The Low Countries' Export Trade in Textiles with the Mediterranean Basin, 1200–1600: A Cost-Benefit Analysis of Comparative Advantages in Overland and Maritime Trade Routes', *International Journal of Maritime History*, 11 (1999), 1–30.

42 G.-G. Dept, *Les influences anglaise et française dans le comté de Flandre au début du XIIIe siècle* (Ghent and Paris, 1928); C. Wyffels, 'De Vlaamse handel op Engeland voor het Engels-Vlaams konflikt van 1270–1274', *Bijdragen voor de geschiedenis der Nederlanden*, 17 (1963), 205–13; and H. Berben, 'Une guerre économique au Moyen âge: L'embargo sur l'exportation des laines anglaises, 1270–1274', in *Études d'histoire dédiées à la mémoire de Henri Pirenne*, pp. 1–17.

were probably hit less hard initially by the English tax policies because their cheaper cloth output made them less dependent upon the English wool supply. But on the other hand, Bruges drapers faced increased competition from other manufacturers, and their less sophisticated products made them more vulnerable. Smaller towns in Flanders, like Diksmuide, Poperinge, Aalst and Oudenaarde, increasingly competed with the cloth entrepreneurs in the larger cities of Flanders and Artois. Regional competitors also emerged in the neighbouring principalities of Brabant and Holland, whose industries succeeded in rivalling Flemish products in both quality and price. Most serious was the rise of textile production in regions to which Flemish cloth was exported. In Normandy, England and Italy, easier access to cheap raw materials and credit, but above all lower transaction costs because of the proximity of markets, conferred distinct advantage on local products, particularly for the cheaper fabrics.[43] Moreover, security along the transportation routes of Europe suffered from political instability and military activity in the late thirteenth and fourteenth centuries causing transaction costs to rise even higher. It was Flemish cloth, and Bruges cloth in particular because of its focus on cheaper fabrics, that lost much of its attractiveness on the international export market.[44]

To avoid decline or even collapse, the Flemish cloth industry reacted to the new market realities of the late thirteenth century in the only possible way. Urban cloth entrepreneurs all but abandoned production of cheaper woollens for export. Instead they concentrated on more expensive woollens for elite customers. Highly expensive and refined fabrics were less subject to demand elasticity. Their value depended, however, much more on the skills of Flemish weavers, dyers and cloth finishers and on the input of expensive raw materials (high-quality English wool and dyestuffs). Entrepreneurs targeted wealthy consumers with textiles manufactured with tight quality standards and 'branding'.[45] During this process of industrial conversion, established cloth centres such as Ypres and Ghent also lashed out at nearby

[43] P. Stabel, *De kleine stad in Vlaanderen: Bevolkingsdynamiek en economische functies van de kleine en secundaire stedelijke centra in het Gentse kwartier (14de – 16de eeuw)* (Brussels, 1995); P. Stabel, 'Les draperies urbaines en Flandre au XIIIe–XVIe siècles', in G. L. Fontana and G. Gayot (eds.), *Wool: Products and Markets (13th–20th Century)* (Padua, 2004), pp. 355–80; R. van Uytven, 'La draperie brabançonne et malinoise du XIIe au XVIIe siècles: Grandeur éphemère et décadence', in M. Spallanzani (ed.), *Produzione, commercio e consumo dei panni di lana* (Florence, 1976), pp. 85–97.

[44] J. H. A. Munro, 'The "New Institutional Economics" and the Changing Fortunes of Fairs in Medieval and Early Modern Europe: The Textile Trades, Warfare and Transaction Costs', *Vierteljahresschrift für Sozial- und Wirtschaftsgeschichte*, 88 (2001), 1–47.

[45] Murray, *Bruges*, p. 279 and bibliography there.

competitors, small towns that imitated the woollens of the larger cities as well as cloth manufacturers in the surrounding countryside.[46] The conversion proved successful and Flemish woollens would remain important until the sixteenth century. Yet of all the big Flemish cloth cities, Bruges was probably the most hesitant in changing its cloth-manufacturing infrastructure and Bruges textile manufacturers would suffer for it.[47]

From a Regional Trading Hub to an International Business Centre, 1100–1250

All larger Flemish and Artesian cloth cities had been centres of regional and even international trade, yet it was Bruges that would finally become the leading market-place of the Low Countries.[48] As we have shown, the first commercial expansion happened because of the city's location in a specialized and flourishing rural economy, and because of its industrial base and importance in comital administration. Located at the crossroads of maritime routes in the North Sea area and the English Channel, the commercial axis from England to the French Champagne fairs, crossing the Alps to the cities of the Italian peninsula, and the route from England to Cologne and the Rhineland, Bruges was well positioned to reap the benefits of trade.[49] Evidence for Bruges trade in the twelfth century is sparse. After the murder of Charles the Good, the short-lived new count, William Clito, withdrew the freedom from tolls which he had granted to the citizens of Bruges five months earlier in return for their approval of his appointment as count in March 1127. This is a clear indication that Bruges burghers were already involved in trade outside their own region.[50] We have seen that in 1134 storm surges helped form the Zwin estuary with direct access to the sea; and that a toll charter shows the existence by c.1160 of the tidal port Letterswerve. In 1174 Count Philip of Alsace expropriated lands around the estuary and had a barrier built to close it off. A new canal connected the Reie in Bruges to the estuary through a sluice in that dam. Water levels could be controlled and a permanent port town, Damme, was created, receiving privileges from the count in 1180. Bruges, however, had paid for the construction works

46 Ibid., p. 281.

47 P. Stabel, *A Capital of Fashion*, forthcoming.

48 For general commercial changes in the Low Countries, see Blockmans, *Metropolen*, pp. 249–58.

49 Ibid., pp. 99–100; Oksanen, *Flanders*, pp. 148–53.

50 Blockmans, *Metropolen*, p. 62; Rider (ed.), *Galbertus Brugensis*, p. 138.

(and the maintenance of the water system) and consequently kept a tight leash on Damme and the other ports that would develop along the estuary: Sint-Anna-ter-Muiden or Mude, Monnikerede, Hoeke and last but not least, Sluis.[51] This cluster of port towns on the left bank of the Zwin was needed because the estuary continually silted up. It also allowed the division of specialized port functions.[52] Damme remained the most important of Bruges' outports until Sluis was founded around 1290. The latter offered a more efficient deep-water harbour. Sluis experienced fast growth both in the volume of commodities and in its population. It outgrew all the other Zwin ports, but like the others, it was also closely monitored by Bruges to the extent that Sluis would be attacked and burnt by Bruges militia in the 1323 revolt of maritime Flanders for violating the city's staple on goods entering the Zwin.[53]

The c.1160 toll charter of Letterswerve reveals more than the existence of a tidal port. It meticulously lists all dues to be paid on goods passing through: salted herring, salmon, mackerel, fish in tons, flatfish and haddock, wine, beer and mead, wool and yarn, grain, beans, salt, turnips, nuts, cheese, soot and grease, lead and copper, but also swords, shields, buckets, drinking cups, plates and messing goods, wax, honey, mattresses, horses, cows, pigs, sheep, wood, manure, fruits, whetstones, millstones, hides, leek, garlic, olives, peat, apples and pears.[54] The attention paid to wine and fish indicates their importance for Letterswerve. These same goods would also be the main staple goods of its successor, Damme. The toll charter also indicates the presence of merchants from Cologne in the Zwin estuary, for it was written after complaints by these merchants about unfair tax collection at Letterswerve; and Rhenish metalware and wine feature prominently in it.[55]

Bruges not only traded through a group of outports, but also participated in the cycle of Flemish fairs at Lille, Ypres and Torhout. Galbert of Bruges described the fairs of Lille and Ypres. At Torhout, a fair had been organized from the eleventh century onwards at the crossroads of the route from Ieper and Diksmuide and the Roman road between Cassel and Bruges, under the protection of the local chapter. The city of Bruges bought a house for

[51] Leloup and Vannieuwenhuyze, 'Damme en Sluis'.

[52] Blockmans, *Metropolen*, p. 252 ; De Smet, 'L'origine des ports du Zwin'.

[53] Murray, *Bruges*, pp. 32–3; Van Houtte, *De geschiedenis van Brugge*, pp. 87–8.

[54] De Groote, 'Het toltarief van Letterswerve'.

[55] A. Verhulst, 'Keulse handelaars in het Zwin tijdens de 12de eeuw en de vroegste ontwikkeling van de Vlaamse zeehavens', *Bijdragen tot de geschiedenis van West-Zeeuws-Vlaanderen*, 81 (1998), 351–8.

its merchants in Torhout in 1294.[56] In 1200 Bruges was granted a fair that would be organized annually between the end of April and the end of May. This fair formally joined the Flemish fair cycle, followed in 1228 by one in the monastic town of Mesen. These five places, each within a stone's throw of the other, formed a yearly cycle of six fairs (two were held at Ypres) from early February to late October. Fairs offered security and concentrated supply and demand, reducing search and information costs for most traders. Local and regional governments secured the roads. They provided safe-conducts and, in return, collected tolls and fees. The fair cycle was relatively close to other large European fairs such as those near Paris (the famous fairs of the 'Lendit'), in southeastern England (the fair of St Ives, where wool was traded), the fairs in the south of Flanders and Hainaut (Valenciennes, Douai, Saint-Omer), and the famous fairs of Champagne. Goods changed hands between fair cycles and merchants visiting the Champagne fairs often travelled to one of the Flemish fairs as well.[57] The Flemish and Champagne fairs succeeded each other, allowing merchants to make deals or credit operations at one fair to be executed at the next. There was intense exchange between the first fair at Troyes and the fairs in Torhout and Lille. In Bruges during the May fair, St Donatian's rented out commercial space around the canons' cloister. The church even hired a security guard for the fair period. The chapter must have valued the revenues, but in 1362 the discomfort of having business on their doorstep proved too much for the canons and they had the merchants frequenting their cloister ejected by the bailiff.[58] Commercial disputes at the Bruges fairs were arbitrated by the city's aldermen (not by a temporary fair court or a specific mercantile court as in many other fair towns).[59] In 1285 the city confirmed that procedures had to be expedient and would not discriminate against foreigners.[60]

Conspicuously absent from the Letterswerve charter, however, is that famous product of Flemish industry, cloth. Yet the essential material for cloth production – wool – was present. After 1100 local Flemish and Artesian wool no longer sufficed: English wool was imported through Bruges.[61] William the Breton described Bruges trade in his *Philippide* (1214) as follows: 'from all corners of the world treasures were sent to

[56] Nicholas, *Medieval Flanders*, p. 117; GVS, *Inventaire*, vol. I, p. 40.

[57] Blockmans, *Metropolen*, pp. 63–4; G. Des Marez and C. Wyffels, *Analyse de reconnaissances des dettes devant les échevins d'Ypres (1249–1291)* (Brussels, 1991), pp. 79–86; and Yamada, 'Le mouvement', pp. 773–89.

[58] Murray, *Bruges*, pp. 68–70.

[59] GVS, *Cartulaire*, vol. I, p. 16.

[60] Ibid., pp. 62–3.

[61] Van Houtte, 'De opkomst', pp. 1–15.

Bruges: silver, gold, exotic fabrics, Hungarian furs, kermes [for dyeing scarlet], wine from Gascony and La Rochelle, iron and other metals, cloth and other goods from Flanders and England'.[62] All goods were sent from Bruges to all quarters of the world.[63] And the undated thirteenth-century list of goods mentioned above hints at the importance already acquired by the Bruges market: the British Isles provided wool and leather, lead, tin, coal, and cheese; Norway falcons, wood, leather, butter, lard and goatskins; Denmark warhorses, leather, lard, ash, herring and hams; Sweden fur, lard, ashes and wood; Russia fur and wax; Hungary, Bohemia and Poland wax, gold and silver, fur and copper; Germany Rhine wine, tar, ashes, wood, grain, iron and steel; Liège and its surroundings copper goods and wood; Bulgaria fur such as ermine and sable; Navarre and Aragon leather from goats and sheep, almonds, wool, furs, sailcloth, saffron and rice; Castile, Leon and Galicia kermes, wax, leather from goats and sheep, wool, furs, quicksilver, lard, cumin, aniseed, almonds, iron and wine; Andalusia and Granada wax, figs, raisins, honey, olive oil, leather, furs, silk and almonds; North Africa and the Balearics wax, leather, fur, cumin, sugar, dates, alum, rice and figs; Sardinia furs; Byzantium alum; the Levant and Egypt pepper and other spices; Armenia cotton and spice; and finally Tartary cloth-of-gold, silks and furs.[64] Many of these goods also feature in a list of fees charged by Bruges brokers in 1303 and in the description of Bruges trade by Francesco Balducci Pegolotti in his merchant manual *Pratica della Mercatura* (1317).[65] The access Bruges enjoyed to foreign goods probably saved lives during the 'great famine' of 1315–17. The city was able to buy grain from Italian merchants and sell it to its citizens at reasonable prices at the height of the dearth.[66]

The twelfth and thirteenth centuries have been characterized by historians of medieval trade as the phase of the 'active Flemish trade'. Flemish merchants carried their trade to foreign markets.[67] Although many foreign merchants, especially those from Cologne, visited the Zwin estuary and the Bruges fairs, Flemings and Bruges traders in particular were active in

62 GVS, *Cartulaire*, vol. I, p. 28.

63 R. van Uytven, 'De overige handelsgoederen te Brugge', in A. Vandewalle (ed.), *Hanzekooplui en Medicibankiers: Brugge, wisselmarkt van Europese culturen* (Oostkamp, 2002), p. 73.

64 GVS, *Cartulaire*, vol. I, pp. 19–21.

65 A. Evans (ed.), *Francesco Balducci Pegolotti, La Pratica della Mercatura*, Medieval Academy Books 24 (Cambridge, MA, 1936). For the brokers' list, see GVS, *Cartulaire*, vol. I, pp. 104–7.

66 Blockmans, *Metropolen*, p. 218; Nicholas, *Medieval Flanders*, p. 207.

67 H. Van Werveke, 'Der Flandrische Eigenhandel im Mittelalter', *Hansische Geschichtsblätter*, 61 (1936), 7–24.

foreign markets, where they were joined by merchants from other Flemish and Artesian cities like Arras, Ypres, Ghent and even Diksmuide.[68] We have seen that Bruges merchants probably already had a merchant guild by 1113 aimed at enhancing mutual assistance when travelling abroad.[69] According to Galbert, several Bruges merchants were doing business in London when they heard of Charles the Good's murder in 1127.[70] Flemish merchants, many from Bruges but also from Saint-Omer, Ypres and Douai, controlled much of England's continental trade in the twelfth century, transferring goods between Flanders, the English fairs, London and the Champagne fairs. They bought wheat and English wool, and sold wine and woollen cloth. Despite or perhaps because of their importance, Flemish merchants often fell victim to English fiscal extortions, confiscations and violence, the result of turbulent politics which continued into the thirteenth century;[71] but this did not hinder Flemish traders from establishing intensive commercial ties with England. They bought wool directly from English monasteries. They were active at the St Ives fairs and developed a sizeable Flemish colony in London.[72] Privileges granted by the king of England mitigated commercial insecurity. King John granted Flemish traders a permit for trade in England in 1213. Flemish merchants were exempted from paying the debts of non-paying countrymen, and from tolls in York and Winchester. More complex systems of credit were operationalized in trade between England and the continent, in which Flemish and Italian merchants were likely involved.[73] The English government, however, expected reciprocity: its subjects were to be treated the same way in Flanders.[74]

Sketching the social profile of these Bruges merchants is difficult because sources do not allow a clear view of urban elites before the thirteenth century. Further analysis of merchants as a social group will appear in Chapter 5; here we should note that social interaction between 'landed aristocracies' and 'commercial elites' seems to have been significant. Galbert

68 Van Houtte, *De geschiedenis van Brugge*, pp. 93–4.

69 Nicholas, *Growth of the Medieval City*, p. 133.

70 Van Houtte, *De geschiedenis van Brugge*, pp. 89–90; Murray, *Bruges*, p. 221.

71 Nicholas, *Medieval Flanders*, pp. 116–18; E. Wedemeyer Moore, *The Fairs of Medieval England: An Introductory Study* (Toronto, 1985), pp. 30–1.

72 Nicholas, *Medieval Flanders*, pp. 164–6; E. Varenbergh, *Histoire des relations diplomatiques entre le Comté de Flandre et l'Angleterre au Moyen-Âge* (Ghent, 1868), pp. 153–5; Wedemeyer Moore, *Fairs of Medieval England*, pp. 13–14; J. A. Van Houtte, *An Economic History of the Low Countries, 800–1800* (London, 1977), p. 35.

73 Van Houtte, *De geschiedenis van Brugge*, p. 90; G.-G. Dept, 'Les marchands flamands et le roi d'Angleterre (1154–1216)', *RN*, 12 (1926), 303–24; T. H. Lloyd, *The English Wool Trade in the Middle Ages* (Cambridge, 1977); Oksanen, *Flanders*, pp. 145–77.

74 Nicholas, *Medieval Flanders*, p. 165.

speaks of the Flemish *pares* or *barones* like Daniel of Dendermonde, Walter of Vladslo, Baldwin and Iwain of Aalst, and the later Bruges castellan, Gervase of Praet.[75] Ranked below this 'feudal nobility' in the 'urban world' were the *milites* – which in this period meant 'warriors' rather than chivalric knights (chivalry in its 'classic' form developing somewhat later in Flanders).[76] Galbert also mentions the leading burghers, who are called 'cives', 'burgenses', 'suburbani' or 'vicini', and he describes their political, legal and diplomatic activities. However, one of the most striking changes in Bruges society was the rise of its merchant class. Their social origins remain a matter of speculation. Before 1100 some may have been traders on the regional agricultural markets or agents of the count's domainal administration. They were perhaps descendants of serfs belonging to the *familia* of the count in his Bruges castle, and of this group of *milites*. Others may have descended from the *coloni* mentioned above (if the term means immigrants into the city).[77] The earliest records indicate that Bruges merchants owned urban land and that they were active in the long-distance trade of luxury goods, salt, metals and other raw materials. Perhaps some had also invested in the developing textile industry.

From the thirteenth century, sources are more forthcoming about the ruling class in Bruges (notably English sources, as the city archives before 1280 have all but disappeared). Most Bruges merchants who traded with England during this period belonged to the same families as those filling the ranks of the city government.[78] Apart from their commercial activities, they also invested in embankment and polders, peat exploitation, brick yards, meadows, fishing rights and tax farming.[79] Just as fundamental to their elite status as communal offices and commerce was their possession of urban landed property. The land the merchants owned in the city or held at fixed rents was divided up and sublet, providing them with further capital to invest in trade.[80] Some of the land was held in feudal tenure. The powerful

75 Warlop, *Flemish Nobility*, vol. I, pp. 136–42.

76 Ibid., pp. 95–101.

77 Nicholas, *Medieval Flanders*, p. 106.

78 The names of Bruges merchants trading with England during the thirteenth century are more easily extracted from the Calendars of Close Rolls and of Patent Rolls than from Flemish sources: see C. Wyffels, 'Peiling naar de sociale stand van een aantal Brugse groothandelaars, inzonderheid op de Britse eilanden (1270–1292)', in *Album Jos De Smet* (Bruges, 1964), pp. 366–7; D. Van den Auweele, 'Schepenbank en schepenen te Brugge (1127–1384): Bijdrage tot de studie van een gewone stedelijke rechts- en bestuursinstelling', 4 vols., unpublished PhD thesis, Catholic University of Leuven (Leuven, 1977), vol. III, pp. 374–5; Häpke, *Brügges Entwicklung*, pp. 189–97.

79 Van den Auweele, 'Schepenbank', vol. III, pp. 385–90; Häpke, *Brügges Entwicklung*, p. 195.

80 Verhulst, *Rise of Cities*, p. 142.

Ram family, for instance, were vassals of the lords of Praet in the quarter of St Giles, and allied to the knightly Tobbin family.[81] But boundaries were blurred. Nobles were equally part of the urban elite and they developed active interests in commerce. The Woestine family held in fief the Great Toll of Bruges, and sold rents on its income to rich burghers. 'Knightly families' like Gruuthuse and Tobbin served as aldermen in the early and mid thirteenth century, alongside merchant families like the Van de Walle, Dop, Bonin, Cant, Van Bachten Halle, Utenzacke, Danwilt, Hubrecht, Calkere, Lam and Priem families. Social distinctions between these groups may not have been important. People like the Voet family were comital officials, who were also active on the land market in Bruges. It is apparent, therefore, that nobles and merchants did not live in separate worlds. Judging by their last names, some of the city's most influential clerics, from St Donatian's or St Saviour's, were also recruited from these families.[82]

The great merchants entered into feudal, commercial and credit relations with the nobility, and certainly by the late thirteenth century many of them also held fiefs in the surrounding countryside from the count or from noble families like the lords of Assebroek and Sijsele. One of the most powerful noble families in thirteenth-century Flanders, the family Van Gistel, held in fief the scales and the Great Toll of Bruges during the thirteenth century, and had close financial relations with leading merchant families such as the Danwilts.[83] Further insight into this ruling class is provided by the records left by the creation of an urban cavalry by the city and count in 1292. Every citizen who possessed more than 300 pound Flemish groat had to own a horse and be ready for combat within three weeks of a call to arms. Those serving as mounted militiamen were merchants, but also hostellers, brokers, butchers and fishmongers.[84] A 1298 charter mentions twelve aldermen and was sealed by fifty-five notable burghers: in total these notables came from forty-five different families, which gives some indication of the relatively restricted character of the Bruges ruling elite. Many of them can

[81] L. Gilliodts-Van Severen, *Bruges ancienne et moderne* (Brussels, 1890), p. 13; Lambert (ed.), *De oorkonden*, pp. 414–15.

[82] The first charters mentioning the Bruges elite show such relations: see A. Schouteet, *Stadsarchief van Brugge: Regesten op de oorkonden*, vol I: *1089–1300* (Bruges, 1973), passim. A detailed study on the thirteenth-century merchant class is still needed, but there are many similarities with the one in Ghent: see F. Blockmans, *Het Gentsche stadspatriciaat vóór 1302* (Antwerp, 1938).

[83] GVS, *Inventaire*, vol. I, pp. 3–4.

[84] J. De Smet, 'De inrichting van de Poorterlijke ruiterij te Brugge in 1292 en haar indeling in gezindheden in 1302', *Verslagen en Mededeelingen der Koninklijke Vlaamse Academie voor Taal- en Letterkunde* (1930), 487–505.

be identified as wool, cloth and wine merchants. The Bonin family, which would remain powerful throughout the Middle Ages, was best represented, with no fewer than six members.[85] This was class rule in its fullest sense: the Bruges merchants monopolized economic, political and social power. Their prestige was also expressed in building campaigns: the paved streets, stone bridges, new churches and hospitals, the Belfry, halls and other commercial infrastructure speak of their dominance. Only at the end of the thirteenth century does evidence appear for greater social mobility, when 'new men,' so called in the narrative sources, entered the ranks of the city magistracy. And only after the political revolution of 1302 would there be a decisive break from the domination of the merchant elite, when for the first years after the revolt at least, new and hitherto unknown names appear in the lists of magistrates.[86]

In 1241 a privilege was given to the city by the countess of Flanders, Joanna of Constantinople, to organize the composition of the town government. It is one of the earliest pieces of evidence for social and political polarization within the city. From a social perspective, its most notable feature was the clause that the aldermen had to be members of the 'Hanse of London' and were not allowed to work with their hands. The 'manual labourer, whoever he may be' ('manuoperarius quicumque fuerit') was excluded from the city government.[87] Almost no other source informs us about the city's manual workers at this time, but this charter strongly suggests their complete exclusion from any power they might have had under the earlier communal regime, even if they were full burghers. The merchants had become ever more dominant.

The history of the so-called 'Flemish Hanse of London' bears witness to this trend. The Hanse was founded between 1212 and 1241.[88] The city of Ypres also had its own London Hanse. Douai joined the association in 1240, followed by Diksmuide, Ghent and Cambrai in 1261. The term *hanse*/*hansa* signified both the duty that had to be paid for mercantile activities abroad and the commercial organization created to organize trade. Hanses generally originated around the mid twelfth century. Their main purpose was mutual assistance when a merchant member was imprisoned

[85] Häpke, *Brügges Entwicklung*, pp. 189–90.

[86] K. Hilderson, 'Schepenbank en patriciaat te Brugge vóór 1302', unpublished MA thesis, Ghent University (Ghent, 1955).

[87] Prevenier, 'La bourgeoisie', pp. 416–17; M. Ryckaert, A. Vandewalle, J. D'hondt et al. (eds.), *Brugge: De geschiedenis van een Europese stad* (Tielt, 1999), p. 40; GVS, *Coutume*, vol. I, p. 196.

[88] H. Van Werveke, '"Hansa" in Vlaanderen en aangrenzende gebieden', *HGG*, 90 (1953), 60–87; C. Wyffels, 'Hanzen in Westelijk Vlaanderen', *De Franse Nederlanden*, 15 (1990), 170–85 (at 178).

or summoned before a foreign court of law. A high membership fee had to be paid to a communal fund and merchants could only become members after having abandoned manual labour for at least a year and a day.[89] After 1241 the Bruges Hanse was either extended to include other Flemish cities, uniting Flemish traders active in London, or became the driving force behind a federation of hanses from different cities. The origins and workings of this federative Flemish Hanse of London are obscure. Only two documents from the third quarter of the thirteenth century offer some insight: a Latin text from Ypres, calling the merchant organization 'Hansa flandrensium, Brugensium scilicet et illorum qui ad hansam illam pertinent';[90] and a French text from Bruges.[91] Both are proposals by Bruges and Ypres as to what the Flemish Hanse of London should look like and how it should function. Its main aim was to defend the interests of Flemish merchants in England. The different members probably realized the strength of inter-urban co-operation in dealing with the king of England and local authorities. By 1250 the federation included traders from many communities: Bruges, Ypres, Diksmuide, Aardenburg, Lille, Oudenburg, Oostburg, Veurne, Orchies, Damme, Torhout, Sint-Winoksbergen (Bergues), Belle (Bailleul), Poperinge, IJzendijke, Sint-Anna-ter-Muiden, and even the bishop's city of Tournai (outside the county of Flanders). Ghent did not become a member as its trade was directed more towards the Rhineland.[92] The Flemish Hanse organized member meetings in England and arbitrated in conflicts between members. Membership fees had to be paid in England. Both texts reveal disagreement between Bruges and Ypres. Bruges sought to control the merchant guild. It claimed the sole right to organize meetings; it wanted its citizens to acquire membership in Bruges and not in England; and it wanted to keep the Hanse's treasury in Bruges. The Flemish Hanse of London was to be directed by a 'hanzegraaf', literally a 'count of the hanse.' He had to be a burgher of Bruges, while his assistant, the so-called 'shield dragon' ('schilddrake') had to come from Ypres.

The Bruges city accounts from 1281 document new entrants to the Flemish Hanse of London, even though Ypres was opposed to buying membership in Flanders. Between 1281 and 1299 no fewer than 199 new

[89] C. Wyffels, 'De Vlaamse Hanze van Londen op het einde van de XIIIe eeuw', *HGG*, 97 (1960), 5–30; C. Wyffels, 'De Vlaamse Hanzen opnieuw belicht', *Academiae Analecta*, 53 (1991), 13–17.

[90] H. Van Werveke, 'Les "statuts" latins et les "statuts" français de la Hanse flamande de Londres', *Handelingen van de Koninklijke Commissie voor Geschiedenis*, 118 (1953), 289–320 (at 311).

[91] Ibid.

[92] H. Van Werveke, 'Das Wesen der flandrischen Hansen', *Hansische Geschichtsblätter*, 76 (1958), 7–20; Verhulst, *Rise of Cities*, p. 132.

members were registered in Bruges. The accounts also allow a reconstruction of the socio-professional profile of members (from Bruges) of the merchant guild. Despite the steep entrance fees for (former) manual labourers, these were nonetheless present. Butchers, bakers, brewers and brokers were among the new members. The lists also provide the first solid data about economic gender relations in the city: women made up 10 per cent of the new Hanse members. The Bruges branch of the Flemish Hanse of London was not entirely monopolized by a few merchant families: it included wealthy craftsmen and retailers too. Perhaps the high entrance fees for manual labourers, and for those whose fathers were not guild members, was not so much an attempt to erect a social boundary, but more a means to guarantee the financial strength of new members. Foreign merchants, such as Flemings in England, were subject to a system of community responsibility.[93] English creditors could seize the goods of any Flemish merchant to recover their losses on a transaction with another Flemish merchant who had defaulted. In order to avoid trade disruptions caused by these seizures, high membership fees kept away adventurers low on capital. (Former) manual labourers may have joined the Flemish Hanse of London to start a trading business in England, but perhaps a more important attraction of the Hanse was its political power. The Bruges branch became a quasi-official urban institution, with the magistracy collecting the membership fees for the communal treasury and the aldermen deciding who was allowed in. The tendency for the urban government also to control 'private' organizations, like the early guilds of the curriers (*leertouwers*) and hosiers (*kousenmakers*), was a general one. They too had to pay entry fees to the urban treasury.[94] Definitely by the end of the thirteenth century, many would have joined the Flemish Hanse of London in Bruges because of its political power and status and not because of their interest in trade with England, where Flemish traders were losing ground. The revolutions of the early fourteenth century, though, ended the political hegemony of the Flemish Hanse of London in Bruges.[95]

[93] A. Greif, 'Impersonal Exchange and the Origin of Markets: From the Community Responsibility System to Individual Legal Responsibility in Pre-Modern Europe', in M. Aoki and Y. Hayami (eds.), *Communities and Markets in Economic Development* (Oxford, 2001), pp. 3–41; L. Boerner and A. Ritschl, 'The Economic History of Sovereignty: Communal Responsibility, the Extended Family, and the Firm', *Journal of Institutional and Theoretical Economics*, 165 (2009), 99–112.

[94] Wyffels, 'De Vlaamse Hanzen opnieuw belicht'.

[95] E. Perroy, 'Le commerce anglo-flamand au XIIIe siècle: La Hanse flamande de Londres', *Revue Historique*, 511 (1974), 3–18; H. Pirenne, 'La Hanse flamande de Londres', in Pirenne, *Les villes*, pp. 157–84.

Bruges took part in another commercial federation too. The Hanse of the Seventeen Cities came into existence between 1185 and 1230, but is not well documented. It seems to have been formed at the Champagne fairs, which had their heyday from the late twelfth to the late thirteenth century.[96] The participation of Bruges merchants seems to have been much less dominant than in the Flemish Hanse of London.[97] In contrast to their colleagues from cities such as Ypres, Arras and Douai, Bruges traders did not often venture beyond the Champagne fairs, although Bruges woollen cloth was marketed in Italy and in the Baltic area.[98]

The era of Flemish active trade came to an abrupt end in the last quarter of the thirteenth century. Flemish merchants generally withdrew from foreign markets. German cities raised tolls for foreigners, while the 1270–4 English–Flemish trade conflict seriously damaged the interests of Flemish merchants. The king of England had demanded increasing taxes from the wool trade and organized a formal wool staple privileging English and Italian merchants. The Champagne fairs went into decline after the French King Philip IV integrated the county of Champagne into his own territories, and clamped down on the fairs by increasing tolls, and by a policy of disruption (arrests and confiscations of tradesmen's goods).[99] The decline of Flemish active trade has perhaps been exaggerated, since some Flemish merchants remained active in France and England in the early fourteenth century.[100] Yet by then a change in the general character of trade and its organization in Bruges cannot be denied. Even so, the change was not necessarily detrimental to the Bruges economy, for foreign merchants had been coming to the city in increasing numbers.

The Letterswerve charter of c.1160 had indicated the presence of Cologne traders in Bruges' vicinity. More foreign merchants appeared in Bruges during the thirteenth century. Bruges changed from a city with native traders on foreign markets into a commercial hub for foreign merchants. By 1230

96 Arras, Saint-Omer, Lille, Douai, Tournai, Ypres, Diksmuide, Bruges, Abbeville, Montreuil-sur-Mer, Cambrai, Valenciennes, Rains and Chalons-sur-Marne. On the Champagne fairs, see J. Edwards and S. Ogilvie, 'What Lessons for Economic Development Can We Draw from the Champagne Fairs?', *Explorations in Economic History*, 49 (2012), 131–48.

97 Van Houtte, *De geschiedenis van Brugge*, p. 92; Blockmans, *Metropolen*, pp. 112–14, 117, 249.

98 Van Houtte, *De geschiedenis van Brugge*, pp. 92–4.

99 E. S. Hunt and J. M. Murray, *A History of Business in Medieval Europe, 1200–1550* (Cambridge, 1999), pp. 160–2; Murray, *Bruges*, p. 190; Nicholas, *Medieval Flanders*, pp. 177–8.

100 Nicholas, *Medieval Flanders*, pp. 287–8; M. De Laet, 'De Vlaamse aktieve handel op Engeland in de eerste helft der 14e eeuw, aan de hand van de Customs Accounts,' in *Economische Geschiedenis van België: Behandeling van de bronnen en problematiek* (Brussels, 1972), pp. 223–31; Van Houtte, *De geschiedenis van Brugge*, p. 179.

Biscayans could be found in Bruges.[101] Traders from Catalonia, Castile, Aragon and Navarre followed, and a few Portuguese were seen on the Bruges markets.[102] In 1253, Hamburg and Lübeck (representing other German cities) obtained an agreement from Countess Margaret of Constantinople on the reduction of tolls, the regulation of the ownership of goods in sunken vessels, arrests in cases of default, and reprisals on the property of foreign merchants. This prefigured the privileged position that the German Hanse came to occupy in the Bruges market in the fourteenth century. Both Hamburg and Lübeck would become key members of the Hanseatic League. Margaret did not grant them an exclusive juridical enclave near Damme, however. The Hanse would never enjoy a privileged territory in Flanders, in contrast to the position they achieved in the London Steelyard or other hotspots, the so-called 'Offices' (*Kontore*) of Hanseatic trade in Bergen or Novgorod.[103] The city of Bremen received similar privileges through the intercession of Gedulf of Bruges, alias of Gruuthuse.[104] French wine traders from Poitou and Saint-Jean-d'Angély were assured of their property rights in 1262.[105] Castilian and Hanseatic merchants received additional privileges in 1280 after they had fled to Aardenburg following a conflict over tolls paid in Bruges; and after civil unrest during the Moerlemaye Revolt, upon receiving the new privileges, they returned to Bruges.[106]

To cater to the needs of this growing group of foreign merchants, a real service economy developed in Bruges. This evolution corresponds

[101] M. P. Rooseboom, *The Scottish Staple in the Netherlands* (The Hague, 1910), pp. 2–3; J. Marechal, 'La colonie espagnole de Bruges du XIVe au XVI siècles', *RN*, 35 (1953), 5–40.

[102] Marechal, 'La colonie espagnole'; F. Miranda, 'Commerce, conflits et justice: Les marchands portugais en Flandre à la fin du Moyen Âge', *Annales de Bretagne et des pays de l'Ouest*, 117 (2010), 193–208.

[103] O. Gelderblom, 'The Decline of Fairs and Merchant Guilds in the Low Countries, 1250–1650', *Jaarboek voor Middeleeuwse Geschiedenis*, 7 (2004), 199–238 (at 200); Murray, *Bruges*, p. 220; and the older studies by W. Stein, 'Über den Umfang des spätmittelalterlichen Handels der Hanse in Flandern und in den Niederlanden', *Hansische Geschichtsblätter*, 23 (1917), 189–236, 'Die deutsche Genossenschaft in Brügge und die Entstehung der deutschen Hanse', *Hansische Geschichtsblätter*, 35 (1908), 409–66, 'Über die ältesten Privilegien der deutschen Hanse in Flandern und die ältere Handelspolitik Lübecks', *Hansische Geschichtsblätter*, 30 (1902), 51–133.

[104] Van Houtte, *De geschiedenis van Brugge*, p. 96; Häpke, *Brügges Entwicklung*, pp. 91–5, 101–4.

[105] Van Houtte, *De geschiedenis van Brugge*, p. 102; J. Craeybeckx, *Un grand commerce d'importation: Les vins de France aux anciens Pays-Bas, XIIIe- XVIe siècles* (Paris, 1958), pp. 87–90, 103–8.

[106] Van Houtte, *De geschiedenis van Brugge*, p. 176; Murray, *Bruges*, p. 220; Häpke, *Brügges Entwicklung*, pp. 227–8; C. Wyffels, 'Nieuwe gegevens betreffende een XIIIde eeuwse "democratische" stedelijke opstand: De Brugse "Moerlemaye" (1280–81)', *Bulletin de la Commission Royale*, 132 (1966), 37–142 (at 51–57, 88–90). The text of the privilege is published in GVS, *Cartulaire*, vol. I, pp. 66–7.

chronologically with the withdrawal of Flemish merchants from foreign markets and has been dubbed a transition from 'active' to 'passive trade'. The Bruges service economy offered foreign merchants the facilities of port infrastructure, brokers and hostellers as intermediaries in trade, money changers and bankers to supply financial needs, but it also included more down-to-earth infrastructure such as taverns, gambling houses, bathhouses and brothels. The services provided by hostellers, brokers and money changers have been evaluated in both a positive and a negative light. Brokers and innkeepers (who also belonged to the brokers' guild) mediated between buyers and sellers, sought out credible counterparties, and offered merchants bundled services (accommodation, food and drink, storage space, payment and agency services and mediation), allowing foreign merchants to trade at low transaction costs. A more pessimistic assessment, however, has pointed out how brokers, through their compulsory presence at wholesale transactions (of more than 5 pounds Flemish *grooten*, three quarters of a master mason's annual wage),[107] were detrimental for freedom of exchange: they were thus harmful rent-seekers.[108] Brokers were mentioned in the 1253 privileges granted to German merchants and their fees were set in a charter of 1262. They were incorporated into a guild in 1293 and officially recognized by the city and the count in 1303.[109] The 1293 guild charter already indicates the dependent ties between brokers and innkeepers, and the stronger position of the latter in relation to the former. By 1302 the brokers' guild was a force to be reckoned with: it supplied fifty-two horses for the Bruges militia; only the weavers and fullers provided more.[110]

It was not only private individuals selling their services to merchants who were fundamental for the development of a service economy: the city government was also committed to the organization of trade through its provision of commercial infrastructure, legislation and justice.[111] The importance of commerce in Bruges was first expressed in stone by the impressive Old

[107] Nicholas, *Medieval Flanders*, p. 298; J. A. Van Houtte, 'Makelaars en waarden te Brugge van de 13e tot de 16e eeuw,' *Bijdragen voor de geschiedenis der Nederlanden*, 5 (1950–1), 1–30, 177–197.

[108] For further debate on this, see Chapter 6; B. Verbist, 'Traditie of innovatie? Wouter Ameyde, een makelaar in het laatmiddeleeuwse Brugge, 1498–1507', unpublished PhD thesis, University of Antwerp (Antwerp, 2014); and a comparison between Bruges and Antwerp in J. Puttevils, P. Stabel and B. Verbist, 'Een eenduidig pad van modernisering van het handelsverkeer: van het liberale Brugge naar het gereguleerde Antwerpen?', in B. Blondé (ed.), *Overheid en economie: Geschiedenis van een spanningsveld* (Antwerp, 2014), pp. 39–54.

[109] Van Houtte, 'Makelaars en waarden'.

[110] Van Houtte, *De geschiedenis van Brugge*, p. 203.

[111] This point is particularly stressed in O. Gelderblom, *Cities of Commerce: The Institutional Foundations of International Trade in the Low Countries, 1250–1650* (Princeton, NJ, 2013).

Hall and attached Belfry (c.1240). The major part of the Hall served to exhibit Flemish woollens and spices to the city's regional and international customers. It also accommodated the stalls of glove makers and mercers. By 1294 the equally impressive 'new hall' or Water Hall was finished, spanning the Kraanrei canal and as such combining loading facilities with a sales venue. Its construction absorbed more than 20 per cent of the city's budget in 1283–4.[112] A city crane for bulky barrels was in place by 1282.[113] The city government also financed two dredging boats, one of which was appropriately known as the 'Mole'.[114] The provision of infrastructure did not always run smoothly. The city scales were a fief held by the Van Gistel and Van der Woestine families and were not always administered transparently. German merchants complained about this in 1280 and requested their own scales from the count, who held the aldermen responsible. When the aldermen refused, the Germans moved to Aardenburg where they received other weighing privileges from the count. They did not return to Bruges for two years, by which time the scales were entrusted to sworn officials appointed by the city.[115] The aldermen also provided a forum for arbitrage in commercial conflicts.[116] The procedures can only be studied, however, for the fifteenth century onwards. They show a great concern to involve the foreign traders themselves in conflict settlement.[117]

In return for the provision of infrastructure and services, the city demanded various tolls on commercial transactions. The 'Small Toll' (*cleene tol*) was essentially a tax on a long list of victuals and articles of daily consumption brought into the city to be retailed on the city's daily and weekly markets. The fee was collected at the city gates. The 'Great Toll' was a due, held in fief from the count, levied on goods imported by boat into the city. It concerned inter-regional and long-distance commerce and was linked to the weighing right. The toll was collected at the official city scale at the end of the Kraanrei where the St John's bridge and the Spiegelrei intersected. Other dues were to be paid on ships entering and leaving the Zwin estuary: ballast due (*oorlof*), passage fee (*leenknechtgeld*), and further taxes to be paid in the Zwin.[118] The city also tried to purchase the rights of lay lords in the city

112 Murray, *Bruges*, pp. 63–7. For more details on these buildings, see Chapter 5.

113 A. Vandewalle, 'De stadskraan', in Vandewalle (ed.), *Hanzekooplui*, pp. 25–6 (at 25).

114 Blockmans, *Metropolen*, p. 254.

115 Nicholas, *Medieval Flanders*, pp. 182–3.

116 Gelderblom, *Cities of Commerce*, p. 106.

117 P. Stabel, 'De gewenste vreemdeling: Italiaanse kooplieden en stedelijke maatschappij in het laat-middeleeuwse Brugge', *Jaarboek voor Middeleeuwse Geschiedenis*, 4 (2001), 189–221.

118 Murray, *Bruges*, pp. 59, 72; Van Houtte, *De geschiedenis van Brugge*, pp. 196, 198–201; G. Renson, 'Het tolrecht te Brugge tot de jaren 1500', in *Misscellanea Jean Gessler* (Antwerp,

which could hinder trade: in 1293 it bought the lord of Gistel's rights on the land where the city crane was located and in 1298 it obtained from the lords of Gruuthuse the right to purchase the tax on imported beers, which were not brewed with *gruut* (the mix of spices used to brew beer before hops were introduced in the fourteenth century, and a fiscal monopoly of the Gruuthuses).[119] In 1324 Bruges obtained formal staple rights for all goods entering Flanders through the Zwin. This implied that all goods had to be offered on the Bruges market before being sent elsewhere. Commerce as such was concentrated at Bruges. The city became a legally enforced central place in the economic network of the county. Damme received a partial exemption from Bruges' staple privileges regarding horses and heavy goods packed in tons such as herring and wine.[120] In Hoeke and Monnikerede, merchants were allowed to sell grain, dried fish, skins and materials for rigging boats. Yet Bruges' staple rights were frequently contested: innumerable staple infringements occurred throughout the late Middle Ages.[121]

The end of the thirteenth century began a period of crisis and conversion: a transition from active to passive trade, the greater influx of foreign merchants and the dawn of a service economy. Bruges became subject to wider economic changes. Wars in and around the Mediterranean and unrest in France signalled the end of the Champagne fairs and may have raised the costs of land transport, making marine transport relatively cheaper.[122] Commerce by sea benefited port towns. Moreover, as Raymond De Roover argued, there was a growing 'sedentarization' of trade, which favoured larger centres where trade was concentrated and conducted throughout the year.[123] Flanders was hit economically by the Anglo-French war of the late thirteenth century with both kingdoms boycotting each other, and by increasing competition in cloth manufacture and declining volumes of English wool reaching Flanders, by lower demand for Flemish cloth in the Mediterranean and as a consequence by large-scale unemployment in

1949), pp. 1044–60. For the various tolls: *oorlof, cleenen oorlof* or *petit congié* in the Zwin estuary and Sluis: GVS, *Inventaire*, vol. VI, p. 40. The Sluis toll was bought by Bruges in 1469: GVS, *Inventaire (Glossaire flamand)*, p. 464 and *Inventaire*, vol. VI, p. 184. For the other tolls: GVS, *Inventaire (Glossaire flamand)*, pp. 394, 482 and 800, and GVS, *Inventaire*, vol. VI, pp. 126, 184.

119 Nicholas, *Medieval Flanders*, p. 131.

120 Blockmans, *Metropolen*, p. 254.

121 B. Lambert, 'Merchants on the Margin: Fifteenth-Century Bruges and the Informal Market', *JMH*, 42 (2016), 226–53.

122 Munro, 'The "New Institutional Economics"'.

123 R. de Roover, 'The Commercial Revolution of the Thirteenth Century,' *Bulletin of the Business Historical Society*, 16 (1942), 34–9; Verbist, 'Traditie'.

textile manufacture.[124] Yet Bruges was well positioned to make the best of this crisis and the resulting structural changes in trade and industry. The city enjoyed a central position in the Flemish urban network, which was still a densely populated area generating a large home demand and producing textiles on an industrial scale which had to be marketed; and the city boasted a legally enforced market by 1323. Bruges was attracting merchants from all over Europe and the city had organized itself into a service economy. Hence, Bruges was well equipped at the dawn of the fourteenth century to embark on its Golden Age. Even so, industrially, the golden age began on a false note.

Failing Industrial Conversion?

While a commercial reorientation was taking place in Bruges, the late thirteenth and early fourteenth centuries witnessed crop failure and famine, industrial conversion and reinvestment, vast unemployment and growing social tensions throughout the Flemish cloth industry. Social unrest and outright revolt were part of the process in the 1280s and 1300s. The events that ultimately led to social revolt and the triumph of the Bruges craft guilds after the Battle of the Golden Spurs in 1302 can be explained with reference to this period of transition. But harsh economic change also stimulated the appearance of new groups in urban society. It restructured cloth manufacture, still by far the main employer in the city, by handing the initiative for industrial manufacture to guild-organized master craftsmen. This would gradually produce a larger and politically more influential middle class, who would become the backbone of the city's economic success half a century later. But the process was disastrous for most textile workers, skilled and unskilled, men and women alike, whose job opportunities must have declined considerably. Labour markets also became more gendered. Perhaps to compensate for falling employment, the craft guilds seem to have pushed out independent female labour from the key stages of textile manufacture from weaving to cloth finishing. Women were increasingly confined to the male-dominated household, their job opportunities limited to tasks within the household and family enterprise or to low-skilled and low-status jobs in manufacture and retail. Whereas they had been active in the twelfth and thirteenth centuries in most stages of textile production except fulling, their involvement became limited to the labour-intensive

124 Blockmans, *Metropolen*, pp. 205–11.

but badly paid preparing stages (spinning yarn, combing wool) or finishing stages (cleaning the finished fabric). Only in these areas were women able to hang on as independent workers.[125]

The process of industrial change at the turn of the fourteenth century was slow and difficult everywhere in Flanders, and probably more so in Bruges. Again this change is poorly documented. The statutes of the Bruges cloth industry of 1282 and 1284 were issued at the beginning of this period of change, after a long process of negotiation between the two stakeholders, the city authorities and the entrepreneurs (*drapiers*), those groups who controlled the manufacturing stages and who were in most cities closely linked to the mercantile elites. The social uprising of the Moerlemaeye in 1280–1 shook the foundations of industrial relations in the city, which might explain the tenacity with which Bruges entrepreneurs held on to their traditional fabrics. Light woollens and says were still the main products of Bruges textile manufacturers, but mention was also being made of more expensive fabrics (*pifelaers, dukerlinghe, pleine lakenen*) and of the newly fashionable striped woollens (*strijpte lakenen*). It is striking how 'liberal' the request of 1282 still is: woollens manufactured outside the city could be finished and marketed without much problem. The *drapiers* at this stage still wanted to avoid interference by craft guild authorities. The statutes forbade drapers to combine their entrepreneurial activities with mastership in the major craft guilds of fullers, dyers and cloth finishers.[126] Only the weavers escaped mention. Some master weavers had probably gained access to entrepreneurship in textile manufacture. The craft guilds in textile manufacture typically consisted on the one hand of a multitude of poor master craftsmen (proletarianized wage-earners in all but name), journeymen and apprentices, and on the other, of a smaller group of wealthier masters, who made their profits less from weaving itself than from entrepreneurship, organizing the stages of textile manufacture and complementing the role of the wool and cloth merchants. Eventually the dominance of the drapers and the ambiguous role they played inside the textile crafts led to a regulatory environment which was a complex mixture of entrepreneurial freedom and strict rules on quality control, labour markets and skill. Hence the drapers insisted in 1282 that every man would be allowed to manufacture cloth, 'from whatever town or village he came' ('van wat porten jof van

125 P. Stabel, 'Working Alone? Single Women in the Urban Economy of Late Medieval Flanders (Thirteenth – Early Fifteenth Century)', in J. De Groot, I. De Vos and A. Schmidt (eds.), *Single Life and the City, 1200–1900* (London, 2015), pp. 27–49.

126 Espinas and Pirenne (eds.), *Recueil*, vol. I, pp. 369–88.

dorpen'), if the right quality of fabric was presented at the Bruges market, where standards set by the Bruges merchants and entrepreneurs could be implemented. At this stage the merchants and drapers wanted to remain in control of what was still a massive industry, and by segmenting labour markets they avoided strong opposition from within the emerging craft guilds. There was a ban on combining various trades within the chain of production. No artisan was allowed to combine two masterships, a practice that previously seems to have been ubiquitous in cloth manufacture. Other statutes reveal a relatively 'free' labour market.[127] Entrepreneurs clearly wanted to stimulate competition among artisans and keep wages down, and the structure of the Bruges cloth industry, with its cheaper output, required such a strategy, perhaps more pressingly than in other towns.

By 1300, however, the inevitable could no longer be put off. Bruges had to fall in line with other Flemish and Artesian cloth cities and focus on high-quality woollens. The manufacture of (semi-) worsteds could no longer be combined with that of the more expensive greased plain and striped woollens. Regulation of quality control at the city's *ramen* (tenter frames), where cloth was finished, became stricter around 1290 as did the monopoly of the Bruges cloth hall on the selling of urban and rural textiles. Independent officers were appointed to supervise control. Urban worsteds were on the way back: the future of cloth manufacture in Bruges now belonged to high-quality cloth, just as it did in the other Flemish cities. But again the social unrest generated by economic conversion burst into the open as competition among old and parvenu elite families led to political friction. As we will see, the revolt of the Bruges middle classes of independent small commodity producers reached its peak in the events of 1301 and 1302, shaking up Bruges society from top to bottom. The victory of the Bruges city militia over the French army at Kortrijk on 11 July 1302 allowed the craft guilds and the new elites of entrepreneurs to brush the old merchant class aside, at least in part and for a time.

Some final light can be shed on the socio-economic changes in Bruges during this transitional period by inferring back from later source material. The draft lists for the city militia from the early fourteenth century allow us to measure, for the first time, the strength of these new groups, and their relative importance in the urban economy.[128] They show that Bruges was still an archetypal medieval industrial city. Some caution is necessary as the lists allow us to assess only the guild-based economy. The guilds,

[127] Espinas and Pirenne (eds.), *Recueil*, vol. I, p. 381.

[128] Dumolyn, 'Population', pp. 49–51.

Table 3.1 *Occupational structure in Bruges and Ghent in the first half of the fourteenth century*

%	Bruges 1302	Bruges 1338	Ghent 1356–8
Textiles	44.7	43.6	56.0
Clothing	14.2	21.2	10.1
Food	10.5	12.3	11.0
Trade and services	11.0	6.6	2.3
Construction	11.3	6.2	5.6
Durables	4.1	6.0	3.5
Transport	2.3	1.6	9.6
Luxury	0.8	1.2	0.7
Health	0.8	0.8	-
Arms	0.4	0.4	-

Source: draft lists without the share of the bourgeoisie in the city militia

together with the bourgeoisie or *poorterij*, provided the backbone of the city militia. In Bruges' political tradition, the *poorters* constituted the class of wealthy city elites, dominated by elite merchants involved in local, regional and international trade,[129] but it was a socially heterogeneous group which also included small retailers, rentiers and others. They had in common the use of the so-called citizens' right (*poortersrecht*) allowing each burgher to be involved in any trade (without further obligations like membership of a guild) and to trade freely up to a maximum of 3 pounds Flemish *grooten* (a substantial sum at the time).

In the early fourteenth century, textile manufacture employed almost half the population. Most textile craftsmen were active in the production of traditional woollen cloth. As such, Bruges did not differ greatly from the other big Flemish cities. In Ghent in the same period over half the population was involved in cloth manufacture and the proportion for Ypres was higher still.[130] But by 1302 cloth manufacture was already a very different industry from its counterpart half a century before. Competition from smaller industrial towns in Flanders caused similar shifts in the nature of

[129] The observations on the *poorterij* in K. Müller-Herrenschwand, 'Brugges Bevölkerung und Wirtschaft zwischen 1282 und 1492 im Spiegel der Einbürgerungsquellen', in R. Schwinges (ed.), *Neubürger im späten Mittelalter: Migration und Austausch in der Städtelandschaft des alten Reiches (1250–1550)* (Berlin, 2002), pp. 479–505, should be used with great care.

[130] Prevenier, 'Bevolkingscijfers'; H. Pirenne, 'Les dénombrements de la population d'Ypres au XVe siècle, 1412–1506: Contribution à la statistique sociale du Moyen Âge', *Vierteljahrschrift für Sozial- und Wirtschaftsgeschichte*, 1 (1903), 1–32.

employment in Eeklo, Diksmuide or Kortrijk.[131] The crisis of traditional cloth manufacture that had started in the late thirteenth century (involving the disappearance in the large cities of the manufacture first of cheaper and then middle-range woollens, as well as the relocation of industrial output to smaller textile towns and the countryside), did not cause immediate disruption to the industry in Bruges, at least not until the mid fourteenth century.[132] But internally, the structure of the industry could not have been more different. By then the cloth guilds, which could guarantee more efficiently the required standard quality for more expensive fabrics, had acquired a pivotal role in this new industrial constellation and slowly the wealthier guild masters, mostly weavers, replaced the capitalist merchant-entrepreneurs as the key organizers of the production chain.

The diminishing share of textile manufacture in Bruges over the following decades implies that a stronger position was being occupied by other sectors in the urban economy. In particular the clothing industries (tailors, leather workers) seem to have been thriving even by 1300. A greater importance for craft guilds involved in food trade, the manufacture of durable consumer goods and of luxuries, albeit still modest, can also be acknowledged. The process whereby Bruges became a centre of luxury and fashion trades and a market for durable consumer goods seems to have been present at this early stage. The occupational structure of Ghent, the largest industrial city of northern Europe, was much less diverse in the 1350s, despite the fact that the number of craft guilds in both cities was nearly identical.[133]

To find evidence for the growth of clothing and fashion in Bruges this early, at the start of the fourteenth century, is surprising. The period is generally described as one of sharp and generalized economic decline across Europe.[134] The 'great famine' of 1315–17 and the end of the long period of Malthusian growth must have gravely affected economic activity and purchasing power, in the countryside and cities. The economic difficulties, which were also felt in Bruges, are confirmed by the apparent decline of transport, international trade and even building industries. Moreover, behind the stability of textiles, shrinking markets for cheaper textiles must have caused massive structural unemployment in the large cloth cities of

[131] Stabel, 'Les draperies urbaines'.

[132] Munro, 'Industrial Transformations'; Chorley, 'Cloth Exports'.

[133] D. Nicholas, *The Metamorphosis of a Medieval City: Ghent in the Age of the Arteveldes, 1302–1390* (Lincoln, 1987); Prevenier, 'Bevolkingscijfers'.

[134] On the crisis of textile manufacture in Flanders, see Stabel, *De kleine stad*, pp. 122–75.

Flanders. Their populations, which had grown almost continuously from the eleventh century onwards, were clearly stagnating by then.[135]

Yet there are other indicators of change to set alongside the evidence for economic difficulty. It has been argued that meat consumption in the cities was increasing in exactly the same period. This suggests stable if not rising purchasing power among particular groups in society.[136] The modest increase in early fourteenth-century Bruges of luxuries, durable consumer goods and food, and the spectacular rise of clothing industries, reveal a similar trend. And even the events surrounding 1302 – the revolt of the Bruges guilds and their victory against the French knights – can be considered in the context of changing social relations in the city, whereby some groups profited from changes in international trade and, above all, in the organization of cloth manufacture.[137] As most demand for durable consumer goods, food (meat and fish, vegetables, oriental fruit) and clothing (dress, purses, belts, hats, stockings, leather) was generated by the urban middle classes, the changing nature of the cloth industry may have been an important catalyst for changing patterns of consumption. As will be argued further on (Chapter 6), the huge success of Bruges, not only as an international commercial city, but also as a place of thriving guild-organized middle classes, active in specialist trades and manufacture, was built on a long process of economic adaptation and experimentation.

[135] Stabel, 'Composition et recompositions des réseaux urbains'.

[136] T. Soens and E. Thoen, 'Vegetarians or Carnivores? Standards of Living and Diet in Late Medieval Flanders', in S. Cavaciocchi (ed.), *Le interazioni fra economia e ambiente biologico nell'Europa preindustriale* (Prato, 2010), pp. 495–527.

[137] On the social background of industrial change in Bruges, see P. Stabel, 'Guilds in Late Medieval Flanders: Myths and Realities of Guild Life in an Export-Oriented Environment', *JMH*, 30 (2004), 187–212; and Stabel, *Capital of Fashion*, forthcoming.

4 Social Groups, Political Power and Institutions I, c.1100–c.1300

JAN DUMOLYN, GEORGES DECLERCQ AND JELLE HAEMERS

Strong economic growth in Bruges during the central Middle Ages needed favourable conditions: chief among these was the rule of law within the urban space. This required city-dwellers to possess a degree of autonomy in order to organize their own economic, social and political life, notwithstanding their contractual relationship with princely authority. The attempt to acquire such autonomy is evident in many European towns from c.1050 onwards, and is generally referred to as the 'communal movement'. During this epoch, urban communities can be characterized as groups of people inhabiting a common space bound by secular justice and by networks of kinship and friendship.[1] Urban justice was delivered according to the laws and customs of what medievalists usually term 'the commune'.[2] This chapter traces the emergence of the commune in Bruges: what it meant, how it developed, but also how it was shaped by the disruptions of social and political unrest from the thirteenth century onwards.

From a legal and political standpoint, forming an urban commune was primarily about townspeople taking measures to protect themselves from oppression and private feuds.[3] From a social-anthropological perspective, the commune may be viewed as a community of labour, markets and solidarity, almost comparable to a large kin group. Towns were constantly filling with newcomers from the countryside, who were often cut off from their places of origin, and in need of substitute kin ties: the commune fulfilled this need. The significance of the city's communal organization cannot be overstated. As later chapters will show, it would generate a lasting set of ideas, expressed through a 'sign language' of buildings, walls, gates and towers, of bells and clocks, of rallying cries and oaths of brotherhood or mutual aid. It would develop within a common space, sanctified by local cults and collective devotion, forming an arena for ritualized expressions of

[1] W. Blockmans, 'Inclusiveness and Exclusion: Trust Networks as the Origins of European Cities', *Theory and Society*, 39 (2010), 315–26.

[2] C. Petit-Dutaillis, *Les communes françaises: Caractères et évolution des origines au XVIIIe siècle* (Paris, 1947); and more recently P. Blickle, *Kommunalismus: Skizzen einer gesellschaftlichen Organisationsform* (Oldenbourg, 2000).

[3] S. Reynolds, *Kingdoms and Communities in Western Europe, 900–1300* (Oxford, 1984), p. 182.

both violence and peace. The commune became the urban authority over a territory of markets and collective properties, controlling infrastructure, streets, roads and canals; and it also became the ideal that justified revenge wrought on enemies outside the city boundaries, and punishment inflicted on violators of city laws within. The beginnings of this communal authority in Bruges become apparent in the twelfth century; yet at the same time so do the social inequalities that also came to characterize the city in the later Middle Ages. The fraught relationship between the communal ideal and social division is also a theme of this chapter.

The Commune and the Count

The earliest examples of the commune are found in northern and central Italy, where communal ideas, institutions and practices developed in conjunction with the administration of common property, markets and port infrastructure, or the farming out of princely tolls and taxes to individuals.[4] The development of the medieval commune, however, was by no means limited to the Italian peninsula: it is also evident in the Holy Roman Empire and the kingdom of France. German historians refer to an *Eidgenossische Bewegung* beginning in the eleventh century, at the heart of which was the *coniuratio*, the sworn oath of city-dwellers.[5] The oath-takers were mostly merchants and artisans, though they often included *milites*, *ministeriales* and clerics. In France, well-known examples are the communes of Le Mans (1070), Noyon (1108–9), Amiens (about 1113) and Laon (1112).[6] In relation to northern France, Petit-Dutaillis defined the commune as an oath made by burghers for mutual aid.[7] Vermeesch emphasized the significance of *pax*, as an extension of the *Pax et treuga Dei*. The idea of a 'peace community' provided an ideological framework in which burghers could express their desire to be liberated from knightly extortion and arbitrary forms of justice such as ordeals and duels so that market peace and freedom from

4 G. Volpe, *Studi sulle instituzioni comunali a Pisa* (Florence, 1970); G. Dilcher, *Die Entstehung der lombardischen Stadtkommune: Eine rechtsgeschichtliche Untersuchung* (Aalen, 1967); J. K. Hyde, *Society and Politics in Medieval Italy: The Evolution of the Civil Life, 1000–1350* (London and Basingstoke, 1973); E. Coleman, 'Cities and Communes', in D. Abulafia (ed.), *Italy in the Central Middle Ages, 1000–1300* (Oxford, 2001), pp. 27–57.

5 Classically formulated by H. Planitz, *Die deutsche Stadt im Mittelalter: Von der Römerzeit bis zu den Zunftkämpfen* (Graz and Köln, 1954), pp. 102–25.

6 A. Vermeesch, *Essai sur les origines et la signification de la commune dans le nord de la France* (Heule, 1966), pp. 105, 113.

7 Petit-Dutaillis, *Les communes*, pp. 80–4.

tolls could be established and trade and industry be developed. This desire for liberation was not revolutionary, however, because the ties of dependence between lords and their subjects were not broken by the commune, and oath-takers continued to pay their land rents to lords.[8]

Galbert of Bruges' description of events following the murder of Count Charles the Good in 1127 appears to show Flemish burghers as emancipated and politically conscious groups, fully prepared to take up arms to protect their rights. In the case of many episcopal cities in northwestern Europe, for instance Cambrai, Noyon, Laon, Cologne and Mainz, the formation of a sworn commune began in the context of revolt against or opposition to the bishop.[9] But in general, the communal movement in Flanders was not characterized by violent upheavals and confrontations with the authority of local lords or the count. The terminology used in the sources for the phenomenon also varies. Thus, in Flanders the word *communio* is only explicitly mentioned in the cases of Saint-Omer and Ghent, but some other terms used for the Flemish communes and for those of neighbouring regions like Hainaut, Brabant and Liège point to their underlying socio-economic, political, legal and ideological features. For instance the term *pax* (attested in Valenciennes with the meaning of 'urban commune') denotes the peace and security that the citizens sought to preserve. The term *amicitia*, used in Aire-sur-la-Lys, implies the mutual aid and free consent of the sworn men. Another keyword is the common term used for an urban privilege or liberty charter: the *cora* or *keure*, that is, the 'chosen law' of the community.[10] Clearly, by 1100 different social groups in the early urban agglomerations had already developed a sense of legal and political community, including the idea of being a burgher.

The origins of communes in Flanders have been the subject of considerable debate. In 1905, the Belgian historian Vanderkindere surmised that legal forms of the commune appeared in the southern Low Countries, the

[8] Vermeesch, *Essai sur les origines*, pp. 177–9; Platelle, 'La violence'; Ross (ed.), *Murder of Charles the Good* (see especially the Introduction); H. Hoffmann, *Gottesfriede und treuga Dei* (Stuttgart, 1964); O. G. Oexle, 'Friede durch Verschwörung', in J. Fried (ed.), *Träger und Instrumentarium des Friedens im hohen und späten Mittelalter* (Sigmaringen, 1991), pp. 115–50.

[9] Planitz, *Die deutsche Stadt*, pp. 102–15; A. Saint-Denis, *Apogée d'une cité: Laon et le Laonnois aux XIIe et XIIIe siècles* (Nancy, 1994); J. Deploige, 'Revolt and the Manipulation of Sacral and Private Space in 12th-Century Laon and Bruges', in P. François, T. Syrjaama and H. Terho (eds.), *Power and Culture: New Perspectives on Spatiality in European History* (Pisa, 2010), pp. 89–107.

[10] L. Vanderkindere, *Choix d'études historique* (Brussels, 1909), p. 254; and see F.-L. Ganshof, 'Le droit urbain en Flandre au début de la première phase de son histoire (1127)', *Revue d'histoire du droit*, 19 (1951), 387–416; A. Derville, *Saint-Omer: Des origines au XIVe siècle* (Lille, 1995); and Verhulst, *Rise of Cities*.

jurés, *jurati*, *coremannnen*, *keurheren* or other similar titles mentioned in later sources being the successors of offices that existed in the early communes.[11] He claimed that the Flemish towns had also originally been communes in the legal sense, governed by 'sworn men'. Henri Pirenne, however, put forward another view. He argued that Flanders was an exception to the trend towards communal self-rule: the Flemish counts soon realized the economic importance of the rapidly growing towns and therefore gave their inhabitants a measure of autonomy, granting them their own 'bench' of aldermen, appointed by the count but composed of burghers, who acted both as city administrators and judges. These aldermen (typically *scabini*, *schepenen* or *échevins*) were already in place in the early twelfth century, or in the case of Bruges were installed after the murder of Charles the Good in 1127.[12] The Flemish urban institutions were an imposition from above rather than a creation from below by the city-dwellers themselves. Yet the precise role of the aldermen and of the count in their creation was not as clear-cut as Pirenne argued. Indeed, Vanderkindere posited that the urban aldermen were originally responsible (between the later eleventh and the mid twelfth century) only for administering criminal justice within the community, whereas the town itself was governed by the 'sworn men' (*jurati*) of the commune. Comital control over these sworn men only came later. The reign of Philip of Alsace (c.1163/8–1191) marked the turning point, transforming urban government in Flanders: in most towns communal institutions such as the *jurati* were eliminated (or marginalized); a new, uniform and severe criminal law was imposed on Flemish towns (the so-called *Grote Keure*); and the aldermen appointed by the count took over their administration. According to Vanderkindere, the urban elites accepted this reform as they recognized the advantages it would bring to their power.[13]

Vanderkindere's arguments were solidly source-based, but the views of Pirenne prevailed, particularly in Belgium. It was only after the Second World War that Belgian historians – among them F.-L. Ganshof, a disciple of Pirenne, who had earlier defended the views of his master – began to question Pirenne's opinion and conceded, in some cases reluctantly, that sworn

[11] Vanderkindere, *Choix d'études historiques*, pp. 251–304, 305–41.

[12] H. Pirenne, 'La question des jurés dans les villes flamandes', *BTFG*, 5 (1926), 401–21; F.-L. Ganshof, 'L'origine des constitutions urbaines en Flandre: A propos d'un livre récent', *Le Moyen Âge*, 26 (1926), 349–68; according to F. Blockmans, 'De oudste privileges der grote Vlaamsche steden', *Nederlandsche Historiebladen*, 1 (1938), 421–46, they existed even earlier, but his reasoning is largely speculative.

[13] Vanderkindere's view was contested, but without really sound arguments, by Pirenne, *Les villes*, pp. 201–18. A general view similar to that of Vanderkindere was defended by R. Monier, *Les institutions judiciaires des villes de Flandre des origines à la rédaction des coutumes* (Lille, 1924).

communes had existed in Flanders and that originally the urban aldermen had only been judges.[14] Yet it was not until 1999 that a Ghent scholar, Adriaan Verhulst, would formulate a view that coincided more or less with that of Vanderkindere's.[15] It will be argued here that Vanderkindere's insights were mostly correct and that the Flemish cities, including Bruges, were no exception to the general tendency in this period towards communal self-rule for which communes possessed institutions of their own. Yet a case can be made to support Pirenne's argument that the strong Flemish counts were generally supportive of urban communities in Flanders (even if the sources are usually vague on this point).[16] By the end of the eleventh century, these dynamic princes seem to have appreciated that liberating merchants from excessive toll tariffs and arbitrary seigniorial violence was also in their own economic interest.[17] Counts Baldwin V (r.1035–67) and Robert I 'the Frisian' (r.1071–93), particularly from the mid eleventh century onwards, found the growing urban communities to be natural allies against the unruly noblemen of the county. These counts promoted 'market peace' to protect commerce and merchants. The earliest traces of this market peace guaranteed by the count date from the late eleventh century: at Torhout (with an annual fair attested in 1084) and at Geraardsbergen (a weekly market in 1067/70). Similarly dated are the earliest indications of urban privileges granted by the counts, albeit for the minor towns of Geraardsbergen (1067/70) and Aire-sur-la-Lys (probably 1093–1111).[18] After an initial impetus

[14] F.-L. Ganshof, 'Einwohnergenossenschaft und Graf in den flandrischen Städten während des 12. Jahrhunderts', *Zeitschrift der Savigny-Stiftung für Rechtsgeschichte. Germanistische Abteilung*, 74 (1957), 98–118; Ganshof, 'Le droit urbain', pp. 389–90; H. Van Werveke, 'De steden: Rechten, instellingen en maatschappelijke toestanden', in *Algemene Geschiedenis der Nederlanden*, vol. II (Utrecht, 1950), pp. 374–416 (at 379–88); R. C. Van Caenegem, 'Galbert van Brugge en het recht', *Mededelingen van de Koninklijke Academie voor Wetenschappen, Letteren en Schone Kunsten van België, Klasse der letteren*, 40 (1978), 34; similar critiques by C. Wyffels, 'Is de Brugse keure betreffende het "poortersgeding", gedagtekend van 1229, in werkelijkheid zestig jaar jonger?', *Legal History Review*, 38 (1968), 525–33.

[15] Verhulst, *Rise of Cities*, pp. 125–31.

[16] The best source material comes from the French-speaking cities of Flanders: see G. Espinas, *Les origines du droit d'association dans les villes de l'Artois et de la Flandre française jusqu'au début du XVIe siècle*, 2 vols. (Lille, 1941–2); P. Bertin, *Une commune flamande-artésienne: Aire-sur-la-Lys des origines au XVIe siècle* (Arras, 1947); P. Rolland, *Les origines de la commune de Tournai: Histoire interne de la seigneurie épiscopale tournaisienne* (Brussels, 1931); Derville, *Saint-Omer.*

[17] K. Schulz, '*Denn sie lieben die Freiheit so sehr...*': *Kommunale Aufstände und Entstehung des europäischen Bürgertums im Hochmittelalter* (Darmstadt, 1992), pp. 101–31; O. G. Oexle, 'Die Kultur der Rebellion: Schwureinung und Verschwörung im früh- und hochmittelalterlichen Okzident', in M. T. Fögen (ed.), *Ordnung und Aufruhr im Mittelalter: Historische und juristische Studien zur Rebellion* (Frankfurt am Main, 1995), pp. 119–37.

[18] Blockmans, 'De oudste'.

given by the Peace and Truce of God movement which had been influential in Flanders from about 1030, the counts, especially Baldwin VII (r.1111–19) and Charles the Good (r.1119–27), increasingly assumed the role of warrantors of the peace. The *pax Dei* now became a *pax comitis*.[19] At the same time, local 'communities of peace' came into existence in towns and rural areas, assuming a de facto legal and semi-autonomous status.[20] In this respect, towns were appropriately called '*loci pacifici*' by Galbert of Bruges, that is, 'places protected by a special peace'.[21] Thus, the picture offered by the scattered documents is that some time between the reigns of Counts Robert the Frisian (r.1071–93) and William Clito (r.1127–8), the Flemish towns became in effect, if not in legal practice, largely autonomous bodies separated from the countryside, having achieved this without any apparent conflict with central power. Comital interest in the urban economies would persist, for subsequent counts, notably Philip of Alsace at the end of the twelfth century, would take many measures to stimulate growth which were mutually beneficial for the cities and comital revenues.[22]

The Rise of a Commune in Bruges

The exact development of the early urban commune in Bruges can only be surmised. One thing is certain: by the time Galbert wrote his chronicle in 1127–8 some form of communal organization was functioning in the city. The indications of this in the chronicle are numerous: in 1127 the urban community had its own customary law; and during the events following Charles the Good's murder, the burghers of Bruges (*cives* or *burgenses*) unmistakably acted as a collectivity, with their own spokesmen and/or leaders (*sapientiores*, *meliores*, *prudentiores*), who were in contact with their counterparts in other Flemish towns. Some sort of mutual solidarity existed within the town, for the burghers not only claimed the exclusive right to

19 Hoffmann, *Gottesfriede*, pp. 143–58.

20 Van Caenegem, *Geschiedenis van het strafprocesrecht*, pp. 3–25, 67–9.

21 Rider (ed.), *Galbertus Brugensis*, p. 7. For towns as 'places protected by a special peace', see R. C. Van Caenegem, 'Notes on Galbert of Bruges and his Translators', in Duvosquel and Thoen (eds.), *Peasants and Townsmen*, pp. 619–29.

22 A. Verhulst, 'Un exemple de la politique économique de Philippe d'Alsace: La fondation de Gravelines (1163)', *Cahiers de Civilisation médiévale*, 10 (1967), 15–28; A. Verhulst, 'Initiative comtale et développement économique en Flandre au XIIe siècle: Le rôle de Thierry et de Philippe d'Alsace (1128–1191)', in D. P. Blok (ed.), *Miscellanea Jan Frederik Niermeyer* (Groningen, 1967), pp. 227–40.

prosecute certain crimes committed by any of their own, but were also sufficiently motivated to take up arms when the castellan sought to infringe this right. Moreover, the king, the count and the nobility recognized this urban collectivity as a full interlocutor: they addressed it through speeches and letters, and granted it a charter of liberties (including toll exemption and freedom from land rents). The counts in return received homage from it as a kind of 'collective vassal'.[23]

Perhaps these manifestations of collective solidarity were recent developments and perhaps communal institutions were still in the process of being formed: after all, Galbert does not explicitly use the terms *communio* or *amicitia* with regard to Bruges.[24] Yet Galbert does not seem to consider the legal and political practices he describes in Bruges to be innovations: they appear as part of daily routine within the town. This may imply that a commune had already formed there in the early twelfth century. Perhaps at some point during the rule of the strong counts (Baldwin V, Robert I, Robert II and Baldwin VII) some sort of 'market peace' was granted to the inhabitants of the urban settlement by the castle and church, informally or through a charter now lost. If small Flemish towns like Geraardsbergen and Aire received privileges around 1070 and 1100, we may assume that an important city like Bruges, visited by foreign merchants in need of security, would also have been granted such recognition by the count well before 1127.[25] And perhaps the townspeople themselves had already established a kind of 'peace community' in Bruges, with or without the count's approval. Ganshof suggested that the *cives* or *burgenses* of Bruges formed a kind of urban community by c.1070, during the civil war between Richildis, mother of Arnulf III, and her brother-in-law Robert the Frisian, who claimed the title of count. The burghers of Bruges possibly fought on Robert's side, as did most men in northern Flanders.[26] All things considered though, it seems unlikely that a true commune in the full legal and political sense came into existence before 1100.

So who held most power within the urban community during this period? We know that Bertulf, as provost of St Donatian's and chancellor

[23] Rider (ed.), *Galbertus Brugensis*, passim.

[24] See above, Chapter 1.

[25] R. C. Van Caenegem, 'Considerations on the Customary Law of Twelfth-Century Flanders', in R. C. Van Caenegem, *Law, History, the Low Countries and Europe* (London, 1994), p. 104. The earliest privilege conserved in the original is the one for Saint-Omer: see G. Espinas, 'Le privilège de Saint-Omer de 1127', *RN*, 29 (1947), 43–8; R. C. Van Caenegem, 'The Borough Charter of Saint-Omer of 1127 granted by William Clito, Count of Flanders', in R. C. Van Caenegem, *Legal History: A European Perspective* (London, 1991), pp. 61–70.

[26] Ganshof, 'Iets over Brugge', p. 290; and on this period in general, see Verlinden, *Robert*.

of Flanders between 1091 and 1127, and as son of the Bruges castellan Erembald, became the most powerful man in Flanders after the count.[27] It appears from Galbert's narrative that the Erembalds had close relations with the townspeople, who considered this clan as their lords and 'friends'. Various members of the family lived inside or close to Bruges. The city-dwellers and the Erembalds also found common enemies in the lords of Straten, who were known to loot merchants coming to Bruges.[28] This association of clan and townspeople may have existed for some time. The text known as the *Miracula sancti Donatiani* provides some clues. It refers to the unrest that broke out in Flanders in 1096 after Count Robert II left on crusade, and that appears to have been principally a conflict among the inhabitants of the Bruges *fines* (borders) – which in this case seems to refer to the castellany rather than to the urban settlement. Bertulf assembled the people before St Donatian's church, and the presence of St Donatian's relics miraculously restored the peace in a *federa pacis*, and served as warrantor to this oath.[29] This kind of 'ecclesiastical peace' may imply that there was as yet no 'communal peace', though perhaps both existed together. We may safely suppose that the Erembalds were protecting a developing urban commune, and that this commune had not existed for long by the time Galbert put quill to parchment, as no earlier source mentions any communal institutions.

Thus, it is plausible to argue that between c.1050 and c.1100 the acceleration of demographic and economic growth in the towns of Flanders led to the development of some sort of communal feeling among their inhabitants, who came to realize that common 'urban' interests could not be upheld solely by their feudal and clerical rulers. As a town of growing importance, Bruges cannot have been an exception to this trend. As to the development in Bruges of a 'true' commune with a significant degree of legal and political autonomy, a *terminus post quem* might be posited as the year 1096 and a *terminus ante quem* as the year 1127. The latter terminus can perhaps even be shifted to 1119, for as we shall see, communal self-rule by that year appears to have been recognized by the count.

[27] Lyon and Verhulst, *Medieval Finance*, pp. 12–19.

[28] Rider (ed.), *Galbertus Brugensis*, pp. 61, 95–6, 128 (chaps. 25, 45, 75).

[29] *Acta Sanctorum, Oct.* (Tongerlo, 1794), vol. VI, pp. 508–9; Holder-Egger (ed.), 'Ex Vita Arnulfi', p. 858; Hoffmann, *Gottesfriede*, p. 150; G. Koziol, 'Monks, Feuds and the Making of Peace in Eleventh-Century Flanders', in T. F. Head and R. A. Landes (eds.), *The Peace of God: Social Violence and Religious Response in France around the Year 1000* (Ithaca, NY, 1992), pp. 239–59 (at 256–7).

Communal autonomy was developing in the context of a close association with the counts. As the earliest known privileges granted to the Flemish towns date from the late eleventh century,[30] it is entirely possible that Bruges had also acquired some privileges by that time. Baldwin VII, count from 1111, continued to strengthen central authority and security in Flanders. He did so, for instance, according to sources favourable to comital power, by inflicting cruel punishments on robber knights.[31] The protection of the urban community from external violence was increasingly maintained through collective defence as well as being guaranteed by the count. But the full extent of communal autonomy is only revealed by Galbert's chronicle. The murder of Count Charles the Good, on 2 March 1127, was followed by events that show the Bruges burghers capable of making political choices. Charles was killed by his opponents, the Erembald clan: Bertulf, his brother Didier Haket the castellan, the many nephews of Bertulf and also some in-laws, members of the local nobility and officials of the count were all involved, seeing their power threatened by the count's growing power. At first the people of Bruges chose to support the Erembalds, but then turned against their former leaders. The burghers sided with another local strongman, Gervase of Praet, chamberlain of Count Charles and perhaps a descendant of Boldran, an earlier castellan of Bruges.[32] Two years of strife followed in which the Flemish townsmen for the first time appear in the sources as self-conscious political actors.

A growing sense of a common space and shared interests reinforced the communal idea. Galbert does not use the term *communio* to describe the political and judicial organization of Bruges, even if he does for Ghent with reference to the Ghent militia. However, he refers frequently to the *sapientiores*, *meliores*, and *prudentiores* of Bruges, the men who took legal and political decisions in the town and negotiated in its name. He also provides us with a vivid impression of a lively culture of political assemblies in Bruges. On 27 March 1127, for instance, the burghers assembled 'in agrum quod suburbio adjacet', and elsewhere in the text 'apud Harenas in exitu suburbia' or 'in aegrum consuetum', but they also convened on the Market Square, then still an unpaved and marshy area.[33] The first known

30 Platelle, 'La violence', pp. 124–7; Verlinden, *Robert*, pp. 35–6; Van Caenegem, *Geschiedenis van het strafrecht*, pp. 240–4.

31 Van Caenegem, *Geschiedenis van het strafrecht*, p. 22.

32 J. B. Ross, 'Rise and Fall of a Twelfth-Century Clan: The Erembalds and the Murder of Count Charles of Flanders, 1127–1128', *Speculum*, 34 (1959), 367–90.

33 A. Demyttenaere, 'Galbert of Bruges on Political Meeting Culture: Palavers and Fights in Flanders during the Years 1127 and 1128', in P. S. Barnwell and M. Mostert (eds.), *Political Assemblies in the Earlier Middle Ages* (Turnhout, 2003), pp. 151–92.

privilege defining relations between the urban community and the count is also mentioned in Galbert's chronicle. On 6 April 1127, a 'chartula conventionis inter comitem et cives nostros factae de telonio condonato et censu mansionum eorundem' was read out before the people. Presented by Galbert as a 'convention' between prince and town, it contained typical economic concessions to the urban commune, to be found in many other cities in Europe, dealing with toll freedom and land rents. He goes on to mention that after the count of Flanders and the king of France, who had been present at the proclamation, had sworn on these privileges, the burghers of Bruges swore allegiance to the count and did homage to him, just as they had done to the count's predecessors ('quoque cives juraverunt fidelitatem comiti, sicut moris erat, et hominia fecerunt ei et securitates sicut prius praedecessoribus suis naturalibus, principibus terrae et dominis'), thus suggesting that this ritual – and hence urban autonomy and its recognition by the count – goes back at least to the time of Baldwin VII (r.1111–19). The count also allowed the burghers to adapt their 'consuetudinarias leges' to changing circumstances, implying that Bruges was developing its own customary law through urban legislation.[34]

The existence of an urban peace association within a confined space is suggested at other points in Galbert's narrative. The Ghent militiamen, who had come to aid Gervase of Praet and the people of Bruges in the siege of the count's murderers hiding in the fortress, were not allowed to enter the *suburbium* before they had sworn to uphold the peace.[35] When Gervase of Praet's men arrested a Bruges citizen who had communicated with the besieged, the burghers turned against their own ally: 'gravis tumultus obortus est inter Gervasium et suos et cives nostros', Galbert writes. The man was captured on the Market Square (the Forum) by a knight of Gervase of Praet. The men of Bruges now turned against Gervase and his knights, and attacked his residence. They said 'it belonged to their power' to judge this crime because the knight had been arrested in the market ('Conclamaverunt enim se nunquam velle pati dominium cujusquam, imo in sua potestate staret hoc malefactum corrigere').[36] The 'tumultus' mentioned here refers to the uprising of Bruges inhabitants because their 'potestas', in other words their legal competence, had been infringed.

[34] Rider (ed.), *Galbertus Brugensis*, p. 104 (chap. 55).

[35] Ibid., p. 77 (chap. 33).

[36] Ibid., pp. 110–11 (chap. 59); R. C. Van Caenegem, 'The Ghent Revolt of February 1128', in Van Caenegem, *Law*, pp. 107–12.

It is almost certain, however, that Bruges did not yet have its own 'bench' of aldermen during the events of 1127–8.[37] Although it has commonly been held, since the work of Ganshof, that aldermen were installed in Bruges during these events, nowhere in his text does Galbert mention any Bruges *scabini*. He uses the term *scabini* only to denote rural aldermen. At one point, however, a 'Folpertus iudex' from Bruges is mentioned, along with an 'Alardus scabinus' from the village of IJzendijke, who seems to have been an alderman of the castellany of Bruges. Was Folpertus perhaps some kind of communal judge? No additional evidence exists to answer this question. Aldermen in Bruges are mentioned explicitly in the Great Privilege given to the city in 1165/77 by Philip of Alsace, but it remains unclear whether they had existed much before this date. The *terminus post quem* is 1115, when the *Flandriae scabini* or aldermen of the castellany of Bruges still had legal competence in the town.[38] The *judices Brugenses* mentioned in a charter dated to 1094 and the *scabini brugenses* or *scabini de Brugis* appearing in documents dated to 1127, 1133, 1153 and 1163 are all aldermen of the Bruges castellany.[39] Thus, at least until 1187, the aldermen of the rural castellany were considered to be the 'aldermen of Bruges' before they became known as the 'aldermen of the Liberty of Bruges' ('scabini de Vria') in thirteenth-century sources.[40] Only in 1198 do urban aldermen appear in a local source. This is the same charter that mentions the city's seal for the first time, of which the oldest surviving and original example dates from 1200.[41] According to a hypothesis first put forward by Vanderkindere and shared by Verhulst and Van Werveke, it was only through the centralizing measures of Philip of Alsace that the aldermen received administrative powers, and communal 'jurors' or 'judges' (or whatever they were then called) disappeared as administrators.[42] This is the most plausible interpretation of the available sources.

The Bruges commune of the early twelfth century was no egalitarian society, for both the very poor and the very rich appear in Galbert's story; but it is likely that around 1100 urban society was less polarized than it would become during the thirteenth century,[43] even if, as the population

[37] Van Caenegem, 'Galbert van Brugge en het recht', pp. 32–5.

[38] Ganshof, 'Anmerkungen', pp. 215–25.

[39] Ganshof, *Recherches sur les tribunaux*, pp. 15–16.

[40] Warlop, 'De vorming'.

[41] Lambert (ed.), *De oorkonden*, p. 82; E. de Ghellinck d'Elseghem-Vaernewyck, *Sceaux et armoiries des villes, communes, échevinages, châtellenies, métiers et seigneuries de la Flandre ancienne et moderne* (Paris, 1935), pp. 82–3.

[42] Verhulst, *Rise of Cities*, pp. 127–30.

[43] Dumolyn, 'Economic Development'.

grew, the oaths and meetings of all free men must have given way by then to smaller groups, to whom power was delegated. These groups were doubtless made up of men who were the richest and most powerful in the commune, and who reasoned and spoke best, men who are sometimes referred to in the sources as, for instance, *prudentes viri* or *probi homines*, and in whose judgement, whether on legal or economic matters, the common burghers could trust. These men probably provided the necessary direction for political action within the early urban community. A strong sense of a communal will, protective of its economic interests, is again reflected by Galbert. For example, he tells us how the people of Bruges were sworn enemies of the lords of Straten who from their stronghold at Sint-Andries obstructed commerce along the road from the west. This was why the people of Bruges supported the Erembald clan when the lords of Straten attacked it.[44]

Communal Law Reformed

The early significance of communal authority is also suggested by the number of violations of the law that came to be considered as specific 'offences against the commune'. The oldest privileges granted to the Flemish communal towns represent a collective response to an established system of criminal law that had emerged from private origins, dealing with *weregeld*, feuding and conflict settlement. In the new, more developed and socially diversified urban community, conflict had to be settled not with the kin group of the victim but with respect to the entire town. Though customary law was often conservative, it was not immutable: medieval customs were adaptable and responsive to change. Communal law was considered 'old law' but even this could be altered: the right to do so, as mentioned above, was recognized for Bruges in 1127.[45] However, this did not imply that a strong government apparatus was in place at the urban level. Members of the commune were still supposed to carry out policing tasks to arrest criminals: failing to do so would risk a fine or exile. All burghers were to act 'like brothers' and come to the aid ('ad auxilium advenire') of their fellows citizens when they cried out ('faire cri') 'bourgesie', 'poorters' or 'communie' to warn that strangers were attacking them.[46] Communal law also had to prevent internal feuds. Through systems of reconciliatory

[44] Van Houtte, 'De opkomst', 44; Rider (ed.), *Galbertus Brugensis*, pp. 95–6 (chap. 45).

[45] Van Caenegem, 'Considerations'.

[46] Van Caenegem, *Geschiedenis van het strafrecht*, pp. 133–6.

justice, the commune forced its members into conflict settlement, known as the *zoenrecht*, a fundamental feature of urban private and criminal law.[47] Communal punishment was also not as sanguinary as one might expect. Exile as a specific urban penalty derives from the idea of the town as a free community of labour and a solidarity within a defined space. Someone who did not collaborate or who sabotaged the town's common welfare was useless and dangerous. Exile made one *vredeloos* or 'outside the peace' of the commune.[48] Another communal consequence of this punishment was the destruction of the house belonging to a city's enemy: the *droit d'arsin*, literally burning down the house, or (since this method put other buildings at risk) the *abattis de maison*, the demolition of a house, were based on another old Germanic legal principle.[49]

The growth of comital authority in Flanders had implications for the development of communal justice, however. Even if princely law was often an ally of communal law, it gradually became its main rival. Thus, the principles of Germanic law that played an important role in the genesis of Flemish communal law were altered and replaced by the direct intervention of the count. This process is evident from the third quarter of the twelfth century, during the rule of Count Philip of Alsace and his advisor Robert of Aire, a shrewd politician,[50] who introduced authoritarian principles favouring princely power.[51] The count still had his representative in the town in the office of castellan. After the events of 1127, the office was briefly occupied by Gervase of Praet, who had taken the initiative in punishing the killers of Charles the Good, principally the Erembald clan. One of them, Haket the son of Erembald, appears in the charters from 1130 to 1133 as castellan (suggesting that some of the clan were restored to comital grace); but after 1134, members of the noble family of Nesle took up this function and the role of the Erembalds in Bruges ended permanently.[52] The office of castellan, however, did not survive. During the second half of the century

47 Van Caenegem, *Geschiedenis van het strafprocesrecht*, p. 5.

48 Van Caenegem, *Geschiedenis van het strafrecht*, pp. 137–55; H. Brunner, 'Abspaltungen der Friedlosigkeit', *Zeitschrift der Savigny-Stiftung für Rechtsgeschichte, Germanistische Abteilung*, 2 (1890), 62–100.

49 Van Caenegem, *Geschiedenis van het strafrecht*, pp. 175–90.

50 H. Van Werveke, *Een Vlaamse graaf van Europees formaat: Filips van de Elzas* (Haarlem, 1976); T. de Hemptinne and M. Parisse, 'Thierry d'Alsace, comte de Flandre: Biographie et actes', *Annales de l'Est*, 43 (1991), 83–113; T. de Hemptinne, 'Robert von Aire, Kanzler von Flandern (†1174), in *Lexikon des Mittelalters*, 9 vols. (Munich, 1995), vol. VII, cols. 899–900.

51 Van Caenegem, *Geschiedenis van het strafprocesrecht*, p. 317; R. C. Van Caenegem, 'L'état de droit dans la Flandre médiévale', in B. Durand and L. Mayali (eds.), *Excerptiones iuris: Studies in Honor of André Gouron* (Berkeley, CA, 2000), pp. 769–72.

52 Warlop, *Flemish Nobility*, vol. I, pp. 209–10, 473–4.

it was stripped of judicial functions when Count Philip introduced a more severe criminal law in all his cities, and delegated these functions to a new type of prosecuting officer, the 'bailiff' (*baljuw*, *bailli*), who did not hold his office in fief and was replaceable.[53] During the early thirteenth century, under Countess Joan of Constantinople, the attempt was made in Bruges and elsewhere to liquidate the office of castellan altogether. In 1224, the countess bought the office in Bruges back from John II of Nesle, whereupon it disappeared for good.[54] Presently, the office of the bailiff was split up into two judicial functions: the bailiff remained the prosecuting officer in the castellany, but within the urban jurisdiction his function would be assumed by the *schout* or 'sheriff' (*scultetus*), an office with older feudal origins and which now became the main representative of princely power in the city. Holders of the office were appointed by the count. During the thirteenth century they were still recruited from the petty nobility but gradually 'new men' would occupy the office. The Bruges burghers also came to demand that their sheriff should no longer be locally recruited to avoid conflicts of interests. This was granted to them in 1228 but apparently not observed as the burghers repeated their demand in 1280, and in 1297 Count Guy de Dampierre reconfirmed it. The sheriff also had a body of 'sergeants' or *beriders* to assist in prosecuting criminals and bringing them before the aldermen.[55]

By c.1170 the new comital dynasty of the house of Alsace had managed to gain more power over the city. Some half century after the events described by Galbert, the law of Bruges and its communal organization were considerably altered on the count's initiative. The 'Great Privilege', the *lex et consuetudo* as it was called in the charter issued between 1165 and 1177 by Philip of Alsace to Bruges and other Flemish cities, was modelled on the 1163 urban charter for Arras – then still in the county of Flanders, and which until well into the thirteenth century remained the most important city in the region. Legal historians have considered these privileges to be very 'modern', given that they imposed a severe criminal law on urban society and cramped urban autonomy.[56] A heavy fine of 60 pounds was introduced and the principle of conciliatory justice which had been typical

53 L. M. de Gryse, 'Some Observations on the Origin of the Flemish Bailiff (Bailli): The Reign of Philip of Alsace', *Viator*, 7 (1976), 243–94.

54 Warlop, *Flemish Nobility*, vol. I, p. 210.

55 Nowé, *Les baillis*, pp. 24–9, 61–2, 82–7, 101–3, 217, 415.

56 R. C. Van Caenegem and L. Milis, 'Kritische uitgave van de "Grote Keure" van Filips van de Elzas, graaf van Vlaanderen, voor Gent en Brugge (1165–1177)', *Handelingen van de Koninklijke Commissie voor Geschiedenis*, 143 (1977), 207–57.

for Flemish towns was strongly restricted. The bailiff appears for the first time in these texts but he is still vaguely described as the *justitia comitis* or *minister comitis*. The right to appoint the aldermen was entirely vested in the count. These aldermen were given both legal and administrative power within the urban territory, and its boundaries were carefully delineated. They were prohibited from changing or adding to urban laws without the consent of the count or bailiff. Only some features of communal law survived this reform, notably the practice of the citizens destroying the house of an enemy of the city. Its survival, despite the challenges to it from a count as powerful as Philip of Alsace, perhaps shows how deeply rooted the notion of communal vengeance was within urban society. Yet, as with other communal practices, it was now brought firmly under the control of the count's aldermen and bailiff. The count also restricted the competence of the aldermen and the town's institutions to within a precisely defined territory, a restriction replicated in the 'Great Privilege' for Ypres. In Ghent, Saint-Omer and Arras, however, urban aldermen could also act in the 'banlieue' around the town.[57] These towns had originated on ecclesiastical domains, not on the count's domain as Bruges and Ypres had done: comital efforts to restrict the scope of urban autonomy were more strenuous than ecclesiastical ones.

The Rule of the Great Merchants during the Thirteenth Century

The development of urban institutions has also to be understood in relation to changes within the town, particularly its social character (as outlined in the preceding chapter). Although comital authority was strengthening, so was the power of aldermen and merchants. After Philip of Alsace's reforms, the comitally appointed aldermen were nominated for an indefinite period, many probably for life: an alderman could only be legally deposed if he issued a false sentence.[58] In all probability aldermen were almost exclusively recruited from the ranks of the great merchants, though some also held knightly titles (and, as seen, a social distinction in the thirteenth century between 'merchants' and 'urban landowners' is difficult to make). As the urban population and economy expanded, particularly as international

57 H. Van Werveke, 'La banlieue primitive des villes flamandes', in *Études d'histoire dédiées à la mémoire de Henri Pirenne*, pp. 389–402.

58 F. L. Ganshof, 'Étude sur le faussement de jugement dans le droit flamand des XIIe et XIIIe siècles', *Handelingen van Oude Wetten en Verordeningen van België*, 14 (1935), 115–40.

commerce rose from the late twelfth century, these city rulers became powerful. They had already made their presence felt on a wider political stage: in 1127, several Flemish cities, notably Ghent, Bruges, Ypres and Saint-Omer, had sworn oaths together, jointly acting as a counterweight to the power of the king of France and the count of Flanders. Although urban autonomy was undermined by the reforms of Philip of Alsace, comital power weakened in its turn after the death of Count Baldwin IX. Countesses Joan (r.1205–44) and Margaret of Constantinople (r.1244–78) suffered under French political pressure and the urban elites exploited this situation to strengthen their power. The political importance of city merchants became more evident, and may explain why the Flemish cities began to appear in charters as political agents. They did so notably in their dealings with their main trading partner, the kingdom of England: in 1208, the burghers of Bruges, Ghent, Ypres, Lille, Douai and Saint-Omer rebelled against the French King Philip II, who had brought Flanders into his direct sphere of influence, and allied with King John of England. Five years later, Bruges, Ghent and Ypres were again crucial in supporting Ferrand, the new husband of their young Countess Joan, against King Philip.[59] To a greater extent than during the succession crisis of 1127–8, the Flemish burghers now appeared as an economic, political and military force to be reckoned with, stronger than the rural nobility and in a position either to support or ignore comital power, and play an autonomous role in international politics. Little is known about political events within Bruges for this period, but when the city and its elites do appear in the sources, their importance is unmistakable.

By the mid thirteenth century, the city governments were joined together in the representative institution of the *scabini Flandriae* which combined the aldermen of the greater cities: this almost set up 'dual power' in the county, especially when it came to dealing with economic matters or conflicts between cities. In 1241, for instance, the *scabini Flandriae* made judgments in a conflict between Bruges and Damme.[60] The Flemish merchant elites now negotiated almost autonomously with the king of England on trade privileges.[61] Their political power was based on their strengthening economic position, notably on the wool imports from England and to a lesser degree from Scotland, which were vital for the growing cloth industry. Anglo-Flemish contacts had increased after Duke William conquered England in 1066 with the help of Flemish knights: in 1127, numerous

[59] Oksanen, *Flanders*, p. 50; Dept, *Les influences*, pp. 54–73.

[60] J. Dhondt, 'Les origines des états de Flandre', *Standen en Landen*, 1 (1950), 3–52 (at 22–7).

[61] Dept, *Les influences*, pp. 68–73.

Flemings were already present in London to buy wool. Civil war during the reign of King Stephen (r.1135–54) caused a crisis in Anglo-Flemish trade, but from the second half of the twelfth century merchants were again present in England. However, as the commercial power of the English cities also began to rise, Flemish merchants became more dependent on the goodwill of the kings of England. The Flemish cities started to broker their own deals with England, which was largely why in 1208 they allied themselves with King John. In 1213, the Bruges merchants obtained a general privilege to trade in England and in 1260 they were freed from confiscation in cases where individual Flemings had not paid their debts.[62]

Although these great merchants were appointed to aldermanic office by the counts, their tendency to monopolize the city government was not a trend welcomed by the comital family. The counts had to acknowledge the greater autonomy of the merchant classes, but tried to maintain their influence. As mentioned above, in 1228 Countess Joan and her first spouse Ferrand of Portugal decreed that the bailiff and sheriff of Bruges could not be someone born in Bruges or married to a woman from Bruges.[63] This was a measure taken to deal with conflicts of interests between the representatives of comital power and the local elites. In January 1241, Joan and her second husband Thomas of Savoy declared that new aldermen were to be appointed every year by the count or his representative on 2 February (Candlemas). If the prince failed to appear on this date the bench of aldermen would remain in place until he did so. Outgoing aldermen could not be directly re-elected and relatives could not serve as aldermen at the same time. Anyone condemned for theft or counterfeiting money could no longer be an alderman. Thus, the system of yearly rotating aldermen (the *wepelganc*) was put in place; but, as magistracy lists seem to show, it was not strictly observed. These measures had been taken earlier in Arras (1194), Ypres (1209), Ghent (1212), Douai (1228) and Lille (1235) and the Bruges outports Damme and Sint-Anna-ter-Muiden also received similar privileges in 1241 and 1242. In this way, the rulers of Flanders hoped to prevent oligarchic concentrations of power at a time when their power was weakening in relation to the large cities. In some cities they failed: in 1228 this rule was abandoned in Ghent under patrician pressure and the college of the thirty-nine *viri hereditarii* was formed.[64] But certainly the clause in the 1241 privilege (discussed in Chapter 3), that

[62] Dept, 'Les marchands flamands'.

[63] Nowé, *Les baillis*, p. 419.

[64] Van den Auweele, 'Schepenbank', vol. II, pp. 156–7; GVS, *Coutume*, vol. I, pp. 196–7; T. Luykx, *Johanna van Constantinopel, gravin van Vlaanderen en Henegouwen: Haar leven (1199/1200–1244), haar regeering (1205–1244), vooral in Vlaanderen* (Brussels, 1946), p. 510.

the aldermen had to be part of the Hanse of London to the exclusion of manual labourers, makes clear that at this point Bruges was ruled by a powerful merchant elite who had excluded lower social groups from political decision-making.[65]

However, notwithstanding the strength of class rule by the great merchants and the poverty in which workers lived, there were tendencies in Bruges society that made it less polarized. It is possible to discern the gradual emergence by the late thirteenth century of a 'middle class', politically still powerless but undoubtedly enjoying a higher living standard than the average textile or leather worker. Until about 1270, the activities of merchant and 'draper' (or entrepreneur in the textile industry) tended to be combined in Bruges. After then, some smaller industrial entrepreneurs developed their activities in the textile industry without at the same time controlling the importing of raw material.[66] During the same period, some artisans became more affluent and managed to rise to the status of merchants as members of the Hanse. Thus, the 'popular class' in late thirteenth-century Bruges was divided into two groups: on the one hand, those who worked with their hands, ineligible therefore to hold political office, and on the other, those who were small retailers such as the weaver-drapers, cloth sellers, wine salesmen, mercers, spice sellers and dyers (at least those who did not dye themselves but acted as drapers). The latter group could become members of the merchant guild but for a hefty entry fee determined by the aldermen. As a result, during the later thirteenth century the Hanse of London no longer consisted merely of international merchants, though the majority of artisans were still excluded. In total, Hanse members made up an elite of some 6 per cent of the Bruges population. Some of these smaller retailers also seem to have become active in international commerce: the few sources we have suggest an increasing degree of social mobility by the end of the thirteenth century.[67]

The effect of these changes on the inner workings of political government is hard to determine. How communal institutions had originally functioned is unclear, so it is difficult to pronounce on what became of them. By the early thirteenth century the 'sworn men' of the Flemish communes probably no longer possessed any real power, for they generally disappear from sources in other cities. In 1236, in a Bruges charter, the word *communitas* does appear in the intitulation of a charter: 'Nos scabini et tota communitas

[65] Prevenier, 'La bourgeoisie', pp. 416–17.

[66] Ibid., p. 409.

[67] Wyffels, 'De Vlaamse Hanze van London'.

oppidi Brugensis'. Yet it probably by then referred to the urban community as a symbolic whole, rather than to an institutional body of the commune that actually governed.[68] A 'consilium villae Brugensis' is mentioned in the 1241 privilege, but its composition is unclear. Was this council the institutional successor of an earlier communal council of sworn men? It seems evident that by 1241 its councillors were appointed not by a popular assembly but by the aldermen, who were themselves comital and not communal judges. No source reveals anything about them, but it does appear that the councillors played primarily an advisory role, forming a group of 'aldermen in waiting', not yet in office, but perhaps with administrative and financial responsibilities. A competence councillors did enjoy, one perhaps inherited from powers that the commune had formerly secured from the prince, was their right to veto the installation of a new bench of aldermen, albeit with the agreement of the count. The councillors also appear with the aldermen in some judicial matters.[69]

This arrangement between councillors and aldermen does seem to be a relic of communal institutions that were in place before the interventions of Philip of Alsace; the councillors having developed from the consultative body that represented the commune, thus becoming distinguished from the aldermen who had originally been princely officers. The composition of the council (of thirteen members) and its competence might also have been changed in 1241. And burgomasters ('burgomastri', 'burghemeesters') are also mentioned for the first time in this charter. Bruges had two of them: a burgomaster of the aldermen and one of the council; and in later sources the latter was also called the burgomaster 'of the *courpse*' or 'of the commune', in other words of the whole body of the city. He had some administrative functions and acted as a public prosecutor representing the commune of Bruges as a whole.[70] This competence also suggests that his function did derive from earlier communal institutions that had formed a counterweight to the comital aldermen in place from the days of Philip of Alsace. So does the fact that in a charter dated 22 July 1299, written in French, the councillors are referred to as the *jurés de le ville*.[71]

68 Monier, *Les institutions judiciaires*, pp. 110–17; GVS, *Coutume*, vol. I, p. 194.

69 Van den Auweele, 'Schepenbank', vol. III, pp. 305–7. A charter of 1235 suggests that the aldermen and the councillors acted together in forbidding the chapter of St Donatian's to rent out its living spaces and cellars: see Lambert (ed.), *De oorkonden*, pp. 205–6.

70 Wyffels, 'Is de Brugse keure', p. 530.

71 GVS, *Inventaire*, vol. I, p. 73.

Growing Social and Political Tensions

From the early thirteenth century, signs of popular discontent appear. In 1225, Valenciennes, Lille, Ghent and Bruges received 'the false Baldwin' as their lost count. Baldwin IX had died in Bulgaria as Latin Emperor of Byzantium; the 'false Baldwin' was an impostor called Bertrand of Rais.[72] The exact social nature of this affair remains obscure but there are indications that the false count was mostly supported by the working people of Flemish towns, who saw him as a messianic figure. The conjunction between social and spiritual unrest was a common phenomenon within the urban environment, and likely therefore in Bruges. During the thirteenth century, the growth of the suburban proletariat (see Chapters 2 and 3) was accompanied by a spiritual enthusiasm for spontaneous forms of religion, voluntary poverty and salvation through manual labour. Some of this enthusiasm was contained within an institutional framework: as discussed above, the movement of the beguines and begards was strong in major Flemish cities. How many beguines were present in Bruges is hard to say, though they must have been numerous. (By the fifteenth century, the largest beguinage, the *Wijngaard*, contained at least 150 beguines.) Apart from the larger convents of the Wijngaard (recognized in 1242 to be under comital protection) and St Obrecht's (1269), at least eight other beguine communities would be created during the fourteenth century, and others may have sprung up and disappeared before that time. The Wijngaard tended to recruit from elitist social circles, though the women in the smaller convents seem to have been generally from more modest backgrounds. The success of the beguine movement in Bruges and in other cities of the Low Countries can be explained partly by the need for cheap and flexible labour in the textile industry and for charitable tasks that were considered suitable for women.[73] A number of these poorer convents of beguines founded in the fourteenth century lived off alms, and perhaps did so in the previous century.[74] The beguine movement may to some extent have channelled spiritual enthusiasm away from social subversion.

Whereas in most other regions of Europe these religious women were considered to be dangerous and heretical, the strategy of Countess Joan and her successors was to take control of this social-religious movement,

72 C. Duvivier, *La querelle des d'Avesnes et des Dampierre jusqu'à la mort de Jean d'Avesnes (1257)*, 2 vols. (Brussels, 1894), vol. I, pp. 92–3.

73 Simons, *Cities of Ladies*, pp. 142, 257.

74 J. Marechal, 'Konventen van arme begijnen in Brugge (1302–1374)', in *Album A. Viaene* (Bruges, 1970), pp. 257–64.

with the help of the mendicant orders, to prevent it from taking more threatening directions. Similarly, the male counterparts of the beguines, the begards (*bogarden* or *begarden*) were working lay brothers whose self-organization was tolerated by the authorities. They had a convent in Bruges from 1252 and were exempted from taxation by the countess. They were active as weavers, and seem to have recruited their members primarily among textile workers. To compensate for this unfair competition, begards had to pay five shillings to the weavers' guild for every new loom they set up. This money was then spent in alms on poor weavers. They did not take religious vows but wore habits of light cloth and lived in community and celibacy. They were affiliated with and under the guidance of the Bruges Franciscans (though another smaller begard convent enjoyed a brief existence affiliated to the Dominicans). Around 1374–6, the Bruges begards were to join the Third Order of St Francis as *Fratres Poenitentiae*.[75] As discussed in Chapter 2 the Bruges ruling class was trying to reduce social tensions through a twin policy of repression and appeasement: introducing the *zestendelen* districts with their captains (*hooftmannen*) to facilitate policing, and investing in charity under the spiritual guidance of the mendicant orders.

In a political context, similar control was also exercised over the craft guilds, who were allowed to exist as professional organizations from the second half of the thirteenth century. They were initially dominated by the city government, which used them for its own benefit to regulate production, market standards and wages. They also played a role in the organization of the city militia. By the end of the century there were some ten 'deans', appointed by the city and recruited from the merchant-entrepreneurs, each overseeing a sector of the textile industry and inspecting its work. Others oversaw the trades of leather, beer and mead, while the butchers also had some form of organization. The Bruges weavers had a charitable organization for mutual aid before 1267 and there were also religious confraternities that grouped Bruges artisans together. Yet craft guild demands for greater autonomy were increasing, and when the first major Bruges revolt, later known as the 'Moerlemaye', broke out in 1280–1, the craft guilds were to form its backbone. The strategies of the political elites had never entirely prevented social unrest. Around 1250, strike actions took place in Douai and Ghent, and similar labour protests probably erupted in Bruges (though

[75] L. Gilliodts-Van Severen, *Inventaire diplomatique des archives de l'ancienne école Bogarde à Bruges* (Bruges, 1899–1900), corrected by W. Simons, 'The Lives of the Beghards', in M. Rubin (ed.), *Medieval Christianity in Practice* (Princeton, NJ, 2009), pp. 238–45.

sources are lacking). Social tensions increased as a result of an economic war with England from 1270–4, conflicts over toll rights within the city, and the poor state of urban finances. But it was the rising demands of the craft guilds that led to the Moerlemaye. In 1280, the guilds demanded autonomy and their own representatives on the benches of aldermen and councillors. Even so, it was not a revolt simply of craftsmen and artisans against the merchant elites, for it also involved the taking of power by an anti-comital group, allied with the popular classes.[76]

The immediate trigger of the revolt was the crisis in the textile industry already sketched above. Certain foreign merchants had been complaining about the abuses they suffered when paying the 'Great Toll' on merchandise imported into Bruges. Against existing custom, families such as the Danwilts, Bonins and Lams had been exacting from these merchants an extra charge for weighing, the *heffeghelt*. This new tax was abolished in 1279 by the countess but not before the conflict had caused factional divisions within the Bruges elites.[77] The problems of importing English wool affected both the manual workers and the drapers. Meanwhile, tensions escalated between Count Guy de Dampierre and the urban elites; accordingly the count gave in to some popular demands to weaken the powerful merchant class. Thus, an ordinance of the French king of 1279, inspired by Count Guy, forced the Flemish cities to have their accounts reviewed every year.[78] After the Bruges Belfry accidentally burnt down in 1280, the count deliberately delayed reissuing the privileges lost in the flames. This event signalled the start of a two-year rebellion in which the artisans sided with the nouveaux riches and with a faction of the merchant elite. The rebel coalition of 1280, calling itself the 'community' (*meentucht*), demanded the right to appoint half of the aldermen and councillors, leaving the count the right to install the other half. They also protested against fraud and abuse of power by the elite and demanded the right to elect their own guild deans and wardens. The rising ended in defeat but clearly demonstrated significant lines of political polarization in the city. These would surface again in 1302.[79]

76 A. A. Bardoel, 'The Urban Uprising at Bruges, 1280–1: Some New Findings about the Rebels and the Partisans', *BTFG*, 72 (1994), 761–91.

77 GVS, *Inventaire*, vol. I, p. 8.

78 G. Espinas and J. Buntinx (eds.), *Privilèges et chartes de franchise de la Flandre*, 2 vols. (Brussels, 1959), vol. I, pp. 6–7.

79 J. Dumolyn and J. Haemers, 'Reclaiming the Common Sphere of the City: The Revival of the Bruges Commune in the Late Thirteenth Century', in J.-P. Genet (ed.), *La légitimité implicite: Le pouvoir symbolique en Occident*, 2 vols. (Paris, 2015), vol. II, pp. 161–88.

According to the *Annales Gandenses*, written by an anonymous Ghent greyfriar around 1308–10 (and the best narrative source on events in Flanders for this period), the two main groups who opposed each other were the 'majores' and the 'scabini' on the one hand and the 'communitas' on the other.[80] The use of the term *communitas* in this context suggests that it had by then acquired a narrower meaning than the urban 'commune'. Even in the early thirteenth century, the term still seems to have meant 'those who are ruled', represented by those who claimed to speak not just for one guild or group but for a unity or *universitas*, the common body of the city. In practice, these representatives were probably notable burghers (*ghoede lieden* or *bonnes gens*) acting as advisors, although they were sometimes assisted by artisans on certain technical matters. Yet as the social gap between *li riches* and *li povres* gradually widened during the thirteenth century, in the wave of revolts in 1280 that struck Bruges, as well as towns like Ypres and Douai, terms like 'commune' began to be deployed in a more divisive sense: in the Moerlemaye revolt in Bruges and Damme, the popular classes formulated their demands in meetings called *meentucht* or *ghemeente*, and could refer to themselves as *li kemuns*.[81] In claiming to speak for the entire urban community, rebel alliances, including craftsmen and factions of the elite, used the political power invested in the 'commune' against the oligarchic misrule of those lineages who controlled the benches of aldermen. Henceforward, 'the commons' or 'the commoners' would increasingly be used to denote a social group in the city. In the fourteenth and fifteenth centuries, *het ghemeen*, *li commun*, *les communes* or similar variants would primarily carry the more restricted meaning of 'the commoners' – in effect 'the popular classes'.[82] At the same time, the term 'commune' (as in *la communaulté* or *de ghemeente*) would always retain the connotation of the political community of those who were ruled, but it would exclude the *poorters* (the 'burghers' in the stricter sense of merchants and landowners) or the *heren* (lords) who usually dominated the city government.[83]

[80] H. Johnstone (ed.), *Annals of Ghent: Translated from the Latin with Introduction and Notes* (London, 1951), pp. 10, 13 and passim.

[81] Prevenier, 'La bourgeoisie'; Wyffels, 'Nieuwe gegevens', p. 43; Bardoel, 'Urban Uprising'.

[82] For instance in J. Lambin (ed.), *Dits de cronike ende genealogie van den prinsen ende graven van den foreeste van buc, dat heet Vlaenderlant, van 863 tot 1436* (Ypres, 1839), p. 213.

[83] For similar developments in Europe, see J. Watts, 'Public or Plebs: The Changing Meaning of "the Commons", 1381–1549', in H. Pryce and J. Watts (eds.), *Power and Identity in the Middle Ages: Essays in Memory of Rees Davies* (Oxford, 2007), pp. 242–60; G. Gleba, *Die Gemeinde als alternatives Ordnungsmodell: Zur sozialen und politischen Differenzierung des Gemeindebegriffs in den innerstädtischen Auseinandersetzungen des 14. und 15. Jahrhunderts. Mainz, Magdeburg, München, Lübeck, Köln* (Vienna, 1989).

After the Moerlemaye was repressed, no concession was granted to the demands of the middle and working classes in the *Keure* issued by Count Guy on 25 May 1281: instead comital authority was tightened by legislative and policing measures that strengthened criminal law, and imposed penalties against clan and factional fighting, and against the hosting of exiles. An extremely heavy fine was imposed on Bruges, worsening the parlous state of public finances.[84] The system of appointing the urban government was slightly changed. The number of aldermen was for the first time explicitly set down, at thirteen. Aldermen had to appoint the councillors within eight days of their election and elect the two burgomasters (mayors).[85] However, the comital privilege granted to the drapery sector in 1284 was more advantageous to the small drapers and artisans and restricted the power of the great merchants.[86] Another statute on 19 December 1298 elaborated on the administrative and financial organization of the city. Previously (from 1241, or perhaps earlier), the two city burgomasters had acted as heads of the finances, but in 1280 their malpractices had been denounced by the rebels. At that point it was decreed that the burgomasters were to be renewed annually on 9 October by the aldermen and councillors, and according to the privilege of 1281 the burgomasters had to be elected by the aldermen.[87] But the statute of 1298, agreed upon by seventy-eight prominent burghers, decreed that the councillors would choose their own burgomaster and the aldermen would choose theirs.[88] Furthermore, new financial officers were installed, and the office of treasurer was created, to be yearly elected on 9 October by the burgomasters, aldermen and councillors. The city accounts were to be controlled by both the representatives of the count and of the commune. In 1299 the college of the so-called 'Twenty Men' was created for this purpose. This was replaced by the Hundred Men after 1302 (though the Twenty Men were to reappear a little later).[89]

84 J.-P. Sosson, 'Finances communales et dette publique: Le cas de Bruges à la fin du XIIIe siècle', in Duvosquel and Thoen (eds.), *Peasants and Townsmen*, pp. 239–57.

85 Van den Auweele, 'Schepenbank', vol. II, pp. 157–8; GVS, *Coutume*, vol. I, pp. 240–54; Wyffels, 'Nieuwe gegevens', pp. 78–9.

86 J. Vermaut, 'De textielnijverheid in Brugge en op het platteland, Westelijk Vlaanderen voor 1800: konjunktuurverloop, organisatie en sociale verhoudingen', 4 vols., unpublished PhD thesis, Ghent University (Ghent, 1974), vol. II, p. 337.

87 GVS, *Inventaire*, vol. I, pp. 240–2.

88 L. A. Warnkoenig and A. E. Gheldolf, *Histoire de la Flandre et de ses institutions civiles et politiques, jusqu'à l'année 1305*, 5 vols. (Brussels, 1835–1864), vol. IV, p. 304.

89 Van den Auweele, 'Schepenbank', vol. II, pp. 158–9, vol. III, p. 308; Warnkoenig and Gheldolf, *Histoire*, vol. IV, pp. 304–8.

The Revolution of 1302

Strife within Bruges, and between Bruges and the count, was exacerbated in the final two decades of the thirteenth century by the increasing tension between Count Guy de Dampierre and his assertive French overlord, King Philip the Fair. The count began to ally himself with the popular classes in the major cities because the Flemish merchant class supported King Philip in weakening comital authority. In June 1296, the king placed Bruges under his protection to reinforce his position among the urban elites.[90] He also announced that he would revise the Bruges *Keure*, on the somewhat self-serving grounds that Count Guy had abolished 'both the good and the bad laws and customs' in 1281. In effect, in January 1297 he re-established the old privileges of Bruges.[91] On 15 May 1297, Guy followed suit, also confirming the old Bruges privileges and revoking those of 1281 in order to gain citizen favour.[92] During this round of political poker it became clear that the French king's ultimate intention was to establish direct control over the county. He bullied his vassal to the point that Guy felt compelled to renounce his feudal oath to his overlord. In retaliation, in June 1297 a French army invaded Flanders, and on 18 September Bruges opened its gates to the French, as the merchant class by then also considered their interests best served by direct French rule. By 1300, after military skirmishes and after the kings of England and France had concluded a separate peace, the county was annexed and incorporated into the crown lands.

This annexation exposed fault-lines in Flemish society: it was supported by the majority of the Flemish urban oligarchs, known as the *Leliaerts* or the 'Lily' party, and also by most Flemish noblemen, but it was opposed by the commoners. Their party called the *amici comitis* or *partie li conte* (not 'the Claws' as is often claimed) began to support more strongly the imprisoned count and his kinsmen and those nobles who remained loyal. In 1301, revolts broke out in Ghent and Bruges. A charismatic weaver called Pieter de Coninck (often mistranslated as 'Peter the King'), who was of modest or middling origins, soon became the rebel leader, perhaps in part because of his rhetorical and leadership skills (to which chronicles throughout Europe were to attest). Another important leader was the butcher Jan Breydel, who acquired a reputation for violent and efficient military action and clearly belonged to the more well-off middle class.[93] The city was liberated but

[90] GVS, *Inventaire*, vol. I, pp. 47–8.

[91] GVS, *Inventaire*, vol. I, pp. 50–1; GVS, *Coutume*, vol. I, pp. 267, 270–3.

[92] GVS, *Inventaire*, vol. I, pp. 51–2; GVS, *Coutume*, vol. I, pp. 274–5.

[93] Van Houtte, *De geschiedenis van Brugge*, pp. 67–71.

again submitted to the French troops led by Jacques de Châtillon. In the meantime the count's sons, John and Guy of Namur, and his grandson William of Gulik waged a guerrilla war to retake the county. They joined forces with Pieter de Coninck, who managed to return to Bruges during the winter of 1301–2, forcing the Lily party and the French to leave. De Châtillon retook the city, but not for long. During the Good Friday Revolt of 18 May 1302 (often romantically called 'the Bruges Matins') the followers of Pieter de Coninck and his companions Jan Breydel and the fuller Jan Heme, massacred some 1,500 occupying French soldiers. This uprising was followed by the celebrated Battle of Kortrijk on 11 July, an event that shocked ruling elites across Europe: a Flemish army of urban militiamen, around 2,380 of whom came from Bruges, and the few Flemish nobles who had remained loyal to the count, defeated and humiliated the French army and their Flemish allies among the urban ruling classes. The popular victory drove the French out and ushered in a new city government structure which included the craft guilds. The next day, a revolt broke out in Ghent, and the artisan class overthrew the Lily faction in that city too.[94]

All the major Flemish cities installed revolutionary regimes, exiled the pro-French Lilies and confiscated their property. A Bruges charter dated 1 July 1302 identified the urban rulers as 'the council and the whole commune of the city' ('*de raed ende al die ghemeentucht van der stede*'). Another document, issued one week later, also omitted the aldermen in its intitulation.[95] Clearly, as in 1280, the revolutionary party was deploying communal institutions and vocabulary as vehicles for political change. The bench of aldermen may have been temporarily stripped of much of its power but, perhaps after members of the Lily party had been removed, it was still functioning.[96] No more mass executions took place. Exile had been the accustomed way of dealing with the commune's internal enemies, as the earliest sources of Flemish urban criminal law show.[97] Accordingly after the popular victory at Kortrijk about 250 Lilies were exiled from Bruges as 'enemies of the city', and their goods were confiscated.[98]

The first demands of the revolutionary regime were also typically communal. A charter issued on 1 August 1302 by John of Namur, acting in place

94 Van Caenegem (ed.), *1302*; J. Dumolyn and J. Haemers, 'Patterns of Urban Rebellion in Medieval Flanders', *JMH*, 31 (2005), 369–93 (at 373–4).

95 SAB, Political Charters, First series, n° 163 and 165; GVS, *Inventaire*, vol. I, pp. 93, 98.

96 GVS, *Inventaire*, vol. I, p. 94.

97 Van Caenegem, *Geschiedenis van het strafrecht*, pp. 22–3.

98 J. F. Verbruggen, *Vlaanderen na de Guldensporenslag: De vrijheidsstrijd van het graafschap Vlaanderen, 1303–1305* (Bruges, 1991), pp. 19–21.

of his imprisoned father, promised that rents on city land, whether built on or not, would never be increased under any pretext, that all inhabitants of Bruges would be allowed to practise without fraud any kind of commerce and industry, and that burghers would be freed from paying tolls in Flanders forever.[99] In a charter of 28 March 1306, the measure on land rents was again confirmed by the new count, Robert of Bethune, son of Guy (who died in 1305). This text also states that 'tout bourgeois ... soient gens de mestier ou autre, soient egalment franc ausi avant li uns li autres'.[100] This meant that every burgher was equal before the law. Other measures taken by the revolutionary regime, and privileges granted to it, dealt with financial, legal and military matters. On 30 October 1302 Bruges temporarily obtained the right to install the city governments of all small towns within its hinterland.[101] Steps were taken to deal with the debt-ridden state of communal finances.[102] The guilds and the popular classes generally had been demanding financial control, believing debts to be the result of corruption and mismanagement. Certainly important burghers had formed syndicates to farm the excises on consumption products together, a situation that had encouraged fraud and corruption because these partnerships came from the same families who populated the benches of aldermen. After 1304 those to whom excises were farmed out, as well as money changers and publicans, were no longer allowed to serve simultaneously as aldermen.[103] The craft guilds also gained significant power: besides the right to possess their own guild banners,[104] after 1302 they also obtained a large degree of military autonomy. The Flemish urban soldiers were renowned as crossbowmen, pikesmen and foot soldiers, but they also realized that military mobilizations while in the service of their prince gave them opportunities to achieve political goals.[105] This sense of possibility was likely solidified in the two years after 1302, when the Bruges militia participated in several more expeditions.[106]

The political goals of the new town government are best characterized as an attempt to move away from rule by a limited number of merchant

[99] GVS, *Coutume*, vol. I, pp. 279–81; GVS, *Inventaire*, vol. I, pp. 111–12.

[100] GVS, *Inventaire*, vol. I, p. 204.

[101] Warnkoenig and Gheldolf, *Histoire*, vol. IV, pp. 313–14; Van Houtte, *De geschiedenis van Brugge*, pp. 74–5.

[102] Sosson, 'Finances', pp. 239–57.

[103] Van den Auweele, 'Schepenbank', vol. III, pp. 269–70.

[104] Already attested in the *Annales Gandenses*, see Johnstone (ed.), *Annals of Ghent*, pp. 12–13.

[105] For a synthesis, see J. F. Verbruggen, *The Art of Warfare in Western Europe during the Middle Ages: From the Eighth Century to 1340* (Amsterdam, 1977).

[106] Verbruggen, *Vlaanderen*, pp. 77–148.

elite families and to return to older communal principles of urban government, supported by a broader representation of the population assembled as a *meentucht* or commune. Rather than a pure 'guild revolution', the social forces in power represented a coalition of different social classes with a programme to establish greater fiscal and social justice and political participation.[107] Members of the nouveaux riches, who had risen from artisanal ranks to become merchants, together with factions of the older merchant class, joined forces with the organized middle and working classes. For some years to come, the weakness of the comital family in relation to King Philip the Fair – especially while the count remained a prisoner in France – forced the dynasty into accepting the urban rebellious 'popular fronts' as allies. In return, the guilds obtained major concessions from the sons of Count Guy and could now for the first time have representatives on the benches of aldermen.

The political momentum did not last, however. In 1309, the multi-class revolutionary alliance of Bruges collapsed under the weight of political opportunism and opposing interests. The butchers, fishmongers and brokers, the three wealthiest craft guilds, joined the Lily party, along with the *poorters* (or *burgenses*, a reference to the merchant class) and wealthy commoners (*ditiores*). Pieter de Coninck and the other leaders of the revolt of 1301–2 were left with the support of the textile workers and other *mechanici vulgares*. They understood that this was a new political phase, in which the popular party would have to face not only the wealthy and powerful within the cities but also the comital family and the nobles of Flanders.[108] While class lines dividing urban society were not clear-cut, and while elite groups and even the ranks of artisans would often be riven by internal splits, a fundamental division had emerged by this period, between the powerful craft guilds and a commercial elite supported by counts and nobles, which would characterize the outline and logic of Bruges' politics for two centuries to come.

[107] K. Czok, 'Zunftkämpfe, Zunftrevolutionen oder Bürgerkämpfe?', *Wissenschaftliche Zeitschrift der Karl Marx-Universität Leipzig, Gesellschafts- und Sprachwissenschaftliche Reihe*, 8 (1958–9), 129–43. For a more recent and nuanced view of the importance of alliances of social groups in revolts, see Patrick Lantschner, 'The Ciompi Revolution Constructed: Modern Historians and the Nineteenth-Century Paradigm of Revolution', *Annali di Storia di Firenze*, 4 (2009), 277–97.

[108] Johnstone (ed.), *Annals of Ghent*, p. 35.

5 | The Urban Landscape II: c.1275–c.1500

JAN DUMOLYN, MARC RYCKAERT, HEIDI DENEWETH, LUC DEVLIEGHER AND GUY DUPONT

By the early fourteenth century the cobweb layout of city streets had come to resemble a form that would last for centuries: many present-day street names can already be found in the city accounts of the 1280s. This relative stasis in street layout partly reflects demographic trends: the city's population explosion came to an end by the late thirteenth century. In the wake of famine in 1315–17 and the Black Death of 1349–50, and despite continuing immigration into the city, the number of people living in Bruges probably declined slightly, to stabilize at around 40,000 to 50,000 (with some variation in years of high mortality or immigration). Thus, during the fourteenth and fifteenth centuries, the general morphology of the city was consolidated (and after 1500, the built-up area within the city would in fact decrease). In general, the areal extent of the later medieval urban landscape remained static, but as we shall see in this chapter, it was continually reshaped by social change: by a greater specialization and diversification of economic activities, by the disappearance of the last social and spatial borders that had existed between the early twelfth-century centre and the thirteenth-century suburbs, and by a greater spatial mix of trades and social groups. These changes were partly the indirect consequence of the development of Bruges into the main commercial hub of the later medieval North Sea area, as well as into a major centre for the textile and luxury industries. This development spatially transformed the city into a genuine medieval metropolis with a great diversity of functionally specialized areas and often sharp social contradictions between and within them. More research needs to be done to grasp fully the complex interactions between material conditions and the changes made to urban space: from the 1280s we enter a period of abundant archival records that have still to be studied more systematically. But a considerable amount of work has been done on particular buildings and on some neighbourhoods: the main lines of development can be sketched with some confidence (see Map 3).[1]

[1] Bibliography on specific buildings and quarters can be found mostly in Ryckaert, *Historische stedenatlas*; and Deneweth, '*Huizen*'. The older work by Duclos, *Bruges*, can still be useful; as can Van Houtte, *De geschiedenis van Brugge*; Ryckaert et al. (eds.), *Brugge*; and N. Geirnaert and L. Vandamme, *Brugge: Een verhaal van 2000 jaar* (Bruges, 1996). For street names: A.

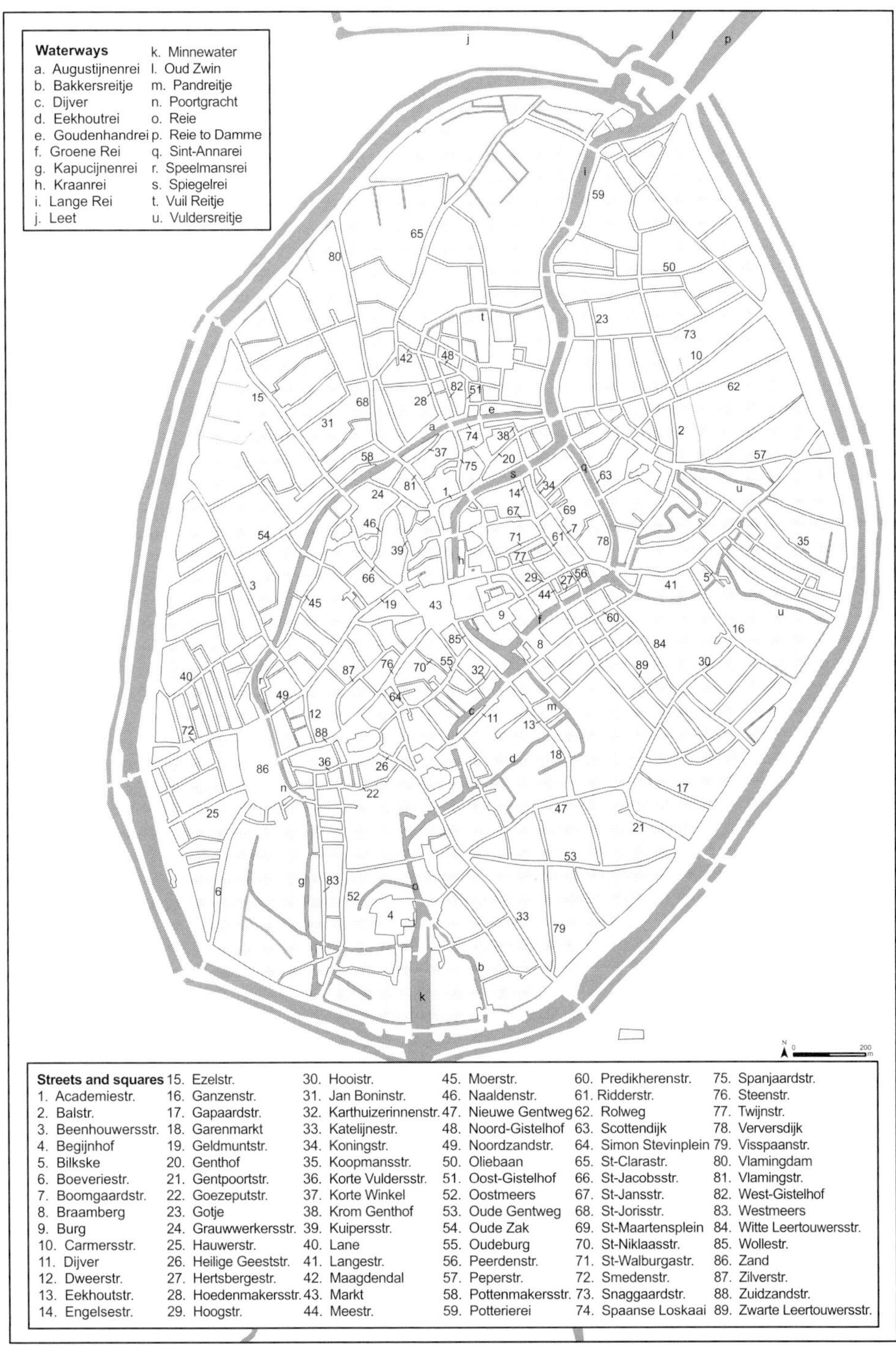

Map 3 Bruges streets, squares and waterways

The Consolidated Territory of the Later Medieval City

At the end of the thirteenth century, urban space was partly shaped by social inequalities: although the distinction between a richer city centre (the area enclosed within the first ramparts) and a poorer periphery (the neighbourhoods *extra muros*) was not rigid, and although the rise of middling groups would temper extremes of wealth, growing social contrasts did express themselves geographically. As in a nineteenth-century industrial town, the working classes of Bruges, especially the still demographically dominant workforce of the textile industry, seem to have lived mostly in the expanding suburbs. In practice these were all city-dwellers, but from a legal point of view, the new immigrants who lived and worked in the thirteenth-century industrial quarters (apart from those in the Braamberg district already incorporated in the city) did not belong to the commune. Large areas just outside the first city wall still lay in the seigniory of Sijsele and its dependent lordships of the Praetse and Assebroek, and many of the suburban workers lived there. Other feudal land around Bruges beyond its 1127 borders was held by the comital dynasty, such as the lordships of the Voormezeelse and the Maandagse, or by the provost and canons of St Donatian.

These separate legal zones created fiscal and social problems for the commune. As the suburbs did not lie under the city's jurisdiction, no urban taxation had to be paid on consumer goods, wages could not be regulated by the urban government, and a 'toll free' black market of commodities probably sprang up. The lords around Bruges thus profited from the surplus created there: this in itself must have been a thorn in the side of the merchant class. The relative lack of communal control over the suburbs also made them potential hotspots of crime and social unrest. Concern about these issues among the ruling merchant groups is apparent in changes made to the urban landscape – strategic changes, driven by a desire to unify

Schouteet, *De straatnamen van Brugge: Oorsprong en betekenis* (Bruges, 1977); buildings and other monuments: L. Devliegher, *De huizen te Brugge*, 2 vols. (Tielt, 1968); L. Snauwaert and L. Devliegher, *Gids voor architectuur in Brugge* (Tielt, 2002); J. Cornilly, *Monumentaal West Vlaanderen: Beschermde monumenten en landschappen in de provincie West Vlaanderen*, vol. II: *De fusiegemeente Brugge* (Bruges, 2003). For almost two decades, the Werkgroep Huizengeschiedenis of the Bruges City Archives has produced reports, in booklets or in short articles, in the journal *Archiefleven*, on the history of particular houses: for a state of the art with further references, including archaeological reports of *Raakvlak*, the Local Archaeological Service of Bruges, see H. Deneweth, J. D'hondt and K. Leenders, *Een huis in Brugge: Vademecum voor de historische studie van woningen, eigenaars en bewoners* (Bruges, 2001).

economically the actual space of urban production and consumption. At a general level, it is possible to detect a concerted spatial strategy pursued by the urban elites, in conjunction with the clergy, to extend their economic, social, political, legal, religious and moral control over the artisans, wage workers and Lumpenproletarians who populated the industrial neighbourhoods around the old town. Spiritual motivations were doubtless at work too, but the city government's efforts in the thirteenth century to patronize mendicant orders and found hospitals, to encourage preaching, charity and pastoral care, may be read partly as efforts to minimize threats to social order. Even so, these efforts were not sufficient for controlling the *classes laborieuses*, that is to say the *classes dangereuses*, of the industrial belt: the Moerlemaye Revolt of 1280–1, during which these classes demanded full burgher rights, made this only too clear. Control over the growing urban territory also had to be enforced by legal and economic means.[2]

Considerable effort was made to strengthen the links between the inner city and the suburbs. The old twelfth-century defensive structures had lost their use so there was less need to preserve the inner city as a walled enclave: thus, during the thirteenth century bridges over the Reie and its arms were built to connect the old city to the expanding suburbs. This programme of bridge building would be continuous: by the end of the fifteenth century, eighty-eight bridges had been built or repaired, thirteen of which, not counting those of the first rampart gates, connected the old city to the suburbs. Not all of these were initially made of stone, but from the fourteenth century wooden ones were gradually replaced with stone structures.[3] Besides eliminating the inner canals as city borders, the expanded urban territory had to be integrated by legal and fiscal means. Feudal and seigniorial structures outside the pre-1127 boundaries were removed. In 1275 the city bought sections of two seigniories, the Maandagse and the Voormezeelse, from Countess Margaret of Constantinople: these were situated somewhere between the first and the future second wall. The countess granted Bruges this favour perhaps because her own fiscal revenues would benefit if economic growth resulted. The city government had a harder task to persuade Wouter Van Sijsele to part company with a large section of his seigniory of *Sijseelse*: it was blackmailed into paying him a higher price than it had first offered.

[2] Dumolyn, 'Economic Development'.

[3] M. Ryckaert, 'Bruggen van Brugge', *In de Steigers: Erfgoednieuws uit West-Vlaanderen*, 10 (2003), 17–27; GVS, *Inventaire*, Introduction, p. 404. Still existing examples are the Augustijnenbrug, close to the Augustinian hermits' convent, with benches and three arches, and the Peerdenbrug and Meebrug, which have a more modest form.

But after this purchase of feudal land on 1 May 1275, the new legal border of Bruges had largely become established.[4] Between 1275 and 1287, an important fief just outside the first city walls was also placed under the city's jurisdiction: this was the Praetse, which by then lay within the new parish of St Giles and also encompassed a large part of the portuary zone. Other seigniorial rights that hindered the socio-economic unification of Bruges were acquired. The tendency in this period for feudal levies to fall perhaps made local lords more willing to sell land to the city for short-term profit.[5]

The lords of Assebroek possessed fishing rights on the Reie as part of their receivership of the so-called Brevia de Roya, part of the old comital domain their lineage had held in fief: the city acquired this vital asset in 1290. The lord of Assebroek was also apparently happy to sell some land near the beguinage on which stood tenter frames for shearing. As with the Praetse, this was a suburban zone into which the textile industry had expanded: the merchant-entrepreneurs must have been eager to establish full legal control over the means of production and over the labour force in these areas and eliminate lordly extraction of surplus from this activity. The city government also tried at the end of the thirteenth century to buy up the Proosse and the Kanunnikse, seigniories that belonged respectively to the provost and canons of St Donatian's, but the attempt failed, and these areas would remain outside the city's jurisdictional grasp: twelve judicial enclaves of these ecclesiastical lordships, the smallest containing only a solitary church or house, would remain enclosed within the city until 1796.[6] The 'Great Toll' of Bruges on imported goods was probably given out originally in fief by the count to the former lords of the seigniory of the Voormezeelse, but by 1200 the lords of Gistel had received it from the count in return for organizing the coastal defence of Flanders. During the thirteenth century there was a struggle (still under-researched) between the town government and noble families of Woestine and Gistel to control it; and the city never fully acquired this vital right, and thus the ability to take

[4] Strubbe, 'Van de eerste'. The seigniories of the Maendagse and the Sijseelse kept their own bailiff for some of the parts that had been incorporated into the city's jurisdiction, and held court in the Burg; so did the aldermen of the Liberty of Bruges and the men of the comital feudal court of the Burg of Bruges.

[5] For the later medieval Flemish agricultural economy, see E. Thoen, 'A "Commercial Survival Economy" in Evolution: The Flemish Countryside and the Transition to Capitalism (Middle Ages – 19th Century)', in P. C. M. Hoppenbrouwers and J. L. Van Zanden (eds.), *Peasants into Farmers? The Transformation of Rural Economy and Society in the Low Countries (Middle Ages – 19th Century) in Light of the Brenner Debate* (Turnhout, 2001), pp. 102–57.

[6] J. De Smet, 'De evolutie van het Brugse stadsgebied', *HGG*, 100 (1963), 90–9.

complete control of the transaction costs of foreign trade. The same was the case with the tax on the gruut. The tax was held in fief by the Van Gruuthuse family, from which they derived their name and riches.[7] However, although not all lordly competitors had been removed, by the end of the thirteenth century the city government had largely assumed control over communal space and its workforce. New ramparts would be erected after 1297 to enclose the expanded urban territory, but even these did not fully encompass the areas brought under the aldermen's jurisdiction: the straight lines between boundary markers demarcated the so-called *paallanden* ('pole' or 'post lands'), including the expanded urban jurisdiction after 1275. These semi-rural lands under the jurisdiction of the Bruges city council stretched beyond the inhabited quarters right up to the village churches of the Holy Cross, St Baaf and St Michael.[8]

The extension of municipal jurisdiction was accompanied by a restructuring of administrative space: at some point during the third quarter of the thirteenth century, the Bruges territory was subdivided into six 'sections' (called *officia* or *ambochten*, and from the 1330s usually *zestendelen* or 'sixth parts'), which served to strengthen the fiscal and policing power of the ruling elite. The earliest history of the *zestendelen* is unclear: at one time there seems to have been seven instead of six, and their borders probably fluctuated while their names became fixed only gradually. The names by which they were eventually known were: (1) the Officium Nord or the Sint-Jans Zestendeel (the section of St John); (2) the Officium Urbis or the Sint-Donaas Zestendeel (the section of St Donatian); (3) the Officium Veteris Urbis or the Onze-Lieve-Vrouwe Zestendeel (the section of Our Lady); (4) the Officium Steenstrate or the Sint-Jacobs Zestendeel (the section of St James); (5) the Officium Cuper or the Sint-Niklaas Zestendeel (the section of St Nicholas); (6) the Officium Vlamingorum or the Carmers Zestendeel (the section of the Carmelites).[9] This division may simply reflect a need to divide the new city into units of roughly equal size, starting from the market-place, and using the main streets or waterways as borders, but their earliest names may not have been chosen at random, and perhaps refer to the types of settlement and activity that had taken place within them. They largely overlapped with (1) the settlement of the earliest elites of merchants, comital officials and soldiers between the axis of the Hoogstraat–Langestraat and the Spinolarei, where the earliest *wic* or

[7] Van Houtte, *De geschiedenis van Brugge*, p. 198.

[8] Ryckaert, *Historische stedenatlas*, p. 82.

[9] Van Werveke, *"Burgus"*, p. 50.

portus had been situated around St Walburga's church and St John's chapel; (2) the area of the comital castle, but stretching further out to the south-east; (3) the suburb of the Oudeburg, around the two main churches of St Saviour and Our Lady; (4) the zone of later westward expansion with a new industrial area and the younger quarter around St James' parish church; (5) the zone of northwards urban growth at the west of the Reie following the development of international commerce towards Damme; (6) the area to the east of the Reie, which had been part of the same twelfth- and thirteenth-century expansion. The *zestendelen*, managed by a captain or headman (*hooftman*) would remain the city's basic administrative districts for policing and tax-collecting until modern times. As we will see below, after 1304, the sections would also become the units for organizing the political 'Member' of the *poorterie* (the merchants and landowners) and the legal districts in which the *deelmannen* (local justices of the peace) operated.

The Second Rampart

The city had long since sprawled beyond the twelfth-century ramparts, but it was only at the end of the thirteenth century, with tensions rising between the kings of France and the counts of Flanders, that the need for a new system of defence became urgent. Ironically, though, it was neither the city nor the count who gave the order to construct new moats around the enlarged urban territory, but the French troops who occupied Flanders after 1297. Between 1297 and 1300, financed by a forced loan imposed on the burghers, workers constructed a defence system of 6,800 metres in length with a double ditch, an earthen rampart, wooden palisades and watchtowers and nine robust city gates made of stone. The moat would not be walled until the early fifteenth century (and then only partially), but it was an immense undertaking; and this second rampart enclosed an area of 430 hectares (the area which still encompasses the old city centre of Bruges today).[10]

Among the most impressive features of this new system were the nine new gates. As in other medieval cities, they were strong signs of urbanity, forming military, fiscal and ideological barriers between urban space and the outside world. Starting from the north, there was the 'Dampoort complex', designed to secure the junction of four waterways vital for maritime

[10] Ryckaert, *Historische stedenatlas*, pp. 91–3; M. Becuwe, B. Beernaert and P. Cardinael, *De Vesten anders bekeken: Een groene wandeling rond Brugge* (Bruges, 2005).

commerce: the Reie river; the Leet or Ieperleet canal leading westward towards Oudenburg, Nieuwpoort and Ypres, connecting Flemish inland trade with the sea; the Oude Zwin (Old Zwin), the older waterway which had connected Bruges to the sea; and the canal to Damme linking the Zwin estuary to the port of Bruges (see Map 4). The Dampoort complex included three gates: the St Nicholas or Koolkerkse Poort, the Sint-Lenaertspoort or Dudzeelse Poort and the Speiepoort (the 'sluice' or 'lock gate'). The St Leonard Gate was added to this three-gated complex in 1305. Some idea of their original and impressive shape can be formed, despite alterations since. The Speiepoort consisted of a rectangular block with a second higher block added on to it and two flanking semicircular towers. In front, and connected to it by two walls, there was a frontal gate with two corner towers corbelling out. The St Nicholas Gate was smaller and rectangular, with two semicircular towers at its outer corners, and had a frontal gate with two semicircular towers. Abutting the gate was the city wall with a covered wall-walk and a semicircular wall-tower. The St Leonard Gate was a round tower through which the entrance led, with a frontal gate and drawbridge. Foreign commerce was channelled into this imposing fortification complex: merchants passing through were undoubtedly made perfectly aware that toll had to be paid on their goods and that the communal authorities would protect them in return.[11]

The remaining gates were the Kruispoort (Gate of the Holy Cross), the Gentpoort (Ghent Gate), the Katelijnepoort (St Catherine's Gate), the Boeveriepoort (next to the Boeverie area, a common field for grazing cattle), the Smedenpoort (Blacksmiths' Gate) and the Ezelpoort (or Donkey Gate, probably referring to the shape of a nearby bridge, rather than, as some have thought, to Christ's entrance into Jerusalem). Their original appearance is unknown: possibly they were simple passageways flanked by two semicircular or rectangular supports, locked with a frontal gate and drawbridge. Their shape and character changed: their history demonstrates the vicissitudes of political fortunes, and their importance, practical and symbolic, to the city and its authorities. In the peace treaty of Athis-sur-Orge in 1305, highly disadvantageous to the Flemish, the king of France ordered that the Bruges fortifications be demolished, though this did not begin to happen until after the defeat of another Bruges rebellion at Cassel in 1328 (see Chapter 7). Even then it seems that the gates were only partially torn down, and ten years later the count of Flanders permitted their restoration. Thus,

11 Ryckaert, *Historische stedenatlas*, pp. 91–6; L. Devliegher, *Beeld van het kunstbezit*, Kunstpatrimonium van West-Vlaanderen 1 (Tielt, 1965), pp. 39–40.

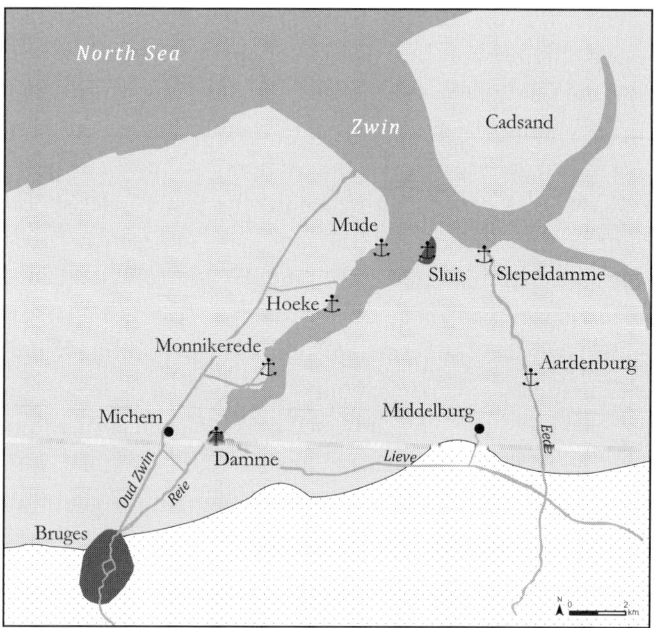

Map 4 The Zwin Estuary

in 1337–8 the Boeverie Gate and the Blacksmiths' Gate were repaired (the latter standing today in its rebuilt form of 1615). During the third quarter of the fourteenth century, it seems that bricks from the communal brickworks (*tegelrie*) in the village of Ramskapelle, twelve kilometres away, were used to reshape them. In 1361–7, the Ghent, St Catherine and Holy Cross gates were reconstructed. And in 1367–70, following a common architectural plan, the Boeverie Gate, the Blacksmiths' Gate and the Donkey Gate (still extant but restored), were also rebuilt with two heavy round towers linked by an overarching passageway. In 1382, the Ghent, St Catherine and Holy Cross Gates were demolished at the order of occupying Ghent rebel troops. The city rebuilt them between 1401 and 1406. Each of these gates consisted of a rectangular block (*zalen*) with an arched-over passage. At their exterior sides they were extended with two stout round towers (*cupen*). At the sides facing the city, they each had a stair turret leading to the upper floor. The passages could be locked with a heavy gate with a portcullis and were also reinforced with loopholes and throw holes in the round towers. The Ghent and Holy Cross Gates are also still preserved, though like the Katelijnepoort and the Speiepoort, the frontal gates added to them as advanced defences in the fifteenth century were demolished in the eighteenth. Other projects intended to increase the city's security were also attempted. At the

Minnewater, two high towers were erected to guard the entrance into the city by water: in 1398, the still extant western Poertoren ('Powder Tower', as the city stored its gunpowder there) and in 1401 the eastern one. During the early fifteenth century, a wall with additional towers was built upon a large part of the moat around the city: this is shown on Marcus Gerards' 1562 map of Bruges. However, walled encirclement of the town was never completed: technological advances in cannon firepower soon rendered the project pointless. Their ideological value, though, had always been as important as their defensive capabilities: in an early fifteenth-century poem written just after their restoration, the gates of Bruges were lauded as the guardians of the city and associated with the central values of urban political discourse, including justice, freedom and unity.[12]

The Commercial Zones

The main commercial buildings of the city were situated on the Markt: at its south side the Old Hall and Belfry and at its east side the Water Hall or New Hall, built over the canal. The earliest reference to the 'Old Hall' appears in a document dated 1211, which mentions one 'Riquardus post Hallam', a cognomen suggesting that the building was erected a generation earlier, perhaps by the later twelfth century. By that time maritime trade was in full expansion, and merchant guildhalls were present in other Flemish commercial cities such as Saint-Omer (mentioned in a charter of 1151)[13] and nearby Aardenburg (its hall mentioned in the comital account of 1187).[14] The Old Hall's four-sided ground construction in masonry dates from the second quarter of the thirteenth century. Originally, it served primarily as a place for the inspection and selling of cloth, but other commodities and products were sold on different floors and rooms and in its inner square. Parts of it functioned as an arms arsenal. Until 1280, the Old Hall with an attached tower known as the 'Belfry' or 'Belfort' (a type of communal building prevalent in northern France and the southern Low Countries), was also the seat of the urban government, and it would continue to serve occasionally as a meeting

[12] M. Coornaert, 'De middeleeuwse vestingwerken van de stad Brugge (deel 3)', *BO*, 32 (1992), 72–7; J. Dumolyn, 'Une idéologie urbaine "bricolée" en Flandre médiévale: Les "Sept Portes de Bruges" dans le manuscrit Gruuthuse (début du 15e siècle)', *BTFG*, 88 (2010), 1039–84; H. Janse and T. Van Straalen, *Middeleeuwse stadswallen en stadspoorten in de lage landen* (Zaltbommel, 1975), pp. 33–4. On this poem, see further Chapter 9.

[13] A. Giry, *Histoire de la ville de Saint-Omer et de ses institutions jusqu'au XIVe siècle* (Paris, 1877), pp. 284–6.

[14] Verhulst and Gysseling (eds.), *Le compte général de 1187*, pp. 123 n. 6, 172.

place for municipal business (see Figure 5.1). The building has four wings grouped around a courtyard. The northern wing, facing the Market Square, was presumably built with the Belfry. The roofing of the southern and the eastern halls dates from the end of the thirteenth century; the cover of the western wing from slightly later. The 'Belfry' itself (*belford*, *belafroid*, *beffredum* or *torre van der halle*, and today often referred to as the Halletoren), is an elegant yet sturdy tower directly connected to the merchant hall. It probably dates to the second quarter of the thirteenth century when the self-conscious and increasingly autonomous merchant elite ruling Bruges decided to erect it, surely in part as a symbol of urban pride. It suffered from a fire in 1280, destroying the city archives which it then housed, and was rebuilt. The thirteenth-century Belfry is made up of two moulds, of which the four corners are completed with an engaged column. The lower stratification has several floors. The ground floor is covered with a cross vault, its ribs supported by bud capitals. On the vault keystone a head is depicted. The first and the second floor also have a cross vault resting on bud capitals. The round vault keystones carry images of (probably) St Martin on his horse and the Lamb of God. Both arches probably date from after 1280 and were adapted to the fourteenth-century stepped tower in the southeastern corner. It seems likely that the 1280 fire destroyed the wooden tower crowning the 'inside belfry' (the wooden scaffold from which the bells hung), as a result of which the bells fell through the dome or the attic of the treasury room on the second floor, thus spreading the fire. In this treasury there are two niches, both closed off with double iron fences, and at its front two more niches with pointed arches, a central pillar and a quatrefoil in the tympanum (on which the fifteenth-century stone cross windows in the hall's northern façade were probably modelled). Halfway along the third floor, the outer walls slightly rebound, creating a gallery, protected by a crenellated parapet. Three of the outer walls of this floor are decorated with large round arched niches, containing three small pointed arches. After 1482 a third storey constructed in Brabantine sandstone, octagonal in shape, was added to the Belfry, probably copying church architecture (perhaps Utrecht cathedral). Every one of its eight sides is cut across by a high light belfry-arch, of which the lower half is closed off by a divided window. Its tower top was burnt in 1493, and was repaired in a different form.[15]

The Belfry served as the city's official bell-tower, to mark important moments in the communal calendar and structure the rhythm of daily

[15] This later tower top would also burn down in 1741, never to be replaced, leaving the Belfry in its current form.

Figure 5.1 The Belfort from the inside quad

life within urban space – as if rivalling the bells of city churches. Its bells were situated in the fourth-floor attic. The communal bell of the Belfry was the *magna campana*, the *campana in halla* or *de clocke*. There was also a *scepenen scelle* (a 'scelle' was a smaller type of bell), a *bruudclocke* or *campana nuntiarum* to announce weddings, and a *clocke van der maeltyt* and a *werc clocke* to organize the rhythm of labour in the city. Bells were rung to announce the yearly market or *Brucghemaerct*, the procession of the Holy Blood (see Chapter 8), visits of the count, and every morning, noon and evening to announce the start and end of the working day.[16] The Belfry and halls also identified the Market Square as the main political space of the city. From its balcony, the comital ordinances and urban bylaws (*hallegeboden*) would be read out to the people, and in times of revolt rebel governments held assemblies in the building while armed guildsmen assembled on the square.[17] It has been questioned whether belfries were communal symbols at all, since they often also carried the arms and symbols of princes; but given the 'contractual' nature of the political relationship between towns and princes in Flanders (outlined above), this argument is difficult to sustain.[18] The ideological significance of belfries, not to mention the economic importance of cloth and other merchant halls for the high medieval towns of Flanders, can hardly be underestimated: the architectural evolution of the Bruges Belfry is an expression of its communal history in the medieval period and remains today the city's iconic landmark par excellence.[19]

Apart from the later octagonal tower-part, the Old Hall and Belfry largely took on their definitive shape at the end of the thirteenth century, a fact which also seems to reflect an economic transition – the decisive shift in Bruges to 'passive trade', in which an elaborate infrastructure for international commerce became the city's lifeline (on which, see Chapter 6). Nowhere is this shift made more manifest than in the building of the so-called 'New Hall' (Nieuwe Halle) or 'Water Hall' (Waterhalle). The Old Hall must have become too small to deal with the quickening pace of commerce: between 1284 and 1294, a new monumental structure covering

16 GVS, *Inventaire*, Table analytique (unnumbered vol.), pp. 48–9.

17 A. Janssens, 'Het Brugse Belfort: Wisselend uitzicht omstreeks 1480 en 1503', *BO*, 44 (2004), 67–84; B. Beernaert, F. Deleu, A. Hemeryck et al., *Het Belfort van Brugge* (Bruges, 2012).

18 R. van Uytven, 'Flämische Belfriede und südniederländische städtische Bauwerke im Mittelalter: Symbol und Mythos', in A. Haverkamp and E. Müller-Luckner (eds.), *Information, Kommunikation und Selbstdarstellung in mittelalterlichen Gemeinden* (Munich, 1998), pp. 125–59.

19 P. Devos, *Brugge, herwonnen schoonheid: Tien jaar monumentenzorg te Brugge* (Tielt and Amsterdam, 1975), pp. 13–26; F. L. Ganshof, 'Les halles et le beffroi de Bruges', *Sessions: Congrès archéologique de France*, 120 (1962), 16–28; L. Devliegher, *25 jaar monumentenzorg in West-Vlaanderen (1950–1975)* (Bruges, 1975), pp. 67–81.

the Kraanrei was constructed at the east side of the Market Square (where wares had probably already been traded in the open air). No building in Bruges better exemplifies the growing importance of commercial traffic. Its main part covered a dock into which barges could enter via the watercourse under the Wisselbrug, where the money changers had their stalls. It marked the final arrival of commodities entering the Bruges portuary zone from the Zwin estuary, hence its name. It was 95 metres long, 24.5 deep and 35 high.[20] During the years 1332–5 and 1366–7, probably because the city tried to improve the market infrastructure (following problems with the wool supply), a covered annex with an upper floor was built against the first structure at the side of the Market Square. In 1419 the roof was renovated and adorned with five coats of arms of the city. This covered market space drew the admiring attention of foreign merchants and travellers and was still considered one of the 'seven marvels of Bruges' in the sixteenth century. Inside there was a quay about 4.5 metres in width. Between this quay and a row of pillars in the middle of the Reie, the width of the watercourse was about 6.4 metres (revealed by archaeology in 1908–10). The Tournai-style pillars in the middle of the water carried round arches. Girders supported the principal beams of the ceiling. The loft was lightened through windows in the façades. This 'upper hall' was covered with an exceptional roof spanning almost 22 metres. The inclined straight principals produced a large storage room. The fourteenth-century annex, facing the Market Square, comprised buttresses with vaults between them. There, stalls were rented out to merchants. The arched-over lower room was connected to the quay along the Reie with round arched openings. At the top, the annex was covered with a terrace and an openwork parapet.[21]

Although these building complexes formed the central commercial section, an expanding zone that reflected the city's international connections also began to give the landscape of Bruges its distinctive character. At the end of the thirteenth century, streets named after foreign merchants increasingly appear in the sources, testifying to a presence that was becoming more prolonged in specialized areas. The city's accounts reveal toponyms

[20] L. Devliegher, *Van Waterhalle tot Provinciaal Hof* (Bruges, 1994), pp. 9–13; L. Devliegher, 'Pero Tafur in Brugge, Sluis en Antwerpen', *HGG*, 140 (2003), 269–87. A translation of Tafur's account appears in Häpke, *Brügges Entwicklung*, p. 13.

[21] As commercial activity in Bruges dwindled during the seventeenth century and was moved to other places in the city, the Water Hall increasingly lost its original function and the building, especially the woodwork, ceased to be well maintained. When in 1786 the Kraanrei was filled up, it was decided to demolish the building, which happened between 1787 and 1791. Devliegher, *Van Waterhalle*, pp. 9–39.

referring to merchants from Lübeck in 1282, to Spaniards and merchants from Bayonne in 1284, and to the English in 1285. As these accounts only date from 1280, it is safe to assume that foreign merchants, the Hanse in particular, had been residing in the city for quite some time. As it became clear that Bruges was developing as a hub for foreign merchants rather than as an active agent in foreign trade, the infrastructure for international commerce was systematically improved. In 1281–2 a weighing house was built on the Market Square and shortly before 1292 a *grue* for unloading heavy objects such as barrels of wine was constructed on the Kraanplaats ('Crane Square') 100 metres from the Market Square on the bank of the Reie. The *grue* became a Bruges landmark, depicted several times by Flemish masters.[22] Fiscality also left its imprint on the infrastructure of the commercial zones. The 'Small Toll', on agricultural and other goods entering the city over land, was exacted at every gate; the 'Great Toll' was imposed on foreign imports (and collected in a house whose location in the thirteenth century is not known precisely). In all likelihood the imported goods were already registered at the Dampoort complex as they entered urban territory and were subjected to the Bruges staple rights. Only in about 1400 was a toll house installed in a former merchant's house at the St John's Bridge. At the beginning of the fifteenth century, the Great Toll became the possession of the lords of Luxemburg, who had a new office built for it in 1477 (which still exists, heavily reconstructed).[23]

During the fourteenth century, foreign merchants and bankers made an indelible impact on the urban landscape, especially its northern part. As Chapter 6 explains, the Ter Beurze Square, becoming known internationally by its French name Place de la Bourse, in many ways formed the heart of international trade and finance in northern Europe. The word 'bourse' was taken up in several European languages to become a term for the 'exchange' and later the 'stock market', but it originally took its name from an inn owned by the Van der Beurze family, a Bruges dynasty of hostellers. The square formed the centre of the commercial area which was a melting pot of foreign merchants, but certain streets and quarters tended to become the particular haunts of some more than others. At the end of the thirteenth century, the Scots were present at one side of the Dyers Quay, referred to as the Scottendijk (Scottish Dyke). In 1315, an English weighing house is

[22] R. Degryse, 'De oudste houten kranen in de Vlaamse en andere havens (13de – 16de eeuw)', *HGG*, 128 (1991), 5–46, 153–87; D. De Vos, *Stedelijke Musea Brugge: Catalogus schilderijen 15de en 16de eeuw* (Bruges, 1979), pp. 47–8, 169–71.

[23] Van Houtte, *De geschiedenis van Brugge*, p. 198.

mentioned in the Engelsestraat, which was shared with the Scottish merchants, even when kings of Scotland and England were at war. During the fourteenth and fifteenth centuries, the Castilians were probably concentrated in the Lange Winkel and Korte Winkel. The Great Square area around the Sint-Jansstraat, the Ridderstraat and the Sint-Walburgastraat, which had early acquired an elite character, mostly remained a quarter inhabited by Bruges nobles, rich merchants and hostellers, and also by foreign merchants, notably some English, Germans and Portuguese. Some streets there temporarily had a broader social mix, but the quarter had recovered its elite character by the end of the Middle Ages. By the fourteenth century, some groups of foreign merchants also obtained their own 'nation houses', used for their internal consular justice, for keeping their common records, and for meetings, dinners and gambling. In 1377 a 'Lucchese Lodge' is mentioned at the corner of the Naaldenstraat and the Grauwwerkersstraat, and in 1394 another nation house was built for the merchants of Lucca at the corner of the Naaldenstraat and the Kuiperstraat. By 1397 at the latest a Venetian Lodge was established in a house formerly belonging to the Van der Beurze family; the Genoese Lodge (still standing) was built in 1399, and by 1420 the Florentines were also renting a house.[24] The Castilian merchants had a house at the Lange Winkel (the current Spanjaardstraat) in 1483 and received another in the same street in 1494. Finally, in 1494, the city bought the house De Gapaert for the Biscay nation and a magnificent building was erected there.

The spatial presence of the Hanseatic merchants in Bruges was also significant, but not as pronounced as it could be elsewhere. They were firmly established in the mid thirteenth century but were unable to secure the extensive privileges granted to them in some other towns, being unable to apply quite the pressure on Bruges and Flanders as they could on weaker and more pliable places. Despite their efforts to obtain an autonomous quarter in the Zwin delta in the thirteenth century, they did not develop their own jurisdictional enclave as they did, for instance, in Bergen or Novgorod. In 1250, Countess Margaret allowed the Hanse merchants to found a new city on the Zwin to be called Nieuwdamme, but for reasons

[24] R. de Roover, 'La communauté des marchands lucquois à Bruges de 1377 à 1404', *HGG*, 86 (1949), 28–89; J. Marechal, *Geschiedenis van de Brugse Beurs* (Bruges, 1949); V. Vermeersch, A. Vandewalle, J. Esther et al., *De Genuese Loge: Van natiehuis tot bankinstelling* (Bruges, 1983); J. Marechal, *Europese aanwezigheid te Brugge: De vreemde kolonies (XIVde–XIXde eeuw)* (Bruges, 1985); V. Vermeersch (ed.), *Brugge en Europa* (Antwerp, 1992); A. Vandewalle, 'De vreemde naties in Brugge', in Vandewalle (ed.), *Hanzekooplui en Medicibankiers*, pp. 34–5.

unknown this plan did not materialize.[25] They therefore held their meetings in the Carmelite convent and resided in the inns of Bruges or in rented houses. Only in 1457, heavily assisted by the city government, would the Oosterlingenhuis be built for the Hanse (to be replaced by a more luxurious towered building in 1478).[26] The city government even had a house on the other side of the street demolished to construct a square for the Hanse merchants. By then, the glory days of Bruges commerce were receding, but municipal investments were still made to persuade foreign merchants to continue residing in the city. However, the fundamental places for international trade were not these nation houses but the network of dozens of often very large inns in which the Bruges hostellers lodged the merchants, stored their goods and also acted as their brokers, trustees, bankers and representatives – which is why the names of Bruges inns are so frequently found in letters and accounts of English, Scottish and German merchants. Many of these hostels had stables, and large attics and cellars for storage of goods, besides functioning as hotels and often restaurants. Apart from living in hostels, merchants also rented houses or rooms when they settled for longer periods in the city.[27]

The accessibility of Bruges from the sea remained of central importance for international commerce: a system of outports, as we saw, assured the city's connection with the flow of merchandise brought by foreign ships. There were difficulties in keeping this access open. Even by 1250, before Bruges became a hub for international merchants, the Zwin had already been reduced to a narrow stream. The reclamation of polder land at both sides of the Zwin gully started in the late twelfth century and lasted until the beginning of the fourteenth, when the city began to resist it. This 'inpoldering' had made the stream ever narrower and limited the natural tidal movements, gradually causing the Zwin, hardly if at all fed by river water, to silt up. From about 1400 pilotage at Sluis was better organized to lead large vessels around the sandbanks; in 1456 a signalization system was installed and during the later fifteenth and sixteenth centuries, the urban authorities would invest in major hydraulic works, such as opening up the polder

[25] Stein, 'Über die ältesten Privilegien'; P. Dollinger, *La Hanse (XIIe–XVIIe siècle)* (Paris, 1964); C. Römer, 'Die Hanse und die niederländische Städtewelt', in *Hanse in Europa: Brücke zwischen den Märkten, 12.–17. Jahrhundert* [exh. cat.] (Cologne, 1973), pp. 121–36.

[26] F. De Smidt [Broeder Firmin], *Het Oosterlingenhuis te Brugge en zijn ontwerper Jan vanden Poele* (Antwerp, 1948); L. Devliegher, 'Het Oosterlingenhuis te Brugge', in N. Jörn, W. Paravicini and H. Wernicke (eds.), *Hansekaufleute in Brügge*, vol. IV: *Beiträge der Internationalen Tagung in Brügge April 1996* (Frankfurt am Main, 2000), pp. 13–32.

[27] Marechal, *Geschiedenis*; Murray, *Bruges*, pp. 73–7, 190–205.

dyke of the Zwarte Gat in 1473, which had no effect.[28] In older historiography, this silting up of the Zwin explained the eventual decay of Bruges (see Chapter 10). Too much importance has been attached to this phenomenon – given that it had been a problem for so long. But sedimentation in the Zwin was a real concern, and access to the sea remained a vital issue.

Local and Regional Market Spaces

Although Bruges became a gateway of international commerce, it remained a central place to its hinterland with numerous local and regional market functions. The exact locations of these markets, their evolution and functional specialization, still need study; but we know that apart from the main market squares such as the Markt, the Vrijdagmarkt/Zand and the Braamberg, there were commercial halls, shopping streets, informal street stalls and places where peddling occurred, spread out all over the urban landscape. The fixed market-places were regulated and controlled by the city government and by craft guilds who jealously guarded their privileges. Food and other utilities were traded in numerous sites. Fish could be bought at the north side of the Markt, near the fishmongers' guild house and St Christopher's chapel, where this guild celebrated mass. Grain was sold on the Braamberg, horses and cattle at the Zand, second-hand clothes at the Vrijdagmarkt (the western part of the Zand); and there were sites, as yet unlocated, where poultry, vinegar, pigs and hay could be purchased. Commercial activity also took place in specialized buildings and halls for marketing consumer goods and services, on an annual, weekly and daily basis. For instance, cheese, butter and milk were sold at the 'butter house' (Boterhuis) next to St Christopher's chapel. Two meat-halls, the Westvleeshuis (mentioned at the beginning of the fourteenth century and situated on the current Simon Stevinplein) and the Oostvleeshuis (appearing in the sources at the end of the fourteenth century, on the Braamberg) were owned by the powerful butchers' guild. The richer butchers controlled the supply and the less prosperous had to cut and sell the meat there. Other retailers, like the spice sellers (*crudeniers*), mercers and linen weavers, had

[28] R. Degryse, 'Brugge en de organisatie van het loodswezen van het Zwin op het einde van de 15de eeuw', *HGG*, 112 (1975), 61–130; Gottschalk, *Stormvloeden*, vol. II, pp. 74, 100; M. Coornaert, *Knokke en het Zwin: De geschiedenis, de topografie en de toponymie van Knokke, met een studie over de Zwindelta* (Tielt, 1974), pp. 55–87; Verhulst, *Landschap*, pp. 57–63; M. Ryckaert and A. Vandewalle, 'De strijd voor het behoud van het Zwin', in V. Vermeersch (ed.), *Brugge en de zee van Bryggia tot Zeebrugge* (Antwerp, 1982), pp. 52–70.

stalls in the Old Hall. These retailers for the local and regional markets were to be found inside the Hall and within the courtyard, together with the cloth sellers (*lakensniders*) who sold Flemish cloth there to foreign merchants, to be marketed all over Europe. At the end of the fifteenth century, close to the Greyfriars' convent, the Pand was built, a cloister-like construction of covered galleries where luxury goods and art were traded. Bruges also had a wide range of shopping streets, usually access roads along which most people passed, with little stalls, or artisans selling commodities from their own shops in front rooms at ground-floor level.[29]

Various individuals and institutions competed to control these markets, organized as a result of private and collective initiatives. Urban commissions of wardens controlled the quality of products in specialized markets ranging from poultry (*de voghelmaerct*) to wax (*de wasse*) or soap (*de zeepe*). Their composition varied and has yet to be studied in detail, but intermittently they included representatives both from the commercial elites and from the guilds who had a direct relationship with the commodities sold.[30] During the twelfth and thirteenth centuries, collective institutions occupying common spaces and buildings were largely responsible for market organization. During the later Middle Ages, these spaces and buildings were still used, but commerce, both for international and local markets, was increasingly organized in private settings such as in the great inns of the hostellers and the shops of artisans in the front rooms of their houses. This did not mean, however, that the brokers' guild, the aldermen and the sheriff were unable to oversee these transactions or to prosecute infractions of the princely privileges granted to foreign merchants, and of urban legislation or guild rules. Women could sell fish on the streets but the fishmongers' guilds, often monopolizing wholesalers like the butchers, contested this practice and the aldermen had to regulate on these matters. In the later fifteenth century, it seems that more collective initiatives became important

[29] P. Stabel, 'The Market-Place and Civic Identity in Late Medieval Flanders', in M. Boone and P. Stabel (eds.), *Shaping Urban Identity in Late Medieval Europe* (Leuven/Apeldoorn, 2000), pp. 43–64; E. Lecuppre-Desjardin, 'Multipolarité et multifonctionnalité des places publiques dans les villes des anciens Pays-Bas bourguignons: Évolution d'une géographie identitaire (XIVe–XVe siècles)', in L. Baudoux-Rousseau, Y. Carbonnier and P. Bragard (eds.), *La place publique urbaine du Moyen Âge à nos jours* (Arras, 2007), pp. 45–52; M. Boone and H. Porfyriou, 'Markets, Squares, Streets: Urban Space, a Tool for Cultural Exchange', in D. Calabi and S. T. Christensen (eds.), *Cultural Exchange in Early Modern Europe*, 4 vols. (Cambridge, 2007), vol. II, pp. 227–53; P. Stabel, 'From the Market to the Shop: Retail and Urban Space in Later Medieval Bruges', in B. Blondé, P. Stabel, J. Stobart et al. (eds.), *Buyers and Sellers: Retail Circuits and Practices in Medieval and Early Modern Europe* (Turnhout, 2008), pp. 79–108.

[30] Vermaut, 'De textielnijverheid', vol. II, pp. 337–64.

once more. While artisans and retailers preferred their own workshops, carrying signs and banners to advertise and setting up wooden stalls in the streets to sell their goods, other items were again more collectively sold: for instance, luxury commodities were marketed in the Pand, or in the Bourse square which had become important for international trade. This kind of collective marketing would continue in Antwerp, Bruges' successor as the hub for international trade.[31]

Market-places functioned primarily as economic spaces, but it is important to recall that they were also the focal points of political, social and cultural life. As Chapter 7 makes clearer, markets and commercial buildings were the scenes of official 'civic rituals': proclamations of new urban and princely ordinances (from the balcony of the Belfry); jousts organized by the elitist White Bear; performances of musicians, street artists and travelling theatre groups on wagons; but also assemblies and collective actions by rebellious guilds.[32]

Artisanal Quarters and Social Topographies

The specialized functions of other quarters of Bruges have been less studied than the conspicuous neighbourhoods associated with international commerce. Yet they deserve to be: after all, thirteenth-century cities were often still clusters of quarters organized along craft lines or shared rural origins.[33] The limited late medieval data for Bruges suggest that by then its neighbourhoods had become more economically heterogeneous. Most toponyms referring to trades, such as 'Potters' Street', may have retained their names from a period when those trades had perhaps been practised there. However, the Grauwwerkersstraat (Furrier Street), formerly the Zacwijnstraat, is an example of this trend in reverse: the furriers seem to have gathered there only from the later fourteenth century. Similarly, the fifteenth-century Zouterstraat (the current Academiestraat) shows a cluster of spice sellers and goldsmiths in what was a zone for the luxury industry, close to the port.[34] During the fifteenth century many mercers evidently lived in the Kartuizerinnenstraat

[31] P. Stabel, 'Public or Private, Collective or Individual? The Spaces of Late Medieval Trade in the Low Countries', in D. Calabi and S. Beltramo (eds.), *Il mercante patrizio: Palazzo e botteghe nell' Europa del Rinascimento* (Milan, 2008), pp. 37–54.

[32] Stabel, 'The Market-Place'.

[33] S. A. Epstein, 'Urban Society', in D. Abulafia (ed.), *The New Cambridge Medieval History*, vol. V (Cambridge, 1999), pp. 26–37 (at 30).

[34] T. De Meester, 'De ontstaansgeschiedenis van de Brugse Poortersloge', *BO*, 53 (2013), 32–54.

behind the Old Hall, close to which there was once a 'Mercer street'.[35] Tax lists of the late fourteenth century show that the smiths were still to be found in large numbers in the Blacksmiths' Street, that many confection workers and coopers occupied the commercial section (*zestendeel*) of St Nicholas, and that many textile workers lived in the poor Westmeers and Oostmeers quarters.[36] Some trades still concentrated their activities in certain areas, though others probably did not: retailers in foodstuffs such as bakers would have spread out over the town to avoid competition with their rivals.

The social topography of the late medieval city was marked by inequality, but lines drawn between rich and poor still need further study. Clearly, some neighbourhoods were richer than others and small side streets often housed more workers than the prominent streets leading from the city centre to the gates; but elites, middle classes and wage workers would also mingle in the same streets and even in the same houses, as attics and basements could be rented out to poorer families.[37] Parcel sizes and the presence of moderate and small types of houses depicted on Marcus Gerards' map (1562) suggest there were poorer quarters north of the Smedenstraat, south of the Langestraat, around the Meers area and around St Giles' church. Unsurprisingly, some of these quarters coincide with the zones occupied by textile workers, but this urban industry, and its impact on the urban landscape, became less important: crisis from the mid fourteenth century (see Chapter 6) reduced the percentage of population employed in it. However, concentrations of textile workers can be found in certain zones as their dwellings would be located near the industrial fields where fulling and shearing took place, and where guilds and warden commissions oversaw production and quality standards on site. The city accounts of 1332 tell us that forty-one tenters at 'ten Freren Ackere', on the communal field where the first Franciscan convent had been erected, were moved to Cattevoorde, another tenter field to the west of the Ezelstraat.[38] A guild book of the shearers c.1416 lists the masters and journeymen in Den Hoye (in the current Bilkske, between the Ganzestraat and the Vuldersreitje), in Den Meersch (between the Capucijnenreitje and the Boeveriestraat) and again in Cattevoorde, the only three main areas for textile activity that were

[35] Ryckaert, 'De Oudeburg te Brugge', p. 160.

[36] I. De Meyer, 'De sociale strukturen te Brugge in de 14e eeuw', in W. Blockmans, I. De Meyer, J. Mertens et al. (eds.), *Studiën betreffende de sociale strukturen te Brugge, Kortrijk en Gent in de 14e en 15e eeuw*, vol. I: *Tekst* (Kortrijk, 1971), pp. 7–78 (at 25–7).

[37] Deneweth, 'Huizen', pp. 56–8: in 1583, 152 families (2 per cent of the population) lived in basements, attics, outbuildings or separate rooms.

[38] SAB, 216, 1332–3, fo. 95r.

left.[39] From the end of the Middle Ages, it appears that some of the grasslands formerly used for the cloth industry, often the property of the city or St John's hospital, were converted to bleaching meadows for the linen industry, which by then had partially supplanted the production of woollens.[40] Industrial quarters were also still poorer than commercial ones or those with more mixed functions. Fiscal sources from the late fourteenth century, preserved for some city sections, also show that the section of Our Lady, between the axis Steenstraat–Zuidzandstraat–Boeveriestraat and the line drawn along the Wollestraat–Eekhoutstraat–Garenmarkt–Nieuwe Gentweg–Gentpoortstraat was full of paupers.[41]

Some areas, by contrast, were the preserve of the wealthy. Large parcels of land and the remains of large private houses indicate the elite status of certain streets and quarters. On the Markt and in prestigious streets like the Sint-Jansstraat, the Vlamingstraat, the Naaldenstraat, the Oudeburg, the Spanjaardstraat, the Wollestraat or the Spinolarei (all contemporary street names) stood the great burgher houses with names: Bouchoute, de Craene, Hof Van Gistel, Hof Bladelin, Hof Van Watervliet, De la Torre, Malvenda or The Patientie. This dynamic elite and merchant neighbourhood around St John's chapel and St Walburga's church, within the area earlier called the Great Square, had been one of the most expensive quarters from the beginning. In the fourteenth century, however, a part of St James' parish where princely buildings were erected from the 1290s also became a highly elite quarter, housing among others the lords of Gistel, the Burgundian courtiers Jean de Gros and Pieter Bladelin, and later the Medici banker Tommaso Portinari, all of whom lived in the Sint-Jacobsstraat and the Naaldenstraat.[42]

Locating the Bruges Sex Industry

Like any thriving port, Bruges was a centre for prostitution.[43] Both the accounts of the city and the *schout* furnish information about the

39 SAB, 324, Guildbook, fo. 1^{r}; W. Baes (ed.), *Van Rame tot Coupure: Geschiedenis van een Brugse wijk* (Bruges, 1997).

40 W. Adriansens, M. Becuwe, P. Cardinael et al., *Groen Brugge* (Bruges, 1987), pp. 44–6; Vermaut, 'De textielnijverheid', vol. I, pp. 199–200; Deneweth, 'Huizen', pp. 59, 66–77.

41 Van Houtte, *De geschiedenis van Brugge*, p. 153.

42 L. Devliegher, 'Demeures gothiques de Bruges', *Bulletin de la Commission Royale des Monuments et des Sites*, 4 (1974), 53–75.

43 For prostitution in Bruges, see G. Dupont, *Maagdenverleidsters, hoeren en speculanten: Prostitutie in Brugge tijdens de Bourgondische periode (1385–1515)* (Bruges, 1996). For figures, see Chapter 6 below.

prostitution scene, its topographical distribution and the changes it underwent during the fifteenth century. In the early fourteenth century, prostitution already flourished in the section of St Nicholas to the northwest. This was a 'recreational zone' in general: it also had courts for *jeu de paumes*, bathhouses and a court of archers.[44] Other concentrations of sex workers could be found in the working-class quarters around the convents of the Franciscans and Dominicans. These were not isolated in particular streets but integrated among other types of houses and buildings, although often in little streets that led the customer towards the houses at the back of a building block.[45] Three types of structure sheltered brothels: 'houses' with several prostitutes, *cameren* or single-room houses where only one prostitute lived and worked, and 'bathhouses' (*stoven*) which offered sexual services as well, mostly operated by women but owned by men.[46] By 1400 nearly two out of three brothels were located in the St Nicholas section, particularly beyond the Augustijnenrei in St Giles. It is no coincidence that prostitutes settled next to, though not in, the zone for international commerce: foreign merchants, sailors and dockworkers must have been customers. On the 'supply side', many poorer families of the neighbourhood may have considered prostitution an addition to income in times of hardship. Another possible reason for the concentration of brothels in St Giles was the higher availability of land and at lower prices than in the city centre. This was why the friars had also settled there – and therefore why the Augustinian, Carmelite and Franciscan convents came to be surrounded by brothels and bathhouses. The friars presumably preached among these fallen women and their clientele of reprobates but it is not inconceivable that some of them succumbed to the sins of the flesh. The most popular haunt in St Giles, and in the entire city, was the ironically named Maagdendal ('Virgins' Valley'). Between 1398 and 1484, in this tiny street with only fifteen to twenty houses, connecting the Sint-Clarastraat with the Hoedenmakersstraat, no fewer than sixty different brothel keepers and prostitutes were registered.

During the fifteenth century the Bruges prostitution landscape underwent some remarkable shifts. The first was a more general spread of brothels over the entire city, and particularly to the western and southern parts (the sections of St James and Our Lady), though in lower concentrations than before. In Our Lady's section there were almost no 'evil inns' registered

44 H. Deneweth, 'Kaatsen in Brugge', *BO*, 44 (2004), 5–18.

45 H. Deneweth, 'Enkele Brugse Schuddeveestraatjes', *Biekorf*, 102 (2002), 193.

46 Murray, *Bruges*, pp. 337–40.

around 1400, but after 1460 they represented 11 per cent of the city's total. In the St James section the number of brothels tripled during the same period from 11 to 33 per cent. The Moerstraat became the most notable red light district in the later fifteenth century, a distinction that had a good deal to do with the presence in the neighbourhood of the Burgundian court. The Prinsenhof had its own bathhouse, though this may not have entertained the kind of women with whom some courtiers wished to keep company (and it must be stressed that not every 'stove' was a brothel and most were respectable). As a consequence, the number of streets with brothels located inside the first city walls increased from 11 to 24. At the same time, the St Nicholas section lost its position as Bruges' most important red light district: its share in the city's brothels was reduced to one-third compared with its heyday in the late fourteenth century (from 63 to 19 per cent). The harbour and the foreign merchants' quarters evidently no longer provided the bulk of the customers. Certainly by the sixteenth century prostitution had spread throughout the city. In an aldermen's ordinance dated 18 September 1542, four 'accustomed' locations were cited. Three were located behind the Augustinian convent in St Giles' parish but the fourth was the Oostproosse: a couple of streets around the Jerusalem chapel (and one of the jurisdictional enclaves of St Donatian's Proosse). As the excises on beer were lower in these ecclesiastical enclaves, many pubs of dubious reputation were encountered there.[47] The neighbourhoods housing most prostitution were probably those that were more generally reputed to be 'bad' or 'dangerous'.

Managing the Urban Ecology

The density of population in Bruges not only stimulated the sex trade but also had obvious consequences for the environment. Problems of sanitation faced all major cities. The absence of city accounts before 1280, and of urban bylaws before 1490, makes it difficult to reconstruct how Bruges dealt with them; but some archaeological and indirect evidence reveals the main measures taken in water supply and waste management. Archaeology and comparison with other cities suggest that 'ecological measures' were undertaken well before the late thirteenth century; costs for maintaining sewers and paved streets, appearing in the earliest city account of 1280, seem already routine. A significant problem in young cities was that while some pollutants were biodegradable, their weight grew in proportion to

[47] Dupont, *Maagdenverleidsters*, pp. 140–57.

population growth. A human annually produces some 50 kilos of faeces: a city the size of medieval Bruges probably had to cope with 2,500 tons of human excrement alone.[48] Animal dung along the streets, and blood and entrails dumped by butchers and fishmongers, further polluted the environment. Surface drainage was inadequate to sewer this away to the rivers and canals: bylaws on street-cleaning and waste collection were doubtless proclaimed long before records for them survive.[49]

From the thirteenth century, several cities had public toilets, situated near market-places or halls where most visitors passed, for instance Lille (1231) and Tournai (1281). Bruges had its public toilets in the city halls. Archaeology has uncovered evidence for thirteenth-century brick cesspits near the back wall of private residences in the city centre;[50] but it was not until the fourteenth and fifteenth centuries that most households had their own latrines. A top-down policy was possibly responsible for this, as in Paris, where the urban authorities in 1374 and 1383 ordered the construction of private latrines.[51] On the other hand, it took until the fourteenth century before brick construction became accessible to the urban middling groups. From then on, households in some areas worked together in groups to construct joint brick cesspits and wells, often on or near the boundaries of their plots.[52] Private toilets were also constructed over waterways or sewers, as was common practice in most religious communities. In the fourteenth century Bruges created the *officie van de Muederaers* (street cleaners or rakers).[53] The *muederaers* were responsible for supervising street-cleaning, the collection of waste and export of dung, and removing cadavers of pigs and dogs from the canals.[54] Bruges, like other medieval urban governments,

[48] C. Monnet, 'Approche historique de l'évacuation des déchets urbains au bas moyen-age: Règlements et équipements', in C. Monnet (ed.), *L'évacuation des déchets en milieu urbain au bas moyen-age: L'exemple des fosses à fond perdu de la Cour Napoléon du Louvre à Paris (XIII–XVe siècles) et mesures diverses pour assainir les villes* (Louvain-la-Neuve, 1992), pp. 327–39.

[49] For Bruges, see H. Deneweth, 'Een riool doorheen het Prinsenhof', in B. Hillewaert and E. Van Besien (eds.), *Het Prinsenhof in Brugge* (Bruges, 2007), pp. 18–21. London already had written regulations governing the positioning of cesspits, removal of rubbish and the maintenance of streets at the end of the twelfth century; see D. J. Keene, 'Rubbish in Medieval Towns', in A. R. Hall and H. K. Kenward (eds.), *Environmental Archaeology in the Urban Context* (London, 1982), p. 26.

[50] Van Eenhooge, 'Middeleeuwse Brugse huizen', pp. 46, 51, 53.

[51] Monnet, 'Approche historique'.

[52] Deneweth, 'Huizen', pp. 414–31.

[53] Street cleaners were appointed in Montpellier (thirteenth century), Lübeck (1336), Brunswick (1354) and Basel (fourteenth century); see Monnet, 'Approche historique'.

[54] Duclos, *Bruges*, p. 218; GVS, *Inventaire*, vol. IV, pp. 417–18; B. Debaenst, 'Historische stront op Vlaamse grond: Een inleidende studie in de historische faecologie', unpublished MA Thesis, Ghent University (Ghent, 1999).

coordinated public sanitation. From the thirteenth century, the system gradually 'evolved into a dispersed model of responsibility with involvement at site-specific, local levels'.[55] The first preserved bylaws of 1490 indicate that neighbourhoods and households were held responsible for weekly street-cleaning. The measures were repeated several times a year, especially in preparation for important religious feasts or commercial fairs, when many people would visit the city.

A network of urban sewers must also have been constructed from the thirteenth century onwards. The first city accounts already include payments for repair works at sewers, called *riotus* (1285), *rivulus* (1290), *ghote* (1331), *grippe verdect* (1341), *riole* (1396) or *wieghe* (1396).[56] The first description of this system dates from the sixteenth century when both the waterworks and the sewers were inventoried, repaired and cleaned after repeated complaints about stench and filth.[57] Bruges had a decentralized system, in which domestic wastewaters flowed into uncovered or covered drains in the middle of the streets. These drains followed the natural slope of the terrain and either debouched into the river or came together in collectors, often at crossroads, from which large brick sewers conducted the water underground to the Reie or the inner ditch of the ramparts. Intact medieval sewers have been uncovered near the Verversdijk and the princely residence (Prinsenhof). From the late fifteenth century (but probably much earlier), individual households were asked to put screens (*yzeren traillen*) between the private waste pipes and the public drains to prevent blockages in the public system. The main sewers, being the canals and rivers, were cleaned at least once a year and in periods of drought. On these occasions, the main locks at the Minnewater were closed while the water was drained at the Dampoort. Adjoining landlords were asked to clean the river next to their plots and remove the dirt; and were given the opportunity to renovate the quays or back walls of their houses. Here again, the initiatives for sanitation works were taken by the urban authorities, though the responsibility for maintenance and repair was localized and partly left to neighbourhoods and individual households.[58]

The urban government also intervened in the construction of 'blood pits'. Butchers and fishmongers were not permitted to dump blood and entrails

[55] For Coventry and Winchester, see D. Jorgensen, '"All Good Rule of the Citee": Sanitation and Civic Government in England, 1400–1600', *Journal of Urban History*, 36 (2010), 300–15 (at 311).

[56] GVS, *Inventaire*, Table Analytique (unnumbered vol.), pp. 535–6.

[57] Deneweth, 'Huizen', pp. 452–65.

[58] Deneweth, 'Huizen', p. 420.

on the streets or in rivers, since river water was also used for brewing or industrial activities. It was only at the end of the Middle Ages and after several plague epidemics, that the miasmas emitted from blood and entrails were deemed dangerous for public health. The first pit was situated between the Boeveriepoort and the Smedenpoort, near the Magdalen leprosarium. It was closed in 1336 and substituted by a pit near the Tillegembos, a nearby forest.[59] Similar sanitary provisions against butchers were taken in cities such as Sens, Meaux, Verdun and Amiens from the thirteenth century onwards.[60]

Thus, public works involving sanitation, organized by the city government, were undertaken well before documented evidence for them appears. Of equal importance was the need to provide fresh drinking water. The construction of a subterranean system of lead water pipes, the *moerbuizen*, for public water supply, and of a network of urban sewers, was under way well before 1280. The *moerbuizen* tapped clean water from the communal Sint-Baafsvijver situated upstream and outside the early urban agglomeration. An engine (*ingenium*) with a water wheel (*noria*) was installed to bring the water up to a level from which it could be drawn down into the city by gravity. To house this machine, the still existing 'Water house' near the Boeveriepoort, with a mill wheel run on horse power, was built between 1384 and 1398. After the second ramparts were built, the main pipes ran from the Boeveriepoort along the Vrijdagmarkt to the Market Square. When the outer ditch was widened at the end of the fourteenth century, it was considered big and safe enough to provide a permanent reservoir to replace the Sint-Baafsvijver. Several brooks, cut across by the new ramparts, fed the outer ditch. Four additional pipes were constructed between the late fourteenth and late fifteenth centuries to serve other parts of the city. The waterworks fed public wells made of brick at regular distances from each other, often situated at street corners or near market-places, where neighbours and passers-by had free access to them. Private use of publicly provided water was clearly differentiated along social lines, as only the rich had domestic access to it. In 1404, only thirty-three houses belonging to the urban elites had direct access to the *moerbuizen*, among them the Hof Van Mouscron near the Schottenplaetse (now the Sint-Maartensplein) and Ter Beke along the Ridderstraat. Breweries were among the first to be connected to the water supply system. In 1510 ninety-six connections were registered, of which fifty-four were made for breweries. While ordinary people

[59] During the sixteenth century, a third pit was provided at the end of the Beenhouwersstraat.
[60] Monnet, 'Approche historique'.

had access to these public wells, several households constructed private wells in their back gardens for underground and rain water, often at the same time as cesspits.[61]

New Urban Landmarks

In the later Middle Ages, especially from the late fourteenth century onwards, further building work made a profound impact on the urban landscape. New churches, convents and charitable institutions were built, and older buildings were made even more imposing. The two main parish churches of St Saviour and Our Lady still had Romanesque forms around 1200 but from the thirteenth century they were gradually transformed into monumental gothic edifices. After an interruption to building activity at the end of the thirteenth century and a fire in 1358, the transepts of St Saviour's were completed and by about 1400 the three-aisled nave was erected. More chapels were added, and at the end of the fifteenth century new projects were begun: the existing choir was reconstructed with an ambulatory and five spacious radial chapels (1481–c.1550). Work on the tower of Our Lady's had continued during the fourteenth century and a chapel dedicated to the Holy Cross was built against the eastern wall of the tower. Additions were made in the fifteenth century: first a northern nave (from the mid fourteenth century), then the 'Paradise porch', a southern nave and a sacristy. St James' had been a small cruciform church with a central tower, but between 1457 and 1478, by then located in a rich neighbourhood near the Prinsenhof, it was expanded at its south side with two new naves and many-sided choirs, transforming the whole of the earlier church into the northern choir and northern nave of the new one. The tower of St Giles' was erected during the fifteenth century, and its body reshaped as a large three-naved hall-church with three many-sided choirs.[62]

The Eeckhout abbey, renovated and embellished during the fifteenth century,[63] and the mendicant houses (whose architectural developments

61 A. Vandewalle, 'De Brugse brouwerijen', in J. Rau and A. Vandewalle (eds.), *De Brugse parochies*, vol. III: *Het leven in O.-L.-Vrouw, Sint-Walburga, Kristus-Koning* (Bruges, 1989), pp. 7–19; Vandevyvere, *Watervoorziening te Brugge*, pp. 33–48, 89–140. Similar waterworks have been documented for Coventry, Provins and Southern France: see A. Guillerme, 'Puits, aqueducs et fontaines: L'alimentation en eau dans les villes du nord de la France, Xe–XIIIe siècles', in *L'eau au Moyen Âge* (Aix-en-Provence, 1985), pp. 185–200; Jorgensen, ' "All Good Rule of the Citee" '.

62 Devliegher, 'De opkomst', 27–43; Devliegher, *De Sint-Salvatorskathedraal te Brugge*, pp. 15–158.

63 N. Huyghebaert, 'Abbaye de Saint-Barthélémy de l'Eeckhout à Bruges', in *Monasticon Belge*, vol. IV, pp. 757–802.

still await detailed study) were complexes that occupied large areas. Their towers, like those of the parish churches, dominated their surroundings. St John's hospital, the large beguinages of the Wijngaard and of Sint-Obrechts (whose beguines were active in health care) and the convent of the begards (Bogaerden) also formed enclaves in the urban landscape, as did many other enclosed areas such as the eight (or more) smaller beguinages, mostly for poor beguines as opposed to the richer women in the Wijngaard, and almshouses. Other small communities of beguines were housed in regular houses or *cameren*. Although these institutions had become more fully integrated into the expanded urban territory, St John's hospital still possessed over three hectares of land within the city, and the Wijngaard formed a separate parish and jurisdiction, and thus separate space within Bruges. Convents and hospitals also used their gardens and meadows within the city for keeping animals, for horticulture and for textile-related activities.[64]

Smaller enclosed spaces, perhaps with houses and a chapel around a courtyard, also appeared, some only for a time. During the fourteenth century, groups of women living in voluntary poverty continued to establish communities, some of which evolved into charitable institutions, forming closed or semi-closed spaces.[65] Several small or middle-sized charitable institutions were founded on the initiative of rich burghers, for instance the houses of Our Lady of Nazareth (in 1327) and of St Joos (1352) for poor travellers, and the shelter of St Nicholas (1394) for impoverished merchants. In 1396–7, the Dulhuus for the mentally ill was created by the city in the Boeveriestraat, testifying to a growing specialization in care for the sick and needy. From 1414 it was staffed by members of the Third Order. Being the site of several other almshouses as well, the Boeveriestraat thus became a street with a high concentration of charitable institutions.[66]

In the fifteenth century, new monastic houses also appeared. In 1430, the small order of the Wilhelmites settled near the Ghent Gate. In 1469, the Colettines, a reform movement within the Clarisses and patronized by the Burgundian dukes, received land from the nobleman Lodewijk van Gruuthuse to build a convent near St Catherine's Gate. In 1488, female Carmelites settled at the Vlamingdam.[67] The last new parish church erected

[64] Marechal, 'Konventen van arme begijnen'; M. Ryckaert, 'Binnenstedelijk onroerend bezit van het Sint-Janshospitaal te Brugge tijdens het Ancien Régime', in *Sint-Janshospitaal Brugge*, pp. 90–111; Ryckaert, *Historische stedenatlas*, p. 205; T. Coomans, 'L'architecture médiévale des ordres mendiants (Franciscains, Dominicains, Carmes et Augustins) en Belgique et aux Pays-Bas', *Revue belge d'archéologie et d'histoire de l'art*, 70 (2001), 3–111.

[65] H. De Bruyne, *De godshuizen in Brugge* (Roeselare, 1994). See further Chapter 7.

[66] Maréchal, *Gebondenheid*, pp. 39–52.

[67] Van Houtte, *De geschiedenis van Brugge*, p. 236; Ryckaert, *Historische stedenatlas*, pp. 181, 196, 204.

in Bruges was St Anne's. In 1497 the urban part of the parish of the Holy Cross, the church of which had fallen *extra muros* following the construction of the second ramparts, received an auxiliary church, though it remained part of the same parish.[68]

Certain buildings occupied by clergy were more luxurious in character: these were the private residences of the top clerics who often resided in Bruges. Major abbeys from outside Bruges had 'refuges' in Bruges, like those of St Pieter and St Baaf of Ghent (respectively next to St Saviour's and at the Garenmarkt), St Peter's abbey of Oudenburg (in the Zilverstraat) or St Bertin's abbey of Saint-Omer (in the Dweersstraat). There the prelates could enjoy a comfortable lifestyle, with access to the best food, wines and luxuries the city had to offer. The Cistercian abbey of the Dunes at Koksijde possessed a building with an imposing thirteenth-century tower in the Snaggaardstraat, called Ten Walle (visible on Marcus Gerards' 1562 map), which had possibly belonged to the burgomaster Hendrik Ram.[69] As buildings of secular rather than religious importance, they proclaimed the elite character of their residents within the urban landscape.

Official spaces and buildings dedicated to communal administration were altered. Significant changes happened at the end of the thirteenth century. The oldest alderman's house had possibly been situated at Oude Burg 13. The fact that a house there carried the name Oud Scepenhuus (old alderman's house) and was in the original Oudeburg settlement seems more than coincidental: the Belfry had been the main building of the urban commune. However, after the fire of 1280, and perhaps intimidated by the popular revolt in 1280–1, the aldermen moved to the Ghiselhuus, a building that had probably functioned formerly as the castellan's house and subsequently as the count's prison. From 1376, this edifice was replaced by a new monumental city hall in the gothic style. An impressive building campaign in the city was begun at the end of the fourteenth century. Besides the nation houses of Italian merchants, the new city hall and the so-called 'burghers' lodge' (see below), many other works were carried out. The Poertoren and another tower east of the Minnewater were built by Jan van Oudenaerde and Martin van Leuvene, then the two principal 'architects' working in Bruges. Jan van Oudenaarde also repaired the city hall and Belfry in the 1390s, and worked on at least half a dozen masonry bridges. In 1398 he constructed a

[68] Strubbe, 'De parochies te Brugge', pp. 361–2; Ryckaert, 'De oorsprong', p. 11.

[69] J. De Cuyper, 'Oudste gegevens nopens het "Huis ten Duinen" op den Houtbrekersdam te Brugge', *HGG*, 70 (1927), 50–4.

city wall between the Minnewater and the Boeverie gate; and had the gates of St Catherine, of Ghent and of the Holy Cross rebuilt.[70]

The new city hall, however, was the most splendid of all the architectural achievements of the period. It is a testimony to municipal power and the evergetism of the Bruges commercial elite (particularly after 1384 when it temporarily gained power over the craft guilds – see Chapter 7).[71] One alderman even used the building to prove his commitment to the city: in a self-justificatory letter drafted in 1407, the treasurer Clais Barbezaen drew particular attention to his own contribution to its refurbishment. Work began in the later fourteenth century. In 1376 payments were made to the 'sculptor' Jan de Valenciennes and his collaborators for the statues and woodwork in the new city hall. Construction was interrupted, presumably because of the political troubles, but from 1401 the city hall was further expanded. An annex was added at right angles to its back wall. Its façade is still rigidly divided vertically by six high and continuous bays comprising the windows of the ground and upper floors. Downstairs there are stone cross windows, and at the upper level the middle post in the windows runs up uninterruptedly to the tracery. The piers between the niches are decorated with tabernacles, resting on corbelstones with baldachins. At the top, the façade is closed off by a parapet with embattlements. In the middle and at the corners there is a small multifaceted tower with dormers. Stylistically innovative, the whole building remains an important monument in the architectural history of the Low Countries. Its high-pointed arch-window niches were borrowed from the church Gothic style and were alternated with piers of similar width. The niches contained sculptures (which in 1434–5 were polychromed by Jan van Eyck). Inside, the hall included a sculptured wooden vault reminiscent of a princely chapel. In 1382–3, the same sculptor and architect Jan de Valenciennes also worked on the chapel vault of the new ducal residence (to be described below).[72] But the Bruges aldermen were not the only political players present in the Burg trumpeting status and wealth. Close by the city chambers in the Burg, from 1434–40 onwards, the castellany of the Liberty of Bruges was also replacing the old *Love*, the seat of its aldermen, with new buildings (parts of which are still preserved).[73]

[70] J.-P. Sosson, *Les travaux publics de la ville de Bruges, XIVe–XVe siècle* (Brussels, 1977), pp. 167–78.

[71] Dumolyn, 'Une idéologie urbaine'.

[72] A. Vandewalle, G. Michiels and A. Michiels (eds.), *600 jaar Brugs stadhuis, 1376–1976* (Brussels, 1976).

[73] L. Devliegher, *De Keizer Karel-schouw van het Brugse Vrije* (Tielt, 1987), pp. 15–27.

The Burg had of course originally been occupied by comital buildings. At some point in the twelfth century, as we have seen, the counts had moved from the Steen to the *Love* (literally 'lodge'). By the thirteenth century, however, all comital buildings on the Burg had been taken over by either the city or castellany: the Steen had become the communal prison and the *Love* (in the fourteenth century) was occupied by the Liberty's aldermen. By then, the counts had abandoned the Burg area. The former princely space within the city became an entirely urban one: during the fourteenth century the comital presence disappeared from the Burg, probably because residences there no longer met with princely tastes and needs, but perhaps also out of a fear of the urban mob. Count Louis of Nevers, after all, had been held prisoner in Bruges in 1325. His son Count Louis of Male (1346–84) initially preferred to reside not in Bruges but in his birthplace, the castle of Male, a mile outside the city. During the later fourteenth century, however, a new *sgraven woninghe* or 'residence of the count' in a different quarter of the city, in the Moerstraat, was gradually expanded by Count Louis. This complex of several buildings would be transformed into the Prinsenhof (the Court of the Prince), where the Burgundian dukes resided when in Bruges. Some partial excavations and a few iconographic sources give clues as to its original shape. The residential quarters were situated at the centre of the complex. Next to a probably older residential tower, a new residence was built with a chapel alongside. The courtyard included buildings that serviced household needs, guesthouses and administrative buildings. The Prinsenhof became one of the most favoured residences of the dukes while itinerating in the Low Countries, and it was there that important political and ceremonial events took place such as meetings of the Order of the Golden Fleece (1432 and 1468). After the death of Mary of Burgundy (1482) and certainly after the revolt of 1488 when Maximilian was held captive in Bruges, however, the Burgundian-Habsburg dynasty would reside far less in the city.[74]

The Prinsenhof was only one, albeit the grandest, of private residences. Members of the nobility had always been firmly present in Bruges;[75] but their dwellings became hard to distinguish from those of rich merchants and hostellers and those of princely officials who during the Burgundian period would all build residences in a similar style. The Clarastraat, a

[74] Hillewaert and Van Besien (eds.), *Het Prinsenhof*; K. De Jonge, 'Bourgondische residenties in het graafschap Vlaanderen: Rijsel, Brugge en Gent ten tijde van Filips de Goede', *HMG*, 54 (2000), 93–134.

[75] F. Buylaert, 'La "noblesse urbaine" à Bruges (1363–1563): Naissance d'un nouveau groupe social?', in T. Dutour (ed.), *Les nobles et la ville dans l'espace francophone (XIIe–XVIe siècles)* (Paris, 2010), pp. 245–74.

less densely built street in the northwest of the city, still included different castles and noble residences of an older and more robust type, such as the early fourteenth-century Hoedemakerskasteel, owned by a rich merchant family, and the later Hof Van Kleef, belonging to a branch of the Burgundian dynasty. There were also smaller 'moated sites' at the edge of town, such as the Boninswal in the Gapaertstraat, belonging to the Bonin family of hostellers, and another on a large parcel enclosed by a wall in the Coopmansstraat (probably built by a family of the same name). During the Burgundian period, however, many new elite residences were built or reconstructed adopting a fashionably new style that included slender towers: for instance, the Court of Gistel, the Court of Gros and the Court of Bladelin in the Naaldenstraat or the Court of Watervliet in the Oude Burg belonging to the noble de Baenst family, the Court of Maldegem and later Claerhout in the Heilige Geeststraat, and Adornes family residence in the Peperstraat next to the Jerusalem chapel founded in the fourteenth century and rebuilt in a distinctive shape after 1427, vaguely reminiscent of the Church of the Holy Sepulchre, to celebrate the family's status as pilgrims to the Holy Land (see Figure 5.2).[76]

The classic example of a noble residence in Bruges is the Gruuthuse palace, still standing although heavily reconstructed in a neo-gothic style. The lords of the Gruuthuse were members of an important noble family, present in the city from the late thirteenth century but who rose to their greatest prominence during the fifteenth. They originally possessed a large demesne along the Sint-Katelijnestraat (which had been cut in two by the second walls of 1297) but later they built a new palace closer to the city centre next to Our Lady's church. Its oldest wing was begun in 1425. It became a complex of buildings that included distinctive and prestigious features. An impressive chimney and the sculptured frieze along the façade are still visible. In 1468 Lodewijk van Gruuthuse began work on a chapel that connected the palace with Our Lady's church, affording the family an elevated view of the high altar (an architectural feature quickly copied by Edward IV of England).[77] Nearby, Lodewijk and his wife Margaret of Borselen also founded the church for the reformed Clarisses of St Coleta. The Gruuthuse

[76] N. Geirnaert, 'De Adornes en de Jeruzalemkapel: Internationale contacten in laatmiddeleeuws Brugge', in N. Geirnaert and A. Vandewalle (eds.), *Adornes en Jeruzalem: Internationaal leven in het 15de- en 16de-eeuws Brugge* [exh. cat.] (Bruges, 1983), pp. 11–49; J.-P. Esther, 'Monumentbeschrijving en bouwgeschiedenis van de Jeruzalemkapel', in Geirnaert and Vandewalle (eds.), *Adornes en Jeruzalem*, pp. 51–81.

[77] L. Devliegher, 'De bidkapel van Gruuthuse te Brugge', *Gentse Bijdragen tot de Kunstgeschiedenis en Oudheidkunde*, 17 (1957–8), 69–74.

palace is well known; less studied are the numerous other noble residences built in fifteenth-century Bruges. The families Van Pittem, Van Maldegem and Claerhout, for instance, successively resided in what is now the episcopal palace. Typical (and surviving) examples are the Bladelin, de Baenst and Adornes houses, which are in a different style to the more traditional Bruges elite residences, and placed at right angles to the street. A gate next to the house gives access into a courtyard with arcades. An upper gallery at the back of the Adornes house leads to the Jerusalem chapel. Several sculptured sole-plates have been conserved in all three of these houses, indicating some degree of architectural splendour. Having gained fortunes in commerce, the families who built these houses needed to assert a noble status they had only recently acquired.[78]

Upper-class residences were not the only new additions to the urban landscape. Houses belonging to guilds were also built from the fourteenth century onwards and perhaps earlier – a reflection of the strengthening role that the middle class of guild masters had come to play in urban government. Guildhouses were often elegantly decorated to display the power and status of their craft. Some were built at prominent locations, such as those of the fishmongers and tilers on the Market Square and of the carpenters, bakers and masons in the Steenstraat, and they were often influenced by the verticalist style of the city hall. During the fifteenth century more appeared at important sites within the city, even when the trade itself was only practised at the edge of town. They served partly as guild meeting places and archives. Craft guilds often rented out rooms in their houses to private individuals, but their main assembly rooms were kept available for guild business. Some houses were large enough to include a separate room for the dean. The more important guilds had their own separate chapel, but most of them installed chapels in one of the parish or mendicant churches. During the later fourteenth and fifteenth centuries some trades also invested in their own almshouses but guilds also helped their members staying in hospitals.[79] As the smaller craft guilds often lacked the resources to construct their own building, some rented a room in another guild house, or made agreements with parish and mendicant churches to hold meetings there and organize their own chapels inside these churches. The shearers and cordwainers established chapels in the side aisles of St Saviour's church. Other guilds were able to build free-standing chapels. Before 1357 the important

[78] L. Devliegher, 'Patrizierhäuser und Adelshöfe des 15. Jahrhunderts in Brügge', *Jahrbuch für Hausforschung*, 44 (1998), 37–53.

[79] P. Allossery, *Het gildeleven in vroeger eeuwen* (Bruges, 1926), pp. 164–209.

Figure 5.2 The Jerusalem Chapel

weavers' guild had a large chapel built at the corner of the Katelijnestraat and the Visspaanstraat; the blacksmiths had a chapel of their own c.1320, which they rebuilt in the mid fourteenth century. In 1371, the bishop of Tournai granted the weavers the right to place crosses on their chapel roof near the St Catherine's Gate and to erect a bell-tower.[80] The fullers had their chapel in the Korte Vuldersstraat, the shippers along the Potterierei, and the mercers in the Sint-Niklaasstraat. A fifteenth-century chapel (still standing at the Speelmansrei) belonged to the minstrels, not a 'craft' guild though a professional organization. Guilds also invested in charitable buildings. By 1376 the blacksmiths had built their own hospice of St Eloi for poor travellers in the Smedenstraat.[81] During the fifteenth century, more guilds would invest in their own property. The coopers, for instance, bought a guildhouse in 1429, as did the bakers in 1458.

Two building complexes in particular catered for the urban elite. Before 1327, the prestigious brokers' guild had built their own chapel in the Sint-Jorisstraat. Next to it lay a 'pleasure garden' (*heester*).[82] The Poorters Loge (Burghers' Lodge) belonged to the elite jousting society of the White Bear. It was erected at the beginning of the fifteenth century in Brabantine sandstone, and was situated in the midst of the commercial quarters (in the present Academiestraat); and it served the leisure activities of this society and of the city's commercial and political elite. During the fifteenth century, the Burghers' Lodge developed into a major venue for elitist sociability, gambling and literary performance among merchants and urban rulers.[83]

The Bruges Style

Innovative types of architecture were increasingly employed by the wealthy elites of Bruges; and these began to influence styles throughout the Low Countries. In the fourteenth century, façades of these residences did not initially have a distinctive style, but in the fifteenth, a 'Bruges style' developed. To the east of the Burg, at Hoogstraat 8, stood the large patrician house 'The Seven Towers'. Under the middle part, it had a two-naved arched-over

[80] Espinas and Pirenne (eds.), *Recueil*, vol. I, p. 583; Van Houtte, *De geschiedenis van Brugge*, p. 145.

[81] Duclos, *Bruges*, pp. 464, 467; N. Geirnaert, 'De oudste klok van de smedenkapel, niet 1489 maar 1357', *Gidsenkroniek Brugge* (1991), 99; M. Ryckaert, 'Ambachtshuizen te Brugge: De huizen van de timmerlieden, de metselaars, de tegeldekkers en de kapel van de smeden', in W. P. Dezutter and M. Goetinck (eds.), *Op en om de bouwwerf* [exh. cat.] (Bruges, 1975), pp. 37–57.

[82] A. Van den Abeele and M. Catry, *Makelaars en handelaars: Van nering der makelaars naar kamer van koophandel in het XVIIde-eeuwse Brugge* (Bruges, 1992), pp. 20–2.

[83] De Meester, 'De ontstaansgeschiedenis'; F. Buylaert, J. De Rock and J. Dumolyn, 'La Loge des Bourgeois de Bruges: Les stratégies de distinction d'une elite commerçante cosmopolite', *RN*, 98 (2016), 37–69; M. Vandermaesen, *Van poortersloge tot Rijksarchief: Een gebouw met inhoud te Brugge (15de eeuw – 1995)* (Brussels, 1995).

basement. In the frontal façade there were masonry cross windows and shutter openings (with middle posts) in round arched niches on continuous drip stone mouldings. The seven towers on the house gave ostentatious testimony to the prestige of the Bonin family, who had made their fortune in international commerce from the thirteenth century onwards. Several mid-fourteenth-century houses of the nations of foreign merchants also had façades with similar breakings: that of Castile (Spanjaardstraat 16, the right hand side) and that of the Florentines (Academiestraat 1) both had a screen façade and turrets. A screen façade is a horizontal wall, sometimes crenellated, hiding a saddle roof, set square, and is quite a rare building form. The exceptional house of the Genoese, built in 1399 (Vlamingstraat 33), had a screen façade at the front and a side façade which both have large pointed windows. In the tympanum above the entrance, there is a sculptured depiction of St George fighting the dragon. The upper floor had sculptured consoles.[84]

Municipal buildings in Bruges also influenced architecture in the Low Countries. The new city hall incorporated artistic innovations that added to municipal splendour: these were copied in other towns in northwestern Europe. The frontage of the new city hall had a window shape which is at the origin of what became the typical façade arrangement of Bruges private residences in the fifteenth and sixteenth centuries. The upper and lower windows of the front of the city hall are in a vertical pointed niche. The windows have tracery at the top in imitation of ecclesiastical buildings. In the façades of houses this principle is further elaborated, but the bay niches containing the windows are usually semicircular and sometimes pointed or horizontal. This type of bay niche is first attested in a private residence, it seems, in the large pointed gable of the Court of the Gruuthuse (c.1425). Three bay niches are captured in a large pointed niche with a trefoil in it. A highlight of this façade type is the Hanse nation house, the Oosterlingenhuis, completed in 1491 (Krom Genthof 1). Its high screen façade with window niches and tracery in the tympanums, towers corbelling out, the graceful main tower and its elaborate interior, proclaimed the status of the German Hanse. Apart from this 'first Bruges type', in which the bay niches are independently placed next to one another, there is a second type in which they are joined together in one large niche, embraced by a composed arch. The oldest example can be found in a back wall of the city hall and in the eastern house front of the Vierschaar room of the Liberty of

[84] Van Houtte, *De geschiedenis van Brugge*, p. 264.

Bruges (both 1523). In a third type of Bruges private house, this composed arch is cut through by piers between the bay niches. The oldest example is the house at Steenstraat 40 (dated 1527). These houses mostly stand at right angles to the street. Their front carries a stepped gable. The large private residences constructed between the thirteenth and fifteenth centuries sometimes have a crenellated screen façade behind which a saddle roof is hidden.[85]

Houses for the Common People

Monumental public and elite buildings dominated the urban skyline, but 80 per cent or more of the built environment was made up of private dwellings for the great majority of the people. We have seen that from 1127 onwards there had been, on the one hand, landowners possessing full allodial property and, on the other, people who were still paying a heritable land rent. This was a source of tension: in 1302, after their victory against the French and the patrician Lily party (*Leliaerts*) one of the first things the Bruges commune demanded of John of Namur, acting for his father the count, was that these land taxes should never be increased again.[86] As rents remained stable after that, over time they lost their real value because of inflation. A positive effect of this was that small owners could now profit from the excess value of their houses by using them as a pledge for mortgages. The productive credit they could thus acquire in its turn stimulated the economy and contributed to the rise of middling groups in the fourteenth century. The effects of this system would not always be unproblematic: in periods of growth, the house values increased so the value of these credits diminished, but after periods of demographic and economic crisis these mortgages could weigh heavily on family incomes.[87]

During the twelfth and thirteenth centuries elite families parcelled out strips of land at the sides of their demesnes for the housing of lower social groups who worked in their households or enterprises; and thus the street pattern became more complex. From the 1280s, the city accounts record a vigorous effort to pave the streets, which had probably begun well before. Not all streets were paved, as those of lesser importance seem to have had

85 Devliegher, 'Het Oosterlingenhuis'.

86 GVS, *Inventaire*, Table analytique (unnumbered vol.), p. 73; Des Marez, *Étude sur la propriété foncière*, pp. 71–2; Warnkoenig and Gheldolf, *Histoire*, vol. IV, pp. 312, 452–3.

87 H. Deneweth, 'Moving Up or Down the House Market? Real Estate and Social Change in Bruges, 1550–1670' (working paper, forthcoming).

merely a strip of paving down the centre.[88] Typical problems arising from rapid urbanization, such as the need to improve traffic circulation, street-planning and housing, were tackled from the top by the city government, although not always systematically, for initiatives were also the result of pressures from below. Plots were divided, construction material evolved, and measures were taken to prevent fires and to solve ecological problems. These efforts made a long-term impact on the urban landscape. Town-plan analysis has often shown how much a modern city can preserve the imprint of its medieval antecedent; and the urban tissue of modern Bruges (its streets and waterways) matches that of medieval Bruges by as much as 80 per cent. Much of the modern layout can be shown to reflect the parcel structure of the late medieval city.[89]

The study of Bruges' later medieval social topography is in its infancy, however. One written source, still underexploited, that affords an impression of housing is the record of properties confiscated from the pro-French Lily party after its defeat in 1302. All the properties in town belonging to its members, and the rents paid by their tenants, were confiscated by the new revolutionary regime and remained so until 1305. Analysis of this record reveals three categories of house. Larger houses or *husen*, about 10 per cent of the houses mentioned, had several floors and were made of durable building materials. These residences were located in elite quarters such as the Hoogstraat and the Naaldenstraat. The group of houses called *huusinghen* consisted of clusters of buildings around the main house. Often more than one house was situated on a plot, and sometimes their owners had the same family name, suggesting that people built additional houses for their family on parcels they owned. Only later, when these houses were bought and sold on the real estate market, were such plots divided and separated from each other with hedges, fences and walls.[90]

A third category comprised the smallest houses, the simple one-room dwellings referred to as *cameren* or *husekins*, originally built on a single sub-plot after larger plots had been parcelled out.[91] These houses for the working classes and the poor receiving charity had a room at the ground floor,

[88] Duclos, *Bruges*, pp. 30, 213–15; the accounts are edited by C. Wyffels et al, *De rekeningen van de stad Brugge*, and entries mentioning the paving of streets are scattered throughout all of them.

[89] For instance, see M. R. G. Conzen, *Alnwick, Northumberland: A Study in Town-plan Analysis* (London, 1960); P. Knox, *Urban Social Geography: An Introduction* (Harlow, 1987), pp. 99–105 on Cologne; Spence, *London in the 1690s*; Deneweth, 'Huizen', pp. 213–52, reconstructs medieval plot structures for five housing blocks in Bruges.

[90] Deneweth, 'Huizen', pp. 465–81.

[91] Boogaart, *Ethnogeography*, pp. 173–8.

in which a single person or a nuclear family would live and work, and an attic used as a bedroom. The surviving houses of this type are usually almshouses: more of these were founded by rich burghers or guilds from the fourteenth century for select groups of needy and elderly. They were built in a row along the street or else gathered around a courtyard forming a small enclosure. Most almshouses also had a small chapel. An example is the row of thirteen houses that form the Godshuis de Moor, in Boeveriestraat 52–76, founded in 1480 by the rich merchant and alderman Donaas de Moor and his wife. Every façade has a basket arch, a window with a middle post and a dormer window in the saddle roof. Another is the group of six rooms east of the Jerusalem chapel in the Balstraat, which probably formed part of twelve almshouses for poor women bequeathed by Anselmus Adornes in his testament of 1470. Clearly, the value of the houses and rents within the old centre was higher than outside, but many of the *cameren* in the 1302–5 confiscation records are also to be found in the inner city.[92]

As explained above, many poor families, newly arrived immigrants and servants were housed in apartments, single rooms, basements and to a lesser extent in attics. Also significant is their distribution. The thirteenth-century suburbs housed more poor and working people than the old centre, but there was no clear socio-topographical separation between an urban core and periphery, and during the later Middle Ages it seems that in most quarters of the city social segregation was the exception, not the rule.[93] Even so, social differences are evident from measurable plot spaces, which range from 750 square metres for residences with gardens in the city centre (such as in the Ridderstraat), to 300 square metres along the entrance roads (for instance in the Eekhoutstraat), and to 25 square metres or fewer in later developed side streets and back alleys. Of course, the available space determined the number of floors and the availability of utilities such as private wells and toilets.[94] During the demographic crisis at the end of the fifteenth century, as population diminished by about a quarter and many smaller dwellings were deserted, the elites took advantage by expanding their houses. This would again lead, by the end of the sixteenth century, to more socio-topographical differences at the level of street blocks, the elites

[92] Devliegher, *De Huizen*, p. 32; V. Vermeersch, *Brugges kunstbezit: Vijftig kunsthistorische opstellen*, 2 vols. (Bruges and Utrecht, 1969–73), vol. I, pp. 35–8.

[93] Deneweth, 'Huizen', p. 88. Descriptive but solid studies of neigbourhoods are C. D'Hooghe, *De huizen van het Zuidproosse te Brugge van ca. 1400 tot 1920* (Bruges, 1997); and C. D'Hooghe, 'Corbie in Brugge: Geschiedenis van een stadsbuurt van 1300 tot heden', *BO*, 31 (1991), 5–54.

[94] Deneweth, 'Huizen', pp. 275–95.

and the upper middle classes living in the main streets and the lower social groups in the side and back streets.[95]

As to the material forms of dwellings, we have little information on common houses. There was no natural stone in Bruges or its immediate surroundings, and the typical greyish, Paniselian, ferriferous, green sandstones of Flanders which were present at 10–20 kilometres from Bruges were small and hard to treat. Hence, as elsewhere in northern Europe, most houses were presumably half-timbered constructions, made of wood and loam, their roofs thatched with reed or straw.[96] Such buildings have left almost no trace in a city where the built environment was constantly evolving. Little is known about the sandstone houses, only some foundations of which have been uncovered (such as those in a basement in the Wollestraat).[97] Demographic growth increased the demand for wood, fuel and construction materials, which had to be imported from elsewhere in Flanders, from the Ardennes and even by the thirteenth century from parts of northern Europe such as Scandinavia.[98] Although in coastal Flanders local wood was already scarce in the twelfth century, stone houses were exceptional in Bruges, certainly when compared to cities like Ghent and Antwerp which could import limestone from the Tournai area via the Scheldt River. However, around 1200, as economic development accelerated, the use of stone for elite houses had become more widespread, especially in the commercial quarter. Natural stone, usually from Tournai, had been used for major buildings such as the castle and the churches of St Saviour and Our Lady but the cost of its transport was high, and it only began to be used for private houses from the twelfth century.[99] As wood supplies grew scarcer and as natural stone was expensive, bricks were being introduced by 1200. These bricks, different in composition from those used in antiquity, had been invented during the twelfth century and had spread rapidly in northwestern Europe.[100]

95 Deneweth, 'Moving Up or Down'.

96 Van Houtte, *De geschiedenis van Brugge*, p. 47.

97 H. Deneweth, J. D'hondt and L. Vandamme, *De Oude Steen: Bouw- en bewoningsgeschiedenis van het huis aan de Wollestraat 29 in Brugge* (Zellik, 1997); B. Hillewaert, 'Het Oude Steen, een steen in de Wollestraat', *Archaeologia Mediaevalis*, 18 (1995), 44–5 (at 44).

98 F. Van Tyghem, *Op en om de middeleeuwse bouwwerf: De gereedschappen en toestellen gebruikt bij het bouwen van de vroege middeleeuwen tot omstreeks 1600: Studie gesteund op beeldende, geschreven en archeologische bronnen* (Brussels, 1966), p. 1; Sosson, *Les travaux publics*, pp. 79–80, 102–12.

99 B. Hillewaert et al., 'Wat de archeologie vertelt'; Devliegher, *De Sint-Salvatorskathedraal*, pp. 15–18, 62–5, 150–6; Sosson, *Les travaux publics*, pp. 83–101; Esther, 'Monumentenbeschrijving en bouwgeschiedenis'.

100 J. Hollestelle, *De steenbakkerij in de Nederlanden tot omstreeks 1560* (Arnhem, 1976), pp. 12–22; L. Devliegher, 'De vroegste gebouwen van baksteen in Vlaanderen', *Bulletin en Nieuwsbulletin Koninklijke Nederlandse Oudheidkundige Bond*, 10 (1957), cols. 245–50.

From the fourteenth century, in line with the relatively high living standards among the more well-to-do Bruges artisans (to be explained in Chapter 6), brick houses would also become available for the middle classes. The city even came to possess its own brickworks at Ramskapelle.[101] Recent demolitions and restorations have allowed further glimpses of these thirteenth-century houses. Side and partition walls have revealed the outlines of windows, piscinas and candle niches, and traces of supporting walls and fireplaces. Evidently these houses often had a vestibule and an outbuilding. Usually, the basements, with roofs of beams and with domes on pillars, are the parts still best preserved. A small façade of a house, exceptionally made of Tournai natural stone, dating from the late thirteenth century, still stands in the Grauwwerkersstraat 2–4, heavily reconstructed, and provides clues for the evolution of window shapes.[102]

Bruges was one of the first northern European cities where so many front walls were constructed in brick, but the introduction of masonry in the city was gradual. Medieval building types originated from so-called *aula* and *camera*, often a combination of a square and rectangular construction connected to each other.[103] In a first phase, a stone crosswall, the so-called firewall, would be constructed, against which the fireplaces were built, as evidenced in the house In Sint Jacobs in the Twijnstraat.[104] In a second phase, brick sidewalls would be raised, making them more capable of supporting the lateral pressure of the tiled roofs. This made it possible to construct chimneys and hearths against the sidewalls.[105] Brick sidewalls required strong foundations and the space between these foundation walls could be used as a cellar. Some of these cellars were installed under the streets to expand available stock space.[106] During a third phase wooden back walls would

101 D. Van Eenhooge, 'De vroegste bakstenen huizen in Brugge', *BO*, 38 (1998), 107–28; D. Van Eenhooge, 'The Archaeological Study of Buildings and Town History in Bruges: Domestic Architecture in the Period 1200–1350', in Gläser (ed.), *Lübecker Kolloquium zur Stadtarchäologie im Hanseraum*, vol. III: *Der Hausbau*, pp. 121–41; M. C. Laleman and P. Raveschot, *Steen voor steen: het onderzoek naar het Middeleeuwse huis in Gent en de bijdragen van Armand Heins* (Ghent, 1988), p. 19; M. Coornaert, *Westkapelle en Ramskapelle: De geschiedenis van Westkapelle en Ramskapelle met een studie over de Brugse tegelrie* (Tielt, 1981), pp. 293–351.

102 L. Devliegher, 'De "nieuwe" 13de-eeuwse huisgevel Grauwwerkersstraat 2–4 te Brugge', *Academiae Analecta*, 49 (1988), 45–63.

103 Van Eenhooge, 'Archaeological Study', p. 138.

104 Van Eenhooge, 'Middeleeuwse Brugse huizen', pp. 48, 51.

105 J. Constandt, 'Het versteningsproces van de Ieperse stadshuizen (16de tot 19de eeuw)', in J. Van Acker (ed.), *Wevend aan het verleden: Liber amicorum O. Mus* (Veurne, 1992), p. 69; R. Tijs, *Tot Cieraet deser Stadt: Bouwtrant en bouwbeleid te Antwerpen van de middeleeuwen tot heden. Een cultuurhistorische studie over de bouwtrant en de ontwikkeling van het stedebouwkundig beleid te Antwerpen van de 13de tot de 20ste eeuw* (Antwerp, 1993), p. 43.

106 Laleman and Raveschot, *Steen voor steen*, p. 149; Van Eenhooge, 'Archaeological Study'.

also be replaced so only the front wall would remain partly made of wood. The increasing use of masonry, predominantly bricks made in the region from the thirteenth century, was accelerated during the fifteenth when relatively high standards of living made its use within reach of the middling classes.[107] Somewhat surprisingly, bricks were often more rapidly introduced in the houses of the lower social classes, as their rich landlords could construct *stenen cameren* using simple brickwork more speedily. During the fifteenth century, wooden façades were often more expensive, and as the middle class of guild masters did not invest their money primarily in their houses, they retained wooden front walls for longer. By the mid sixteenth century almost half of Bruges houses had brick façades, more than most other towns in this region of Europe. Middling groups would cooperate by sharing common facilities such as wells and cesspits.[108]

The use of thatched roofs was probably discouraged from the beginning of the thirteenth century: in a charter dated 5 December 1232, Count Ferdinand of Portugal authorized the aldermen of Aardenburg to forbid the construction of thatched roofs, referring to an existing bylaw on fire protection in Bruges, which required roofing with tiles, lead or wooden boards for all buildings on both sides of the main streets to a depth of 40 feet.[109] The measure was not strictly imposed, but it forbade construction of new thatched roofs and the renovation of existing ones. After major fires in 1361, 1412, and 1415, burning entire quarters of the city, the authorities in 1417 introduced a subsidy of up to a third of the costs to replace straw roofs with tiles. When more than 200 households applied for a grant between 1417 and 1422, the measure was extended to the entire city. In 1467, tile roofs were made compulsory for every building in the main streets and for newly constructed houses above a certain value.[110] In 1535 roofing with thatch was finally prohibited.[111]

By the end of the thirteenth century Bruges had reached its greatest areal extent, but although its street layout was to change little in the following

[107] This was also the case in Antwerp and Ghent: F. De Smidt [Broeder Firmin], 'De burgerlijke bouwkunde te Brugge in de XVIe eeuw', in *Handelingen van het 4e congres voor algemeene kunstgeschiedenis* (Ghent, 1938), pp. 11–22; Tijs, *Tot Cieraet*, p. 108; J. Dambruyne 'Het versteningsproces en de bouwactiviteit te Gent in de zeventiende eeuw', *TG*, 102 (1989), 33–5.

[108] Deneweth, 'Huizen', p. 362. Of these many wooden façades only two now remain, Genthof 7 and Korte Winkel 2 (the right hand side): hundreds of these façades were prohibited by the city and demolished, particularly during the seventeenth century.

[109] Dezutter and Ryckaert, 'Brandgevaar'.

[110] Van Houtte, *De geschiedenis van Brugge*, p. 266, GVS, *Inventaire*, vol. IV, pp. 407–9.

[111] A. Janssens, 'Over brand, blussen en brandpreventie in Brugge tijdens de laatbourgondische tijd (1450–1500)', *BO*, 50 (2010), 219–38.

centuries, its landscape was continually reshaped: economic changes, social ambitions and political agendas (to be examined in the following chapters) gave late medieval Bruges its particular morphology. The wealth generated in the city was partly channelled by individual benefactors and corporate groups, for many reasons, into ecclesiastical and secular monuments that dominated the skyline. The expansion of the city's function as a hub of international commerce, as well as the diversification of local trade, drove the erection of large commercial buildings and the proliferation of market spaces. Great social divisions and mobility were given expression in the contrasts that developed between richer neighbourhoods and more artisanal or industrial zones, and between the scale, layout and style of wealthy residences compared with those of poorer dwellings; yet the diversity of housing and the absence of strict social segregation between areas of the city point to the importance of middling groups whose rise tempered the more extreme divisions of power and wealth in late medieval Bruges. Also apparent is the consolidation of the city as a single unit. The jurisdictional control that the city magistrates finally achieved over most of the city territory and over its more unruly social groups, the extension of their authority over public sanitation, charity and building, the investment in municipal grandeur and in gates and walls that encompassed the city, produced an urban landscape that was less a collection of spaces and more an urban space that could be imagined as a coherent whole.

6 Production, Markets and Socio-economic Structures II: c.1320–c.1500

PETER STABEL, JEROEN PUTTEVILS, JAN DUMOLYN, BART LAMBERT, JAMES M. MURRAY AND GUY DUPONT

In 1438, the Castilian traveller Pero Tafur was able to marvel at the goods available in Bruges: 'oranges and lemons from Castile … fruits and wine from Greece … confections and spices from Alexandria, and all the Levant'.[1] Since its first attestation in the eleventh century, Bruges' reputation for commercial abundance had become a commonplace. The city's brokers' fee tariff list of 1303 already recorded more than sixty different commodities, some listed with a place of origin, among them Ireland, Norway, Spain, Burgundy, Normandy, Frankfurt and the Hanseatic town of Zwolle.[2] In 1425 the Florentine Dominican preacher Bernardino of Siena referred in a sermon to Bruges as the place par excellence where merchants converged with their wool, cloth, gold, silver and other splendid goods.[3] The Zwin town had become a metaphor for the metropolitan city where profit and riches were to be found – and so too the sins associated with commerce. And in spite of its prosperity, Bruges was also beset with deep social and economic contradictions, which regularly surfaced in conflict and revolt, usually driven by the middle classes of artisans and supported by the unskilled workers and urban poor. When Pero Tafur encountered exotic abundance in 1438, Bruges was in fact recovering from civil war and beginning to suffer famine and plague.[4] Duke Philip the Good in 1438, after the revolt against his authority, was severe in punishing the rebel ringleaders and restricting the power of craft guilds; yet mindful of his own fiscal interests, he also confirmed his will to protect the city's economy, calling Bruges 'la plus renommée par tout le monde par le fait de marchandise'.[5] To merchants, travellers, clerics and princes alike, Bruges was known as one of

1 Pero Tafur, *Travels and Adventures 1435–1439*, trans and Intro. M. Letts (London, 1926,) pp. 200–1.

2 Van Uytven, 'De overige', p. 73; A. Greve, 'Brokerage and Trade in Medieval Bruges: Regulation and Reality', in P. Stabel, B. Blondé and A. Greve (eds.), *International Trade in the Low Countries (14th – 16th Centuries): Merchants, Organisation, Infrastructure* (Leuven, 2000), pp. 37–44. And see also the 1441 Zwin staple rules in GVS, *Cartulaire*, vol. I, p. 644.

3 Murray, *Bruges*, p. 259.

4 See Chapter 7, and J. Dumolyn, *De Brugse opstand van 1436–1438* (Kortrijk, 1997), pp. 270–2.

5 GVS, *Inventaire*, vol. V, p. 345.

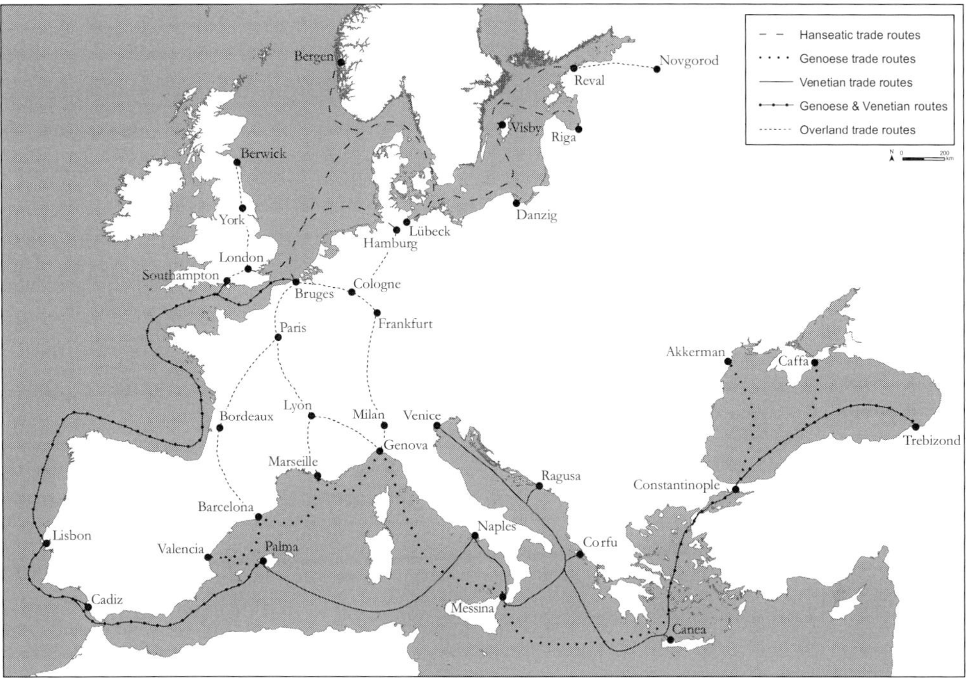

Map 5 European trade routes

the great market-places of Europe, and certainly the most important in the North Sea area (see Map 5).

By the late thirteenth century, the decline of the Champagne fairs and the reorientation of trade flows towards maritime routes had turned Bruges into a crossroads for commercial traffic, connecting northern Europe with the Mediterranean area and indirectly with the Islamic world. The resulting diversity of commodities available in Bruges was precisely the feature that struck contemporary observers as the city's hallmark. Wealth, abundance, rarity and luxury: all could be found in the Bruges markets and workshops. The city had become one of the most market-driven towns in northern Europe. At the same time, artisanal production was gradually converted from domination by textiles to diversification and specialization in luxury products and confection. How this came to be is the subject of this chapter. But the story of late medieval Bruges is not one only of glamour. The success of the new guild-organized middle classes cannot hide the fact that job opportunities in textile manufacture, which as late as the 1330s was still the city's main employer, must have plummeted at a staggering rate from the 1340s, and probably led to massive unemployment and misery. Even the subsequent success of Bruges' commerce and specialist crafts had its downside. Economic conversion to trade and manufacture of high added-value commodities were always going to be fragile, especially when commercial trends turned against the city. From the second half of the fifteenth century Bruges experienced growing competition from fairs in Antwerp and Bergen-op-Zoom, and luxury crafts and skilled craftsmen, being highly mobile, would move to new centres of production and consumption. Skill and access to capital and information were the major assets of Bruges artisans, and commercial competitors were quickly able to offer similar, if not better, economic conditions.

Even Pero Tafur, awestruck as he was by the magnificence of commerce, had a keen eye for Bruges' downsides. He observed that 'the goddess luxury has great power there … but it is no place for a poor man.'[6] As in any medieval town, structural poverty afflicted a substantial part of the population, and despite (as we shall see) the relatively advantageous position of the 'middling sort' in Bruges compared with many other European cities, the social position of most artisans was never secure. Organized in their guilds, the craftsmen and retailers claimed political participation (see Chapter 7), but most of all they wanted their say in the city's economic policies. All guildsmen would collectively take to the streets to defend their privileges and standard of living.[7] Anthonis de Roovere, the principal rhetorician writing in late fifteenth-century Bruges but also a master stonemason, expressed their sentiments well. In several poems, Anthonis laments the fact that artisans had to work hard for small rewards and were despised by the elites, even if their honest work would bring them eternal salvation in the end.[8] However, their economic well-being depended on shifting economic cycles and on political stability. In his 'Dialogue between War and Peace', these two allegorical figures try to refute each other's arguments. Peace states: 'I make commerce grow in the meantime / And you chase industry from the land' ('Ick doe coopmanschap wassen onderhande / Ende ghy iaecht neeringhe uut den lande');[9] and Peace even shows insight into the financial markets when he blames War for high interest rates: 'Yes, ten per cent, that is what you bring us' ('ia tiene voor thondert dat brengt ghy by').[10]

6 Tafur, *Travels*, pp. 201–2.

7 Dumolyn and Haemers, 'Patterns of Urban Rebellion'.

8 J. Dumolyn, 'Het corporatieve element in de Middelnederlandse letterkunde en de zogenaamde laatmiddeleeuwse burgermoraal', *Spiegel der Letteren*, 56 (2014), 123–54. For Anthonis, see Chapter 9.

9 Anthonis de Roovere, *De gedichten van Anthonis de Roovere*, ed. J. J. Mak (Zwolle, 1955), p. 377.

10 Ibid., p. 380. On interest rates in Bruges, see Murray, *Bruges*, pp. 136–7.

Becoming a Trading Hub: The Mature Bruges Market of the Later Middle Ages

The roller-coaster ride of political and social change in Bruges from 1280–1306 was driven in part by changes in the European economy. The wool trade was threatened by the Anglo-French war of 1294–7 that resulted in a wool embargo.[11] Flemish cloth entrepreneurs often had to deal with the king of England's political use of English overseas commerce. The king used wool exports as a major source of fiscal income. Embargoes and trade disruptions occurred, most notably in 1336. Stability in trade relations – but also an end to the active wool trade by Bruges merchants in England – came with the establishment of the English wool staple in Calais in 1363. The English king's need for money also led to a preference for Italian merchants in royal finance, for which the collateral was often English wool. Italian merchant capital had largely driven out Flemish merchants from direct trade in English wool by 1300. Moreover, the Flemish textile industry was forced to change its products in the face of intense international competition. All this brought a reorientation of the Bruges urban economy towards a role as a centre of trade and exchange (see Map 5).[12]

Great change seldom arises out of nothing. Bruges had long been a meeting place and residence for foreign merchants (see Chapter 3). The Germans were increasingly prominent from the 1240s and 1250s. The English had long been visitors, probably becoming more numerous in the thirteenth century while Bruges was a prime market for English wool. By the 1260s and 1270s, the 'Biscayans', merchants from the Basque country and northern Spain, and also traders from Castile and Aragon, appeared as visitors and residents. The Genoese first appear in the sources in 1277, though only came regularly around the time when the Venetians established their maritime link with London and Bruges in 1314.[13] It was this relative shift

11 Lloyd, *English Wool Trade*, p. 75.

12 H. Van der Wee, 'Structural Changes and Specialization in the Industry of the Southern Netherlands, 1100–1600', *Economic History Review*, 28 (1975), 203–21; H. Van der Wee, 'Industrial Dynamics and the Process of Urbanization and De-Urbanization in the Low Countries from the Late Middle Ages to the Eighteenth Century: A Synthesis', in H. Van der Wee (ed.), *The Rise and Decline of Urban Industries in Italy and in the Low Countries (Late Middle Ages – Early Modern Times)* (Leuven, 1988), pp. 307–88; Munro, 'Medieval Woollens: The Western European Woollen Industries and their Struggles for Markets, c. 1000–1500', in Jenkins (ed.), *Cambridge History of Western Textiles*, vol. I, pp. 228–324.

13 Häpke, *Brügges Entwicklung*; and in general, see R. Doehaerd, 'Les galères génoises dans la Manche et la Mer du Nord à la fin du XIIIe siècle et au début du XIVe siècle', *Bulletin de l'Institut historique belge de Rome*, 19 (1938), 5–76; G. Yver, *Le commerce et les marchands dans l'Italie méridionale au XIIIe et au XIVe siècle* (Paris, 1903); A. Schaube, 'Die Anfänge

from overland to maritime trade that favoured maritime gateways such as Bruges.[14] Long-distance trade became more concentrated in a few port cities, and land-locked fairs (as at Champagne) lost ground. Italian merchants were, of course, interested in the wool trade in Southampton or London, but the Low Countries offered more: at the margins of growing European states such as England and France, combined with a large, urbanized domestic market and a specialized industrial infrastructure, the Low Countries with Bruges as its commercial epicentre offered economic possibilities few other regions could match.[15]

From the beginning of the fourteenth century, Bruges functioned as the natural gateway-market for most export commodities produced in the Low Countries, especially woollen cloth. Although markets and cloth halls in the cloth-manufacturing cities of Flanders, Artois and Brabant still functioned as depots for locally manufactured textiles which (foreign) merchants could visit, Flemish, Artesian and Brabantine entrepreneurs and cloth merchants, followed by those from Holland, Hainaut and other manufacturing regions, increasingly used the Bruges market (and from the fifteenth century the Brabantine fairs in Antwerp and Bergen-op-Zoom) to sell their textiles.[16] Flemish cloth entrepreneurs found their clientele on the Bruges market, to be more precise in the 'Old' Hall or in specialized, smaller halls often owned by the merchant guilds of cloth towns for the sale of their woollens in places such as Kortrijk, Wervik, Menen, Tourcoing, Poperinge and Saint-Omer. They also acquired raw materials in Bruges like English wool from the Calais Staple, and from the fifteenth century onwards Spanish merino wool, regionally grown dyestuffs like madder or woad, or imports from the Mediterranean like kermes and alum.[17] Some foreign merchants even established direct relations with producers. The Tuscan merchant Francesco di Marco Datini from Prato (whose account books and correspondence are famously preserved) had an agent in Bruges who single-handedly acquired most of the cloth output of Wervik in western Flanders

der venezianischen Galeerenfahrten nach den Nordsee', *Historische Zeitschrift*, 101 (1908), 28–89; R. Cessi, 'Le relazioni commerciali tra Venezia e le Fiandre nel secolo XIV', *Archivo Veneto*, 27 (1914), 5–116; E. H. Byrne, *Genoese Shipping in the Twelfth and Thirteenth Centuries* (Cambridge, MA, 1930).

[14] For references, see Chapter 3.

[15] P. Stabel, 'Kooplieden in de stad', in Vandewalle (ed.), *Hanzekooplui en Medicibankiers*, p. 85; Hunt and Murray, *History of Business*, p. 146.

[16] P. Stabel, 'Marketing Cloth in the Low Countries: Manufacturers, Brokers and Merchants', in Stabel et al. (eds.), *International Trade*, pp. 15–36.

[17] Stabel, *Dwarfs among Giants*, p. 142.

to be sold in Mediterranean markets.[18] Telling details appear in the Datini correspondence about the popularity of Wervik cloth and how it was marketed. In 1397 a fire seriously damaged the centre of the town. The Alberti in Bruges reported on the fire to Datini's agent in Valencia, saying that most of the cloth in production and many stored pieces had been destroyed, and thus a serious price increase could be expected. This indeed materialized and the Bruges Datini agent, Deo Ambrogi, wrote to Valencia to say that he had prepared a shipment of 50 woollens to be transported by the Venetian galleys of Flanders on which a large profit would be made. He added that he had purchased the cloth for cash since the inhabitants of Wervik needed it to rebuild their houses, and everyone offering cash was bound to get a better price from the weavers.[19] Hanseatic merchants organized similar monopoly contracts with cloth towns such as Poperinge, Menen and Oudenaarde in the fifteenth century for all woollens woven from Spanish wool.[20] The city of Bruges even guaranteed those monopoly contracts with textile towns and the quality standards of the cloth.[21] The participation of Bruges and its industrialized hinterland in long-distance trade would have profound effects: the manufacturing towns and their commercial gateway of Bruges were to be increasingly subject to trends on the international market, to changing patterns of demand and to price volatility.[22]

The major commodity flows in Bruges were as follows. Hanseatic merchants acquired cloth, metals, luxuries such as Mediterranean silks and brocades, French and Mediterranean wines, and spices. They sold furs, metals, forest products like wax, honey and wood, amber, Rhenish wine, and cured, salted or dried fish (especially cod and herring).[23] Bruges imported Poitou wine, salt from the bay of Bourgneuf and Normandy cloth, wool and wheat, and the city exported cloth, Castilian wool, alum from Tolfa, Baltic

18 F. Melis, 'La diffusione nel Mediterraneo occidentale dei panni di Wervicq e delle altre città della Lys attorno al 1400', in *Studi in onore di Amintore Fanfani*, 6 vols. (Milan, 1962), vol. III, pp. 217–43.

19 F. Guidi Bruscoli, 'Trade with Northern Europe', in G. Nigro (ed.), *Francesco di Marco Datini: The Man, the Merchant* (Florence, 2010), p. 488.

20 Stabel, 'Marketing Cloth', p. 19; H. Van Werveke, 'Die Stellung des hansischen Kaufmanns dem flandrischen Tuchproduzenten gegenüber', in H. Van Werveke, *Miscellanea Medievalia. Verspreide opstellen over economische en sociale geschiedenis van de Middeleeuwen* (Ghent, 1968), pp. 123–30; H. Ammann, 'Deutschland und die Tuchindustrie Nordwesteuropas im Mittelalter', *Hansische Geschichtsblätter*, 72 (1954), 1–63.

21 S. Abraham-Thisse, 'De lakenhandel in Brugge', in Vandewalle (ed.), *Hanzekooplui en Medicibankers*, p. 67.

22 Stabel, *Dwarfs among Giants*, p. 143.

23 W. Paravicini, 'De Hanze als Europees verschijnsel', in Vandewalle (ed.), *Hanzekooplui en Medicibankers*, pp. 11–24.

wood and herring from France (especially from Norman ports). From the second half of the fifteenth century contacts with Bordeaux became intensive (for the export of French *pastel* or woad).[24] The few Portuguese traders active in Bruges from the late fourteenth century onwards brought wine, olive oil, dried fruit (figs and raisins), cork, Portuguese salt from Setubal, honey, wax, fat, silks and leather. The discovery and exploitation of the Atlantic islands and the west African coast supplied the Portuguese with sugar, a new strategic and much sought-after commodity which previously had come in smaller quantities from Mediterranean trading partners. Mid-fifteenth-century accounts of the Portuguese royal agent, who often visited Bruges from 1416 onwards, show how he sold goods subject to royal monopoly at Bruges: spices, pepper from Guinea (probably malagueta pepper or grains of paradise) and ivory.[25] The royal agent also purchased goods for the Portuguese court, the military and the fleet, or for re-export to Africa: jewellery, sable and marten furs, Italian silks, Lille cloth, Lille and Tournai tapestries, serges, linen from Holland and France, parchment for the Portuguese chronicler Gomes Eanes de Zurana, tournament lances, books of hours, breviaries and other liturgical books, armour, chainmail, cannons, tar, ship planks, gunpowder, copper, brass wire and rope.[26] Merchants from Barcelona sailed to Bruges in the fourteenth century, bringing spices, dyestuffs, precious metals, paper, dried fruits, sugar, spices, oil, soap, leather, silk and cotton. Not all of these goods were produced in Spain: Spanish merchants also re-exported Mediterranean, Italian and French commodities. Flemish cloth, clothing, linen, tapestries, sculptures, paintings, furniture, mercery goods, crystal, books and copper goods functioned as return cargo. Goods from the Low Countries profoundly influenced Spanish fashion and demand at the end of the Middle Ages. In the fifteenth century, merino wool – for use in Flemish textile production – was added to the imports from Spain. The Castilian nation was even granted a fully fledged staple for oil, iron and wool at Bruges in 1494.[27]

[24] J. Craeybeckx, *Un grand commerce*, pp. 144–8.

[25] The fact that there was already a Portuguese royal agent in fifteenth-century Bruges is significant since the presence of such a royal factor has been adduced as one of the key causes of the rise of Antwerp: W. Brulez, 'Brugge en Antwerpen in de 15e en 16e eeuw: Een tegenstelling?', *TG*, 83 (1970), 15–37 (at 30).

[26] J. Paviot, 'Brugge en Portugal', in Vandewalle (ed.), *Hanzekooplui en Medicibankers*, pp. 45–9 (at 45–6).

[27] J. Finot, *Étude historique sur les relations commerciales entre la Flandre et l'Espagne au Moyen Âge* (Paris, 1899); H. Casado Alonso, 'Brugge, centrum van uitwisseling met Spanje', in Vandewalle (ed.), *Hanzekooplui en Medicibankers*, pp. 51–7.

Italian merchants from Genoa, Florence, Venice, Lucca and Milan, who after the German Hanse were the most important trading communities in Bruges, similarly imported both Italian and transit goods: Italian silks, linen, south German fustians and weapons, alum from Chios and Phocaea (and later in the fifteenth century from Tolfa in the Papal State[28]), Greek wines, eastern spices and silks, African gold, Spanish sugar and fruits. Italian traders took English wool, cloth, fur, tin, grain, luxuries and fashion articles back home.[29] Bruges has often been portrayed as the meeting place of northern and southern Europe, of Mediterranean and Baltic trade. Data on the trading volumes of Lübeck and Genoa around 1380 show that Mediterranean trade was in monetary terms vastly more important than that of the Baltic (by a factor of nine). Bruges and the Low Countries financed their Mediterranean (and especially Italian) trade deficit with a surplus from commerce with the Baltic and central Europe, a surplus created by the craving for expensive Low Countries woollens among the elites of central and eastern Europe.[30] From England, wool, leather, tin, lead, coal, grain, beer and cheese were imported and Flanders exported Flemish and Brabant cloth, Rhenish wine and other transit products available on the Bruges market to the British Isles.[31]

Conspicuously absent on the Bruges market were English textiles: these had been banned from Flanders since at least the 1350s in an attempt to shield the Flemish cloth industry from English competition. Bruges' competitor Antwerp, however, welcomed English merchants and their broadcloth and lesser quality kerseys and worsteds; historians have pointed out that this would prove to be a crucial advantage to Antwerp trade vis-à-vis Bruges at the end of the fifteenth century. The Flemish ban on English cloth may have helped Flemish textile entrepreneurs in the short run but it also

[28] J. Delumeau, *L'alun de Rome, XVe–XIXe siècles* (Paris, 1962).

[29] G. Petti Balbi, *Mercanti e nationes nelle Fiandre: I Genovesi in età bassomedievale* (Pisa, 1996); G. Petti Balbi, 'Brugge, haven van de Italianen', in Vandewalle (ed.), *Hanzekooplui en Medicibankers*, pp. 58–63; G. Petti Balbi, 'Le nationes italiane all'estero', in F. Franceschi, R. A. Goldthwaite and R. C. Mueller (eds.), *Commercio e cultura mercantile: Il Rinascimento italiano e l'Europa*, (Vicenza, 2007), pp. 397–424; R. de Roover, *The Rise and Decline of the Medici Bank, 1397–1494* (Cambridge, MA, 1963); R. A. Goldthwaite, *The Economy of Renaissance Florence* (Baltimore, MD, 2009); B. Lambert, *The City, the Duke and their Banker: The Rapondi Family and the Formation of the Burgundian State (1384–1430)* (Turnhout, 2006).

[30] P. Spufford, *Power and Profit: The Merchant in Medieval Europe* (London, 2002), pp. 342–62, 376–89; Blockmans, *Metropolen*, p. 263.

[31] J. H. A. Munro, *Wool, Cloth and Gold: The Struggle for Bullion in Anglo-Burgundian Trade, 1340–1478* (Brussels, 1973); D. Nicholas, 'The English Trade at Bruges in the Last Years of Edward III', *JMH*, 5 (1979), 23–61; M.-R. Thielemans, *Bourgogne et Angleterre: Relations politiques et économiques entre les Pays-Bas Bourguignons et l'Angleterre, 1435–1467* (Brussels, 1966).

caused Bruges merchants to miss out on one of the staple goods that would eventually assist the rise of Antwerp as an international market.[32] The distribution of the 384 stalls in the Old Hall in 1398–9 demonstrates the characteristics and amplitude of the Bruges market: 70 booths were reserved for the cloth trade, 19 for hosiery, 21 for hats (including wide hats for the clergy), 24 for glove makers, 28 for purse makers, 49 for mercers, 12 for belt makers, 8 for tapestries sellers, 50 for linen traders, 8 for arrow makers, 17 for makers of wooden shoes, 25 for knife sellers and 53 for the spice sellers or grocers.[33] However, it remains difficult to provide a quantitative overview of international commerce chronologically, as a lack of data prevents measuring the ups and downs of Bruges' trade. The tax farms of the Great Zwin Toll provide some insight: the tolls were leased for 7,800 pounds par. in 1384 and 1403, for 8,400 in 1432 and 1440, and 6,800 in 1464, after which a continuous decline of the lease price set in.[34]

The general characteristics of the late medieval Bruges market have been disputed. Van Houtte has characterized Bruges as a 'national' market and Antwerp as an 'international' market.[35] This is mostly based on a strict definition of an international market as one where merchants from different regions intensively interact.[36] In Bruges, commercial contacts between foreign traders – especially Mediterranean traders and Hanseatic merchants – did take place, but Van Houtte's (unstatistical) analysis of judgments of the Court of Aldermen (*Civiele Sententiën*), yielded far more disputes between foreign merchants and Brugeois or other subjects of the count of Flanders than between foreigners. Italian merchants, for example, could do without Bruges in establishing direct relations with England and southern Germany (over the Alps). Yet one cannot deny the scale and scope of the Bruges commodity market and the presence in Bruges of the key players in European commerce. Bruges was the major market north of the Alps; interaction between foreign merchants was possible through the mediation

[32] J. H. A. Munro, 'Bruges and the Abortive Staple of English Cloth', in J. H. A. Munro, *Textiles, Towns and Trade: Essays in the Economic History of Late Medieval England and the Low Countries* (Aldershot, 1994), pp. 1138–59 (at 1145); Munro, *Wool, Cloth and Gold*, pp. 7–27.

[33] GVS, *Inventaire*, vol. IV, pp. 162–3.

[34] R. van Uytven, 'La Flandre et le Brabant, "terres de promission" sous les ducs de Bourgogne?', *RN*, 43 (1961), 282.

[35] Most pronounced in J. A. Van Houtte, 'Bruges et Anvers, marchés "nationaux" ou "internationaux" du XIVe au XVIe siècles', *RN*, 34 (1952), 89–108; J. A. Van Houtte, 'The Rise and Decline of the Market of Bruges', *Economic History Review*, 19 (1966), 29–47 (at 37).

[36] For this critique of Van Houtte's characterization, see W. Brulez, 'Bruges and Antwerp in the 15th and 16th Centuries: An Antithesis?', *Acta historiae Neerlandica*, 6 (1973), 1–26.

of locals, and the city acted as a redistribution centre for a wide range of commodities.

Locals catered to the needs of foreign merchants, whether they visited the town for a couple of weeks or resided more permanently. Many merchants stayed in one of the many hostels; several of these lodged guests from a particular region, sometimes the region of origin of the hosteller (if he or his ancestors were foreign and had become burghers of Bruges). Some of these innkeepers were major power holders in Bruges: Filip Van Aartrijke, a Bruges burgomaster, had a hostel for Portuguese merchants from 1443 onwards; he mediated between Bruges burghers and Portuguese traders in fruit transactions, acting as guarantor for the contracts.[37] A hostel often offered more than eating, drinking and sleeping: there, deals were struck, legal sanctuary was often offered, merchandise stored, currencies changed, and above all credit and payment could be organized via the hosteller's account with a local money changer.[38] Hostels were common in medieval towns, but Bruges was exceptional in the density and number of hostels and in the complexity of the financial networks organized around them.[39]

The Bruges Commercial Elite: Hostellers and Merchants

As noted, until the thirteenth century Bruges' ruling elite had been a class of international merchants who were also strongly engaged in the organization of textile production. But as the commercical elite reoriented from 'active' to 'passive' trade, it underwent significant changes. From the fourteenth century, the innkeepers or hostellers (*waarden* or *hosteliers*) merged with the traditional merchant class. The hostellers dominated the brokers' guild to which they belonged by monopolizing the offices of dean and wardens. However, prosopographical study suggests that many hostellers and their families also overlapped with the *poorterie* which now grouped all who were not organized in a formal craft guild. As a 'member' of the body politic of Bruges, the *poorterie* was in some respect the institutional successor of the former Hanse within the city's political structure.[40] The hostellers had now joined the merchant class as the most powerful social group

37 Paviot, 'Brugge en Portugal', pp. 46–7.

38 Murray, *Bruges*, pp. 181–210; A. Greve, *Hansische Kaufleute, Hosteliers und Herbergen im Brügge des 14. und 15. Jahrhunderts* (Frankfurt am Main, 2012).

39 Hunt and Murray, *History of Business*, pp. 163–4.

40 See above, Chapter 4; and for the sharing of political power between *poorterie* and craft guilds, see below, Chapter 7.

of Bruges, and some of the thirteenth-century families, like the Bonins, joined their ranks. Many seem to have combined active and passive trade. Moreover, during the early fourteenth century growing tensions arose in the brokers' guild between, on the one hand, the common brokers, who were the obligatory intermediaries for transactions between foreign merchants and often men of more modest middle-class backgrounds, and, on the other hand, the hostellers who were often their employers, and some of whom belonged to the city's wealthiest families.[41]

A systematic portrait of the Bruges hostellers has yet to be undertaken but these men were clearly overrepresented in the city government and they appear more than other groups among the city's excise farmers, the city's greatest creditors, the most frequent buyers of annuities, the most important house owners – several streets were named after them because they possessed the majority of the buildings – and among the fief holders in the surrounding countryside. Some innkeeper families acquired noble status; all of them had power, social prestige and access to capital. They were also among the most important benefactors of charitable institutions and patrons of art. Although wool, cloth, spice, grain and timber merchants still appear in the tax lists of late fourteenth-century Bruges as the wealthiest burghers, the restructured Bruges commercial elite was primarily defined in terms of the services it could offer to international merchants. Hosteller lineages – the Bortoens, Gheerolfs, Honins, Ruebs, Scutelares, Van Aartrijkes, Van der Vlamincpoortes, Van de Vaghevieres, Van de Walles or Van der Beurzes – developed complex commercial, financial, industrial and political networks. They married each others' daughters and into families from the petty nobility and princely officers. The hostellers were the spiders in the web of international commerce and the power brokers to conflict settlement, judicial security and economic, fiscal and financial legislation in the city; they acted as rent seekers on international trade and as risk-taking investors and entrepreneurs. During the fourteenth and fifteenth centuries they thus formed the main economic and political counterbalance to the corporate world of organized artisan labour and, as will be seen in Chapter 7, they constituted the core of the Bruges ruling class together with some active Bruges merchants. They derived their wealth and power from Bruges' position as a hub for the flows of international trade and finance, and from their ability to institutionalize their involvement and regulate these flows to their own advantage as well as to that of the prince,

[41] J. A. Van Houtte, 'Les courtiers au Moyen Âge', *Revue Historique de Droit Français et Étranger*, 15 (1936), 105–41; Van Houtte, 'Makelaars en waarden'.

who skimmed off profits through taxation. Yet the activities of brokers and hostellers were not limited to milking the profits of commerce: their intervention in international trade was also crucial for the foreign merchants.[42]

Many hostellers either doubled as brokers or employed a broker for the settlement of business transactions in their hostel. From 1293 the presence of an official broker was compulsory for every transaction of foreign merchants in Bruges.[43] Mediation by brokers allowed the matching of business parties unacquainted with each other, and offered valuable local knowledge.[44] Several historians have argued that this compulsory brokerage hampered market exchange and raised transaction costs for all parties; in short that brokers acted as parasites.[45] This is an exaggeration. There were complaints by Hanseatic merchants about the brokers' tariffs, which was one reason for a Hanseatic boycott in 1307. The city government reacted by lowering the brokerage fees for the German merchants.[46] But in general brokerage costs were not a real barrier for efficient and lucrative trade opportunities. Brokers' fees remained very low. They accounted for less than 0.15 per cent of the purchase value of wheat in Bruges between 1360 and 1500; the Medici bank paid less than 1 per cent for brokers' fees in a series of transactions in almonds and cardamom, and fees for cloth transactions were no higher.[47] Brokers and hostellers increasingly acted as agents on behalf of merchants who were not physically present in Bruges and this despite the prohibition of associations between brokers and their clients.[48] They started to buy and sell commodities, to arrange payments, to pay tolls, and they stood surety and acted as guarantors, organized transportation and insurance and they provided legal expertise and acted as witnesses in court cases.[49] The account books of Wouter Ameyde, a broker who also acted as factor and merchant in his own right from the end of the fifteenth century, show that merchants

42 Hostellers appear prominently in prosopographical studies with a primary focus on the political elites: see Dumolyn, *De Brugse opstand*; K. Vanhaverbeke, 'Het stadsbestuur in Brugge in de periode 1375–1407: Een sociaal-institutionele studie aan de hand van de prosopografische methode', *HGG*, 135 (1998), 3–54; A. Mattheus, 'Prosopografie van het Brugse stadsbestuur 1467–1477', 2 vols., unpublished MA thesis, Ghent University (Ghent, 2011).

43 SAB, 299, Cartularium (1250–1792), fos. 1[r–v]. For more on the rules and realities of brokerage, see Verbist, 'Traditie ', pp. 59–127; Greve, *Hansische Kaufleute*; Van den Abeele and Catry, *Makelaars en handelaars*.

44 J. Boerner and D. Quint, 'Medieval Matching Markets' (Discussion paper, Free University Berlin, School of Business and Economics, 2010).

45 Van Houtte, 'Makelaars en waarden'.

46 Gelderblom, *Cities of Commerce*, p. 47.

47 Stabel, 'Marketing Cloth'.

48 Van Houtte, 'Makelaars en waarden', pp. 23–4; Murray, *Bruges*, pp. 196–210.

49 Murray, *Bruges*, pp. 190–215.

not only used the services of a broker when they were absent from Bruges, but also relied on them even when they were present in the city.[50] The books kept by hostellers, brokers and money changers were also testimonies in court cases. A recent analysis of Ameyde registers has stressed the documentary and discursive nature of such brokers' accounts.[51] Through a broker, merchants had access to the Bruges payment system based on book transfers in an integrated system of brokers, hostellers and money changers who maintained mutual clearing accounts. Ameyde's Italian and Iberian clients made frequent use of book transfers via Ameydé, to finance their transactions.[52] This is not to say that the institution of brokerage remained unaltered throughout the fourteenth and fifteenth centuries. When more and more merchants established themselves for longer periods in Bruges, the demand for brokers' and hostellers' services must have declined. The 'guest system' or *Gastrecht* – the hosteller's liability for his guest – also changed. A hosteller was held liable for the commodity transactions of his guests, and visiting merchants were often identified by the name of their hosteller.[53] In the fifteenth century creditors made less use of this form of liability and directly attached the goods of their debtors or had them arrested, followed by summary proceedings at the 'court' of aldermen.[54]

Fourteenth- and fifteenth-century Bruges is often called a centre for passive Flemish trade: by then, it was foreign merchants who came to the city to trade, not Flemings who went abroad.[55] However, this picture needs nuancing, and it does seem that Bruges' active trade made a comeback in the fifteenth century at the latest. A substantial number of Bruges merchants (as we shall see) traded in fashion items and textiles in fifteenth-century Rome, while other more renowned merchant families were active in France or in the Mediterranean, for example Martin van der Beurze who traded in Valencia.[56] Flemish vessels, financed by Flemish entrepreneurs,

[50] O. Mus, 'Wouter Ameyde, een Brugs makelaar op het einde van de 15de eeuw', in Buysse (ed.), *Album*, pp. 117–32; P. Stabel, 'Entre commerce international et entrepreneurs locaux: Le monde financier de Wouter Ameide (Bruges, fin 15e – début 16e siècle)', in M. Boone and W. Prevenier (eds.), *Finances publiques et finances privées au bas Moyen Âge* (Leuven, 1996), pp. 75–96.

[51] Verbist, 'Traditie', pp. 293–346.

[52] Stabel, 'Entre commerce', pp. 83–90.

[53] Gelderblom, *Cities of Commerce*, p. 49.

[54] Ibid., p. 51.

[55] See Van Werveke, 'Der Flandrische Eigenhandel'; Van Houtte, 'Rise and Decline'; Stabel, *Dwarfs among Giants*, p. 47.

[56] C. Verlinden, 'Le registre du marchand brugeois Martin van der Beurse aux archives de Valence (1414–1427)', in *Les Espagnes médiévales: Mélanges offertes à Jean Gautier Dalché* (Paris, 1983), pp. 153–8.

remained active in trade along the French coast.[57] At least five Bruges traders (Rombout de Wachtere, Pieter Metteneye, Lievin vander Mersch, Zegher Parmentier, Maarten Lem and João Esteves, perhaps Portuguese for Joost Stevens) were involved in a court case about the sale of jewellery in Lisbon and Seville in 1449–50.[58] Maarten Lem, a key figure in Bruges during the later fifteenth century, became a major trader in Lisbon. For a time he held the monopoly on cork, granted to him by the Portuguese king in 1456, and traded in Mediterranean fruits and sugar from Madeira where he set up large farms. A sales register for 1478–99 shows the intensive commercial contacts between Portugal and the Bruges firm of the brothers Jacob and Wouter Despars. They imported Madeira sugar, fruits and olive oil to Bruges and sold Flemish cloth and tapestries and south German fustians in Lisbon, and also brass rings used in the Portuguese trade with western Africa.[59] Bruges merchants were not only active in distant markets; they also acted as intermediaries within the Low Countries. Several rented or owned large houses near the central market square in Antwerp to accommodate guests and store goods. They sold wool and spices (many of them were grocers) and they bought cloth.[60] Indeed, Bruges and Antwerp were complementary markets throughout much of the fifteenth century. The Brabant fairs held in Antwerp and Bergen-op-Zoom attracted many merchants, including those residing in Bruges. The city of Bruges tried to forbid these visits, to no great avail, but it remained the leading market for much of the fifteenth century.[61]

The 1438 ledger of the bank of Filippo Borromei and Company, with its branches in Bruges and London, demonstrates this complementarity. While established in Bruges, the bank's operations predominantly took place at the Brabant fairs where it bought large quantities of south German fustians and other goods, and made available large amounts of cash for

57 R. Degryse, 'De Vlaamse westvaart en de Engelse represailles omstreeks 1378', *HMG*, 27 (1973), 193–239; W. Brulez, *De firma Della Faille en de internationale handel van Vlaamse firma's in de 16e eeuw* (Brussels, 1959), pp. 445–51; Brulez, 'Brugge en Antwerpen', pp. 27–8. As such, they anticipated the growing group of merchants from the Low Countries who, out of Antwerp, conquered European markets in the sixteenth century: see J. Puttevils, *Merchants and Trading in the Sixteenth Century: The Golden Age of Antwerp*, Perspectives in Economic and Social History 38 (London, 2015).

58 J. Paviot, 'Les Portugais à Bruges', in Stabel et al. (eds.), *International Trade*, pp. 55–74.

59 O. Mus, 'De Brugse compagnie Despars op het einde van de 15e eeuw', *HGG*, 101 (1964), 5–118.

60 G. Asaert, 'Gasten uit Brugge: Nieuwe gegevens over Bruggelingen op de Antwerpse markt in de vijftiende eeuw', in G. Hansotte and H. Coppejans (eds.), *Album Carlos Wyffels* (Brussels, 1987), pp. 23–41.

61 Gelderblom, *Cities of Commerce*, pp. 26–8.

its customers in Antwerp. The bank's activities may have shifted back to Bruges after the 1436 Bruges revolt, however. The ledger reveals another financial network besides that of the Bruges money changers. The Borromei kept in contact with other major commercial and financial centres: London, Cologne, Florence, Genoa, Venice, Geneva, Palermo, Pisa, the papal court at Avignon, Valencia, Barcelona and Seville. Most of the bank's account holders were other Italians, either resident in Bruges or in other cities. The Borromei bank was also firmly rooted in the Low Countries: its network fanned out from Bruges and included men and women from Antwerp, Bergen-op-Zoom, Middelburg, Damme, Mechelen, Lier, Kortrijk, Tournai, Wervik, Ghent and Hainaut who made use of the bank's payment services. To that end, the partners and staff of the bank regularly travelled in the circuit shaped by Bruges, Antwerp, Bergen-op-Zoom and Calais. A cash account was opened for the Brabant fairs at Antwerp and Bergen-op-Zoom to allow clients and third parties – Italians, Germans and Catalans from Bruges but also local bankers such as Jan Finai from Mons, the Bruges grocer Diederic de Roovere, clothiers from Lier and Mechelen – to pay or be paid for goods and services.[62]

The Foreign Merchants and their Communities

The presence and social profile of Bruges' foreign merchants are hard to characterize, given the absence of any representative statistical series of records. The lists of individuals who, according to the Bruges city accounts, were exempted from paying excise taxes, mainly on beer and wine, suggest that between 1360 and 1390 at least 1,020 Hanseatic merchants resided in Bruges, with a maximum of 205 at any one time.[63] A total of 990 foreign merchants of various origins have been counted in the first two volumes of the ledger of the Bruges money changer Collard de Marke, active between 1366 and 1370, a number which must be considered a bare minimum.[64] Drawing on notarial records, Giovanna Petti Balbi estimated that about 150 Genoese lived in the city during the fifteenth century.[65] Between 1331 and

[62] J. L. Bolton and F. Guidi Bruscoli, 'When Did Antwerp Replace Bruges as the Commercial and Financial Centre of North-Western Europe? The Evidence of the Boromei Ledger for 1438', *Economic History Review*, 61 (2008), 360–79.

[63] K. Krüger and W. Paravicini (eds.), *Hansekaufleute in Brügge*, vol. I: *Die Brügger Steuerlisten 1360–1390* (Frankfurt am Main, 1992).

[64] J. M. Murray, 'Of Nodes and Networks: Bruges and the Infrastructure of Trade in Fourteenth-Century Europe', in Stabel et al. (eds.), *International Trade*, pp. 1–14 (at 9).

[65] Petti Balbi, *Mercanti*, pp. 82–3.

1479, 12,939 people became Bruges citizens, 25 per cent of whom came from outside the county of Flanders. As merchants did not need citizenship to engage in international trade, this is only an indirect indicator of foreign commercial presence.[66] Chroniclers also mention numbers of foreign merchants at ceremonial entries of the Burgundian dukes. In 1440, Philip the Good was greeted by over 300 of them, including 136 Hansards, 48 Castilians, 40 Milanese, 40 Venetians, 38 Genoese, 22 Florentines, 12 Lucchese and an unspecified number of Portuguese and Catalans.[67] In 1468, 310 merchants welcomed Charles the Bold, consisting of 108 Hansards, 108 Genoese, 60 Florentines, 24 Castilians and 10 Venetians.[68] These numbers are minima, indicating only those who were present on these occasions, and they omit the English, the Scots, all those who were not part of foreign merchant guilds and the hundreds of factors, servants and sailors employed by the merchants who doubtless milled around in the streets, markets and inns of Bruges. What is certain, however, is that even though Bruges' unequalled range of networking institutions made it possible to make use of its business opportunities in absentia,[69] the city harboured a great number of foreign traders, which, according to contemporaries, was exceptional in a European context. Pero Tafur also stressed that trade in Bruges was more international than in Venice, that other commercial metropolis of the fifteenth century.[70]

There were differences between foreigners besides the obvious ones of origin. The diversity of commercial and financial services offered in Bruges meant that the economic capital of the individuals involved in international trade and banking varied accordingly. The Italian community in the city consisted just as much of Dino Rapondi, the Lucchese banker who, at the turn of the fifteenth century, effected transfers of up to 200,000 francs on behalf of the Burgundian dukes,[71] or Felice de Fagnano, who managed a Milanese bank with a total turnover of nearly 275,000 pounds Flemish in 1438,[72] as it did of Domenico Macetti, a Lombard who, in 1448, issued a

[66] E. Thoen, 'Immigration to Bruges during the late Middle Ages', in S. Cavaciocchi (ed.), *Le migrazioni in Europa: Secc. XIII–XVIII* (Florence, 1994), pp. 335–53 (at 342–6).

[67] Nicolas Despars, *Cronijcke van den lande ende graefscepe van Vlaenderen*, 4 vols., ed. J. De Jonghe (Bruges and Rotterdam, 1839–42), vol. III, pp. 431–2.

[68] Olivier de la Marche, *Mémoires d'Olivier de la Marche: Maitre d'hôtel et capitaine des gardes de Charles le Téméraire*, 4 vols., ed. H. Beaune and J. d'Arbaumont (Paris, 1883–8), vol. III, pp. 113–14.

[69] Murray, 'Of Nodes and Networks', p. 14.

[70] Tafur, *Travels*, p. 198.

[71] Lambert, *The City*, p. 116.

[72] Bolton and Guidi Bruscoli, 'When did Antwerp Replace Bruges', p. 368.

petty loan of 4 pounds groten to an artisan secured on the latter's movables.[73] As economies of scale dictate that cost advantages increase according to the volume of trade, differences in economic capital also affected an ability to take advantage of Bruges' concentration of merchants and commercial institutions, and their cost-reducing effects. This was reflected in the use of urban space: whereas the doyens of international trade and banking flocked and traded assets in the Bourse Square, the financial epicentre of the city,[74] an alternative market based on small-scale commercial exchange and the absence of a regulatory framework developed on the margins of the urban economy and, not coincidentally, outside the urban jurisdiction. In Sluis, the foreign merchant communities' lesser personnel and those involved in the much less capital-intensive carrying trade, such as Bretons and Hollanders, met with locals to net their share of Bruges' economic success.[75]

These huge inequalities in terms of economic capital often corresponded with differences in social capital. The Venetians, who were among the most commercially active in the Bruges market, relied on a state-sponsored trade infrastructure and a vast network of commission agents, which made it unnecessary for them to be personally present in the Low Countries and even discouraged them from any active integration with local networks in Bruges.[76] There are exceptions: the Venetian Giovanni Bembo bought Bruges citizenship in 1451.[77] At the other end of the social spectrum, the Genoese compensated for the passive role of their home state by adopting local commercial infrastructures, obtaining Bruges citizenship, marrying Flemish women and buying local real estate significantly more than any other group. Thus, most of the foreign commercial dynasties who settled permanently in Bruges were Genoese: the Adornes (or Adorni in Italian), the Spingheles (Spinola), the Lommellins (Lommellini) and the Oliviers (Oliveri).[78] Merchants were aware of these differences in social capital and their commercial implications. It is no coincidence that, when looking for

[73] J. Marechal, *Bijdrage tot de geschiedenis van het bankwezen te Brugge* (Bruges, 1955), p. 20.

[74] Blockmans, 'Urban Space'.

[75] Lambert, 'Merchants on the Margin'.

[76] P. Stabel, 'Venice and the Low Countries: Commercial Contacts and Intellectual Inspirations', in B. Aikema and B. L. Brown (eds.), *Renaissance Venice and the North: Crosscurrents in the Time of Bellini, Dürer and Titian* (New York, 1999), pp. 31–43.

[77] A. Jamees, *Brugse poorters opgetekend uit de stadsrekeningen*, 3 vols. (Handzame, 1980), vol. II, p. 247.

[78] B. Lambert, 'De Genuese aanwezigheid in laatmiddeleeuws Brugge (1435–1495): Een laboratorium voor de studie van de instellingen en hun rol in de economische geschiedenis', unpublished PhD thesis, Ghent University (Ghent, 2011), pp. 111–12.

someone to safeguard their privileges, the Scots preferred a well-positioned Genoese, Anselmus Adornes, over one of their own.

Within groups of foreign merchants, social capital also varied, certainly between the minority who resided permanently in the city and the majority who came and went with the commercial seasons. The Genoese community included men such as Haran Galice, a 'poor man who knows nothing', arrested in 1403 for selling some figs and raisins without paying taxes,[79] but also members of the mighty Doria and Spinola families and the Giustiniani, who controlled the alum trade from the eastern Mediterranean.[80] Even though most of these traders only stayed temporarily, some made remarkable careers in the Low Countries. Bonnore Olivier, a member of a bastard line of one of the most important Ligurian noble families, who made good money on the Bruges market, married a local alderman's daughter, worked as an officer for the Burgundian duke, married a noblewoman and returned to his homeland, where he acquired a seigniory. His case also highlights the pragmatic way in which these foreign merchants often used local citizenship: originally from the Ligurian town of Finale, Olivier became a Bruges citizen when his commercial interests in the city grew stronger but re-emphasized his Italian origins once his noble aspirations came within reach. Not wanting to lose his advantages in Flanders, he now presented himself as 'Bonnore de Carrette named Olivier of Finale of the city of Bruges'.[81] His colleague Egidio Lomellini bought Bruges citizenship for himself and his ten children in 1463 though his son Lazarro renounced it in 1467.[82]

Some foreign merchants interacted more with the local population than others.[83] Foreigners lived among Bruges citizens and owned houses scattered over the city, although they preferred the districts around the Bourse Square. The same is true for the Hanseatic merchants who, along with other temporary visitors of all origins, were the most frequent customers of the city's hostellers.[84] The use of local brokers as intermediaries was obligatory for each transaction between foreigners, although many, with local

[79] ADN, B 6094, fo. 3r.

[80] N. L. W. Streeton, 'Jan van Eyck's Dresden Triptych: New Evidence for the Giustiniani of Genoa in the Borromei Ledger for Bruges, 1438', *Journal of Historians of Netherlandish Art*, 3 (2011) (online publication).

[81] J. Braekevelt and B. Lambert, 'Bonnore Olivier, courtier ligurien de la fiscalité bourguignonne (1429–1466)', *BTFG*, 90 (2012), 1155–91.

[82] R. A. Parmentier, *Indices op de Brugsche poorterboeken*, 2 vols. (Bruges, 1938), vol. II, pp. 614–15.

[83] Stabel, 'De gewenste vreemdeling', pp. 207–9.

[84] P. Dollinger, *The German Hanse*, ed. and trans. D. S. Ault and S. H. Steinberg, p. 103; Greve, *Hansische Kaufleute*.

knowledge, tried to avoid them. In 1420 the Genoese Jacopo Spinola pretended to be a Bruges citizen in order to evade brokerage fees.[85] The 1438 ledgers of the Borromei bank reveal that merchants dealt in a direct way with these and other professionals who earned their living in Bruges' trade, such as pilots, carriers, money changers or translators.[86] Some people of foreign origin were active in Bruges' commercial service industries: Clais Barbezaen, a descendant of the Lucchese Barbagialla family, worked as a broker; Pieter Adornes (Adorno) ran an inn at the end of the fourteenth century.[87] Language was no barrier for integration into Bruges society or for interaction between different merchants. The Bruges aldermen in their judgements quickly shifted to languages other than Dutch, mostly to French, the common language of merchants in northern Europe, but also to Latin and even Italian. English and Scottish merchants were addressed in Latin, while they communicated with Italians, French and Spaniards in French. Hanseatic merchants had no problem with Dutch.[88] A conversation manual-cum-dictionary, the so-called *Livre des mestiers* (c.1360–70), provides sentences in Dutch, French, English and German, often with a reference to products and transactions common to the Bruges market.[89]

Social relationships could be capitalized in commercial partnerships. Patronage structures bridged considerable differences in economic and social capital and, for reasons of trust, were often restricted to members of the same geographical group, such as the Genoese *commenda* contract between an active and a passive partner and the Tuscan merchant–factor relationship, frequently built on kinship. Yet, as merchants did not come to Bruges solely to deal with their fellow townsmen, partnerships with other foreigners or local citizens were more important. In the 1440s, for example, the Florentine Antonio de Francesco engaged in the salt trade with Jan Losschaert and Gillis van der Vlamincpoorte from the Bruges commercial elite.[90] Women were also part of the commercial strategies of foreign merchants in Bruges. 'Trade endogamy' meant that merchants tended to marry within their own social class.[91] But some groups like the Genoese and

[85] AGR, Chambers of Accounts, 13771, fo. 20ʳ.

[86] They can be consulted at www.queenmaryhistoricalresearch.org/roundhouse/default.aspx.

[87] Marechal, *Bijdrage*, p. 68.

[88] A. Carlier, 'Taaldiversiteit in de kosmopolitische stad: Taalgebruik, migratie en integratieaspecten in Brugge in de 15[de] eeuw', unpublished MA thesis, Ghent University (Ghent, 2002).

[89] J. Gessler (ed.), *Het Brugsche Livre des mestiers en zijn navolgingen: Vier aloude conversatieboekjes om Fransch te leeren*, 6 vols. (Bruges, 1931). More on this text in Chapter 9.

[90] SAB, 11, fo. 294ᵛ–5ʳ.

[91] M. C. Howell, 'From Land to Love: Commerce and Marriage in Northern Europe during the Late Middle Ages', *Jaarboek voor Middeleeuwse Geschiedenis*, 10 (2007), 216–53 (at 233–4).

Castilians were inclined to find a partner among locals. Others, certainly Florentine and Lucchese merchants, preferred to look for a spouse within their own group. In 1419, Filippo Rapondi married off his two daughters to members of the Trenta and the Burlamacchi families, fellow Lucchese who were also active in the Bruges market.[92] Most visitors from abroad, however, were in the city too briefly to consider marriage strategies; which possibly made them more likely than others to procreate illegitimate offspring[93] or figure in the prostitution statistics.[94] The Venetian Francesco da Canal and the Genoese Nicolao Giustiniani managed both. They fathered a child with the same woman, probably a prostitute – a rare example of common social behaviour in the city among Genoese and Venetians.[95]

Some foreign merchants integrated with the local political elites. Clais Barbezaen was one of the city's treasurers and an important politician when, in a stormy political episode (see Chapter 7), he was banished from the city by John the Fearless in 1407.[96] Anselmus Adornes rose to the rank of burgomaster in 1475–6.[97] Leon Spinghele (Spinola) acted as alderman and councillor before and after the political unrest of 1477–92.[98] Merchants did not have to take up office to invest in political capital. A succession of Italian bankers, employed by the Burgundian dukes, influenced the balance of power in the city in the fifteenth century.[99] In 1407, a loan from the Lucchese Rapondi Company enabled the faction favoured by John the Fearless to take control of the Bruges city hall. The city's inhabitants were fully aware of the operation's political effects and showed their dissatisfaction four years later. Returning from a campaign in 1411, the Bruges militia refused to enter the city unless, among other things, Dino Rapondi's goods were confiscated.[100] In the late 1470s and early 1480s, a network comprising the Genoese Lazarro Lomellini, the Lucchese Pietro Carincioni, the

92 E. Lazzareschi and L. Mirot (eds.), 'Lettere di Mercanti Lucchesi da Bruges e da Parigi', *Bollettino Storico Lucchese*, 1 (1929), 166–99 (at 191–2).

93 M. Carlier, *Kinderen van de minne? Bastaarden in het vijftiende-eeuwse Vlaanderen* (Brussels, 2001), pp. 78–87.

94 Dupont, *Maagdenverleidsters*, pp. 124–5.

95 Carlier, *Kinderen*, p. 83.

96 Dumolyn, *De Brugse Opstand*, pp. 133–4.

97 Geirnaert, 'De Adornes en de Jeruzalemkapel', p. 22.

98 SAB, 114, 1468–1501, fo. 78^{r-v}, 177^{r}, 195^{r-v}.

99 B. Lambert, '*Se fist riche par draps de soye*: The Intertwinement of Italian Financial Interests and Luxury Trade at the Burgundian Court (1384–1481)', in B. Lambert and K. A. Wilson (eds.), *Europe's Rich Fabric: The Consumption, Commercialisation and Production of Luxury Textiles in Italy, the Low Countries and Neighbouring Territories (14th–16th Centuries)* (Ashgate, 2016), pp. 91–106.

100 Lambert, *The City*, pp. 133–5.

Florentine Giovanni Cambi and the Venetian Alberto Contarini financially backed the politician Willem Moreel while he still enjoyed the favour of Archduke Maximilian.[101] Possibly instrumental in the accumulation of political capital were networks such as the exclusive confraternity of the Dry Tree, where foreign merchants, mainly Tuscans and Castilians, joined with Burgundian courtiers and members of the Bruges urban elites.[102]

The differences in economic, social or political capital were often expressed through investments in cultural capital. Precious clothes and accessories were used as markers of status: silks, brocades and velvets were worn by wealthy courtiers and Italian merchants, expensive and fashionable woollen garments usually by Bruges elites and foreign merchants. In general all inhabitants wore similar types of dress and many also had clothing lined with furs, though these could denote status: simple furs for the poor, and hugely expensive sable and Russian squirrel furs, imported by Hanseatic traders, for wealthy burghers and merchants.[103] These vestimentary features appear in portraits commissioned by foreign merchants during their stay in Bruges. In the later fifteenth century, Italians copied Burgundian courtiers by displaying their social status through paintings commissioned from local artists. They were followed more reluctantly by Hanseatic merchants.[104] Bricks served social differentiation too: Tommaso Portinari ran his branch of the Florentine Medici bank from a city palace that had previously been the residence of a Burgundian courtier.[105] Bonnore Olivier possessed a sumptuous mansion with a tower, situated along Bruges' most important commercial artery.[106] As we have seen, the Adornes enriched Bruges' cultural pedigree with their own private Jerusalem chapel and necropolis (see Figure 5.2).[107]

Although Bruges' foreign merchants were socially heterogeneous, a more homogeneous collective identity among them is detectable. Many

[101] J. Haemers, *For the Common Good: State Power and Urban Revolts in the Reign of Mary of Burgundy (1477–1482)* (Turnhout, 2009), pp. 81–2; and see Chapter 7 below.

[102] On this fraternity, see further Chapter 8.

[103] F. Piponnier and P. Mane, *Se vêtir au Moyen Âge* (Paris, 1995); and more particularly for Bruges: P. Stabel, 'Dressing the Poor in Bruges: Clothing and Social Identity in a Late Medieval City', *Social History*, forthcoming.

[104] L. Campbell, 'Bruges, Jan van Eyck, Early Netherlandish Painting and Southern Europe', *Burlington Magazine*, 144 (2002), 367–71.

[105] W. De Clercq, J. Dumolyn and J. Haemers, 'Vivre Noblement: The Material and Immaterial Construction of Elite-Identity in Late Medieval Flanders: The Case of Pieter Bladelin and William Hugonet', *Journal of Interdisciplinary History*, 38 (2007), 1–31.

[106] Braekevelt and Lambert, 'Bonnore Olivier'.

[107] Geirnaert, 'De Adornes en de Jeruzalemkapel'.

were grouped as merchant guilds or nations, based on their geographical origins. Apart from the German Hanse, Bruges had Venetian, Genoese, Florentine, Lucchese,[108] Castilian,[109] Catalan-Aragonese,[110] English and Scottish nations. The Biscayans seceded from the Castilian guild in 1455 and a Portuguese one was fully established in 1438.[111] The few Placentines in the city associated with the Genoese,[112] and the Bolognese with the Lucchese. Yet here too, merchants adopted these identities in a loose and opportunistic manner. Bonnore Olivier was considered a Genoese before he became a Bruges citizen; Antonio de Francesco came from Volterra[113] but presented himself as a Florentine. Nations negotiated commercial franchises with the prince, which allowed their members to trade in Flanders. They played a key role in the organization of commercial conflict-solving in Bruges. Presided over by their consuls, nations judged disputes between nation members. Cases between foreigners of different origins or between foreigners and locals were handled by the Bruges aldermen, to whom nation members could appeal against their consuls' decisions. Foreign merchant guilds also boosted collective consciousness through festivities or through religious services organized with the city's mendicant orders, and they participated in civic ceremonies together with the rest of the Bruges population. They liaised with the home government and, to a varying extent, defended their members' commercial and financial interests abroad. As the Venetians were less permanently present in the city than were most other groups, their consul in Bruges played an active part in representing fellow citizens. When glancing through the consulate register of the Lucchese merchant guild, the only surviving record of its kind,[114] it is striking how the more powerful families, such as the Rapondi or Forteguerra, participated in the ceremonial activities of their nations but, unlike their colleagues with more

108 De Roover, 'La communauté des marchands Lucquois'.

109 H. Casado Alonso 'La nation et le quartier des Castillans de Bruges (XVe et XVIe siècles)', *HGG*, 133 (1996), 61–77; Marechal, 'La colonie espagnole'.

110 D. Pifarré Torres, *El comerç internacional de Barcelona i el Mar del Nord (Bruges) al final del segle XIV* (Barcelona, 2002), passim.

111 J. Paviot, 'Les Portugais à Bruges au XVe siècle', *Arquivos do Centro Cultural Calouste Gulbenkian*, 38 (1999), 1–122.

112 G. Petti Balbi, 'I Piacentini tra Genova e i Paesi Bassi', in *Precursori di Cristoforo Colombo: Mercanti e banchieri piacentini nel mondo durante il medioevo* (Bologna, 1994), pp. 69–88.

113 G. Biscaro, 'Il banco Filippo Borromei e compagni di Londra (1436–1439)', *Archivio Storico Lombardo*, 19 (1913), 37–126, 283–386 (at 39–40).

114 E. Lazzareschi (ed.), *Il libro della communitá dei mercanti Lucchesi in Bruges* (Milan, 1947), passim.

modest means, hardly ever resorted to these bodies to sort out their commercial problems. The Lucchese merchant guild might thus have functioned as a tool of sociability, allowing the lesser merchants to benefit from the economic and social capital amassed by the grander ones, who had more effective tools of trade at their disposal.

Occasionally, these nations joined together and defended their common interests with either the urban or the princely authorities. Throughout the thirteenth and fourteenth centuries, they repeatedly complained about the improper use of the urban weight.[115] In 1457, the Florentines, Lucchese, Genoese, Catalans and Castilians wrote to the Lübecker city council to persuade the German Hanse to give up its embargo and return to Bruges.[116] In 1460, all nations forgot their mutual competition and campaigned for the abolition of a ducal tax on Catalan goods.[117] Still, even this 'foreign merchant community' left out the Lombards and the Breton shippers, the representative of the German Order and the Sienese bankers, and many others involved in the city's international trade. In short, the richness and diversity of foreign commercial presence in medieval Bruges are difficult to apprehend.

The Bruges Money Market

Money and its use reflect many of the communities and complexities in any market-driven city, as do trade goods and the sometimes long-distance economic systems that brought them to the Bruges market-place. Goods were exchanged for silver coins, and increasingly in the fourteenth century bulk and expensive commodities were sold for gold coins, but these simple statements conceal a complex reality for merchants. While the silver coinage of Flanders was modelled on the French example, it was issued by the count, who in the fourteenth century took ample advantage of his sovereign rights to debase the silver coinage multiple times. Imitation coins were also produced in large numbers, especially English sterling, and a variety of gold coins. The Burgundian dukes intervened in the money supply themselves, both increasing the value of the coins (a *renforcement*) in 1433 and renewing a tradition of debasement across the fifteenth century. In short, merchants in

[115] GVS, *Cartulaire*, vol. II, pp. 27–8.

[116] V. Henn, 'Der *dudesche kopman* zu Brügge und seine Beziehungen zu den *nationes* der übrigen Fremden im späten Mittelalter', in N. Jörn, D. Kattinger and H. Wernicke (eds.), *'Kopet uns werk by tyden': Walter Stark zum 75. Geburtstag* (Schwerin, 1999), p. 141.

[117] GVS, *Inventaire*, vol. IV, pp. 343–4.

Bruges faced a highly challenging monetary environment.[118] Export restrictions of bullion, insecure transport of specie, shortage of petty coins, and constant debasement were just a few of the challenges faced by the medieval merchant and it was in this context that Bruges excelled in becoming what modern historians have called a banking centre. But the modern term gives a poor idea of the social complexity of the fourteenth and fifteenth centuries, for 'banking' was not an institutionalized single business but a social cooperative shared among the various merchant communities of the city who brought with them not only trade goods but also financial practices and networks. These made Bruges a node in networks stretching from Ireland to Novgorod, from Iceland to the Mediterranean, allowing the merchant to effect payments and collections in ways that could defeat distance and unstable currencies.[119]

The lynchpin of the Bruges credit/payment network was the book transfer system developed by brokers/hostellers and money changers in the city. Bruges money changers were originally to be found in the rear arcades of the Halletoren, or Old Cloth Hall, which as we have seen above was a crossing point of a significant commercial street, the largest urban cloth market, the Burg, and Bruges' first commercial neighbourhood, the Oudeburg. This location underlines the affinity of cloth and money in the towns of the medieval Low Countries, as it was an almost invariable rule that where cloth was traded, so too was money.[120] By 1300, the place of exchange or *Wissel* had moved about a hundred yards north to the northern arcade of the aptly named 'New Cloth Hall', later commonly called the Waterhalle, where it would remain for the next hundred years or more. This move placed the changers at the new nexus of cloth sales and imports flowing into Bruges via its outports of Damme and Sluis. This of course resulted from the shift to seaborne trade and the decline of overland transport noticeable by that time. Thus the link with cloth remained, but to it was added the complexities of new commodities.[121]

[118] Murray, *Bruges*, pp. 123–38. And for the fifteenth century, Munro, *Wool, Cloth and Gold*, pp. 77–81; R. de Roover, *Money, Banking and Credit in Medieval Bruges* (Cambridge, MA, 1948), pp. 220–39.

[119] H. Van der Wee, 'International Finance and Monetary Policy in Western Europe', *Business History Review*, 43 (1969), 372–80; Murray, 'Of Nodes and Networks'; E. Aerts, 'The Absence of Public Exchange Banks in Medieval and Early Modern Flanders and Brabant (1400–1800): A Historical Anomaly to be Explained', *Financial History Review*, 18 (2011), 91–117.

[120] Most prominently in Ypres (Ieper) where changer stalls were located in the great Cloth Hall: see de Roover, *Money, Banking and Credit*, p. 100.

[121] Murray, *Bruges*, pp. 31–8; H. Van der Wee, 'Un modèle dynamique de croissance interséculaire du commerce mondiale (XIIe–XVIIIe sièces'), *Annales: Économies, Sociétés, Civilisations*, 25 (1970), 100–26.

And the slow creep northwards continued when in the fifteenth century at least some money changers moved two hundred yards to the Bourse square, which had become the customary meeting place of foreign and native merchants for purposes of exchange. There the city supervised the conduct of the Bourse, keeping time, keeping out undesirables, and generally ensuring good order. We know of at least one money changer who owned a small house just around the corner from the Bourse square. Other changers continued to operate from the St Peter's or Wissel bridge, at the Waterhalle. Thus urban space reflected the changes in the market and the necessary adaptations of those who dealt in money and commercial paper.[122]

A persistent problem in the study of merchant professions is to understand their variety and instability across time and space. For example, money changers often bore the same name (indeed they famously figure in the New Testament, being expelled collectively by an outraged Jesus), but often all they had in common was the manual exchange of one coin type for another. In Bruges, as elsewhere, the thirteenth-century money changers (those lodged behind the Halletoren) combined this simple exchange with duties as caretakers of the currency and officers of the comital mint. The four so-called 'free' changers were in fact enfeoffed as such by the count or countess of Flanders, and appended the additional title of 'mint master' to that of changer. It appears that money changing in thirteenth-century Bruges was a relatively humble affair of public service and meagre profits. However, around the time of the first northwards move of the Exchange to the north end of the Waterhalle, money changing appeared in its most complex of forms, combining coin exchange, deposit accounts and commercial investment. By 1305 there were roughly twelve to fourteen exchanges either on the Wissel Bridge or, in at least one case, being wheeled around the city's market-places like a modern food cart. Five of these were held as fiefs; the remaining were in effect franchisees who paid a small fee to the fief holders for the right to operate. All the changers probably accepted deposits, made book transfers and operated on a fractional reserve principle from this date. And most likely, this expansion in the number of operators was a result of the growth of the commercial economy of Bruges, especially its shift in emphasis to brokering and finance.[123]

Thus commenced the golden age of money changing which lasted until about 1390, aided and abetted by a number of external factors. The first

[122] De Roover, *Money, Banking and Credit*, p. 332; Marechal, *Bijdrage*, pp. 64–5.

[123] Murray, *Bruges*, pp. 148–55; Marechal, *Bijdrage*, pp. 47–56.

was the extreme currency instability caused by the debasement policies of the count of Flanders. This gave changers considerable leverage over the market as arbiters and arbitragers of sound and unsound coins. The legal circulation of a whole host of gold coins also added to the authority of the changer as he or she would be the only trustworthy source of the current exchange value of the Venetian ducat, Florentine florin, many varieties of French and English gold coins, not to mention imitations and counterfeits. In other words, the more complex the monetary regime, the better it suited the devices and desires of the money changers. The peak of complexity was undoubtedly reached during the reign of Count Louis of Male, a notorious debaser of his coinage. In the period from 1337 to 1364 he reduced the bullion content of the Flemish groot by half across some nineteen different coin issues. The differences between issues were often so minute as to be detectable only by money changers apart from the mint masters. Similar chaos reigned in gold coinage as well, since foreign coins circulated as legal tender, especially in Bruges, and the count imitated many of these foreign coins (especially the Florentine florin, English noble and French écu). In Louis of Male's reign no fewer than fifteen different gold coins were struck in the count's mints, both originals and imitations. So active and profitable were Louis' mints that in some years 20 per cent of the count's revenues were derived from mint profits.[124]

Yet the variety of business activity pursued by individual changers could be considerable, going far beyond manual exchange or coin arbitrage, making generalizations about the profession difficult even in the limited context of Bruges, not to mention other cities. As a rule, the largest and perhaps most successful changers held the bulk of their investments in trade and manufacture. Collard de Marke, whose ledger books survive, falls into this category. His business encompassed trade in bullion with correspondents in northern France, with an active presence at the comital mint in Ghent. His money on deposit there was used to pay for purchases made in the Ghent market. His other major side business was cloth importing from northern France, which he conducted with a partner until 1368. Thereafter his son took over the operation of the business, with receipts posted to the general ledger of the exchange. Other Bruges changers seem also to have invested heavily in cloth manufacture and trade.[125]

124 Munro, *Wool, Cloth and Gold*, pp. 18–34; H. Van Werveke, 'Currency Manipulation in the Middle Ages: The Case of Louis de Male, Count of Flanders', *Transactions of the Royal Historical Society*, series 4, 31 (1949), 115–27; Aerts, 'Absence of Public Exchange Banks', pp. 96–8.

125 Murray, *Bruges*, pp. 174–6.

The exchange of Willem Ruweel offers a second example of the structure of a money exchange based upon an examination of his accounts and other surviving documents. What is clear from these sources was a gender-based division of labour between Willem and his wife Margaret, who had inherited the licence to hold an exchange from a maternal aunt. She and her sons and a male relative operated the day-to-day business of the exchange, while Willem occupied himself with investments. His preferences ran to real estate and tax farming, quite unlike de Marke's for trade, and it was probably miscalculations in his leasing of the right to collect the wine assize that brought down his exchange in 1370. This was as much a result of social class as of finance, however, since the Ruweels were not of the hosteller elite, which controlled both the auction process and purchase in most cases. Thus Ruweel was deprived of essential information that might have resulted in a more rational bid for the assize. Yet gender proved to be stronger than bankruptcy in the Ruweel case, as Margaret's possession of the licence to operate the exchange was exempt from claims against her husband's failure, so that two of her sons operated the family business until the 1390s.[126]

Yet despite abundant kinds of silver and gold coins, there was a persistent shortage of trading specie. This was true from top to bottom, from the mites used for small purchases in the bakeries and beer halls of the city, to the gold coins used for large transactions. This lack resulted in a vast and thinly documented system of credit buying, and more significantly it led to a payment/financial system based on money changers. They allowed individuals to open bank accounts through deposit of coin or bullion, whose balances could be transferred either directly if the beneficiary also had an account with that changer, or via clearing accounts held by Bruges innkeepers. This system had considerable advantages for foreign merchants, who could entrust money to either their innkeeper or a particular changer and leave it there until it was needed to complete a business deal. Changers and hostellers could retain only a portion of those deposits in ready money, thus creating a pool of 'bank money' to provide liquidity for investment in the Bruges economy, thus remedying somewhat the chronic shortage of coin. This payment system was backed to a certain extent by the Bruges city government, which acted as a guarantor of last resort in case of the bankruptcy of a money changer and in some instances of innkeepers. Considering the number of changers and hostellers whose specializations complemented each other, this made Bruges one of the most successful solvers of the

[126] Murray, *Bruges*, pp. 170–5.

drawbacks of medieval monetary systems in Europe.[127] Yet however troubled the money supply, the real transformation of the exchange business came with the integration of accounts held at the Exchange into the broader commercial world of Bruges. Crucial to this were not only the bank accounts of the changers, but also the vast sums amassed by Bruges hostellers, which came from their customers, partners and other clients, but often circulated through the accounts they held with the money changers. This massive pool of capital was made available for the great variety of investment opportunities presented by the Bruges market, opportunities that included investment in wool imports, cloth production, cloth imports, commercial real estate, tax farming and trade in precious metals, to name but a few. The reach of this payment/financial system extended considerably beyond Bruges, either through cooperative accounts with money changers and hostellers in other cities – Antwerp and Ghent were prominent – or by providing a payment vehicle for foreign merchants who could swap their account balances for trade goods anywhere in the trading sphere of merchants who visited the Bruges market.[128]

Even this remarkably elegant system to soften the inefficiencies of medieval coin did not exhaust the significance of Bruges as a banking city. For Bruges, by hosting permanent communities of foreign merchants within its walls, also served thereby as a node where a variety of credit/payment systems intersected. Bruges in effect became an essential collecting point for the credits accumulated by trade in spices, wool, textiles and other commodities, from where they could be remitted to another banking place or traded in furtherance of some other business deal. Bruges was the first northern international banking centre in European history and it retained that role even after it was surpassed by Antwerp. Italian merchants, especially those from Florence and Lucca, were specialists in long-distance remittances and finance through the devices of the multi-branch trading company and the bill of exchange. The bill served to transfer balances from branch to branch, or company to company, and it did so in a form that supplied a need for short-term credit without violating usury prohibitions. The papacy was an important customer of this system through Bruges, as remittances from the Scandinavian and Polish churches were brought to Bruges as bullion and sent via bills of exchange on to Rome or Avignon. Italian companies specializing in the spice trade also remitted a good deal

[127] P. Spufford, *Money and its Use in Medieval Europe* (Cambridge, 1988), pp. 370–9; J. H. A. Munro, 'Deflation and the Petty Coinage Problem in the Late Medieval Economy: The Case of Flanders, 1334–1484', *Explorations in Economic History*, 25 (1988), 387–423.

[128] E.g. Murray, *Bruges*, pp. 210–15; Greve, 'Brokerage and Trade'.

of money either to Italy or Barcelona as well as English wool acquired in Calais and trans-shipped through Bruges.[129]

The most obvious and long-standing trade/credit network through Bruges was with England. It was made possible by two factors. The first was the domination of the export of English wool by Italian companies as well as the import of spices from the Mediterranean, both commodities intersecting in Bruges. With London as the predominant urban market in England by the mid fourteenth century, it was London grocers who bought up the credits owed to English wool producers in Bruges to turn around and purchase spices (including dyestuffs and alum) on the Bruges market. All this was effected through book transfers on the accounts of Bruges money changers and innkeepers. A secondary English market through Bruges existed in the north of England through York, though it gradually declined in importance by the fifteenth century.[130] The third and final example of a credit/payment network was that of the German Hanse, which made Bruges a *Kontor*, or headquarters, for their entire trading operation in northwest Europe. Hanse merchants were intensely involved with Bruges innkeepers in particular as partners and factors, which often resulted in a Bruges innkeeper acting as the sedentary partner in joint trading ventures with Hanse merchants. This often resulted in payments effected in far-off corners of the Hanse trading realm by means of signing over balances held in Bruges via charter or other promissory note. These could be redeemed upon presentation to the Bruges innkeeper or money changer in question.[131]

Indices of decline for the Bruges financial system are much more difficult to detect than are those of growth. Overall numbers of changers do not offer firm evidence because the transition to money changing as banking had trimmed their number before 1305. The decline of Bruges as a commercial centre also does not coincide with indications of decline in money changing, for the city was still thriving until c.1490 when a combination of politics and economic change struck with disabling force. Yet if we consider the success of money changing to be the result of a series of contingent, changeable advantages – an economic ecology, if you will – then we are able to provide at least a plausible hypothesis until further research can add to our rather meagre data. One important ecological change to note was the new monetary regime launched by the Burgundian dukes after 1390. In December 1389, Philip the Bold began this new era with a drastic strengthening of the silver coinage,

[129] Nicholas, 'English Trade'.

[130] J. Kermode, *Medieval Merchants: York, Beverley and Hull in the Later Middle Ages* (Cambridge, 2002).

[131] Murray, *Bruges*, pp. 247–57.

increasing its bullion content by 32 per cent, and ordering a general recoinage. For the remainder of his reign and that of his successor, gold and silver bullion became tools in a trade war with the English, in which money changers were forced to become instruments of ducal policy in the control and inspection of coins used in trade. They were also subject to more and tighter oversight by ducal officials, who confiscated illicit coins and imposed fines on miscreant money changers far more often than had their predecessors. These changes struck a double blow to the money changing business both by reducing or eliminating the ability to profit by arbitrage, and by increasing the costs of oversight of the coinage imposed by the government.[132]

Official hostility must have also contributed to troubles with money changing, beginning with a ducal ordinance of 1399, which forbade the payment of bills of exchange by assignment on an account with a money changer and ending in 1489 with the prohibition of all banking activity. Yet the most serious change that undermined the foundation of money changing probably came from within Bruges and not without. The organization of the Bruges Bourse is still a murky and little-known history. Its origins lay with the city's hostellers and their efforts to control and profit from their foreign merchant guests and business partners. As we have seen in Chapter 5, some of these foreign merchants established their own 'nation houses' in the vicinity of the square where the old Van der Beurze Inn stood. Early descriptions of the square as a meeting place for merchants point out its accessibility and use as a forum for information exchange, including financial information published by the Burgundian government. But the Bourse itself came to transcend these origins by becoming more than a trading venue of information and contracts, becoming something resembling a capital market at some point in the fifteenth century. Here, too, the money changers offer a window into important changes in the overall urban economy. Money changers certainly declined in number, even while the Bruges economy continued to flourish, so on the one hand 'decline' might suitably describe this stage in money changing's history. On the other hand, however, the profession seems to have bifurcated, with some changers remaining at the traditional site near the central market, while a small contingent migrated to the Bourse square. Those who moved called themselves 'changers and bankers', the first linkage of those terms in the history of the city. Clearly, these changers differed from the traditional and not only in their spatial link to the developing Bourse.[133]

[132] De Roover, *Money, Banking and Credit*, pp. 339–41.

[133] Marechal, *Bijdrage*, p. 126; Marechal, *Geschiedenis van de Brugse Beurs*, pp. 37–42.

Another aspect for future research is to investigate the loss of money changing's 'nodal' role in the Bruges economy. A public Bourse for trading in bills of exchange and other payment instruments may have deprived the changers of their key role as the gatekeepers of all the payment systems that converged in Bruges. Thus instead of tapping into the Italian exchange system via one's hosteller and his inn house or retained money changer, a merchant needed only to frequent the Bourse square during business hours. Recent research into the account books left by the broker/hosteller Wouter Ameyde shows that the financial cooperation of changers and brokers continued into the sixteenth century. At least two money changers show up in these records, though we do not know if these changers had their offices in the traditional location on the Wisselbrug (Exchange Bridge) by the New Cloth Hall, or had migrated northward to the Bourse square.[134]

The Institutional Framework of Socio-Economic Life: Town Government and Craft Guilds

During a major revolt in 1488,[135] the complaints formulated by the Great Council of Bruges (which included the deans of the city's fifty-four craft guilds) reveal a discourse, similar to the views expressed by the poet and master mason Anthonis de Roovere cited at the beginning of this chapter, that artisans and commercial elites shared a common interest in sustaining a favourable climate for investment.[136] For the city-dweller the idea of a 'free market' was a market regulated by privileged institutions and incorporated groups describing themselves as 'free' (*vry*). Apart from those specifically involved in the organization of international commerce and finance, the institutions that organized and oversaw markets and production included the princely and city governments and the guilds. But less formal institutions such as the family and the household also played a crucial role in economic production. The count of Flanders defended the city's welfare and guaranteed peace and safety on land and at sea. The prince's role was to secure a stable climate of investment in industry and trade, including military, political, legal, fiscal and monetary stability. His role in economic life was to keep down what theorists of 'New Institutional Economics' or

[134] Verbist, 'Traditie', pp. 97–102.

[135] See Chapter 6.

[136] J. Dumolyn, '"Our Land is Only Founded on Trade and Industry": Economic Discourses in Fifteenth-Century Bruges', *JMH*, 36 (2010), 374–89.

'Transaction Cost Economics' call 'policing and enforcement costs', and to limit factors of uncertainty for investors.[137] Harmonious relations with the nations of foreign merchants and respect for their privileges, and protection of the city's own staple rights, depended upon his policies. Contracts had to be enforced and monetary stability maintained within a volatile international market. A coherent study of the economic policy of the Bruges city authorities and initiatives in creating market infrastructure and legal security for merchants is still lacking, but we know that the Bruges aldermen handled commercial disputes if these could not be settled by arbitration within the nations or with the help of their brokers and hostellers.[138] The city government was also active in ensuring a business infrastructure: port and market, halls, canals and dykes.[139]

Immediately under the level of the urban government, the most crucial institution for regulating manufacture and markets was the craft guild. From the successful revolution of 1302, guilds had become essential in defining the social, economic, political and even some of the cultural relations in the city. The range of craft guild activities increased considerably during the fourteenth century. As we have seen, by 1280 textile workers had already participated in meetings in which wages and other matters were discussed; but in addition to advising on industrial and commercial regulations, they soon acquired their own financial organizations (often serving charitable purposes among guild members), and they served in the city militia. Apart from delegating representatives to the bench of aldermen and councillors, the boards of the guilds also served as *smalle wetten* ('small courts of law') to judge on infringements of production and marketing regulation. Guild wardens, usually called the deans (*deken*) and the 'finders' (*vinders*, 'the men who find a judgment'), were responsible for punishing violations of their privileges (*keuren*). Guilds were institutions that enforced and guaranteed quality standards in manufacture and

137 J. Dumolyn and B. Lambert, 'Cities of Commerce, Cities of Constraints: International Trade, Government Institutions and the Law of Commerce in Later Medieval Bruges and the Burgundian State', *Low Countries Journal of Social and Economic History*, 11 (2014), 89–102; P. Stabel, 'Economic Development, Urbanisation and Political Organisation in the Late Medieval Southern Low Countries', in P. Bernholz, M. E. Streit and R. Vaubel (eds.), *Political Competition, Innovation and Growth: A Historical Analysis* (Berlin, 1998), pp. 183–204.

138 Stabel, 'De gewenste vreemdeling', pp. 214–15.

139 Hunt and Murray, *History of Business*, p. 161. There is an overview of the literature on infrastructure of trade in Ryckaert, *Historische stedenatlas*, pp. 160–73. There are few recent references of the legal aspects of trade in medieval Bruges and a balanced view is still lacking. Gelderblom, *Cities of Commerce*, rightly focuses on the importance of the urban court but neglects other institutional levels, while Murray, *Bruges*, primarily discusses the role of hostellers.

retail: they controlled the quality of raw materials, tools and finished products; they inspected weights and measures and oversaw techniques and methods of production. By reducing 'search and information costs' for entrepreneurs and consumers, they lowered information asymmetries in market-places while contributing to (or in some cases hampering) innovation and productive efficiency.[140] As interest groups they protected their members to a degree from exploitation by merchant elites; managed conflict and tension between competing guild members; and saw to it that hours and conditions of labour, membership obligations and monopoly regulations were respected.[141]

After 1304 the guilds became an integrated part of the urban body politic. Their primary concerns were obviously economic policies. Although guilds were usually at the centre of popular revolts, in most periods they collaborated with the city council in promoting a favourable business climate. In relation to their specific trade, some of them could also elect members who served as wardens in urban commissions overseeing different markets (spices, mercery, soap or poultry) or exercising quality control (for example the wardens of the 'Rame' or tenter frames for cloth finishing). De facto or de iure, guilds also operated as consultative bodies, especially for economic policy and in financial or fiscal matters. They sometimes had the power to reject new taxes or to present petitions to the city government to change policy.[142] The urban and guild authorities were jointly responsible for the specific functioning of the industrial process, industrial and market relations (including financial transactions), the reduction of bargaining costs, the basic infrastructure for transport and market space, price regulation, weights and measures and similar competences that influenced the price mechanisms, and the general performance of the Bruges market. This quality control and the guaranteed 'quality label' it produced was a prerequisite for functioning markets and stable incomes for small commodity producers, providing a basis

[140] Stabel, 'Guilds in Late Medieval Flanders', pp. 197–8. For a more updated interpretation of guild agency in late medieval Bruges, see P. Stabel, *Capital of Fashion*, forthcoming.

[141] S. R. Epstein, 'Craft Guilds, Apprenticeship and Technological Change in Pre-Industrial Europe', *Journal of Economic History*, 58 (1998), 684–713; S. R. Epstein and M. Prak (eds.), *Guilds, Innovation, and the European Economy, 1400–1800* (Cambridge, 2008); B. de Munck, S. L. Kaplan and H. Soly (eds.), *Learning on the Shop Floor: Historical Perspectives on Apprenticeship* (New York, 2007).

[142] Vermaut, 'De textielnijverheid', vol. II, pp. 337–64; J. Dumolyn, 'De Brugse ambachtsbesturen tijdens de late middeleeuwen: enkele institutionele en rechtshistorische aspecten', *HGG*, 147 (2010), 309–27; J. Dumolyn, 'Guild Politics and Political Guilds in Fourteenth-Century Flanders', in J. Dumolyn, J. Haemers, H. R. Oliva Herrer et al. (eds.) *The Voices of the People in Late Medieval Europe: Communication and Popular Politics* (Turnhout, 2014), pp. 15–48.

for high fiscal revenues and therefore for the welfare of the whole urban community.[143]

Yet as Anthonis de Roovere also noted, apart from these areas of common effort, guildsmen had interests that diverged from those of the commercial elites. In most periods these elites still dominated the city government, even if artisans were represented among the aldermen and councillors. The most influential and well-off artisans were usually the 'small commodity producers': petty masters who possessed their own means of production but employed few labourers. They were a group distinct from the merchant class, other guilds and their own wage workers.[144] Indeed, the diversity and internal contradictions within corporately organized labour should caution us against generalizing about their potential for 'class solidarity'.[145] A retailer had different interests from a textile worker manufacturing for export and a master entrepreneur and his family from his workers. But interests could also differ among the workers: journeymen were skilled assistants, but there were also younger apprentices and even unskilled assistants, men or women. An artisan from a luxury craft would generally possess far more capital than a minor shoemaker or tailor, but some of the industrial crafts allowed concentration of capital, as well as vertical and horizontal industrial relations among masters, journeymen and even people outside the guild. Systems of subcontracting were ubiquitous. In contrast to its egalitarian ideals, the corporate system therefore did not exclude internal hierarchies and differences of class and status, while it also partly excluded 'outsiders' such as unskilled workers and increasingly from the 1300s women too. But in spite of these social inequalities between artisans, they all shared a concern to make a decent livelihood in return for their 'honest labour'. Their ideological language centered on the value of their skilled labour, fundamentally expressed as the desire of a *pater familias* to maintain himself, his family and his place in society. Even outside the guild they upheld this identity of the hard-working craftsman and a subject loyal to the prince.[146]

143 Epstein, 'Craft Guilds'; for the Low Countries, see C. Lis and H. Soly (eds.), *Werelden van verschil: Ambachtsgilden in de Lage Landen* (Brussels, 1997); and M. Prak (ed.), *Craft Guilds in the Early Modern Low Countries: Work, Power, and Representation* (Aldershot, 2006).

144 R. S. Duplessis and M. C. Howell, 'Reconsidering the Early Modern Urban Economy: The Cases of Leiden and Lille', *Past and Present*, 94 (1982), 49–84.

145 C. Lis and H. Soly, *Worthy Efforts: Attitudes to Work and Workers in Pre-Industrial Europe* (Boston, 2012), p. 327.

146 A. De Meyer, '"Tot synder goeden fame ende name". De "self-fashioning" van Mechelse en Brugse stedelingen in de laatmiddeleeuwse en vroegmoderne genadebrieven', unpublished PhD thesis, University of Antwerp (Antwerp, 2014).

The Institutional Framework of Socio-Economic Life: Households and Families

The social position of artisans cannot be understood without also considering family and household structures, age and gender. A guild master was usually a married householder who stood in a patriarchal relationship to the other household members, not only his wife and children but also his apprentices, who started learning their trade between the ages of eight and fifteen. They acquired their skills on the shop floor and lived in the household of their masters, aspiring to reach the master's position.[147] Journeymen remained in a liminal state, working as wage labourers for their masters and hoping to start a workshop of their own, which many never achieved. Their level of income depended on their skill, and on the business structure and the relation between demand and supply of skill in each of the economic sectors.[148]

The nuclear family generally became a common feature of northwestern Europe in the thirteenth and fourteenth centuries, and Bruges seems to match this pattern.[149] In Flemish towns, the nuclear family gradually became more important than extended family networks. For the artisanal class it was a basic economic institution that aimed at providing subsistence and it became closely intertwined with small commodity production itself. For the great majority of the urban population, marriage usually meant setting up a separate household in the economic sense as well (the so-called 'neolocality'). The household, often referred to as *mesniede* in the Bruges sources, was in many cases also the physical site of the business

[147] P. J. P. Goldberg, 'Masters and Men in Later Medieval England', in D. M. Hadley (ed.), *Masculinity in Medieval Europe* (London and New York, 1999), pp. 56–70; on apprentices in the Low Countries, see B. de Munck, 'Corpses, Live Models, and Nature: Assessing Skills and Knowledge before the Industrial Revolution (Case: Antwerp)', *Technology and Culture*, 51 (2010), 332–56 (at 337); and B. de Munck, 'From Brotherhood Community to Civil Society? Apprentices between Guild, Household and the Freedom of Contract in Early Modern Antwerp', *Social History*, 35 (2010), 1–20 (at 2).

[148] On the success rate of Bruges apprentices and journeymen, see P. Stabel, 'Social Mobility and Apprenticeship in Late Medieval Flanders', in De Munck, Kaplan and Soly (eds.), *Learning on the Shop Floor*, pp. 158–78. On journeymen, see generally J. Dambruyne, 'Journeymen, Social Rise and the Urban Labour Market in the Southern Netherlands during the Transformation from the Middle Ages to the Early Modern Period', in N. Peeters (ed.), *Invisible Hands? The Role and Status of the Painters' Journeymen in the Low Countries, c.1450–c.1650* (Leuven, 2007), pp. 105–32; and C. Lis and H. Soly, 'An Irresistible Phalanx: Journeymen Associations in Western Europe, 1300–1800', in C. Lis, J. Lucassen and H. Soly (eds.), *Before the Unions: Wage Earners and Collective Action in Europe, 1300–1850* (Cambridge, 1994), pp. 31–4.

[149] Stabel, 'Working Alone'.

of an artisan or retailer. Artisanal *mesnieden*, possibly including domestic servants and apprentices, served as the basic production units. All family members beyond early childhood were integrated in the process. All shared in its earnings, though not everyone to the same degree. The Flemish urban guild economy was fundamentally based on these family units under the supervision and control of the head of the household. As a basic unit of production, the patriarchal household set out the limits for women's participation in skilled labour. Households also developed common strategies for consumption. And the artisanal household provided the setting for training and disciplining youths who had not been born into the family. Working as an apprentice was an experience common among a great number of Flemish children. Elite families but also many artisan households employed young male servants or maids for domestic work. We lack figures for Bruges; but in late medieval Ypres, up to 10 per cent of the population worked as domestic (usually living-in) servants and almost 60 per cent of these were women. As Ypres was a textile city with many proleterianized workers, percentages of servants in commercial Bruges may have been considerably higher.[150]

As the research stands, it seems that in a city like fifteenth-century Bruges an average non-elite couple married only at about the age of twenty-five, when they had become or were becoming financially independent from their parents or guardians. They were of roughly equal age and social class, or even in the same kind of trade. For upper-class families, for whom more was at stake symbolically and materially, the male age of marriage might have been higher and the age gap with women more important (though empirical studies on this are lacking). Urban families in Flanders were on average smaller than those in the countryside.[151] An urban-living parent was survived perhaps by only two or three children, though by more among elite and better nourished families. In Bruges, however, there was also a large group of singles, including young servant men and women,

150 Stabel, 'Working Alone'. See also J. De Groot, 'Zorgen voor later? De betekenis van de dienstperiode voor jonge vrouwen in het laatmiddeleeuwse Gent herbekeken', *Stadsgeschiedenis*, 6 (2011), pp. 1–15; P. Hoppenbrouwers, 'Comparing Medieval Households from a Legal Perspective', in M. Carlier and T. Soens (eds.), *The Household in Late Medieval Cities: Italy and Northwestern Europe Compared* (Leuven and Apeldoorn, 2001), p. 53; M. C. Howell, 'The Social Logic of the Marital Household', in Carlier and Soens (eds.), *The Household*, pp. 187–202; M. C. Howell, *Women, Production and Patriarchy in Late Medieval Cities* (Chicago, IL, 1986), pp. 27–30; D. Nicholas, 'Child and Adolescent Labour in the Late Medieval City: A Flemish Model in Regional Perspective', *English Historical Review*, 110 (1995), 1103–31.

151 Stabel, *De kleine stad*, pp. 72–5; and Stabel, *Dwarfs among Giants*, pp. 122–5.

widows and widowers, clerics and people without the means to support a family. Widowed men and women usually remarried, and among them age differences were sometimes more marked (often fifteen to twenty years). Widows from the middle or upper classes attracted new husbands by providing assets, business experience and economic networks, enabling them to maintain their deceased husband's social position. Remarriage even to a guild member was, however, often regarded with suspicion in urban society, certainly if a journeyman or, worse, an apprentice were involved.[152]

We have no figures for Bruges, but sex ratios in other cities of the Low Countries from the sixteenth century show a market surplus of women, probably because more female than male immigrants settled to find employment as domestic servants or in low-wage and low status occupations in textile manufacture or petty retail.[153] Aside from upper-class families who aspired to form noble-like lineages and invest in feudal property, extended families seem to have had little direct influence on the lives of Bruges citizens. However, kin and friends (in Middle Dutch *vrienden ende maghen* or in French *parens et amis*), but also neighbours, played a crucial role by supporting orphans, bastard children and the elderly, by protecting the family possessions in times of crisis or by assisting family members who ran into juridical trouble. The extended family had an important legal role in the guardianship of orphans by keeping in check the interests of the surviving parent and defending those of the child. Wider family networks would still maintain some influence in the later Middle Ages, even though the nuclear family had become the basic structure of organization.[154] Children were taken care of, but not all of them were born in wedlock. Calculations based on orphanage registers (which underrepresent the lower social groups) suggest more than 8 per cent of Bruges families included illegitimate children. These were often taken care of by their kin, and because they could not inherit from their father without a difficult procedure of formal recognition, they received gifts as their inheritance.[155]

152 Examples in Stabel, *Capital of Fashion*, forthcoming.

153 Stabel, 'Working Alone'.

154 J. Hajnal, 'European Marriage Patterns in Perspective', in D. V. Glass and D. E. C. Eversley (eds.), *Population in History* (London, 1967), pp. 101–43; M. Carlier, 'Solidariteit of sociale controle? De rol van vrienden en magen en buren in een middeleeuwse stad', in M. Carlier, A. Greve, W. Prevenier et al. (eds.), *Hart en marge in de laat-middeleeuwse stedelijke maatschappij* (Leuven, 1997), pp. 71–91; M. Danneel, 'Vrienden en magen in de bronnen van de laat-middeleeuwse Brugse weeskamer', *HKZM*, 36 (1982), 33–9; Howell, 'Social Logic', pp. 193–4; Simons, *Cities of Ladies*, pp. 7–8.

155 Carlier, *Kinderen*, p. 47.

The role of women in later medieval Bruges still awaits a thorough study. Relative to many other European regions and certainly to Italian cities, legal traditions in Flanders show that Flemish women enjoyed a favourable position in society. They probably possessed greater autonomy in matters of private law such as inheritance, property rights, legal guardianship and commercial capacity. Husbands acted as the legal guardians over their wives and minor children, but the laws of succession decreed that sons and daughters inherited equal shares of their parents' property. Legally, both parents, not just the father, had authority over their children. Movable or semi-movable goods mostly belonged to households in their entirety but immovables, typically land, often remained the individual property of a spouse. However, property would be transmitted in the patrilineal line in the end, even if community property resided with the conjugal household while the marriage lasted. This tendency increased towards the end of the Middle Ages, especially among higher-status families. Women could not, of course, hold political or guild offices, though they were sometimes active in credit activities and property management. In general, women enjoyed more economic rights outside the guild system, either as manual workers or as entrepreneurs. Inside the guild system their role was limited by the status of their husbands. Girls do not appear as apprentices in the Bruges craft guilds, although outside the system many women, married or not, were involved in retail or manufacture. Strangely, women seem to have had more freedom of movement in high-status commerce than in low-status but guild-associated retail. Beguines and especially their headmistresses, nuns, women in the tertiary orders, hospital sisters and certainly noblewomen also held prestige and authority. Many of them were active professionally, even in sectors that were guild organized. This often led to friction with the guilds.[156] In short, though women in Flemish cities still held a subordinate position in society, they were not totally excluded from the public sphere, and as will be seen below, they also played a key role in economic life.[157]

[156] Examples in N. Mazeure and P. Stabel, 'Zusters in getouw, ambachten in verweer: Een conflict over kloosterarbeid in Brugge en Sluis in de 15de eeuw', *Bijdragen tot de Geschiedenis*, 87 (2004), 107–25.

[157] Key references on women in medieval Flanders and Bruges in particular include Murray, *Bruges*, pp. 300–43; M. Danneel, 'Weduwen en wezen in de late Middeleeuwen: Een juridische en sociografische benadering vanuit het Brugse voorbeeld', 2 vols., unpublished MA thesis, Ghent University, (Ghent, 1981); M. Danneel, *Weduwen en wezen in het laatmiddeleeuwse Gent* (Leuven, 1996); S. Hutton, *Women and Economic Activities in Late Medieval Ghent* (New York, 2011); Howell, *Women, Production and Patriarchy*; M. C. Howell, *The Marriage Exchange: Property, Social Place, and Gender in Cities of the Low Countries, 1300–1550* (Chicago, IL, 1998); E. Bousmar, 'Neither Equality nor Radical Oppression: The Elasticity of Women's Roles in the Late Medieval Low Countries', in E. E. Kittell and M.A. Suydam (eds.),

Demographic Decline?

While household size (and therefore the age of marriage and level of fertility) had a significant impact on population levels, the most crucial demographic factor in the late medieval period was mortality. Following a period when neo-Malthusian pressures were at their strongest – the heavy blows dealt by the dearth of 1315–17 in cities like Bruges and Ypres were symptomatic of this – plague struck Europe from 1348. One-third of the population in many places, half in some, suddenly died. The European economy entered a deep crisis. Though it is hard to calculate 'normal' death rates, it seems that in the fifteenth century the average urban mortality rate was about 3.4 to 4.5 per cent per year (with child mortality reaching levels of 6 per cent). In the countryside this was slightly lower with 3.3 to 3.8 per cent per year.[158] During the Black Death, which arrived in Bruges shortly before August 1349 and lasted until 1351, this rate possibly reached about 30 per cent or more.[159] As elsewhere in Europe, the initial outbreak of the plague caused deep emotional trauma. It inspired religious movements, sometimes of a quasi-heretical nature. In 1349, the chronicle of Gilles li Muisis from Tournai recorded no fewer than 650 flagellants arriving from Bruges. At first, the religious and secular authorities left them alone, though persecution began when the movement lost momentum. But the social and economic consequences in the long run were even more crucial. After the Black Death recovery proved difficult when successive epidemics raged at regular intervals and a deflationary spiral took hold as demand declined, particularly for agricultural products. In Bruges, further outbreaks of epidemic disease occurred in 1360–1, 1368–9, 1399–1400, 1438–9, 1456–9

The Texture of Society: Medieval Women in the Southern Low Countries (New York, 2004), pp. 109–23.

[158] The crude urban death rates were calculated for the smaller towns of Hulst and Kortrijk: see Stabel, *De kleine stad*, pp. 54–62; P. Stabel, 'Mourir au quotidien: Réalités démographiques et sociales de la mort au Moyen Âge', in S. Balace and A. De Poorter (eds.), *Entre paradis et enfer: Mourir au Moyen Âge* (Brussels, 2010) pp. 18–29. For the rural death rates for the region of Oudenaarde, see E. Thoen and I. Devos, 'Pest in de Zuidelijke Nederlanden tijdens de middeleeuwen en de moderne tijden: Een status quaestionis over de ziekte in haar sociaal-economische context', in *De pest in de Nederlanden: Medisch-historische beschouwingen 650 jaar na de Zwarte Dood* (Brussels, 1999), pp. 19–43.

[159] According to the recent research by J. Vandeburie, 'De Zwarte Dood te Brugge: Een status quaestionis en enkele nieuwe beschouwingen', *HGG*, 147 (2010), 269–308 (at 292–3). Earlier estimates were more optimistic and estimated numbers between 10 and 15 per cent, e.g. W. Blockmans, 'The Social and Economic Effects of Plague in the Low Countries, 1349–1500', *BTFG*, 58 (1980), 833–63; G. Maréchal, 'De zwarte dood te Brugge (1349–1351)', *Biekorf*, 80 (1980), 377–92.

and 1481–5. Their demographic impact still has to be determined.[160] In the meantime, chronic warfare and rising transaction costs also hit European trade. When all these blights coincided, the short-term impact on the urban economy was devastating. During the epidemic in 1400–1 and especially the one in 1438–9 (when disease followed a revolt, economic blockade and bad harvests), at least 20 per cent of the population may have been lost on both occasions.[161]

The great later medieval crisis was long-lasting and structural but it was triggered by population decline. However, this also meant that equilibria in society changed as wealth shifted relatively from landowners and farmers towards manufacturers and traders of consumer goods. Death redistributed income, and per capita income seems to have grown in some areas: real wages rose and income from investment in trade and crafts was stimulated. There were winners and losers. Few historians currently would argue that the Black Death did not affect the densely urbanized Low Countries, and even fewer would claim that subsequent epidemics bypassed the region. But many would agree that the first wave of plague did not completely disrupt the region's economy, that the southern principalities of Flanders and Brabant were remarkably resilient throughout the crisis, and that the northern areas, like Holland or the Campine region, even experienced growth. What is more, in contrast to Italy, the urban system did not collapse; wage increases, as we shall see below, were less sharp than in other European regions like England or Italy (and real wages around 1300 may even have been higher than after the Black Death);[162] and most of all, many cities of the Low Countries, despite the crisis of their leading industry, were able to alter their economic infrastructure. Bruges, as the main trading hub, would lead this trend.

In Chapter 3, we proposed a minimum figure of 46,000 inhabitants in Bruges for the 1330s (and a recalibrated figure of perhaps even 57,000 when non-guild and non-bourgeois households are added). These figures rely on the draft lists of the city militia. A second more or less reliable assessment of the Bruges population dates only from the late fourteenth century, four decades after the outbreak of the Black Death. Unlike the

160 Murray, *Bruges*, p. 106; W. Blockmans, G. Pieters, W. Prevenier et al., 'Tussen crisis en welvaart: Sociale veranderingen, 1300–1500', in *Algemene Geschiedenis der Nederlanden*, vol. IV (Haarlem, 1980), pp. 42–86 (at 56, 59).

161 Blockmans, 'Social and Economic Effects of Plague'.

162 E. Thoen and T. Soens, 'The Family or the Farm: A Sophie's Choice? The Late Medieval Crisis in Flanders', in J. Drendel (ed.), *Crisis in the Later Middle Ages: Beyond the Postan–Duby Paradigm* (Turnhout, 2015), pp. 195–224.

Table 6.1 *Population estimates of Bruges and incoming citizens, 1330–1530*

Minimum assessments based on guild-organized inhabitants

	Population estimates	New citizens (yearly average)
1330–50	46,000	145
1350–70		112
1370–90		94
1390–1410	37,000	68
1410–30		196
1430–50	35,000 (before plague) 25,000 (shortly after plague)	183
1450–70		162
1470–90	40,000	114
1490–1510		59
1510–30	35,000	51

figures for the 1330s, these figures are calculated from tax lists for three of the city's six sections.[163] Including groups enjoying tax immunity, the population can be estimated at about 37,000, suggesting only a slight population decline after the Black Death.[164] The first wave of plague seems not to have seriously affected the Low Countries cities long term, but the second wave in the 1360s hit the region hard.[165] Combined with the general economic crisis in Flanders during and after the revolt of 1379–85, a decline of about 20 per cent is likely, but the population of the large cities throughout the county remained more or less stable. This stability hides the spikes of crisis mortality; but it shows that despite the general European crisis and the crisis of woollen cloth manufacture (the main source of urban employment in Flanders, Brabant and Artois), cities succeeded in remaining attractive for newcomers, who to some extent replenished the population.[166]

Trends in the number of new citizens confirm this assessment. Indeed the number of newcomers is a good way to investigate, indirectly, the

[163] Numbers based upon the data in I. De Meyer and W. Vanderpijpen, *Studiën betreffende de sociale strukturen te Brugge, Kortrijk en Gent in de 14e en 15e eeuw*, vol. II: *Tabellen* (Heule, 1972).

[164] Heidi Deneweth has argued that this estimate is probably too optimistic and a population of about 32,000 should be considered: 'Een demografische knoop ontward? Brugse bevolkingscijfers voor de vroegmoderne tijd', *HGG*, 147 (2010), 3–48.

[165] Blockmans, 'Social and Economic Effects of Plague'.

[166] Stabel, 'Composition et recompositions des réseaux urbains'.

economic cycles of medieval cities. Their demography was characterized by the 'urban graveyard effect'. Even in normal years, cities could only retain their size if newcomers arrived to compensate for losses. The number of unskilled immigrants from the countryside, and specialized artisans from further afield, indicates a city's attractiveness – though movement from the countryside could also mean that opportunities there were declining or population levels there were growing unsustainably. Immigration to Bruges can be partially traced through the *poortersboeken* (the matriculation lists in which new burghers were registered). Many newcomers went unrecorded in the registers: beggars, thieves, prostitutes or the destitute and seasonal wage workers seeking jobs as unskilled workers, may not have had the money to buy burghership, or had less to gain from obtaining it. But burghership was of interest to those wishing to benefit from the economic structures of guilds and commerce. Skilled workers wanting to enter a craft guild were obliged to become burghers. Some sectors, like the ready-made clothing industry, stand out in attracting skilled labour.[167]

In normal years, from the 1330s, there were more than 100 officially registered immigrants in Bruges. Out of a total of 4,836 new burghers arriving during the fourteenth century, the origins of 2,140 are known: 1,897, almost 40 per cent, were Flemish, and almost half of them came from the Liberty of Bruges; 207 came from the northern Low Countries and only 36 came from 'abroad'.[168] Numbers from the places where Bruges seemed to attract skilled craftsmen before the Black Death (many of these probably textile workers) dropped sharply in the 1350s. Once the first demographic shock had passed, numbers recovered, despite plague epidemics in the 1360s. In the following decades immigration of skilled artisans remained high with about 120 to 150 newcomers each year. In the 1380s the tide turned again. Disease, grain shortages and political turmoil caused a sharp decline of new citizens and only from the 1400s were there signs of improvement, modest at first (since a severe plague raged in Flanders in 1405), but later the annual immigration of skilled labour gradually rose to a medieval peak of more than 230 in the 1420s and 1440s. After the crisis of 1436–40 many new skilled workers were attracted by the cheaper tariffs allowed by the Burgundian duke.[169]

In the 1430s the total population of Bruges can again be reconstructed from the draft list for the city militia. It is also possible to combine this data with a 1440–1 tax list for one of the city's six sections, St John's.[170] This period

[167] Murray, *Bruges*, pp. 107–10; Thoen, 'Immigration to Bruges'; Boogaart, *Ethnogeography*, pp. 180–2.

[168] Van Houtte, *De geschiedenis van Brugge*, pp. 156–7.

[169] Thoen, 'Immigration to Bruges'.

[170] Dumolyn, 'Population', pp. 58–62.

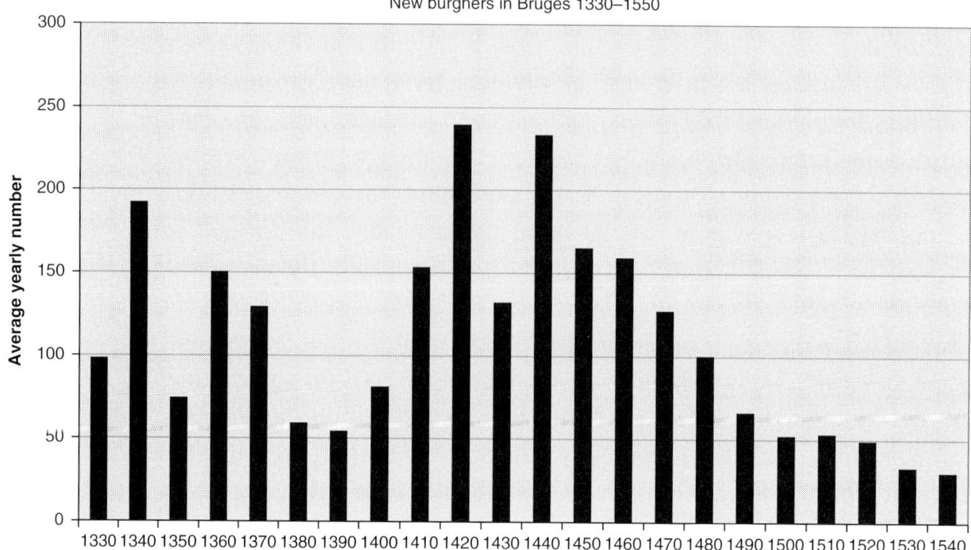

Figure 6.1 New burghers in Bruges, 1330–1540
Source: matriculation lists of new citizens[171]

may be atypical compared with the earlier ones. Bruges was in revolt against the duke. Plague and grain shortages ravaged the city. Standards of living were hit hard, possibly diminishing the city's attractiveness for newcomers. An extrapolation based on St John's section records suggests a mere 22,000 to 28,000 inhabitants. In the short term, plague and revolt perhaps reduced the population by one-third, so before the revolt, the total population in the 1430s may have been between 30,000 and 37,000.[172] As these figures are not just based on the city militia, since non-guild members with enough means were listed, they do not need to be adjusted; though as the source is fiscal, it excludes the very poor and inhabitants not obliged to pay the tax. But despite these caveats, the general impression remains that population decline, even before the revolt of 1436, was setting in. Whether this decline, as yet modest, was linked to general economic decline or whether the downturn of cloth manufacture reduced the need for a large labour force, needs to be investigated. But the rise of immigration figures in the 1440s demonstrates the continuing vitality of the Bruges economy. The deliberate lowering of entrance fees was a success and even occupational groups who

[171] The data are based on the entries in the city accounts: Jamees, *Brugse poorters*; and on the matriculation lists in Parmentier, *Indices*.

[172] Deneweth, 'Een demografische knoop ontward'.

had not wanted citizenship before were interested in acquiring it. After the peak of the 1440s, in the 1450s and 1460s immigration figures subsided, with yearly averages of between 160 and 170 new burghers. Surprisingly figures remained relatively high in the turmoil of the 1480s, but the last years of conflict with Maximilian (see Chapter 7) proved disastrous. The slow decline in immigration accelerated in the 1490s and Bruges would never recover: it dropped to an annual average of 50 in the early sixteenth century and fell further from the 1530s onwards.

For 1477, another population estimate, less reliable because it depends not on draft lists but on paid members of the Bruges militia in the city accounts (one in seven Bruges inhabitants can be assumed to have been enlisted), suggests a population between 38,000 and 47,000.[173] Only during the 1480s and early 1490s did the population of Bruges decline sharply, though there is little consensus over numbers. Van Uytven and Dambruyne suggested a figure then of about 30,000 inhabitants.[174] In the early 1490s, Bruges must have suffered particularly. Apparently, no fewer than 4,000 to 5,000 houses stood empty (equivalent to about 16,000 inhabitants). The city tried hard after 1492 to encourage citizens who had fled Bruges to return, and to attract newcomers by again lowering the entrance fee for new citizens.[175] But this time, the number of new citizens remained low and continued to decline afterwards. Bruges only partly recovered and was not repopulated with skilled artisans quite as it had been in the 1440s. When the population again reached about 35,000 inhabitants in the 1520s,[176] fewer than before had the status of 'burgher', and thus fewer were skilled or incorporated in a guild system.

Industrial Conversion in a Time of Crisis

So despite the late medieval crisis, the sources suggest that the population of Bruges remained relatively stable, recovering for a time even after 1440. The city's economic strength was a strong pull factor. Research on the

173 A. Janssens, 'Het Brugse bevolkingsaantal in 1477', in *Van middeleeuwen tot heden: Bladeren door Brugse kunst en geschiedenis* (Bruges, 1983), pp. 29–35.

174 Dumolyn, 'Population', p. 62.

175 Van Houtte, *De geschiedenis van Brugge*, p. 293; Deneweth, 'Een demografische knoop ontward', pp. 22–3.

176 J. Mertens, 'De bevolking van het Brugse Vrije rond 1520', in C. Vandenbroeke and W. Prevenier (eds.), *Demografische evoluties en gedragspatronen van de 9de tot de 20ste eeuw in de Nederlanden* (Ghent, 1977), pp. 145–66 (at 155); and Deneweth, 'Een demografische knoop ontward', pp. 24–6.

agrarian organization of coastal Flanders also indicates push factors. The structure of the rural economy in the polders of Flanders around Bruges, the city's natural source of semi-skilled and unskilled migrants,[177] changed dramatically during the late medieval crisis. The traditional small-scale peasant farms came under increasing pressure and were gradually absorbed by larger mid-scale holdings, often owned by city-dwellers and leased out to large-scale farmers using labourers to work their fields.[178] This change of the agrarian economy from smallholding to leaseholding may have caused particular migration patterns as labour became more mobile and seasonal. The cities probably profited from this development by becoming receptacles for agrarian labour, allowing them to maintain a downward pressure on unskilled or semi-skilled wages. It is probably no coincidence that despite a stagnating population, evidence for wages of building workers in Flanders articulates less upward pressure than it does for example in England.

The demographic resilience of Bruges and the high number of skilled craftsmen that continued to migrate to the city (particularly between 1410 and 1470) demonstrates its success and its attraction to newcomers. Despite the decline of its woollen cloth industry, Bruges merchants, entrepreneurs and craftsmen were able to develop new markets for their products, and from the 1430s the city would even become a leading art centre in Europe. The new counts, the dukes of Burgundy, did not hesitate to use the city as their most important market for luxuries and items of fashion.[179] Foreign merchants not only bought textiles manufactured in the Low Countries at the Bruges market, but also developed interests in some of the export consumer goods and luxuries from Bruges. And Bruges merchants began again to enter foreign markets, be it on a more limited scale than their thirteenth-century predecessors. In mid-fifteenth-century Rome, Bruges merchants were importing significant numbers of Bruges-manufactured hats, sleeves and other fashionable goods.[180] Most importantly, Bruges was able to cater for the rising middle groups of urban society of the Low Countries. Their purchasing power had not suffered from the medieval crisis; on the contrary, demand for industrial goods was rising because of higher standards of living. Furthermore, these groups were willing to invest in consumer goods,

177 Thoen, 'Immigration to Bruges'.

178 Soens, *De spade in de dijk?*

179 P. Stabel, 'For Mutual Benefit? Court and City in the Burgundian Low Countries', in S. Gunn and A. Janse (eds.), *The Court as a Stage: England and the Low Countries in the Later Middle Ages* (Woodbridge, 2006), pp. 101–17.

180 A. Esch, *Economia, cultura material ed arte nella Roma des Rinascimento: Studi sui registri doganali romani 1445–1485* (Rome, 2007).

dress and luxuries to display their newly acquired status. Despite its role as an international trading hub, Bruges' industrial growth in this period seems to have been primarily homespun. While elite demand triggered fashion cycles or attracted high-flying artisans to the city – not least the painters Jan van Eyck and Hans Memling – it was the demand generated by urban middle groups that allowed the necessary concentration of manufacture, capital and information flows for framing a 'knowledge economy'. The craft guilds, the associational organizations of the middle groups, proved crucial in adopting and adapting labour markets, information flows, product innovation and capital pooling.[181]

Paradoxically, the success of the Bruges economy was built on the disastrous failure to convert textile manufacture. Drastic changes in the organization of cloth production had occurred in the early fourteenth century. As entrepreneurs geared their textile production towards increasing specialization and higher quality (first in Ypres, Ghent, Douai in Flanders, then also Mechelen and Brussels in Brabant, and in secondary manufacturing towns like Kortrijk or Wervik), the skill required in the organization of production increased as well, and drapers (usually guild-organized master weavers, fullers, dyers, etc.) took over from the traditional merchants.[182] As we have seen, the appearance of this new middle class of small-scale entrepreneurs encouraged not only political aspirations and defiance of traditional urban elites, but also changes in patterns of consumption, whereby access was improved to particular goods, such as meat, dress, furniture and even luxuries. The result was a shift in the urban economy, and probably a self-sustaining one, as most groups involved in the manufacture of consumer goods, clothing and luxuries also entered the same middle class of skilled craftsmen. The overall effects on the Bruges economy at this point must not be exaggerated, however. Textiles continued in the early fourteenth century to meet shrinking export markets, and industrial change towards luxury textiles must have caused the economic demise of a massive number of proletarianized workers. At the same time the mercantile elites suffered from growing competition on the international market, and faced a difficult period of change in trying to attract international trade while their political dominance was being eroded. As we have seen, the era of Flemish 'active trade' had mostly gone, and that of 'passive trade' in Bruges was only emerging.

181 The crucial transition is discussed in Stabel, *Capital of Fashion*, forthcoming.

182 Van Werveke, 'De koopman-ondernemer'; and more recently R. Holbach, 'Some Remarks on the Role of "Putting-out" in Flemish and Northwest European Cloth Production', in M. Boone and W. Prevenier (eds.), *Drapery Production in the Late Medieval Low Countries: Markets and*

Table 6.2 *Occupational structure in Bruges, 1338–1436*

	1338	1394	1411	1436
Textiles	43.6	15.1	18.1	17.3
Clothing	21.2	14.3	26.9	26.4
Food	12.3	11.9	11.4	10.3
Trade and services	6.6	20.8	9.3	9.7
Construction	6.2	14.5	12.8	12.5
Durable consumer goods	6.0	14.3	10.2	13.4
Transport	1.6	1.9	1.7	1.8
Luxury	1.2	4.6	6.5	4.3
Health care	0.8	1.7	1.2	2.1
Arms	0.4	1.0	1.8	2.1

Source: draft lists for 1338, 1411, 1436, without the share of the *poorters* (bourgeoisie), and taxation list for 1394

The change in relative importance of guilds in the Bruges militia lists shows that the traditional occupational pattern of a cloth-manufacturing city, still the hallmark of Bruges before the Black Death, was undermined in the later fourteenth century. The textile industry lost its dominant position and fell back to a mere 17 per cent of all economic activity, and the figure hides, as we shall argue, an even more drastic structural change in the industry's organization. Clothing, the internationally reputed confection industry, and the fastest growing sector in the first half of the fourteenth century, seems to have stagnated, recovering slightly in 1394, to return in full force during the fifteenth century, when more than one quarter of the city's skilled craftsmen were employed as tailors, hatters, glovers, manufacturers of belts or purses, shoemakers, fine-leather workers, furriers, etc. Also managing well in the later fourteenth century were the manufacturers of durable consumer goods (cabinet makers, manufacturers of tableware, lantern makers, saddlers, iron workers, pewterers and the increasingly numerous coopers), of luxuries (painters, silversmiths, rosary makers) and of arms (armourers, bowyers), and this time also the construction industry (although the source material tempts to an overestimation of their importance in 1394).[183] The

Strategies for Survival (14th–16th Centuries) (Leuven and Apeldoorn, 1993), pp. 207–50; and Holbach, *Frühformen*.

183 Some sources for these guilds are discussed in older literature, for instance A. Van de Velde, *Het kuipersambacht te Brugge historisch beschouwd* (Bruges, 1909). Far more insightful is the study on the rosary makers by J. A. Van Houtte, 'Ambernijverheid en paternostermakers gedurende de 14e en 15e eeuw', *HGG*, 82 (1939), 149–84. The most important studies are more recent: J. P. Sosson, 'Corporation et paupérisme: L'exemple des métiers du bâtiment

move towards fashion, luxury and durable consumer goods at the expense of textiles was probably even more pronounced than the figures suggested by the draft lists. Many of the new and highly successful trades were not necessarily organized in guilds: book illuminators seem to have been included in the imagers' guild in the fourteenth century, but they had always enjoyed a distinct status, and from 1454 were organized in a separate fraternity; embroiderers had no proper guild structure, although grand-scale commissions for the Burgundian dukes were often organized logistically by Bruges craftsmen, and the number of embroiderers must have been high.[184]

Food processing and trade remained stable, as did all trades involved in the organization of the Bruges trade hub (transporters, carriers and other harbour facilities).[185] The mercantile elite had already partially recovered from the blows of the early fourteenth century, by concentrating on regional trade networks and by acting as middlemen in international trade. They had partly succeeded in regaining control over the city magistracy, which they had lost to the craft guilds after 1302. Their role in local and regional trade and in brokering and financing international trade, allowed them to profit from Bruges' growth as an international commercial centre. Traditionally this is linked to the importance of brokers and hostellers in the city, yet the tax lists of the 1390s suggest that most profits were made in trade itself (in particular regional trade in cloth, wool, wood and grain) and not in brokerage in the first instance. Brokers generally belonged to the prosperous middling group, not to the city's financial elite, although as we have seen hostellers were often very wealthy.[186]

The best-known examples of the new middle groups of highly skilled craftsmen that defined Bruges' economic success in the late Middle Ages are the painters. Their artistic production will be further considered in Chapter 9, but the names of Jan van Eyck, Petrus Christus, Hans Memling

aux XIVe et XVe siècles,' *TG*, 92 (1979), 557–75; and J.-P. Sosson, 'La structure sociale de la corporation médiévale: L'exemple des tonneliers de Bruges de 1350 à 1500', *BTFG*, 44 (1966), 457–78; A. Vandewalle (ed.), *De Brugse schoenmakers en timmerlieden: De ambachten en hun huizen 14de–20ste eeuw* (Bruges, 1985).

184 M. Smeyers, *Vlaamse miniaturen van de 8ste tot het midden van de 16de eeuw* (Leuven, 1998), pp. 231–55; and P. Trio, 'L'enlumineur à Bruges, Gand et Ypres (1300–1450): Son milieu socio-économique et corporatif', in M. Smeyers and B. Cardon (eds.), *Flanders in European Perspective: Manuscript Illumination around 1400 in Flanders and Abroad* (Leuven, 1995), pp. 721–29.

185 A. Vandewalle, 'Hafen und Hafenarbeit im spätmittelalterlichen Brügge', in K. Friedland (ed.), *Brügge-Colloquium des Hansischen Geschichtsvereins 26. bis 29. Mai 1988* (Cologne, 1991), pp. 13–24.

186 Greve, *Hansische Kaufleute*; Verbist, 'Traditie'.

and Gerard David also stand *pars pro toto* for the whole economic process that changed the foundations of the urban economy. Of course, the relative share of these luxury industries cannot compare with that of cloth production or even clothing. In the 1420s, Bruges counted only sixteen illuminators' workshops and about fifty 'librarians' (booksellers, parchment makers and scribes).[187] These numbers were dwarfed by the 500 or so cloth weavers still active in Bruges in the 1390s. In general, luxury industries rose from less than 2 per cent to about 5 per cent of all guild-related economic activity. The share of the imagers' (*beeldemaeckers*) guild dedicated to St Luke, which brought together the panel and canvas painters, and some smaller crafts like saddle makers, rose slowly during the fourteenth century and reached its peak in 1411. The silversmiths followed the same trajectory, but unlike the St Luke guild, their share stabilized in the first half of the fifteenth century. The cycle of the specialist (and protectionist) guild of the rosary makers – rosaries were another much exported speciality from Bruges – was more capricious, with a more pronounced growth until 1411 and a sudden decline between the 1410s and 1430s.[188]

Like many other cities in Flanders, Artois and Brabant, Bruges was an important cultural centre throughout the high and late Middle Ages.[189] It was an active centre of book production and illumination, partly stimulated by book production in the Flemish monasteries of coastal Flanders, many of which had a refuge in the city.[190] The imagers' guild was already important in the early fourteenth century, when the Bruges craftsmen faced the French knights at Kortrijk, and a handful of Bruges painters and illuminators were so successful that they received commissions for works of art from the royal courts of Europe.[191] As will be seen in Chapter 9 these early Bruges masters laid the foundations for a new 'pre-Eyckian', 'realistic' style of art. But it was in the second quarter of the fifteenth century that production accelerated, turning Bruges into the most important centre of

[187] R. van Uytven, 'Splendour and Wealth? Art and Economy in the Burgundian Netherlands', *Transactions of the Cambridge Bibliographical Society* 10 (1992), 101–24; and R. van Uytven, 'Stages of Economic Decline: Late Medieval Bruges', in Duvosquel and Thoen (eds.), *Peasants and Townsmen*, pp. 259–70.

[188] Van Houtte, 'The Rise and Decline'; and Van Houtte, 'Ambernijverheid'.

[189] J. Oosterman (ed.), *Stad van koopmanschap en vrede: Literatuur in Brugge tussen Middeleeuwen en Rederijkerstijd* (Leuven, 2005). See also the recent surveys of Middle Dutch literature: F. van Oostrom, *Wereld in woorden: Geschiedenis van de Nederlandse literatuur, 1300–1400* (Amsterdam, 2013); and H. Pleij, *Het gevleugelde woord: Geschiedenis van de Nederlandse literatuur, 1400–1560* (Amsterdam, 2007).

[190] Smeyers, *Vlaamse miniaturen*, pp. 269–78.

[191] Ibid., pp. 231–55.

the *ars nova*. These art trades were in this respect representative of Bruges' economic transformation. The city boasted many comparative advantages. It was an international commercial city, where clients from all over Europe gathered and networks of information and communication were relatively compact. The city was by far the wealthiest in the Low Countries and the centre of a densely urbanized region where a substantial middle class of landowners and small nobility added to demand. The city could also profit from advantages of agglomeration: nowhere else were so many art forms and types of luxury production concentrated in the same spot.

However, Bruges had no monopoly on art production and trade. As in the case of export industries (especially textiles), Bruges was only the top of a pyramid of numerous manufacturing centres. Practically all large cities of Flanders, Artois, Hainaut and Brabant were part of this network and even smaller towns could often perform surprisingly well in organizing niche markets for art.[192] It is probably no coincidence that the artists who worked for the Burgundian court in late fourteenth- and early fifteenth-century Dijon and Paris came from all over the Low Countries. Even at the height of the *ars nova* in Bruges around the mid fifteenth century, the city never totally eclipsed cities like Tournai (for painting and tapestry weaving), Ghent (for book illumination), Arras and Brussels (for tapestry weaving).[193] Even so, Bruges was arguably the leading and trend-setting centre of this explosion of creativity in the southern Low Countries. Besides the important domestic market, it was in Bruges that demand from all over Europe for products of the 'new art' was centralized and that international merchants and agents of foreign princes gathered to commission illuminated manuscripts, tapestries, paintings, sculptures, brass memorial slabs and so on. Local elites tuned into the same marketing pattern as did many Italian and Hanseatic merchants, German bishops, English and Spanish wool dealers, and French, Polish and German noblemen.

In Bruges, painters normally had to be members of the imagers' guild. There were exceptions: court painters did not require membership if they respected the customary arrangements and technical requirements of the guild. Jan van Eyck was exempted from becoming a master guildsman of St Luke. From 1453 onwards prestigious members did not need to be

192 Stabel, *Dwarfs among Giants*, pp. 226–35; and J.-P. Sosson, 'Le statut du peintre', in R. Van Schoute and B. De Patoul (eds.), *Les Primitifs flamands et leur temps* (Brussels, 1994), pp. 75–87.

193 P. Stabel, 'Organisation corporative et production d'œuvres d'art à Bruges à la fin du Moyen Âge et au début des Temps modernes', *Le Moyen Âge*, 113 (2007), 91–134.

apprenticed when acquiring the status of guild master.[194] Not all Bruges painters were, therefore, regular guildsmen, but not all the guildsmen of St Luke were painters either, for they included a wide range of occupations – panel painters, but also *cleederscrivers* (canvas painters), and the different occupations of saddlers, glaziers and mirror makers. This does not necessarily mean that guild regulation was uniform for all these groups, or that different branches of the same guild had much contact with each other. Guild members often paid their contribution to their own branch alone and most of the guild's social, economic and even cultural and religious activities took place within each branch, rather than within the framework of the wider guild. Boundaries within and between the guilds were also permeable. Craftsmen could be active in more than one branch or they could switch occupations easily from one branch to another, without requiring full training or having to pay a full entrance fee. In many cases the masters wanting to be active in another branch could do so: they had only to promise not to employ journeymen in this process. Double membership was ubiquitous.[195]

The quantitative evidence for the St Luke guild allows us to assess the cycle of membership from the mid fifteenth century. Generally it is assumed that it was only with the arrival of Jan van Eyck, perhaps from Maaseik in the Prince-Bishopric of Liège, and in his wake Petrus Christus, who came from Baarle in Brabant, that Bruges came to lead the *ars nova* in the Burgundian territories. After the mid fifteenth century, on average six masters and ten apprentices yearly entered the imagers' guild. This relatively high number of new guildsmen continued in the following decades; and even in the 1480s, when political turmoil hit the Bruges economy hard, numbers kept rising. It is only at the century's end that a significant downward pressure on new entries seems to be present. The number of new masters and apprentices appears to decline from the late 1480s and early 1490s, though they still remained at a high level. The breakdown in the 1490s, observed by many art historians, is only an illusion, as the matriculation lists were no longer completed in these years. In fact, Bruges remained an important centre of art production well into the sixteenth century (see Chapter 10) and shortly after 1500 the number of new masters would even surpass the number in the 1470s.[196] Numbers of new apprentices, however, seem to have been

194 J.-P. Sosson, 'La production artistique dans les anciens Pays-Bas méridionaux, XIVe–XVIe siècles', in S. Cavaciocchi (ed.), *Economia e arte secc. XIII–XVIII* (Florence, 2002), pp. 675–701.

195 Stabel, 'Guilds in Late Medieval Flanders'.

196 M. P. J. Martens, 'Some Aspects of the Origins of the Art Market in Fifteenth-Century Bruges', in M. North and D. Ormrod (eds.), *Art Markets in Europe 1400–1800* (Aldershot, 1998),

Table 6.3 *Occupational analysis of incoming citizens in the fifteenth century*

	fourteenth century	1418–34	1434–1450	1479–1492	Total
N		531	884	703	
Construction	11.9	7.5	10.0	10.4	9.5
Services	10.2	10.7	3.1	6.7	6.2
Health care	2.2	1.9	3.5	2.8	2.9
Retail	–	1.5	3.8	1.4	2.5
Trade	6.5	0.0	0.1	0.0	0.0
Transport	–	3.6	5.1	6.0	5.0
Luxury	13.4	7.0	6.7	4.6	6.0
Durables	11.5	10.2	10.0	7.3	9.1
Clothing	26.2	38.8	32.1	25.0	31.4
Textiles	18.7	7.5	7.7	23.8	13.0
Food	10.1	11.1	16.1	10.1	12.8
Arms	–	0.2	1.9	2.0	1.5

Source: citizens' registers, fifteenth century

declining earlier, which suggests a changing balance between training and the economic cycle. Only from the 1520s did the attraction of Bruges painting apparently fade for good.

The registration of new citizens confirms the trend towards a more diversified economy built on skill and added value. Sadly, only in the register of 1479–94 are almost all occupational titles recorded. In earlier periods the share of known occupations varied from less than 10 per cent in the fourteenth century to 17 per cent in the register of 1418–34 and 33 per cent in the period 1434–50. Moreover, for a substantial number of the occupations (>15 per cent) only the qualification 'to do a burgher's job' ('omme poortersneeringhe te doene') is recorded. This qualification is linked to the 'burgher's right' mentioned above, and these newcomers were probably involved in trade, services or non-guild organized manufacture, but above all in retailing: in contrast to most other cities in the Low Countries, Bruges lacked a well-established and inclusive mercers' guild, which might explain the very low figures of retail-related occupations among new citizens.

Since Bruges had developed into an international commercial city during the fourteenth century, and remained so during the fifteenth, employment

pp. 19–28; J.-P. Sosson, 'A propos des aspects socio-économiques des métiers d'art aux anciens Pays-Bas méridionaux XIVe–XVe siècles', *Revue Belge d'Archéologie et d'Histoire de l'Art*, 51 (1982), 17–25. For a detailed analysis of the matriculation lists of the Bruges painters, see Stabel, 'Organisation corporative'.

in services and transport accounted for a significant part (around 10–12 per cent) of all incoming citizens. These occupations included shipping, harbour facilities (crane workers, carriers and carters) and fiscal officers (measurers, toll collectors), but also clerks and policemen (the so-called *scerewetters*).[197] Numbers entering for construction work were also remarkably stable throughout the period (>10 per cent). The low figure for the 1420s is probably due to the fact that relatively few occupational titles are preserved and as such these tend to list more specialized labour that did not originate from the immediate hinterland, from where most building craftsmen came.[198]

For other economic sectors, fluctuations seem much stronger. They can be linked both to long-term trends and a changing occupational structure of the city, but also to short-term changes in the economic or political cycle. The remarkable growth of food-processing and food retail trades in the 1430s and 1440s seems to have been the direct consequence of ducal economic policy, after the revolt, of lowering income fees and attracting newcomers to Bruges.[199] As a result, occupations outside the guild framework that did not include many citizens, like the *beurdenaers* (mobile fish sellers), suddenly started to count many citizens in their ranks. Otherwise food trades remained relatively stable. The situation for the principal economic activity in Bruges was completely different. Textile occupations declined from about 19 per cent in the fourteenth century (data stemming primarily from the second half of the century when the industry was already suffering) to merely 7 per cent in the fifteenth century. Towards the end of the century the share of textiles increased again to almost a quarter. The manufacture and trade of durable consumer goods seems to remain stable until the mid fifteenth century, and to decline towards the end.

Surprisingly the share of luxuries (including arms) declined slowly during the fifteenth century,[200] while that of clothing industries was extremely high in the first half of the fifteenth century (30–40 per cent), returning to a more normal one-third of all occupations in the century's final decades,

197 The port and transportation infrastructure of Bruges is discussed in Vandewalle, 'Hafen und Hafenarbeit'.

198 For the history of construction in late medieval Bruges, see Sosson, *Les travaux publics*.

199 M. Boone and P. Stabel, 'New Burghers in the Late Medieval Towns of Flanders and Brabant: Conditions of Entry, Rules and Reality', in Schwinges (ed.), *Neubürger*, pp. 317–32. On the food trades, see H. Van Werveke, *Ambachten en erfelijkheid* (Antwerp, 1942).

200 The relatively sharp decline compared with the data for the fourteenth century may be linked to a different categorization in Thoen, 'Immigration to Bruges'. But as this study does not contain detailed surveys of occupations, it is impossible to calculate the share of the different occupational groups.

when Bruges again attracted more textile workers. But the pattern that seems to emerge is that woollen cloth production lost out during the heyday of the Bruges market, when Bruges was the staple market in northwest Europe for Low Countries textiles, while in the ascendant were clothing industries (confection of all kinds) and to a lesser extent the manufacture of luxury items (art), arms (armour) and durable consumer goods (furniture). Bruges became a centre for the manufacture of finished goods, catering above all for local and regional consumers. Hence there is a paradox. As we will see later, Bruges became an international outlet for textiles from other manufacturing centres. Bruges merchants were also involved in exporting luxury and fashion (paintings, funeral slabs, but above all items of clothing such as dresses, hats, purses and sleeves) to places like Rome, and probably elsewhere as well. Yet the bulk of Bruges manufactured goods remained in the Low Countries. The capital available on the Bruges market and the knowledge about trade flows, fashion and taste came in with the foreign merchants (and the regional noble elites who tended to indulge more and more of their luxury consumption in Bruges), yet for the fundamental industrial change to have taken place, the direct impact of foreign demand cannot have been that important. The change to luxuries was, therefore, above all a homespun change caused by rising elite and upper middle-class demand in the urban world of the Low Countries. Bruges was paradoxically at the same time the international market-place for textiles manufactured elsewhere in the Low Countries, and a manufacturer of goods catering for local and regional demand.

Death and Resurrection of an Industry: Textiles in a Specializing Economy

The move towards an economy of specialized crafts and skill came at a great cost. The Bruges cloth industry sank into ever deeper trouble during the fourteenth century and was on the point of disappearing in the fifteenth. In contrast to its main competitors – Ypres, Ghent, Douai, Brussels and Mechelen – its change to luxury cloth had not been a great success. With respect to middle-range woollens, the secondary Flemish towns, like Poperinge, Armentières, Oudenaarde, Kortrijk, Menen, Wervik and others, were fiercely competing for export markets.[201] Even the new demand for cheaper worsteds and

[201] Munro, 'Medieval Woollens: Western European Woollen Industries'; E. Coornaert, 'Draperies rurales, draperies urbaines: L'évolution de l'industrie flamande au Moyen Âge et au XVI siècle', *BTFG*, 28 (1950), 60–96; Stabel, *De kleine stad*, pp. 122–55.

semi-worsteds, the niche that Bruges had claimed in the thirteenth century, could not be secured, as throughout the fifteenth century says from Hondschoote (in western Flanders) started to flood the export markets. Even the pivotal role of Bruges in the international cloth trade could not stop the decay of its industry.

Figures are revealing. As numbers of skilled artisans rose, the share of textile workers fell spectacularly from almost 50 per cent around 1300 to 15 per cent after 1400. This general figure hides an even more profound change. Within the sector of textile manufacture, woollen cloth production dropped from more than 96 per cent in the first half of the fourteenth century to 87 per cent, as the share of tapestry weavers and above all linen weavers rose. Bruges became, together with Kortrijk, an important manufacturing centre for urban linens (table and bed linen).[202] This almost cataclysmic decline of what had been the major industry during the city's growth in the twelfth and thirteenth centuries did not pass unchallenged. Throughout the fourteenth and early fifteenth centuries, Bruges entrepreneurs tried to turn the tide by focusing, like their Flemish competitors, on increasingly refined fabrics. Sometimes these attempts led to higher numbers of new textile workers in the city (in particular in the 1410s and 1420s when the registration of new master weavers rose from less than two per year to ten), but these periods of relative success were extremely short-lived.[203]

In the end it was a more drastic change in textile manufacture that bore some fruit. The manufacture of woollen cloth was gradually abandoned, and Bruges entrepreneurs focused instead on finishing woollens manufactured elsewhere. This must have had profound consequences for the labour force. The preparation of wool and the weaving of the fabric had been the most labour intensive stages of production in the industry's heyday, while fulling, dyeing and shearing were more capital and skill intensive. In the fifteenth century the change seems to have worked. Developing the city's role as a centre of commercial knowledge, manufacturing skill and capital accumulation paid off, as it had done for the manufacture of fashionable dress and clothing accessories, of luxuries and of durable consumer goods. In the mid fourteenth century cloth entrepreneurs (the 'drapers') already used

[202] P. Stabel, 'Urban Markets, Rural Industries and the Organization of Labour in Late Medieval Flanders: The Constraints of Guild Regulations and the Requirements of Export Oriented Production', in Blondé et al. (eds.), *Labour and Labour Markets*, pp. 140–57. Most linen production in Flanders was organized by proto-industrialized peasants in interior Flanders.

[203] See also Vermaut, 'De textielnijverheid', although the author's conclusions are sometimes outdated in light of recent research and should be interpreted cautiously. The history of the cloth industry in medieval Bruges remains an important lacuna in historical research.

Table 6.4 *Textile industries in the late medieval Bruges draft lists (1302–1436) and taxation records (1394)*[204]

	1302	1338	1394	1411	1436
Preparation of wool (only guild activities)	5.8	0.9	5.5	4.8	5.3
Cloth weavers	42.0	45.3	33.1	24.2	24.6
Fullers	29.7	30.2	22.0	24.2	24.6
Shearers	13.3	15.1	13.4	24.2	24.6
Dyers	5.7	4.7	7.1	9.7	8.8
Cloth (totals)	96.5	96.2	81.1	87.2	87.7
Tapestry weavers	0.9	1.4	4.7	1.6	1.8
Linen weavers	2.6	2.4	14.2	11.2	10.5

the complex financial system of money changers and hostellers in Bruges to facilitate access to capital and counter problems of cash-flow.[205] These mechanisms probably not only allowed drapers to remain in business, but also influenced the developments in textiles that occurred later on. Around 1500, the Bruges broker Wouter Ameyde controlled a complex network of cloth trade with Florentine financiers and suppliers of wool, and textile entrepreneurs from cloth-manufacturing towns in the Leie basin (Kortrijk, Menen and Wervik). Ameyde not only acted as a commercial go-between, but also played a part in organizing networks for finishing and dyeing these woollens.[206] The cloth trade was still, even in the autumn of Bruges' role in international trade, the mark of success for the Bruges economy.

The roots of specialization reached back to the thirteenth century, when woollens manufactured elsewhere were finished by Bruges shearers and dyers. A willingness to attract half-finished fabrics and finish them in Bruges probably explains why the finishing capacity of the Bruges textile industry was able to resist the general decline of cloth weaving. How it did so, is not well documented. At first, the shift seems to have been hesitant. In the militia lists of the early fourteenth century almost half of all textile workers were weavers and one third were fullers. This balance between textile manufacturers and finishers changed after 1350, at first slightly, but by 1400 dramatically. The share of cloth weavers declined to a quarter of all

[204] The data stem from Dumolyn, 'Population', 64; and De Meyer, 'De sociale strukturen', pp. 30–2. The latter makes no distinction between the linen weavers and the tapestry weavers. In order to allow comparison, the proportion of ¾ linen and ¼ tapestry weavers based upon the data in the militia lists was used.

[205] Murray, *Bruges*, pp. 285–7.

[206] Mus, 'Wouter Ameyde'; Stabel, 'Entre commerce'; and more recently Verbist, 'Traditie'.

Table 6.5 *Textile occupations among new Bruges citizens, 1418–96*

	1418–34	1434–50	1479–96
Cloth	**48.6**	**52.9**	**74.9**
Weavers	18.9	13.2	5.4
Fullers	10.8	11.8	18.6
Dyers	5.4	7.4	20.4
Shearers	13.5	17.6	11.4
Say weavers	–	–	19.2
Wool preparation	**10.8**	**10.3**	**2.4**
Other textiles	**40.5**	**36.8**	**22.8**
Linen weavers	21.6	13.2	13.8
Tapestry weavers	18.9	22.1	3.0
N	37	68	167

Source: burgher matriculation registers

textile workers, while the share of fullers stabilized and that of dyers and shearers rose significantly. This development is confirmed by the registration of new citizens in the same period.

Cloth weaving had clearly lost much of its appeal for newcomers after 1400. Many of the new citizens listed themselves rather as linen or tapestry weavers. However, this was a short-lived upsurge of a new textile sector as numbers of newcomers started to dwindle a couple of decades later. Bruges linen weavers were probably no match for the competition of coarse linens from the countryside in Hainaut and interior Flanders, or of refined table linen from new manufacturing centres like Kortrijk, where wages were generally lower and guild organization less tight.[207] In cloth manufacture, the share of new immigrant weavers steadily declined. By contrast cloth finishers, like shearers and dyers (and even fullers), became increasingly important. The shift towards luxury cloth had not produced the results that Bruges drapers had hoped for when they adapted the regulatory environment of cloth manufacture from the late thirteenth century onwards. It had been too little and much too late compared with Bruges' competitors. Traditional cloth weaving was now well beyond the city's capabilities. In sharp contrast to the ill fate of the weavers, the finishing industries fared much better.

In the last quarter of the fifteenth century, when the occupational titles are known for practically all incoming citizens, the cloth industry experienced a surprisingly positive turn: three quarters of all new textile workers

[207] Stabel, *De kleine stad*, pp. 176–90.

were employed in it. But weaving of traditional cloth was still in full decay. The share of cloth weavers fell to a historic low. In the same period the share of shearers declined as well, although it remained at a relatively high level. This time the Bruges cloth industry attracted important numbers of say weavers (a quarter of all cloth workers), many of them coming from the booming say manufacturing town of Hondschoote.[208] As Bruges entrepreneurs finally realized that their switch to high-quality cloth had not been successful, they returned to manufacturing worsteds, which had made the city's cloth industry successful in the twelfth and thirteenth centuries. This switch was made elsewhere in Flanders, and had met with great success (as in Hondschoote).[209] It is, however, surprising that Bruges chose to revive its traditional production of worsteds, a sector that could only thrive in places where wages could remain relatively low. It was, moreover, a deliberate choice. The city administrators attracted craftsmen from Hondschoote to kickstart the industry by giving them subsidies. In a city where finishing industries were so dominant and where dyers seemed to be thriving, the arrival of cheaper fabrics, which did not require much finishing, may seem a paradox. But, surprisingly, the attempts had some success. In the final decades of the fifteenth and the early sixteenth centuries many say weavers arrived in the decaying commercial city to settle down as craftsmen.[210]

Women in the Labour Market

The economic possibilities for women in the labour market, whether active in the market-place or in the artisanal sector, varied considerably and in ways that were gendered. Class, wealth, marriage status and household position affected opportunities for women in the labour market. Tax lists show relatively high numbers of single (young and unmarried) women and widows, for instance respectively 18.5 per cent and 11.3 per cent in the St Donatian's section in 1383. These single women can mostly be found in the lower fiscal classes and their lives are unlikely to have been comfortable. There were substantially more widows than widowers in fifteenth-century Bruges. At the end of the fourteenth century widows were more equally divided between all

[208] E. Coornaert, *Un centre industriel d'autrefois: La draperie-sayetterie d'Hondschoote. XIVe–XVIIIe siècle* (Paris, 1930); and Van der Wee, 'Industrial Dynamics', pp. 321–36.

[209] J. Vermaut, 'Structural Transformation in a Textile Centre: Bruges from the Sixteenth to the Nineteenth Century', in Van der Wee (ed.), *Rise and Decline*, pp. 187–205; Stabel, 'Les draperies urbaines'.

[210] Vermaut, 'Structural Transformation'.

fiscal classes than single women but it is impossible to calculate the number of single men for comparison. In the tax lists from 1394–6 in the sections of St James, St Nicholas and Our Lady, households headed by women account for 14 per cent of the total number of households. Single unmarried women represent 11 per cent of the population. Some of these were upper-class women described as *vrouwe* or *joncvrouwe* but on average the fiscal assessment of these households of single women or widows is much lower than the neigbourhood's average and they mostly seem to have lived in backstreets. Middle-class widows tended to marry sooner than wealthier or poorer women, allowing them to enter a new household for economic survival.[211]

As described above, in the export-oriented textile industry of the twelfth and thirteenth centuries, relatively free labour markets had been controlled by merchant capital. At that point women seem to have played an important role in cloth production. When the textile industry converted during the fourteenth century towards guild-controlled production of more expensive woollens, job opportunities for unskilled workers and also for women declined. Women largely disappeared from the key industrial functions in the industry (from weaving to cloth finishing) and their role as independent workers was gradually limited to spinning. Recent historiography has emphasized that, overall, female labour became more limited to jobs with lower status and pay and that the general social and economic position and autonomy of women were gradually restricted. In many manufacturing towns in the Low Countries during the fifteenth and sixteenth centuries, women lost access to occupations they had once practised.[212] In Bruges, as in Ghent, they were pushed to the lower-paid stages of cloth manufacture and wool processing: washing, combing, carding and spinning the wool and cleaning woollens. Moreover, women became very rare in the male-dominated world of guilds. Only occasionally does the *mestrigghe* or female guild master still appear in the sources, mostly in retailing occupations, and most late medieval craft guild matriculation lists contain no women at all. If they are present in guild-organized occupations, it is in the context of the male-dominated household and their role is visible in mercantile activities rather than in manufacture itself.[213]

[211] Stabel, 'Working Alone'; P. Stabel, 'A European Household Economy?', in Carlier and Soens (eds.), *The Household*, pp. 121–6 (at 121); W. Prevenier, 'Fiscale repartitie en familiale situaties in het Sint-Donatiaanszestendeel te Brugge in 1383', in M. Van der Eycken and E. Houtman (eds.), *Liber Amicorum Coppens Herman* (Brussels, 2007), pp. 775–99; Danneel, 'Weduwen en wezen', vol. II, pp. 140–1.

[212] Hutton, *Women*, pp. 5, 128–30.

[213] P. Stabel, 'Women at the Market: Gender and Retail in the Towns of Late Medieval Flanders', in W. Blockmans, M. Boone and T. De Hemptinne (eds.), *Secretum scriptorum: Liber*

Some richer women were active independently in money changing or brokering or as hostellers. They would have had small pawnshops and been engaged in petty credit. But some women from more important families were also involved in money changing for merchants and in international hostelling.[214] Others seem to have played a role in the luxury trades, particularly those organized outside the regular guild framework. A number of female scribes were active in Bruges; highly skilled, they were engaged in the production of quality books for the export market; 25 per cent of the scribes' fraternity of St John the Baptist were women.[215] Women were also involved in the formal guild economy: the rosary makers' records reference female servants or *joncwiven*.[216] However, as a rule, the only way a woman could become a guild master, and achieve active entrepreneurship, was as a master's widow. As in many medieval towns, widows were allowed to continue the trade of their deceased husband. Fifteenth-century guild statutes in Bruges, with the exception of the shippers and some guilds in the building industry, decree that the master's widow was entitled to practise the trade until she remarried outside the trade. In most guilds women could only be active either as members of the master's household or as unskilled servant girls, but some statutes were more lenient. The addition to the bakers' statutes in June 1464 is less clear about gender restrictions when it states that all masters, men or women, could draw lots for the market stalls.[217] That said, even widows met with serious restrictions: those who were *meestrigghe* (female guild masters) could often not hire new apprentice boys. In the textile industries, journeymen who married the widow of a master only paid half the sum of another new master, thus restoring patriarchal domination of the household within the guild.[218]

In less normative sources, women do sometimes appear in guild matriculation books acting on behalf of their husbands, or as widows, as masters (without widowhood being specified) or perhaps as apprentice girls (the

alumnorum Walter Prevenier (Leuven, 1999), pp. 259–76 (at 262); Stabel, 'Working Alone'; Hutton, *Women*, pp. 11, 112, 119.

214 Murray, *Bruges*, pp. 308–26.

215 T. de Hemptinne, 'Des femmes copistes dans les Pays-Bas au bas Moyen Âge (14e–15e siècle) : Approche d'une activité féminine mal connue', in Blockmans, Boone and De Hemptinne (eds.), *Secretum scriptorum*, pp. 129–43.

216 Van Houtte, 'Ambernijverheid', p. 171.

217 RAB, Ambachten, 1, fo. 280v.

218 Danneel, 'Weduwen en wezen', vol. II, pp. 169–75; M. Danneel, 'Weduwen en sociale mobiliteit: Het juridisch statuut van de weduwen in Vlaanderen in de 14e–15e eeuw, in het bijzonder te Brugge', in J. De Belder, W. Prevenier and C. Vandenbroeke (eds.), *Sociale mobiliteit en sociale structuren in Vlaanderen en Brabant van de late Middeleeuwen tot de 20e eeuw* (Ghent, 1983), pp. 19–21.

distinction is not always made in the sources) – for example, in the furriers' guild,[219] among the *culkstikkers* (manufacturers of stuffed dress and bed-covers, like doublets and quilts), the shearers and the coopers.[220] Records of the retailing guilds mention women as active partners of their husbands within the household. Wives of mercers, cloth merchants and spice sellers in Bruges were often involved in their husbands' business as *coopwijven*.[221] Some guilds could not enforce monopolies or left certain activities to non-guild members. Hence the old-clothes sellers, organized in one of the most successful guilds of late medieval Bruges, allowed the activities of *uutdraghen*, women outside the guild framework who were active in the low-status trade of worn dress and accessories. Consequently, women were most active economically within their husband's household, and at the margins of the guild-controlled economy, especially in retailing; or they were forced to look for independent employment as maid servants or tavern girls. But despite these restrictions on independent labour, women seem to have dominated food markets, especially markets for fruits, vegetables and mussels. They were also present but less prominent in marketing wine and beer. Even so, the most profitable sectors of meat and fish were firmly controlled by the guilds of butchers and fishmongers who jealously protected their monopolies from female retailers.[222]

The few women who asked for burghership on their own often indicated that they wanted to practise a 'burgher's trade' or to open a bathhouse or wine tavern. On one sector of female employment, we are disproportionately well informed. Prostitution in the city, as we have seen, was widespread and tolerated by the urban authorities: the annual fines for brothel keeping or owning were seemingly not intended to discourage prostitution itself. In lists of those paying fines, both in the accounts of the city and of the sheriff who split the income, the same people returned year after year. Fining became a form of taxation: sex was just another commodity with income opportunities for the authorities too.[223] The number of brothels and bathhouses or inns that received prostitutes was impressive, especially in the later fourteenth century. While the figure rose slowly from about 25 per year in the early fourteenth century and 35 in the 1330s–1340s, from

219 For instance SAB, 345, Furriers' Guild book 1399–1523, fo. 5^{r}.

220 For instance SAB, 337, 1452–61; SAB, 324, Shearers' guild book 1413–1786, fo. 12^{r} and passim; SAB, 336, passim.

221 Howell, 'Social Logic', p. 192; Stabel, 'Women at the Market', pp. 271–2.

222 Murray, *Bruges*, pp. 307–8; Stabel, 'Women at the Market', pp. 263, 271; M. Danneel, 'Handelaarsters in oude kleren in de 16de eeuw te Brugge', *BO*, 25 (1985), 203–18.

223 For what follows, see Dupont, *Maagdenverleidsters*.

the 1350s a boom began. In 1352–4 there were 93, and in 1369, no fewer than 139. Ten years later, revolt interrupted the policing of prostitution and possibly also the market for women. After 1385, the sex business partially recovered, and in the 1390s there were on average 48 houses (though with fluctuations between years), though inefficient collection of fines and fraud mean the number was probably higher. Also, the figure only applies to the urban territory under the jurisdiction of the aldermen, and not to St Donatian's juridical enclaves (for which no similar contemporary sources survive). In the fifteenth century, the Bruges sex industry slowed down, though it is hard to quantify: the reported number of brothels cannot be equated to the real number of prostitutes, because the fine payers were variously innkeepers casually renting rooms to prostitutes, professional brothel or bathhouse operators, self-employed sex workers, or women combining both latter roles or occasional prostitution with a more 'respectable', low-paid job. Information about the number of women employed in a brothel is not abundant. In the early fifteenth century, Katelijne Boomgaerds ran a brothel at Boninswalle, an enclave of St Donatian's: she was assisted by one or two maids, one of whom eventually took over the business. Three other 'wivekins', probably prostitutes, lived in the house.[224]

From the 1360s onwards, the Bruges sex market was principally managed by women. In the period 1385–1515 they represented no less than 85 per cent of the fine-paying brothel operators. As for their mobility, all we know about the origin of migrant sex workers is based upon geographical nicknames, and this applies only to one fine payer in eight. Half of these names point at places outside Flanders and this immigration seems to have followed the movement of trade: the geographical area of recruitment was international in the early fifteenth century and this shrank from the middle of the century onwards (a change also evident among other social groups). A small group of sex businesses, representing 9 per cent of fine payers, stayed at least five years in Bruges. In contrast to their operators and staff, three quarters of the brothel owners were, not surprisingly, male. In at least 30 per cent of cases they belonged to the city's elites and were linked by family and/or professional ties. For these men, brothels must have fitted into their portfolio of profitable investments, without causing too much moral distress (until perhaps the last decades of the fifteenth century). Some members of craft guilds (like the curriers) even owned brothels in the streets where they lived and worked (the Witte and Zwarte Leertouwerstraat). Even if the gender distribution among the brothel owners favoured men, a quarter were

[224] RAB, *Proosdij*, 1619, fo. 7ʳ. Cited by Dupont, *Maagdenverleidsters*, pp. 86, 100, 114.

madams. This surprisingly high figure cannot be fully explained by the fact that a dozen successful female brothel keepers and/or prostitutes came to possess their own house. The involvement in the Bruges real estate market of female investors (especially widows, who represent more than one female owner out of four) is likely more important than commonly acknowledged.

Standards of Living

In a typical household budget of the lower classes, some 70 to 80 per cent was spent on food, 5 to 15 per cent on rent, and the rest on heating, light, clothing and other utensils.[225] A promising source on houses and their contents, as yet not systematically analyzed, is the confiscation records following a late fourteenth-century revolt: these provide information on the furniture, household articles and housing among different social groups, from relatively poor weavers and various modest trades to wealthy brokers, butchers and a few rich burghers. Many of those whose properties were confiscated had debts, but many also possessed their own reasonably well-furnished houses.[226] Little is known about the housing market, the use of fuel or the importance of gardens, livestock and fishing for the urban middle and lower classes, but it is clear that after the monotonous grain-based diet of the twelfth and thirteenth centuries, food during the later Middle Ages became more varied. More of the population could afford meat and fish. This observation fits with the generalized picture of post-plague Europe as a 'golden age for wage workers', and post-1350 Bruges as a period of the 'rise of the middle classes'. These generalizations need to be made cautiously, but it does appear from the accounts of charitable institutions in Bruges that meat and fish gained importance in the diet from the second quarter of the fourteenth century and again during the early fifteenth. There was also a shift in consumption from predominantly mutton and pork to beef. More meat was eaten in Bruges during the fifteenth century it seems than, for instance, in Antwerp. Commercialized farms in coastal Flanders must have provided the Bruges butchers, some of whom were wealthy monopolists, with a steady supply of meat.[227] Mead

[225] Blockmans et al., 'Tussen crisis en welvaart,' p. 76. Compare with C. Dyer, *Standards of Living in the Later Middle Ages: Social Change in England c.1200–1520* (Cambridge, 1989).

[226] J. De Smet, 'De repressie te Brugge na de slag bij West-Rozebeke (1382–1384): Bijdrage tot de kennis van de sociale en economische toestand van de Brugse bevolking', *HGG*, 84 (1947), 71–118.

[227] Soens and Thoen, 'Vegetarians or Carnivores?'; see varieties in meat, wine, dairy and vegetables in S. Dehaeck, 'Voedselconsumptie in het Brugse Sint-Janshospitaal tijdens de Middeleeuwen (1280–1440)', *HGG*, 141 (2004), 332–64.

and cider were drunk, but Flanders was primarily a land of beer, the daily drink for men, women and children. Beer was brewed with *gruut*, a mixture of herbs, but from the fourteenth century also with hops, first in beer imported from north Germany and Holland, and later also in beer brewed in Bruges. In 1441 Bruges counted fifty-four breweries. Wine, preferred by the upper social strata, was imported from the Rhineland, the Mosel or Alsace regions, and from French regions like Gascony and Burgundy, while sweet liqueur wines were imported from the Mediterranean. Damme had a staple market for wine. For 1420 an impressive total consumption of 70 litres of wine per head can be calculated. This may say little about the consumption habits of a wider population. The lower and middle classes could only drink wine from time to time, for instance during guild or fraternity meals.[228] The above figures are indicative and do not accurately reflect the varieties of consumption habits between social groups; but we can safely suppose that living standards in the city were relatively high compared with elsewhere, and not only among the elites. The middling sort of people in guilds could often achieve a reasonable standard of living in Bruges: there were many worse places in medieval Europe to live and work.

Compared with other European cities, real wages in Flemish cities were surprisingly high at the end of the period of medieval growth, and Bruges wages were higher than those in most other towns in Flanders. Wages were even relatively high by 1300 and they were only slightly disturbed by the calamities of the fourteenth century. When population diminished after famine and plague, migration filled gaps in the labour force with relative ease.[229] Wage levels probably plummeted during and after the grain shortages of 1315–17, but they seem to have recovered. After the mid fourteenth century, they only rose slowly despite recurrent demographic crises. Real wages climbed to their c.1300 levels at the end of the century and then followed a cyclical pattern with only slight growth during the fifteenth century. When in England, wages increased after 1350 because of labour shortages, in Bruges real wages of master building craftsmen, for instance, fell by 31 per cent between the intervals 1346–50 and 1351–5. Sharp inflation following coinage debasements wiped out the gains in nominal wages. They then slightly increased until 1386–90 and faster until 1401–5, as a consequence of deflation following the monetary reform of 1389–90. Even if nominal

[228] A. Janssens, 'Wijn in Brugge tijdens het laatste kwart van de 15de eeuw: Hoeveelheden, prijzen en consumptie', *HGG*, 146 (2009), 141–68; R. van Uytven, 'Le combat des boissons en Europe du Moyen Âge au XVIIIe siècle', in S. Cavaciocchi (ed.), *Alimentazione e nutrizione secc. XIII–XVIII* (Florence, 1997), pp. 53–83.

[229] Stabel, 'Working Alone'.

wages were cut by a quarter, consumer prices dropped to a greater extent. Real wages decreased afterwards by 31 per cent until 1436–40 to rise again to a peak in 1461–5, and during this time purchasing power rose significantly. The last quarter of the fifteenth century was again a time of deteriorating living standards as unrest damaged the urban economy. In 1481–2, the price of a loaf of bread took away half the daily wage of a skilled worker. Jean-Pierre Sosson has shown that even skilled journeymen in construction often lived at the edge of subsistence in the fifteenth century. For unskilled workers the situation would often have been worse, and even master carpenters and bricklayers (without the capital for involvement in large-scale building activity and working as artisans for building entrepreneurs) were often at the lower levels of income tax.[230] Independent artisans and retailers who did not work in wage-labour relations must have been vulnerable to cyclical movements in specific economic sectors.

Journeymen and the unskilled workforce had a harder time in years of famine.[231] Maximum daily wages in the building industry, for instance, varied between 6 pennies Flemish groten a day for a journeyman and 12 pennies for a guild master.[232] An unskilled digger only received between 2 and 5 pennies a day, and waste collectors mentioned in the city accounts sometimes only received half a penny.[233] It is impossible to quantify the percentage of people engaged in wage labour and those working as independent retailers or small commodity producers, and many wage labourers received piece wages rather than time wages (usually paid at the end of the week in Bruges). For instance, a tailor could sell a so-called *journeye* (an overcoat without sleeves) for 3 pennies Flemish groten, which meant he had to produce at least four to reach the daily wage of a master carpenter or mason, without taking into account the cost for raw materials and tools.[234]

[230] Sosson, *Les travaux publics*. For other towns, see B. Blondé and J. Hanus, 'Beyond Building Craftsmen: Economic Growth and Living Standards in the Sixteenth-Century Low Countries: The Case of 's-Hertogenbosch (1500–1560)', *European Review of Economic History*, 14 (2010), 179–207.

[231] J. H. A. Munro, 'Builders' Wages in Southern England and the Southern Low Countries, 1346–1500: A Comparative Study of Trends in and Levels of Real Income', in S. Cavaciocchi (ed.), *L'edilizia prima della rivoluzione industriale secc. XIII–XVIII* (Florence, 2005), pp. 1013–76, and the references there cited, provides a methodological overview; Sosson, *Les travaux publics*, pp. 225–31.

[232] E. Scholliers, 'Lonen te Brugge en in het Brugse Vrije (Xve–XVIIIe eeuw)', in C. Verlinden (ed.), *Dokumenten voor de geschiedenis van prijzen en lonen in Vlaanderen en Brabant*, 4 vols. (Bruges, 1965), vol. II, pp. 87–160 (at 94–5); Sosson, *Les travaux publics*, pp. 225–7.

[233] A. Janssens, *Middeleeuws Brugge door de ogen van Hans Memling (1465–1494)* (Leuven, 2012), p. 103.

[234] Ibid., p. 91.

The poorest people have left few historical or archaeological traces. As we have seen, they often lived in one-room apartments (*camerkins*) or temporary houses, if they had a roof above their head at all. Years of high grain prices included 1382–3, 1408–9, 1415–17, 1423–4, 1436–8, 1455–7, 1481–3 and 1488–92:[235] bread shortages must have been disastrous not only for the urban poor and unskilled, including many single women, but also for many journeymen, apprentice boys and the poorer guild masters. The poorest faced hunger and the middle classes were threatened with downward social mobility. However, to prevent social unrest and sharply rising poverty, the urban government took measures against speculation, and imported large amounts of foreign grain. This strategy worked: not a single rebellion in Bruges or in any other Flemish town can really be classified as a 'hunger revolt'. As early as 1280 it was forbidden to organize monopolies to drive up food prices. Bruges also became integrated into a growing international food market. Most of the grain consumed in Bruges came from the fertile plains of Artois and Picardy, but during famine it was also imported from overseas. In 1317, when the 'Great Hunger' was almost over, the city government bought 20,000 hectolitres of grain from Italian merchants. In 1369–70, the city bought large quantities of wheat, mostly from Hanseatic merchants who had shipped it to Sluis. In 1432, 1480–3 and 1488–9 the urban government bought massive stocks of grain and stored it in rented attics.[236]

When the urban poor appear in legal sources, little is mentioned beyond stereotypical discourse about their living conditions, and many of them do not figure in the fiscal sources, being too poor to pay any contribution. The tax registers of 1394–6 show that 12 per cent of the population paid less than one penny; and they were luckier than the beggars on the streets. Historians have often called this group of taxpayers the 'fiscal poor' though this calculation depends on the tariff used for taxing. It is difficult to calculate the number of poor people whose ranks increased in times of crisis when the working poor were pushed into destitution. Data from charitable institutions provide only a rough idea of the number of 'deserving poor', and tell us more about community ideologies than about actual poverty. The Potterie hospital, for instance, gave bread, meat, herring, clothes and shoes to between twenty-four and thirty-six poor people

[235] Murray, *Bruges*, pp. 99–106; Grierson (ed.), *Les annales*, p. 112; Van Werveke, 'De middeleeuwse hongersnood'; Van Werveke, 'La famine'; Van Werveke, 'Bronnenmateriaal'.

[236] GVS, *Inventaire*, vol. II, p. 346, vol. V, p. 61; Janssens, *Middeleeuws Brugge*, p. 78. GVS, *Coutume*, vol. I, p. 235; Murray, *Bruges*, p. 40.

on church holidays, a number with little meaning for assessing the real number of poor.[237]

As already seen, most institutions of poor relief were homes for elderly people, who did not usually belong to the poorest strata in society; and they were controlled by the town government and the elites.[238] These have left important archives; but we are far less well informed about the women and men in various beguinages, almshouses or hospitals affiliated with the 'Third Orders'. They often seem to have received poor relief, and most of these institutions were very small. The mendicant orders supervised some of them, the Franciscans for instance the *tertiaries* of St Barbara in the Ganzestraat (founded before or in 1342–3) and the Goezeputstraat (by 1391).[239] Even so, the urban elite kept a firm grip on the governance and finances of hospitals and other charitable houses. However, during the fourteenth and fifteenth centuries, in some less institutionalized smaller convents or almshouses, pious women lived together in voluntary poverty, for instance in the convent *ten Hamerkine*.[240] These women were probably active in charity (as research in other cities has shown),[241] but their impact is hard to measure and many of these communities were ephemeral. In the fourteenth century no more large-scale hospitals were set up, though many smaller almshouses were created, most of which have left little trace.

The lepers too poor to live in the official Bruges lepers' house were the *akkerzieken* (literally 'the field sick'). They lived in four different locations outside the city but within its jurisdiction, and were organized as a guild-like institution, with their own dean and sworn men.[242] In the late fourteenth century the Dulhuus was established for the poor and dangerous mentally ill and there were also night shelters for 'poor travellers', like the ones of St Julian, Our Lady of Nazareth, St Justus and St Nicholas. Less well-off travellers were welcomed in St Julian's house, but they were only allowed to stay for one night, in the evening receiving *potagie*, a pea soup with butter, and some bread.[243] In 1402, a house for abandoned infants was

237 See M. T. Galvin, 'Credit and Parochial Charity in Fifteenth-Century Bruges', *JMH*, 28 (2002), 131–54; W. Blockmans and W. Prevenier, 'Armoede in de Nederlanden van de 14e tot het midden van de 16e eeuw: bronnen en problemen', *TG*, 88 (1975), 501–37.

238 Maréchal, *Gebondenheid*.

239 GVS, *Inventaire*, vol. I, p. 27; Simons, *Bedelordekloosters*, pp. 161–2, 181–2; Simons, *Cities of Ladies*, pp. 268–9.

240 N. Geirnaert, 'Het "Convent ten Hamerkine" te Brugge (14de–15de eeuw)', *Biekorf*, 82 (1982), 220–4.

241 K. Overlaet, 'Replacing the Family? Beguinages in Early Modern Western European Cities: An Analysis of the Family Networks of Beguines Living in Mechelen (1532–1591)', *Continuity and Change*, 29 (2014) pp. 325–47.

242 Maréchal, *Gebondenheid*, pp. 81–3.

243 Ibid., p. 253.

created in the Boeveriestraat. Infanticide as a sign of poverty, however, is not often reported in the sources.[244] In 1459 the Bethany convent was founded for repentant prostitutes by the bishop of Tournai.[245] The larger guilds also played a role in charity for their own members (or for their widows and orphans) who had lost their ability to work during work accidents or because of disease: they were considered to be the 'deserving poor' par excellence. By 1327 the brokers' guild had its own almshouse;[246] in 1346 the weavers created St James' almshouse at the Katelijnepoort for their sick guild masters ('verweecte meesters').[247] During the fifteenth century, an increasing number of guilds invested in almshouses and 'boxes' for mutual assistance, although in times of crisis the lodging and alms they could distribute never sufficed. Many of these initiatives seem to have been aimed primarily at reinforcing the corporatist ideology of guild solidarity rather than solving problems of poverty.[248]

Aside from urban government, elite and guild initiatives, most of the charity in this period was run through the parish poor tables or *dissen*. Each of the six major parishes had a poor table or 'table of the Holy Spirit' for the 'house-poor', as householders and wage workers with insufficient income were called. The poor tables of St Saviour, Our Lady, St Walburga and St James are first mentioned in 1307, though the one of St Giles seems to be half a century older. They appear to have replaced the House of the Holy Spirit, which probably dated from the early 1200s and was controlled by the city government. Poor tables were in theory under the authority of the parish priest, though in practice they were governed by the notable parishioners. They took their name from the tables set up near the church entrance where the parishioners could donate money and goods. They relied on donations, though the bulk of their income came from gifts invested in annuities and immovable property. Gifts came from rich parishioners but also to a large degree from the middle classes. These served to benefit the souls of donors, but also to discipline the lower classes in the parish. In the fifteenth century, the poor tables provided regular assistance to some 180 paupers, perhaps representing 700 to 900 'privileged' poor with their families, distributing food once or twice a week and on major feast days. The

244 Carlier, *Kinderen*, pp. 264, 270.

245 N. Geirnaert, 'De eerste jaren van het zusterhuis Bethanië te Brugge', *Sacris Erudiri*, 26 (1983), 249–73.

246 A. Brown, *Civic Ceremony and Religion in Medieval Bruges, c.1300–1520* (Cambridge, 2011), p. 135.

247 Maréchal, *Gebondenheid*, p. 293.

248 E. Huys, *Duizend jaar mutualiteit bij de Vlaamsche gilden* (Dendermonde, 1923) gives an overview of guilds' investments in charity, for instance pp. 167–9.

paupers received bread and some meat, fish, cheese, eggs or peas, sometimes also shoes and clothing (usually linen underwear and breeches). If it is assumed that the poor on average made up 10 per cent of medieval urban dwellers, only one fifth of the poor in Bruges would have received such benefits and these were limited.[249] Even supposing that the other charitable institutions in Bruges kept a further few hundred to a thousand people alive in times of hardship, when the rural poor also flocked to the city (as studies on medieval poor relief have shown), the entire charity sector of the city was probably about as effective as a drop of water on a hot plate. And at the end of the Middle Ages, as elsewhere in Europe, charitable assistance in Bruges was increasingly restricted to local paupers, and begging became more tightly regulated.[250]

The Economic Heyday of the City

Bruges changed dramatically during the course of the later Middle Ages. Before 1300, members of its patriciate were actively involved in international trade, while the city's economy thrived on wool and cloth. Almost half of the population was involved in the manufacture of woollens of all kinds, which flooded the European markets (particularly Mediterranean markets in the case of Bruges and its lighter woollens). By c.1400 the cloth industry had all but vanished. Instead textile entrepreneurs, no longer the archetypical capitalistic merchant-entrepreneurs but small-scale drapers, focused on refining and finishing cloth imported from the Flemish small towns and the countryside. Woollen cloth was still dominant, but it was manufactured mostly elsewhere in the Low Countries.

Bruges merchants were also no longer present at the international trading posts: foreign merchants frequented Bruges instead. The city had become the main hub of international trade in northern Europe. Instead of proletarianized textile workers making fabrics, small commodity-producing specialist craftsmen now manufactured fashion items (such as dress, belts, sleeves, hats, purses, gloves, shoes), but also furniture, arms and armour, mirrors, glass, pottery and hollowware. Bruges merchants specialized in regional supply systems of wood, grain, wool and cloth; they imported German and Dutch beer and luxury goods, such as spices, exotic fruits

[249] M. T. Galvin, 'The Poor Tables of Bruges, 1270–1477', unpublished PhD thesis, Columbia University (New York, 1998), pp. 2–3, 179–210; Galvin, 'Credit and Parochial Charity'; Murrray, *Bruges*, p. 89.

[250] Maréchal, *Gebondenheid*, pp. 310–11.

and wine. Craftsmen and traders were involved in decorating the houses and feeding the bodies of an affluent and hungry domestic market. Its products gradually conquered some foreign markets and supplied the demand for luxuries among European noblemen and elites. Bruges was also on the verge of becoming the centre of the 'new art', where painters, embroiderers and jewellers from all over the Low Countries and beyond gathered and found a new clientele among wealthy townsmen, the Burgundian nobility and the ducal court, and among the hundreds of foreign merchants in the city, eager to satisfy the demand for manufactured goods of their customers at home.

Throughout the late fourteenth and fifteenth centuries, this changing pattern was Bruges' key to success. Successive revolts and political turmoil were only minor setbacks and the remarkable stability of its population levels throughout the late medieval crisis is a sign that economic conversion had been a success. But it is also a deceitful indicator, as the social composition of the city must have changed dramatically. The revolutionary masses of textile workers and capitalistic merchant-entrepreneurs of 1302 were replaced by self-conscious middle classes of skilled craftsmen, brokers and regional traders. These groups would feed the city's political and social ambitions and an ambivalence towards Burgundian centralization.[251] But the change also defined a new social balance based on several elements: relative population stability, rising real wages, a greater importance of guild-organized middle groups in urban society, a greater stress on manufactured goods for those groups who were more ready than before to consume them, short information lines on clothing and material goods because of the presence of foreign merchants and noble consumers (especially courtiers), shorter fashion cycles because of these flows and the subsequent flexibility of manufacture geared towards the export of textiles (colour, finishing) and clothing.

These circumstances generated a 'creative environment'. The massive immigration of skilled craftsmen from towns of the Low Countries added to the phenomenon, but did not cause it. Jan van Eyck, Petrus Christus, Hans Memling and Gerard David were lured to Bruges because of its dynamic economy of skill and the presence of wealthy customers. The changing social balance and the increased purchasing power stimulated demand for luxury goods, dress, tableware, jewellery and furniture. Burghers and noblemen alike wanted to invest in these goods, and material culture responded accordingly. The post-plague period was less a golden age for

[251] Dumolyn, 'Our Land is Only Founded on Trade and Industry'.

the wage earner than it was for the specialist craftsman, who could capitalize on a revived emphasis on consumption. The key to explaining these dramatic changes lies in the increasing demands of the new groups who were themselves products of these changes: the urban middle classes. The new economic activities encouraged the rise of a new middle class. Higher income stimulated demand for goods and services which were probably more closely related to local dynamics (building, food, services of all kinds) than to Bruges' international business community. This benefited not only the dynamic sectors aiming at the export market, but also other, locally oriented activities.

Hence, the city's corporative framework was able to cushion economic downturn by specializing in existing economic sectors with high added value, which required particular flows of raw materials (cloth and other fabrics, precious metals and stones) and labour. No new guilds had to be founded. Economic change was integrated into the existing guild framework. But Bruges was able to grasp these new opportunities more than its Flemish competitors. The city's pivotal role in the north European trade network offered opportunities to bypass difficulties of supply and labour shortage, and link demand to manufacture in sectors where fashion cycles were of crucial importance. Good access to raw materials, comparatively low information costs and changed opportunity costs for investment of capital and labour gave the city's specialist activities a cutting edge over competitors. Bruges' expertise in finance not only favoured cloth entrepreneurs, but probably also allowed specialist craftsmen to invest in capital-intensive workshops. In fourteenth-century Bruges, craftsmen had already been able to enter the banking facilities of exchangers like Collard de Marke; but credit networks in mid-fifteenth-century Bruges also seem particularly dense.

The two crucial developments were the long-term decline of textiles and the rise of clothing and luxury industries. Their chronologies, though, do not run completely parallel. Whereas the cloth industry lost out towards the mid fourteenth century, the clothing industry seems to have taken off somewhat later. As a consequence the latter part of the thirteenth and the first half of the fourteenth centuries must have been a period of great stress and difficult adaptation of the local economy. It is a strange paradox, that the beginnings of Bruges' success as a commercial hub in European trade probably took place in a city racked with unemployment and poverty.

The dynamic pattern of the supply side of the Bruges economy more or less confirms the assessment made by most contemporary observers. They failed to see a marked decline in the Bruges economy until the end of the fifteenth century.[252] When considering the city's industrial output, contemporary observers were probably more accurate in their assessment than some present-day historians. There is, of course, little doubt that moments of political tension caused trade difficulties, and Bruges was vulnerable to economic cycles like any other premodern market (sixteenth-century Antwerp also encountered adversities). But the nuances added to the debate by Wilfrid Brulez in 1970 need taking into account.[253] Even amidst political chaos and structural change of trade routes, as Italian and Hanseatic commerce in Bruges declined and English, south German and Portuguese trade in Antwerp flourished, Bruges proved resilient and, as we will see further on, throughout the sixteenth century and the golden age of Antwerp, it remained an important financial and commercial centre. In the end, the events in the late 1480s and early 1490s were to prove fatal to the city's international role. Its industrial infrastructure relied too heavily on the intricate density of the networking and financial capabilities of international trade and luxury consumption. Specialization in luxury and clothing was a wonderfully successful strategy as long as information on patterns of demand and consumption was readily available and relatively cheap. These were, however, also industries that could easily be relocated to competing commercial cities, and Antwerp guildsmen would gradually take over the role of Bruges craftsmen, who themselves often moved to the Scheldt metropolis. Once the comparative advantage was gone, the specialist craftsmen and cloth finishers began to leave. But this was a slow process – as the number of new masters in the St Luke guild suggests. In all likelihood, the Bruges aldermen and entrepreneurs realized the structural weakness of their city. At the end of the fifteenth century, they reacted by investing in a revival of their old strength, the textile industries and more specifically the successful Hondschoote-type worsteds. As it turned out, this strategy did not work well, and the gradual decline of what had been in the late medieval context an exceptional industrial capacity would turn Bruges in the sixteenth century into a more normal pre-industrial society.

[252] Van Uytven, 'Stages of Economic Decline', pp. 259–61.
[253] Brulez, 'Bruges and Antwerp'.

7 | Social Groups, Political Power and Institutions II, c.1300–c.1500

JAN DUMOLYN, FREDERIK BUYLAERT, GUY DUPONT, JELLE HAEMERS AND ANDY RAMANDT

At the turn of the fourteenth century, the character of political rule in the major cities of Flanders changed decisively. Around 1280, the manual workers who during the thirteenth century had been systematically excluded from the city government, finally entered the political stage. After the popular victory of 1302 the craft guilds, especially in the larger urban centres of Bruges and Ghent, gained access to the arenas of political decision-making. The cities emerged with new constitutions in which control of the urban government was shared between the old merchant class and the guilds, which were now given new liberties, though the equilibrium between the two would always remain precarious.[1] Guild power became a prominent feature of social and political life, so much so that the late medieval period in Bruges can be justly termed the age of 'corporatism', with the city being regarded as a body politic strongly influenced by the 'political guilds'. While this development partly emerged from longer-term economic change, the momentous events around 1300 altered the nature of communal politics. While corporatist ideas and practices of governing the urban body politic borrowed from an earlier communal ideology, after 1302 the craft guilds would become, or would at least present themselves as, the embodiment of the urban commune. For centuries to come, the guilds would also be the main political bodies around which popular demands would mobilize. Their sign languages and practices – their banners, slogans, meetings, armed gatherings and strikes – came to dominate the processes and course of popular politics.[2]

Yet as 'political guilds', the Bruges crafts were also Janus-faced: they functioned both as instruments of popular political participation or even rebellion and also as tools of urban government, delegated with military, political and legal tasks. They also developed their own internal elites, who were economically powerful and politically active, though they were connected

[1] The best synthesis on the events and aftermath of 1302, with references to older works, is Van Caenegem (ed.), *1302*.

[2] M. Boone, 'La construction d'un républicanisme urbain: Enjeux de la politique municipale dans les villes flamandes au bas Moyen Âge', in D. Menjot and J.-L. Pinol (eds.), *Enjeux et expressions de la politique municipale (XIIe–XXe siècles)* (Paris, 1997), pp. 41–60.

still to other social groups. An examination of the city's political history needs to consider the changing nature of Bruges society, and the difficulty of categorizing the social groups involved in political processes. Even so, one of the main underlying sources of tension, perhaps the major fault-line in Bruges society throughout the later Middle Ages, was between two main groups: the commercial elites (rentiers, merchants, bankers, brokers, hostellers and the richer retailers, including butchers and fishmongers) on the one hand, and the producing classes and small shopkeepers from the local market (small entrepreneurs, middle-class guild masters and wage workers), on the other. The commercial elite was constantly trying to restore its power and eliminate corporatist rule of the city. Yet while this main fault-line is often visible, it was complicated and obscured by other social and political networks and solidarities. A full picture of late medieval politics and society in Bruges has to take account of other alliances: between families, between textile workers and merchant factions siding against ruling regimes, or between the rich and their clients among poorer people.[3]

From the Commune to the Corporatist Body Politic: Institutions and Administration

The institutional bases of guild authority were many. Essential to their flexing of political power was their military muscle. In 1302, the Bruges city militia had shown itself to princes and nobles as a force to be reckoned with, and by 1340 it counted more than 6,000 people, the majority of whom were artisans. The division of each guild or section of the *poorterie* in the militia, the *voud*, was directed by a captain or *hooftman* recruited from its own ranks, and artisans also took part in the shooting guilds of the longbowmen, later known as St Sebastian's guild, and of the crossbowmen, eventually organized into two guilds of St George, the Oudhof (Old Court) and the Jonghof (Young Court). During the fourteenth century these shooting guilds became strongly associated with the urban government and urban identity, though the crossbowmen would always retain a more socially elitist profile than the longbowmen.[4] By 1349, the craft guilds had successfully lobbied to receive

[3] Dumolyn, 'Guild Politics'.

[4] J. F. Verbruggen, 'De Brugse effectieven van de slag bij Kortrijk', *Bijdragen voor de Geschiedenis der Nederlanden*, 2 (1948), 241–7 (at 242–3); Verbruggen, *Het gemeenteleger van Brugge*; J. F. Verbruggen, 'De organisatie van de militie te Brugge in de XIVe eeuw', *HGG*, 87 (1950), 163–70; an example of the military expenses of a specific guild can be found in the accounts of the Bruges weavers 1372–3: see Espinas and Pirenne (eds.), *Recueil*, vol. I, p. 589.

a salary during campaigns, the so-called 'monthly money' (*maendgheld*).[5] Apart from the regular militia mobilized by the guilds and the merchants, a paramilitary group in the service of the town also developed, known as the Red Hoods (Rode Kaproenen), an elite corps of between 40 and 100 men led by a captain, the *upperhooftman*. First mentioned around 1360, its subsequent history suggests strong connections with guild aspirations, for it would be abolished after the 1436–8 revolt and then re-established in 1477, both dates when guilds lost and reasserted their authority (see below). The city's military organization was thus a mixture of corporatist and professional elements, the exception being the urban cavalry which was the preserve of rich burghers who possessed their own horses and armour. The Flemish urban militias have sometimes been unfairly dismissed as inefficient and ineffective compared with professional armies. The militia was makeshift in so far as many citizens kept arms at home, but it also had professional artillery specialists to handle a considerable arsenal of heavy guns, and the guilds also stocked weapons in their guildhouses.[6] But the militia's military capabilities were of less significance than its political importance: its military strength primarily served to bolster urban autonomy and to add political weight to artisans within the body politic.

Capitalizing on their power after 1302, the Flemish artisans forced their allies of the comital family to grant privileges to their guilds and cities. These charters made concessions to many popular demands that had been voiced from the first major wave of Flemish revolts in 1275–80. In 1302, having exiled their adversaries of the pro-French Lily party to which the majority of the merchant class belonged, the popular alliance of artisans and entrepreneurs – who were then still known as the *amici comitis* or *partie li conte* ('friends' or 'party' of the count) – occupied approximately 75 per cent of governmental offices in Bruges. After 1304 this number began to decrease and a new balance was sought between the different social groups.[7] On 4 November 1304, Philip of Chieti, a son of Count Guy de Dampierre (the latter still held prisoner by the French king) granted Bruges a new charter of privileges. Like its predecessors of 1165–77 and 1281, this

[5] GVS, *Inventaire*, vol. IV, p. 180.

[6] Van Houtte, *De geschiedenis van Brugge*, pp. 327–32; De Smet, 'De inrichting'; P. Stabel, 'Militaire organisatie, bewapening en wapenbezit in het laatmiddeleeuwse Brugge', *BTFG*, 89 (2011), 1049–73; J. Haemers and B. Verbist, 'Het Gentse gemeenteleger in het laatste kwart van de vijftiende eeuw: Een politieke, financiële en militaire analyse van stadsmilities', *HMG*, 62 (2008), 291–326; F. Buylaert and B. Verwerft, 'Urban Militias, Nobles and Mercenaries: The Organisation of the Antwerp Army in the Flemish-Brabantine Revolt of the 1480s', *Journal of Medieval Military History*, 9 (2011), 146–66.

[7] J. F. Verbruggen, 'Beschouwingen over 1302', *HGG*, 93 (1956), 38–53 (at 43).

'urban constitution' mostly covered matters dealing with criminal and private law, and with procedures for the administration of justice. However, testifying to an increased degree of urban autonomy, new stipulations set out how relations between the city and the count and his officers were to be run, and how the city government was to be elected. The textual tradition of the 1304 privilege is confusing. The document exists in different versions. Only the copies from the 'urban point of view', and not from the 'comital', explicitly describe how the city government was to be elected. Every year on 2 February (Candlemas), thirteen aldermen (*scepenen*) and thirteen councillors (*raeden*) were to be appointed. Significantly, the craft guilds had the right to appoint nine of the thirteen aldermen and councillors while the four other ones were to be appointed by the count from the ranks of the *poorters* (burghers). The term *poorter* had been used to denote anyone with burgher rights, but now it was also used more narrowly to refer to merchant families, other property owners and rich burghers. The *poorterie*, a group that now formed a separate institution and in effect the legal successor to the former merchant Hanse, would continue to operate as a political counterweight to the guilds in Bruges. Following the election of the aldermen and councillors, the aldermen were to choose a burgomaster (*burchmeestere van scepenen*) from their ranks, and subsequently the aldermen and councillors together would elect the burgomaster of the council, also called the burgomaster 'of the body' (*burghemeester van den courpse*) or 'of the commune' (*van den commune*). Another type of city officials, the treasurers, already introduced as distinct officers in 1297–8, reported on urban finances. Their number was eventually settled at two for each yearly jurisdiction.[8]

Institutionally, the city government and the administration of justice were closely intertwined. Many of the councils, commissions and boards in Bruges exercised both administrative and judicial powers. Elected or appointed politicians normally served no more than one consecutive year on a particular council, although they could be – and were often – re-elected after a compulsory one-year lapse. They were assisted by professional city clerks, who built their career in the city administration and who guaranteed

[8] G. De Poerck, 'Note critique sur le grand privilège brugeois de 1304 et le règlement d'élection du magistrat', *HGG*, 74 (1931), 139–57; GVS, *Coutume*, vol. I, pp. 286–307, 316; D. Berten, 'Un ancien manuscrit flamand de la bibliothèque de Vienne', *Bulletin de la Commission Royale pour la Publication des Anciennes Lois et Ordonnances de Belgique*, 9 (1913), 443–4, is the version stating that nine aldermen and councillors would be elected by the *ambochters* (guildsmen); and see the critical reflections on this textual tradition in Van den Auweele, 'Schepenbank', pp. 159–61; and D. Van den Auweele, 'Varia juridica ex manuscriptis: Bronnen van het oude Brugse recht', *Standen en Landen. Nieuwsbrief*, 2 (1992), 6–19.

its continuity. The council of aldermen (*den ghemeenen college van scepenen*) – in historiography commonly referred to as the 'bench' of aldermen although this term never occurs in a medieval source – acted both as the supreme council for the daily political administration of the city and as the highest court of law in criminal matters, including both penal and reconciliation justice, and in civil matters, including contentious and voluntary justice. Acts of private law, such as inheritances, sales and other contracts were sealed by the aldermen (for although notaries existed in Bruges and Flanders, they were less prominent than in Italy). It was the urban court that acted as a warrantor for property rights and business contracts, including those involving foreign merchants. In spite of contemporary references to the council as 'the aldermen' or 'the common council of aldermen', the city government was composed not only of twelve aldermen, but also of twelve councillors (*raeden*), each with a burgomaster. Hence, the city council's full title, often used in its sentences and deeds, was 'the council of burgomasters, aldermen and councillors'.[9]

The precise competencies of the 'councillors', who in origin may have emerged from older communal institutions (see Chapter 4), still need further investigation. Contrary to a persistent myth in Bruges historiography, the councillors did not constitute a second 'bench' of magistrates separate from the aldermen (as was the case in Ghent, where the aldermen of the *keure* and those of *gedele* constituted two benches, each with its own organization and even assembly hall).[10] The collective name for the councillors in contemporary sources was indeed 'council' (*raed*), but this is not the same as '*the* council'. In fact the councillors acted as assessors in the council of aldermen and in its commissions and deputations, but they had a lesser role as their votes were not taken into account when reaching a verdict or establishing a quorum. In contrast to the aldermen, the councillors did not take part in the judgment of criminal cases, but in civil cases only. Moreover, the burgomaster of the council, apart from also imposing arbitration and reconciliatory justice on conflicting parties, acted as public prosecutor defending the interests of the commune.[11] However, certain executive powers

[9] Dutch: 'Wij buerchmeesters, scepenen ende raed van de stede van Brugghe' (SAB, 157, no. 3, reg. 1447–53, fo. 55^{v} –29 August 1448); French: 'Bourgmaistres, eschevins et conseil de la ville de Bruges' (SAB, 157, no. 3, reg. 1447–53, fo. 24^{r} – 27 January 1448 n.s.); Latin: 'Burgimagistri, scabini et consules ville Brugensis' (SAB, 164, reg. 1439–41, fo. 44 – 4 March 1440 n.s.).

[10] For the institutions of Ghent, see M. Boone, *Gent en de Bourgondische hertogen ca. 1384 – ca. 1453: Een sociaal-politieke studie van een staatsvormingsproces* (Brussels, 1990); and numerous other publications by the same author.

[11] See above, Chapter 4. A useful source for the urban institutions remains the treatise by the Bruges jurist Joos de Damhouder, *Van de grootdadigheyt der breedt-vermaerde regeringhe van*

remained in the hands of the count. Another prosecutor was the 'sheriff' (*schout, scouteete, escoutete* or *scultetus*). The sheriff was directly appointed by the prince and was not to be a burgher of the town. He upheld public peace, the rule of law and the interests of the count. He was lodged at the *Love* on the Burg square and had his own police force of twelve sergeants (*'s heren cnaepen*). The sheriff summoned perpetrators of crimes and other transgressors of the law before the aldermen.[12]

The council of aldermen generally assembled every morning, except on Sundays, in their chamber in the aldermen's hall (*scepenen huus*), in the Burg square. During the assemblies, behind closed doors, the aldermen, often jointly with the councillors, dealt with matters of city government and with judicial cases that were brought to them. Unlike the legal proceedings and verdicts, of which records were kept as early as 1361 (no registers of the chamber survive from before 1423 and those preserved cover only thirty years of the fifteenth century), the political discussions by their council were for a long time kept secret from the outside world.[13] They presumably also remained unrecorded, as the registers of the resolutions of the aldermen only start in 1535 and no reference is made to them before that date.[14] Hence, little is known about political decision-making by the city government, beyond that it was to be kept secret by those participating (observing the so-called *secreet van scepenen* or 'secret of the aldermen') and that there was an established order in which the council members were allowed to voice their opinion (first came the aldermen, then the senior clerks and finally the councillors). Prior to 1490, except for some decisions copied into the city's cartularies of privileges, there are no surviving records of the council's political decisions, the *hallegeboden*, which were made public in proclamations at the Belfry.[15]

By 1304, the main apparatus of urban administration was established, although in line with many towns, it grew in size and became further professionalized during the fourteenth and fifteenth centuries. The policemen

de stadt Brugge (Amsterdam, 1684), pp. 484, 491, 503, which is the Dutch translation of his original *De magnificentia politae amplissimae civitatis Brugensis* (Antwerp, 1564).

12 The development of the princely judicial officers in Bruges and Flanders, from *burggraaf* (castellan) to *baljuw* (bailiff) and, particularly in the case of Bruges, the *schout* (sheriff) may be traced in Ganshof, *Recherches sur les tribunaux*; Nowé, *Les baillis*; J. Van Rompaey, *Het grafelijk baljuwsambt in Vlaanderen tijdens de Boergondische periode* (Brussels, 1967); and see above, Chapter 4.

13 SAB, 157, 164, 165 and 166 contain registers of the chamber dating from the fifteenth century (but no earlier than 1423), that have sometimes been mixed up with registers of the *vierscare* (as is the case with series 157).

14 SAB, 118.

15 SAB, 120 (injunctions issued at the halle of *Hallegeboden*) starts in December 1490.

in the service of the city (the *scarwetters*) had their headquarters in the Groenevoorde house at the market-place and were charged with upholding public order and protecting the members of the town government. Apart from its political members, who were annually renewed (from 1241 onwards, as we have seen), the urban administration was also composed of a varying number of salaried clerks, who advised on city governance and in trials, and who registered the council's political and legal proceedings: they formed the most stable and professional element within the administration. There were four to eight 'senior clerks' (*upperclercken*) in the fourteenth century, rising to thirteen in the busiest years of the fifteenth century, and stabilizing at around ten in the sixteenth. They included the *pencionarissen* or *clercken pencionarissen*, who acted as senior political and legal advisors to the aldermen and who were often legally, or at least academically, trained, as indicated by their university title of master (*meester*). (Confusingly, the term *pencionarissen (van der stede)* could be used to refer to all city personnel who were on the city's payroll.) The *clerck pencionaris* who was first in rank had no specific function title before the sixteenth century, when he was called the '(first) secretary' (*secretaris* or *eerste secretaris*) or the first *pencionaris*. Besides the senior advisors, who had no specific responsibilities, the category of city clerks also included the *greffiers* or *clercken* who acted as the registrar or administrative head of one of the aldermen's offices (*greffies*) or commissions. They comprised – in order of importance – the registrar of the (aldermen's) chamber, later known as the civil registrar (*greffier civil*); the registrar of the *vierscare*, in the fifteenth century also called the clerk of the blood (*clerc van den bloede*) or simply the registrar (*greffier*), and in the sixteenth century the registrar of the blood (*greffier van den bloede*) or the criminal registrar (*greffier criminel*); his *onder greffier*; the clerk of the treasury (*clerc van der tresorie*); his *onder clerc*, who acted also as the collector of the heritable rents; and the clerk of the orphans' chamber (*clerc van den wesen*). Moreover, *taelmannen* or lawyers served the city to defend its interests in princely and ecclesiastical courts. From the end of the thirteenth century there was also an official city surgeon, and engineers (*engienmeesters*) responsible for the locks and water infrastructure. The *mudderaers* were of much lower rank, responsible for cleaning the streets and canals. The city employed many messengers, and twelve trial servers who also served as bodyguards for the magistrates (*stede garsoenen*). Other official urban offices included cloth measurers, wine carriers and other types of porter, profitable offices which were often leased to a limited number of people. The urban prison (the Steen), was run by a warder (*steenwaerder*). By the end of the fourteenth century, the city administration comprised some fifty paid officials in total, a considerable number. Other urban offices, often with lucrative incomes attached to them, were farmed out to private investors, as was the collection of excises on consumption products in most years.[16]

The precise control that guildsmen exercised over the urban government is not easy to document; and in the early fourteenth century it was not even certain that guild dominance would prevail, still less that the earlier communal model of mass assemblies, in which every sworn member of the commune had been able to participate, would be replaced by a guild system of popular participation. This system had to be gradually worked out and the artisans' impact on Bruges' institutions would continue to depend on the particular socio-political balance of forces in any given period.[17] The Moerlemaye Revolt of 1280–1 tried in vain to revive the memory of the old communal assemblies, and by 1302 it had become clear that the guilds, asserting a greater military and economic power, were in the best position institutionally to represent the mass of the urban population. Even

[16] SAB, 216 (city accounts): yearly entries of expenditure for salaries; GVS, *Coutume*, vol. I, pp. 286–323; Van Houtte, *De geschiedenis van Brugge*, pp. 319–44. On the urban prison, see B. Beernaert, 'Het Steen: Een benadering van de vroegere Brugse gevangenis', in *Van Middeleeuwen tot heden*, pp. 20–8. On various urban officers, see the works of A. Vandewalle, 'De stadsofficiën van Brugge: openbaar ambt of commercie (15e–18e eeuw)', in G. Macours (ed.), *Cornua legum: Actes des journées internationales d'histoire du droit et des institutions 1986* (Antwerp, 1987), pp. 217–25; A. Vandewalle, 'De stedegarsoenen, boden in dienst van de magistraat in de Nieuwe Tijd', in G. Asaert (ed.), *Recht en instellingen in de oude Nederlanden tijdens de Middeleeuwen en de Nieuwe Tijd. Liber Amicorum Jan Buntinx* (Leuven, 1981), pp. 391–404. On the aldermen, see J. Mertens, 'Bestuursinstellingen van de stad Brugge (1127–1795)', in W. Prevenier and B. Augustyn (eds.), *De gewestelijke en lokale overheidsinstellingen in Vlaanderen tot 1795* (Brussels, 1997), pp. 323–32 (at p. 327); J. van Leeuwen, *De Vlaamse wetsvernieuwing: Een onderzoek naar de jaarlijkse keuze en aanstelling van het stadsbestuur in Gent, Brugge en Ieper in de Middeleeuwen* (Brussels, 2004), passim. On clerks and messengers, see H. Dendooven, 'De Brugse klerken in de veertiende eeuw', unpublished MA thesis, Ghent University (Ghent, 2007); H. Lowagie, *Met brieven an de wet: stedelijk briefverkeer in het laatmiddeleeuwse graafschap Vlaanderen* (Ghent, 2012), passim.

[17] J. Mertens, 'De verdeling van de Brugse schepenzetels op sociaal gebied (XIVde eeuw)', *Wetenschappelijke tijdingen*, 21 (1961), cols. 451–66; J. Mertens, 'Brugge en Gent: De vertegenwoordiging van de "leden" in de stadmagistraat', in J. De Zutter, L. Charles and A. Capiteyn (eds.), *Qui Valet Ingenio, Liber Amicorum Dr. Johan Decavele* (Ghent, 1996), pp. 385–91; Van den Auweele, 'Schepenbank', passim; A. Vandewalle, 'De Brugse stadsmagistraat en de deelname van de ambachten aan het bestuur, 14de–15e eeuw', in W. Prevenier and B. Augustyn (eds.), *De Vlaamse instellingen tijdens het Ancien Régime: Recent onderzoek in nieuw perspectief* (Brussels, 1999), pp. 27–40; Dumolyn, *De Brugse opstand*, pp. 105–20; Vanhaverbeke, 'Het stadsbestuur in Brugge in de periode 1375–1407: Sociaal-institutionele benadering aan de hand van een prosopografische methode', unpublished MA thesis, Catholic University of Leuven (Leuven, 1997); Vanhaverbeke, 'Het stadsbestuur in Brugge'; A. Janssens, 'Macht en onmacht van de Brugse schepenbank in de periode 1477–1490', in *HGG*, 133 (1996), 5–45; Haemers, *For the Common Good*, passim.

so, the charters granted to Bruges and other cities in Flanders between 1301 and 1304 referred to liberties granted to 'the commune' and 'commoners' (*ghemeentucht*, *ghemeente*, *ghemeen* or *li commun*) rather than explicitly to 'guilds'. However, shortly after, Bruges charters began to name the guilds as the groups with the exclusive right to represent the commoners.[18] Other institutional experiments in these early years also seem designed to frame the increased political influence of a larger portion of the population. Shortly after 1302, the Bruges guildsmen took control of an institution known as the 'hundredmen' (*hondertmannen*). On 25 April 1303, these hundredmen were appointed as justices of the peace (*paisieres*), to mediate in conflicts and feuds between citizens. Earlier in that year they had already been checking the city accounts, a long-standing popular demand to prevent fraud and corruption by the ruling oligarchs, replacing the ephemeral 'twentymen' whom the king of France had installed during French occupation. However, the competences of the hundredmen were also short-lived and they were ultimately replaced by the colleges of the 'partitioners' (*deelmannen*) and of the 'headmen' (*hooftmannen*). The 'hundredmen' are not mentioned after 1337–8. The college of *deelmannen* was given a formal structure in 1305 and by 1311 they seem to have gradually replaced the 'hundredmen' in most of their responsibilities. Initially, there were three to seven *deelmannen* per section (*zestendeel*) but their number ultimately settled at six, each led by a dean. They were appointed by the aldermen and councillors within three days of a new city magistracy being established. As decreed in their regulations around 1305, these 'partitioners' dealt with the succession of goods in small inheritances, the settlement of minor debts, the supervision of marriages and priestly ordinations (to prevent too lavish parties and gifts being given), the removal of fire hazards and the resolution of border issues between properties. The aldermen also charged them with other kinds of neighbourhood inspection.[19]

The exact relationship between the 'revolutionary' institution of the hundredmen and the older one of the headmen (*hooftmannen*) of the *zestendelen* (the six sections, usually called *ambochten* or *official* before the 1330s)[20] had also to be clarified, as the one potentially rivalled the other. The headmen were selected only from the *poorters* (the merchants and property

[18] Dumolyn and Haemers, 'Reclaiming the Common Sphere'. A similar example is the 'constitutional' charter of Senlis granted to Ghent in 1301: M. Boone, 'Het "Charter van Senlis" (November 1301) voor de stad Gent: Een stedelijke constitutie in het spanningsveld tussen vorst en stad (met uitgave van de tekst)', *HMG*, 57 (2003), 1–45 (at 44): 'ceus du commun'.

[19] Van Caenegem, *Geschiedenis van het strafrecht*, p. 304; GVS, *Coutume*, vol. I, pp. 348–9.

[20] See Chapter 2.

owners), while the hundredmen appear to have been recruited largely from guild ranks. Surviving sources suggest that the headmen originally operated only within their own section, with some responsibilities over its policing, guarding its part of the city defences and leading the contingent of the *poorterie* of their district in the militia. In the mid-fourteenth century the college of the headmen developed into a collective institution that represented the interests of the *poorterie* as a whole, as a corporatist counterweight to the power of the craft guilds. The headmen assembled under the presidency of the St John's section, the richest section in the town. In 1359 the hundredmen controlled the accounts for the last time and in 1363 the headmen appear in the sources as a fully functioning college. At this point their responsibilities become clearer: they dealt with crimes against public morality and family affairs, areas of jurisdiction the aldermen had appropriated from ecclesiastical courts. They also assumed the *paisierer* function of the hundredmen in the early 1360s. In 1384, under Burgundian rule, they would temporarily obtain more responsibility as 'governors' of the city when the guilds were again deprived of their military and political autonomy, and from 1399 they were directly appointed by the prince.[21]

Other courts also had jurisdiction in Bruges or over Bruges citizens, notably the comital court of the *Audiencie*. From 1386 it was known as the *Raedt van Vlaenderen* (Council of Flanders), competent for instance on crimes relating to princely jurisdiction such as *lèse majesté*, and from the 1450s it would also handle civil cases from Bruges as a court of appeal. The feudal court of the 'Burg of Bruges' dealt with transactions and inheritances of fiefs held from the count in both the city and the castellany.[22] From the late thirteenth century, Bruges also had its own ecclesiastical court under a *sigillifer* or 'seal carrier', a decentralized delegation of the official of Tournai with limited competence, so that Flemings did not have to travel to Tournai for every case.[23] As we have seen, there were also seigniorial courts operating within enclaves of the Bruges territory that had resisted the unification

21 Verbruggen, *Vlaanderen na de Guldensporenslag*, p. 19; GVS, *Coutume*, vol. I, pp. 281–4, 327–62; Van den Auweele, 'Schepenbank', vol. III, pp. 296–7.

22 On these comital institutions, see J. Buntinx, *De Audiëntie van de graven van Vlaanderen: Studie over het centraal grafelijk gerecht (c.1330 – c.1409)* (Brussels, 1949); J. Van Rompaey, *De Grote Raad van de hertogen van Boergondië en het Parlement van Mechelen* (Brussels, 1973); D. Heirbaut, *Over heren, vazallen en graven: Het persoonlijk leenrecht in Vlaanderen ca. 1000–1305* (Brussels, 1997); J. Dumolyn, *De Raad van Vlaanderen en de Rekenkamer van Rijsel: Gewestelijke overheidsinstellingen als instrument van de centralisatie (1419–1477)* (Brussels, 2002).

23 M. Vleeschouwers-Van Melkebeek, 'De mazen van het net: Samenwerking tussen de kerkelijke rechtbanken van Doornik en Brugge in de late Middeleeuwen', *Bulletin de la Commission Royale pour la publication des Anciennes Lois et Ordonnances de Belgique*, 43 (2002), 167–96.

of the city: the *redenaers*, magistrates of the Proosse who also administered justice, at least in criminal cases, in the Kanunnikse.[24] Despite these other courts, the development of administrative and judicial processes in Bruges largely reflected the increasing institutional hold that the guilds had begun to exert over urban government, as well as the strong tendency towards legal and political autonomy, an aspiration shared by both the commercial elites and the guildsmen. This aspiration would be gradually crushed as the dukes of Burgundy built up a more centralized state apparatus in the fifteenth century, but the types and competences of city offices and councils that had emerged by the mid-fourteenth century would largely remain.[25]

The Guilds as Urban Institutions

Between the early fourteenth century and the 1370s, during a period of constant strife, the craft guilds developed into institutions that became fully integrated into the urban political system. They emerged, in effect, as a political force that counterbalanced the vested interests of the ruling oligarchic families of merchants, hostellers, bankers and landowners and represented the interests of the productive classes in society and the petty retailers. In many or most cases their delegates may well have belonged to an upper group of wealthier guild masters, yet these men could not disregard the wider interests of other craftsmen, and acted to channel the economic and political opinions of their members, who were consulted in assemblies of the entire membership or at least of the masters, where the views of the rank and file would be voiced. We have seen above how the guild wardens, the dean and the 'finders' also served as *smalle wetten* (small courts of law) to judge on infringements of market regulations; how, de facto or de iure, the craft guilds also operated as consultative bodies for economic policy; how they had the power to reject new taxes or to deliver petitions to the city government.[26] But the guilds' jurisdiction extended beyond economic

[24] J. Marechal, *Inventaris van het Archief van de Proosdij van Sint-Donaas te Brugge* (Brussels, 1960); L. Gilliodts-Van Severen (ed.), *Coutume de la prévôté de Bruges*, 2 vols. (Brussels, 1887).

[25] On Burgundian judicial and institutional centralization in Flanders, see D. Lambrecht, 'Centralisatie onder de Bourgondiërs: Van Audiëntie naar Parlement van Mechelen', *Bijdragen voor de Geschiedenis der Nederlanden*, 20 (1965–6), 83–109; W. Blockmans and W. Prevenier, *The Promised Lands: The Low Countries under Burgundian Rule, 1369–1530*, trans. E. Fackelman (Philadelphia, 1999); J. Dumolyn, *Staatsvorming en vorstelijke ambtenaren in het graafschap Vlaanderen (1419–1477)* (Leuven, 2003); R. Stein, *De hertog en zijn staten: De eenwording van de Bourgondische Nederlanden, c.1380–c.1480* (Hilversum, 2014).

[26] Vermaut, 'De textielnijverheid', vol. II, pp. 337–64; Dumolyn, 'De Brugse ambachtsbesturen'.

matters, for the task of organizing their own members, and of working with other crafts in city government, required them to promote harmony at all political levels. In both guild and city-wide legislation, certain ideal goals became stressed above all others, even if they were difficult to achieve in times of crisis: peace, brotherly love, unity and justice, including economic justice, the possibility of securing a livelihood through honest labour. These goals amount to a 'corporatist ideology' that dominated political discourse within the city. Artisans would hold the urban government accountable for defending the 'common weal' (*ghemenen oerboer*) of the city which they defined within this ideology.[27]

The guilds also increased their political autonomy, but in the teeth of opposition. For a brief period after 1302, while the alliance held between the artisans and the comital family, they managed to obtain the most favourable privileges they would ever have regarding their internal organization and autonomy. They gained the right to elect their own leaders, a demand that the Damme guildsmen had articulated in 1280 and one that had surely also been circulating in Bruges. Evidence for the precise functioning of election procedures is fragmentary for some guilds and non-existent for others, however. The privileges of the fullers and shearers, probably granted in 1303 (although the texts preserved may only have been draught documents never issued), laid out a complicated procedure for internal elections but did not eliminate the role of the city government entirely. The guilds had to present two lists in which they nominated candidates for the office of warden, from which the magistrates would make the final selection. In the fullers' privilege, journeymen also obtained the right to be represented among the wardens. The brokers' privilege, dated 8 May 1303, apparently did not then have such autonomy: a later charter, dated 8 June 1306, stated that 'from now on, they shall choose their sworn men themselves'. Probably the first Flemish guild to gain the right to elect new guild wardens was the Bruges butchers in their privilege of 2 December 1302, secured only a few months after the victory at Kortrijk (11 July). This charter highlights the complexity of our picture of these early election procedures. The newly elected leaders were to share electoral power with four men appointed by the 'community' (*meentucht*) of the craft guild, in other words the assembly

[27] Dumolyn, 'Het corporatieve element'; Wyffels, *De oorsprong*, pp. 47–8, 75; J.-P. Sosson, 'Die Körperschaften in den Niederlanden und Nordfrankreich: Neue Forschungsperspektiven', in K. Friedland (ed.) *Gilden und Korporationen in den nordeuropäischen Städten des späten Mittelalters* (Cologne, 1984), pp. 79–90 (at 82); M. Boone, 'Armes, coursses, assemblees et commocions: Les gens de métiers et l'usage de la violence dans la société urbaine flamande à la fin du Moyen Âge', *RN*, 359 (2005), 7–34 (at 20–4).

of all the guild masters. Together, they were to choose six men, one to be the 'shield bearer' (military leader), and five to be 'finders', with the offices to be apportioned by lot. It seems that these six men were then to select the dean together with the whole guild, or at least with the approval of all members gathered at a meeting. Though the charter does not describe the process exactly, it involved seeking consensus rather than using ballots.[28]

However, there were limits to full participation of guild members in elections, and to the autonomy of their procedures. Where consensus was sought in elections, the voices of the most wealthy and socially prestigious guild members probably dominated. It is unclear which guilds allowed journeymen to participate in meetings, but the majority probably did not; while apprentice boys and female members had no say in internal guild politics. Socio-economic and political hierarchies existed within guilds, as we shall see: we need to avoid too rosy a picture of 'guild democracy'. And guild autonomy was also opposed. When artisan revolts were suppressed, the count and urban authorities would typically substitute the dean elected by the guild masters (sometimes also by the journeymen) with a *maenre* (translatable as 'summoner') or a *beleeder* (although this could also refer to an outside military leader of the guilds in the militia). *Maenres* or *beleeders* were recruited from the urban elites, and were often imposed on the Bruges guilds after corporatist revolts had failed, for instance (as we shall see) in 1328, 1348, 1380 and 1384.[29]

Guilds were not simply economic and political organizations: the corporatist values they promoted encompassed other aspects of urban life. They regulated moral behaviour according to the guild ethos of brotherly love and they organized charitable activities in ways that helped maintain social order. They promoted festive social events and ceremonies to reinforce their solidarity. An integral part of their assumption of greater political power was the manner in which they established a religious and architectural presence in the urban landscape. Information about guild buildings is fragmentary, and some guilds may have possessed chapels at an early date: the carpenters had a chapel in the Franciscan church by 1300. But during the fourteenth century, as we have seen (Chapter 6), the more important craft guilds certainly began to construct new guild houses and chapels.

[28] These charters are edited in Espinas and Pirenne (eds.), *Recueil*, vol. I, pp. 532–52; see also C. Wyffels, 'Twee oude Vlaamse ambachtskeuren: De vleeshouwers van Brugge (2 december 1302) en de smeden van Damme (eerste helft 1303)', *HGG*, 87 (1950), 93–109 (at 94–5, 105–6, 109); Van Houtte, 'Makelaars en waarden', p. 7.

[29] R. Demuynck, 'De Gentse oorlog (1379–1385): Oorzaken en karakter', *HMG*, 5 (1951), 305–18 (at 306–7).

Guild altars would be furnished with the guild's own liturgical objects and vestments adorned with its symbols, and every guild would have had a coffer containing devotional artefacts. Stained glass windows in side chapels of major churches could include the images of craft guilds and of their patron saints. The guild chapel also had an administrative function, particularly before the fifteenth century when the majority of guilds did not have their own guildhouse: a chapel could serve as a guild meeting place, or storage space for the guild archives and silverwork.[30]

This increasingly visible presence of guilds in the urban landscape, and within its sacred spaces, no doubt helped to strengthen their political status in relation to commercial and noble families who were similarly active in prestige constructions. But this distinction between 'guild' and 'commercial' interests was not hard and fast (as later comment on factions in Bruges will show); and despite guild promotion of corporatist ideals, attempts by workers to establish new guilds were not often welcomed by existing guilds. By the end of the fourteenth century the number of Bruges craft guilds stabilized at fifty-four, and any new trade could only take the institutional form of a *poortersnering* (burgher trade), whose members would be politically represented by the *poorterie*.[31] The porters at the Old Mill Bridge, for instance, were prevented from organizing themselves into a proper craft guild, and in their case, the religious fraternity they founded, devoted to Our Lady and approved by the city government in 1425, may have served as a surrogate craft organization: the regulations of this fraternity included ones on work and morality that were similar to other craft guilds, yet they had no political rights.[32] Moreover, corporatist discourse did not eliminate competition between guilds, and there often remained a gap between the ideals of unity and the many conflicting interests and identities that the world of the craftsmen represented.

A Century of Social and Political Struggle

Guild power in fourteenth-century Bruges in some aspects reached a level found in few other European cities outside the southern Low Countries

[30] On the collective devotion of the guilds, see also Chapter 8.

[31] Parmentier, *Indices*, vol. I, passim; Vandewalle, 'De Brugse stadsmagistraat'.

[32] L. Gilliodts-Van Severen (ed.), *Mémoriaux de Bruges* (Bruges, 1913), vol. I, pp. 9–14; on the various associations of Bruges porters, see A. Vandewalle, 'Arbeiders aan de kade', in Vandewalle (ed.), *Hanzekooplui en Medicibankiers*, pp. 105–6; and Vandewalle, 'Hafen und Hafenarbeit'.

and the Rhineland. But its growth was sporadic and took place amidst great political uncertainty. The Flemings may have won the Battle of Kortrijk in 1302 and survived the Battle of Mons-en-Pévèle in 1304, but they were forced in 1305 to accept the humiliating treaty of Athis-sur-Orge.[33] The French king imposed a massive fine on the Flemings, and ordered a punitive pilgrimage to be undertaken by no fewer than 3,000 male burghers. The exiled 'Lilies' (the pro-French party which included the majority of the merchant class) returned to their hometowns and recovered their confiscated property. With their return, the fragile compromise between the propertied classes and the guilds, within the newly established political system, was put under pressure. A fear that the old ruling families would reassert their authority in Bruges probably caused artisans to wring from Count Robert a decree, dated 28 March 1306, that testifies to their aspirations to legal and political equality: the decree stated that all burghers of Bruges 'whether guildsmen or others, should all be equally free' ('soient gens de mestier ou autre, soient également franc, aussi avant li uns ke li autres').[34]

The history of fourteenth-century Bruges, until the Valois dukes of Burgundy assumed comital power in 1384, would be marked by frequent rebellion and other forms of collective action. The guilds, and especially the four textile guilds of the weavers, fullers, shearers and dyers, were at the forefront of these movements. It must be emphasized, however, that the artisans only rebelled when they saw their privileges and economic welfare seriously threatened. In most cases the Janus-faced guild organizations played a stabilizing role, seeking compromise between warring groups rather than stirring up class antagonisms. But their efforts were vitiated by the limited nature of their political power: guild participation in the urban government was often more theoretical than real. But at least the common artisans preferred it over the oligarchic rule that had existed in the thirteenth century. The principle that nine of the thirteen aldermen and councillors had to be nominated by the craft guilds operated only in some periods (as the prosopographical research thus far undertaken suggests).[35] The fragile nature and changing roles of institutions like the hundredmen and the headmen, and the severe restrictions sometimes imposed on the autonomy and the influence of the craft guilds, should also be explained by alterations in the balance of power within the city. As stated above, one of the main underlying causes of unrest in Bruges politics throughout the

[33] R. Lesaffer, 'Cedant arma togae: De vrede van Athis-sur-Orge (1305)', in P. Trio, D. Heirbaut and D. van den Auweele (eds.), *Omtrent 1302* (Leuven, 2002), pp. 161–81.

[34] GVS, *Coutume*, vol. I, p. 366.

[35] See the references in note 17 in this chapter.

later Middle Ages was, broadly speaking, the structural fracture between two main groups: the commercial elites and rentiers, on the one hand, and the producing classes and smaller retailers for the local markets, on the other. While the latter tended to support a corporatist approach to ruling the city, the former made continual efforts to eliminate it and restore their power, even if the commercial families were themselves often divided by business and factional interests.[36] This generalization will need to be qualified, but it provides a useful guideline for understanding the main tensions in Bruges politics from the fourteenth century onwards. The Flemish political revolution of 1302 was a victory for the middle and working classes, but the merchant elites also retained much of their power, especially because the count of Flanders soon sided with them again, abandoning his temporary coalition with the commoners against the king of France. Very soon cracks appeared in the united front of guildsmen. By 1309, in Bruges and in Ghent, some prosperous commercial guilds, such as the brokers, butchers and fishmongers, were siding with the pro-French Lily faction against the textile workers.[37]

As the Bruges 'popular front' of 1302 withered away, the new count, Robert de Béthune, lost the support of the common guildsmen as a result of his increasingly autocratic policies. Other members of the comital family sided with the French again and the Lily party regained much of its influence.[38] Between 1310 and 1320, the initial success of the guilds in gaining positions in city governments ran up against a reaction from the old commercial elite. In 1316, 25 per cent of the Bruges aldermen once again came from the top 5 per cent of taxpayers.[39] On 26 March and 24 April 1309, Pieter de Coninck and Jan Heme, a fuller who had also played an important role in 1302, led many artisans in risings against the provisions of the treaty of Athis-sur-Orges. Their guild banners were deployed, and their armed followers turned on the *poorters*, the brokers, the butchers and fishmongers.[40] During the two centuries to come, artisan revolts would continue to

[36] J. Braekevelt, F. Buylaert, J. Dumolyn et al., 'The Politics of Factional Conflict in Late Medieval Flanders', *Historical Research*, 85 (2012), 1–31.

[37] Johnstone (ed.), *Annals of Ghent*, p. 95.

[38] J. Sabbe, 'De opstand van Brugge tegen graaf Robrecht van Bethune en zijn zoon Robrecht van Kassel in 1321–1322: Het laatste politieke optreden van de volksleiders Pieter de Coninc en Jan Breidel', *HGG*, 107 (1970), 217–49.

[39] R. van Uytven, 'Plutokratie in de "oude demokratieën der Nederlanden": Cijfers en beschouwingen omtrent de korporatieve organisatie en de sociale struktuur der gemeenten in de late middeleeuwen', *HKZM*, 17 (1962), 373–409 (at 390–2).

[40] B. Schotte, 'Beroering in Brugge en de moorden op Michiel van Lo en Pieter uten Sacke, 1309', *HGG*, 144 (2007), 5–27.

use a fixed set of rituals of mobilization: ringing bells and shouting rallying cries, attacking the houses of enemies within the city, and organizing armed assemblies (*wapeninghe* or *auweet*) at the Market Square. Their actions were preceded and accompanied by a vibrant culture of political speech acts ranging from muttering in inns and workshops, formulating petitions in meetings and shouting defiant slogans against rulers they considered unworthy to lead the city.[41] This was the fundamental character of 'popular politics' in Bruges: even in times when the middle and lower classes had no say in the town government, they would continue to put pressure on the elites by voicing their opinions and threatening instability.[42]

During the early decades of the fourteenth century, tensions in Bruges sharpened as Count Robert de Béthune and the king of France continued their hostilities, while the burghers tired of the conflict and the heavy financial toll it imposed on them. In 1318 conflict arose between Bruges and Robert de Béthune, and in 1321–2 an open revolt against the count broke out, led by radical textile workers. This time the divisions cut right through social groups and guilds. The butcher Jan Breydel now opposed his erstwhile comrade Pieter de Coninck (the latter supporting the count), and he was followed by most (though not all) of the textile workers.[43] In 1323 the count, never enthusiastic about the political role his family had been forced to grant the guilds, reacted with new election rules. The date for appointing the magistrates was to be changed to 11 October; and a college of eight electors was to be set up, four of them chosen by the count and four by the city, who would then choose the new aldermen. In 1324 the new count, Louis of Nevers, issued a further regulation, reserving to himself the exclusive right to appoint the magistrates; although failure to do so within eight days after 2 February, would give the outgoing aldermen the right to appoint them.[44] It seems, however, that this charter was never put into effect, for by then a

41 Boone, 'Armes'; R. Verbruggen, *Geweld in Vlaanderen: Macht en onderdrukking in de Vlaamse steden tijdens de veertiende eeuw* (Bruges, 2005); J. Haemers, 'A Moody Community? Emotion and Ritual in Late Medieval Urban Revolts', in E. Lecuppre-Desjardin and A.-L. Van Bruaene (eds.), *Emotions in the Heart of the City (14th–16th Century)* (Turnhout, 2005), pp. 63–81; J. Dumolyn and J. Haemers, 'A Bad Chicken Was Brooding: Subversive Speech in Late Medieval Flanders', *Past and Present*, 214 (2012), 45–86; J. Dumolyn, 'The Vengeance of the Commune: Sign Systems of Popular Politics in Medieval Bruges', in H. R. Oliva Herrer, V. Challet, J. Dumolyn et al. (eds.), *La comunidad medieval como esfera publica* (Seville, 2014), pp. 251–89.

42 C. Liddy and J. Haemers, 'Popular Politics in the Late Medieval City: York and Bruges', *English Historical Review*, 128 (2013), 771–805.

43 Sabbe, 'De opstand'; Verbruggen, *Geweld*, pp. 32–40.

44 Van den Auweele, 'Schepenbank', vol. II, pp. 163–4; T. de Limburg-Stirum (ed.), *Codex Diplomaticus Flandriae*, 2 vols. (Bruges, 1889), vol. I, pp. 365–6.

major revolt had broken out in Flanders. The attempt of the count to pacify the revolt in 1324 failed, and hostility to his rule escalated between 1324 and 1326 in western Flanders, and in Bruges itself.[45]

The chronology, causality and social character of the 'revolt of Maritime Flanders' (1323–8) still needs further study (which is made difficult by the disappearance of many documents for these years from the Bruges archives).[46] As with most rebellions in Flanders, the revolt was not a straightforward clash of social classes. At first, the protests of the rebels of the castellany of Bruges and other rural districts in coastal Flanders were aimed at the abuses in tax collection by the ruling elites – and more specifically members of the castellany's noblemen who were thought to be exploiting the commoners to line their own pockets. Factional divisions among these ruling elites (some of whom were excluded from political participation) also played a small but crucial part. However, the rising was soon joined by a Bruges coalition of artisans and some disgruntled members of the city's commercial elite. Discontent with Count Robert, who died in 1322, and then with his son Count Louis of Nevers, was reinforced by the policies of John of Namur (Louis' uncle): he held the Bruges outport of Sluis as a fief and had tried to draw away the foreign merchants from the city to Sluis' more accessible harbour. As a result, on 1 August 1323, the Bruges militia put Sluis to the torch (see below). In February 1324, a full-scale rebellion broke out in the city and the merchant-dominated government was overthrown. Willem de Deken, a moderately rich broker who was burgomaster of the commune during the revolt, was sent to England on a diplomatic mission to gather support. He led a rebellious coalition uniting various social groups though with the textile workers as its backbone.[47] Peasants and artisans joined forces and until 1328 a large part of the county resisted the young count's weak political authority. At one point in 1325, Count Louis was taken prisoner in Kortrijk and brought over to Bruges, from where he eventually managed to escape. After a failed peace treaty in 1326, on 23 August 1328 the rebellion was finally crushed by a French army at Cassel. Bruges had to send 500 hostages to Paris, among whom were many textile workers, a number of veterans from the struggles of 1302 and the subsequent conflicts, but also some rich burghers who had supported

[45] Sabbe, 'De opstand', p. 24.

[46] On this revolt, see in general J. Sabbe, *Vlaanderen in opstand 1323–1328: Nikolaas Zannekin, Zeger Janszone en Willem de Deken* (Bruges, 1992); W. TeBrake, *A Plague of Insurrection: Popular Politics and Peasant Revolt in Flanders, 1323–1328* (Philadelphia, 1993).

[47] A. Vandewalle, 'Willem de Deken (†1328): Volksleider en makelaar', *HGG*, 115 (1978), 207–11.

the revolt. The rebel leader Willem de Deken was executed in Paris.[48] The new 'privilege' of 1329 severely limited Bruges' autonomy from the count, and the power of the guilds. Many of the gains of 1304 were now reversed, and the terms of the *Keure* of 1281 were reinstated. The city government could no longer tax or make laws without the bailiff's permission; the craft guilds could no longer choose their own leadership; and the judicial competence of the aldermen was reduced while the role of the central officers and comital justice was reinforced. Most importantly, the count demanded that he alone would have the sole right to appoint the aldermen.[49]

In the years after 1330, however, Louis of Nevers began to moderate these regulations. Comital power weakened, especially because of the outbreak of war between the kings of France and England. Louis was caught between his vassalic loyalty to the French crown, and the economic interests of his Flemish townsmen, who were dependent on English wool. King Edward III used this dependence to force Louis' hand, while the Flemings exerted pressure on their count. In 1336 the English banned the export of wool to the county, thus causing a severe crisis in its textile centres. Ghent and Bruges despatched their militias to help Louis of Nevers block the entrance into Sluis and the Westerscheldt stream at the island of Cadzand but they were defeated by an English fleet. To obtain the favour of Bruges, Count Louis acquitted the fine he had imposed after the 1323–8 revolt and revoked the order to demolish the urban fortifications (which, as we have seen, had not been properly carried out). On 6 January 1338, the count also restored an important Bruges privilege prohibiting the confiscation of burghers' properties, and on 24 April he restored all other privileges that had been abolished in 1329 'because of the good conduct' of the city. The 1304 *Keure* again obtained the force of law.[50] Amid the political turmoil and comital concessions, guild power in Bruges was quickly re-established; and without the least gratitude to the count for his concessions, between 1338 and 1348 the city joined with Ghent in its revolt against the count, led by the famous rebel captain James of Artevelde.[51] During the first Artevelde years, comital

[48] R. C. Van Caenegem, 'Nota over de terechtstelling van Willem de Deken in Parijs in 1328', *HGG*, 90 (1953), 140–2.

[49] J. Van Rompaey, 'De Brugse Keure van 1329 en de aanvullende privileges', *Bulletin de la Commission Royale pour la publication des Anciennes Lois et Ordonnances de Belgique*, 21 (1965), 35–105.

[50] GVS, *Coutume*, vol. I, pp. 405–9.

[51] On the 'Artevelde period in Bruges', see L. Gilliodts-van Severen, 'Jacques van Artevelde', *La Flandre: Revue des Monuments d'Histoire et d'antiquités*, 10 (1879), 257–314, 375–443; H. S. Lucas, *The Low Countries and the Hundred Years' War (1326–1347)* (Ann Arbor, 1929); P. Rogghé, *Vlaanderen en het zevenjarig beleid van Jacob van Artevelde, 1338–1345: Een critisch-historische studie*, 2 vols. (Brussels, 1942); H. Van Werveke, *Jacob van Artevelde* (The Hague,

rule was all but at an end: this is the period that some historians have called 'the age of the Flemish city states', when in practice Bruges co-ruled the county with Ghent and Ypres (though Ghent tended to dominate).[52]

Further light needs shedding on internal events in Bruges around this period; but it is clear that the crisis in the Flemish textile industry had hit Bruges especially hard, and that the same groups who had ruled the city in 1323–8 went on to support Artevelde.[53] For half a century to come, the textile workers would grow increasingly radical in their struggle but they also became isolated from most other guilds: small retailers tended to be more conservative and prudent, preferring to side with the commercial elite and rentiers. Bruges would now lose its reputation as Flanders' most rebellious town to Ghent, its larger and more industrial neighbour. The crisis of the Bruges textile industry meant its workers lost political influence, though they continued to voice their grievances. For instance, in 1344 the shearers went on strike to demand higher wages. The political situation remained tense until Artevelde's death in 1345.[54] In 1348, the pro-comital party in Bruges regained the upper hand, and the city was reconciled with the new count, Louis of Male.[55] Louis confirmed all Bruges' privileges, forgiving the city for its rebellion, probably because he considered Ghent a more dangerous threat and needed Bruges as an ally.[56]

Louis of Male, a far shrewder politician than his two predecessors, soon mastered Ghent and Ypres, and established firm rule in Flanders. Politics remained turbulent, however. The period after 1348 witnessed the Black Death, popular religious upheaval with the 'flagellants', and crises within the textile industry. The weavers, fullers, shearers and dyers attempted to maintain their political power. The ideal of more popular and representative rule, the political heritage of 1302, was now threatened by the oligarchic

1982); D. Nicholas, *The Van Arteveldes of Ghent: The Varieties of Vendetta and the Hero in History* (Leiden, 1988). Until now, these revolts and this period in the history of Bruges have not been sufficiently studied. For a state-of-the-art survey, see J. Dumolyn and M. Lenoir, 'De sociaal-politieke verhoudingen binnen het Brugse stadsbestuur tijdens het midden van de veertiende eeuw (1329–1361)', *HGG*, 151 (2015), 323–76.

52 Rogghé, 'Vlaanderen', vol. II, pp. 13–15; and in general D. Nicholas, *Town and Countryside: Social, Economic, and Political Tensions in Fourteenth-Century Flanders* (Bruges, 1971); W. Prevenier and M. Boone, 'The City-State Dream', in J. Decavele (ed.), *Ghent: In Defence of a Rebellious City: History, Art, Culture* (Antwerp, 1989), pp. 81–105 (at 101–5).

53 Dumolyn and Lenoir, 'De sociaal-politieke verhoudingen'.

54 Vermaut, 'De textielnijverheid', vol. II, pp. 339–40.

55 P. Rogghé, 'Gemeente ende Vrient: Nationale omwentelingen in de XIVde eeuw', *HGG*, 89 (1952), 101–35 (at 114–17).

56 GVS, *Coutume*, vol. I, pp. 410–14; T. de Limburg-Stirum (ed.), *Cartulaire de Louis de Male, comte de Flandre*, 2 vols. (Bruges, 1898–1909), vol. I, pp. 13–15.

tendencies of merchants, brokers and richer craftsmen who did not espouse the corporate ideal as much as the textile workers did. There were riots and revolts in which textile workers played the main role. In 1351, 1359, 1361, 1367 and 1369 collective actions broke out in Bruges. Most were unsuccessful as they seemed unable to forge the necessary alliances between different social groups to achieve victory; but between 1359 and 1361 (though the events are unclear) the textile workers and the guilds in general were briefly able to restore their political power. In May 1359 there were heavy riots on the Market Square. In July the textile guilds faced the other crafts in a violent struggle, and changes of government followed. On 2 March 1360, an agreement was sealed by 'all the commoners' ('al tcommun ghemeenlike van der stede van Brucghe') to maintain the peace, but after April 1360 new conflicts broke out. Ultimately in September 1361 a peace was concluded. A new compromise was established between commoners and the *poorterie*, similar to the one after 1302. On 3 September 1361, Louis once again forgave the city for its rebellions, illegal meetings and violence, clearly because he lacked the power to intervene more aggressively. This charter of peace was sealed by all the guilds.[57]

After the events of 1359–61, the city's representative institutions – those that included larger groups of people than the aldermen and councillors – assumed a more stable form. During the early 1360s efforts were apparently made to restore the fragile social and political balance that had existed within the city since 1304, and to develop a clearer constitutional framework that could encapsulate the ideal of the city as a corporate entity and channel the political voices of the guilds. During the decades that followed 1360, the city's body politic was increasingly referred to as 'the common body' (*de ghemeene buke* or *den gheheelen lechame ende ghemeente van der stede*). Depending on the particular balance of forces in place after political upheavals, from this period onwards the principle of guild representation on the 'bench' of aldermen (established in 1304 but in practice often neglected) gradually became institutionalized in the system of the 'Nine Members' in which every 'member' of the body politic comprised either a certain group of craft guilds or the *poorterie*. The Nine Members, a terminology fixed in

[57] For this period, see J. Mertens, 'Woelingen te Brugge tussen 1359 en 1361', in Hansotte and Coppejans (eds.), *Album Carlos Wyffels*, pp. 325–32 (at 326–7); M. Boone, 'Le comté de Flandre dans le long XIVe siècle: Une société urbanisée face aux crises du bas Moyen Âge', in M. Bourin, G. Cherubini and G. Pinto (eds.), *Rivolte urbane e rivolte contadine nell' Europa del trecento: Un confronto* (Florence, 2008), pp. 17–47; J. Vuylsteke, 'De Goede Disendach', *HMG*, 1 (1894–5), 9–47; Demuynck, 'De Gentse oorlog'; GVS, *Coutume*, vol. I, pp. 416–21; GVS, *Inventaire*, vol. II, pp. 107, 119.

the later fifteenth century but already apparent as an organizing principle, were divided according to economic sectors. The first Member was the *poorterie*, representing the interests of the commercial and landed elites. The second brought together the four textile guilds. The third assembled the butchers and fishmongers. The fourth was called 'the Seventeen Small Guilds', mainly from the building industry. The fifth was known as 'the guilds of the Hammer' (*van den haemere*), and grouped the metal workers together. The sixth included the guilds 'of the Leather' (*van den ledere*), the various leather workers. The seventh, 'the guilds of the Needle' (*van den naelde*), comprised the clothing workers. The eighth included the bakers, millers and some subordinate guilds. The ninth and last Member consisted of the large brokers' guild. As we have seen, the first Member, the *poorterie*, was led by the headman of the St John's section, while the other eight were all led by what would eventually be called a 'heavy dean' (*zwaerdeken*, a term encountered in 1464) who was the dean of the principal guild of the Member in question, for instance the weavers' dean for the textile guilds and the blacksmiths' dean for the 'Hammer'. From 1363 onwards, the registers of 'the new laws' (*wetsvernieuwinghe*) appear in the Bruges archives, listing for each year all the burgomasters, aldermen, councillors, treasurers, headmen, *deelmannen*, members of urban commissions for quality and market control, and all the deans and finders of the fifty-four guilds. After 1361 (or 1363) the Nine Member system, even if not referred to, was probably used to nominate the aldermen and the councillors, meaning that the *poorterie* would obtain four of the thirteen seats (including the burgomasters') in each institution, and the guilds the other nine. In practice, though, its application continued to depend on whether the guilds or merchants were dominant in the city and was thus discarded at various times during the following century and a half.[58]

The term 'common body' and its variants were also used for a new government institution known as the Great Council (*grote raed*): its membership included all the guild deans and the six captains of the sections, the latter as representatives of the *poorterie*. Assemblies representing the entire commune and advising the city government had doubtless gathered earlier, though their forms are ill recorded. The *meentucht* had gathered in 1280; during the Artevelde Revolt (1338–45), a 'Great Council' of the city made decisions alongside the college of aldermen. Evidence for others has to be gleaned from the city accounts as they did not produce reports before the later fifteenth century. For instance, in 1357 the headmen, guild deans and

[58] Vandewalle, 'De Brugse stadsmagistraat'.

finders met to deal with a weighty financial issue, and represented the entire commune.[59] Assemblies of the 'commune' or *ghemeente* were probably also formalized during the reforms of the early 1360s to become meetings of the Great Council, and these would include the captains of the burghers and all the guild deans. Taxes and troops would only be granted to the prince by meetings of 'den ghemeenen van den stede' (the commoners of the city), or 'al tghemeente' (the whole commune), but it is not always clear whether such meetings meant an assembly of the entire Great Council in its embryonic or developed form. More restricted consultative meetings also continued to take place, those of 'good people' (*bonnes gens* or *goede lieden*), usually members of the commercial class of merchants, hostellers and brokers, with only six headmen and the nine or eighteen most important deans present, along with former aldermen and burgomasters. Nonetheless, in its varying forms the Great Council would remain a part of the city's institutions, even if its political weight and frequency of meeting varied. In 1388 and 1399, for instance, meetings of the urban government and 'toute la communaulté' are mentioned. In the fifteenth century we encounter meetings of the headman with all the guild deans and sworn men or at least the nine or eighteen principal deans. The Great Council, by then often referred to as 'de ghemeene buke van der stede' (the common belly of the city), appears to have assumed competence over all important financial and fiscal matters. During the revolts of 1436–8 and in the years 1477–85 and 1488, it played a major role in ruling the city. From then on, it became a more subservient institution.[60] While further research is needed, it is clear that the creation of the Nine Members and the Great Council were institutional attempts to resolve political instability within the city: they offered popular forms of representation for guilds and artisans that could act as counterweights to the power of the city government, which without pressure from below usually acted in the interests of the propertied elites and the prince.

The City and its Hinterland

The economic, social and political development of Bruges did not take place in isolation from the surrounding countryside; an understanding of the city's internal history must take account of Bruges' relations with its

[59] GVS, *Inventaire*, vol. II, p. 28.

[60] W. Blockmans, *De volksvertegenwoordiging in Vlaanderen in de overgang van middeleeuwen naar nieuwe tijden (1384–1506)* (Brussels, 1978), pp. 81–7.

rural neighbours and the Zwin ports. The relationship between the city and the rural district (castellany) of the 'Liberty of Bruges' (*Brugse Vrije*, *Franc de Bruges*), a fairly prosperous area, was ambivalent at best. As we have seen, when the castellany was first installed under Count Baldwin IV (r.988–1035), the *castrum* of Bruges became its administrative centre, and for about a century, town and countryside were governed as a single, inseparable whole. Probably just before 1100, when Bruges developed as a legal and political entity, the city was institutionally detached from the castellany. The two remained linked, however, because the principal seat of the Liberty aldermen remained in Bruges (and from their residence in the Burg square these aldermen would continue to govern the castellany until the end of the ancien régime).[61] But the institutional separation of town and castellany did not prevent tensions between them. Violent clashes, arising from court cases between the citizens of Bruges and inhabitants of the Liberty, evidently took place in the Burg square, for on 22 July 1289, the count was moved to condemn them.[62] As both Bruges and the castellany relied primarily on their respective customary laws and their writs of privilege to determine their rights of jurisdiction, marking out their rights in relation to each other was an ongoing process. A formal agreement between Bruges and the Liberty was first chartered in 1318. It would become known as 'the seventeen points' and it dealt with conflicts of judicial competence, criminal law, taxes from toll rights, local legislation, mobilization in wartime and burgher rights.[63] In 1322 new tensions arose over textiles, and at the request of Bruges, the count forbade the sale of textiles in the Liberty, outside of the smaller privileged cities, except those produced in the villages themselves and in free annual fairs. In 1342, during the Artevelde period, this measure was extended to a ban on rural cloth production except for small-scale and domestic use. This charter was enforced by Bruges militias who destroyed looms, fulling tubs and shearing tenters in the villages.[64] Throughout the later Middle Ages several points of contention dogged relations between

[61] A. C. F. Koch, *De rechterlijke organisatie van het graafschap Vlaanderen tot in de 13de eeuw* (Antwerp and Amsterdam, 1951), pp. 124–35, E. Huys, 'Kasselrij van het Brugse Vrije', in Prevenier and Augustyn (eds.), *De gewestelijke en lokale overheidsinstellingen*, pp. 461–78 (at 461–4); Warlop, 'De vorming'. The aldermen of some other seigniories, like the one of the Sijseelse, would also assemble in Bruges, and so did the comital feudal court of the 'Burg of Bruges'.

[62] On this so-called practice of 'burgstorm', see, GVS, *Coutume*, vol. I, pp. 257–8.

[63] W. Prevenier, 'Het Brugse Vrije en de Leden van Vlaanderen', *HGG*, 96 (1959), 5–60; Nicholas, *Town and Countryside*, pp. 59, 69–71, 102–8, 142–7; Blockmans, *De volksvertegenwoordiging*, pp. 126, 129–35; Dumolyn, *De Brugse opstand*, pp. 101–2; GVS, *Coutume*, vol. I, pp. 379–92; GVS, *Inventaire*, vol. I, pp. 325–8.

[64] GVS, *Inventaire*, vol. I, pp. 337–9; Van Houtte, *De geschiedenis van Brugge*, p. 119.

the two legal entities: political and military issues, trade and commerce, the production of cloth and its marketing in the villages (a direct threat to the Bruges textile guilds), and the particularly thorny problem of 'outburghership'. This was the right to burghership (typical in Flemish towns) that a non-resident could acquire when he or she resided for a certain period in town. In Bruges, they were called the *hagepoorters* (hedge burghers). Outburghership was often acquired by rural elites to avoid paying taxes in their own castellany. Many of them lived elsewhere, away from the city, but some of the Bruges outburghers lived in the city's immediate vicinity, outside its ramparts but still within the judicial authority of the aldermen.[65]

Although relations with the Liberty were frequently tense, they did not become as divisive as relations could sometimes be with Sluis, Bruges' outport in the Zwin estuary. The conflict in 1323 involving John of Namur was particularly serious. In 1305 John had become lord of Lamminsvliet or Sluis which had only recently been established. Because of the gradual silting of the Zwin, Sluis rapidly became important as the place where seagoing ships had to stop to unload freight into, or receive it from, smaller boats that could pass further upstream. It was vital for Bruges to control full access to the sea with minimal lordly interference. It managed to assert this control over its nearest outport Damme (certainly by the mid fourteenth century) but the larger port of Sluis remained a potential threat to its commercial interests. From the 1320s tensions escalated. Bruges pressured the count to obtain a staple privilege on 4 April 1324 stating that most goods of foreign merchants could only be stapled in Bruges. When, in July, John obtained the judicial office of 'water bailiff' in the Zwin, including the right to police all traffic on the estuary, the Bruges commune reacted immediately: on 31 July, the urban militia marched on Sluis and burned it to the ground.[66]

These events coincided with the peasant revolt of 1323–8 and were the direct cause of Bruges' participation in it.[67] During such revolts townsmen and peasants, especially the less affluent, could unite in common interest. Indeed, the rural communes of the coastal plain of Flanders had similar

[65] For Bruges, it is impossible to quantify their numbers but in general see Nicholas, *Town and Countryside*, passim; J. Decavele, 'De Gentse poorterij en buitenpoorterij', in Asaert (ed.), *Recht en instellingen*, pp. 63–83; and E. Thoen, 'Rechten en plichten van plattelanders als instrumenten van machtspolitieke strijd tussen adel, stedelijke burgerij en grafelijke gezag in het laat-middeleeuwse Vlaanderen: Buitenpoorterij en mortemain-rechten ten persoonlijken titel in de kasselrijen van Aalst en Oudenaarde, vooral toegepast op de periode rond 1400', in *Machtsstructuren in de plattelandsgemeenschappen in Belgie en aangrenzende gebieden* (Brussels, 1988), pp. 469–90.

[66] Sabbe, *Vlaanderen in Opstand*, pp. 19–20. See further above.

[67] Ibid., pp. 24–5.

political aspirations to urban communes and similar traditions of popular meetings and assemblies. The internal dynamics of rural assemblies are less well documented; but it seems that during mobilizations, captains were elected in each rural district. The captains also played other roles in popular politics, for instance in authorizing the local levy of taxes. The rural communes were led not by the most downtrodden peasants but by the more important farmers and those of middling wealth. These were people who resisted rising rents and taxes imposed by the local nobility and the princely government; and who could also articulate a communal sense of politics and aspirations to liberty and self-rule.[68] So it was that farmers and peasants could cooperate with urban rebels against landed and commercial elites – as they were to do during rebellions in Bruges in 1436 and 1477. However, on other occasions, the interests of countrymen and townsmen diverged. The men of the Liberty could become incensed by attempts of townspeople – guildsmen and merchants – to subject them to the authority of the city (though apparently not in 1477, as we will see). Certainly during the Artevelde years (1338–45), Ghent, Ypres and Bruges strove to create hinterlands similar to the *contadi* surrounding Italian city-states,[69] and aroused opposition from country-dwellers: in 1342 Louis of Nevers had to order that any inhabitant of the Liberty who would 'ring the bell upon those of Bruges', that is, mobilize a popular assembly or riot against the city ('dat niemene clocke of scelle en sla in tVrije up die van Brucghe'), would be exiled.[70]

There were areas of political cooperation between city and Liberty within the county of Flanders. Relations between them became more complex in the later fourteenth century when the Liberty began to take its place within the county's system of representative assemblies. During the fourteenth century representatives from Ghent, Bruges and Ypres began to assemble in negotiations with the count over matters of taxation and legislation, and became known as the 'Three Members' of Flanders, serving as the representative body for the county (rather different from the model of the 'three estates' common in most other European regions). In the later fourteenth century, the political elite of the Liberty gained recognition as the 'Fourth Member'. A crucial factor in its eventual acceptance, and consolidation under the rule of the dukes of Burgundy in Flanders after 1384, was the economic significance of the castellany, most strikingly manifested in its

68 TeBrake, *Plague of Insurrection*, pp. 57–8, 135.

69 Boone and Prevenier, 'City-State Dream'.

70 Verbruggen, *Geweld*, pp. 103–4 (1342) and 141 (1380).

contribution to subsidies (*aides*) granted to the prince. It was in acting as the 'Fourth Member' that the Liberty showed a remarkable solidarity with the cities, cooperating with or resisting the count as mutual goals shifted and realigned. During the Burgundian epoch, therefore, the issues that divided Bruges and the Liberty did not prevent them from presenting a unified front when necessary. In fact, Bruges and the Liberty conferred almost daily on matters affecting their interests, as well as on their relations with the other two Members. Bruges and its hinterland had a complex relationship, which was complicated still further (as we shall see) by relations between their elites.[71]

The Burgundian Dukes and the New Balance of Power

The peace of 1361 solidified constitutional arrangements within the city, but was not a permanent solution to political divisions. In 1379 a new revolt erupted in Ghent, and the Bruges textile workers soon took sides against the elite of their own city. The 'Ghent war', lasting until 1385, began as a conflict between the two cities, when Bruges began to dig a canal to link itself with the Lys River, having been granted permission to do so by Count Louis of Male: this allowed barges carrying grain to bypass Ghent, undermining the interests of the Ghent shippers and the grain staple of their city. In retaliation, the Ghent urban militia of the 'White Hoods' attacked the Bruges canal workers in the village of Sint-Joris-ten-Distel, and Ghent rebelled against the count. The weavers and some other artisans in Bruges and Ypres allied with their 'brother' artisans from Ghent. In Bruges, the count's representatives tore up the peace charter of 1361. In February 1380, a Bruges alderman was killed in a riot but the pro-comital party reasserted control and the rebel textile workers were punished, and were forced to swear never to serve in the city government again. In May 1380, following

[71] W. Prevenier, *De leden en de staten van Vlaanderen (1384–1405)* (Brussels, 1961), pp. 41–5; M. Boone, 'Elites urbaines, noblesse d'état: Bourgeois et nobles dans la société des Pays-Bas Bourguignons (principalement en Flandre et en Brabant)', in J. Paviot (ed.) *Liber Amicorum Raphaël De Smedt* (Leuven, 2001), pp. 61–85; F. Buylaert, 'Edelen in de Vlaamse stedelijke samenleving: Een kwantitatieve benadering van de elite van het laatmiddeleeuwse en vroegmoderne Brugge', *Tijdschrift voor Sociale en Economische Geschiedenis*, 4 (2007), 29–56 (at 56); J. Dumolyn and F. Van Tricht, 'De sociaal-economische positie van de laatmiddeleeuwse Vlaamse adel: Enkele trends', *HGG*, 137 (2000), 3–46 (at 23); Dumolyn, *Staatsvorming*, pp. 148–50; W. Prevenier and W. Blockmans, *Prinsen en poorters: Beelden van de laat-middeleeuwse samenleving in de Bourgondische Nederlanden (1384–1530)* (Antwerp, 1998), p. 89.

another uprising, the comital party regained the upper hand; and a new attempt by the weavers to take power in December also failed. However, the count's partisans were unable to gain enough support among other artisans, and the blacksmiths also joined the rebel party in the city. In May 1381, forces from Ghent marched on Bruges, and defeated the Bruges city militia at the Beverhoutsveld. As the Ghenters occupied their rival city, rebels in Bruges cheered them in. On 20 May 1382, a new revolutionary regime was installed. However, this came to an end after the Battle of Westrozebeke (27 November 1382), where the Ghent rebels were defeated by a combined French and comital army. Reprisals were crueller than for any previous repression of a Bruges rebellion. In 1383 and 1384, 224 rebels (not all from Bruges) were executed. In all likelihood the count reinstated the repressive privilege of 1329; and even after his death in 1384 the guilds were unable to recover their power.[72]

The balance of forces between guilds and commercial elites, and between city and prince, had begun to change. The new count of Flanders, Duke Philip the Bold of Burgundy, who succeeded to the county *de jure uxoris* as husband of Count Louis' sole heir, Margaret of Male, began an era of more assertive comital rule. Ghent capitulated to him in 1385 (though on advantageous terms), but in Bruges it was not the guilds that emerged victorious, but the commercial elites and rentiers: they assumed full power in the city, backed by the new dynasty. The charter imposed on Bruges by Duke Philip on 26 April 1384 included clauses that were anti-communal in nature and weakened guild authority in decisive ways: the policing of the commune and the leadership of the militia were transferred to the captains or headmen of the *poorterie*. In effect, this eradicated the role of the guilds from the body politic, returning the political system to the regime that had existed in the 1270s. The guilds were stripped of political and military power. Symbols of their corporate identity were removed: their banners were seized (on the pretext that that this would stop guilds fighting each other); and the candles they carried during the annual civic procession of the Holy Blood (see Chapter 8) were confiscated.[73]

[72] Demuynck, 'De Gentse oorlog'; A. Holsters, 'Moord en politiek tijdens de Gentse opstand, 1379–1385', *HMG*, new series, 37 (1983), 89–111; M. Vandermaesen, M. Ryckaert and M. Coornaert, 'De Witte Kaproenen: De Gentse opstand (1379–1385) en de geschiedenis van de Brugse Leie', *Kultureel Jaarboek voor de Provincie Oost-Vlaanderen*, 10 (1979), 9–17.

[73] De Smet, 'De repressie te Brugge'; A. Van Oost, 'Sociale stratificatie van de Brugse opstandigen en van de opstandige ingezetenen van de kleinere kasselrijsteden en van de kasselrijdorpen in Vlaanderen van 1379–1385: Kritische benadering van konfiskatiedokumenten', *BTFG*, 61 (1978), 830–77; Espinas and Pirenne (eds.), *Recueil*, vol. I, p. 176; GVS, *Inventaire*, vol. IV, p. 8, and see vol. II, pp. 467–71 for a charter issued by this communal government, not mentioning

For the next twenty-five years, Bruges was run by an oligarchy, mostly belonging to rich hosteller families. The measures repressing guild power were challenged but without success: in 1387 a 'revolt, alliance and conspiracy' ('upset, verband ende vergaderinghe'), a plot by the weaver Jan Groeninc to kill the 'goede lieden' of the city, was put down. The dominance of a hostellers' faction headed by Clais Barbezaen, the son of an immigrant from Lucca, and by the Honin family, could not be broken. Another uprising of textile workers failed in 1391: it showed how the power of the textile guilds was fading. Riots in 1392 and 1394, caused by divisions between city and prince in the wake of the Papal Schism, did not undermine the authority of the ruling faction. Further unrest occurred in 1398–9. In the end the faction's grip on power was loosened not by the guilds but by the prince. Duke Philip grew dissatisfied with the ruling faction because of its unwillingness to support his ambitions at the French court. The unrest in 1398–9 led to ducal legislation on 26 October 1399 ruling that the appointment of aldermen could only be made by the princely 'commissioners of the renewal of the law' (*commissarissen van wetsvernieuwinghe*), usually high ducal officials, often including the bailiff, and important clerics.[74] In the first years of the fifteenth century, more than in any previous period of Bruges' history, the elites began to turn against one another, their divisions encouraged by the machinations of a new and more ambitious prince.

In 1407, Duke John the Fearless, Philip's successor, supported a coup to replace the Barbezaen faction and tighten the Burgundian grip on the politics and finances of Bruges. Its circumstances reflected other familiar tensions within the city and between Bruges and the Liberty. In that year, the men of Bruges refused to allow a comital arbiter to judge on certain differences between themselves and the Liberty. This was a classic conflict of interest between, on the one hand, the urban working and middle classes, who wanted to suppress the rural textile industry, and, on the other, the Bruges merchant elites who wished it to continue, since they could 'put out' textile work to villagers and pay them lower wages. Duke John decided to draw up a compromise and to grant the Liberty of Bruges and Sluis some minor new rights for the sale and production of cloth. The prince cleverly used the resulting discontent among the popular classes to arrange a coup and to replace the Barbezaen faction with another political clan led by

the aldermen and emphasizing the freedoms and equality of all burghers; GVS, *Coutume*, vol. I, pp. 434–6.

74 GVS, *Inventaire*, vol. III, p. 233; J. Mertens, 'Twee (wevers)opstanden te Brugge (1387–1391)', *HGG*, 90 (1973), 5–20; Van Leeuwen, *De Vlaamse wetsvernieuwing*, pp. 142–53; Van den Auweele, 'Schepenbank', vol. II, pp. 164–5.

the Scutelare family. The coup resulted in some advantages for the guilds. They were given back their banners, their right to carry candles in the Holy Blood procession, and to elect their own wardens. The Scutelare family, though also hostellers and merchants, were more favourable towards the guilds: over the previous century, they had often sided with the guilds and must have enjoyed some popularity among them. However, the policies of the new regime were as disadvantageous to the lower orders as those of the preceding one. A charter soon issued by the duke, known as the Calf Skin (*Calfvel*) decreed that a seventh part of Bruges' annual revenues was to be directly paid to him. In order to finance this burden, a 'cueillote' was introduced – a new consumption tax on grain that weighed heavily on the middle and working classes, who were also suffering from higher grain prices. It was soon alleged that the Scutelare faction had promulgated this Calf Skin 'without the knowledge of the commune', and that the guild deans had been forced by threats to seal the charter without knowing its contents.[75]

In October 1411, the Scutelare regime was overthrown by the guilds, who reinstated the previous faction and regained many of their privileges as a reward. A dramatic demonstration of re-emerging guild power had precipitated this regime change. The militia of Bruges, returning from a Burgundian expedition against the Armagnac enemies of Duke John in Picardy, struck camp on a field just outside Bruges. They refused to put down their arms and enter the city unless the Calf Skin were given to them, and the tax house demolished with hammers and thrown into the canal. On 19 October 1411, the Calf Skin was duly handed over to the guild deans. Every dean tore off the seal of his guild and the whole parchment was then shredded by the artisans using their teeth. Also at stake during the turbulent years of 1407–11 were other special privileges possessed by the Bruges commune. One highly sensitive issue that touched on the original communal emancipation from servility was the prince's right to confiscate the material goods of burghers. Louis of Nevers had abdicated this right in 1338. In 1384, Philip the Bold had made an exception to exemptions from confiscation for those who rebelled against him; and in 1407, the Calf Skin charter stated that those who brought their guild banner to the marketplace before that of the count would have their goods confiscated. In 1411, however, the restrictive measures of 1407 were abolished.[76]

[75] V. Fris, *Het Brugsche Calfvel van 1407–1411* (Antwerp, 1911); Dumolyn, 'Une idéologie urbaine'.

[76] Braekevelt et al., 'Politics of Factional Conflict', pp. 24–5.

On this issue, the duke gambled and lost. Nevertheless, ducal power was in the ascendant. The 'Burgundian state' was gradually reinforcing the power of the central institutions it had created in Flanders: the judicial court of the Council of Flanders, which sought to tighten its grip over urban justice as a court of appeal and by handling cases in the first instance; and the Lille-based Chambre des Comptes, which assumed general financial and administrative control in the county. Although the Burgundian grip on the Bruges elite should not be overstated, within the city notables belonging to pro-Burgundian political factions increasingly formed marriage alliances and networks with ducal officials and important noblemen.[77] Thus, notwithstanding guild successes, the events of 1407–11 principally demonstrated the strength of developing ties between the commercial and political elites of Bruges and the Burgundian state apparatus.[78] Internal politics in Bruges would be increasingly shaped by the rulers' dynastic interests. Compared with the fourteenth-century Flemish counts, the Valois dukes had far more resources at their disposal, enjoying the means to discipline urban politics and control the often dangerous turns these could take when under the influence of corporatist ideology. As some elite factions were autonomist, tending to side with the guilds, ducal strategy was often cleverly tactical rather than confrontational. Thus, on 30 September 1414, in a trade-off for subsidies for his campaigns in France, John the Fearless once again granted the privilege of non-confiscation and also imposed the *wepelganc*. This meant that burgomasters and treasurers could not be reappointed for two years after they had left their offices, while the aldermen, councillors and captains had to wait one year. This was a concession to the popular classes, but it was also motivated by a princely interest in preventing monopolies of power among the Bruges elites. However, the new privilege also stated that only native-born Flemings who were burghers of Bruges could become members of the city government, reflecting suspicion in Bruges towards a duke keen to install his own cronies from outside in urban offices.[79]

The following period, until the 1430s, was relatively peaceful, although tensions between Bruges and variously the Liberty of Bruges, Sluis and Ghent were rising, and Duke Philip the Good, who succeeded John the Fearless in 1419, was augmenting his power and unifying the principalities of the

[77] J. Dumolyn, 'Nobles, Patricians and Officers: The Making of a Regional Political Elite in Late Medieval Flanders', *Journal of Social History*, 40 (2006), 431–52.

[78] As illustrated by the case of the Italian Rapondi family: see Lambert, *The City*.

[79] GVS, *Coutume*, vol. I, pp. 475–8; GVS, *Inventaire*, vol. IV, pp. 323–4.

Netherlands.[80] The commercial elite continued to dominate the city government but the guilds, or at least the guild elites, were not entirely excluded from power. Political rule was relatively stable after the 1414 privilege had returned some autonomy to the city government. The city could still issue its own decrees without the intervention or presence of the *schout*, a privilege that the Burgundian dukes had not changed.[81] For some time, politics remained a matter of compromise between the prince and the Flemish urban elites who negotiated with princely central power in the assemblies of the Four Members of Flanders. A number of 'power brokers' also acted as intermediaries between the Burgundian court, or state apparatus, and the commercial and financial milieu of Bruges. Urban finances were subject to the influence of financiers with links to the duke – often financiers of Italian origin, such as Dino Rapondi from Lucca. Notable citizens from Bruges like Pieter Bladelin and Pauwels van Overtvelt rose to the highest levels of princely administration, acting on behalf of the duke in the city and of the urban elite at court. The wealth they amassed – expressed in the purchase of grand residences, luxury goods and fashionable artworks – was acquired less as a result of their social origins (which lay among the lower segments of the commercial class) and more through their service to the prince.[82] Other important Bruges families, such as the de Baensts, Adornes and Van Gruuthuses, however, combined urban and princely politics without becoming fully dependent on the Burgundian dynasty, and looked primarily after their own interests.[83]

80 R. Vaughan, *John the Fearless: The Growth of Burgundian Power* (London, 1979); and B. Schnerb, *Jean sans Peur: Le prince meurtrier* (Paris, 2005); R. Vaughan, *Philip the Good: The Apogee of Burgundian Power* (London, 1970).

81 GVS, *Coutume*, vol. I, pp. 436–7.

82 De Clercq et al., 'Vivre Noblement'; M. Boone, 'Un grand commis de l'État burgundo-habsbourgeois face à la mort: Le testament et la sépulture de Pierre Lanchals (Bruges, 1488)', in F. Daelemans and A. Kelders (eds.), *Miscellanea in memoriam Pierre Cockshaw (1938–2008): Aspects de la vie culturelle dans les Pays-Bas méridionaux (XIVe–XVIIIe siècle)*, 2 vols. (Brussels, 2009), vol. I, pp. 63–88.

83 F. Buylaert and J. Dumolyn, 'L'importance sociale, politique et culturelle de la haute noblesse dans les pays bourguignons et habsbourgeois (1475–1525): un état de la question', in J. Haemers, C. Van Hoorebeeck and H. Wijsman (eds.), *Entre la ville, la noblesse et l'État: Philippe de Clèves (1456–1528), homme politique et bibliophile*, Burgundica 13 (Turnhout, 2007), pp. 279–94; and F. Buylaert, 'Sociale mobiliteit bij stedelijke elites in laatmiddeleeuws Vlaanderen: Een gevalstudie over de Vlaamse familie De Baenst,' *Jaarboek voor Middeleeuwse Geschiedenis*, 8 (2005), 201–51.

Criminal Justice during the Fifteenth Century

In a medieval city, politics and justice were two sides of the same coin. During the fifteenth century (when sources for the administration of justice become more abundant), the exercise of criminal justice in Bruges reflected the growing impact on society of public power, both urban and princely. Princely power especially under the Burgundians was eventually to prevail, but its extension over criminal justice was not a straightforward or linear process. As with urban politics, the administration of criminal justice was a joint affair (as shown above) between the town government and the *schout*, the comital sheriff and public prosecutor. Since the beginning of the urban commune in its legally recognized form, criminal justice had occupied the larger part of any privilege Bruges obtained, as was also the case for other cities. Communal space had to be one of 'peace' and security in order to guarantee the well-being of city-dwellers and a sound climate for investment, and during the later Middle Ages, public authority was to strengthen.

The criminal justice system in Bruges, as elsewhere in Flanders, had both public and private aspects. The public dimension of criminal law became dominant from the twelfth century onwards in conjunction with the centralization of comital power. We have seen above that the charters issued by the counts, starting with the Great Charter of Philip of Alsace from 1165–77, and later adapted in 1281, 1304, 1329, 1338 and 1384, constituted the legal basis for the prosecution and the punishment of criminal offences, particularly acts of violence labelled illegal by the counts. The creation of an urban 'bench' of aldermen that acted as a panel of judges on the count's behalf, and of a comital officer, the bailiff, who acted as a public prosecutor, along with the burgomaster of the commune, and as the executor of criminal sentences involving fines, corporal punishment or the death penalty, set the organizational framework for the local criminal justice system. The older privileges of 1281 and 1304 had been preoccupied with preventing feuds between warring families. By that time, the last remnants of 'irrational' methods of proof such as the judicial duel were abolished and replaced by testimonies of witnesses and an inquisitorial procedure (which included the use of torture). Outside the ecclesiastical courts, imprisonment was never used as a punishment; only those awaiting their trial, or who could not pay off debts, were incarcerated in the *Ghiselhuus* and later in the *Steen* as the urban prison. The usual communal punishments were exile, forced pilgrimages, execution, mutilations and shaming punishments but also a great many fines.[84]

The sustainable settlement of violent conflicts among citizens and between families, clans, factions or corporations could not be achieved, however, by the mere punishment of criminal acts. The pacification of those conflicts by (private) arrangements between offenders and victims was equally important in order to recognize the rights of all parties involved and to restore the social equilibrium. Bruges had no reconciliation court separate from the criminal court, in contrast to Ghent (which was unique in the county in this respect). Admittedly, the panels of partitioners (*deelmannen* or *partiseurs*), which were lower courts subordinate to the aldermen, were given the competence of peace makers (*paisierders*) in 1305. These panels numbered six – one for each of the city sections – until 1525, when they merged into a single panel for the whole city. But their power was limited, by statute, to imposing legal 'truces' which were (in theory) only temporary cessations of hostilities, and which did not include 'reconciliations' (or sustainable commitments of friendship). The Bruges aldermen, who constituted a single bench together with the councillors, dealt with criminal affairs both in criminal trials, where they acted as a panel of judges, and in reconciliation cases, where they simply acted as a panel of notaries. A reconciliation procedure between offenders and victims was conducted largely outside the courtroom, because it was seen essentially as a private lawsuit that did not offer a valid legal alternative for a criminal procedure (a rule which, exceptionally again, did not operate in Ghent). However, a successful reconciliation could – and often did – interfere with the criminal procedure, as it could serve as a motive for the public prosecutor, the bailiff, to drop the charge in exchange for the payment of a composition.[85]

The procedure of 'composing' (*composeren* or *verdingen* in Dutch) by the bailiff was often applied in the resolution of criminal cases during the fourteenth and fifteenth centuries, as evidenced by the Bruges sheriff accounts. Most criminal offences were eligible for composition, though some crimes, for instance homicide, could not be 'composed' without prior advice from a higher-ranking comital officer or court (the bailiff sovereign, the receiver general, the comital Chamber of Accounts, the Council of Flanders or an individual master of accounts or comital councillor). Only the most

[84] Van Caenegem, *Geschiedenis van het strafrecht*, passim; Van Caenegem, *Geschiedenis van het strafprocesrecht*, passim.

[85] Van Rompaey, *Het grafelijk baljuwsambt*; J. Van Rompaey, 'Het compositierecht in Vlaanderen van de veertiende tot de achttiende eeuw', *Tijdschrift voor Rechtsgeschiedenis*, 29 (1961), 43–79.

serious crimes, including murder, armed robbery or *lèse-majesté*, were excluded from composition. Initially, the compositions concluded by the Bruges sheriff concerned in the first place acts of violence, punishable by fixed fines (of 3 pounds, 11½ pounds or 60 pounds parisis), as listed in the comital charters, including physical assault, threats with weapons, and complicity to homicide. The second most important category of 'composed' offences included those linked to the organizing or facilitating of prostitution (brothel keeping or ownership, fined respectively with 3 pounds and 10 pounds parisis). From the late 1430s on, the formerly minor category of 'various offences' ('diverses calaenges et aventures' in French, the language of the Burgundian administration normally used in the sheriff accounts) increased exponentially, thus widening dramatically the range of criminal cases (including economic and property crimes) that were resolved by a composition with the sheriff.

It is important to note that composition, as a legal term and technique, designated not only the financial arrangement with the bailiff or sheriff in his capacity as the public prosecutor on behalf of the count in order to buy off prosecution (thus avoiding trial), but also the partial cancellation (or remission) of the criminal fines imposed by the aldermen, or more exactly, of the comital part of the revenues of those fines, by the same sheriff, but in his capacity as an executor of the court's criminal sentences. In both cases, by making use of his jurisdictional power to compose with an accused or convicted offender, the sheriff played an important role in the exercise of both criminal justice and the right of pardon. This was especially true for the charges of violent crimes punishable with the huge fine of 60 pounds (the equivalent of 120 days' wages of a skilled labourer in fifteenth-century Bruges), which were in 99 per cent of all 2759 cases between 1385 and 1550 composed by the sheriff, either before or after trial. Also the much lower, but still substantial, fine of eleven and a half pounds was in 83 per cent of the cases (numbering 1469 in total) not entirely composed by the comital officer. For the fourteenth and fifteenth centuries, we are ignorant about the ratio between the number of criminal charges that resulted in a pre-trial composition with the sheriff and those that led to an actual conviction by the aldermen. No registers of criminal sentences by the *vierschaar*, the main chamber of the aldermen's court for criminal cases, survive before 1520 (except the register for 1491–2, filled mainly with charges of rebellion following the Flemish Revolt). Until 1530, the sheriff accounts give no clue either as to whether the financial arrangements occurred before or after trial. In the period 1530–50, around 70 per cent of all charges of violent crimes punishable with fines of 60 pounds or 11½ pounds resulted in a pre-trial composition, and about 30 per cent in a post-trial composition (or partial cancellation). Besides, post-trial composition was not the exclusive province of the sheriff. The burgomasters, particularly the burgomaster of the commune, had the same power to compose a fine – or more exactly, the city's part in the revenues of a fine – imposed by the court of aldermen. By 1480 the treasurers had taken over that competence from the burgomasters. The power to compose *before* trial, however, was reserved to the sheriff only.

Whether composition by the sheriff had a positive or negative effect on the fairness and quality of the criminal justice system in late medieval Bruges is hard to decide. It is true that the sheriff could abuse the right of composition for personal gain, by forcing alleged suspects into accepting a composition on his terms, or by siphoning off a part of the compositions' revenues. The sheriff did indeed embezzle the revenues of 25 to 50 per cent of all compositions he concluded, either by not registering them or by booking a lower sum than he actually received. After all, the sheriff of Bruges received no salary (unlike most other comital bailiffs), which compelled him to generate his own revenues. For a long time, the central authorities did not have the power or the will to clean up the sheriff's financial administration. The only effective way to change this proved to be the farming out of the office of sheriff, which began to occur from 1469. But leaving aside the risks of abuse, composition was nevertheless a means to add flexibility and leniency to the rigid system of fixed fines by taking into account the distinct elements of every case and the financial means of every suspect. Composition allowed for a more balanced judgement of an offence or crime, especially in those cases where the judging panel had no discretionary power, and it encouraged offender–victim reconciliation. It was a pragmatic solution for justice to be applied in cases where either a lack of evidence or legal means of coercion to bring the suspect before the court jeopardized the chance of conviction. From 1385 until 1485 the number of charges that resulted in a fine imposed by the aldermen or a composition concluded by the sheriff fluctuated around a yearly average of 93, with peaks in the 1390s and 1440s (yearly averaging 120–5) alternating with troughs in the 1410s (yearly averaging 60) and 1460s (yearly averaging 75).

In the long run, fines and compositions declined in number. By the 1530s – no information survives for 1495–1530 – the yearly average had shrunk to 22, and one decade later to 11. The amounts paid slowly declined too. In the late fourteenth century, a violent crime punishable with the fine of 60 pounds was composed for an average of 30 pounds; by the end of the fifteenth century, the average suspect of that type of crime paid in reality no more than 5 pounds. This amounts to saying that the late medieval criminal justice system was oriented towards the private settlement of offences through reconciliation and its concomitants, composition with the sheriff, and towards financial punishment; but that by the mid sixteenth century this system had collapsed. From 1465 onwards, as the central Burgundian state grew stronger, a new, 'early modern' system of criminal justice, based on public humiliation, corporal punishment, and banishment outside the county, had begun to take its place. The number of sentences to the pillory, whipping and/or mutilation doubled from a yearly average of 7 in the period 1385–65 to 13.5 in the period 1465–1500. In the first half of the sixteenth century this yearly average doubled again to 26. At the same time, the traditional focus of the criminal justice policy on violent crimes shifted towards property crimes, vagrancy and begging, as evidenced by communal and princely ordinances (from 1496 onwards), the expenses for executions in the sheriff accounts and the sentence registers of the aldermen.[86]

Politics at the End of the Middle Ages

Relative political stability after 1414 came to an end in the 1430s. An unfavourable commercial climate and tensions between Bruges and the Liberty and between Bruges and its unruly outport Sluis were the primary causes of a large-scale uprising in 1436–8. It started with a strike – what a Burgundian charter called a 'ledichganc' (a going idle) – by the urban militia. As in 1411, the militiamen were returning after a campaign in the service of the prince, in this case a failed attempt to besiege Calais in support of Duke Philip the Good's war with England. Once back in Bruges, the guildsmen refused to start work. The familiar pattern of mobilization for collective action then followed. On 19 October 1436 the Belfry bell was rung and a crowd gathered before it on the Market Square. The rebel government proclaimed its ordinances before the urban community, liberating from banishment those who had been exiled for petty crimes by the former, unpopular, sheriff and allowing all men of the Liberty of Bruges to become burghers of the city. All

[86] G. Dupont, 'Le temps des compositions: Pratiques judiciaires à Bruges et à Gand du XIVe au XVIe siècle (Partie I)', in B. Dauven and X. Rousseaux (eds.), *Préférant miséricorde à rigueur de justice: Pratiques de la grâce (XIIIe–XVIIe siècles): Actes de la journée d'études de Louvain-la-Neuve, 15 octobre 2007* (Louvain-la-Neuve, 2012), pp. 53–95; G. Dupont, 'Le temps des compositions: Pratiques judiciaires à Bruges et à Gand du XIVe au XVIe siècle (Partie II)', in M.-A. Bourguignon, B. Dauven and X. Rousseaux (eds.), *Amender, sanctionner et punir: Histoire de la peine du Moyen Âge au XXe siècle: Actes des journées d'études de Louvain-la-Neuve, 19–20 octobre 2009* (Louvain-la-Neuve, 2012), pp. 15–47.

those who had been in the city government within the last thirty years were ordered to come to the Market Square to justify why the privileges had not been respected. The crisis escalated as the elite fled the town, but burgomaster Morissis van Varsenare was caught and lynched. As in 1323–8, the effects of the revolt reverberated around the countryside and in the smaller towns of western Flanders. In 1437 the militia laid siege to Sluis, although failed to destroy the town as it had done in 1323. Another familiar pattern of rebellion also emerged. Once again, the city was ruled by a wider cross-section of society, in which guild power was prominent. During the two years of revolt, authority was exercised through a Great Council: all guildsmen and captains of the six sections, bound together by sworn oath, ruled the city, thus in practice restricting the power of the aldermen, and in theory opening up political decision-making to the rank-and-file of all guilds. The ideal of 'the commune', as a wider community of all burghers and guilds, had triumphed again.[87]

Triumph was fleeting. An economic blockade imposed by Duke Philip the Good, lack of support from Ghent and eventual exhaustion among the rebels, caused the revolt to fail. In 1438 a harsh repression followed, including the imposition of a massive fine on the city, and the execution of some forty ringleaders of the rising. A punitive charter issued at Arras on 4 March 1438 granted greater autonomy for Sluis from Bruges, and prohibited so-called 'bad customs' in the city, including any form of strike. The Liberty of Bruges also emerged from the rebellion with greater prestige: it had already been formally recognized as the Fourth Member of Flanders by Duke Philip in 1437. Further misery was visited on Bruges with plague and famine between 1439 and 1441. Between 1441 and 1445, all the guild statutes were systematically revised by the duke and the urban elite, though Philip did not make the mistake of stripping the guilds entirely of their power, which would have provoked fresh revolts.[88]

By the 1440s, then, it seemed that the age-long struggle of the guilds (and their allies among the elites) to maintain or restore the communal privileges of Bruges had been dealt a fatal blow by their opponents. Chief among these, by this time, were the elite groups in Bruges society who had begun to hitch their ambitions to the coat-tails of Burgundian power or simply to enjoy relative stability and economic prosperity that characterized the second half of Philip the Good's reign.[89] Ducal authority, and its

[87] Dumolyn, *De Brugse opstand*; J. Dumolyn, 'The "Terrible Wednesday" of Pentecost: Confronting Urban and Princely Discourses in the Bruges Rebellion of 1436–1438', *History: Journal of the Historical Association*, 92 (2007), 3–20.

[88] GVS, *Inventaire*, vol. V, pp. 151–4.

[89] See above, Chapter 6.

state apparatus, were in the ascendant. By 1440 Duke Philip had at his disposal more men and finances than any of his comital predecessors and he was a major player on the European political scene. The path was open to pursue more centralizing measures to reduce the autonomy of the city and to reinforce the strength of oligarchic groups within it in relation to the guilds. Philip did not remove the remaining privileges of the city entirely; even so, several were eroded. For instance, appeal against verdicts of the aldermen in civil cases with the Council of Flanders, the provincial comital court of law, became a general phenomenon from the 1450s. Such was the strength and success of Burgundian rule that for almost forty years after 1438, no new revolts broke out in the city. Even during the major Ghent Revolt of 1449–53, there were no real troubles in Bruges. Some chroniclers suggest that the Ghent rebels had their supporters in the city, but powerful representatives of the Burgundian government such as the nobleman Lodewijk van Gruuthuse and the financier Pieter Bladelin, with the help of other elite groups, kept Bruges firmly in line.[90]

This political stability is also explained by favourable economic conditions between c.1445 and c.1475 that ushered in the classic 'Burgundian' high point of medieval Bruges, when living standards for middling groups were at their peak (see Chapter 6). Yet the relative urban prosperity did not necessarily make for greater social equality. Inequalities became especially visible in the mechanisms used to finance the city government. As in most other medieval cities, urban taxation was dependent on indirect taxing of daily necessities, especially of beer, wine and grain: at least 60 per cent of the city's income in the fifteenth century came from this regressive system that was by its nature socially unjust. In addition, the wealthy were able to purchase the farms of these forms of taxation. Only during times of financial hardship were the wealthiest groups asked for voluntary loans to the city. The burden on the lower and middle classes was made heavier still by the cost of annuities that had to be paid out of city income: the city finances also depended on selling life and heritable annuities and the selling of these began to spiral from the mid-fifteenth century onwards. Some annuities were sold to artisans, but it was mostly the upper classes, including the foreign merchants, who invested in them. Therefore, wealthier groups profited thrice over from this financial system: they were made to pay less taxation than others relative to income, they farmed the various forms of the indirect tax system, and they were the city's principal creditors. The same groups

[90] J. Haemers, *De Gentse opstand (1449 – 1453): De strijd tussen rivaliserende netwerken om het stedelijke kapitaal* (Kortrijk, 2004), p. 302.

formed part of the elite who ran or had close connections with the urban government. Thus, the intermingling of the city's fiscal income and the public debt strengthened the political position of a small group of investors.[91]

During the reign of Charles the Bold (1467–77), the commercial elite and rentiers were still dominant in Bruges. Fiscal pressure was mounting and this caused growing discontent among the popular classes who paid the bulk of taxes. Moreover, on average, a third of taxation raised in Bruges was transferred to the treasury of Duke Charles. In the accounting year of 1475/6, a record of 83 per cent of urban revenues was directed towards his wars and the repayment of annuities and debts. In August 1475, under the pretext of budget cuts, the Bruges political elite composed an ordinance, ratified by the duke, declaring that the aldermen would no longer receive salaries. The effect was to make the city government even more oligarchic (and the artisans would revoke this law when they revolted in 1477). Prosopographical study of city government offices in this period demonstrates how few of them were in the hands of guild representatives. The *poorters* occupied about 22 per cent of the magistracy; the hostellers and brokers made up almost 20 per cent of the burgomasters, councillors and aldermen, while the butchers and fishmongers filled another 10 per cent of all municipal offices. The textile guilds, however, contributed 2.5 per cent and the various small guilds a mere 12 per cent. The remaining 33 per cent are more difficult to identify: they would have included some guildsmen, but probably also many *poorters*, who are often more difficult to identify than artisans in terms of their professions.[92] These inequities were very likely a cause of tension; and the city was suffering from the growing financial demands of the princely government while economic conditions were worsening.[93] The crisis point came in 1477 after the death of Duke Charles at the Battle of Nancy: it precipitated a period of internecine civil war that touched the whole of Flanders, and other parts of the Netherlands. Once again the guilds asserted their power and political aspirations. An alliance of rebels in Ghent, Bruges and Ypres took advantage of the weakness of Charles' heir, the young Countess Mary of Burgundy, to win back their former privileges and political position.[94]

91 Haemers, *For the Common Good*, pp. 152–3, 195–9; L. Derycke, 'The Public Annuity Market in Bruges at the End of the 15th Century', in M. Boone, K. Davids and P. Janssens (eds.), *Urban Public Debts: Urban Government and the Market for Annuities in Western Europe (14th–18th Centuries)* (Turnhout, 2003), pp. 165–81.

92 Mattheus, 'Prosopografie', vol. I, p. 20.

93 Haemers, *For the Common Good*, pp. 146–7.

94 J. Haemers, *De strijd om het regentschap over Filips de Schone: Opstand, facties en geweld in Brugge, Gent en Ieper (1482–1488)* (Ghent, 2014).

The Bruges craft guilds mobilized in 1477 following the customary pattern of popular politics, breaking into the Belfry to examine the city's privileges, assembling and arming themselves in their guild houses, raising their banners there, drawing up a petition in the Great Council, and assembling in a *wapeninghe* (armed gathering) through a *roepinghe* (call for action). Much of their programme was a traditional communal one: demanding the removal of obstacles to trade and industry such as tolls and market restrictions, the restoration of guild political and military rights, the ratification of urban privileges, the eradication of corruption among the political elites, the introduction of high standards of justice, and the elevation of the representatives of the commune, the deans and captains, to a position of greater power. The 1438 charter of Arras was ritually destroyed by the Bruges nobleman and princely councillor Lodewijk van Gruuthuse as a concession to the rebels. On 30 March 1477, Mary of Burgundy granted Bruges a new privilege. The old election system was restored: nine out of every thirteen members of the 'bench' of aldermen and the councillors were to be elected by the eight Members of the guilds and the remaining four by the Member of the *poorterie*. The rebels also sought to weaken the privileges of the Liberty of Bruges: the Liberty was to lose its position as Fourth Member of Flanders, and any mention of the Fourth Member was to be removed from every copy of the General Privilege for Flanders which had been issued on 11 February that year. The political and judicial administration of the castellany was reorganized and on many points made subordinate to Bruges. The years 1477–85 and 1488–90 were to be the only periods, from the early eleventh century when the castellany was set up until 1795 when it was abolished, that the Liberty was de facto (if not quite de jure) subordinate to the city. The Bruges militia was also strengthened: the peasants of the Liberty joined the communal army of the city, while the militia of the Red Hoods, counting 100 men, was also re-established.[95]

As in the past, though, these victories for the guilds were achieved in coalition with certain members of elite groups, and in opposition to others. The guilds were allied with a faction led by the wealthy spice merchant Willem Moreel against another party favourable to the princely dynasty. The Moreel faction survived the death of Mary of Burgundy in 1482, when her husband, the Habsburg Maximilian of Austria, assumed

[95] Haemers, *For the Common Good*, passim.

power in Flanders as the guardian of their son Philip. Considered an unjust and illegitimate regent, Maximilian found his rule strongly contested by most of his Flemish subjects, including some Flemish nobles. Regime changes in different Flemish cities began to occur. In 1485, the Moreel faction was overthrown; and even though the privileges won in 1477 remained in place, the new faction loyal to Maximilian imposed a reign of harsh repression on the city under the leadership of the sheriff Pieter Lanchals. After 1485 the guilds were no longer represented in the city government.

Early in 1488, however, a vigorous revolt erupted in Bruges while Maximilian was in the city. The guildsmen once again occupied the market-place, and installed a new magistracy. Famously, they imprisoned Maximilian himself. Reprisals were visited on members of the old regime: the hated Pieter Lanchals was hunted down and executed. His head was attached to the Ghent gate. After five months, the humiliated Habsburg prince was released after he had sworn to restore all Bruges' privileges. Unsurprisingly he did not keep his word, and waged war on the city: Bruges was finally subdued at the beginning of 1490. In the summer of that year, a final uprising took place when the Bruges rebels allied with the nobleman Philip of Cleves, who was resisting Maximilian's authority from Sluis and other strongholds, and with Lodewijk van Gruuthuse; but on 6 December 1490 the 'peace of Damme' was sealed and the city finally submitted to the Habsburg dynasty. The provisions of the 1438 charter of Arras were reinstated and the privileges of 1477, including those regarding the Liberty, lost all legal authority.

The guilds would never completely lose their social and political power, but from then on, and throughout the sixteenth century, they were to be cowed by a political system that was elitist and oligarchic, ruled by local merchants, jurists and nobles who were usually more unconditional in their loyalty to the Habsburg rulers of Flanders than their predecessors had been. After 1490 there were to be no more major social and political upheavals in Bruges until iconoclasm broke out in 1566, and even in that period Bruges would remain a relatively stable city.[96]

[96] Haemers, *For the Common Good*, pp. 156–73; R. Wellens, 'La révolte brugeoise de 1488', *HGG*, 102 (1965), 5–52; J. van Leeuwen, 'Rebels, Texts and Triumph: The Use of Written Documents during the Revolt of 1477 in Bruges', in P. Schulte, M. Mostert and I. van Renswoude (eds.), *Strategies of Writing: Studies on Text and Trust in the Middle Ages* (Turnhout, 2008), pp. 301–22 (at 313); Van Uytven, 'Stages of Economic Decline'; GVS, *Inventaire*, vol. V, pp. 121–38, 146–52, 297–8.

The Bruges Political Elite

The previous discussion has outlined a political and institutional history of Bruges in which an underlying dynamic was the debate and conflict over the corporate nature of the city. The guilds were often the institutions at the forefront of agitation for more popular representation, while members of the 'commercial elites', increasingly allied to princely authority, acted to check guild power. But it is quite apparent that political conflicts were never a straightforward contest between guilds and so-called 'elites', or between 'lower' and 'upper classes'. There was also a complex institutional entwining of the urban magistracy with the craft guilds. To offer a more balanced approach to politics in later medieval Bruges, some further questions need to be addressed: who exactly were the 'commercial elites' and 'guildsmen'? Who became members of the urban magistracy and why?

The difficulty with answering these questions partly stems from difficulties with terminology. For a start, we should only use the notion of 'patricians' as a term of convenience; in fact, it is an anachronism that ill fits the situation in Bruges. Those who became aldermen and councillors were hardly a homogeneous group with legal prerogatives akin to those of the senatorial families of the Roman republic, to whom the term 'patricians' was first applied. Surviving evidence is sufficiently rich to show that in the thirteenth century the Bruges magistracy in control of the judicial system and city finances was dominated by a relatively small number of families; but the members of this group undoubtedly had a mixed background, ranging from successful merchants living in the city's oldest commercial district to rural landowners and *milites* who were attracted by the opportunities offered by the burgeoning urban economy.[97] The early presence of such lordly landowners can be deduced from Marcus Gerards' 1562 map of Bruges: it shows, within the city area enclosed by the second line of city ramparts (begun in 1297), what appear to be several fortified houses and moated sites. Perhaps some of these landowners had not initially been interested in commerce or urban finance, but found their properties gradually absorbed into the expanding space occupied by the city. Moreover, owning landed property outside the city limits had become a defining characteristic of the Flemish urban elites from the thirteenth century onwards. Studies of the Bruges elite family of de Vos, for instance, have shown that it continued to invest heavily in the countryside for centuries. The same family also took

[97] See the general discussion in A. B. Hibbert, 'The Origins of the Medieval Town Patriciate', *Past and Present*, 3 (1953), 15–27.

up several comital offices, illustrating that a certain number of elite Bruges lineages had an active interest in serving the prince even before Burgundian power made this an ever more appealing career path.[98]

At the turn of the fourteenth century, as we have seen, the traditional power of the merchant class and aldermanic families was challenged by the craft guilds, and the social make-up of the magistracy and the *poorterie* became more complex. A number of the traditional ruling families of the twelfth and thirteenth centuries certainly continued to participate in the city council: some had joined the party of the guilds; others returned during the years of reaction after 1309. Many of the representatives of the *poorterie* still came from the same families who had belonged to the thirteenth-century political elite. Nevertheless, many others were 'new men'. During the fourteenth and fifteenth centuries, the *poorterie*, as a 'Member' in the new constitution, constituted around 20 per cent of city inhabitants. Evidence from the early fifteenth century shows that when the Bruges militia was in the field, roughly 20 per cent of the monthly expenses went to the *poorterie*.[99] Even if we concede that a member of the *poorterie* may have received a higher monthly stipend than a fellow combatant from the craft guilds (especially as some wealthy merchants fought as fully armoured horsemen, requiring higher outlays) it is clear that the *poorterie* was a much larger group than the handful of families who had once dominated the Bruges city council. Moreover, not all of them were rich merchants engaged in international commerce, for the *poorterie* also represented the *poortersneringen* or 'burgher trades' which were not organized in formal guilds (such as landlords of wine taverns, bonnet makers and a number of other specialized professions mostly in the smaller retailing sector). Other *poorters* were merchants involved in local or regional trade; still others came from professions like jurists or schoolmasters who enjoyed some prestige but who could be relatively poor. In fact, the social make-up of the Bruges magistracy can be quite difficult to categorize even with detailed prosopographical study. For instance, some families and individuals who served in the urban magistracy did not consistently take up office via the same route: in one year they can appear to serve as members of the *poorterie* and in another they are listed as hostellers, serving as members of the brokers'

98 C. D'Hooghe and E. Balthau, 'Een bijdrage tot de studie van het stadspatriciaat in de late middeleeuwen: De Brugse familie De Vos in de 14de–15de eeuw', *Castellum*, 5 (1988), 4–81 (at 4–36).

99 This figure tallies with an older estimate that the commercial elite of mid-fourteenth-century Bruges comprised about 20 per cent of the population: Dumolyn, *De Brugse opstand*, pp. 57–8; Prevenier, 'Bevolkingscijfers'.

guild. And as we have noted, certain kinds of guildsmen, while representing their guilds in city government, shared the same social milieu and political outlook as *poorters*: butchers, fishermen, stone masons and carpenters were wealthy contractors, while many members from the luxury trades such as goldsmiths or furriers were well off. Thus, it is difficult to determine the precise social standing of the members of the city council and draw up clear statistics.

Moreover, not all richer merchants aspired to political office. For instance, Wouter Ameyde (see Chapter 6) was a typical representative of the Bruges commercial elite at the end of the Middle Ages. He combined the trades of broker, international banker and entrepreneur in the textile industry and he was also active as a merchant in wool, cloth and dyeing materials. His business network included Spanish and Italian merchants, Bruges money changers, merchants of Ghent and Lille and drapers of the smaller Flemish textile towns of Kortrijk, Menen, Hondschoote and Harelbeke.[100] On the political level, however, the Ameyde family would never rise to great prominence. In other words, the holding of political power, after 1300, was not a necessary constituent of social prestige. Contemporaries had no clear-cut social criteria for determining access to exclusive groups of men dedicated to the direct wielding of political power as aldermen, treasurers or headmen. However, this does not mean that certain cliques were unable to establish their power in urban government over long periods, or that the inhabitants of late medieval Bruges were unaware of their existence. Prosopographical research shows the continuing dominance, within all kinds of regime in the late medieval period, of a number of great hostellers' families, such as Honin, Bonin, Metteneye, Van der Beurze, Van de Walle or Scutelare.[101] Indeed, there were networks in Bruges fully geared to the accumulation of an inordinate amount of status and power. This may be illustrated with the example of the Metteneye family, who were active in hostelling and international commerce, and who provided no fewer than 108 aldermen and councillors between 1351 and 1500.

The genealogical reconstruction of this prominent family is tentative but revealing: it shows that, among the elites, marriage was not only shaped by individual preferences, but also – and perhaps primarily – by collective concerns. All the marriage partners of this family originated from the top layers of Flemish society, belonging either to noble lineages (marked in black in Figure 7.1) or to the world of hostellers, wealthy merchants, rentiers

[100] Stabel, 'Entre commerce', pp. 75–90; Verbist, 'Traditie'.

[101] Dumolyn, *De Brugse opstand*, pp. 105–20.

and large landowners. Furthermore, this marriage network was closely tied to the wielding of urban political power. Of the twenty-six known families who provided a marriage partner to the Metteneye family, no fewer than nineteen had provided at least one alderman or councillor to the Bruges magistracy. Marriage functioned as part of an overarching strategy to preserve and expand the family's fortune and political influence, a function best illustrated in the alliance of the brothers Jacob and Jan Metteneye, in the later fourteenth century, with women from the Breydel family, which owned extensive properties in the Bruges hinterland and often provided the representatives of the butchers' guild in the city council. A similar double marriage occurred again in the generation of their grandchildren, when Christoffel Metteneye and his sister Agnes Metteneye respectively married a brother and sister of the Van Nieuwenhove family, who combined long-distance trade with an increasingly frequent participation in the city council. In sum, the Metteneye family not only accumulated a large number of mandates in the city council, but also maintained strong ties with other families who were themselves exceptionally influential in Bruges society.

While it is impossible to measure the precise political power wielded by such a closely knit network of fathers, sons, brothers-in-law, cousins, friends and business partners, it was surely a force to be reckoned with.[102] A quantitative analysis of the surviving lists of aldermen indicates that families such as the Metteneye were no rarity and that their political power far exceeded their numerical strength. Figure 7.2 shows the social balance of power in the city council: it seems that the Bruges political community was structurally shaped by two seemingly contradictory developments, namely a relatively low threshold for entrance into the urban political arena, on the one hand, and the formation of strong networks within that arena, on the other.

Put briefly, there was a strong and structural imbalance in the political community of late medieval Bruges, in which during every quarter-century period, the top 20 per cent of the families usually claimed around half of all available offices of aldermen and councillors. While, as we have seen, no information survives on the actual process of decision-making within those councils, it is likely that much of it was shaped by an aggregate of strongly interrelated 'political dynasties', like that of the Metteneye family. In this sense, one might say that the structure of the political elite hardly

[102] For a detailed case study, see J. Haemers, 'Factionalism and State Power in the Flemish Revolt (1482–1492)', *Journal of Social History*, 42 (2009), 1009–39.

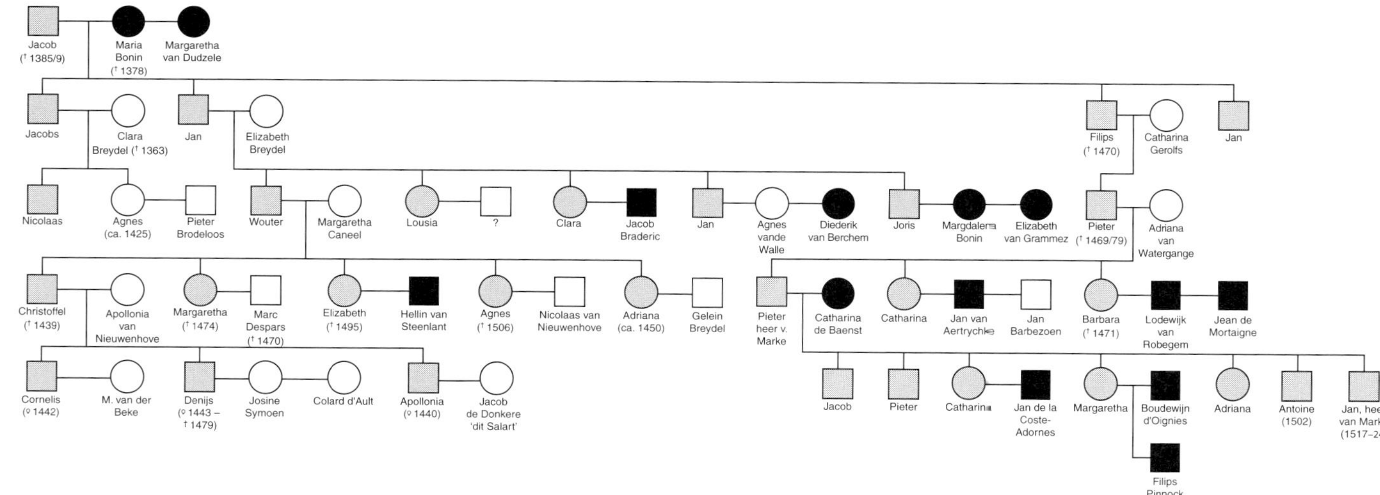

Figure 7.1 The Metteneye family genealogy in late medieval Bruges

Key: Squares represent males, ovals females; black indicates marriage partner with noble status; blank squares/circles are marriage partners with commoner status; shaded squares/circles are the individuals bearing the Metteneye family name.

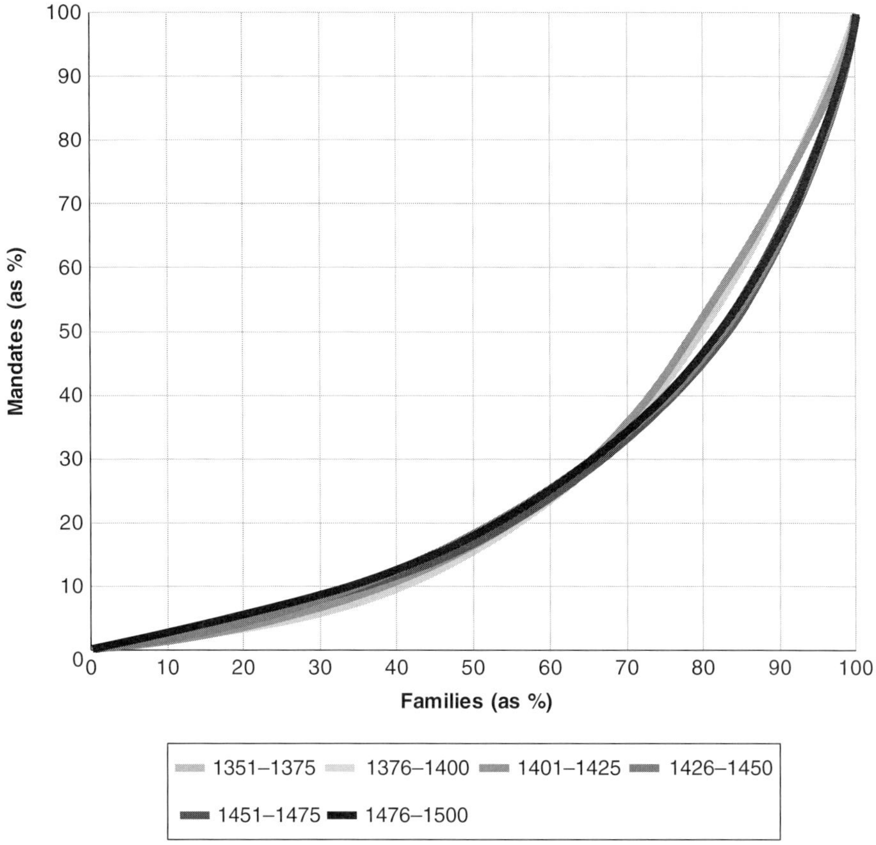

Figure 7.2 Lorenz curve of the distribution of mandates in the Bruges city council between 1351 and 1500 (per 25 years)

changed between 1351 and 1500, despite all the upheavals and despite the political influence of the guilds. That said, this structural feature of Bruges urban politics does not imply that the city was dominated by a fixed set of families, as was the case for example in the city-state of Venice.[103] There was always a considerable turnover within the political community in the long run, simply because not all families managed to reproduce themselves in a biological and social sense. The prominence of the Metteneye lineage spanned the entire fourteenth and fifteenth centuries, but in this they were rather exceptional. If the turnover rate within the contemporary Flemish nobility is anything to go by (and the Metteneye marriages show that leading political families were closely tied to that social group), then it is likely

[103] See A. Cowan, *Manners, Marriage and Mobility in Early Modern Venice* (Aldershot, 2007).

that the Bruges political elite would have lost more than half its members per century: other ambitious families were thus constantly given opportunities to take their place.[104]

Clearly, the revolts that so frequently punctuated Bruges politics only temporarily interrupted the political domination of wealthy merchants and moneyed landowners. The groups who led these revolts mostly originated in what can be considered 'the middle class of small commodity producers': independent guild masters who possessed their own means of production and had a comparatively good standard of living.[105] Their social inferiors among the artisans who did not possess their own means of production, such as the weavers working in subcontracting and fullers or the wage workers not organized in guilds, had no political power at all. However, clear distinctions between these various social layers are often difficult to make because they were to some extent interconnected through social networks and ties of patronage. Professional links between richer guild masters and common artisans must have been legion, as they made daily contact, economic partnerships and friendships, but these ties are often difficult to reconstruct. It is harder to trace in surviving sources the marriage networks that existed among these social groups than it is for those made between families such as the Metteneyes. Marriages generated trust between trade partners, created social networks functioning as a kind of social security system, and allowed the assimilation of outsiders into Bruges society: foreign merchants, for instance, often married local tradesmen in Bruges; several descendants from the Adornes, the commercial family originating from Genoa, married important banker and merchant families in the city.[106] Though the elite was bound together by this kind of 'trade endogamy', marriages of elite children with sons and daughters of middle-class members often occurred, which made social mobility possible for guild masters. Social networks within the city were many and diverse, and to some extent the sharpness of social divisions must have been softened by an overlap between these networks.[107]

The career of Boudin Petyt in the late fifteenth century reveals the connections that could exist between social networks and political power.

[104] F. Buylaert, 'The Late Medieval "Crisis of the Nobility" Reconsidered: The Case of Flanders', *Journal of Social History*, 45 (2012), 1–18.

[105] H. Soly, 'The Political Economy of European Craft Guilds: Power Relations and Economic Strategies of Merchants and Master Artisans in the Medieval and Early Modern Textile Industries', *International Review of Social History*, 53 (2008), 45–71.

[106] On this family, see Geirnaert and Vandewalle (eds.), *Adornes en Jeruzalem*.

[107] Haemers, *For the Common Good*, pp. 174–5.

Boudin did not belong to the urban 'elite', but he was a master bonnet maker (*mutsemaker*). The bonnet makers were often small entrepreneurs, as Bruges was well known for its fashionable confection products, which often had large markets, so Boudin might have belonged to the more well-to-do middle class. Since he was related to the Adornes family, whose family archives have survived, much can be retrieved about his social background. He was married to Kateline Losschaert, the sister of Jan, a wealthy hosteller who belonged to the Bruges political elite.[108] With this marriage, Boudin made a remarkable social leap, as Jan Losschaert was married to Adriana Despars, the daughter of the international merchant Mark Despars and Margriete Metteneye. Boudin's marriage contract sheds light on the economic background of both partners. When Boudin Petyt married Kateline in December 1476, the Losschaerts provided her with a dowry of money and fiefs in Oostduinkerke, Kaaskerke, Diksmuide and Cadzand (small villages in the Liberty of Bruges). From his mother, Boudin had inherited some annuities, houses in Bruges, and money from 'diverse trading ships' belonging to his father.[109] Boudin himself owned annuities on properties in Nieuwpoort and Bruges, where he held property too.[110] Evidently, Boudin had accumulated some economic and financial resources in the years preceding his marriage. This made him a more eligible prospect for a marriage into a really elite family. Two other powerful members of the commercial elite, Jan de Boot and Donaas de Moor, were witnesses at Boudin's wedding.[111] Boudin's marriage to Kateline brought grist to his mill in another respect, as his wife would turn out to be the principal (but not sole) heir to the Losschaert estate.[112] In short, Boudin came from a prosperous upper

108 SAB, Adornes, 361; AGR, Chambers of Accounts, 17412, fos. 1^{v}–2^{r}; and R. Opsommer, *Omme dat leengoed es thoochste dinc van der weerelt: Het leenrecht in Vlaanderen in de 14de en 15de eeuw* (Brussels, 1995), p. 348. The father of Jan, Antonis, possessed many fiefs, namely in Koolkerke, Westkapelle, Cadzand, Sint-Anna-ter-Muiden, Oostkerke, Wenduine, Zuienkerke, Leffinge, Esen, Loppem and Oostkamp (AGR, Chambers of Accounts 17404, fos. 1^{v}–2^{v}; and SAB, 64, fos. 17^{v}–18^{r}, 40^{r}, 64^{v}, 70^{v}, 89^{r-v}, 92^{r}, 93^{v}, 107^{r-v}, 115^{r}, 139^{v}, 143^{r}, 198^{v}, 227^{v}, 237^{v} and 276^{v}; compare with SAB, 519, fos. 7^{v}, 30^{r-v}, 46^{v}, 56^{r-v}, 67^{v}–68^{r}, 70^{r}–71^{r}, 80^{r-v}, 104^{r-v}, 110^{r}, 139^{v}–140^{r}, 162^{r-v}, 187^{v}, 205^{r}, 223^{r}).

109 The marriage contract gave Boudin Petyt annuities worth 23 pounds Flemish gros, 414 pounds Flemish gros in cash (129 pounds from 'diversche coopmanscepen'), four houses in the Rechtestraat and land in the Sint-Jansdijk (SAB, Adornes, 361).

110 He owned annuities from Nieuwpoort (ADN, B 5392, fo. 27^{v}), and several parts of houses in the Zouterstraat and Vlamingstraat in Bruges (SAB, 360).

111 SAB, Adornes, 361. The social background of these people is discussed above.

112 The other heir was Kateline's sister Jozijne Losschaert, married to Jacob Boulengier. Upon Kateline's death in 1538, her son Francois f. Boudin Petyt inherited from her three fiefs with a combined area of 55.5 measures (24.6 ha) and two additional fiefs in kind. Prior to her death she also bequeathed two fiefs to her granddaughters Margriete and Kateline f. Francois Petyt

middle-class family, acquired social capital among the urban elite through his marriage, and then expanded his property holdings with a lucrative marriage contract. His career reads as a story of upward social mobility.

And then a sudden opportunity offered Boudin a unique chance to acquire political power. In April 1477, only a few months after his marriage, Boudin was elected as councillor during the turbulent period after the death of Charles the Bold. The city government that had been installed in April 1477 united representatives of the craft guilds which had recently gained power, and members of the elite faction of Willem Moreel.[113] It seems that Boudin was an excellent candidate for this office because he had social and political ties to both power networks in the newly appointed magistracy. His brother-in-law Jan Losschaert, who had become burgomaster, probably supported him as a candidate. It is quite possible that the officials of the guild to which Boudin belonged had a decisive voice in his election. Perhaps the guild officials thought that Boudin's connections with the leading networks of the urban elite made him useful to them as a candidate for city office; or perhaps (since they also appointed him guild dean in September 1478) they considered him politically and intellectually able, talents that he certainly needed to fulfil the task of political office.[114] Briefly, Boudin was not a common craftsman, but neither did he belong to the higher circles of the socio-economic elite of Bruges. He developed social ties with the merchant elite through his marriage, which made him a 'rising star'. He might already have aspired to political office, but it was the revolt of 1477 that launched his political career.

The Lorenz graph confirms that a large part of the political community never achieved a long-term presence in the city government; and that access to the system remained relatively open, even if the men who served infrequently were liable to become pawns in the games of the more powerful or acted primarily as spokesmen for their guild or for another economic interest group. Clearly, if the top 20 per cent of the politically active families claimed half of the available mandates, the other half was filled by a large group of men who were not the products of 'dynasties,' but individuals representing families who rarely provided members to serve in the city magistracy. These individuals, some of whom only served once, made up a broad and ever-changing satellite group around a stable core of well-established

with a combined area of 112 measures (49.6 ha). In 1503, Francois had already inherited a fief of 34.5 measures (15.3 ha) upon his father's death. See SAB, 64 (feudal register 1468) and SAB, 519.

113 Haemers, 'Factionalism'.

114 SAB, 114.

Table 7.1 *Number of families providing aldermen and councillors to the Bruges magistracy, 1351–1500*

Time span	Number of families providing aldermen and councillors to the Bruges magistracy
1351–75	138
1376–1400	144
1401–25	115
1426–50	158
1451–75	164
1476–1500	237

families. That some ambitious and talented individuals could rise to become councillors and aldermen, despite lacking the social connections that were so central to dominant families such as the Metteneyes, is undoubtedly a consequence of the shift in power that occurred in the early fourteenth century: the successful bid for power made by the craft guilds in 1304, and the collapse of the monopoly enjoyed by the thirteenth-century oligarchy, had allowed many newcomers to enter the magistracy as representatives of one of the Nine Members. This relative openness of the political arena was maintained throughout the Burgundian and Habsburg eras (from 1384 onwards) – this despite the gradual dismantling of guild political power.

One might imagine that the growing influence of the princely state would have allowed the fifteenth-century commercial elite to re-establish the level of control over the urban government which the thirteenth-century merchant oligarchy had lost in the early fourteenth century with the rise of the craft guilds. Yet, an analysis of the recruitment base of the urban government reveals that the socio-political history of late medieval Bruges was more complicated than that, as table 7.1 shows.

Initially, in line with the political development outlined above, the late fourteenth century did see a trend towards oligarchy, with the temporary elimination of the guilds from power. Indeed, the first quarter of the fifteenth century saw a marked drop in the number of families who populated the city magistracy (from 138 families in 1351–75 to 115 families in 1401–25). This observation tallies with the vigorous conflicts between prominent factions who sought to oust each other from the political arena at the beginning of the fifteenth century. Yet, this trend was reversed when the Bruges craftsmen rebelled against Duke Philip the Good in 1436 in an attempt to reclaim their political rights. Although the duke eventually crushed the revolt, the repression that followed did not cause the recruitment base of the city council to shrink. Both the revolt and its repression included purges of the city council, so that no fewer than 158 families provided a magistrate in 1426–50. Yet this figure was even higher for the period 1451–75 (164 families), which was not subject to such drastic upheavals. Thus, the number of families that provided one or more members of the city government essentially remained stable and even climbed higher during the new urban uprisings and repressions of the late fifteenth century, when control over the social composition of the city council shifted to and fro between princely factions and the craft guilds. These figures contradict the hypothesis that a closed oligarchy was restored in the fifteenth century. When resuming control after a rebellion, the prince and his representatives must have felt some pressure to establish a stable urban government, and thus to encourage the recruitment to it of individuals and families who had not been tainted by previous ideological association with craft guilds or with partisans of the prince. Of course, it is quite likely that in the wake of repressions, new aldermen from higher socio-economic strata than before were put in place, yet this did not necessarily imply a complete closure of the political arena.

Hence, the Lorenz curve showing distribution of political office among families sets up yet another problem: the image of structural stability that it presents seems to contradict the recurrent phenomenon of intense political crisis. After all, the distribution of mandates over the participating number of families was as unequal at the end of the fifteenth century as it had been in the middle of the fourteenth. The underlying reason seems to be that the presence of powerful family networks could be found both among the *poorterie* and the craft guilds. It was not the case that the cluster of 'political dynasties' who claimed about half the available seats in the city council was strictly recruited from the *poorterie* whereas the craft guilds furnished the hundreds of isolated individuals who appear as an alderman or a councillor without ever constituting a durable political network. So, whichever political ideology held sway at a given moment – either the ideal of a corporately structured commune or that of a city entwined with the burgeoning princely state – there were always strong networks of intermarried families who had a long-standing tradition of having representatives in the college of aldermen.

Various developments contributed to this phenomenon. Firstly, the ranks of guilds were themselves to some degree joined by leading families of the *poorterie*: these sometimes purchased guild membership, even if they had little to do with the guild's economic activity. Some of those families took up leading positions in the guild's government and represented the guild in the city government. Secondly, as we have seen, many of these guilds were not egalitarian institutions, but had their own internal hierarchies. In 1477 the demand that the aldermen should be elected from each Member of the city, showed that the principle of fixed guild representation had long been abandoned.[115] Since at least the end of the fourteenth century it had become the case that only some representatives from the richer guilds – such as the butchers, fishmongers and luxury trades, or those of the weavers or stone masons who were actually big entrepreneurs – managed to become aldermen. In any case, membership of the butchers and fishmongers had effectively become hereditary at the turn of the fifteenth century, and they were dominated by status-conscious families whose power, social networks and sense of lineage were equal to those of the leading families of the *poorterie*.[116]

Within some other crafts there was also a pronounced trend towards oligarchy during the fifteenth century. Guild membership was kept scrupulously accessible to newcomers, but the guild dean, members of its government and representatives in the city council were increasingly recruited from a cluster of prominent families who usually enjoyed a privileged position within the guild economy. The well-documented case of the construction guilds provides a telling example: the politically active guild masters were also the richest members of the guild and they seem to have used their influence in the city council to exert a monopoly over contracts for public construction works in the city. A similar polarization was present in the textile crafts, where a large number of relatively poor guild masters seem to have worked as subcontractors for wealthy drapers who controlled the capital necessary for the production process.[117] During the fifteenth century, the powerful dean of the weavers' guild and their representative in urban government was always an important draper.[118] The leading families in these guilds did not monopolize the guild government or the guild's representation in the city council completely; nor could they ignore their rank and file during guild assemblies; but their dominating presence in craft guilds shows that they contributed to the exclusive network of families that claimed so many seats in the city magistracy.

A sense of social hierarchy penetrated even the most communal occasions of guild activity. The seating arrangements at the annual banquet of

[115] Haemers, *For the Common Good*, pp. 159–60.

[116] Dumolyn, *De Brugse opstand*, pp. 85–7, 355.

[117] Sosson, 'La structure sociale', pp. 472–6; Sosson, *Les travaux publics*, passim; Stabel, 'Entre commerce'; Stabel, 'Guilds in Late Medieval Flanders', p. 209; and J. Brys, 'Sociale gelaagdheid binnen het laatmiddeleeuwse Brugse weversambacht: Een prosopografische studie', 2 vols., unpublished MA thesis, Ghent University (Ghent, 2009).

[118] Vermaut, 'De textielnijverheid', vol. II, p. 340.

the shooting confraternity of St Sebastian (one with broad social appeal, bringing together members of many craft guilds, and well attended by the majority of members), were carefully calibrated to highlight gradations of status within the confraternity: the table of honour was presided over by prominent urban politicians, some of whom belonged to the craft guilds; the second table was reserved for prominent craftsmen and younger members of established political dynasties; all the other guild members were relegated to three other tables – where they seem to have been served beer instead of wine.[119] In these kinds of festive occasion, the leading members of craft guilds manifested their social aspirations. Indeed, they and their families often married into the political dynasties of the *poorterie* whose wealth was probably based not on craft activity but on a mix of commerce, rents and landownership. Little wonder, then, that angry craftsmen often targeted their own representatives in the city council when they rebelled to restore, in effect, the ideal of corporate equality.[120]

These reflections help clarify the nature of the Bruges 'elite'. It is clear that the *poorterie* itself did not form a coherent 'patriciate' of elite families; and that many powerful families of the Bruges magistracy came from the craft guilds. Less clear is whether the aggregate of the powerful families from both craft guilds and *poorterie* can be categorized as a coherent urban 'patriciate'. The balance of evidence suggests not. There obviously existed powerful and thoroughly intermarried families of which middling and lower groups in Bruges society were acutely aware: the frequency of urban revolts shows that craftsmen were highly sensitive to the dangers presented by political oligarchies to which their own guild leaders often belonged. Yet it is not self-evident that these political oligarchies constituted coherent social groups. The frequent intermarriages between the mighty dynasties of the *poorterie* and the craft guilds (such as the Metteneyes and the Breydels), may well have appeared to members of lower social strata to be the alliances of a single social group bent on consolidating their exclusive political power, but it does not follow that those dynasties would have shared that view. First, although there was certainly a strong tendency for politically active families to intermarry, political office was not in itself their sole concern. Although the majority of Metteneye marriage partners came from families with representatives in the city council, and while all of them belonged to the top layers of the socio-economic hierarchy, some of them had little to do

[119] L. Crombie, 'Honour, Community and Hierarchy in the Feasts of the Archery and Crossbow Guilds of Bruges, 1445–81', *JMH*, 30 (2011), 102–13.

[120] Dumolyn, *De Brugse opstand*, pp. 75–6, 115.

with urban politics. Secondly, and more importantly, the aggregate of families that historians so readily term a 'patriciate' or the 'urban political elite' was not closed at the top. The aspirational sights of most prominent families in late medieval Bruges were trained less on a seat in urban government than on a place within the Flemish nobility. The marriages of the Metteneye family into noble lineages were replicated by many similar families.

Intermarriage between nobles and citizens had long taken place. In the wake of the increasing urbanization of the county from the high Middle Ages onwards, a growing number of noble lineages had established themselves in the large cities and opened up their ranks for marriage to those citizens who were particularly notable. From the mid fourteenth century onwards, this growing proximity to nobles enabled some of those citizens to acquire the hallmarks of nobility for themselves, namely the ownership of a lordship or a knightly title. By 1500, at least twenty-three lineages of Bruges citizens had been ennobled. The Metteneye family can serve once more as an example: one Jan Metteneye appears in the sources as a knight in the 1380s, and in the fifteenth century the family held the lordship of Marke (a village near Kortrijk). The end result was a growing noble presence in Bruges: whereas in the mid fourteenth century, there had only been six noble lineages established in the city, by the mid fifteenth there were at least thirty. Thus, the world of politically active individuals in Bruges did not constitute a self-contained *social* category. The widespread desire among leading families in Bruges to join the Flemish nobility superseded any desire to enter and dominate the city council: for many of them municipal office was only one constituent of the family's power and prestige, behind more important social markers such as the acquisition of seigniorial lordship or service to the prince.[121]

There were pressures on the Flemish nobility as well as gradations within it. In Bruges, men such as Roeland van Uutkerke and Lodewijk van Gruuthuse stood out from the rest of the nobility within towns because of the sheer extent of their prestige and riches, and the sheer number of their offices and courtly positions.[122] They represented a pinnacle towards which other noble families aspired to climb. Lineages such as the Metteneyes felt the pressures exerted by a strengthening ambition to acquire noble lordship. The branch of the Metteneye lineage that held the lordship of Marke – and thus with

[121] Buylaert, 'La "noblesse urbaine"'.

[122] M. Boone, 'Une famille au service de l'État bourguignon naissant: Roland et Jean d'Uutkerke, nobles flamands dans l'entourage de Philippe le Bon', *RN*, 77 (1995), 233–55; M. P. J. Martens (ed.), *Lodewijk van Gruuthuse: Mecenas en Europees diplomaat (ca. 1427–1492)* (Bruges, 1992).

a stronger claim to noble status than the other branch – was increasingly inclined to marry into other noble families; and so in the fifteenth century they gradually developed a social perspective that was somewhat different from that of the lower-ranking family branch, and from that of many other families in Bruges who were otherwise their equal in terms of wealth and clout in urban politics. In other words, a process of social differentiation is evident within what had formerly been a cohesive milieu within Bruges society.

This trend seems to have been reinforced by the unusually frequent presence of Duke Philip the Good's court in Bruges between 1440 and 1467. The more prolonged residence of noblemen associated with the court had an effect on the social character of the city that is visible in one of Bruges' most prominent social occasions. Since the fourteenth century, the city had had its own jousting confraternity, known probably from the 1370s as the society of the White Bear, which had its own annual event; and the available evidence suggests that this exclusive society became even more elitist. In the 1420s and 1430s, this club was completely dominated by scions of local families of great power and wealth, of which roughly 20 per cent had become ennobled. From the 1440s onwards, the number of individuals allowed to participate in the jousts declined, largely at the expense of those with commoner status, while a growing number of high-born nobles from the ducal entourage now started to participate in their stead. The confraternity seems to have become the club of an increasingly small and socially conscious clique that distinguished itself from its urban peers by basking in the social glow produced by intensified interactions with the high nobility.

The quest for pre-eminence within noble society had another geographical dimension: pressures within Bruges society had implications for the Liberty of Bruges. The world view of their respective elites was not bounded by the city's walls. The upper groups of city and countryside, while possessing their own distinctive characteristics, were all part of the same heterogeneous top layer of late medieval society; 'boundaries' between the Bruges merchant elite and the local nobles in the countryside had always been porous. From the twelfth century onwards, the gap between the nobility and other groups in the top social layer (such as burghers and large landowners who lacked noble status) narrowed. As we have seen, during the thirteenth century the merchant class reached a certain *modus vivendi* with important noble families in the vicinity, such as the lords of Assebroek, the lords of Gistel and of Praet: the city gradually bought up their toll rights and landed property. Not all local lords were compliant: the lord of Sijsele 'had always been an enemy of the city', according to the *Annales Gandenses*. After the victory of the Flemish army at the Battle of Kortrijk – largely made up of the Bruges and Ypres militias but also with a strong contingent of peasants of the Liberty of Bruges – Bruges seized all his territories in the immediate vicinity of the city.[123] In most cases, however, the relations between the elites of Bruges and the Liberty, and between the nobility and the burghers, had not been so tense. From the thirteenth century onwards they were drawn closer by the effects of two complementary processes: the growing tendency of nobles to gravitate towards the cities, and of burghers to buy property in the countryside. Both of these were closely tied up with the renewal of late medieval elites and interrelated trends in social mobility.[124]

While landownership remained a staple of nobility throughout the ancien régime, from the fourteenth century onwards new nobles frequently hailed from social groups with a basis very different from rural landownership. In turn, most nobles became less dependent on seigniorial revenues. The trend towards greater social differentiation and mobility within the ranks of the nobility and burghers was intensified by the arrival of the Valois Burgundian dynasty in Flanders and the integration of the county into a burgeoning state apparatus: princely service opened up more career opportunities to noblemen, burghers and aspiring commoners alike. By the end of the fifteenth century some 25 per cent of the noble families in Bruges and its environs were from the ranks of the urban elite. We must be wary of picturing this too readily in terms of a social melting pot, though. Those groups as a whole did not completely lose their distinctive characteristics. Burghers who invested in extensive rural properties did not necessarily abandon their business interests; the purchase of fiefs could be driven by a desire for social recognition but also by a hard-nosed decision to diversify assets. A noble lifestyle and commercial enterprise were not necessarily incompatible pursuits. Overall, while there was considerable interaction between elements of rural and urban elites, the exchange between them was not reciprocated equally. As the nobility remained the class with the highest social prestige, the upper part of burgher society was more strongly drawn to the nobility than vice versa. As such, this rapprochement between burghers and nobility did not result in the creation of a group that can be labelled an 'urban nobility': to suggest that the nobility in general became virtually indistinguishable from the upper groups of Bruges citizens would be to stretch a point too far.[125]

123 Johnstone (ed.), *Annals of Ghent*, pp. 8, 14.

124 Buylaert, 'Late Medieval Crisis'; F. Buylaert and A. Ramandt, 'The Transformation of Rural Elites in Late Medieval Flanders: Oligarchy, State Formation and Social Change in the Liberty of Bruges (ca. 1350 – ca. 1525)', *Continuity and Change*, 30 (2015), 36–69.

125 Buylaert, 'La "noblesse urbaine"'.

Moreover, towards the end of the Middle Ages some of the most prominent families of Bruges were increasingly inclined to expand their social horizons beyond the city and its direct hinterland. In the fourteenth century, Bruges had still been more or less a political entity that was contained within a political framework involving relations with the count of Flanders and the two other urban giants, Ghent and Ypres. During the later Middle Ages, the county of Flanders was first incorporated into the political union of the Burgundian Low Countries, and subsequently into that of the vast Habsburg empire. This development opened up new vistas of opportunity for local elites. Consider the Metteneye family again: in the mid fourteenth century its activities were limited to Bruges and its environs, but in the early sixteenth century, the family extended its marriage ties out to noble lineages from Hainaut, Walloon Flanders and other more distant regions. Jan Metteneye, lord of Marke, spent several years in Spain as a chamberlain of Emperor Charles V. The Metteneye lineage did remain committed to the world of Bruges politics, but this was not the case for all families. Consider the example of the Braderic family (see Figure 7.3), which had combined interests in high finance with a long-standing participation in the city council. This family also became noble in the fourteenth century, and came to possess a growing number of properties in eastern Flanders as a consequence of marriages with lineages from the environs of Ghent and Malines (such as the families Vilain, Van Massemen and Van Voorhoute). In the second half of the fifteenth century, the family lost interest in Bruges politics in favour of other arenas and never again provided an alderman or a councillor after 1447. Perhaps for most families the spires of the Bruges Belfry and the city churches continued to remain the dominant landmarks on their mental landscape; but for some the pursuit of power and prestige made them peer beyond the local horizon, and thus lose touch with the upper echelons of Bruges society.

So to what extent was position within the social hierarchy of late medieval Bruges determined by position in the political *cursus honorum* of urban government? The answer to this question must be nuanced. Political power undoubtedly bestowed social status on its holder: access to the decision-making arenas of both the urban magistracy and of guild government was restricted and thus exclusive. Only a small part of the male urban population was ever actively involved in policy-making, and those who were must have acquired considerable social standing within the urban community. Beyond that, however, there is little reason to assume that the aggregate of politically active individuals and families ever corresponded to a relatively stable and coherent social group. Oligarchies were able to form

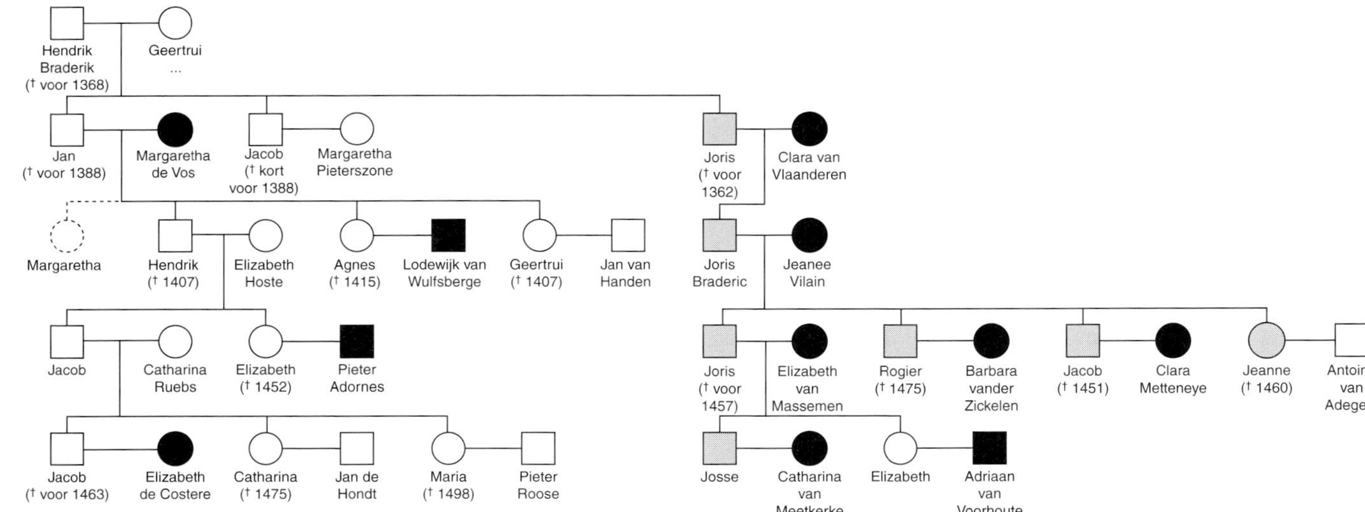

Figure 7.3 The Braderic family genealogy in late medieval Bruges

Key: Squares represent males, circles females; black indicates marriage partner with noble status; shaded squares/circles are the individuals bearing the Braderic family name.

and reform despite the political revolt of the early 1300s, but the city and guild governments were never dominated exclusively by cliques of powerful families. Such cliques did exist, and the political 'dynasties' that constituted them, especially the hosteller families who profited from Bruges international commerce, could have a disproportionately loud voice in the Bruges polity, but they always co-existed with a relatively broad and unstable assemblage of individuals whose calling to politics was more muted and perhaps more personal in nature. The total number of families who provided office-holders gradually grew, especially because repeated urban risings continued to bring about regime changes in the city magistracy. Thus, members of the 'urban political elite' became an increasingly heterogeneous group in the later Middle Ages: some remained commoners, others became noble, while still others, the most prominent of families, turned their gaze to opportunities far beyond the city walls. Whereas in 1300 the marriage networks and social aspirations of Bruges' most august families had been geared principally around the city's government and politics, by 1500 this was no longer the case.

8 Religious Practices, c.1200–1500

ANDREW BROWN AND HENDRIK CALLEWIER

In 1564 Joost de Damhouder described the annual procession of the Holy Blood relic on 3 May as one of Bruges' defining events.[1] A procession on that day had begun probably in the late thirteenth century, and it had first acquired official civic funding in 1303.[2] Expanding considerably in scale during the fourteenth century, it became an event that no other ceremony in Bruges rivalled as a public occasion, nor received such regular municipal funding, nor brought together so many in an ordered hierarchy of magistrates, guilds and clergy. The Holy Blood procession seems an obvious place to begin a study of religious practices in Bruges: in its regular repetition, it appears to encapsulate the communal and religious priorities of its inhabitants. Yet characterizing these priorities is a harder task than first appears. As preceding chapters have shown, the procession's origins lay in a period of intense political crisis, and its later development occurred in a dynamic society in which the communal ideal was both cherished and threatened. The procession has also to be set within a wider religious setting. It took place as one event during the liturgical year that throughout late medieval Christendom was undergoing considerable alteration, preserving a form of devotion when other forms changed around it. Interpretations of these changes also differ depending on the perspective adopted: notions of 'civic religion', 'space' and 'memory' have been variously applied to religious practices in late medieval towns and may be applied to Bruges, in so far as the available sources allow. These are full in certain respects, but scarce in others and weighted to the late medieval period: evidence before c.1200 largely relates to the early history of religious institutions (discussed in Chapter 2). This chapter begins by outlining the main features and trends of religious life that emerge from surviving evidence, before situating them within wider social and political contexts.

[1] De Damhouder, *Van de grootdadigheyt*, pp. 484, 491, 503 (de Damhouder, *De magnificentia politae*, pp. 555–73).

[2] A procession on that day may not originally have carried the Holy Blood relic; see further below for problems of dating its origin.

Sacred Space

The most imposing landmark of the urban landscape, especially from the tenth century onwards, was the church of St Donatian: its alignment with comital power, and its investment with saintly relics, established a primacy over other churches and over the urban settlement which its clergy was tireless in promoting. The shrine of St Donatian was cultivated as the conduit of miracles at a local and regional level in the eleventh century, and in ways that appear to have encouraged loyalty to the saint from the inhabitants of Bruges – although description of such loyalty is encased within hagiographical and clerical topoi. Miracles in 1089 were announced by bell-ringing that brought the 'burghers' inside the 'principal church'; and in 1096, the provost Bertulf gathered the people in front of relics before the church in order to restore peace, and had St Donatian's body translated to a new shrine.[3] Galbert of Bruges also emphasized the significance of St Donatian's relics to the growing town during the troubles of 1127 and 1128: the church bells were rung to call on burghers to prevent the body of St Donatian being taken away; the oaths of the counts were sworn on relics brought out of the church in procession before the assembled people.[4]

The dominance of St Donatian's church over all the inhabitants of Bruges was never unrivalled. Bruges lay within the bishopric of Tournai, and although bishops had no jurisdiction over St Donatian's, they exercised authority throughout the later Middle Ages over parishioners and clergy in Bruges through a resident 'dean of Christianity', who occupied a house near St Saviour's church.[5] The two original mother churches of the city, Our Lady's and St Saviour's, dating back probably to the ninth century, were also prominent; and outside the comital castle, they served the pastoral needs of the earliest areas of settlement, assisted by St Walburga's and later by the smaller dependent chapels of St Peter's, St Christopher's, St John's and St Basil's (see Chapter 2). Our Lady's church may have acquired the important relics of St Boniface in the early twelfth century, sent from Utrecht. But the rapid growth of the city in the thirteenth century changed the ecclesiastical landscape, and began to enclose St Donatian's within a territory encompassing a greater diversity of religious

[3] For the sources for a miracle in 1011 (relating to a woman from West Frisia), and further miracles between 1070 and 1089, and 1096 to 1100, see Meijns, 'Hoe een heilige verdienstelijk werd'.

[4] Rider (ed.), *Galbertus Brugensis*, chaps. 22, 35, 52, 55.

[5] H. Callewier, *De papen van Brugge: De seculiere clerus in een middeleeuwse wereldstad (1411–1477)* (Leuven, 2014), pp. 1–3.

life. The establishment of four major charitable institutions and at least five mendicant houses, as well as the creation of three new parishes, testify to changing pastoral and social needs, particularly in the areas that sprawled beyond the first city ramparts built in 1127. By the close of the thirteenth century, however, the great expansion in the number of sizeable ecclesiastical buildings, such as collegiate and parish churches, mendicant houses and hospitals, had virtually come to a halt. By then, the city had reached its demographic peak and its geographical limits (with the virtual completion of the second walling in 1297), although vested interest also explains why the founding of large religious houses became less frequent. The Carmelites established their house only after tough negotiation in 1260 with the canons of St Donatian's who were anxious to prevent encroachment on their ecclesiastical rights.[6]

Yet despite these restrictions, and despite demographic reversals in the fourteenth century, the number of places where mass was celebrated or daily offices and prayers performed, increased dramatically, especially between 1360 and 1480. While large mendicant houses with full ecclesiastical rights were no longer founded, smaller tertiary foundations continued to be set up (five by 1400, four more between 1450 and 1470). The Wilhelmite order was represented by a small foundation set up in 1430. Reforming currents within the mendicant orders made a notable impact, with four observant houses being founded in the city between 1460 and 1488: the Observant Franciscans, the Bethany sisters (following the rule of St Augustine), the Poor Clares (Colettines) and the Carmelites of Sion (see Chapter 2). Daily regimes of prayer were practised in another kind of semi-religious house that proliferated during the later Middle Ages, in Bruges as elsewhere: the almshouse or 'house of God'. At least twenty were founded between 1300 and 1480.[7] Such houses usually lacked the ecclesiastical rights of hospitals – they had no chapels or members of the clergy attached to them – and catered for a small number of inmates, often the old or widowed, who were supported in return for living a life of prayer.

Only one new parish church with full parochial rights was founded after the thirteenth century, which itself reflects ecclesiastical reluctance to alter parish boundaries. This was St Anne's in 1497, which finally resolved an anomalous situation for those parishioners of St Cross who lived within the

6 Archives of the Discalced Carmelites of Brugge, Liber Oblongus, fo. 4$^{r–v}$. This is followed by several folios detailing later 'compromises' with other churches in Bruges.

7 At least four '*godshusen*' were founded before 1350, five in the 1360s and 70s, six between 1400 and 1450, and five between 1450 and 1480.

city walls, but whose parish church lay outside them.[8] Yet at a sub-parochial level, chapels proliferated, especially in the fifteenth century. Most new free-standing chapels were set up by guilds – the brokers and prestigious craft guilds – that had come to form the institutional basis of corporate life in the city (see Chapter 5), and they also established almshouses for their indigent members. Some negotiated privileges that gave them a distinctive presence in the city. Between 1370 and 1470 the chapels of the brokers, weavers, mercers, shippers, smiths and bakers all acquired bell-towers to summon their members to mass. Other substantial chapels were built by individuals. The most impressive was the Adornes family chapel (founded after 1427), loosely modelled on the Holy Sepulchre of Jerusalem, to which was attached an almshouse for twelve poor widows (see Figure 5.2).[9] The local noble Lodewijk van Gruuthuse had his lofty oratory bridging the gap between his townhouse and parish church completed in 1472.[10] The rulers of Flanders made their own domestic arrangements for divine service. The Dampierre counts had a chapel within their new townhouse by 1324; the Valois Burgundian dukes expanded the residence and built a new chapel complex within it, complete with a bell-tower by the 1440s.[11]

Thus, by the end of the fifteenth century, the city was visibly occupied by more sacred buildings than ever before. But besides being filled with holy spaces, a sense also grew that the city landscape as a whole was a numinous territory. The notion of the city as a sacred association or body, analogous to the body of Christ, had long formed part of a stock set of ideas defining the ideal city. It was present in the association of towns with the Peace of God movement, and it informed the language of the 'commune' in the twelfth century (see Chapter 2). But in the later Middle Ages, it flourished with vigour and in a variety of new contexts. The city ramparts after 1297 enclosed a territory that gradually came to be marked out as hallowed ground. The impressive city gates built during the fourteenth century, decorated with images of saints, and later celebrated in a poem from the Gruuthuse collection as bastions of communal virtues,[12] gave notice of entry into a rarefied landscape. From the early fourteenth century the Holy Blood procession

[8] RAB, Sint-Anna, 308, 309. See Chapter 2. The parishioners of St Catherine also had their church outside the city walls.

[9] Geirnaert, 'De Adornes en de Jeruzalemkapel'.

[10] M. P. J. Martens, 'Religieuze stichtingen en overeenkomsten met de Onze-Lieve-Vrouwekerk', in Martens (ed.), *Lodewijk van Gruuthuse*, pp. 39–42.

[11] T. De Meester and B. Schotte, 'De woning van de graaf in de 14de eeuw', in Hillewaert and Van Besien (eds.), *Het Prinsenhof*, pp. 15–16 (at 15); de Jonge, 'Bourgondische residenties', pp. 109–26.

[12] See above, Chapter 3, and below, Chapter 9.

also began to take its processors annually around the perimeter of the new city walls, their progress announced by the chimes of the Belfry bells, and interrupted by pauses before each city gate to sing psalms or antiphons.[13] The wagon-plays added to the procession by the late fourteenth century included a representation of Jerusalem; and direct analogies between Bruges and the celestial city also came to be drawn at entry ceremonies in the fifteenth century.[14]

Sacred Time

In 1419, the Feast of the Invention – the day on which the main Holy Blood procession fell – was elevated to the rank of great double within the church of St Donatian.[15] While this reflected the day's importance for the inhabitants of Bruges, it also followed wider devotional trends. The expansion of divine service increased from the thirteenth century: sacred time as well as sacred space came to be marked out in new ways. The enrichment of the liturgy happened all over Christendom, and nowhere more so than in large collegiate churches. In Bruges, the three main churches had sufficient clerical staff to celebrate the daily offices, and in the fourteenth century these were accompanied by a rising level of polyphonic singing. In the 1370s, smaller parish churches (St Walburga's and St Giles') began to provide for the 'seven hours with special solemnity'. In 1403 a large endowment from Niclaas Barbezaen, the wealthy broker and politician, made provision for St James' clergy to sing the seven hours on five Marian feast days. By the 1420s, endowments had been amassed to allow the daily celebration of the seven hours.[16] Votive offices 'with special intention' were founded with greater frequency and elaborateness from the 1360s. In St Donatian's the singing of the *Salve*, in praise of the Virgin Mary, can be traced back to the 1220s, but later foundations increased its scale considerably. In 1365 Boudin de Vos, mint master to the count, gave 550 pounds par. for *Salve regina* to be sung every Saturday in procession after Vespers, for the antiphon of St Donatian to be sung at the station point, and for the bell 'Naes' (Donatian) to be

[13] For reference to bell-chiming as the processors passed certain gates, see Jan Crayscieter's foundations dating to c.1360 (Bruges, Archives of the OCMW, Register 178, fo. 64^{r}); and for psalm-singing before the gates, see the processional dated to the sixteenth century (Archives of the Confraternity of the Holy Blood, Register 15).

[14] See for instance G. Kipling, *Enter the King: Theatre, Liturgy, and Ritual in the Medieval Civic Triumph* (Oxford, 1998), pp. 33, 59, 111, 117.

[15] BAB, A50, fos. 36^{r}, 63^{r}, 64^{r}–5^{v}; SAB, 96, 11, fos. 92^{v}–3^{r}.

[16] RAB, Sint-Jacob, 151, charter 136; 377, fos. 1^{r-v}, 6^{v}.

rung until the end of the antiphon.[17] Smaller parish churches like St Giles' in the 1380s also began provision for *Salve* singing. At St James' in 1416, Nicolas van der Beurze (later an alderman) provided for the 'community of the choir' ('commuun') to sing the vespers of Our Lady on the first Friday after midwinter and a Marian mass on the Saturday. Over the next nine years, a further thirty-five benefactors added to each successive Friday and Saturday, until a systematic programme of Marian vespers and masses had been built up to cover the whole year.[18]

The daily offices were complemented with other elaborations of the liturgical year. The inflation in ranks of feast days was a trend common throughout late medieval Christendom, but the capacity to support the weight of liturgical complexity demanded by higher-ranking feasts could only be met by the wealthiest of institutions. Between 1220 and 1520, within six of the main collegiate or parish churches (but especially in the three largest) 145 separate feast days were enhanced, many of them more than once, the result of 709 foundations made by 415 benefactors; 110 foundations increased divine service on 17 feast days of the *temporale*, from Advent to Trinity; an even greater number of foundations – 599 in total – were dedicated to enriching feast days of the *sanctorale*; 128 feast days of saints or cults were liturgically elevated, many more than once even within the same church. The process had begun in the thirteenth century, but the majority of foundations were set up from 1360 onwards. The high point was reached between 1440 and 1486, when 212 foundations (from 123 benefactors) were set up (see Figure 8.1).

Feast days were enhanced in manifold ways. Before the mid fourteenth century, the largest endowments tended to scatter provision over many feast days.[19] After 1360, benefactors concentrated investment on fewer feasts but in greater depth and with finer precision (which Figure 8.1 is unable to show). Many more – like Boudin de Vos in 1360 – began to specify what they required. The ringing of bells was demanded during processions and mass on an unprecedented scale. 'Wishing to excite the faithful in memory of Christ's Passion', the burgomaster Jan Camphin asked the canons of St Donatian's in 1395 for the great bells to be rung on the eve of the Annunciation, and then five times on the following day at the moment when the body and blood of Christ were elevated at mass.[20] By the end of

17 BAB, A141, fos. 1^{r-v}, 101^{r}; BAB, A47, fo. 174^{v}; BAB, D42, 25. See Murray, *Bruges*, p. 292.

18 RAB, Sint-Jacob, 377, fos. 1^{v}–20^{v}.

19 See for instance Jan de Gruuthuse's provision in 1311 for pittances for clergy to attend mass on eight feast days in Our Lady's church: RAB, Onze-Lieve-Vrouw, 735, fos. 30^{v}, 93^{r}, 106^{v}, 127^{v}, 133^{r}, 200^{r}.

20 BAB, A49, fos. 6^{r}–17^{r}; SAB, 96, 20, fos. 30^{r}–1^{r} (1397).

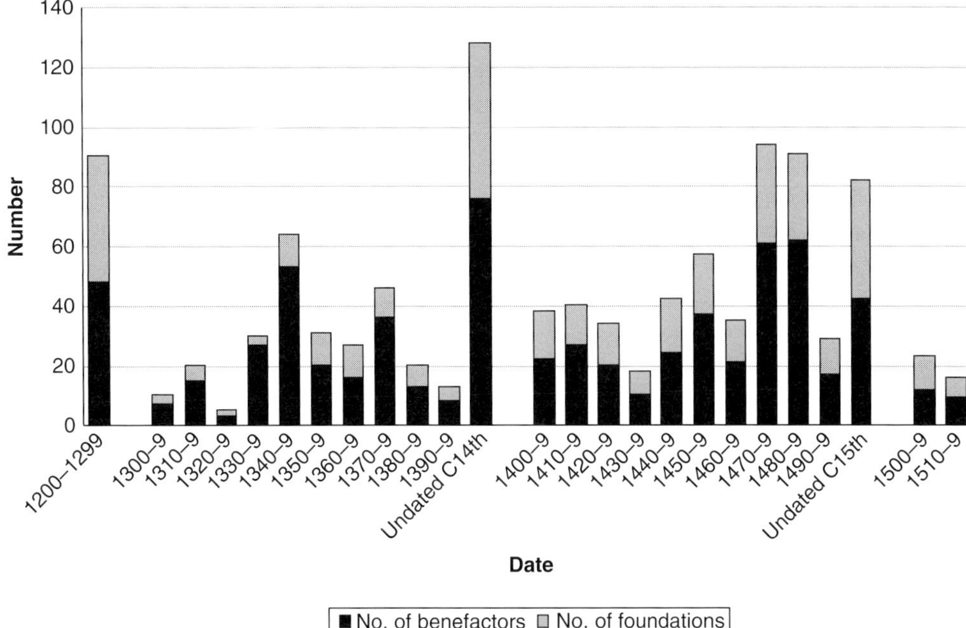

Figure 8.1 Feast day foundations in Bruges churches, 1200–1510
The figures for this table are derived mainly from the *planarii*, cartularies and charters of the three largest churches in Bruges (St Donatian's, Our Lady's and St Saviour's), and from the records of the three of the other main parish churches, St James', St Walburga's and St Giles'. For more on these sources and problems with dating foundations, see Brown, *Civic Ceremony*, pp. 101–6, 309–10.

the fifteenth century, many more elaborate arrangements had been made. So 'deeply moved' was the merchant Jan Moscron in 1499 by the Feast of Our Lady of the Snow (on 5 August) that he made an endowment in Our Lady's church to elevate the feast to the rank of great double. He also specified bell-ringing on other Marian feast days: on the eve and day of the Assumption, the bell 'Boniface' was to ring out 150 times, 'Kateline' 200 times, and 'Maria' 250 times.[21] Feast days also began to be celebrated with a level of polyphonic singing never previously sustained. Especially from the 1370s, more benefactors specified antiphons to be sung during processions; more elaborate mass settings were required; requests for motets began to multiply, among the earliest in St Donatian's being for the twinned feast days of the Exaltation of the Holy Cross (1415) and of

[21] RAB, Onze-Lieve-Vrouw, 1350, fos. 182^r–4^r, 203^v–5^r; 735, fo. 119^r.

the Invention (1419).[22] Feast days were enhanced visibly as well as audibly. Some benefactors requested the presence of relics, Jan Moscron asking for those of Our Lady's church to be shown on the Feast of Our Lady of the Snow. More processions of clergy were conducted on feast days, with and without relics, inside and outside churches. Traditional processions were newly endowed. The three days of Rogation, when clergy from the three mother churches processed in turn to station churches outside the city walls, had attracted benefaction from the early fourteenth century, but were re-endowed extensively in the 1480s by the alderman Lodewijk Greffinc.[23] The flood of such investment in divine service reached a high-water mark in the 1480s.

The visual impact of such foundations on church fabrics and fittings must have been striking. Though much of this has been lost, it may be partially visualized from documentary sources. St Donatian's was destroyed during the French Revolution, but the references in the surviving chapter act-books and fabric accounts speak of a liturgical splendour that few churches in Christendom could have matched: investment in service books (such as a 'book of motets' referred to in 1377 when twelve new leaves were added);[24] the filling up of *planarii* (leading to replacements around 1320, and again in 1418 and 1481) detailing the services on feast days; the founding of new bells and the strengthening of the bell-tower (under alarming strain in the early fifteenth century);[25] the addition of new chapels, altars and altarpieces, or the improvement of windows, walls and reliquaries. In other parish churches demand for new liturgical space stimulated building work: at St James', major rebuilding took place from 1454, resulting twenty years later in the addition of two more aisles, several chapels and a new choir.[26] By the late fifteenth century, benefaction of all kinds had expanded sacred space and embellished the marking of sacred time to an unprecedented degree.

[22] On motets in Bruges, see R. Nosow, *Ritual Meanings in the Fifteenth-Century Motet* (Cambridge, 2012), pp. 105–34.

[23] BAB, A56, fos. 71v, 78v, 79v–80r; BAB, A141, fo. 99v; RAB, Onze-Lieve-Vrouw, 1017; 735, fos. 199v, 202v, 204v; BAB, S289, fos. 102v–3r.

[24] A. Dewitte, 'Gegevens betreffende het muziekleven in de voormalige Sint-Donaaskerk te Brugge', 1251–1660, *HGG*, 111 (1974), 129–74; A. Dewitte, 'Iconen en ritueel in de Brugse Donaaskerk, 1200–1550', *Biekorf*, 99 (1999), 44–53.

[25] Serious work began on the bell-tower in 1404 (BAB, A49, fos. 74v–5r; BAB, G2, 1405/6, fo. 8r); the town council contributed 100 pounds par. in 1413 (SAB, 216, 1413/14, fo. 81r); and the main bell was entirely replaced in 1432, at the cost of over 613 pounds par. (BAB, G3, 1431/2, fo. 16v).

[26] According to the churchwardens' accounts, the building effort was in its tenth year in 1464: RAB, Sint-Jacob, 98 (Rekeningen 1464–78).

Commemoration of the Dead

Church *planarii* that set out the cyclical passage of liturgical time also recorded the names of benefactors who invested in its celebration. Part of the purpose of such investment was the generation of suffrage for souls: the multiplication of the number and type of services for the dead, and their request by a widening spectrum of social groups, were among the most characteristic features of late medieval religion, nowhere more so than in Europe's largest towns. One of the most exclusive types was the perpetual chantry (*kapelanie*). This had emerged from a monastic tradition of service for the dead, but the dedication by benefactors of an endowment for the specific purpose of celebrating daily mass for their souls, at altars set aside for the purpose, began in the twelfth century. The earliest chantries in Bruges were founded in St Donatian's by rulers (such as Countess Margaret in 1190) or by highly ranked clergy (such as Gerard the provost, chancellor of Flanders c.1237). A few were founded in the other collegiate churches before 1250, but the pace of foundation quickened from the late thirteenth century, increasingly involved prominent citizens, and spread to other parish churches. There was another intense period of foundation in the 1360s and 1370s. Fewer individual chantries for daily mass were founded after then, but many mass services, especially between 1460 and the late 1480s, were founded in all churches of Bruges (in St James' notably during its period of rebuilding). Most of these were for weekly masses and proportionally more were the result of collective foundations by guilds.

The foundation by an individual of a perpetual chantry remained the preserve of the exceptionally wealthy, but the anniversary mass (or obit) was within purchasable reach of a less exclusive clientele. The obit had an even longer history within monastic tradition, and it was a service performed by collegiate clergy. St Donatian's *planarius* indicates obits for the counts and countesses of Flanders dating back to the tenth century (though the earliest were probably added retrospectively).[27] It would appear that from the late twelfth century, the number of obits founded began to increase. At least 343 benefactors – canons, great lords but also citizens – had their names included by c.1320. In St Saviour's over one thousand benefactors had founded obits by c.1340. Throughout the later Middle Ages, the scribes of *planarii* were kept busy adding names for obits. Still active in this task

[27] For the obits of Arnulf (d.965), Charles the Good (d.1127), Philip (d.1191) and his wife Matilda, Margaret of Alsace (d.1194), Joanne (d.1244) and Louis of Nevers (d.1346), see BAB, A141, fos. 19^{r}, 19^{v}, 26^{v}, 43^{v}, 64^{v}, 76^{v}, 90^{r}.

were the scribes of religious houses: friaries and older religious houses continued to be valued as suppliers of commemorative services.[28] But for most lay people, the parish remained the principal source for the sacraments, in life as in death; and what many demanded was increasingly intricate in form. Most of the early obits simply required pittances to be distributed to the clergy for their attendance at the service. References in *planarii* to candles (*stallichten*) being set out around the tomb and to distributions to the poor at obits first appear in the early fourteenth century.[29] The spelling out of specific requirements became more frequent from the 1360s, and heavier endowments swelled the number of those attending services.[30] In the fifteenth century, there was further inflation in the number of priests who were required to attend anniversaries. The number of poor required to attend (collecting doles in return for their prayers) also rose, though the maximum number was generally held at sixty. Some obits were more distinctive than others. A spectacular display of light was to illuminate the obit of the canon Jan Meurin (who had been secretary to Archduke Maximilian, and to the previous two Burgundian dukes). From 1470 he endowed a mass service for which 150 candles were to be lit in specific places, including eight before the main feretories and seventy before other reliquaries.[31] Other benefactors linked their obits with further services. The obit foundation of the painter Cornelius Bollaert in St Giles' church in 1477 included a request to hold the Feast of the Visitation as a principal double, with the seven hours to be celebrated daily between the feast day and the octave.[32]

Suffrages for the departed also involved commemoration of the special dead: intercession from saints was a fundamental part of the penitential process. The increasing endowment of feast days meant a growing range of saintly intercessors (see Table 8.1). A high proportion (over 72 per cent) of the 114 saints or cults whose feast days received endowments (excluding foundations made on days in the *temporale*) were universal ones with

[28] The *Liber Oblongus* (Archives of the Discalced Carmelites of Bruges) lists a large number of post-obit services, particularly in the fifteenth century.

[29] One of the earliest such arrangements in St Donatian's was made for Alard Lam in 1314 (BAB, A141, fo. 5ᵛ; D41, 49). He also set up a chantry in 1300 in the Potterie hospital, where he wanted the serving priest to be of 'Flemish origin' to serve (Bruges, Archives of the OCMW, Potterie, charter 150).

[30] For an early example, see the obit of Jan Hoste and his wife in St Donatian's, founded c.1364, who required the attendance of canons, other clergy and poor people. Jan had been the choir doorkeeper, and he also endowed a chantry and the singing of the Magnificat on the eve of the Immaculate Conception; see BAB, A141, fo. 18ʳ; BAB, A47, fo. 167ʳ; BAB, D42, 12).

[31] BAB, A54, fos. 19ᵛ, 40ʳ, 151ᵛ; BAB, A55, fo. 93ʳ⁻ᵛ; BAB, A141, fos. 113ʳ–14ʳ.

[32] RAB, Sint-Gillis, 273, fos. 110ʳ–13ᵛ.

Table 8.1 *Feast day foundations in six Bruges collegiate and parish churches, 1220–1520*

Christ – Temporale				**Old regional**	
Easter	15	St Quintin	6	St Donatian	8
Christmas	11	Sts Philip, James	5	St Eligius (Tournai)	8
Trinity	9	St Agatha	5	St Boniface	7
Epiphany	8	Sts James, Christopher	5	St Godelieve	6
Lent	8	St Anne	5	St Judoc/Josse	5
Invention HC	7	Sts Simon, Jude	5	Sts Amand, Vedast	4
Exaltation HC	7	St Jerome	5	St Giles	4
All Saints	7	St Gregory	5	Sts Remigius, Bavo	4
Rogation	6	Mary Egypt	5	St Eleutherius (Tournai)	3
Pentecost	6	St John Evangelist	4	St Livinus	3
Circumcision	5	Sts Fabian, Sebastian	4		
Ascension	5	St Paul	4		
Advent	5	St Blaise	4		
Transfiguration	4	St Matthew	4		
All Souls	3	St Margaret	4		
Holy Innocents	3	St John Latin Gate	4		
Palm Sunday	1	St Lawrence	4		
		St Matthew	4		
Sanctorale:		St Benedict	4		
Mary		St Cecilia	4		
		St Augustine	4		
Salve/ masses	27	St Nicasius	4		
Assumption	23	St Vincent	3		
Annunciation	22	St George	3		
Conception	19	St Bernard	3		
Nativity	17	St Luke	3		
Purification	16	Sts Crispin, Crispinian	3		
Our Lady of Pity	1	St Leonard	3		
		St Clement	3		
Old Universal (pre 1200)		St Maximus	3		
		St Lucy	3		
St Katherine Alexandria	14	St Barnabus	2		
St Peter ex cathedra	13	St Martha	2		
St John Baptist	11	St Hippolitus	2		
St Barbara	11	St Firmin	2		
St Thomas Apostle	11	St Denys	2		
Sts Peter, Paul	10	St Apollonia	2		
St Martin	10	St William	2		
St Michael Archangel	9	St Stephen	2		
11, 000 virgins	8	St Valentine	1		
St Mark	7	St Demetrius	1		
St Mary Magdalene	7	St Severinus	1		
St Basil	7	St Theodore, martyr	1		
St Bartholomew	7	St Silvester	1		
St Andrew	6	St Macarius	1		
St Anthony	6	St Euphemia	1		
St Nicholas	6	St John Chrysostom	1		
St Agnes	6	10,000 martyrs	1		
St Adrian	6	Divisio Apostolorum	1		
St Ambrose	6	St Pantaleon	1		

long-established credentials in the Christian calendar, the Virgin Mary above all. Most of the others favoured were among the early church fathers and martyrs. A further 12 per cent were saints that were regional but also venerable: early saint-bishops of Tournai (Eligius and Eleutherius) and apostles of Flanders (St Livinus, St Amand, St Willibrord), martyrs or bishops in the wider region (St Boniface, and especially St Donatian). The same pattern is evident in the choice of saints or cults that guilds chose to patronize (see Table 8.2). Of the 180 known dedications, 67 different saints or cults were chosen. Those most favoured (73 per cent) were old universal saints, the Virgin Mary especially; a further 15 per cent were regional (6 per cent of these being associated with Flanders in particular).

These figures may tell us more about the devotional preferences of citizens, as we shall see; but in terms of post-obit commemoration, not all forms available to the laity can be best studied using evidence from Bruges. Funeral customs and choice of burial places are most fully documented in wills and testaments, but there is a relative dearth of such sources for Bruges. Perhaps some tendencies can be observed, such as a growing demand for burial inside churches rather than outside in cemeteries.[33] That obits in Bruges were becoming more elaborate suggests a similar trend in funerals, obits being repetitions of burial services. Some funerals that are recorded were flamboyant. Duke Philip the Good's burial in St Donatian's in 1467, which required the burning of at least 6,000 lbs of wax, doles to 100 poor people and bell-ringing in all the churches of Bruges, was only the most magnificent example of a type already familiar in the city.[34] Ducal counsellors and highly prominent citizens could generate similar intercession immediately after death. The body of the sheriff Pieter Lanchals, despite his unpopularity and execution at the hands of vengeful commoners in March 1488, enjoyed an astonishingly splendid send-off: services in the three mother churches, the four orders, five further 'houses of God', and at the altars of the brokers' and of the two rhetorician guilds, a procession of sixteen poor householders dressed in black cloth carrying torches, mass in Our Lady's with the full choir, and doles to 100 poor people.[35] The funeral formed only a small fraction of the massive endowments

33 See references to burials in St James' church below.

34 For references and context, see A. Viaene, 'Bij een vijfhonderdste verjaring: De grote dode van het Prinsenhof: Uitvaart en bijzetting van hertog Filips de Goede. Brugge 1467', *Biekorf*, 68 (1967), 321–32; A. Brown, 'Exit Ceremonies in Late Medieval Bruges', in W. Blockmans, T.-H. Borchert, N. Gabriëls et al. (eds.), *Staging the Court of Burgundy* (Turnhout, 2013), pp. 113–19.

35 For Lanchals' will and funeral expenses: RAB, Onze-Lieve-Vrouw, 1062, 1273. The chaplain Lodewijk Witkin accounted for over 72 pounds groten (the equivalent of paying the daily wage to 286 skilled craftsmen) for the funeral expenses on the day alone, which included a substantial funeral feast. Boone, 'Un grand commis de l'État'.

Table 8.2 *Guild dedications to saints and cults in Bruges, c.1270–1520*

Old universal (pre 1200)		**Old regional (pre 1200)**		**'New' regional (post 1300)**	
Our Lady:		Flanders (or nearby)		St Wilgefortis	1
Our Lady	20	St Eligius (Tournai)	3		
Assumption	2	St Bavo	2		
Christ:		St Amand	2		
Holy Cross	4				
Trinity:					
Holy Ghost	4	St Livinus	2		
Trinity	4	St Drogo	1		
St Katherine Alexandria	12	St Godelieve	1		
St Nicholas	8				
St Barbara	7	France:			
St Anthony	5	St Hubert	3		
St George	4	St Judoc	2		
St Anne	4	St Ghislain	2		
St John Baptist	4	St Genevieve	2		
St James	3	St Arnulf of Metz	1		
St Victor	3	St Denis	1		
St Adrian	3	St Leodegarius	1		
St Lawrence	3	St Leonard	1		
St James	3	Sts Crispin, Crispinian	1		
St Blaise	2	St Fiacre	1		
St Christopher	2				
St Daniel	2	**New universal (post 1200)**			
St John Evangelist	2				
St Luke	2	Our Lady:			
St Sebastian	2	Presentation	2		
St Agnes	1	Milan	1		
St Andrew	1	Visitation	1		
St Benedict	1	Seven Sorrows	1		
St Cecilia	1	'Loretten'	1		
St Clement	1	Snow	1		
St Cornelius	1	Grace	1		
Sts Cosmus/Damian	1	Angels	1		
Sts Crispin/Crispinian	1	'Lichtmesse'	1		
St Elisabeth	1	Rozebeke	1		
St Erasmus	1	Conception	1		
St Jerome	1	Dry Tree	1		
St Job	1	Hoedekin	1		
St Joseph	1	Hulsterlo	1		
St Lucy	1	Christ:			
St Mark	1	Corpus Christi	4		
St Martin	1	Holy Blood	1		
St Michael	1	Name of Jesus	1		
St Ninian	1	Flagellation	1		
Sts Peter and Paul	1	Volto Santo	1		
St Philip	1	Other:			
St Roche	1	St Francis	3		
St Silvester	1	St Dominic	1		
St Zacharius	1	St Ivo	1		
10,000 martyrs	1	St Thomas Becket	1		
11,000 virgins	1	St Nicholas of Tolentino	1		
Four crowned martyrs	1				

Lanchals wished to set up for his soul. The most distinctive among these was a double chantry chapel in Our Lady's, and endowments to elevate the Feast of the Presentation in the three main collegiate or parish churches to the rank of great double. Lanchals' untimely demise made it difficult for his executors to carry out his wishes, but most of his foundations were finally in place by the late 1490s. They illustrate how far, by this period, individuals with means could harness commemoration of their souls to the cycle of liturgical time.

Lay and Clerical Activism

Lanchals' benefactions were more lavish and meticulous than most, but were like those of other citizens by this period in specifying what, when and how intercessory service was to be performed. Like others, Lanchals also required the intercession of many individuals and groups. His benefactions thus point to another trend: the growing number of ways in which the urban laity, individually and collectively, made it their business to increase divine service. Yet they also point to the continuing necessity of clerical mediation. Lanchals depended for his commemorative needs on priestly direction and sacramental suffrage which the clergy alone could provide. The chaplain Lodewijk Witkin served as his confessor and executor, doubtless guided him on choice of feast days, steered the performance of his post-obit gifts, and became his posthumous employee as the priest in his chantry foundation.[36] The significance of lay activism and choice needs to be set alongside evidence for the influence of the clergy in the religious life of the city.

The clerical presence within the late medieval city was as considerable as it was varied. Canons and parish priests formed an elite, but chaplains, sacristans, singers and lower functionaries also filled the main collegiate, parish churches and twenty smaller chapels within the city; the religious and semi-religious inhabited the thirty or so monastic houses, tertiaries and beguinages; clerics staffed hospitals and houses of God. With the expansion of the number of religious houses and other ecclesiastical offices, the number of clergy within Bruges must have increased substantially by the fifteenth century. In total some 1,000 to 1,200 people, at least 3 per cent of the population, were members of the secular or regular clergy. Yet this

[36] H. Callewier, 'De papen van Brugge: De seculiere clerus in een middeleeuwse wereldstad (1411–1477)', unpublished PhD thesis, Catholic University of Leuven (Leuven, 2011), pp. 340–1, 527.

does not include those who occupied a twilight zone between clergy and laity: the *clerici tonsurati*, who had received the tonsure as a child, but had afterwards led a lay existence, perhaps marrying, yet regarded by the church as clerics, with immunity from lay jurisdiction. As much as one third of the male population may have enjoyed this status.[37]

Although the number of clergy and clerical institutions grew, the involvement of the laity in the management of sacred activity also increased substantially. The organization of parish life became more complex and more susceptible to lay influence, though St Donatian's remained less so than the two main parish churches. In Our Lady's and St Saviour's the 'communes' of clergy were the sole recipients of endowments in their parishes in the thirteenth century, and continued to be the main receivers of benefactions for feast days thereafter, but the role of the laity in commemorative services began to increase. The emergence of fabric funds supervised by a lay officer or churchwarden is evident in many places in Europe during this period, though difficult to chart in Bruges. The role of lay officials in the management or oversight of post-obit foundations certainly grew.[38] By the fifteenth century, when records of fabric funds start to survive, the lists of receipts and expenditure concerning obits occupy a large part of annual accounts, and show the extent of lay integration into the economy of post-obit foundation. Greater lay involvement in commemorative service is evident in poor-table accounts that also survive from the fifteenth century. The beginnings of five parish poor tables, with their own lay masters by the fifteenth century, receiving gifts of rents specifically to set up doles to the parish poor, can be dated to the early 1300s.[39] These poor tables began to replace the charitable work of hospitals, notably the Potterie, to the 'shamefaced house poor'. Endowments for distributions, usually of clothing or food, were built up: these became more frequent in the 1330s, reaching peaks in

[37] Callewier, *De papen van Brugge*, p. 25.

[38] For the Low Countries, see J. Kuys, 'Secular Authorities and Parish Church Building in Late Medieval Towns in the Netherlands', in M. De Smet, J. Kuys and P. Trio (eds.), *Processions and Church Fabrics in the Low Countries during the Late Middle Ages* (Leuven, 2006), pp. 109–33. There are references to 'provisores' receiving gifts in Bruges churches in the early fourteenth century, but it is unclear whether these were clerics or lay people: St Walburga's in 1310; St Saviour's in 1321, St Giles' in 1321 and St James' in 1339 (RAB, Sint-Walburga, 396, fo. 201^{v}; BAB, S718, fo. 21$^{r–v}$; RAB, Sint-Gillis, 26, fos. 76^{v}–80^{r}; RAB, Sint-Jacob, 20, chap. 15). In St Cross parish, there is reference to a lay 'churchwarden' involved in a foundation in 1336, when a gift was assigned to the curate, poor table and churchwarden to have a requiem mass and a name placed in the 'libro anniversarium' (RAB, Sint-Anna, 5, fo. 107^{v}).

[39] See Galvin, 'Poor Tables'; P. Van Zeir, 'De armenzorg te Brugge', *Biekorf*, 61 (1960), 357–79; and P. Van Zeir, 'De inrichting van de armendissen van de oude Brugse stadsparochies vóór 1526', in *HGG*, 97 (1960), 104–53.

the 1360s and the 1390s, and were then sustained for most of the fifteenth century. The names of benefactors were recorded in calendars, managed by poor-table masters, and resemble the liturgical arrangements set out in clerical *planarii*. Many of these benefactions were linked to the elaboration of the liturgy, such as the enhancement of feast days, and often required the involvement of both the 'communes' of clergy and churchwardens. The full extent of collective activity by lay parishioners only becomes apparent in the fifteenth century. The rebuilding of St James' detailed from 1454 demonstrates the mechanisms and the persistence of their efforts: weekly collection of small contributions in boxes placed in eight streets within the parish, and in addition the regular and more substantial gifts of parish 'notables'.[40] Some benefactors gave handsomely to secure burial places or even chapels within the new parts of the building.[41] The coordination of collective effort that went into the rebuilding work for over twenty years, testifies to the strength of lay attachment to the local parish church.

Visible at an earlier date is another characteristic phenomenon of collective lay activity in the later Middle Ages: the guild or fraternity. At least 170 guilds are known to have existed in Bruges between c.1270 and 1520; and what is remarkable besides their profusion, is the variety of their membership, size and purpose.[42] But common to virtually all, even those designed to protect the economic interests of a particular craft or those limited to a certain social group, was the provision of spiritual insurance for their members. This is already evident in the late thirteenth century.[43] Many craft guilds probably had their own altars in various churches by 1300;[44] while there are traces of guilds whose membership was not apparently restricted to a particular craft. Pilgrimage fraternities, in which lay people were active in a defined religious purpose, have been identified as significant early indicators of lay initiative in sacred activity within Flemish towns.[45] In Bruges,

[40] RAB, Sint-Jacob, 98 (Rekeningen 1464–78).

[41] W. Rombauts, *Het oud archief van de kerkfabriek van Sint-Jacob (XIII–XIXde eeuw)* (Brussels, 1986), pp. 10–32. Among the most prominent benefactors were brokers, furriers, butchers and coopers. For the chapels of Tommaso Portinari, Florentine banker, Willem Moreel, burgomaster, and Donaas de Moor, see further below.

[42] Compare with similar trends in Ghent: P. Trio, *De Gentse broederschappen (1182–1580)* (Ghent, 1990); and P. Trio, *Volksreligie als spiegel van een stedelijke samenleving: De broederschappen te Gent in de late middeleeuwen* (Leuven, 1993).

[43] The guild rules of the black-leather workers c.1300 refer to torches to be lit for funerals of members, and attendance at masses for all members departing on long-distance ('verre') pilgrimages (Huys, *Duizend jaar mutualiteit*).

[44] For a list of guilds in Bruges, see Brown, *Civic Ceremony*, Appendix 5.

[45] P. Trio, 'The Emergence of New Devotions in Late Medieval Urban Flanders (Thirteenth–Fifteenth Centuries): Struggle and Cooperation between Church/Clergy and Urban

the brotherhood of Our Lady of Hulsterlo existed by 1339, and some of its members annually assembled the day after Pentecost outside Damme to make a pilgrimage to a miracle-working image that lay in a chapel in the nearby forest. The fraternity had strong associations with the furrier guilds, though its membership included many others.[46] At a similar date there existed other fraternities with more specialist functions, such as the St George crossbowmen. The evidence is too patchy to determine how many guilds were in existence before 1350. But there are strong indications that guild foundation – or at least foundations of divine service made by guilds – increased after that date. Some of the cartularies and *planarii* of Bruges churches record properties and endowments from the thirteenth century; but from the mid fourteenth century they begin to register more efforts by guilds to establish altars or increase their level of divine service. The peak of such guild activity was reached between 1450 and 1490 (see Figure 8.2). This may reflect the greater availability of source material on guilds; but it also matches the pattern of benefaction made by individuals for post-obit or liturgical service (see Figure 8.1).

These figures do justice neither to the complexity of guild activity, nor to the multiple ways in which guilds accumulated links with the divine. While the wealthiest of associations, like the brokers, established their own almshouses and free-standing chapels (with bell-towers, indulgences and burial rights), less prestigious groups in the fifteenth century also sought to improve the services offered to their members as their means allowed. By then, many guilds of middling rank were adorning their altars with paintings commissioned from fashionable artists (the tanners, for instance, from Hans Memling), equipping their priests with costly vestments, and stocking their guild chests with relics and letters of indulgence. According to their inventory (c.1476), the smiths owned a relic of St Eligius, their patron saint, as well as the blood – 'it is said' – of St Cornelius.[47] Lesser guilds also strove to acquire marks of sacred distinction. A 'confraternity' of St Francis existed in the church of begard tertiaries, apparently by the mid fourteenth century, for guilds that did not have their own 'oratories'; one of them, the carters, withdrew in 1435 in order to found their own

Government/Bourgeoisie', in S. Ehrich and J. Oberste (eds.), *Städtische Kulte im Mittelalter* (Regensburg, 2010), pp. 327–37.

46 An indulgence granted in 1474 rehearses the legend of a monk from Thérouanne who brought a miraculous statue to the forest of Hulsterlo and had it placed in a tree, whereupon two doves settled there: SAB, 524, Gilden Hulsterloo. See H. Brinkman, 'De Brugse pelgrims in het Gruuthuse handschrift', in Oosterman (ed.), *Stad van koopmanschap en vrede*, pp. 9–39.

47 RAB, Ambachten, 386, Register, before foliation, and fo. 1^{r-v}; SAB, 96, 14, fo. 204^{v}.

altar elsewhere.[48] The apprentices of several crafts formed brotherhoods with their own altars in churches of their choosing, those of the shoemakers (the *elsenaars*) for instance first within St James' in 1415 before moving to St Saviour's in 1448.

The most common guilds to be found in Bruges were ones associated with particular occupations and crafts. These usually imposed obligations on their members, such as attendance at annual feasts, funerals and obits. But in the later fourteenth century another type of association came to be founded. The 'confraternity' of Our Lady of the Dry Tree, established by 1396 in the Franciscan friary, was one of several that were focused around new devotional cults (others being dedicated to Corpus Christi, the Holy Blood, the Trinity and later the Name of Jesus), but it was different in the kind of involvement demanded of its members.[49] Active participation in guild affairs was not necessarily required: in return for modest fees, members could expect an impressive suite of suffrages, especially on the Assumption. Membership of this fraternity was exclusive: the ninety or so who were members of the Dry Tree c.1496 were made up largely of courtiers, highly ranked citizens, foreign merchants and important clergy. Other devotional fraternities had a wider social catchment. Membership of the guild devoted to Our Lady of the Snow mushroomed following news in 1464 of a miracle effected through the guild's image in Our Lady's church. By the early 1470s, 1,300 people from every walk of urban life, lay and clerical, were paying a small fee in return for prayers at low mass during the week and at high mass every Sunday at the altar.[50] The proliferation of such guilds shows a desire among townsmen and women to choose specific cults to venerate, or to respond to new forms of devotion, even though they did not involve most members in active forms of piety. Other guilds appearing in the early fifteenth century did demand a more considered exploration of religious life. The first chamber of rhetoric in Bruges – and one of the first in the region – was reputedly founded by a small group of well-connected laymen in 1428 or 1429 under the inspiration of the Holy Ghost. The involvement of rhetoricians in composing devotional poems, organizing poetry competitions and staging morality plays was to become a highly distinctive feature of urban life throughout the Low Countries (see Chapter 9).

[48] SAB, 96, 11, fo. 236^{v}.

[49] On the significance of these 'confraternities', and for similar trends elsewhere in the Low Countries, see Trio, *Volksreligie*, pp. 100–2.

[50] See A. Brown, 'Bruges and the "Burgundian Theatre-State": Charles the Bold and Our Lady of the Snow', *History*, 84 (1999), 573–89, and references cited there.

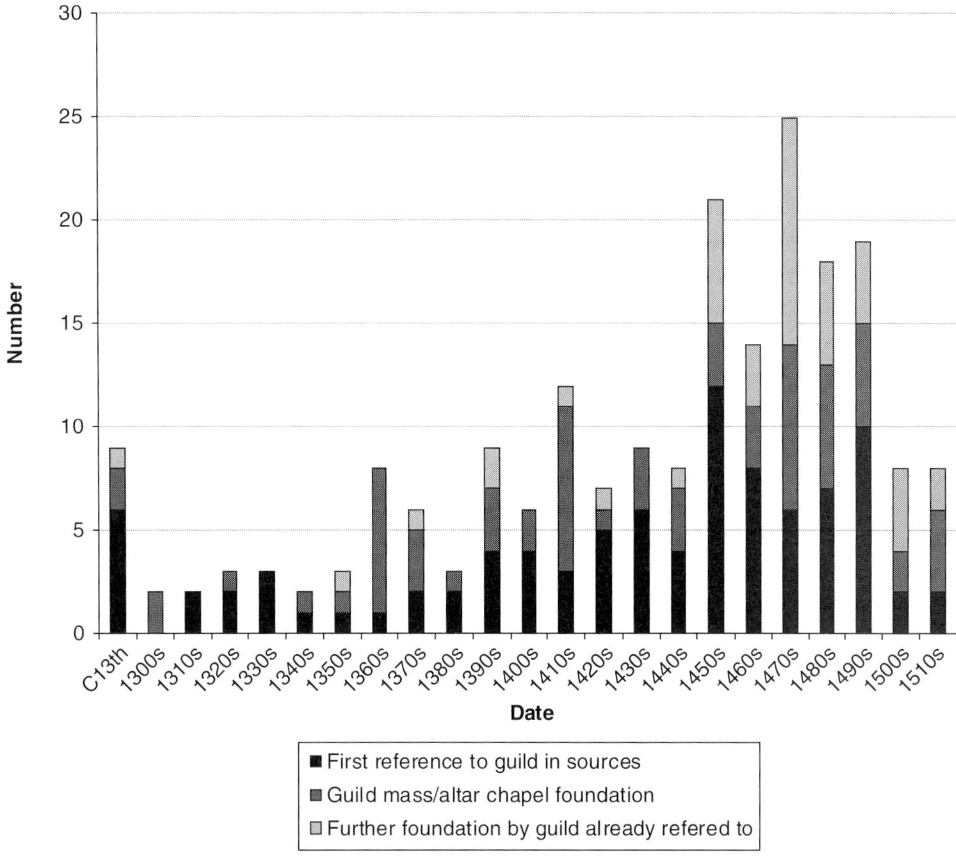

Figure 8.2 Guild foundations in Bruges churches, c.1270–1520

While all types of guild primarily served the interests of their own members, most also made a devotional impact within or beyond the churches in which they maintained altars. In 1420 the armourers agreed with the churchwardens of St Saviour's to display their relic of the True Cross for the benefit of 'all the inhabitants of Bruges'.[51] Substantial contributions were made by guilds to the liturgy. The barber surgeons contracted with the clergy and churchwardens of St James' in 1432 to celebrate the feast day of Sts Cosmas and Damian (26 September) as a 'small principal feast', which included a procession to the guild altar with children singing a motet. The guild also contributed to the singing of daily offices on an additional seven days following their feast day, thus adding to the programme of

[51] K. Verschelde, *De kathedrale van S. Salvator te Brugge* (Bruges, 1863), p. 230.

such investment that had been underway in the church for twenty years.[52] Enrichment of the liturgy was only one of the ways in which guild activity became linked with divine service. From the 1420s onwards the number of foundations that required the participation of guilds increased considerably. More benefactors began to require guild governors to oversee the fulfilment of their services, particularly regarding distributions to the poor during their anniversaries. Such use of guilds was even made by courtiers and nobles. Lodewijk van Gruuthuse's post-obit arrangements with Our Lady's church included doles to prisoners at his four anniversaries, supervision of which he entrusted in part to the shippers, tailors and mobile fish-sellers.[53] Lanchals required the performance of his chantry to be overseen by the leather workers; the goldsmiths were to attend Jan Meurin's obit. By 1490, almost fifty guilds were performing such commemorative duties. With these arrangements benefactors thus generated wider suffrage for their souls, while guilds became enmeshed in an increasingly complex network of intercession managed by citizens.

Growing lay involvement in sacred activity, however, did not necessarily mean a diminishing role for the clergy. Evidence for lay activism points in two apparently contradictory directions: on the one hand, to increasing lay control over the clergy; on the other hand, to continuing dependence of the laity on clerical mediation. The provision of sacramental suffrage was a task that ultimately remained a clerical preserve. The proliferation of mass services and the enrichment of liturgical life expanded employment opportunities for clerics. The foundation of smaller religious houses and the remarkable diversity in types of religious life, including the novel Observance, reflected clerical initiatives of reform as well as lay interest in it. The elaboration of feast days was also promoted by the clergy: Lanchals' chaplain, Lodewijk Witkin, had sufficient wealth to augment feast day and other liturgical celebration in Our Lady's church on a scale that exceeded even his master's foundation there.[54] Within the more clerical institution of St Donatian's, most of the major feast day or obit foundations (like Jan Meurin's) were made by the canons themselves.

Particularly active within urban society were the friars. Their specialist vocation as preachers was valued by a wide range of Bruges' inhabitants.

52 RAB, Charters with blue numbers, 8128.

53 SAB, 196, 9, fo. 4^{v}; SAB, 333, fos. 1^{r}–6^{r}, 7^{r}–19^{r}; RAB, Onze-Lieve-Vrouw, 735, fo. 40^{v}.

54 Among several feast days that he augmented in Our Lady's Church, Witkin founded a double feast for the 11,000 Virgins, a feast day he also augmented in St Donatian's (RAB, Onze-Lieve-Vrouw, chap. 358; Reg. 735, fo. 157^{v}; 1350, fo. 214^{r}; 250, fo. 70^{v}; and for his 'singular devotion' to the cult, BAB, A57, fo. 175^{r}).

In 1236, the Dominicans formally agreed to deliver a public sermon after processions conducted five times a year by St Donatian's church; from 1312, the Carmelites were obliged to preach once a year in Our Lady's. Relations between the secular clergy and the friars were sometimes troubled, but a certain modus vivendi between them had been reached by the end of the fourteenth century, even if tensions caused by mendicant preaching continued into the fifteenth.[55] Mendicant relations with the city authorities were smoother. Virtually all the city accounts, from 1280 onwards, contain payments to friars; the chaplain of the city prison, the Steen, was a friar; and mendicants were regularly employed as preachers during general processions in the fifteenth century. The friars also served a wider clientele; Franciscans were confessors to the beguinage; while mendicant churches housed the altars and chapels of certain craft guilds, and of foreign 'nations' in Bruges.

Within the ecclesiastical landscape, the church of St Donatian retained a redoubtable presence. It comprised a powerful group of clergy who jealously guarded its liberties against the encroachments of townsmen and clergy, including the bishop of Tournai.[56] Its canons (numbering thirty-one by 1368) were wealthy, mobile, cosmopolitan and highly connected; many were local in origin, but educated in prestigious schools and universities, and especially by the fifteenth century a majority of them owed promotion to their benefices to the Burgundian dukes. Their sense of corporate identity was encouraged by gatherings such as the annual *Crepelfeest* pilgrimage to Aardenburg (which also brought out the clergy of Our Lady's, St Saviour's and St James'). The numerous chaplains and other clerics of St Donatian's served in various capacities within the church, but were also employed as singers in other city churches, and in a range of activity, religious and secular, that required their highly developed levels of literacy. The influence of St Donatian's on the particular religious character of the city remained significant, even if other collegiate bodies within the city were also influential. Their *esprit de corps* was strengthened by the formation of 'brotherhoods of the choir' dedicated to the daily singing of the seven hours, and which also continued to be the main beneficiaries of benefactions, lay and clerical, for other commemorative services in their parishes. In 1428, the brotherhood of the choir at Our Lady's also opened its membership to the laity, though it remained clerically dominated.[57]

[55] Simons, *Stad en apostolaat*, pp. 169, 186–7; J. De Smet, 'De vestiging van de vier bedelorden te Brugge in de XIIIde eeuw', *Biekorf*, 52 (1951), 233–7; W. Simons, 'Mendicant Collaboration in the Fourteenth Century: The Bruges Pact of 1370', in P. Chandler and K. J. Egan (eds.), *The Land of Carmel: Essays in Honor of Joachim Smet, O.Carm* (Rome, 1991), pp. 171–87.

[56] For the following, see Callewier, *De papen van Brugge*, passim.

[57] RAB, Onze-Lieve-Vrouw, 2003, fos. 13^{v}–15^{r}.

Relations between clergy and laity were often perceived as amicable and mutually beneficial. Clerics joined and served in fraternities that were mostly lay in membership: Lodewijk Witkin was a member of the two rhetorician guilds. Lay rhetoricians valued clerical roles: de Roovere wrote a poem in praise of the priestly office, as well as one praising the holy sacrament.[58] Yet the same poem criticizes clergymen who prioritized other things over celebrating the mass; and clerics in the service of lay people could find their employers exacting. Failure of priests to perform spiritual duties caused complaint. The archery guild of St Sebastian on more than one occasion took the Carmelite friars to task for neglect of their intercessory services.[59] When two priests of St John's chapel were called to account for creating a disturbance in 1470, they were reprimanded by one Adrianus de Hoofsche, a tonsured cleric but also an alderman, in a way that shows both lay demands on the priestly role, and respect for it (even if double-edged): 'you are priests,' he told them, 'you must go about peacefully and speak Latin!'[60]

Wider events in Christendom affected relations between clergy and laity: the Papal Schism (1378–1417) was particularly damaging for clerical authority and was divisive in Bruges. Even the Holy Blood relic was made to serve factional purpose: one bishop in 1388 claimed that it represented God's promise that Flanders would never separate itself from obedience to Rome. In 1392 many citizens refused to accept the sacraments of priests supporting the Avignon pope, and churches were left empty even on feast days.[61] But the status of the priestly office may not have been undermined by the Schism in the long term. Lay criticism of the clergy was voiced most often when individual clerics fell short of standards expected of the clergy – and when relations between clerics and lay people became a touch too amicable. Concubinage and drunkenness in city taverns were the priestly peccadilloes that the canons of St Donatian's were most frequently called upon to correct in their colleagues, especially their younger clerics.[62] The opportunities and entanglements faced by some clergy in Bruges are

[58] Anthonis de Roovere, 'Lof van den priesterlijcken staet', in De Roovere, *De gedichten*, pp. 148–61. On de Roovere, see Chapter 9.

[59] Archives of head guild Saint-Sebastian, Bruges, charters 10 (1456), 12 (1491).

[60] BAB, A53, fo. 367v (see Callewier, *De papen van Brugge*, p. 178).

[61] J. Gaillard, *Recherches historiques sur la chapelle du Saint-Sang à Bruges* (Bruges, 1846), pp. 60–2, 229–31; Jan van Dixmude, *Chronicke van den prinsen ende graven van Vlaenderen en Brabant van 1377 tot 1443*, ed. J. Lambin (Ypres, 1835), p. 283. Within Bruges, St Donatian's followed the Burgundian duke in declaring for the Avignon pope, against the majority of citizens who sided with Rome.

[62] For figures, see Callewier, *De papen van Brugge*, pp. 127–40, esp. 127.

illustrated by the career of Gillis Joye (d.1484). Gillis moved from Kortrijk to St Donatian's in Bruges in 1448, developing a reputation as a singer but also as a brawler and brothel-creeper; service to the duke of Cleves and connections with the Burgundian court landed him benefices, affording an opulent lifestyle which funded several foundations and his portrait from Hans Memling, but which bankrupted him in 1474. He became a canon of St Donatian's, as well as a composer of secular songs, the lyrics of which were sometimes blatantly obscene.[63] The worldliness of priests, despite their theoretical separation from the world, was a source of perennial criticism, and the exceptional wealth of some clergymen in Bruges allowed them a lifestyle that was perceptibly less imitative of Christ than of the noblest laymen. Some of the shortcomings of younger clerics in St Donatian's were brought to the attention of the canons by lay people. However, the sharpest criticism of clerical failings came from within the ranks of the clergy: the chronicle of Romboudt de Doppere, himself a canon of St Donatian's and a rhetorician, is vituperative about the sins of late fifteenth-century clergy.[64] Moreover, although de Doppere placed the blame for these on clerical immorality, the worldliness of clerics was also the result of pressures that were not of their making. The multiplying ways that the clergy were drawn into service of the laity and into worldly matters placed formidable obstacles in the path of fulfilling the ideals of the priestly office. The same pressures are also evident in clerical relations with civic government.

Public Worship and Civic Government

The initiative taken by the laity in sacred matters is apparent in the most distinctive forms of lay activism in late medieval towns: those that involved urban government. The authority that the city council in Bruges exercised over its citizen body came to be expressed in sacred terms. This partly built upon earlier links formed between the commune and its aspiration towards peace; and it also developed in tandem with the expansion of municipal jurisdiction over the economic and social life of the city during the thirteenth century. For instance, immigration into the city prompted legislation

[63] H. Callewier, '*What You Do on the Sly … Will Be Deemed Forgiven in the Sight of the Most High*: Gilles Joye and the Changing Status of the Singers in 15th-Century Bruges', *Journal of the Alamire Foundation*, 1 (2009), 89–109.

[64] Romboudt de Doppere, *Fragments inédits de Romboudt de Doppere … chronique Brugeoise de 1491 à 1498*, ed. P. H. Dussart (Bruges, 1892), pp. 23, 44, 70, 72; H. Callewier, 'Leven en werk van Rombout de Doppere', *HGG*, 150 (2013), 219–44.

to control its effects (see Chapter 2), but management of the poor, as a work of mercy, developed a religious aspect to municipal business. Dispensing alms to the urban poor was a responsibility expressed in communal oversight of St John's hospital, founded in the late twelfth century, and of hospitals and leper houses during the thirteenth.[65] Poor tables supplanted hospitals in the fourteenth century as the principal means of organized charity to the parish poor: over these too the municipal government placed itself as their overseer.

The sacred dimension of civic authority was reinforced in more deliberate ways. Municipal responsibility for another work of mercy – help to prisoners – was enshrined in the foundation of the civic prison, located in the Burg, close to the magistrates' townhouse (*scepenhuis*). From the mid fourteenth century, the Dark Room (*donkere kamer*), which was part of the Steen for poorer prisoners, began to receive endowments or indirect gifts through the parish poor tables, for distribution to prisoners. By the end of the fifteenth century, the accumulation of endowments from fifty-one benefactors allowed distributions to prisoners on more than sixty days of the year.[66] The absence of city council minutes makes it difficult to chart the development of civic initiatives, but other evidence suggests effort to strengthen the sacred aura surrounding the exercise of municipal rule. In 1397 the city treasury directly funded the foundation of a new almshouse, the Dulhuus, for the mentally ill. Other endowments confirmed the special responsibility that the city magistracy had assumed towards the urban poor. In 1395 the citizen Jan Waghenare provided for a *mandatum* ceremony to be held every Maundy Thursday in St Donatian's. Five poor men were to sit at high mass near the sanctuary and have their hands and feet washed by the celebrant (in imitation of Christ): two of these five were to be selected by the aldermen.[67] Waghenare's foundation also provided for a Holy Ghost mass to be sung during the annual election on 2 September of alderman and councillors, so that 'grace might be given' while the new council was being formed. By the fifteenth century, aldermen could also meet as another kind of devotional body, as members of the Holy Blood fraternity. Its twenty-six members mirrored the number of men serving

[65] Maréchal, *Gebondenheid*.

[66] A benefaction from Jan de Wec c.1390 reputedly supplied the prisoners with a daily bowl of soup. These benefactions (like those for poor tables) began to be recorded systematically in a calendar or *bezettebouck*: SAB, 196, 9 and 11; P. Allossery, 'De oudste giften en fondatiën ten bate der arme gevangenen te Brugge (ca. 1300–1475)', *HGG*, 79 (1936), 67–130, and 80 (1937), 155–73.

[67] GVS, *Inventaire*, vol. III, pp. 302–4.

as aldermen and councillors, and its membership was almost exclusive to those who had held these offices.[68]

This fraternity had particular responsibilities towards the relic and procession of the Holy Blood. It thus embodied the city magistracy's special association with a cult that had become the most important in Bruges. The relic was present in Bruges by 1256, and by 1297 it was being identified with the protection of the city's liberties: when the army of King Philip IV of France was poised to invade Flanders, the Bruges magistrates petitioned the king not to remove the relic from the city.[69] Quite when the relic came to be carried in an annual procession is not certain. A distinctive feature of many towns from the later thirteenth century was the annual civic procession, in honour of the town's principal patron saints or cults. The Holy Blood procession in Bruges, as a city-wide event involving guilds, probably evolved from processions held on Holy Cross day (3 May), but the first official civic subsidy of the occasion began in 1303, and the first certain contemporary record of the carrying of the Holy Blood relic on that day occurs in 1304.[70] After episcopal blessing and a papal indulgence had been acquired in 1310, the level of civic funding of the procession mounted, much of it directed towards enhancing the visual and auditory impact of the event. Systematic payments are recorded from the 1330s for gifts and hospitality for attending clergy from within and outside the city, for crossbowmen and later archers to accompany the relic, for the liveries of official participants, and for pipers and trumpeters. These expenses increased substantially from the mid fourteenth century. From around 1350, the city also began to contribute to an expansion of the processional period: the city's clergy were paid to take it in turns to process during the fifteen days after 3 May. In 1396, the city began to subsidize 'plays' or dumbshows to be acted out during the main procession.[71] It was the city council in 1419 that petitioned the canons of St Donatian's to elevate Holy Cross day to the rank of great double, basing their case on the 'popular devotion' to the procession and the large number of prelates who attended it.

Holy Blood day came to be twinned with another annual procession on Corpus Christi day which included all the craft guilds by the fifteenth century. It remained a lesser event, and did not receive specific civic

68 The earliest references to the fraternity are found in 1405 and 1406: SAB, 114, 1397–1422, fo. 64r; SAB, 216, 1405/6, fo. 121v. Membership was increased to thirty-one in 1471: Archives of the Confraternity of the Holy Blood, Register 5, fo. 9r.

69 SAB, 96, 2, fo. 29r–v.

70 Boogaart, *Ethnogeography*; but see N. Geirnaert, 'De oudste sporen van het Heilig Bloed in Brugge (1255–1310)', *HGG*, 147 (2010), 247–55.

71 SAB, 216, 1395/6, fo. 91v.

funding,[72] but it also fell under the city magistrates' authority. For instance, in 1475 the council ordered the plumber Reynoud Willems, for failing to wear the correct livery on Holy Blood day, to appear correctly attired with his guild on Corpus Christi.[73] St Donatian's day (15 October) was also of city-wide significance: in 1493, the city magistrates petitioned Philip the Fair to allow them to hold a procession with magistrates and guilds.[74] But Holy Blood day remained the most important day of the city's calendar. It set out the hierarchical order of the craft guilds, and intervened in disputes between them (see further below). It also allowed city governments to exercise a degree of legislative authority over members of the clergy. They too had a processional order to follow, and took turns in carrying the Holy Blood reliquary. The order could be disputed: great disturbance occurred on 3 May 1500, when a canon of St Donatian's apparently clouted the Eekhout prior as he attempted to wrestle the Holy Blood relic from the prior's grip. In June 1501, the city council pronounced the prior to have been in error for resisting the relic change-over, and referred participating clergy to a schedule that would henceforward be placed in the civic chambers, which presumably set down the order of relic-carriers. The council also added (somewhat imperiously) that this would prevent future 'scandals and dangers' that might occur because of the 'carelessness of clerics'.[75]

The city government directly sponsored other liturgical events. The singing of *Salve* attracted multiple benefactions in Bruges parishes; and in 1480 the city magistrates began to contribute to the singing in St Donatian's of a *Maria lof ende salve*, which by 1483 became a daily event supported by city minstrels and trumpeters. The civic magistrates considered attendance beneficial for every 'devout person'.[76] Other festive occasions had already fallen under municipal auspices. During the fourteenth century, more public money was directed towards the ludic events of jousters and shooters, which began to be concentrated in the summer months, especially around Holy Blood day. The high point of such investment was in the middle decades of the fifteenth century.[77] Connections between civic government and rhetorical activity were also being established. The first rhetoric chamber in Bruges may have emerged partly in the context of municipal sponsorship of 'plays', perhaps

72 For sources on this, see Brown, *Civic Ceremony*, pp. 115, 127–8.

73 OBB, Ms. 437, fo. 364^{r-v}; SAB, 157 (Register 1461–1519), fos. 144^{v}–7^{r}.

74 ADN, B 1705, fos. 10^{r}–11^{v}.

75 BAB, I12; A57, fos. 144^{v}, 165^{r}, 167^{v}, 225^{v}; SAB, 96, 13, fos. 317^{v}–19^{r}.

76 SAB, 216, 1479/80, fo. 174^{v}; 1480/1, fo. 174^{r}; 1482/3, fo. 157^{v}; 1483/4 fo. 172^{r}; BAB, G6 (1470–86), 1483/4, fo. 9^{r}; A55, fo, 210^{r}. See R. Strohm, *Music in Late Medieval Bruges*, 2nd edn (Oxford, 1990), pp. 33, 39, 85–6.

77 See Brown, *Civic Ceremony*, pp. 171–4.

even those of the Holy Blood procession. A Jan van Hulst was one of the reputed founders of the Holy Spirit chamber; a man of the same name was paid by the city in 1394 for plays performed before Duchess Margaret, and for those put on during the Holy Blood procession in 1396.[78] By the 1440s, rhetoric competitions were becoming part of civic festivity (see Chapter 9). From the mid fifteenth century, rhetoricians were being employed in more events, including the *Salve* concerts at St Donatian's.[79] The services of the most prolific of Bruges' rhetoricians, Anthonis de Roovere, were held in such regard that in 1466 the city magistrates awarded him an annual emolument of 6 pounds groten to deter him from leaving the city (see Chapter 9).

De Roovere's skills were prized partly because they were employed on occasions that added lustre to civic honour in relation to the outside world. Rhetoric competitions proliferated, especially in the mid fifteenth century, and Bruges was active in sending its representatives to other towns or hosting events within its walls. One of the most distinctive characteristics of urban society in the Low Countries was the degree of ceremonial interaction between towns.[80] Rhetoric events had emerged partly from a tradition of festive competition involving jousters and archers: these also reached a height in the mid fifteenth century. A competition between the White Bear jousters of Bruges and Epinette jousters of Lille lasted until 1487.[81] The religious activities of other guilds were also deemed to play a part in upholding civic honour. Some guilds organized annual pilgrimages to places outside the city. By 1396, the fraternity of Our Lady of Rozebeke (a group comprising the 'principal and most notable men of the town') was undertaking an annual pilgrimage to a chapel in Westrozebeke, where it joined guilds from other small towns in the region.[82] Some craft guilds sent delegates to regional shrines, the glovers for instance to the illustrious image of Our Lady in Aardenburg at Pentecost possibly by the 1350s.[83] These pilgrimages were certainly regarded later as occasions that had brought prestige to the city.[84]

78 SAB, 216, 1393/4, fo. 64r; 1396/7, fo. 92r.

79 Alianus de Groote, succentor of St Donatian's and a Holy Ghost rhetorician, was paid in 1480 for his contribution to the *lof* (SAB, 216, 1480/1, fo. 174r).

80 A.-L. Van Bruaene, *Om beters wille: Rederijkerskamers en de stedelijke cultuur in de zuidelijke Nederlanden 1400–1650* (Amsterdam, 2008), pp. 208–10.

81 A. Van den Abeele, *Het ridderlijk gezelschap van de Witte Beer* (Bruges, 2000).

82 SAB, 509, Gilde Roosebeke.

83 SAB, 96, 14, fo. 177v; Gilliodts-Van Severen (ed.), *Mémoriaux*, pp. 360–2.

84 See Zegher van Male's lament in 1590 at their passing: Zegher van Male, *De Lamentatie van Zeghere van Male, Brugge na de opstand tegen Spanje 1590*, ed. A. Dewitte and A. Viaene (Bruges, 1977), p. 74.

Craft and shooting guilds were given responsibilities to uphold civic honour at the entries of princes into the city. These had become more elaborate from 1440, when for the first time dumbshows, often adopting biblical themes, were staged lining the ceremonial route. Their performance could be delegated to guilds, and was sometimes aided by payments from civic coffers.[85] But the coordination of these events increasingly devolved onto rhetoricians, which was another reason why their skills became highly valued. De Roovere was rewarded his emolument at the behest of Duke Charles the Bold, pleased at the rhetorician's efforts. The dumbshows could indeed be designed to gratify princely visitors: those of 1468, after the marriage of Charles and Margaret of York, flattered the newlyweds entering the city with nine tableaux (staged by various guilds) that made reference to biblical or antique couples. De Roovere, who probably directed the programme, himself recorded that these signified the good that the marriage would bring to the lands of the duke.[86] Dumbshows on other occasions, however, notably the 1440 entry of Duke Philip following the suppression of revolt in Bruges, were more penitential in tone. The words of John the Baptist (used at Advent) greeted the duke as he entered the city gate: 'I am the voice of one crying in the wilderness: make straight the way of the lord.' The meaning of these tableaux may be debated.[87] In this context it is worth noting that entries offered yet another arena of civic activity in which municipal authorities felt able to deploy the language of liturgy and scripture.

While Holy Blood day remained the most important civic event in which clergy, magistrates, guildsmen, shooters, rhetoricians, painters and a host of other citizens were brought together most inclusively, the city treasury also began at the beginning of the fifteenth century to fund a type of procession that required a different kind of participation from citizens.[88] The ad hoc or 'general' procession, in which relics were processed for a specific supplicatory purpose, had a long liturgical tradition (associated particularly with the litanies of Rogation). Galbert of Bruges recounted how the canons of St Donatian, in the aftermath of Charles the Good's murder in 1127, called for a universal fast within the town, and encouraged the people

[85] For instance when Duke Philip the Good entered Bruges in March 1455: SAB, 216, 1454/5, fo. 51v.

[86] A. J. Enschedé, 'Huwelijksplechtigheden van Karel van Bourgondië en Margaretha van York', *Kronijk van het historisch genootschap gevestigd te Utrecht*, 22 (1866), 26–31.

[87] Kipling, *Enter the King*, pp. 49–60, 102–14. But see also B. A. M. Ramakers, 'Multifaceted and Ambiguous: The *tableaux vivants* in the Bruges Entry of 1440', in R. Suntrup, J. R. Veenstra and A. Bolleman (eds.), *Medien der Symbolik in Spätmittelalter und Früher Neuzeit* (Frankfurt am Main, 2005), pp. 163–94.

[88] For the following, see Brown, *Civic Ceremony*, pp. 73–98.

to appease God by following them in procession with crosses and relics.[89] The canons were apparently prime movers of such supplicatory processions for two mentioned in 1380 and 1381, but in 1408 the city itself began to contribute to them, paying a friar to preach two sermons during a 'general procession' for Duke John the Fearless' expedition against the rebel city of Liège. Thereafter, most of the references to such processions occur in city accounts rather than clerical sources; and the chapter act-books of St Donatian begin to record an increasing number of requests for relic processions from the 'city legislators'. The general procession differed from the Holy Blood chiefly in its penitential aspect. It was deliberately purged of the pomp – the plays, trumpets and banquets – that attended the 3 May event. It could also require all citizens on the day to go to church and confess as they would do at Easter, so that their prayers might be 'better heard and received by almighty God'.[90]

Municipal effort to encourage piety among citizens was matched by effort to discourage impiety. Penitential behaviour could be enforced during general processions. Viewing the sacrament when carried on these occasions was considered beneficial to citizens, if not compulsory: in January 1491 a man was banished from Flanders for wilfully covering up his eyes with nutshells as the sacrament passed during a general procession.[91] From the 1470s, chronicles begin to record the appearance of miscreants in general processions as a form of punishment.[92] Municipal appetite for these processions sharpened from the 1440s onwards, and was almost insatiable during the political upheavals of the 1480s when an average of twenty processions a year were dispatched, a number of them by then carrying the Holy Blood relic. Although demand diminished after the period of crisis had passed, the continued regularity of their calling in the early sixteenth century shows that they had become an indispensable expression of the authority vested in the city's magistracy.

These processions also demanded much of the clergy, especially St Donatian's, who were asked to process with specific relics or the sacrament from their churches. But the impression of municipal ascendancy over

89 Rider (ed.), *Galbertus Brugensis*, chaps. 35, 114, 116.

90 For example, SAB, 120, II (1490–99), fos. 63^{v}–4^{v}.

91 P. Fredericq (ed.), *Corpus documentorum inquisitionis haereticae pravitatis neerlandicae: verzameling van stukken betreffende de pauselijke en bisschoppelijke inquisitie in de Nederlanden*, 5 vols. (Ghent and The Hague, 1889–1906), vol. II, pp. 279–80.

92 In July 1477 a man who had spoken 'bad words' about the people of Bruges and Ghent was made to walk bareheaded in a general procession, carrying a candle (OBB, Ms. 437, fo. 392^{r}). Certainly by the 1490s this kind of punishment was a standard procedure: SAB, 157, fos. 2^{v}–3^{v}, 8^{v}, 12^{v}–13^{r}, 15^{r}–16^{r} and passim.

processions, relics and clergy may be qualified. The canons of St Donatian's had cause to resent the demand for their relics: the same period of high demand for general processions in the 1480s was also the period in which the canons disputed management of these processions most frequently. During rebellions that pitted citizens against each other or against their princely rulers, the canons often proved equivocal, even divided among themselves, in supporting one side or the other.[93] As members of the most prestigious clerical institution in Bruges, they continued to retain a strong sense of their own identity and agenda in the face of lay demands.

Currents of Spirituality, Devotion and Morality

Lay involvement in processions, parishes and pilgrimages was involvement in what clerics described as an 'active' form of life, one appropriate for people who lived in the world. Retreat into a superior 'contemplative' form of life had traditionally been available only to the religious. In Bruges, there were no monastic institutions founded before the twelfth century (see Chapter 2); and the older orders such as the Benedictines and Cistercians were never established within the city. But in the twelfth century, during a wider period of church reform, a new variety of religious communities began to find a niche within the expanding urban environment, and not always as a result of official encouragement. The Eekhout abbey originated as a hybrid community of men who coalesced around veneration of a local hermit. In the thirteenth century, the Rich Clares also began as a group of women devoted to a female hermit; and the Wijngaard beguines initially formed a community without institutional affiliations. The relative merits of the 'active' and 'contemplative' life were more sharply debated with the appearance of friars who were active in the world, while other kinds of spiritual life, more accessible to lay people, began to multiply.

The greater involvement of the laity in a religious life and in more personal forms of devotion is often considered another characteristic trend of late medieval religion.[94] It is most apparent in the *Devotio moderna* that emerged first in the towns of the northern Netherlands within the houses of the Common Life, under the inspiration of Geert Groote (d.1384).[95] These

93 See Callewier, *De papen van Brugge*, pp. 280–4.

94 R. N. Swanson, *Religion and Devotion in Europe c.1215–c.1515* (Cambridge, 1995), pp. 102–16, 177–82.

95 For the following, see J. Van Engen, *Sisters and Brothers of the Common Life: The Devotio Moderna and the World of the Later Middle Ages* (Philadelphia, 2008).

houses were distinctive by virtue of their emphasis on meditation on the life of Christ, their accessibility to lay people, and their claim to live a communal religious life but without a Rule. In many ways, they supported rather than undermined the institutional church (especially when they adopted a Rule); and the theology of the *Devotio*'s most famous exponent, Thomas of Kempen (who valued meditation on the Eucharist), was entirely orthodox. But they raised suspicions, not least because the Common Life was implicitly critical of the church, given its emphasis on reform, the inner life and the merits of daily work, rather than on clerical mediation and performance of good works. These suspicions were intensified partly because of wider alarm at other explicit and heretical criticisms of religious practices that were voiced more stridently in late fourteenth-century Europe, especially in the wake of the Papal Schism from 1378.

No houses of the Common Life were founded in Bruges. Seemingly little heresy appeared in the city during the later Middle Ages. But absence of certain kinds of evidence (especially the loss of the episcopal archives at Tournai) makes it difficult to detect the presence of alternative forms of spirituality.[96] In any case, both *Devotio* and 'deviance' need to be placed within a wider context of late medieval devotion and its many interconnecting trends. The absence of houses of the Common Life in Bruges does not in itself indicate antipathy to the kind of spirituality that these houses espoused.[97] Too sharp a distinction can be drawn between this devotional spirituality and the other religious practices discussed so far. For all its novelty, part of the popularity of the Common Life lay in its similarity to broader currents of spiritual reform, in which the clergy were as involved as the laity. These evidently appealed to residents of Bruges. Groote himself had been a Carthusian cleric, and the austere piety of his order was well regarded in Bruges as elsewhere, by individuals and governments. The Carthusian priory of Genadedal, outside the city walls, received occasional civic subsidy for its building works,[98] and was given the oversight of the Adornes Jerusalem chapel and almshouse. In 1454 Pieter Adornes left

[96] The city accounts in 1420/1 mention the imprisonment of a man accused of spreading things 'contrary to our belief' (SAB, 216, 1420/1, fo. 107^{r}). A merchant of Spanish origin was accused in his absence of 'heresy' or 'diabolic Judaic rites' in 1460 (SAB, 96, 2, fos. 171^{v}–3^{r}). However, a public meeting called by the bishop before Our Lady's church to ask for witnesses apparently raised no interest.

[97] For traces of this influence, see N. Geirnaert, 'Sporen van Windesheimse invloed in en rond het laatmiddeleeuwse Brugge', in W. Verbeke, M. Haverals, K. De Keyser et al. (eds.), *Serta devota in memoriam Guillelmi Lourdaux: Pars prior: Devotio windeshemenis* (Leuven, 1992), pp. 115–32.

[98] SAB, 216, 1432/3, fo. 83^{v}.

civic office and a worldly life, after his wife's death, to become a lay brother attached to the Carthusian house by St Cross church.[99]

The absence of houses of the Common Life in Bruges may be partly explained by the strong presence of the collegiate clergy and the friars. In other towns, friars could be hostile to the activities of the 'devout' on their patch; in any case, the desire among lay people to live a more religious life was to some extent accommodated within the mendicant framework of tertiary foundations which were in plentiful supply in Bruges.[100] Not all reforming initiatives were warmly received: initial attempts from outside Bruges, led by John of Capistrano (with ducal support), to found a new observant house within the city were resisted by the civic magistrates and the conventual friars. But admiration for the observant lifestyle may finally have caused the magistrates to relent: the observant friars were granted land by the Ezel gate to build a house in 1468.[101]

Lay interest in meditation and theological matters was fomented in several contexts. The first rhetoric chamber in Bruges, which claimed inspiration from the Holy Spirit, encouraged literary exploration of religious truths among its members. Many of de Roovere's poems focus on the grace and salvation offered through the Virgin Mary or Christ's Passion. They were also intended to edify a wider audience, and some of their themes suited the needs of public worship. *Lof van den heijlighen sacramente* focuses on the Eucharist's miraculous efficacy and its prefiguration in the Old Testament. It borrows from Ruusbroec's *Mirror of Salvation*, an influential text of the *Devotio*. It may well have been displayed for the benefit of parishioners on a pillar in St Saviour's church (see Figure 8.3), where the main civic procession of Corpus Christi was held.[102] Another poem translated the words of

[99] Geirnaert, 'De Adornes en de Jeruzalemkapel', pp. 18, 20. Admiration for a reclusive lifestyle, like that of the Carthusians, was also expressed in the support of anchorites and anchoresses, but their presence in Bruges is obscured by relative absence of evidence (such as wills, or bishops' registers) where they might have been mentioned. See, though, the payment of alms by the city to the 'clusenesse' of St Saviour's in 1399 (SAB, 216, 1388/9, fo. 110^{r}); and reference to certain women 'in reclusagiis' in St Saviour's cemetery in 1458: M. Vleeschouwers-Van Melkebeek, 'Het archief van de bisschoppen van Doornik: Een inventaris uit 1477,' *Handelingen van de Koninklijke Commissie voor Geschiedenis*, 199 (1983), 121–375 (at 330).

[100] For the hostility of certain friars to the devout of Common Life, but also the eventual approval of them from Jan Brugman, leading luminary of the observance in the region, see Van Engen, *Sisters and Brothers*, pp. 212–18, 234–5.

[101] See M. De Smet and P. Trio, 'The Involvement of the Late Medieval Urban Authorities in the Low Countries with Regard to the Introduction of the Franciscan Observance', *Revue d'histoire ecclésiastique*, 101 (2006), 37–88.

[102] De Roovere, *De gedichten*, pp. 136–44. Eduard de Dene in his *Testament Rhetoricael* in 1555 refers to de Roovere's prayers hung up 'openly' for all to read in the chancel of the church; a more general practice visible in the Seven Sacraments painting by Rogier van der Weyden: J.

Figure 8.3 Anthonis de Roovere's *Praise of the Holy Sacrament* (as poster in St Saviour's)

the *Salve Regina,* making more accessible to citizens an antiphon that was sung in the civic-sponsored concerts from 1480, and in a growing number of processions on feast days in Bruges, including that of the Holy Blood. The motets and other polyphonic music sung on ceremonial occasions were also intended to encourage contemplative meditation.[103]

Devotional images – altarpieces, books of hours and other illuminated manuscripts – found a ready market in fifteenth-century Bruges (see

Oosterman, 'Anthonis de Roovere: Het werk: Overlevering, toeschrijving en plaatsbepaling', *Jaarboek De Fonteine* (1995/6), 9–88 (at 47).

[103] Nosow, *Ritual Meanings*, pp. 135–66.

Chapter 9). These also illustrate the interconnected nature of 'public' and 'private' piety. Objects made to satisfy a demand for inner contemplation were also commodities of commercial value and targets of civic legislation. The importing of detached images from Utrecht had to be banned more than once.[104] Painters too were subject to the demands of the market. Petrus Christus moved to Bruges in 1444, perhaps enticed by the lowering of burgher (*poorter*) entry fees. Besides commissions from prominent citizens and guilds, Christus was employed by the city council to work on arrangements for the Holy Blood procession: in 1463, he was entrusted with renovation of the structures that represented the Tree of Jesse and the City of Jerusalem.[105] Dramatic performances on Holy Blood day were intended to induce spiritual responses in spectators. They may also have inspired devotional painting: the panel of *Christ Bearing the Cross*, c.1470 (attributed to a Utrecht painter), appears to make reference to the procession of the Holy Blood and its suite of plays centring on the Passion. It depicts the agonies suffered by Christ being led to the Cross, and thus perhaps gave pictorial expression to the mental journeys encouraged by guidebooks of spiritual pilgrimage.[106]

Contemplation of books and images was associated with a quietist kind of piety, but emphasis on inner renewal could take on a more vigorous form. Revivalist calls for reform inspired crowds to take radical action. Flagellant movements first sprang up in north Italian towns, and were associated with mendicant preaching and penitential spirituality. They appeared in northern France in the wake of the first outbreak of plague in 1349.[107] In August and September, a large crowd of flagellants, including hundreds from Bruges, descended upon Tournai, listened to apocalyptic sermons in the market square and enacted public penances, to the consternation of clerical and civic authorities.[108] Flagellant movements were short-lived, but urgent calls for renewal continued to be made, especially by preachers associated with the observance. Their impact is less apparent in the towns of Flanders than it is in those of northern Italy. Unlike Siena or Florence,

[104] See further below, Chapter 10.

[105] SAB, 216, 1462/3, fo. 53^r (according to GVS, *Inventaire*, vol. VI, p. 563).

[106] M. Trowbridge, 'Jerusalem-Transposed: A Fifteenth-Century Panel for the Bruges Market', *Journal of Historians of Netherlandish Art*, 1 (2009) (online publication). For links between the *Devotio* and Corpus Christi processions elsewhere, see B. A. M. Ramakers, *Spelen en figuren: Toneelkunst en processiecultuur in Oudenaarde tussen Middeleeuwen en Moderne Tijd* (Amsterdam, 1996), p. 22. For de Doppere's pilgrimage guide, see further below.

[107] E. Delaruelle, 'Les grandes processions de pénitents de 1349 et 1399', in E. Delaruelle (ed.), *La piété populaire au Moyen Âge* (Torino, 1975), pp. 280–313.

[108] Gilles Li Muisis, 'Chronica Aegidii li Muisis', in J.-J. De Smet (ed.), *Corpus Chronicorum Flandriae*, 4 vols. (Brussels, 1837–65), vol. II, pp. 93–448 (at 348–9, 354–9).

Bruges was apparently untroubled by a Bernardino or a Savonarola.[109] But in both regions the interest among urban authorities in the mobilizing and management of public preaching was similar. The Bruges magistrates were paying for a Good Friday sermon in the Burg by the later fourteenth century, and after 1408 for sermons during general processions.[110] In times of crisis, exceptional numbers of sermons were subsidized. Between February and May 1485, besides sermons delivered during general processions, the city accounts itemize a further 159 sermons, virtually one a day, preached by 'diverse brothers of the four orders' in various churches 'following orders of the magistrates'.[111] The content of these sermons is not known, but the kind of piety that the authorities wished to induce among citizens is evident from other sources. General processions themselves, when asking for God's grace, were intended to be conducted within a town placed in a heightened state of penitence – though one that encouraged conformity to appropriate liturgical forms rather than radical excesses of devotion.[112]

The moral reform of its citizens was a task that by the late fifteenth century the city government felt fully equipped to undertake. Municipal decrees (*hallegeboden*) surviving from the 1490s demonstrate an ingrained habit among the magistrates of correcting citizens, rooted in a perception of government as a sacred duty. The failure of citizens to fulfil their obligations on feast days was a failure, according to a decree in 1493, to obey both the 'orders of town councillors' as well as 'the commands of God'.[113] Upholding 'moral' standards of behaviour had long mattered to wider groups of citizens. In the fifteenth century, guild rules approved by the city magistrates encouraged exemplary social conduct among young and old, and between men and women. The youthful members of a junior crossbowmen guild (founded by 1397) risked punishment if caught wearing guild livery inside a brothel or bathhouse. The senior crossbowmen were forbidden to share a house with any woman besides their 'good and true wife', as were other guildsmen in the collection of craft guild rules put together in the 1440s.[114]

109 Though note the impact of Jan Brugman's words in Dutch towns or the preaching tour in northern France by Vincent Ferrer (d.1419). R. Rusconi, 'Public Purity and Discipline: States and Religious Renewal', in M. Rubin and W. Simons (eds.), *The Cambridge History of Christianity*, vol. IV: *Christianity in Western Europe* (Cambridge, 2009), pp. 458–71 (at 459–64).

110 SAB, 216, 1408/9, fo. 85^{v}, 86^{r}.

111 SAB, 216, 1484/5, fos. 157^{r}, 158^{r}, 158^{v}, 160^{v}, 162^{v}.

112 A. Brown, 'Devotion and Emotion: Creating the Devout Body in Late Medieval Bruges', *Digital Phililogy: A Journal of Medieval Cultures*, 1 (2012), 210–34.

113 SAB, 120, I, fo. 122^{v}–3^{r}.

114 SAB, 96, 11, fo. 241^{v}; RAB, Ambachten, 1.

The importance of ordered households – obedience to elders or the good wife devoutly going to church, for instance – is stressed in some of de Roovere's poems.[115]

Municipal concern with the pious behaviour of citizens and clergy may have become more acute in the later fifteenth century. De Roovere's own poems could be critical of earthly values, while his contribution to the Chronicle of Flanders assumes a darker tone when describing the city's woes in the late 1470s. The political divisions and economic crises of the late 1470s and 1480s (see Chapter 7) prompted a heightened anxiety with perhaps increasing delinquent behaviour. Attitudes to those who deviated from social norms also became harsher. The poor may have been treated with less benevolence.[116] There is evidence for greater intolerance of prostitution, and a new determination to prosecute the crime of sodomy.[117] Calls for general processions and sermons reached a peak; and anxieties may also explain the beginning of municipal support for *salve* concerts in the 1480s. And if citizens were being urged to listen more often to sacred words, so they were punished for uttering profane ones: references to the prosecution of blasphemy first appear during the same decade.[118] Some of the city's festive events also fell under a cloud of disfavour. The last annual event of the White Bear jousters was subsidized in 1487, and although its demise was the result partly of political crisis, its activities were already being probed for immorality. At Lille, friars and theologians were consulted in 1484 as to the value of the jousting in the city, which (it was noted) involved jousters from Bruges: there were strong doubts whether these activities 'could not be pursued without sin'.[119] Other burlesque activities were looked upon by city authorities with an icier eye. On 26 December 1483, the burgomaster Willem Moreel appeared before the dean and chapter of St Donatian's to demand the abolition of the Feast of the Ass-Bishop that took place annually between 7 and 13 January.[120] This was a rumbustious occasion, its processions of choristers and profane songs having already caused disquiet

115 De Roovere, *De gedichten*, pp. 248–51, 252–4.

116 For harsher treatment of poor beggars within St Donatian's in the 1480s, see BAB, A55, fos. 90v, 165r–v, 178r–v; A56, fo. 76r; G6, 1489/90, fo. 18r.

117 Dupont, *Maagdenverleidsters*, pp. 70–9; M. Boone, 'State Power and Illicit Sexuality: The Persecution of Sodomy in Late Medieval Bruges', *JMH*, 22 (1996), 135–53.

118 SAB, 157, 1490–2, fos. 36r, 39v, 96r–7r. Cases of blasphemy (in chronicles) are first recorded in 1484, see C. Carton (ed.), *Het boeck van al 't gene datter gheschiedt is binnen Brugghe sichtent jaer 1477, 14 februarii, tot 1491* (Ghent, 1859), pp. 67–8.

119 ADN, B 7662 (9); B 1616.

120 BAB, A56, fos. 21v–2r. H. Callewier, 'De omgekeerde wereld van de Brugse ezelspaus: Een omstreden aspect van de laat-middeleeuwse kerkelijke feestcultuur', *Jaarboek voor Middeleeuwse Geschiedenis*, 12 (2009), 175–95.

among the canons.[121] But Moreel's complaint that it created 'great scandal', and that it provoked the people into 'petulant' behaviour, began a period of more consistent hostility to the event that was to end with its disappearance in the early sixteenth century.

Continued complaints about 'scandalous' behaviour, however, may only indicate its persistence. Moreel's objections did not deter a young clerk, two weeks later, from defiantly dressing up as the 'priest of asses' and appearing unsuitably clad in the choir. City authorities were keenly aware that they were attempting to sow the seeds of respectable behaviour on potentially stony ground: in April 1493 they lamented that 'the common people spend feast days and holy mass days badly and irreverently', while craftsmen indulged in commerce and other 'bad habits'.[122] The surviving court records, civil and ecclesiastical, reveal irreverence and sacrilege. St Donatian's clergy suffered thefts from the collection box of St Machut and even from the feretory of its principal patron saint.[123] The Holy Sacrament was never entirely safe from thieves; not all citizens repaired devoutly to church or stayed indoors on Corpus Christi day.[124] Had more such records survived, an impression of greater delinquency and disobedience within the city might have been left to us, to counterbalance the weight of sources that tilt so heavily towards an impression of conformist piety.

Religion in Urban Society

The nature and diversity of religious practices in Bruges were not peculiar to the city: they need to be explained within wider contexts, religious, social and political. Some practices reflect the pastoral efforts of the church and were driven by the internal dynamics of church doctrine: the proliferation of masses, feast day endowments or processions from the late thirteenth century flowed from the importance assigned by the church to the penitential process of salvation, and the generation of suffrages to reduce punishment in purgatory, pronounced official doctrine in 1274. Clerical emphasis

121 See the concerns of the canons about possible disturbances caused by the event in 1436 and 1452: BAB, A50, fo. 230^{r}; A51, fo. 290^{v}.

122 SAB, 120, I, fos. 122^{v}–3^{r}.

123 RAB, Charters with blue numbers, 7721. A thief who stole a gold image and other things from the feretory of St Donatian in 1374: BAB, A48, fo. 41^{r}; and for another theft from the feretory in 1489: BAB, A56, fo. 181^{r}; also a crime of poverty in 1474 (AGR, Chambers of Accounts, 13780, fos. 35^{v}–6^{r}). For other sacrilegious thefts: SAB, 192, fos. 26^{r}, 27^{v}–8^{r}, 38^{r}, 45^{r}–6^{r}, 49^{v}–50^{v}.

124 For example: SAB, 216, 1401/2, fo. 94^{r}. For a case of 'ruudhede' committed near the Bouverie gate on Corpus Christi day 1510: SAB, 192, fo. 55^{v}.

on recourse to the sacraments, to good works, and to limited forms of spiritual self-help, undoubtedly stimulated lay initiatives in religious matters.

The proliferation of good works has been identified as a highly characteristic feature of late medieval religion, although description of it has long been clothed in pejorative rhetoric. Venerable traditions of Protestant historiography condemned the medieval Catholic Church for peddling a mechanical kind of piety that failed to meet the spiritual needs of the people.[125] The same confessional tradition touched Johan Huizinga's *Autumn of the Middle Ages*, written in 1919. Huizinga also introduced a view of late medieval religion that has never entirely lost its appeal. For him, the defining features of religious practices sprang from an 'autumnal' spirit that ran to excess in all areas of life.[126] Few historians since have agreed with such a reductionist explanation, but it has been hard to resist Huizinga's image of late medieval piety as shrouded in melancholia or prone to obsessive multiplication of liturgical worship. Toussaert could not shake off an oppressive sense of gloom from his overview of Flemish piety in the period, which he also cast over processions in Bruges.[127] Devotion in the Low Countries has been said to show a tendency to 'ritualise and externalise' Christian belief.[128] In specific instances, these comments are hard to deny, and were even shared by some late medieval churchmen when expressing concern with contemporary practices; but as generalizations they appear too much informed by an unspoken assumption that ritualized actions are empty of inner piety.[129] On the other hand, certain currents of spirituality are traditionally perceived as counteracting these generalizations: to Huizinga, the brothers and sisters of the Common Life offered a new devotional path, and a way out of oppressive formalism.[130] While the *Devotio* has since been placed within longer traditions of Catholic spirituality, it has often been made to sit uncomfortably alongside the outward forms of religion

[125] For commentary on this tradition in relation to the clergy and 'anticlericalism', see Callewier, *De papen van Brugge*, pp. 15–17.

[126] J. Huizinga, *The Autumn of the Middle Ages*, trans. R. J. Payton and U. Mammitzsch (Chicago, IL, 1996).

[127] J. Toussaert, *Le sentiment religieux en Flandre à la fin du Moyen Âge* (Paris, 1963), esp. pp. 129–59, 259–66, 340–1. See also the 'obsessive' malaise falling over 'flamboyant' processions in northern France: J. Chiffoleau, 'Les processions parisiennes de 1412: Analyse d'un rituel flamboyant', *Revue historique*, 114 (1990), 37–76 (at 40, 46, 71, 74–5).

[128] Ramakers, *Spelen en figuren*, p. 18 but see also p. 22; J. van Herwaarden, *Between St James and Erasmus: Studies in Late-Medieval Religious Life: Devotion and Pilgrimage in the Netherlands* (Leiden, 2003), p. 120.

[129] For ritual viewed as 'thoughtless action', see C. Bell, *Ritual Theory, Ritual Practice* (Oxford, 1992), p. 19.

[130] Huizinga, *Autumn*, pp. 203, 222–3, 265–7.

practised by the majority.[131] Yet the 'privatization' of devotion and the elaboration of 'public' ritual seem to have developed simultaneously during the later Middle Ages, and perhaps even in tandem: there were many circumstances in Bruges, as we have seen, when 'inner' spirituality complemented 'outer' performance of religious practices.

Huizinga tended to regard the 'extremes' of late medieval piety as the result of a declining spirit. Others since have viewed the apparent dysfunctions in late medieval religious culture as products of a dysfunctional society. The traumatic effects of plagues seem quite sufficient to explain descent into melancholy or recourse to 'frantic' accumulation of masses. Studies for other towns have pointed to an increasing need among testators to shore up suffrage for their souls in the wake of plague, particularly in the 1360s following its second major visitation.[132] The relative dearth of wills in Bruges prevents a comparative study, but the evidence in other sources for obit and feast day foundations makes for more equivocal conclusions. There was an acceleration of more precise foundations in the 1360s: a sharpened fear of mortality and oblivion may well be an explanation. But a trend towards more specific conditions of endowment began in the late thirteenth century, which indicates longer-term developments; and the high point in foundation occurred in the middle decades of the fifteenth century – for which other explanations besides a plague-induced need for commemoration are required.

The study of post-obit commemoration, however, does help to revise description of late medieval piety as obsessively morbid. It focuses attention on the preferences of testators and the strategic calculations that benefactors made. As shown, when endowing feast days or selecting patron saints, Bruges citizens chose some saints over others, particularly the Virgin Mary and early church fathers and martyrs; a smaller proportion favoured cults that were more regional (see Tables 8.1 and 8.2). Almost none of the saints favoured by guilds or feast day benefactors, incidentally, were those particularly associated with powers to cure plague.[133] The choices made by

[131] Van Engen, *Sisters and Brothers*, pp. 2–10.

[132] S. K. Cohn, *The Cult of Remembrance and the Black Death: Six Renaissance Cities in Central Italy* (London, 1992). For more indirect effects of plague on post-obit 'flamboyance': J. Chiffoleau, *La comptabilité de l'au-delà: Les hommes, la mort et la religion dans la region d'Avignon à la fin du Moyen Âge (vers 1320 – vers 1480)* (Rome, 1980), p. 274. See also S. K. Cohn, 'The Place of the Dead in Flanders and Tuscany', in B. Gordon and P. Marshall (eds.), *The Place of the Dead: Death and Remembrance in Late Medieval and Early Modern Europe* (Cambridge, 2000), pp. 17–43.

[133] St Roche and St Sebastian were particularly favoured as protectors against plague. For their apparent popularity elsewhere, see D. Herlihy, *The Black Death and the Transformation of the West*, ed. S. K. Cohn Jr (Cambridge, MA, 1997), p. 80.

benefactors and guilds may also point to what was distinctive about devotional sensibilities in Bruges. Compared with citizens of north Italian towns, those of Bruges (and perhaps of many other towns in northern Europe) seem more conservative in their religious choices. In Perugia a greater tendency for its citizens to adopt newer cults has been identified; and most of the new saints came from the ranks of the mendicant orders.[134] In contrast, of the new cults augmented in Bruges – fewer than 13 per cent of the total number – most were new universal feasts associated with Christ or the Virgin Mary, and only 3 per cent of them were mendicant, these being the founders of the main orders – St Francis, St Dominic and St Clare – rather than later celebrities such as Bernardino of Siena.[135] One reason for this apparent difference between Italian and northern European towns lies in the relative influence within them of the mendicant orders. Bruges was exceptional among towns of Flanders and Brabant in the number of friars resident within its walls, but their activities were perhaps more carefully circumscribed than those of their counterparts in Italy by the powerful presence of older collegiate churches. Bruges did not lack for new observant houses, but their appearance in the city was not immediately welcomed by the civic government; nor was it aligned as closely in Bruges as it could be elsewhere with a drive towards the spiritual reform of citizens.[136] It is harder to find examples in Bruges and other towns in the region of the revivalist preaching of such as Bernardino of Siena. The kind of enthusiastic spirituality inspired by mendicants in Italy was generally more muted north of the Alps.

The difference between these two regions of Europe, however, is more apparent than real. The number of new canonized saints from Italy had more to do with mendicant access there to the papal curia than differences in spirituality.[137] In terms of the number of different saints chosen as patrons

[134] G. Dickson, 'The 115 Cults of Saints in Later Medieval and Renaissance Perugia: A Demographic Overview of a Civic Pantheon', in G. Dickson (ed.), *Religious Enthusiasm in the Medieval West* (Aldershot, 2000), pp. 6–25.

[135] A partial exception is the cult of the Augustinian friar St Nicholas of Tolentino, canonized in 1446, devotion to whom was cultivated at the Augustinian church in Bruges: see A. Keelhoff, *Histoire de l'ancient couvent des ermites de Saint Augustin à Bruges* (Bruges, 1869), p. 112.

[136] For such a case in Bologna, see N. Terpstra, *Lay Confraternities and Civic Religion in Renaissance Bologna* (Cambridge, 1995), pp. 4–5, 17–37, 45–67. However, for the importance of mendicant influence on Flemish towns, see W. Simons, '"Dieu, li premierz, plus anchiiens et souverains bourgois de tous": Sur la place de la religion dans les villes flamandes (XIIIe–XVe siècle)', in Crouzet-Pavan and Lecuppre-Desjardin (eds.) *Villes de Flandre et d'Italie*, pp. 77–103.

[137] A. Vauchez, *Sainthood in the Later Middle Ages*, trans. J. Birrell (Cambridge, 1997), pp. 74–5, 207–12, 336–54.

(Tables 8.1 and 8.2), citizens of Bruges ranged as widely as those of Perugia, just as the proliferation of altar space in Bruges churches was as extensive as that in Florence.[138] Many different strains of devotion were available in Bruges, whether flagellant, observant, Carthusian or Common Life, even if their influence is more difficult to detect in the sources. Bruges inhabitants were also susceptible to new cults, such as the wonder-working image of Our Lady of the Snow. Conversely, the heightened sensitivity in Perugia to a newly elevated mendicant saint like Bernardino, may reflect an intense local loyalty among citizens there to a friar who had been associated with their city. The 'localization' of cults of saints, whether universal or regional in origin, is another trend often identified in late medieval piety;[139] and in Bruges too, devotion even to the most universal saints perhaps reflects their embedding within the local landscape. The city's churches (especially St Donatian's) boasted a large number of relics of these saints.[140] Most of the feast days associated with the relics in Bruges were elevated during the later Middle Ages. Of the 709 foundations that enhanced feast days in the six collegiate or parish churches (Figure 8.1), over 73 per cent of them were on days for saints or cults for which physical remains existed in the city.

The preference in Bruges for universal saints, whether new or old, may have had less to do with any devotional conservatism than it had with the city's position as a centre of international banking and trade, and its potential openness to trends from all over Christendom. The commercial dynamism of Bruges undoubtedly had a significant bearing on the character of religious life in the city. It partly explains why the city initially came to support so many friaries, compared with neighbouring towns. A growing artisanal population, and consequent pastoral problems, attracted the friars to Ghent as well as Bruges; but Ghent's more industrial nature was less well equipped to sustain the infrastructure and endowments needed to support the Franciscan vow of poverty and the mendicant vocation of preaching or teaching. The demand for post-obit suffrage among the commercial elite of Bruges inexorably drew the conventual friars into the social networks of the city.

[138] Note the contrast that Goldthwaite makes between a greater 'expansion of liturgical space' in Italian towns compared with those in northern Europe, based on comparison between Florence and the cities of Lyon, Cologne and Frankfurt: see R. A. Goldthwaite, *Wealth and the Demand for Art in Italy, 1300–1600* (Baltimore, MD, 1993), pp. 131–4.

[139] A. Vauchez, 'Saints and Pilgrimages: New and Old', in Rubin and Simons (eds.), *Cambridge History of Christianity*, vol. IV, pp. 324–39.

[140] For lists of relics belonging to St Donatian's c.1200 and in 1463, see BAB, A130, fo. 14^{r-v}; A52, fo. 246^{v}. Combined, these lists produce a total of 92 saints, although this excludes the many relics associated with Christ or the Virgin Mary that the church also possessed.

There were also links between the massive investment in feast days and the availability in Bruges of disposable wealth. The trends in investment correlate best with the ebb and flow of economic prosperity: dips in foundations during periods of warfare and disruption (the late 1370s and 1380s, the late 1430s, the 1490s); the high points occurring in the middle decades of the fifteenth century, when the Low Countries as a whole seemed a 'promised land'.[141] Greater investment in such foundations can be found elsewhere in the region, such as in Brussels, though even the prosperity of this city did not compete with that of Bruges.[142] The specialization of the Bruges economy in the production of luxury goods and services by the end of the fourteenth century (see Chapter 6) gave those involved the means to make larger investments. A good proportion of lay people who set up foundations with poor tables can be identified as craftsmen who had profited from the demands of 'fashion' (such as furriers, tailors, hosiers and second-hand clothes dealers).[143] Moreover, the variety of choices made by citizens of Bruges in matters of religious practice would seem to match their commercial enterprise. The complicated arrangements made in the fifteenth century by benefactors – particularly the hostellers and brokers – to ensure continuation of post-obit services mirror the sophistication of their financial dealings and the dense networks of credit within which they operated (see Chapter 6). The multiplication of masses was less the result of melancholy than of confidence in an ability to plan strategically for the afterlife.

Availability of capital does not explain the forms of its disposal; and disposal of it was determined by needs that were otherworldly. But the ways chosen to commemorate the dead reflected social phenomena and had social consequences.[144] Endowment of post-obit services, especially when they resulted in impressive tombs, altars or chapels, was an investment in 'symbolic' capital that contributed to social identity.[145] In the thirteenth century some of the families who dominated the property market and aldermanic

[141] The high level of investments in the 1480s, a decade of serious crisis, may be explained by the high mortality rate of benefactors who had built up their wealth in previous years. Compare with similar trends in Ghent: Trio, *Volksreligie*, pp. 200–3.

[142] For investment in offices, obits and masses in Brussels, though it seems not quite at the same level as in Bruges, see B. Haggh, 'Music, Liturgy, and Ceremony in Brussels, 1350–1500', unpublished PhD thesis, University of Illinois (Urbana-Champaign, 1988), pp. 383–408.

[143] Galvin, 'Poor Tables', pp. 183–7.

[144] O. G. Oexle, *Memoria als Kultur* (Göttingen, 1995), p. 12; M. Borgolte, 'Die Stiftungen des Mittelalters in rechts- und sozialhistorischer Sicht', *Zeitschrift de Savigny-Stiftung für Rechtsgeschichte: Kanonische Abteilung*, 74 (1988), 71–94.

[145] See the conceptual apparatus of P. Bourdieu, *Distinction: A Social Critique of the Judgement of Taste*, trans. R. Nice (Cambridge, MA, 1984).

office attended to the security of their status and souls by becoming prominent benefactors of divine service: Hendrik Ram, as the principal founder of the first Franciscan church in Bruges, positioned himself alongside local lords and members of the comital dynasty who endowed other mendicant houses (see Chapter 2). The aspiration to the noble life among the commercial elite remained a powerful one throughout the later Middle Ages (see Chapter 7), and was reflected in foundations that emulated those of the higher nobility. Interest in the newer observant orders attracted the attention of the ducal household in the mid fifteenth century, and those close to it, such as the Gruuthuse family.

Other trends in post-obit foundation also bear the imprint of social change. The proliferation and variety in forms of divine service reflect the growing social complexity of urban society, which became both more strongly polarized and more finely gradated. The dominance of aldermanic families was challenged from the late thirteenth century by other social groups, particularly those represented by craft guilds; a commercial elite continued to dominate political office in the fourteenth and fifteenth centuries, but as we have seen in Chapter 7, was under greater pressure to negotiate power with producing classes and shopkeepers; yet within all these groups hierarchies also developed. The pressure to assert status among individuals and families was particularly intense, and was brought to bear even within the higher echelons of Bruges society. The distinctive Adornes chapel modelled on the Holy Sepulchre, or the unusual Gruuthuse family oratory that literally elevated its noble occupants above other worshippers in Our Lady's church, were partly the product of social competition from below. Yet even these families did not cultivate isolation from lesser social groups: the glovers' craft established an altar in the Adornes chapel, while Lodewijk van Gruuthuse employed the services of three craft guilds to oversee his anniversary.

The pressures to express social status affected clergy and laity. In the case of some clerics, splendid foundations in later life may have compensated for lowly origins or illegitimate births.[146] Some of the most distinctive investments were made by 'new' men of modest backgrounds whose rise to wealth and prominence had been swift.[147] Boudin de Vos' promotion to mint master of the count found social confirmation in the large and (at that time) distinctive foundation he made in St Donatian's in the

[146] Callewier, *De papen van Brugge*, pp. 192–4.

[147] J. Dumolyn and K. Moermans, 'Distinctie en memorie: Symbolische investeringen in de eeuwigheid door laatmiddeleeuwse hoge ambtenaren in het graafschap Vlaanderen', *TG*, 116 (2003), 332–49.

1360s. In the fifteenth century, choices of commemorative service were even more varied. The elaborate tomb of Pauwels van Overtvelt placed in Our Lady's church, the spectacular anniversary of Canon Jan Meurin in St Donatian's, or the lavish funeral arrangements for Pieter Lanchals (and his endowment of a fashionably new Marian feast day) belong to men whose social elevation followed from service to the prince. Those who owed their status more to commerce made equally impressive bids for long-term suffrage. Extensive arrangements were made in St Donatian's after 1477 by the burgomaster Martin Lem, an associate of Willem Moreel, and a 'magnificus vir' in the canons' estimation.[148] His foundation in the choir ambulatory of a chantry chapel or 'oratory' dedicated to Our Lady of Pity, with seating and burial places there for his wife and family, continued a tradition of chantry foundation in the church, begun by the clergy and officers of the count's household in the twelfth century; but it was built on the mercantile wealth he had accumulated, notably by the importing of sugar from Madeira.[149] There must have been some pressure on families like the Lems to establish these foundations. The desire to acquire symbolic capital could overstretch capital of a more prosaic kind. Martin Lem's sudden death in Leuven in 1485 (like that of his rival Pieter Lanchals three years later) landed his successors in difficulties. His widow struggled to bring his body back for burial in Bruges, and his executors were unable to build his chapel quickly or to fund his chantry endowment fully. In 1499 the canons bluntly informed Martin's son that there was little money left for the foundation, and the number of masses sung for his soul would be cut back.

The collective efforts among those of similar status, at every level of society, might also be explained as efforts to mark out distinct social identities within a devotional framework. Membership of some devotional fraternities was exclusive. Only those of the highest status, linked with service on the city council, were admitted to the fraternities of the Holy Blood and the Holy Trinity. The Rozebeke guild was more numerous but its members still comprised city 'notables'. The appearance in the late fourteenth century of such elite groupings suggests a particular social need then for markers of exclusivity. The most prestigious craft guilds also demonstrated a need for public distinction in their building of almshouses, bell-towers and chapels – which marked them out from lesser guilds who acquired only altar or chapel space

[148] For the following, see BAB, A55, fos. 104^{v}, 135^{r}, 186^{r}, 196^{v}, 203^{v}; A56, fos. 82^{v}, 97^{v}, 100^{v}, 112^{v}, 119^{v}, 139^{r}; A57, fos. 9^{r}, 70^{r}, 71^{v}, 85^{v}, 102^{r}, 117^{r}.

[149] On Martin Lem's career, see Haemers, *For the Common Good*, pp. 82–9.

within churches. The apprentices of guilds in the fifteenth century could also found altars separate from the crafts to which they belonged, perhaps giving expression to a sense of collective identity that a protectionist guild structure did not directly allow them.[150]

At a parish level, the pressures of hierarchy and status competed with a sense of community. Parishioners arranged themselves in life and death in ways that befitted their status. Quite when fixed seating became regular in Bruges churches is not known, but certainly by the end of the fourteenth century, families were able to purchase seating places.[151] These purchases sometimes caused disputes that required solutions of considerable ingenuity to avoid further conflict between families.[152] Clearly some positions within the church were more prestigious than others. In St Donatian's, a place beside a pillar in the nave, before an image of Our Lady, was where 'the notables of the city' were 'accustomed to gather'.[153] Space for burial places within the church could also be bought, and it appears that this was becoming more common in the fifteenth century. Some places, especially the choir, were more prestigious than others, and churchwardens fixed prices accordingly.[154] The collective endeavour to extend St James' church, for instance, opened up new opportunities for the upwardly mobile. Many more burials within the church were permitted from the 1450s than had been the case in the previous three decades, and some individuals (Tommaso Portinari the Florentine banker, Willem Moreel the burgomaster, and Jean de Gros the treasurer of the Order of the Golden Fleece) and guilds (the barber surgeons, coopers and furriers) bought chapels for burial and chantry masses around the choir ambulatory.[155] The prestigious craft of butchers had their own chapel in the church before 1447, but individual craft members (like

150 Brown, *Civic Ceremony*, pp. 139–40, 151–8.

151 In 1409, Victor Cekaerd could claim that a seat by a pillar in the northeast side of the church of St Giles had been purchased by his grandfather (SAB, 96, 11, fo. 23r).

152 In a case involving two parishioners of St Saviour's in 1408, the aldermen ordered an inquest, and required the disputed seat to be dismantled, and two new seats to be built outside the choir, each at the same place relative to each other within the two lateral side aisles. Ownership between the two parties would be settled by lot (SAB, 96, 11, fo. 22r).

153 According to a case before the court of the *proosdij* in 1466 (RAB, Proosdij, 1508, fo. 204r).

154 A sense of hierarchy in burial places in St Donatian's is suggested by the sliding scale of payment made to the 'grave maker'. In 1487, the canons agreed to pay him 6 pounds. par. for a grave in the choir, but less for other specified areas: the outer choir and ambulatory (4 pounds), the parish altar (3), the nave (2), cloister (20 s) and church house (12 s) (BAB, A55, fo. 197r–v).

155 From the 'begraving boek' of St James' church 1426–80 (RAB, Sint-Jacob, 197), the number of burial places purchased within the nave or choir was as follows: in the 1420s there were five; 1430s five; 1440s six, 1450s twelve, 1460s (most after 1464) ten, 1470s thirty-eight.

Frans Bassevelde in the 1470s) secured burial places by or within the choir. The building of the new choir prompted some to relocate their planned place of ultimate rest. The original choice in 1453 of Donaas de Moor (a furrier who rose to great wealth and prominence on the city council), had been a spot in the Lady chapel, but in 1475 after the rebuilding he was upgraded to a site before the sacristy in the 'high' choir.[156]

Urban society in Bruges was made distinctive by the presence of two other groups: foreign merchants and (particularly in the mid fifteenth century) the princely household. These groups in different ways contributed both to financial capital and to social competition, although their effect on the religious character of the city is hard to assess. The foreign merchants who established altars within Bruges churches brought with them devotion to their native saints: the English merchants had an altar dedicated to St Thomas Becket, the Scottish to St Ninian, the merchants of Lucca to the Volto Santo.[157] Others (like the Catalans), however, chose universal saints such as the Virgin Mary. Arguably, the strong tendency in Bruges to favour universal saints or cults as heavenly patrons, was strengthened by the international connections promoted by the city's foreign merchants. The cult of Our Lady of the Snow originated in Rome. Jan Moscron had his altar adorned by an image of the *Pietà* sculpted by Michelangelo. On the other hand, it is hard to detect much direct influence of foreign merchants on local practices. The city minstrels adopted the cult of the Volto Santo, but there is little sign that the cults of St Thomas Becket or St Ninian inspired wider followings among native townspeople.[158]

Influence of native practices on foreign merchants is easier to discern. Those resident in the city were drawn in a limited way into its religious mores. Most 'nations' founded their altars in friaries rather than the parish churches of Bruges, but foreign merchants who bought rights of burghership could become as involved as their Flemish peers in parish life,[159] and as attached as they to localized saints. The rebuilding of St James' church in

[156] RAB, Sint-Jacob, 197, fo. 11^{r}. For comment on the 'moderate' nature of social differentiation in grave positioning, see K. Goudriaan, 'Ownership of Graves in Medieval Parish Churches in Holland', in W. Blockmans and A. Janse (eds.), *Showing Status: Representations of Social Positions in the Late Middle Ages* (Turnhout, 1999), pp. 197–226.

[157] Marechal, *Europese aanwezigheid*. See the agreements between the Carmelites and the English (in 1344) and the Scots (in 1366): Archives of the Discalced Carmelites of Brugge, Liber Oblongus, fos. 18^{r}–22^{r}, 48^{v}–51^{r}. The Castilian merchants paid for five windows to be put into the new Observant friary in 1474, one of them representing their 'native' St James (SAB, 304, charter 27).

[158] The corn measurers and corn carriers did have an altar dedicated to St Ninian in St Giles' church by 1474 (RAB, Sint-Gillis, 27, fo. 121^{v}).

[159] For members of the Hanse who contributed to the parish poor tables, see R. Rössner, *Hansekaufleute in Brügge*, vol. V: *Hansische Memoria in Flandern* (Frankfurt am Main, 2001).

the mid fifteenth century profited from the wealth of 'diverse nations', some Spaniards and Italians (such as Giovanni Arnolfini, whose wife paid for a seat before the tower door) making substantial contributions; others such as Tommaso Portinari founded their own chapels.[160] Portinari was later to pay for the canopy at St James' to be carried over the sacrament on Corpus Christi day, and embroidered with the arms of Florence and the Medici family.[161] Yet besides promoting universal cults, he also helped foster more local ones. When preparations began in Our Lady's church in 1469 to fund the translation of St Boniface's relics to a new shrine, he was also among the 'diverse nations' who contributed.[162]

As a financier, Portinari was one of many residents in Bruges who hoped to profit from the presence of the ducal household in the city, and from the growing needs of princely government. The increasing importance in the fifteenth century of service to the state as an avenue of social advancement has been already noted (see Chapter 7). Moreover, the ducal court has been regarded as a trend-setter, establishing modes of cultural behaviour on which aspirants to social status modelled themselves. From the perspective of cultural developments in Italy, however, these courtly modes have not always been considered creative.[163] Whereas in northern Italy autonomous 'patriciates' developed new consumption habits, their counterparts in northern European towns were apparently still dominated by the 'feudal ethos' of princely courts.[164] In fifteenth-century Bruges, the presence of the Burgundian court loomed ever larger, with the refurbishment of the Prinsenhof from the 1390s, the lengthening stays there from 1440 of the duke and his family members, and the residence of an increasing number of household personnel. Arguably, this presence made an impact upon city life, religious and social. Burgundian grip on ecclesiastical appointments tightened, while the presence of the princely household acted as a magnet on clerics, who found employment within as councillors, secretaries, singers or almoners. The arrival of the Observant friars in Bruges, and the foundation of the Poor Clares in 1477, were courtly as well as clerical initiatives.[165] Perhaps the stone-clad Prinsenhof, complete with its chapel and

160 RAB, Sint-Jacob, 98 (Rekeningen 1464–78), fos. 38^{r}, 67^{r}, 81^{v}, 98^{v}, 99^{v}, 106^{r}, 134^{r}, 136^{r}.

161 SAB, 216, 1486/7, fos. 173^{v}–4^{r}.

162 RAB, Onze-Lieve-Vrouw, 1271 (1464–71), fo. 261^{r}.

163 For a summary, see M. Belozerskaya, *Rethinking the Renaissance: Burgundian Arts Across Europe* (Cambridge, 2002), pp. 4, 32–46.

164 Goldthwaite, *Wealth*, pp. 159–92.

165 The house of Poor Clares was consecrated in the presence of Maximilian, Margaret of York and Mary of Burgundy: see OBB, Ms. 437, fo. 397^{v}.

bell-tower by the 1440s, was the model for the houses built by court functionaries, the oratories of urbanized nobles, and the chapels of high-status guilds (see Chapter 5). On the other hand, the impact of courtly households on the religious landscape of the city should not be exaggerated. The particular liturgical arrangements and cults favoured by the Burgundian dukes and their chapel did not noticeably change patterns in the city. The involvement of the ducal family, household or court functionaries in the devotional life of the city was more conservative than trend-setting. They spread their largesse widely but often in well-established forms, to some extent following comital tradition of benefaction, but also adopting the devotional habits of contemporary citizens. In the early years of his rule, Duke Charles the Bold made multiple offerings to see the relics belonging to churches and guilds (such as Our Lady of the Dry Tree), contributed to the rebuilding of St James' church, and joined the guild of Our Lady of the Snow. Ducal endowments exceeded those of citizens but for the most part were adapted to existing devotional structures. Duke Philip's endowment in Our Lady's church for mass and bell-ringing on the morrow of the Assumption in 1451 was impressive, but joined one of many services that augmented feast days in this church by this time.[166]

Social aspirations shaped the expression of religious practice in Bruges, but in complex ways. The expansive foundations of benefactors associated with the court or civic elites – observant houses, feast day endowments, chantries, large funerals and obits and exclusive burial sites – served as markers of exalted identity, and this in turn may have driven their social inferiors to emulate their foundations. The forces of social competition in Bruges help to explain the pace of liturgical elaboration and change. Yet social pressures worked in other directions: in such an affluent society, the services established by lesser citizens propelled their social superiors to take grander steps to distance themselves from them. Moreover, the extent to which other Bruges citizens, in their religious practices, were simply emulating a courtly or noble 'culture' can be exaggerated. A 'feudal' ethos is hard to disentangle from a 'civic' one. The foundations that even the dukes made in Bruges differed more in scale than in kind from those of other citizens, while efforts by the urban nobility or court functionaries to distance themselves from lesser citizens did not mean isolation from them: their foundations invariably used the services of city guildsmen, as other citizens had begun to do, in order to secure their endowments and increase intercession for their souls.

[166] For details, see Brown, *Civic Ceremony*, pp. 247–52.

Religion and Political Power

The presence of the ducal court in the city had both social and political aspects. The growth of state power, and the extension of princely over civic government, is a much developed theme of historiography in the Low Countries.[167] Inevitably this had implications for religious practices: it is possible to show princely government encroaching on ecclesiastical affairs, arrogating divine authority, and appropriating sacred ceremony – even creating for itself a 'liturgy of state'.[168] The performance of the great set-pieces of court ritual in towns, such as the processions to church of the knights of the Golden Fleece (in Bruges in 1432, 1468 and 1478), duly recorded in urban chronicles, imposed courtly ceremony on urban landscape and memory. The presence of princely authority also appears to set Bruges (and other towns in northern Europe) most clearly apart from their counterparts in northern Italy, in both a political and religious context. The strength of civic autonomy in Lombard and Tuscan towns is often viewed as having a direct bearing on the character of their religious practices. Perhaps Italian citizens, freer than their north European counterparts from 'feudal' forms of lordship, were more likely to develop a sense of their cities as sacred bodies, and a 'civic' kind of religion in which public welfare was celebrated, and where municipal authorities exercised control over multiple forms of religious life, cultic, devotional or institutional.[169] However, the cultivation of cults and saints, the use of processions, the erection of chapels associated with town councils, and the extension of municipal government over other city churches and hospitals are all detectable in the larger cities of northern Europe.[170] So too is another phenomenon that has more recently been linked to 'civic religion': a 'cult of memory' identifiable in post-obit foundations with specific connections to notions of public welfare and expressions of civic authority.[171]

167 See notably, Boone, *Gent en de Bourgondische hertogen*.

168 E. Lecuppre-Desjardin, *La ville des cérémonies: Essai sur la communication politique dans les anciens Pays-Bas bourguignons* (Turnhout, 2004), pp. 278, 324, 326.

169 See generally A. Vauchez, 'Introduction', in A. Vauchez (ed.), *La religion civique à l'époque médiévale et moderne (Chrétieneté et Islam)* (Rome, 1995), pp. 1–2; and P. Boucheron, D. Menjot and M. Boone, 'La ville médiévale', in Boucheron and Menjot, *Histoire de l'Europe urbaine*, pp. 374–81.

170 See E. Bünz, 'Klerus und Bürger: Die Bedeutung der Kirche für die Identität deutscher Städte im Spätmittelalter', in G. Chittolini and P. Johanek (eds.), *Aspetti e componenti dell'identità urbana in Italia e in Germania (secoli XIV–XVI)* (Bologna and Berlin, 2003), pp. 351–89; and for consideration of 'civic religion' (in all but name) in German towns, see G. Signori, 'Religion civique – patriotisme urbain. Concepts au banc d'essai', *Histoire Urbain*, 27 (2010), 9–14.

171 M. Staub, *Les paroisses et la cité de Nuremburg du XIIIe siècle à la Reforme* (Paris, 2003), pp. 251–79; S. Rüther, 'Entre intégration et distinction: La logique sociale des fondations pieuses

Developments in religious practices in Bruges can be similarly placed in these contexts. Links were made between individual foundations and city government. On the one hand, the city council played an increasing role in the post-obit economy. Its ratification of property transactions, including rents that supported foundations, and arbitration of disputes that arose, contributed to a perception that the city government was the ultimate protector of liturgical commemoration. Its oversight of the growing number of 'houses of God' and poor tables in the fourteenth century, strengthened an image of the city magistracy as a fount of charity. On the other hand, individual foundations contributed to services that were linked to municipal authority either directly – such as Jan Waghenare's foundation – or indirectly by their promotion of cults that enjoyed city-wide patronage. The significant number of aldermen, especially from the late fourteenth century onwards, who enhanced feast days associated with Christ or the Virgin Mary indicates a preference that reflects more than personal piety: the Holy Blood, and devotion to the Virgin, were cults universally venerated but associated locally with municipal authority.[172] The growth of the Holy Blood procession from the early fourteenth century, from modest funding by the civic treasury to heavier investment in a much larger ceremony by the 1390s, suggests a growing municipal will, commensurate with its expanding bureaucratic power, to manage religious life and to encourage the notion of the city as a sacred space and community.

It remains a moot point, however, whether such processions served as a vehicle for civic authority, or even for uniting the wider civic community.[173] The nature of 'civic' authority in Bruges was complex, its development uncertain, and its exercise frequently challenged, especially from the 1280s onwards (see Chapter 6). A notion of the 'commune', encompassing all

des couches dominantes à Lübeck', *Histoire Urbaine*, 27 (2010), 43–58; H. Brand, 'Mémoire individualisée et conscience communautaire – souvenir, charité et representation au sein des élites de Leyde à la fin du Moyen Âge', in H. Brand, P. Monnet and M. Staub (eds.), *Memoria, Communitas, Civitas: Mémoire et conscience urbaines en occident à la fin du Moyen Âge* (Ostfildern, 2003), pp. 87–116; O. Richard, *Mémoires bourgeoises: Memoria et identité urbaine à Ratisbonne à la fin du Moyen Âge* (Rennes, 2009).

172 See Brown, *Civic Ceremony*, pp. 108–12, 115–16. For similar investment in Corpus Christi day and processions in German towns, such as Augsburg, see A. Löther, *Prozessionen in Spätmittelalterliche Städten: Politische Partizipation, obrigkeitliche Inszenierung, städtische Eintracht* (Cologne, 1999), pp. 59–70. For a more pronounced case in which memorial practices among the 'patriciate' shifted in the fifteenth century from ones that promoted dynastic grandeur, to ones that promoted civic cohesion and memory, see the example of Regensburg (Richard, *Mémoires bourgeoises*, pp. 189–214, 287–91).

173 For methodological debate on this question, see Brown, *Civic Ceremony*, pp. 22–8, 50–7, 84–92.

denizens of the city, survived throughout the later Middle Ages, as repeated reference to the 'common body' testifies, but the questions remained as to what it meant and who was best fitted to represent it. Even the representative authority of the elected city magistrates could be undermined by appeal to a wider Great Council. At times, attempts made by those in power to invest in religious ceremony were the product of particular political circumstances. The faction of wealthy hostellers and brokers that gained ascendancy over the city between 1385 and 1407 (see Chapter 7) was strongly associated with the efforts at this time to surround municipal rule with an aura of spiritual authority: Holy Ghost masses to celebrate elections to the magistracy; the funding of plays for the Holy Blood procession and general processions; the beginnings of the Holy Blood fraternity (whose members wore a livery that depicted the pelican, the Eucharistic symbol of self-sacrifice).[174] Faction members such as Niclaas Barbezaen, who in his self-justificatory letter to the duke in 1407 trumpeted his own sacrifices for the communal good of the city, were particularly prominent as founders of services that promoted devotion to Christ and the Virgin Mary. During the same period, restrictions were placed on guild display during the Holy Blood ceremony: their right to carry candles during the procession was rescinded, and it seems that the citizens were grouped according to their sections (*zestendeelen*) and not within their craft guilds.

Yet while communal religious ceremony could be bent to the narrower demands of oligarchies, it nevertheless remained responsive to wider political interests. The very beginnings of the Holy Blood procession in the early fourteenth century must be placed within the turmoil that resulted in a political voice being granted to wider social groups, represented by the craft guilds. The first reference to municipal funding of a procession on Holy Cross day (in 1303) and to the carrying of the Holy Blood on that day (in 1304) occurred in the immediate aftermath of the 'guild revolution' of 1302 (see Chapter 6). It is not known whether the craft guilds became officially represented in the procession at this point, and it was perhaps not until the 1360s that processional order of craft guilds was developed to match the constitutional arrangements in place by then for electing city council members; but certainly, guild representation in the procession was later guarded

[174] Many of these developments can be found elsewhere – for instance the ceremonies surrounding civic elections in German or English towns: see D. W. Poeck, 'Rituale der Ratswahl in westfälischen Städten', in B. Stollberg-Rilinger (ed.), *Vormoderne politische Verfahren*, Zeitschrift für historische Forschung 25 (Berlin, 2001), pp. 207–62; C. M. Barron, 'Mass at the Election of the Mayor, 1406', in Rubin (ed.), *Medieval Christianity in Practice*, pp. 333–8.

with jealousy. Being stripped of it by the ascendant ruling faction in 1385 was resented: as soon as the faction was overturned in 1407, the craft guilds regained their privileges in the Holy Blood procession, and retained them throughout the fifteenth century. Their power within the city was gradually undermined by the commercial elite, but their growing involvement in post-obit arrangements may reflect their continuing political status; while political upheavals between 1477 and 1492 demonstrated their potential threat to oligarchic assumptions of power (see Chapter 7). The Holy Blood procession could never quite become a vehicle for oligarchy or faction. City magistrates processed closest to the relic, suggesting a 'natural' link between earthly and celestial authority; yet it potentially created a sense of disjuncture between the artifice of ceremonial form and the realities of political life.[175] In any case, the political aim of craft guilds was not to undermine municipal authority so much as to establish a louder voice within it. On Holy Blood day, the ideals of corporatism, as represented by the crafts and their position within the city, were most visibly displayed: in this sense the annual procession in Bruges is more accurately described as an expression not of 'civic' but of 'communal' religion.

Municipal authority over the city's sacred landscape was tightened but never closed within the hands of a 'patriciate' (see Chapter 7). In any case, straightforward distinctions between guildsmen and commercial elites were cut through by social and family networks. In enforcing their rulings, city councils usually required a wider consensus or at least the appearance of deference to the common good. The Holy Blood procession was sometimes disrupted with squabbles over precedence between guilds. While solving these disputes provided opportunities for the city magistrates to assert their authority, they also reaffirmed the constitutional place of guilds in the civic order.[176] On some occasions, magistrates were reacting to the demands of guildsmen: their decision to punish Reynoud Willems for donning an incorrect livery on Holy Blood day in 1475, followed initial complaints against him by guildsmen, and 'murmurings' that had almost provoked a riot. The wider efforts by city councils to promote public worship and enforce standards of morality and charity were also efforts that chimed with

[175] M. James, 'Ritual, Drama and the Social Body in the Late Medieval English Town', in M. James, *Society, Politics and Culture: Studies in Early Modern England* (Cambridge, 1986), pp. 16–47; M. Rubin, *Corpus Christi: The Eucharist in Late Medieval Culture* (Cambridge, 1991), pp. 267, 270–1, 288.

[176] In 1446 the aldermen delivered a solution worthy of Solomon to the quarrel between the tilers, plumbers and plasterers, in relation also to four other guilds, regarding their relative positions in the procession: SAB, 96, 11, fo. 297^{r-v}; Brown, *Civic Ceremony*, pp. 53–7.

the corporatist values of guilds. Municipal management of the communal dungeon, the Dark Room, with its increasing number of doles to prisoners, demonstrated the city government's expanding capacity to work for the common good by the simultaneous correction of malefactors and exercise of communal charity.[177] Punishment of other miscreants could also take on forms that made specific connections between municipal good works and sources of sacred authority. For uttering certain 'injurious words', one Jooris Ram was ordered by the aldermen to gift half a *hoet* of bread each to the Dulhuus inmates and the Dark Room prisoners, and also to offer three pounds of wax before the Holy Blood relic.[178]

Other forms of punishment inflicted on those perceived to have violated these values reaffirmed the perception that the city occupied a sacred territory. Malefactors could be ejected from its protective boundaries: Reynoud Willems was banished from Flanders for fifty years. Punitive pilgrimage imposed by city governments, and endorsed by guild regulations, temporarily expelled others.[179] The earliest records of the glovers' guild in the 1340s already show use of this practice. Penitents were sent to a wide selection of local places (Hulsterlo, Brussels, Ghent) and further afield (Vendôme, Rouen, Rocamadour); and a favoured place for longer distances imposed by other guilds (with the aldermen's approval) was St James of Compostela.[180] Yet there was a growing tendency by guild deans and city aldermen to dispatch their pilgrims to the Holy Blood of Wilsnack (a cult that began in 1388).[181] The canons of St Donatian's preferred to send miscreants under

177 For parallels with prisons in north Italian towns, see G. Geltner, *The Medieval Prison: A Social History* (Princeton, NJ, 2008), pp. 4, 28, 54–5.

178 SAB, 157, fo. 37^{v}.

179 Some sources from St Donatian's, and the smattering of guild judgements, suggest trends, although without continuous records of civic justice a comprehensive list of pilgrimage destinations cannot be constructed, as it has been for some other towns, e.g. J. van Herwaarden, *Opgelegde bedevaarten. Een studie over de praktijk van opleggen van bedevaarten (met name in de stedelijke rechtspraak) in de Nederlanden gedurende de late middleeuwen (ca. 1300–1550)* (Amsterdam, 1978).

180 A. Viaene, 'Onse Vrauwe te Rutsemadoene (Rocamadour): Een bedevaart uit het oude Vlaamse strafrecht', *Biekorf*, 67 (1966), 193–99 (at 195); A. Viaene, 'Vlamingen op strafbedevaart naar Compostella 1300–1450', *Biekorf*, 75 (1974), 379–95; A. Viaene, 'Sinte Niklaus in Warangeville: Een bedevaart in het oude Vlaamse strafrecht', *Biekorf*, 71 (1970), 321–5. For municipal punishment, see cases in 1434, 1457, 1487, 1492 (in SAB, 157, 1434, fos. 19^{r}, 69^{v}; 1455–9, fos. 172^{v}–3^{r}; 1487/8, fos. 42^{v}–3^{r}; 1490–2, fos. 26^{v}, 29^{v}); 1424 and 1455 in civic cartularies (SAB, 96, 11, fos. 163^{v}–4^{r}; 14, fo. 65^{r}). For pilgrimage punishment in guild records: 1351 (brokers: SAB, 291, cartularium, fo. 51^{r}); 1378 (chandlers: RAB, Charters with blue numbers, 8098); 1455 (goldsmiths: RAB, Ambachten, 64, goudsmeden cartulaire); 1458 (coopers: SAB, 336, fo. 96^{v}).

181 A. Viaene, 'Het heilig Bloed van Wilsnack: Een bedevaert uit het oude Vlaamse strafrecht', *Biekorf*, 69 (1968), 5–17. See cases in 1462 (SAB, 96, 14, fos. 131^{v}–2^{r}), 1491, 1492 (SAB, 157,

their jurisdiction to Our Lady of Aardenburg;[182] but the judges of the provost's court of St Donatian (from the 1470s) also showed a distinct preference for Wilsnack.[183] The bleeding hosts of Wilsnack were a popular if controversial destination of voluntary pilgrimage, and were another miraculous kind of holy blood;[184] but the preference for Wilsnack as a punitive destination affirmed the special association of the city magistracy and of its constituent groups with Bruges' blood of Christ. The municipal desire to present the city as occupying hallowed ground is also apparent in the prosecution of sodomy in the late fifteenth century. Evidently sodomy was regarded as a crime that might contaminate the city in a way few others did: whereas other criminals condemned to death were executed in the Burg, those convicted of this 'horrible crime' were taken for execution 'to the accustomed place' outside the Cross gate, beyond the city walls.[185] If the route followed by the Holy Blood procession marked out the parameters of a holy city, so punishment of the unclean outside its walls reinforced a sense of Bruges as a sacred space within.

It is thus possible to map out the landscape of a 'communal' religion in Bruges without reference to the demands of court or state. Yet the political pressures exerted by princely power undoubtedly shaped its contours. The growing influence of the prince over election to city offices meant that municipal government was increasingly aligned with princely government. Prosecution of sodomy in Bruges, for instance, also interested state authorities in the later fifteenth century as a crime of *lèse-majesté*.[186] Moreover, the growing demand for general processions came from both civic and princely needs. These could be harnessed in support of ducal causes: in 1465, for the first time, both the Holy Blood and the Holy Sacrament were transported on general processions, in order to petition divine protection for Charles the Bold during his campaigns in France. After 1477, the Habsburg

1491–2, fos. 8^{v}, 97^{r}, 104^{v}); guild records in RAB, Charters with blue numbers, 8127 (handlers in 1432), 8185 (carpenters in 1457), 8205 (tanners in 1463).

182 Between 1387 and 1490, the chapter act-books mention Aardenburg twenty times as the place to which miscreants were sent, Cologne twelve times, St Adrian of Geraardsbergen ten, Our Lady of Halle seven. Wilsnack was the destination in only two cases (Callewier, 'De papen van Brugge', pp. 413–14).

183 Between 1470 and 1500, the *proosdij* court (RAB, Proosdij, Vierschaar, 1509–1513) refers to Wilsnack eight times as a place to which malefactors were sent, Rome twice, Cologne twice, and once each to Aardenburg, Compostela, St Adrian of Geraardsbergen, and Our Lady of 's-Hertogenbosch.

184 See C. Walker Bynum, *Wonderful Blood: Theology and Practice in Late Medieval Northern Germany and Beyond* (Philadelphia, 2007).

185 SAB, 192, fos. 38^{v}, 47^{r}, 60^{v}, 75^{r}, 77^{r}.

186 See Boone, 'State Power'.

regime made even greater use of the Holy Blood in support of its rule.[187] In other walks of religious life, the heavy tread of princely authority began to make a deeper impression, especially from the 1440s onwards. Punishment inflicted on the city for rebellion against Duke Philip in 1436–8 included the establishment of a commemorative service for the murdered ducal counsellor Lord L'Isle Adam, which the city was to fund in perpetuity. In 1440, as part of the process of reconciliation, the duke made an entry into the city which for the first time included elaborate dumbshows. On the face of it, these emphasized the penitential submission of city to prince. Arguably John the Baptist's words declaimed before Duke Philip arriving outside the Cross gate – 'make straight the coming of the lord' – turned the duke into a Christ-like figure. Use of dumbshows became common in ducal entries, responsibility for which was turned over to the rhetoricians; and their activities seem to have become more attuned to the needs of rulers, all the more so under Habsburg rule.[188] The interweaving of state with civic authority in religious practice became tighter; and is seamless in the sequence of eleven dumbshows put on by the city to mark the entry of the young Habsburg prince, Charles, in 1515. Most of them presented an episode of Flemish history or myth that linked the city with its ruler, and two of the scenes recalled the reputed gifts to the city by former counts of the Holy Blood relic and St Donatian's body.[189]

The foundation in 1493 within St Saviour's church by Jan van Coudenberge, secretary to Philip the Fair, of a fraternity dedicated to the Seven Sorrows of Our Lady seems another example of state encroachment on urban devotion. Whereas previous princely involvement in the city's fraternities had been limited to membership of existing groups, here the initiative for foundation came from the court itself. This was one of several similar fraternities founded in regions under Habsburg control. Like the new rosary confraternities on which they were modelled, they aimed to draw in a wide membership, but they also explicitly linked compassion for the Virgin Mary with sympathy for the Habsburg dynasty that claimed finally to have united the Low Countries in peace.[190] In Bruges, the fraternity quickly received official

[187] See Brown, *Civic Ceremony*, pp. 260–7, 295–6.

[188] Van Bruaene, *Om beters wille*, pp. 58–76.

[189] Remi du Puys, *La tryumphante entrée de Charles prince des espagnes en Bruges 1515*, ed. S. Anglo (Amsterdam and New York, 1973); and Jan de Scheereres, 'Jan de Scheereres *Triumphe ghedaen te brugghe ter intreye van Caerle*: Teksteditie met inleiding en aantekeningen', ed. S. Mareel, *Jaarboek De Fonteine* (2005), 79–143.

[190] S. Speakman Sutch and A.-L. Van Bruaene, 'The Seven Sorrows of the Virgin Mary: Devotional Communication and Politics in the Burgundian-Habsburg Low Countries, c. 1490–1520', *Journal of Ecclesiastical History*, 61 (2010), 252–78 (at 265–6).

civic patronage. On 22 April 1493, the city council agreed to organize a general procession to celebrate its foundation 'in the name of Prince Philip'. The procession would pray for the prosperity of Maximilian and Philip, and for 'the welfare of all their lands'.[191]

It is possible therefore to enclose the history of religious practices in Bruges within a grand narrative that emphasizes their growing submission to state control. However, it is not a narrative that flows without digressions. Obedience of city to ruler was never complete; princely involvement in civic ceremonies did not amount to an appropriation of them. The drama of entry ceremonies was better suited as a vehicle of civic rather than courtly agenda: at the very least it allowed townsmen to make oblique reference to the limitations of the ruler's authority. Allusions to the city's subservience in biblical scenes during the 1440 entry were double-edged, for they pointed also to the city's aspirations to be a sacred city, and to the wider history of salvation against which the duke was invited to consider his own actions. In 1515, the history of the ties between city and ruler played out in the dumb-shows was a reminder to Charles that his rule in Flanders was based on his title of count, and that it was linked to a divinely arranged pattern: most of them showed scenes that twinned the count's obligations to Bruges with episodes of biblical or sacred history.

It may well be difficult to distinguish a 'civic' from a 'courtly' agenda, given the increasing ties that bound city magistrates to state government. Drawn into the apparatus of state bureaucracy, city elites were likely to favour the extension of princely rule. Yet the decade that followed Charles the Bold's death in 1477 shows how divided in loyalty these elites could be. Men such as Willem Moreel or Maarten Lem, however implicated in the structures of Habsburg rule, formed a faction, bound by a social network of commerce, that opposed men like Lanchals whose basis of power rested on service to the prince (see Chapter 7). It was in the same decade of faction and crisis that general processions were used more than ever before: the calls by Maximilian or his supporting faction for such processions were the result of crisis in Habsburg rule, not its success. Moreover, the purposes of these processions did not entirely serve immediate political needs. Rulers could not simply require citizens to pray for their 'welfare' against their enemies, unless these enemies were directly attacking Flanders. A more delicate approach was often required. Invariably prayers for the 'welfare of the prince' in general processions had to be linked with prayers for 'peace'.

191 SAB, 120, I, fo. 124^{r}. The city council boosted the cult on 20 December 1522, with mass and bell-ringing, following the death of Jan van Coudenberge (SAB, 120, III, fo. 343^{v}).

The call for peace was one of the fundamental liturgical purposes of such processions, as well as being a core value of communal society. The cooperation of citizens was sought with promises of peace, and these began to look parchment-thin during the 1480s. The endless repetition of prayers 'for peace' shows the limits to princely use of civic processions, and the need to work with the grain of communal values and traditions.[192] The effect of Habsburg sponsorship of the cult of Seven Sorrows from the 1490s was limited in similar ways. The cult's popularity had less to do with the ability of state power to impose its will, than with the widespread appeal of Marian cults, so many of which had spread in Bruges over the previous century. As with other Marian cults, devotion to the Seven Sorrows may also have become localized, losing touch with its original message of territorial unity.[193]

The relationship between religious and secular authority was not always a mutually supportive one. Miraculous events, like many other religious phenomena, were difficult for earthly authorities to harness, and might even be corrosive of secular power. The shape of religious practices in Bruges is not explicable simply by reference to the demands of secular authority and the conflict between 'city' and 'state'. It is as well to recall the continuing power of ecclesiastical authority and tradition to influence and limit lay initiatives. Municipal management of processions in Bruges, for instance, worked through the mediation of St Donatian's canons, who claimed an authority over processional procedure that neither citizens nor state officials could dispense with entirely, and who insisted on adherence to liturgical traditions regardless of political circumstance. For all the changes in the religious landscape that occurred during the later Middle Ages, some features remained constant. Devotion to St Donatian, which the canons had encouraged at an early date, continued to be promoted; and lay attachment to the cult developed from its original appearance as a clerical topos. St Donatian's body, given a new shrine in 1096, was again translated in 1186 before Count Philip – an event recalled by the canons in 1463, when a new translation was made before the ducal household as well as 'a multitude of people'.[194] In 1493, the city magistrates petitioned Philip the Fair to be

[192] For consideration of the need for legitimacy in the appropriation of symbolic power, and the need to preserve the formalities of ritual etiquette, see P. Bourdieu, *Language and Symbolic Power*, ed. and intro J. B. Thomson, trans. G. Raymond and M. Adamson (Cambridge, 1991), esp. pp. 113, 123.

[193] See the passing comments on this in Speakman Sutch and Van Bruaene, 'Seven Sorrows', p. 272.

[194] BAB, A52, fo. 246^{v}.

allowed to institute a procession on St Donatian's day; and in 1515, civic memory re-enacted the count's original gift to the church of St Donatian's body, in one of the dumbshows that celebrated the history of Bruges' close ties with the count.

Thus, the history of urban religious practices in the later Middle Ages can be plausibly written with a focus on the growing involvement of the laity in all areas of devotional life. It is a focus easily magnified in the study of a city such as Bruges, where exceptionally wealthy citizens founded large endowments to suit their intercessory, social and political requirements, or where city magistrates came to manage sacred ceremonies with some confidence. It seems a small step to take to describe increasing lay involvement in religion as a process of 'secularization' or 'laicization'– and to see the growth of municipal authority or 'communal religion' as the urban equivalent of this same process.[195] But these are anachronistic shorthands, albeit convenient ones, that disguise more complicated processes; and if they are meant to imply a lay desire to bring the divine and sacred down to earth, to bypass the mediation of the clergy or to construct forms of Christianity divergent from ecclesiastical traditions, they can mislead altogether. The religious practices most visible in Bruges – the great expansion of sacred spaces, the deliberate efforts to construct a holy city, or the continual references made by citizens in ceremonial events to the history of salvation above human affairs – point in another direction: towards an impulse among the urban laity, with clerical aid, to draw their community on earth closer to heaven.

Similar processes were at work elsewhere: the promotion of public worship, the investment in divine service, and the diversification of religious life are apparent in other late European towns, large and even small.[196] But in few other towns were such promotion, investment and diversity as developed as they were in Bruges. In this sense, Bruges was different in degree more than in kind. All towns were in theory part of a universal church, and it is a comment on the relative uniformity of practices within late medieval Christendom that foreign merchants residing in Bruges could be accommodated within the devotional and sacramental life of the city with apparent ease. Yet the localism of these practices, the way they were made subject to local forces and loyalties, is an equally salient aspect of urban religious life.

[195] For application of these terms in Italian towns, see for instance Goldthwaite, *Wealth*, pp. 129, 142; A. Thompson, *Cities of God: The Religion of the Italian Communes 1125–1325* (Penn State University Park, 2005), pp. 3, 107, 136.

[196] For generally smaller towns in England, Scotland and Wales, see G. Rosser, 'Urban Culture and the Church 1300–1540', in D. M. Palliser (ed.), *The Cambridge Urban History of Britain*, vol. I: *600–1540* (Cambridge, 2000), pp. 335–69.

What made Bruges distinctive was the unique way in which many of these practices were brought together, and in the case of its most prized relic, the Holy Blood, turned into events that were familiar to many European towns yet marked Bruges out from all other communities.

The diversity of late medieval religious practices precludes simple summary, especially if examined within a city as wealthy and cosmopolitan as Bruges. The multiplicity of practices and choices in towns, or the many focuses of loyalty besides the 'civic', seem to render questionable any search for a specific religious identity peculiar to one or any town.[197] Nevertheless, this diversity did not necessarily cause identities or loyalties within the city to fragment: one trend that appears to emerge most strongly in evidence from Bruges is the growing number of links that were forged, especially from the end of the fourteenth century onwards, between the myriad forms of religious life and the authority of municipal government. Venerable clerical institutions, lay guilds, new cults and foundations flourished: many arose independently of civic authority, some of them resisted or undermined it, but very few were untouched by it. The tight management of urban life in Bruges – and the increasingly close ties between municipal and state government by the sixteenth century – is a characteristic that also explains how the early upheavals of the Reformation were successfully weathered by Catholic authorities in the region (see Chapter 10).

In the end, an overview of religious practices in Bruges as for any city must acknowledge the fragmentary nature of its sources. What does survive may well show devotional diversity and pressures to conform, but it does not provide a complete picture. Wealth and cosmopolitanism bred diversity but not always piety. It may have been difficult for the clergy, let alone the laity, to resist the earthly temptations that were so readily available in Bruges society: the Cordoban traveller Pero Tafur claimed that the city's inhabitants were given to all kinds of luxury, and that they regarded men and women bathing together to be as respectable as churchgoing.[198] Even the Holy Blood relic and its annual procession, the great set-piece of communal religion, did not command universal obedience, nor did it mean one

[197] See C. Caby, 'Religion urbaine et religion civique en Italie au Moyen Âge. Lieux, acteurs, pratiques', in Crouzet-Pavan and Lecuppre-Desjardin (eds.), *Villes de Flandre et d'Italie*, pp. 105–20; J. Oberste, 'Gibt es eine urbane Religiosität des Mittelalters?', in Ehrich and Oberste (eds.), *Städtische Kulte*, pp. 15–36; Signori, 'Religion civique'. For emphasis on diversity, see J. Chiffoleau, 'Note sur le polycentrisme religieux urbain à la fin du Moyen Âge,' in P. Boucheron and J. Chiffoleau (eds.), *Religion et société urbaine au Moyen Âge* (Paris, 2000), pp. 227–52.

[198] Tafur, *Travels*, p. 200.

thing to all citizens. The city magistrates in 1297 associated the relic with the protection of civic liberties; but a bishop in 1388 linked it with obedience to Rome. A grieving mother in 1470 thanked the relic for a miracle that revived her stillborn child; a wealthy owner of a prayer book could focus contemplation on the 'sweet blood' that flowed from Christ's side;[199] yet an artisan, Hannekin van Uphove, found 'Holy Blood' to function particularly well as a blasphemous swear-word.[200] While craft guilds or clergymen could use the Holy Blood procession to assert their own agendas, some townsmen paid it scant respect: in 1530 three drunkards saw fit to parody the procession by following its route around the walls in reverse, one of them riding on a donkey.[201] The religious landscape of the city was to be ruptured in other ways during the Reformation, but it had never been uniform. Conformity and unquestioning belief within late medieval Bruges are the impressions most often left by available sources, but alternative attitudes can just occasionally be glimpsed. Perhaps there were others who agreed with the claim, also attributed to the blaspheming artisan, that 'there was no God'.

[199] OBB, Ms. 437, fo. 346^{r-v}; Bruges, Grootseminaire, Handschriften, 72/125, fos. 94^{v}–5^{r}. This prayerbook may be dated to the mid fifteenth century.

[200] He was accused in 1491 of 'customarily' swearing by the Holy Blood as well as by the head and five wounds of Christ; and was punished by having a piece of his tongue removed: SAB, 157, 1490–2, fos. 36^{r}, 39^{v}.

[201] SAB, 157, 1521–30, fo. 50^{r}. The city magistrates decided that this escapade was the result of drink rather than malice or Protestant inclinations, but the three were fined and sent off to the Holy Blood of Wilsnack as penance.

9 Texts, Images and Sounds in the Urban Environment, c.1100–c.1500

MAXIMILIAAN P. J. MARTENS, JOHAN OOSTERMAN, NELE GABRIËLS, ANDREW BROWN AND HENDRIK CALLEWIER

No single event in medieval Bruges was recorded by so many as the marriage festivities of Charles the Bold and Margaret of York in 1468; and no event brought so much artistic talent together. More than 150 artists (painters, sculptors, embroiderers and others), including some of the most celebrated of the day, were drafted in from all over the duke's territories to work on the decoration and staging of the *pas d'armes* on the Markt and the banquet entertainments in the Prinsenhof that took place between 3 and 12 July. The singing sirens who emerged during the last banquet from the jaws of a 60 foot model whale – which had mirrors for eyes and moved to the sound of trumpets and shawms – were among the countless singers and musicians who performed during the event. The cost to the ducal household of these expenses (which included building work on the duke's residence) came to more than 13,000 pounds (of 40 groten), the equivalent of paying a daily wage to 52,000 skilled craftsmen. Local artists were also employed by the city aldermen for the couple's entry into the city. The rhetorician Anthonis de Roovere was paid for staging the dumbshows forming part of the entry ceremony, of which he also wrote the most detailed account.[1]

The festivities of 1468 illuminate several aspects of 'cultural' activity in Bruges that form the themes of this chapter. They serve to highlight the scale of resources available to Burgundian rulers in Bruges, the capacity of the city to supply such magnificence, and therefore the need to set the event within a wider context of the city's development and its links with the outside world. The festivities also brought many media together: the event was a true *Gesamtkunstwerk*, intended to dazzle with sight and sound. Different media may have had their own genres, patrons, audiences and means of production, but they were often linked within an urban landscape

[1] For recent comment on contemporary writers on the event, see J. Oosterman, 'Scattered Voices: Anthonis de Roovere and Other Reporters of the Wedding of Charles the Bold and Margaret of York', in Blockmans et al. (eds.), *Staging the Court of Burgundy*, pp. 241–7. For ducal expenses, see L. de Laborde, *Les ducs de Bourgogne: Étude sur les lettres, les arts et l'industrie pendant le XVe siècle*, 3 vols. (Paris, 1849–52), vol. II, pp. 293–381. These by no means represent the total cost of the event. For the city's expenses: SAB, 216, 1467/8, fos. 14^{v}, 37^{r}–8^{v}, 73^{v}–4^{v}, 76^{v}–7^{v}.

that shaped them all. Moreover, not many of them in 1468 (least of all the mirror-eyed whale) would earn accolades as 'great art': most served purposes that were more decorative and ephemeral, yet they were highly valued by contemporaries nonetheless. Much of what follows will inevitably deal with the texts, images and sounds that are typically labelled as 'literature', 'fine art' and 'music',[2] but even these features of 'high culture' have to be placed within a context of activities and beliefs that were cultural in a broader sense, and part of social practices within the urban context.

As an environment where occupations, potential patrons and social contacts were so numerous, the city may well be considered the ideal arena for cultural variety and exchange.[3] As a source for urban culture in Bruges, the 1468 festivities can therefore mislead as well as illuminate: they indicate but also exaggerate the importance of princely patronage within the city, since the abundance of evidence for an event that lasted less than two weeks overshadows the significance of other cultural activity that was more regular and less well recorded, and not all of which was supportive of those in authority. A great deal even of 'high' art and text has been lost; echoes of oral culture such as songs and plays are faint. The ceaseless noise created by the hubbub and daily rhythms of a metropolis are only partially recorded in the non-sounding media of text and image; even the context and sound of the most carefully notated music cannot be recreated with any certainty. Particularly unfortunate is the relative dearth of evidence (non-literary especially) before c.1400 compared with the later period. Bruges emerges as a 'creative environment' in the fifteenth century, but the conditions for this had been long in the making.

Literature and the Visual Arts, c.1100–c.1300

A history of literate culture in Bruges necessarily begins with the church of St Donatian, and with the tremulous pen of Galbert of Bruges: 'It was in the midst of so many calamities and in the most constrained circumstances that I began to compose my deeply unsteady mind … and to subdue it to the discipline of writing.'[4] A notary and cleric, but one fully acquainted with his urban environment, Galbert produced a poignant and well-crafted account

[2] For city architecture, see Chapters 2 and 5.

[3] See generally, Calabi and Christensen (eds.), *Cultural Exchange*, vol. II, esp. pp. xxvi–xxvii, 3–5, 12, 28–31, 229, 331.

[4] On Galbert of Bruges, see Rider, *God's Scribe*; J. Rider and A. Murray, *Galbert of Bruges and the Historiography of Medieval Flanders* (Washington, DC, 2009).

of the murder of Charles the Good, count of Flanders, in 1127 and of all related developments, shortly after these tumultuous events took place (see Chapters 2 and 4). As 'the first recognizable writer we have from the Low Countries',[5] Galbert himself created no school; but St Donatian's became a centre of learning and culture. In the vicinity of the church and within its famous chapter, a written culture flourished: catalogues show that the chapter had a well-stocked library (with 136 codices by 1274).[6] While a tradition of chronicle writing did not develop within its walls, or at least not before the end of the fourteenth century, Galbert's style of annalistic notations at the end of his record of events was perhaps continued in the canons' series of chapter act-books, which were begun long before their first surviving example in 1345.

Galbert also records echoes and glimpses of other forms of cultural life. The city already generated various noises, though most of them were troubling: 'tumult' and 'clamour' dominate the soundscape of Galbert's Bruges. But there are sounds that articulate purpose. The ringing of St Donatian's bells called the 'citizens' to arms in 1127 (though it appears that a 'trumpet' was used to the same effect; and trumpets, 'straight and crooked', were used by the lookouts for those besieged in the castle). At Saint-Omer, in April 1127, the new count of Flanders, William, was received by the clergy and their 'harmonies of sweet singing', applauded by the 'citizens'; as well as by youths 'singing his praises' and 'sounding the signal for their dances'.[7] Galbert omits mention of any similar customs in Bruges when the count arrived there; but other evidence suggests their existence by at least the thirteenth century. The collegiate church had a choir school well established by 1312 when the succentor was instructing eight 'chorales' who sang at mass, matins and vespers.[8] A more secular tradition of May songs, for which there is evidence by the fourteenth century, dates back perhaps to the thirteenth.[9] Galbert gives more attention to the architecture of St Donatian's, the castle and other dwellings (see Chapter 2); and he also alludes to the capabilities of local craftsmen who were already well established in the thriving market

[5] F. van Oostrom, *Stemmen op schrift: Geschiedenis van de Nederlandse literatuur vanaf het begin tot 1300* (Amsterdam, 2006), p. 37.

[6] A. Dewitte, 'Boek- en bibliotheekwezen in de Brugse Sint-Donaaskerk XIIIe–XVe eeuw', in Meulemeester (ed.), *Sint-Donaas*, pp. 61–95.

[7] Rider (ed.), *Galbertus Brugensis*, chaps. 45, 66.

[8] Strohm, *Music*, p. 13.

[9] Ibid., pp. 99–100; J. Oosterman, 'Ik breng u de mei: Meigebruiken, meitakken en meibomen in Middelnederlandse meiliederen', in B. Baert and V. Fraeters (eds.), *Aan de vruchten kent men de boom: De boom in tekst en beeld in de middeleeuwse Nederlanden* (Leuven, 2001), pp. 166–89 (at 167–70).

centre: the murdered count's sepulchre had to be constructed hastily, but it was achieved with 'decent craftsmanship'.[10]

Other cultural forms in Bruges become clearer in the thirteenth century. The diversity of influences on them is apparent in the career and works of Jacob van Maerlant, who was born near or in Bruges, and who is considered to be the 'father of all Dutch poets'. It was probably at the school attached to St Donatian's, around 1250, that Maerlant received his education – a good one according to his own testimony.[11] He was familiar with the current canon of classical writers (Virgil, Ovid, Statius), with the Bible and with its basic exegesis, and also with the large compendia that distilled the learned knowledge of his day. All this is apparent in his first work, *Alexanders geesten* (c.1260), a voluminous romance, based on the *Alexandreis* by Walter de Châtillon, and filled out, for instance, with cosmographical detail drawn from Honorius' *Imago mundi*.[12] Maerlant's literary career initially followed the path of romance, though it never strayed too far from the didacticism that later became so characteristic of his work. He relates stories about historical figures (Alexander, the Trojan heroes, King Arthur), striving to write accurately about them; and he sharply rebukes itinerant storytellers, who often told stories about the same heroes. Similar criticism of storytellers and reciters by a literary elite can also be found in other contemporary texts, some from Flanders but others from elsewhere: it reveals the significance of orality in the dissemination of stories, and how far from marginal such storytelling was in this period.

From 1270 Maerlant, now in Damme near Bruges, probably served as a town clerk.[13] He wrote three major works, all in rhyme, and all based on authoritative Latin sources: the *Rijmbijbel* (c.1271) is derived from the *Historia scolastica* by Peter Comestor, the *Spieghel Historiael*, his greatest work (c.1280–85), one he dedicated to Count Floris V of Holland, was a translation and edition of the *Speculum historiale* by Vincent of Beauvais; and in 1281 he completed *Van de naturen bloeme*, an adaptation of *De natura rerum* by Thomas of Cantimpré (a work which Maerlant thought

[10] Rider (ed.), *Galbertus Brugensis*, chap. 24.

[11] For much of what follows on Maerlant, and the older bibliography on him, including references to his edited works, see F. van Oostrom, *Maerlants wereld* (Amsterdam, 1996), and esp. pp. 19–80 for his education.

[12] Jacob van Maerlant, *Alexanders geesten*, ed. J. Franck (Groningen, 1882); P. Berendrecht, *Proeven van bekwaamheid: Jacob van Maerlant en de omgang met zijn Latijnse bronnen* (Amsterdam, 1996), pp. 13–85.

[13] E. van den Berg and A. Berteloot, 'Waar kwam Jacob van Maerlant vandaan?', in *Verslagen en mededelingen van der Koninklijke Academie voor Nederlandse taal- en letterkunde*, 103 (1993), 30–77.

was by Albert the Great). He translated the compendia of the academic curriculum for a lay audience, and accordingly often edited his texts thoroughly, unable to resist showing that sometimes he knew a little better than his learned predecessors. 'According to Aristotle the sparrow lives no longer than a year,' Maerlant writes. 'This may be so in his country, but here is otherwise. I suppose it is the result of the cold here. ('*Dat mach sijn inden lande daer, Mar hier nest niet, des siwi vroet. Ic waent onse coude lant doet*'). Maerlant's own voice rings out most vibrantly in his strophic poems. In three of them, he conducts a dialogue with the probably fictional Martin, following the form of a university *quodlibeta* (the written record of a *disputatio*). Grand issues are addressed, such as the nature of love or of the Trinity. Many of Maerlant's works resonate with concern about social injustice and the state of the church: *Van der naturen bloeme* takes the side of the people against the injustices inflicted by the nobility. The state of the church and Christian life is questioned in *Vanden lande van oversee*, a poem written shortly after news arrived in Flanders that the city of Acre had fallen and the crusaders had suffered an ignominious defeat. In a powerful appeal to anyone who will listen, he begins the poem with the words, 'Kersten man wats die geschiet, Slaepstu? Hoe ne dienstu niet Jhesum Christum, dinen here?' (Christian man, what happened to you, are you asleep? Why are you not serving Jesus Christ, your lord?).[14] The poetic virtuosity of his late poems is exceptional, but Maerlant's work forms part of a west Flemish tradition in which, as we shall see, an attention to form and style is often conspicuous.

Maerlant's works were written almost entirely for noble circles in the northern Netherlands, although there is evidence for their reception in Flanders, and among a wider group beyond the nobility. During the later Middle Ages his works circulated widely in urban milieus.[15] Maerlant also translated and embroidered French romances, such as the *Roman de Troie*. His audience must have been familiar with reading and listening to literature: however dominant his presence in the thirteenth century, Maerlant did not stand alone, nor did he emerge from nowhere. In the first half of the thirteenth century, Bruges and Flanders must already have enjoyed a lively literary climate, in which knightly tales figured prominently. An important part of the Middle Dutch Charlemagne and Arthurian romances were written and distributed in Flanders, although how much of this took

[14] Jacob van Maerlant, *Strophische gedichten*, ed. E. Verwijs (Groningen, 1879), p. 124.

[15] On the reception of his magnum opus *Spieghel Historiael*, see J. Biemans, *Onsen Speghele Ystoriale in Vlaemsche: Codicologisch onderzoek naar de overlevering van de Spiegel historiael* (Leuven, 1997).

place in Bruges is not known. The seeds of knightly tales, both in French and Flemish, apparently fell on fertile soil. Indirect evidence, such as the criticism of storytellers, entries in catalogues, and naming habits (parents in the upper echelons of society calling their sons 'Gawain'), makes it clear that chivalric romances were widely known and loved.[16] These doubtless contributed to the spread of courtly and chivalric ideals, not only within the nobility, but also among the urban elites, who eagerly embraced and imitated models of noble living. An early and important link with such ideals, although not exclusive to Bruges, is the romance *Perceval*, written between 1181 and 1191 by Chrétien de Troyes, the principal writer of his generation, for Philip of Alsace, count of Flanders. The central location of the Grail in this work has associations with the crusades. Whether this would have evoked association with the Holy Blood in Bruges is doubtful, since it is only in the fourteenth century that legend began to assign the relic's arrival in Bruges to the mid twelfth century (see below). Yet interestingly, the Dutch translation of *Perceval* that survives in only fragmentary form, made at the beginning of the thirteenth century, contains a long section on the entry of Gawain into a city that, although not named, may well have conjured Bruges to mind. In few other cities would Gawain have encountered such commerce and industry:

> Hi sach die wisselbancke lecghen
> Vul van silver ende van goude,
> Dar bi die munte menechfoude.
> Hi sach liede van ambachten,
> Die missielike ambacht vrachten,
> Alse misselike ambacht sin.
>
> . . .
>
> Dese weven, die gene vollen,
> Dese carden, dese wieden.
>
> . . .
>
> Ghene strate in allen sinnen
> Was vul van comanscapen binnen,
> Alse ofmen daer alle daghe
> Vulle marct te houdene plaghe.

He saw the exchange counters piled with silver and gold, and all kinds of coins. He saw craftsmen carrying out as many crafts as there are crafts . . . He saw one weaving

[16] Van Oostrom, *Stemmen op schrift*, pp. 216–332; F. Willaert, *De ruimte van het boek: Literaire regio's in de Lage Landen tijdens de Middeleeuwen* (Leiden, 2010).

and another fulling, a third carding and another yet combing ... The streets were very crowded with merchants, as if a busy market was held every day.

This passage is absent from the original French text.[17]

Gawain's submergence in city life seems to plunge us back into thirteenth-century Bruges, in its state of rapid expansion (as described in Chapter 2). Besides the crafts that produced or provided for mundane necessities, were those that supplied more cultural needs. A corporation of tapestry makers was mentioned in 1302, and its activities must have predated this.[18] The production of illuminated psalters was thriving in the second and third quarters of the thirteenth century. Burghers demonstrated an increasing interest in illustrated texts for private devotion, influenced by mendicant preaching – a demand that Jacob van Maerlant had also met by translating Bonaventura's Latin life of St Francis (as well as a life of St Clare). These psalters opened with calendars embellished with the labours of the months, and full-page miniatures liturgically divided the psalms with scenes from the infancy and passion of Christ, and sometimes scenes from the lives of St Francis or St Dominic (see Figure 9.1).[19] The style of these miniatures betrays the influences of northern France, but is distinguished from the refined elegance of the Parisian gothic by its greater attention to convincing movement. Wider influences on visual and literate culture in Bruges are apparent at an early date.

The city was already an environment where levels of literacy were high, and uses of the written word were valued, not least pragmatically in guild and municipal activity.[20] Jacob van Maerlant's probable position as town clerk at Damme is an indication of the level of literacy required by town governments in the region, even those much smaller than Bruges. The need for written records within the early commune in Bruges, generated by a desire for self-government, is already apparent in Galbert's account of the burghers' demand for a charter of liberties. The need to preserve such

17 Van Oostrom, *Stemmen op schrift*, pp. 228–9; S. I. Oppenhuis de Jong, *De Middelnederlandse Perceval-traditie: Inleiding en editie van de bewaarde fragmenten van een Middelnederlandse vertaling van de Perceval of Conte du Graal van Chrétien de Troyes, en de Perchevael in de Lancelotcompilatie* (Hilversum, 2003), p. 84.

18 On tapestry weaving in Bruges, see G. Delmarcel and E. Duverger (eds.), *Brugge en de tapijtkunst* [exh. cat.] (Bruges and Mouscron, 1987); and J. Versyp, *De geschiedenis van de tapijtkunst te Brugge* (Brussels, 1954).

19 See K. Carlvant, *Manuscript Painting in Thirteenth-Century Flanders: Bruges, Ghent and the Circle of the Counts* (Turnhout, 2012); Smeyers, *Vlaamse miniaturen*, pp. 136–45.

20 For the links between urban literacy, government and 'literate mentalities', see for instance M. Mostert and A. Adamska (eds.), *Writing and the Administration of Medieval Towns: Medieval Urban Literacy I* (Turnhout, 2014).

Figure 9.1 St Francis preaches to the birds: Psalter, Bruges, c.1270 (Bruges, Grootseminarie 55/171, fo. 95)

records – to create a repository of communal 'memory' – was met by the building of the Halle that housed the city archive. Its destruction by fire in 1280 was more than a material loss to communal identity. The Bruges city accounts which survive from 1281 (in Latin interspersed with Middle Dutch terms that were 'untranslatable') are evidently products of long practice; and from 1302, in the midst of political crisis and craft guild ascendancy, they began to be written down in the vernacular. This period of turmoil marks the work of Van Maerlant too. His criticism of the social order perhaps reflects a mendicant response to the problems of poverty, as well as the ambivalent view of the poor among his elite audience of lords, local nobles and merchants who patronized the mendicant orders for socio-political as well as penitential reasons.[21] As city clerk, moreover, Van Maerlant had an ear close to the aural world of communal politics: he may even have been present in 1280 to record the petition made to the count by the people of Damme, angered by 'patrician' abuses of power.[22]

The Fourteenth Century: The Development of Urban Culture

Evidence for urban cultural production in the visual arts and literature is scarce before c.1300, and fragmentary even in the fourteenth century. Distinguishing a distinctly 'urban' culture from other forms remains difficult: the registers of 'clerical' and 'noble' cultures still had a dominant influence on works of art produced in Bruges, although they also entered into a dialogue with more vernacular and popular traditions. After Maerlant's death, probably shortly before 1300, the focus of Middle Dutch literature seems to have shifted to Brabant. All we have of Bruges as a literary centre are isolated texts and fragments. On the back of a manuscript from Ter Doest, a large Cistercian monastery at Lissewege near Bruges, are listed two love poems (songs perhaps), probably dating to the late thirteenth century. They attest to new poetic perceptions of love, and they are written in forms that are derived from both Latin and French traditions. The imagery they employ is sometimes close to the metaphors used in Marian poetry.[23] Not unlike literature found in Bruges in the late medieval period, they are often strikingly positioned at the interface between secular and religious literature, and are innovative in poetical phrasing. The freedoms that poets permitted themselves, and the experiments they made with style and form, are typified by the West Flemish translation of the *Roman de la rose*, only part of which survives. The original French text is never fully jettisoned, but the translator, 'a poet of exceptional stature', gives himself great interpretative freedom to adapt the tale.[24] A century later, the translator of the *Speculum humanae salvationis*, who almost certainly worked in Bruges, would also

21 For the significance of mendicant houses to patrician elites in dealing with an expanding urban proletariat, see Chapter 2.

22 Van Oostrom, *Stemmen op schrift*, pp. 530–6.

23 F. Willaert, *De poëtica van Hadewijch in de strofische gedichten* (Utrecht, 1984), pp. 67–74.

24 D. E. van der Poel, 'A Romance of a Rose and Florentine: The Flemish Adaptation of the Romance of the Rose', in K. Brownlee and S. Huot (eds.), *Rethinking the Romance of the Rose: Text, Image, Reception* (Philadelphia, 1992), pp. 304–15.

freely adapt his text to create his own *Spieghel der menscheliker behoudenisse*. The tight composition of the Latin text is loosened, and the typological compendium is turned into a narrative, into which the writer's own concerns are inserted. The text contains an increased focus on the Virgin Mary compared with the original, and its fierce criticism of mendicants, occupying more than 100 verses, is absent from the original text: it is a unique version of a work that was spread throughout Europe, and was often copied and illuminated in Bruges.[25]

As the medieval Flemish urban elites – both nobles and the highest-ranking among the commercial groups – were generally to some degree bilingual in their cultural outlook and shifted between Romance and Dutch or German influence, French romances continued to find an audience in Bruges. The poem *Baudouin de Sebourc* (datable to a period after 1358, and quickly translated into Middle Dutch) has been attributed to a poet from Hainaut, but it is worth emphasizing the references within it to Bruges.[26] Parts of the poem may well have appealed to local pride: the poet addresses 'seigneurs' and 'barons', but the first term did not necessarily exclude an audience of merchant elites; and the poem is one of the first recorded legends concerning the arrival of the Holy Blood in Bruges. Reference to the attempts to bring a phial of the Holy Blood to Bruges shortly after the First Crusade, initially by Eustace (III) of Boulogne, and then successfully by the eponymous and legendary Baldwin (partly based on King Baldwin II of Jerusalem), rivalled similar legends associated with Boulogne and Fécamp. A different account of the relic's arrival, this time attributing it to the efforts of Thierry of Alsace after the Second Crusade, appears at much the same time in the chronicle of the abbot of St Bertin. This version was to gain more traction in Bruges itself.[27] While these accounts derive from sources outside Bruges, they perhaps reflect a need within the city to find an illustrious pedigree, linked to the highest social circles, for the city's principal relic – at a time in the late fourteenth century when municipal investment in the annual procession of the relic was particularly increasing (see Chapter 8).

25 J. Oosterman, 'Vertaler of verteller? Het "Speculum humanae salvationis" en de Westvlaamse "Spieghel der menscheliker behoudenesse"', in P. Wackers et al. (eds.), *Verraders en bruggenbouwers: Verkenningen naar de relatie tussen Latinitas en Middelnederlandse letterkunde* (Amsterdam, 1996), pp. 169–88, 322–7.

26 J. F. van der Meulen, 'Bruges, Brendan et Baudouin de Sebourc', *Queeste: Tijdschrift over middeleeuwse letterkunde in de Nederlanden*, 3 (1996), 1–17 (see n. 48 on the audience); N. Huyghebaert, 'Iperius et la translation de la relique du Saint Sang à Bruges', *HGG*, 100 (1963), 110–87.

27 N. Geirnaert, 'Het Heilig Bloed en Diederick van de Elzas: De fascinatie voor een taaie legende', *HGG*, 150 (2013), 397–410.

Latinity and vernacular literature also enjoyed a close relationship, as shown in two other, totally idiosyncratic works from late fourteenth-century Bruges. The *Life of St Amand* (*Leven van Sinte Amand*) was written by a certain Gillis de Wevel in a year (1366) and a place (Bruges) that are both mentioned in the text: 'Ghescreven xiij ondert jare, Ende lxvj daer toe mede. Te Brugghe, in die goede stede Was dese legende eerst ghemaect' (Written in the year thirteenth hundred and sixty-six. In Bruges, in the good city, was this legend first composed). While making full use of the Latin *vita* of St Amand, the text is nevertheless modelled on the courtly romance. Storytelling techniques, motifs and a so-called King's Game are directly derived from the secular narrative genre, but are effortlessly integrated into the discourse of a holy life. It is a 'parody' that shows that Gillis de Wevel knew his literary classics – and that his audience was familiar with knightly romances.[28] Jan Praet (who is thought to have been an inhabitant of West Flanders, probably Bruges, although where and when he lived is not known) wrote *Speghel der wijsheit* (Mirror of Wisdom), a large allegorical and catechetical work, strongly rooted in Latinity, both in terms of content and of poetic forms used.[29] The poet of this 'masterfully controlled undertaking' was well schooled, but his language usage shows him to be conversant with popular idiom. And with sublime self-deprecation, within his high-minded text on the attaining of eternal salvation, he admits that his own life has not always been distinguished by piety:

> In cabarette ende in taverne
> so ben ic milde[r] te verterne
> eens anders gheldekijn dan tmijn.
> Up scone vrouwen sie ic gherne;
>
> ...
>
> Als ic bi hen ben gheseten,
> hemelrike hebbic vergheten;
> so doe ic ooc der hellen wrake.[30]

In pubs and taverns I am liberal in consuming other people's money more than my own. I like to look at beautiful women ... When I dally in their company, I forget the kingdom of heaven as much as I do all the punishments of hell.

28 P. Blommaert (ed.), *Leven van Sinte Amand, patroon der Nederlanden: Dichtstuk der XIVe eeuw*, 2 vols. (Ghent, 1842–3); W. Verbeke, 'La "Vie de Saint Amand" par Gillis de Wevel et ses modèles', in W. Verbeke, L. Milis and J. Goossens (eds.), *Medieval Narrative Sources: A Gateway into the Medieval Mind* (Leuven, 2005), pp. 107–37.

29 Van Oostrom, *Wereld in woorden*, pp. 528–34; J. Reynaert, *Jan Praets Parlament van Omoed ende Hoverdye* (Nijmegen, 1983).

30 Jan Praet, *Speghel der wijsheit of Leeringe der zalichede van Jan Praet, Westvlaemschen dichter van 't einde der XIIIe eeuw, voor de eerste maal uitgegeven van wege de Koninklijke Akademie van België*, ed. J. H. Bormans (Brussels, 1872), lines 1779–87.

Jan Praet's *Speghel* was written in order that spiritual priorities would not be neglected; and many of the works extant from this period answer to similar concerns. Dozens of prayer books, produced in Bruges, survive particularly from the end of the fourteenth century, in which Marian devotion is manifest. Within them are older Latin hymns, but also prayers in French and Latin which are sometimes placed alongside each other. Those in rhyme were often meant to be read out, like the lyrics of songs, and many of them were illuminated. Liturgical needs were also reflected in book production: the expansion of the liturgy, particularly in Bruges' three principal churches from the mid fourteenth century (see Chapter 8), generated music and books as well as services for mass. The main musical ingredient of these services consisted of monophonic chant or plainsong, delivered by the clerical staff, and was often accompanied by or alternated with the organ. The fabric accounts of St Donatian's record an increasing number of new and repaired liturgical choirbooks in the second half of the fourteenth century.[31] The earliest mention of a book of polyphony dates from 1377, when twelve leaves were added to an existing 'book of motets', and in 1402 a new 'book of motets' was acquired.[32] Polyphonic compositions might serve liturgical and ceremonial occasions, but they also met a demand for contemplative devotion.[33]

While polyphonic music and the services that generated it were contained within church walls, their performance was announced to town-dwellers outside. The bells of St Donatian's were made to chime for the main monastic hours of the day, but also for many new foundations, particularly from 1360 onwards, the distinctions between them signalled by the tones of different bells and the number of strikes (see Chapter 8). Extensive repairs were required on an over-strained bell-tower and on the principal bell 'Donaas' by the early fifteenth century.[34] These bells were also tolled on occasions that involved citizens as well as clergy. In 1306, the scribe of the fabric accounts already records that St Donatian's bells were being rung on Holy Blood day (though he considered it a 'bad custom'),[35] and the involvement of St Donatian's clergy in the procession was to increase during the fourteenth century. Even by then, however, the municipal government had its own auditory resources, building sound into civic architecture. Whereas in 1127 a call to arms within the city had been raised by the bells of

31 Dewitte, 'Gegevens betreffende het muziekleven'.

32 Strohm, *Music*, p. 14.

33 Nosow, *Ritual Meanings*, pp. 135–66.

34 BAB, A49, fos. 37^{r}, 74^{v}–5^{r}; A50, fo. 187^{r}.

35 BAB, G1, roll 4.

St Donatian's, by the late thirteenth century the Belfry had its own system of bells that synchronized with those of St Donatian's. Three new bells were installed after the fire of 1280, one of which was a *werckclocke* that chimed the hour; and towards the end of the fourteenth century its tolling was announced by a pre-signal or strike (*voorslag*) through an automated system, regulated by a clock: a drum with metal pins set a hammer in motion to hit the side of another bell.[36] There were other sounding elements on the Belfry tower (see Chapter 5): city waits (three of them by 1331) kept watch over the city and blew their trumpets in times of danger. By the early fourteenth century some of them received extra fees for performing music: in 1310 'Lammekin Spetaerde en Fierkin en Heinric de Gartere' played 'te hoghetiden'; in 1331/2 'Fierkin de trompete' and 'Coppin Zeghaerd' performed with other minstrels at the count's castle of Male.[37] A tradition of minstrel music had already been established at Bruges: in 1318, Bruges organized one of the earliest known international 'schools' for minstrels.[38] These gatherings took place in Lent, when minstrels were not allowed to perform publicly. The city subsidized musical production on many occasions, particularly during the Holy Blood procession, which was amplified considerably during the fourteenth century: by 1389, no fewer than eighteen paid 'trumpeters and pipers' accompanied the cortege. This, however, may also reflect political strife: these musicians were placed in front of the six 'headmen' of the city's sections, thus displaying the ascendancy asserted during this period by the Honin/Barbezaen faction, which had demoted the role of the craft guilds in the procession.[39]

The vibrancy of city streets in the fourteenth century is captured in another book, entirely different from the chivalric or devotional works discussed above: the *Boec van den ambachten*.[40] Whereas the earlier Middle Dutch translation of *Perceval* described impressionistically a quasi-fictional town, this work details the bustle of Bruges more directly. It is a schoolbook: 'It

[36] P. Andriessen, *Die van muziken gheerne horen: Muziek in Brugge 1200–1800* (Bruges, 2002), p. 38.

[37] L. Gilliodts-Van Severen, *Les Ménestrels de Bruges* (Bruges, 1912), p. 30; SAB, 96, 1331/2, fo. 109^{v}.

[38] SAB, 96, 1318, fo. 47^{r}; Strohm, *Music*, p. 78.

[39] SAB, 96, 1388/9, fo. 109^{r}. In 1392, 9 of the 18 came from 'outside the town'; in 1393 extra pipers came from Ghistel (SAB, 96, 1391/2, fo. 94^{v}; 1392/3, fo. 96^{r}). The eighteen playing before the six 'headmen' of the town, appears to be a recent innovation; but from 1407 this number was reduced (to four trumpeters and one piper with a 'riethoorne'): SAB, 96, 1406/7, fo. 111^{r}. For the Honin/Barbezaen faction, in power between 1385 and 1407, and the taking away of craft guild representation during the procession in these years, see Chapters 4, 8.

[40] Gessler (ed.), *Het Brugsche Livre des mestiers*.

is very useful for children to learn from it', writes a schoolmaster in the epilogue; and a book that seems a distant ancestor of modern popular guidebooks that teach basic foreign words by giving sample phrases. The oldest version of this text that survives from Bruges dates from about 1380 and places French and Dutch texts side by side. Later versions appeared with English, German and Italian phrases. The book shows how important multilingualism was to an international city (and how widespread literacy was); and it provides colourful examples of the people, activities and crafts in Bruges. It tells of 'Goris the bookseller, who has more books that anyone else in the city'; of 'Olivier the innkeeper who has many good guests: Germans, Spaniards and Scots'; of 'Nathalie, that beautiful woman, who has a good bathhouse'. And it mentions 'Ysabelle of Roeselare'. She sells parchment, 'but she sold me a sheet that was slippery so I was not able to write well on it'.

The production of parchment and books, and indeed a whole range of craft activity, also begin to be visible in other sources. The gradual shift in the local economy, as explained in Chapter 6, from textile manufacture to the production of more sophisticated and luxury goods, was under way. By 1350, local artistic life was already well organized. Bruges was becoming an international centre for the production of sculpted retables, brass tomb plates,[41] tapestry,[42] embroidery, and canvas painting.[43] A corporation of image makers (*beeldenmakers*) was first mentioned in 1358.[44] Little of this specialized artisans' work has been preserved. Besides a large polychromed sculpture representing St Cornelius, usually dated to c.1360,[45] a

[41] R. Van Belle, 'La production tournaisienne de dalles plates à figuration XIIIe siècle – 1566', unpublished PhD thesis, Ghent University (Ghent, 2012); and V. Vermeersch, *Grafmonumenten te Brugge vóór 1578*, 3 vols. (Bruges, 1976).

[42] Delmarcel and Duverger, *Brugge en de tapijtkunst.*

[43] D. Wolfthal, *The Beginnings of Netherlandish Canvas Painting: 1400–1530* (Cambridge, 1989); M. Smeyers, B. Cardon and S. Vertongen (eds.), *Naer natueren ghelike: Vlaamse miniaturen vóór Van Eyck (ca. 1350 – ca. 1420)* [exh. cat.] (Leuven, 1993); S. Kemperdick and F. Lammertse (eds.), *The Road to Van Eyck* [exh. cat.] (Rotterdam, 2012).

[44] Some painters' guilds were established earlier: one in Brussels by 1306, another in Ghent before 1339. In towns of the southern Netherlands, painters appear in the fourteenth century: Tournai in 1364, Antwerp in 1382. In many other towns, painters' guilds do not appear until the fifteenth century. On the Bruges corporation of image makers, see D. Van de Casteele, *Keuren 1441–1774, Livre d'admission 1453–1574, et autres documents inédits concernant la ghilde de St-Luc de Bruges, suivie des keuren de la corporation des peintres, sculpteurs et verriers de Gand* (Bruges, 1867); C. Van den Haute, *La corporation des peintres de Bruges* (Bruges, 1913); and A. Schouteet, *De Vlaamse primitieven te Brugge: Bronnen voor de schilderkunst te Brugge tot de dood van Gerard David* (Brussels, 1989–99).

[45] R. Didier, L. Kockaert, H. Lobelle et al., 'Le saint Corneille sculpté de l'hôpital Saint-Jean à Bruges (XIVe siècle): Étude et conservation', *Bulletin KIK-IRPA*, 20 (1984/5), 99–136.

few examples of monumental sculpture can still be found. The sculpted vault keys of the assembly hall at the new city hall (see Chapter 5) are attributed to Jean de Valenciennes,[46] who in 1376 also began the series of sculptures of the façade, of which a few corbels survive (see Figure 9.2). The tympanum and stone corbels of the Genoese loggia are generally dated to around 1400 (see Figure 9.3). Preserved in greater quantity are the many illuminated manuscripts; and they indicate that by 1400 their production was professionally organized and large-scale. The image makers, under the patronage of St Luke, gathered different professions within their corporation: the image makers themselves (who were panel painters), canvas painters (*cleerscrivers*), glass painters, mirror makers and artisans involved in making saddles and horse harnesses. It did not include sculptors (as the equivalent guild in Antwerp was to do): wood sculptors formed a separate corporation with the carpenters (cabinet makers), while stone sculptors gathered with the stonemasons.[47] All these specialized trades were probably attracting significant numbers of people from elsewhere in Flanders and beyond by 1400. Certainly the conflicts already surfacing in 1402 between the image makers and the librarians or book producers (see below) indicate groups striving to protect their monopolies and status.

The production of luxury goods involved craftsmen and artisans as producers rather than consumers. As becomes more apparent in the fifteenth century, craft guilds could also be patrons of art and polyphonic music, even if these were the preserve of more high-ranking circles of patrons. Little survives, however, to indicate what artisans listened to or might have read. But remnants of street cries appear in some polyphonic compositions,[48] and by happenstance one street song survives. 'Claeuwaert claeuwaert Wacht hu voorden lelyaert' are the opening lines of a venomous ditty that locals sang after the victory in 1380 of the count's forces over Ghent (with the help of the Bruges militia), which alludes to the devices that both

46 A. Janssens de Bisthoven, 'Het beeldhouwwerk van het Brugsche Stadhuis', *Gentse Bijdragen tot de Kunstgeschiedenis en Oudheidkunde*, 10 (1944), 7–81; P. Coremans et al. (eds.), *Flanders in the Fifteenth Century: Art and Civilization: Catalogue of the Exhibition Masters of Flemish Art: Van Eyck to Bosch* (Detroit, 1960), pp. 229–31; J. W. Steyaert and M. Tahon-Vanroose (eds.), *Late Gothic Sculpture: The Burgundian Netherlands* (Ghent, 1994), especially no. 38, pp. 187–9.

47 On woodworkers, see A. Van de Velde, *De ambachten van de timmerlieden en de schrijnwerkers te Brugge* (Ghent, 1909); and Vandewalle (ed.), *De Brugse schoenmakers en timmerlieden*. On the stonemasons, see Sosson, *Les travaux publics*.

48 A fragment of a three-voice *quodlibet* of such cries dating back to c.1400–40 appears in Utrecht, University Library ms. 1846 (fo. IIA^{v}–IIB^{r}), which may have originated in Bruges, though this is disputed (Strohm, *Music*, pp. 105–6; Andriessen, *Die van muziken gheerne horen*, pp. 166–7).

Figure 9.2 Jean de Valenciennes (attr.), Tristan, Isolde and Brangien, original corbel of the façade sculpture, sandstone, Bruges, 1376–80

Figure 9.3 The Portal sculpture (consoles) at the Genoese Loggia (or 'Witte Saaihalle'), Bruges, c.1400

parties had worn: Ghent the lion's claw, Bruges the lily. According to one source in which it was written down, it was sung throughout the city; and in another source it seems almost to have become a nursery rhyme. Mockery stings most when it issues from the mouths of children: 'Omme dat die van Brugghe dese victorye hadden zo zonghen de kinderen dit naervolghende liedeken…'[49] But not all locals applauded the victory, and another chronicle, written in rhyming French by a Fleming, probably a Bruges burgher who tried to write in the language of the princely court and the noble elite, makes it clear how divided the city was in these years: 'Leliaarts' supported the count, weavers the rebels of Ghent, while 'li commun' complained against the harm done to the goods of city by the 'seigneurs'.[50]

The Gruuthuse Manuscript: A Monument of Medieval Dutch Literature, c.1400

Late fourteenth-century Bruges was troubled by social revolt, political faction and shifts in the economy, but it was also to yield a remarkable collection of texts that brings us closer than any earlier work to the social and cultural outlooks of its elite and 'upper middle-class' citizens. With the so-called Gruuthuse manuscript, put together around 1405 to 1410, we are dealing with an early example of patronage among burgher circles, in which links between the commercial elite and the luxury trades are evident.[51] It contains 172 texts, all written in Bruges and, according to recent research, probably by one author, Jan van Hulst, who lived from about 1360 to after 1428. Jan Moritoen was long regarded as the most important poet of the manuscript, but his role seems to have been more one of patron than author. The handwriting looks somewhat crude and even sloppy in places, but this simple appearance distracts from the true significance of this collection, as does the connection to Lodewijk van Gruuthuse, from whom the name of

[49] On the children singing in Bruges, OBB, Ms. 437, a manuscript of the *Excellente Cronike van Vlaanderen*. The song is attested within an older Latin version of this chronicle tradition: see Braekevelt et al., 'Politics of Factional Conflict', p. 16.

[50] The chronicle was probably begun after 1384, in support of the new Valois-Burgundian count, but the surviving portion relates to the years 1379–80: see H. Pirenne (ed.), *Chronique rimée des troubles de Flandre en 1379–1380* (Ghent, 1902).

[51] H. Brinkman (ed.), *Het Gruuthuse-handschrift: Hs. Den Haag, Koninklijke Bibliotheek, 79 K 10* (Hilversum, 2015). For the following, see F. Willaert (ed.), *Het Gruuthuse-handschrift in woord en klank: Nieuwe inzichten, nieuwe vragen* (Ghent, 2010); and J. Koldeweij, I. Geysen and E. Tahon (eds.), *Liefde en devotie: Het Gruuthusehandschrift: Kunst en cultuur omstreeks 1400* (Bruges, 2013), with older references cited.

the collection derives. In its current form, the collection does not look as neat as it would have done originally, since a few of its prayers, poems and songs were later additions. The original codex opened with a poem, followed by two or three prayers and about 150 songs. It was extended in several stages, and the manuscript now consists of three parts, with seven rhymed prayers, 147 songs and eighteen poems.

The songs are mostly about love (including five May songs), and many of them evidently circulated within a group of friends, among whom the winning of love was both a game and a serious matter. Many contain an acrostic, and in one of them we read the name Liegaert, who from 1395 was the wife of Jan van Hulst. Other female names mentioned probably referred in many cases to real people, but the stories behind these names are now lost to us. While love songs occupy the lion's share of the collection, some of the other songs have achieved canonical status in Dutch literature. This applies to a song of fools (*zot lied*), about the chaplain from Oedelem, a village not far from Bruges, who has an affair with the sexton's wife, and predictably is caught by the husband. Better known still is the *Kerelslied*, a satirical song in which peasant rebels, or perhaps rebels in general, are ridiculed. The most famous song from the collection is a lament on the death of Egidius, a good friend who died young. It begins with a dramatic exclamation: 'Egidius, waer bestu bleven? Mi lanct na di gheselle mijn'. Within the short space of a roundel it expresses the deep crisis into which the friend has been plunged by the death of Egidius, who had been a singer. The melody that accompanies the song was newly composed; and it seems the Gruuthuse manuscript contains stroke notation for many new melodies.[52] The notation is disconnected from the text and may have served instrumentalists (fiddle, harp or lute players) when accompanying a singer who knew the melodies by heart. While such notation seems simple, it need not point to limited musical knowledge. The melodies refer both to French and German traditions. The poetic form of these songs also betrays the influences of a wider world. The songs' poet made use of *formes fixes*, which were dominant in late medieval French poetry, though he stretched the possibilities of these forms to their limits. The familiar shape of the rondeau, usually with a refrain of two or at

[52] The essence of this notation is not the shape of the symbols (i.e. the 'strokes') but rather its arhythmic nature: I. De Loos, 'Het Gruuthuse-liedboek en de muziek van zijn tijd', in Willaert (ed.), *Het Gruuthuse-handschrift*, pp. 113–47. On the *Kerels*, see H. Brinkman, 'Een lied van hoon en weerwraak. "Ruters" contra "Kerels" in het Gruuthuse-handschrift', *Queeste*, 11 (2004), 1–43. On a possible identification of Egidius, see N. Geirnaert, 'Op zoek naar Egidius. Het laatmiddeleeuwse Brugge in het Gruuthusehandschrift', in Willaert (ed.), *Het Gruuthuse-handschrift*, pp. 169–80; and Brinkman (ed.), *Het Gruuthuse-handschrift*, who disputes Geirnaert's interpretation.

most five verses, is in one case here given a refrain of thirteen verses. But the songs also lean towards German poetry, not least because the West Flemish language was continually being coloured by German words. The lyrics have a cosmopolitan flavour, but they achieve their own distinctive character by their experimentations in style and form.

The eighteen poems do not fall into a single category. An important group is formed by those in which a first person narrator tells of a dream, the journey that he makes and the struggle between allegorical characters such as Hope, Hate, Beauty and Virtue. They contain numerous elements that occur in the *Roman de la rose*, and in late medieval literature, especially the works of French poets such as Guillaume de Machaut and Eustache Deschamps. The emphasis on virtue characterizes almost all the poems, and especially the spiritual poems that conclude the manuscript. They amount to an appeal to the reader or listener not to choose pleasures of the moment but instead to take the difficult path to God, through fasting and prayer, and the practice of virtue and love – the path to spiritual rather than worldly love. In the poem that would have opened the original codex is a long allegory that tells of a young man in love (the 'I' narrator), melancholic in temperament and talented as a poet. His talent brings him fame, but he loses sight of virtue and has to leave the castle. A bitter farewell is his lot. The moral weight of this poem is strengthened by the prayers that follow, and it espouses an ethical approach to literature – and of course, encourages moral behaviour in the world. The ideals expressed here are lofty and stoical. In comparison, the songs that follow seem quite airy. However, within many (even if not all), a tone is struck that is less carefree than in the troubadour lyrics of an earlier period.

The complexities of the Gruuthuse poems would have required an audience well-versed in a wide range of literature to appreciate them. The prologue of the first poem declares: 'He who is not civilized, has no idea how a work of art should be rewarded for its value. I want my wagon to be driven before those who are familiar with the way of art, so my effort will be finally rewarded in a fitting way.' It is an audience au fait with the literature of French noble and chivalric circles, which was known in Bruges: around 1375 Deschamps visited Bruges to offer Count Louis of Male a copy of Machaut's *Voir dit*, and in later years the works of both poets were present in Bruges libraries. It was also an audience linked with the highest ecclesiastical circles. The contrast set up between the poems on women and love, and those emphasizing moral and ethical virtues, seems to echo the contrasting positions taken up in the *Querelle de la rose*, the fierce debate on the morality of the *Roman de la rose* that took place around the University of Paris.[53] Jean Gerson, the university chancellor and one of Christine de Pisan's supporters in this debate, arrived in Bruges in 1396 to become dean of St Donatian's. A tentative link can also be made between the Eekhout abbey in Bruges and the duke of Berry's court: the abbot Lubertus Hauscilt (d.1417) had strong cultural associations with the court.[54]

Gerson spent some time reforming liturgical procedures within St Donatian's, while Hauscilt enriched the sung liturgy of his abbey. The poems in the Gruuthuse manuscript evince similar ecclesiastical concerns: we learn from a second, more dispassionate song on the dead Egidius, that he made his living as a tenor singing polyphonic works; and the high point of Marian devotion in the manuscript is a prayer that comprises a paraphrase of the *Salve regina.* Vocal music was identified as producing the kind of sound most closely linked with the divine. Other aspects of the collection are redolent with the many currents of spirituality within Bruges and elsewhere (see Chapter 8). Jan van Hulst, whose name appears as an acrostic to this poem, performed a polyphonic mass at the order of the town magistracy for Duke John the Fearless with his companions of the confraternity of Our Lady of the Dry Tree in 1410.[55] The pilgrim's prayer (the fourth of the manuscript) may be linked to the annual pilgrimage made to Our Lady of Hulsterlo. The last poem is a manual for the spiritual life: its I-narrator, his mind divided between worldly and spiritual love, is instructed by a hermit whose ideals reflect those of the Carthusians. The tensions between the 'active' and 'contemplative' life, or between the virtues of spiritual love and the vices of immorality, are explored in several poems and reflect wider attitudes of ecclesiastical elites, though they may also have had a particular poignancy in a metropolis as opulent as Bruges.

Although the content of the manuscript suggests an audience connected to the highest social echelons, it nevertheless reflects the interests of a small circle of burghers. Jan van Hulst and Jan Moritoen can be placed among the aspiring middling groups of Bruges. Jan Moritoen, of Scottish origin, was a furrier who achieved a more prominent position within his craft, as master of the poor table in St Giles' parish, as a member of the Hulsterlo brotherhood of pilgrims and finally as a member of the Bruges city council. Jan van Hulst was active in many fields, as an organizer of festivities (including

[53] See for instance V. Greene, 'Le débat sur le *Roman de la rose* comme document d'histoire littéraire et morale', *Cahiers de Recherches Médiévales et Humanistes*, 14 (2007), 297–311.

[54] M. Smeyers, 'Lubert Hautscilt, abt van de Brugse Eekhoutabdij (1393–1417): Over handschriften, planeten en de toekomst van Vlaanderen', *Academia Analecta*, 55 (1995), 39–104.

[55] SAB, 216, 1410/11, fo. 107v.

plays for the Holy Blood), as a singer, and as clerk of the *vierschaar*. The people who shared these songs and poems must have been a small group of insiders, with similar sensibilities, forming part of a cultural as well as a social elite within the city. Still, there is at least one poem that must have been recited before a larger group. It is a New Year's poem in which the king of the White Bear, the jousting company, is addressed. The king for the year in this poem is to receive a gift: a model of the city of Bruges with its ramparts and seven gates. All seven of them represent virtues and qualities that were desired by the city. The poem on the seven gates can be dated to a period following the restoration of the ramparts in 1406 (see Chapter 3). It is one of the last poems in the collection. The poet and the other members of the group are now among the elite of Bruges and emphasize their position with the offer of both poem and gift.

This poem in particular seems to reflect the factional strife that had disrupted the city between 1384 and 1411, when 'love and friendship' seemed in short supply. The city gates that enshrine desirable values also point to the particular concerns of the city's magistracy, and its other efforts during this period to bolster the sense of the city as a sacred space.[56] The poems that ridicule the boorishness of country-dwellers outside the city confirm the stereotype of the city as a haven of civilization. The prologue of the poem of forty lines that originally opened the codex points in a similar direction: it gives an Aristotelian-flavoured exposition of the essence of art, simultaneously said to involve skill, will and predisposition. It thus flatters the sophistication of its audience, and it also seems to offer a 'theoretical' underpinning for the exceptional level of artistic skill that was developing in the city. One of the love poems describes a woman's neck as a 'pillar of clear, white alabaster' as though carved in a 'masterly' ('meesterlijk') fashion: it is a metaphor that belongs to the market-place of luxury production and craftsmanship in early fifteenth-century Bruges.

Bruges as a European Centre of Artistic Production, c.1420–c.1480.

From the 1420s, but perhaps particularly from the 1440s after the upheaval of rebellion in 1436–8, Bruges enters a period celebrated as the peak in its cultural creativity.[57] The 'inventor of oil painting', the genius painter Jan van

56 Dumolyn, 'Une idéologie urbaine'; and see also above, Chapters 5 and 7.

57 W. Blockmans, 'The Creative Environment: Incentives to and Functions of Bruges Art Production', in M. W. Ainsworth (ed.), *Petrus Christus in Renaissance Bruges: An Interdisciplinary Approach* (New York, 1995), pp. 11–20.

Eyck, first appears in Bruges in 1425,[58] and was settled there more permanently by 1432, when he was already attracting the attention of the burgomaster and the city government to his workshop.[59] A new kind of literary association was also born, apparently with divine inspiration. On Maundy Thursday in 1428, as later legend had it, thirteen men were gathered in the house of Jan van Hulst in Bruges, when a dove fluttered in, a speech scroll in its beak, bearing the words 'Mijn werc is hemelic' ('My work is hidden' or 'My work is heavenly'). This event purportedly initiated the first chamber of rhetoric in Bruges and in the Netherlands, establishing a tradition of literary competition that became a highly characteristic feature of urban culture in the region.[60] The tempo of musical production may also have been quickening. In 1421, St Donatian's significantly increased its capacity for polyphony by endowing a new choral foundation: four choirboys were to sing a daily *Missa de Salve* in descant and participate in high mass and vespers, while another nine schoolboys were to be trained in plainsong and, if sufficiently skilled, in descant. Polyphony began to be used for other liturgical forms besides the mass from the 1430s.[61]

The scale of artistic production in Bruges, especially in the middle decades of the fifteenth century, though not unique, was without rival in the Low Countries. But as we have seen, this cultural efflorescence emerged from soil that had already proved fertile. This is most obvious in relation to polyphonic music and the elaboration of mass settings and foundations that had been well under way since the mid fourteenth century. St Donatian's daily *Missa de Salve* in any case was modelled on the example of the cathedrals of Tournai and Cambrai. The voices of rhetoricians also did not burst from silence. The conception of the Holy Spirit chamber as a spiritual brotherhood makes it comparable to devotional fraternities already in existence; and its formation in the house of Jan van Hulst (probably the Gruuthuse poet) places it in exactly the same social milieu as those who produced the Gruuthuse manuscript, that is, the more well-off burghers and artistically talented guild masters. The Holy Spirit chamber resembled

58 In August 1425 Philip the Good ordered him to leave Bruges, to which he had fled from the politically unstable Hague.

59 SAB, 216, 1431/2, fo. 78r.

60 See L. Derycke and A.-L. Van Bruaene, 'Sociale en literaire dynamiek in het vroeg vijftiende-eeuwse Brugge: De oprichting van de rederijkerskamer De Heilige Geest ca. 1428', in Oosterman (ed.), *Stad van koopmanschap en vrede*, pp. 59–96; Van Bruaene, *Om beters wille*; on the links between literary production and guilds, see Dumolyn, 'Het corporatieve element'.

61 Strohm, *Music*, pp. 22–3, 29.

earlier northern French *chambres de rhetoriques* and *puis marial*,[62] and the inter-town competitions that developed between rhetoric chambers mirrored the earlier festive events of shooting guilds and jousters.

Jan van Eyck's art emerged from earlier work in which Bruges artists had been involved. Prolific Netherlandish artists of the previous generation often went to Paris or Dijon to work in the service of the Valois court. The Bruges artists Jean Bondol (Jan Baudolf) and Jacob Coene, and artists from elsewhere in the Netherlands, like the sculptor Claus Sluter (originating from Haarlem) and the illuminators the Limbourg brothers (from Nijmegen), merged the Parisian late gothic tradition with local influences and thus stood at the cradle of what has been termed the *ars nova*.[63] Swaying, elegant figures received increasingly more convincing mass and volume and were set in an illusionistic space conceived as an extension of the beholder's one. Van Eyck's art was also prefigured in earlier book illumination and panel painting produced in Bruges.[64] This 'pre-Eckyian' art has been praised for its 'realism' – which might be defined as 'an attempt to evoke the proper nature of humans and objects with respect to proportions, physical presence and individual traits, and to situate them in a three-dimensional space'. In comparison with the prevailing international court style, this art was more expressive, appealing to the emotional empathy of the viewer, and did not shrink from representing ugliness, death or the lower strata of society.[65] Bruges books of hours from c.1400 also feature a number of iconographical innovations that would become more popular. Besides standardized cycles, such as the infancy of Christ and the Passion, new motifs were used, such as the Man of Sorrows, the Trinity in which God the Father bears the Cross with his dead Son, the True Face (Vera Icon), the Madonna of Humility,

62 See for instance C. Symes, *A Common Stage: Theater and Public Life in Medieval Arras* (Ithaca, NY, 2007).

63 S. Nash and T.-H. Borchert, *No Equal in Any Land: André Beauneveu, Artist to the Courts of France and Flanders* (London, 2007). On Jacob Coene (hypothetically identified with the so-called Boucicaut Master), see M. Meiss, *French Painting in the Time of Jean De Berry: The Late Fourteenth Century and the Patronage of the Duke*, 2 vols., 2nd edn (London, 1969); and A. Châtelet, 'Le miniaturiste Jacques Coene', *Bulletin de la Société Nationale des Antiquaires de France* (2000), 29–42. On Claus Sluter, see S. N. Fliegel and S. Jugie (eds.), *L'art à la cour de Bourgogne: Le mécénat de Philippe le Hardi et de Jean sans Peur (1364–1419)* [exh. cat.] (Dijon, 2004); on the Limbourg brothers, see R. Dückers and P. Roelofs (eds.), *The Limbourg Brothers: Nijmegen Masters at the French Court 1400–1416* (Antwerp, 2005).

64 See also pre-Eyckian representations of St Donatian (viz. Van Eyck's *Madonna with Canon Van der Paele*, 1436) for instance in the *planarius* of St Donatian's church, c.1419: D. Vanwijnsberghe, 'Une représentation inédite de saint Donatien et sa place au sein de l'enluminure dite "pré-eyckienne"', in C. Rabel (ed.), *Le manuscrit enluminé: Études réunies en hommage à Patricia Stirnemann* (Paris, 2014), pp. 167–90.

65 Smeyers et al. (eds.), *Naer natueren ghelike*, pp. 9–10.

Figure 9.4 Shrine of Saint Ursula, c.1400–15 (Bruges, St John's hospital)

and the Madonna with the Inkpot or the writing Christ child, as well as the Death of the Virgin. As for panel painting, systematic study of examples from the southern Netherlands from c.1400 has only recently been made.[66] The number of surviving works is small, heterogeneous and difficult to localize. Only two of them seem to have a provenance old enough to suppose that they were originally made in Bruges: the Shrine of St Ursula (Figure 9.4) and the so-called *Calvary of the Tanners* (Figure 9.5).[67] In general terms, these two objects are stylistically related to contemporaneous miniatures. Based on iconographical comparisons with book illuminations, the Shrine is now dated c.1400–15. The *Calvary*, which used to be dated to a similar period, has been redated on the basis of dendrochronology to c.1420–5, tantalisingly close to the earliest documented stay of Jan van Eyck in Bruges. But they are traditional in several respects – for instance in their use of a gold background with relief applied in brush, or gold on blue and red paint in gowns of female saints in the *Calvary*. The *ars nova* in painting was anticipated within an urban environment that had long been favourable to artistic production of all kinds; but aspects of it would be innovatory and its scale unprecedented.

[66] C. Stroo (ed.), *Pre-Eyckian Panel Painting in the Low Countries*, 2 vols. (Turnhout, 2009).

[67] For the altarpiece of the Tanners and the first reliquary of St Ursula, see Stroo (ed.), *Pre-Eyckian Panel Painting*, vol. I, pp. 124–95.

Figure 9.5 Anonymous, so-called *Calvary of the Tanners*, Bruges, c.1420–5 (Bruges, Cathedral of St Saviour's)

The Rhetoricians and Anthonis de Roovere

As later evidence shows, the rhetoricians practised literature in competition between individual poets and between groups: honours and prizes were given out for poems written and dramas staged. They became the opinion leaders and culture bearers of urban society; their appearance is part of a European pattern of corporatism in the literary field (of which the German *Meistersänger* also form a memorable part). Little is recorded about the early history of the Holy Spirit chamber in Bruges. The first known organized contest in Bruges was a drama competition in 1442, when companies from other towns visited Bruges, staging plays in French and Dutch. The city magistrates were apparently keen to be present.[68] The shorter rhetorician poems and the plays dominated literary production in the fifteenth century, and many were written in Dutch by poets whose names are known to us only in the archives or through a handful of poems: Master Fransois Stoc, a priest who graduated in Rome (and who would have informed lay poets on theological matters), wrote four known poems in the rhetorician style.

Some of these poems demonstrate the lively diversity of the literary scene. In the 1430s Jan van den Berghe wrote *Dat Kaetspel Ghemoraliseert* (The *Jeu de Paume* Moralized), following the model of the older *Moralized*

[68] SAB, 216, 1441/42, fo. 62ʳ. See Van Bruaene, *Om beters wille*, p. 43.

Game of Chess. This text was presented to a literary circle in Bruges under the patronage of the nobleman Roeland van Uutkerke.[69] In 1466 the Bruges goldsmith Jacob Vilt finished his rhymed translation of a French version of Boethius' *Consolation*. The bilingual drama competition in 1442 reflects the close connections between French-speaking and Dutch-speaking poets in these years. French poets were known in Bruges, and some of their works were even situated there. The works of Jean Regnier, who must have been in Bruges for a period in 1449, include many references to locations and situations in Bruges. An actor in one of his poems declares:

> Se ce n'eust esté Mimequine,
> Nostre meschine,
> Qui se tenoit en la cuysine
> Et Calquin, fille de l'hostesse
>
> ...
>
> Et puis la belle Brodaresse
>
> ...
>
> Et Drogue la bonne maistresse,
> Qui point ne cesse
> De monstrer aux amans l'adresse
> En son hostel au Puis d'Amours,
> Ung bien peu au dessus de l'Ours[70]

Is that not Mimekijn, our maid, who resides in the kitchen, and Calekijn, daughter of the hostess, and the beautiful embroiderer, and Drogue, the lovely hostess who gives all lovers the address of the *hotel au Puis d'Amours*, next to the Bear [the jousting company of the White Bear]?

Part of this poem was probably written in Bruges when Regnier was there in the entourage of Duke Philip the Good. The presence of the Burgundian court in Bruges meant other acclaimed writers came to Bruges. Among them was George Chastelain (b.1415), son of a Ghent shipper, who graduated as Master of Arts at the Leuven University and became *indiciaire*, the official court chronicler: he must have been in Bruges several times as member of the ducal retinue (to which his chronicle bears witness).[71]

[69] Jan van den Berghe, *Dat Kaetspel ghemoralizeert*, ed. J. A. Roetert Frederikse (Leiden, 1915); and for the link with the Bruges nobleman Roeland van Uutkerke who acted as a patron of this literary circle, see Boone, 'Une famille au service'.

[70] Jean Regnier, *Les fortunes et adversitez de Jean Regnier*, ed. E. Droz (Paris, 1903), p. 205. On Regnier and Bruges, see J. Oosterman, 'Tussen twee wateren zwem ik: Anthonis de Roovere tussen rederijkers en rhetoriqueurs', *Jaarboek De Fonteine* (1999–2000), 11–29 (at 20–1).

[71] G. Small, *George Chastelain and the Shaping of Valois Burgundy: Political and Historical Culture at Court in the Fifteenth Century* (Woodbridge, 1997).

The most visible connection of the court with the Flemish city is *Les douze dames de rhétorique*, a poem on rhetoric written in 1463 and presented as a poetical exchange in Bruges between George Chastelain, Jean Robertet and Jean de Montferrant.[72]

Little is known about the many local poets; but with the appearance of Anthonis de Roovere, rhetorician activity in Bruges, and in the Netherlands as a whole, acquires a face.[73] De Roovere lived from about 1430 to 16 May 1482. He was probably the son of one of the founders of the Holy Spirit chamber, and he won great fame at a tender age: at seventeen he became Prince of Rhetoric, a title he retained throughout his life. By profession, de Roovere was a stonemason, almost certainly a guild master and perhaps a building contractor. He was an artisan himself who knew the daily life of working people around him. De Roovere's artistic activities were very diverse. Judging from what survives of his work, particularly because more than 100 of his poems survive,[74] he might principally be considered as a distinguished poet; but in his own time, he was primarily known for his drama. Little of this survives. There is one long and serious piece, in which the Creed is retold and expanded with commentary, but in which a foolish character repeatedly pops up to disrupt the play's serious tone. The sincerity of priests is, for example, sharply questioned with heavy irony:

> Ghy en vynt ooc gheen ghebreck jnde clergye
> Hier jn Vlaendren / Tsus spreict al scoonekins.
> Sy en willen gheen / meyskins houden / noch doonekins
> Maer houden matroonekins / versufte grielkens
> Aerme houde vraukins / met gheluwe dielkens.
> Sy en doen metten lyfue niet / zy en winnen gheen kynderkens.
> Sy leuen jn zuverhede.[75]

72 George Chastelain, Jean Robertet and Jean de Montferrant, *Les douze dames de rhétorique*, ed. D. Cowling (Paris, 2002).

73 On de Roovere, see J. Oosterman. 'Oh Flanders, Weep! Anthonis de Roovere and Charles the Bold', in M. Gosman, A. Vanderjagt and J. Veenstra (eds.), *The Growth of Authority in the Medieval West* (Groningen, 1999), pp. 257–67; J. Oosterman, 'Imprint on your Memory: An Exploration of Mnemonics in the Work of Anthonis de Roovere', in F. Willaert, H. Braet, T. F. C. Mertens et al. (eds.), *Medieval Memory: Image and Text* (Turnhout, 2004), pp. 161–75; J. Oosterman, ' "Si mes paroles avaient le son des cordes de vielle": Les rhétoriqueurs considérent le langage comme le comble de la musique', in J.-M. Cauchies, *Poètes et musiciens dans l'espace bourguignon: Les artistes et leurs mécènes: Rencontres de Dordrecht (23 au 26 septembre 2004)*, Publications du centre europeen d'etudes Bourguignonnes (XIVe–XVI s.) 45, pp. 81–91; J. Oosterman, 'Anthonis de Roovere, Dichter aus Brügge: Die Präsenz des Autors und die Aufführung seiner Gedichte', *Zeitschrift für deutsche Philologie. Sonderheft*, 130 (2011), 301–14.

74 De Roovere, *De gedichten*; and Oosterman, 'Anthonis de Roovere: Het werk'. A new edition is in preparation by E. Strietman and J. Oosterman.

75 L. Scharpé, 'De Roovere's spel van "Quicunque vult salvus esse" ', *Leuvensche Bijdragen*, 4 (1900–2), 155–93 (at 184).

There is no lack at all in the clergy, / here in Flanders. So be aware of what you're saying. / They don't long for nice girls and models. / They have [as housekeepers] widows, washed out dolls, / Poor old women with barren genitals. / They don't do any corporal exercise, they don't make children. / They live in purity.

The only other surviving play involves a short dialogue between a young man and a married man. It is a striking development of a popular and topical theme: the relationship between men and women in the urban environment where economic transaction is dominant. And thus we are thrown right into the middle of subjects to which de Roovere often returns: everyday society, social abuses, concern for the working man and the poor, and anger over the abuse of power. But the largest group of poems is religious in character. The hymns to Mary form the core of them; and it is within these that de Roovere displays his poetic virtuosity at its best. While they may be the least favoured of his poems today, in his own time they elevated him to the status of a master of poetry. Within the literary culture of the 'Burgundian world', he can surpass the virtuosity of his contemporary Jean Molinet, who as a writer in French is far better known today.[76]

It is difficult to pigeonhole de Roovere's work. Besides the themes he addressed, the novelty of his poetry lies in the forms he chose. Few other poets experimented as de Roovere did. His work offers a sampling of complex poetic forms, artfully woven acrostics, complex rhyme schemes and surprising – sometimes affected – imagery. It suggests kinship with a wider literary world, and perhaps knowledge of contemporary theories of writing. Several French treatises written in the fifteenth century instruct poets on the writing of poetry, and on what forms, rhymes and metaphors they might deploy. One of the best known is the *Art de seconde rhétorique* by Jean Molinet, with whom de Roovere may have been acquainted since the Burgundian court poet was often present in Bruges.[77] Lodewijk van Gruuthuse quickly acquired a copy of this work for his library. Earlier, in 1432, Baudet Herenc wrote *Le doctrinal de la seconde rhétorique*. The poetics in this work are based on poetry from northern French cities, and it describes many forms that de Roovere himself came to use. De Roovere's work seems almost to constitute a Flemish realization of the possibilities that Herenc had outlined. It suggests again that an intimate relationship existed between French and Dutch literature in the cities of Burgundian Flanders.

[76] Oosterman, 'Tussen twee wateren zwem ik'.

[77] On the relationship between de Roovere and French literature, see ibid.

It is also difficult to pin a precise social label on de Roovere. He appears in many guises: slavish to authorities, but cynical, and also sensitive to the conditions of the common people of Bruges. He was a craftsman, but moved in circles that were in direct contact with the Burgundian rulers. It is therefore not surprising that in 1466 de Roovere received an annual stipend from the city of Bruges at the instance of Duke Charles the Bold. In his surroundings we might situate the translator of Christine de Pisan's *Book of the City of Ladies*, *Stede der vrauwen*, which was presented to Jan de Baenst, member of the Bruges nobility, who was de Roovere's patron when he acquired the stipend in 1466. De Roovere earned honour and income with his work, so he was not shy in praising the duke and the Bruges city council. But in his work another voice can be heard, that of compassion and fierce social criticism, echoing a longer tradition of such criticism within the urban environment. In this he seems to reflect the opinions of the 'middling groups', men like himself who were independent craftsmen, neither among the commercial elite nor among wage workers, critical of those who wielded power, but also of those who demanded its overthrow, advocating instead the guild and corporate ideals of charity and brotherhood.[78] But de Roovere's audience was diverse, and differently constituted for different works. This also explains the seemingly contradictory messages that are sometimes expressed. For a small circle of friends, he wrote New Year poems in which his audience is given personal encouragement. His audience was broader when he wrote poems for processions and other urban events.[79] His drama was often intended for a wider public, though there were also performances given within the restricted circle of a brotherhood. In 1474 de Roovere wrote a play for the brotherhood of Our Lady of the Snow for the annual guild meal held that year on 7 August.[80] Often we do not know for whom certain texts were intended. This applies to the *Excellente cronike van Vlaanderen*, largely the work of de Roovere. It is a fascinating mixture of a comprehensive genealogy of the counts of Flanders combined with a chronicle in which from about 1465 Bruges occupies a central place. The content seems particularly focused on the circle around the Bruges city council, a connection that is also suggested by the manuscript tradition: subsequent continuations

[78] J. Dumolyn and J. Haemers, '"Let Each Man Carry On with his Trade and Remain Silent": Middle Class Ideology in the Urban Literature of the Late Medieval Low Countries', *Cultural and Social History*, 10 (2013), 169–89. O. S. H. Lie, M. Meuwese, M. Aussems, H. Joldersma, Christine de Pizan in Bruges. Le Livre de la Cité des Dames as Het Bouc van de Stede der Vrauwen (Hilversum, 2015).

[79] S. Mareel, 'Politics, Mnemonics and the Verse Form: On the Function of the Poems in the *Excellente cronike van Vlaenderen*', in Blockmans et al. (eds.), *Staging the Court of Burgundy*, pp. 249–54.

[80] RAB, Onze-Lieve-Vrouw, 1531, fo. 135^r.

indicate involvement of later rhetoricians; and in the preserved copies and in the printed version that appeared in 1531, the chronicle was explicitly attributed to de Roovere.[81]

In the later fifteenth century, the printing press arrived, and in Bruges particularly, the possibilities of this new medium were soon explored. By 1474, Colard Mansion and William Caxton had set up a printing workshop. Mansion, originating from France, was active for years in Bruges as scribe and illuminator and had an elite clientele. He produced beautifully calligraphed and decorated books. He was very likely the first to experiment with the new medium. Caxton was secretary of the Merchant Adventurers in Bruges from 1462 and literary advisor of Margaret of York, and from 1471 to 1473 resided in Cologne where he must have learned the essentials of printing. Back in Bruges he produced the *The Recuyell of the Historyes of Troye* (c.1475), a book that catered for a cosmopolitan clientele. So did Mansion's de luxe French edition of Ovid's *Metamorphoses* (1484). Mansion printed sixteen incunabula between 1476 and 1484 but his output remained rooted in the tradition of the luxury book.[82] And while Caxton published in Latin and English – his *Recuyell* was the first printed book in the English language – and Mansion in Latin and French, a third printer in Bruges published in Latin and Dutch. Jan Bartoen, as the register of his guild tells us, came as a scribe from Brittany to Bruges: 'Jean Brito, escripvans, né de Bretagne'. From 1455 he was member of the St John's guild and from the mid 1470s onwards he experimented with the printing press. Only a few books have been preserved, but other sources show he must have collaborated

[81] J. Oosterman, 'De "Excellente cronike van Vlaenderen" en Anthonis de Roovere', *Tijdschrift voor Nederlandse Taal en Letterkunde* 118 (2002), 22–37; J. Dumolyn, J. Oosterman, T. Snijders et al., 'Rewriting Chronicles in an Urban Environment: The Middle Dutch 'Excellent Chronicle of Flanders' Tradition', *Lias: Journal of Early Modern Intellectual Culture and its Sources*, 41 (2014), 85–116.

[82] 'Willem Caxtoon' was gifted wine by the magistracy on 13 August 1469 (SAB, 277, 1468/9, fo. 82ᵛ). On Mansion's edition, see Bruges, OBB, 3877; L. Vandamme, 'De verzameling Mansion-drukken van de stadsbibliotheek Brugge', *Jaarboek van het Nederlands genootschap van bibliofielen*, 6 (1998), pp. 50–7; J.-C. Moisan and S. Vervacke, 'Les Métamorphoses d'Ovide et le monde de l'imprimé: La Bible des poëtes, Bruges, Colard Mansion, 1484', in E. Bury (ed.), *Lectures d'Ovide, publiées à la mémoire de Jean-Pierre Néraudau* (Paris, 2003), pp. 217–37; L. Vandamme, 'Colard Mansion et le monde du livre à Bruges', in P. Aquilon and T. Claerr (eds.), *Le berceau du livre imprimé: Autour des incunables* (Turnhout, 2010), pp. 177–86. For the relation between Caxton and Mansion, see L. Hellinga, 'William Caxton, Colard Mansion and the Printer in Type 1', *Bulletin du Bibliophile*, 1 (2011), 86–114. See also P. Saenger, 'Colard Mansion and the Evolution of the Printed Book', *Library Quarterly*, 35 (1975), 405–18. On the role of the early printing press in Bruges, see J. Oosterman, 'Discovering New Media: Anthonis de Roovere and the Early Printing Press', in A. Brown and J. Dumolyn (eds.), *Medieval Urban Culture* (Turnhout, 2017), pp. 171–82.

with rhetorician circles. His elegy on the death of Anthonis de Roovere is a moving proof of this. The first living Dutch author to see his work in print was in fact de Roovere himself. In 1478, not long after the first Dutch book was printed, a booklet by Gerard Leeu appeared in Gouda containing the *Lof van het Heilig Sacrament* by de Roovere, his most famous poem, that had a wide circulation, probably helped by the official consent given it by the Bruges clergy. Of all the versions, the printed one was the most special: it was a novelty that is difficult to appreciate today. De Roovere recognized immediately the possibilities of this new medium: he must have appreciated its potential to expand his audience greatly. The printing press flourished in Bruges, and for a while it was the most internationally oriented centre in Europe after Venice. But it lasted only for a short period. After Caxton left for Westminster and after the death of Bartoen around 1483, Mansion was the only printer in Bruges and his production sharply decreased. In the long run the printing press did not become successfully established in Bruges. The three men pioneering with a new medium knew perfectly the requirements of their elite clientele, but were not able to find the new public needed for the 'mass production' of printed books.[83]

De Roovere's connection with the early days of print might have heralded a new era of literary culture; but the work of another rhetorician recalls the textual traditions of a much earlier period. Romboudt de Doppere (d.1502) was a member of the Holy Spirit chamber in 1494, and a chronicler in his own right, but he was also a public notary, with a *scryfcamere* (scriptorium) in the Burg, and like Galbert of Bruges before him, he was associated with St Donatian's. He received an early education at the chapter's school and became a chantry chaplain (*kapelanie)* within the church. In his vernacular 'Complaint about the Land of Flanders' (1490), he bewailed the divisions of this time, and like other rhetoricians, called for charity and upholding of the common good; while in his Latin account of the period 1482 to 1498 he lamented, as Galbert had done, the tribulations and immorality that reigned in the Bruges of his day.[84]

Rhetoricians and the values they upheld tend to dominate textual production in Bruges in the fifteenth century, but there were other influences. Bruges did not become a significant centre of humanist learning until the sixteenth century (see Chapter 10), and it was not home to any early pioneers of Christian humanism: such men were often associated with the *Devotio moderna*, which was underrepresented in Bruges (at least in institutional

[83] Oosterman, 'Discovering New Media'.

[84] De Doppere, *Fragments*, e.g. p. 37; Callewier, 'Leven en werk'.

terms – see Chapter 8).[85] But other strands of humanism caught the attention of members of the lower and regular clergy in Bruges or its surroundings. The schoolmaster Jan van de Veren, active in nearby Oudenburg, was a proponent of free love, and in 1463 discussed Latin grammar with his Bruges colleague Nicasius Weyts. Weyts adhered to the teaching of Priscian, favoured at the Sorbonne, while Van de Veren preferred the *Elegantiae linguae Latinae* of Lorenzo Valla, which only appeared in print in 1473.[86] Johannes Crabbe, Cistercian abbot of the nearby Duinenabdij, and Rafael de Mercatellis, abbot of Oudenburg in Ghent but who spent his last years in Bruges, were important patrons and collectors of humanist manuscripts.[87] St Donatian's too included clergy who had interests in humanist scholarship: the school and singing masters Godefridus de Dommele and Alianus de Groote were responsible for the performance of Latin adaptations of Greek plays in the 1480s and 1490s.[88]

Jan van Eyck, Master Craftsmen and 'Mass Production'

Jan van Eyck (act. Bruges 1432–41) bought a house in Bruges in 1432, and shortly afterwards must have married Margaret, whose portrait is still preserved. His known dated paintings, such as the *Portrait of Arnolfini and his Wife* (1434) or the *Madonna with Canon Van der Paele* (1436), were therefore all executed in his Bruges workshop, where he must have worked with assistants.[89] His place within the canon of great painters has been secure ever since he was credited with the invention of oil painting by the Italian biographer of artists Giorgio Vasari.[90] Oil had already been used centuries

85 A. Dewitte, 'Het humanisme te Brugge: Een overtrokken begrip?', *HKZM*, 27 (1973), 5–26.

86 G. G. Meersseman, 'L'épistolaire de Jean van der Veren et le début de l'humanisme en Flandre', *Humanistica Lovaniensia*, 19 (1970), 119–200.

87 N. Geirnaert, 'Vlaamse cisterciënzers en Europese stadscultuur: Abt Johannes Crabbe en het cultureel leven in de Duinenabdij tijdens zijn bestuur (1457–1488)', unpublished PhD thesis, Catholic University of Leuven (Leuven, 2001).

88 Callewier, *De papen van Brugge*, pp. 315–17.

89 The scholarship on Van Eyck is vast, but see notably A. Châtelet, *Jean van Eyck enlumineur: Les heures de Turin et de Milan-Turin* (Strasbourg, 1993); P. Coremans (ed.), *L'agneau mystique au laboratoire, examen et traitement* (Antwerp, 1953); E. Panofsky, *Early Netherlandish Painting:Its Origins and Character*, 2 vols. (London, 1954), vol. I, pp. 178–264, vol. II, pp. 109–69; E. Dhanens, *Hubert and Jan van Eyck* (Antwerp, 1980); C. Harbison, *Jan van Eyck: The Play of Realism* (London, 1991); and O. Pächt, *Van Eyck and the Founders of Early Netherlandish Painting* (London, 1994).

90 The best edition is Giorgio Vasari, *Le vite de' piu eccellenti pittori, scultori e architettori: Nella redazioni del 1550 e 1568*, ed. R. Bettarini and P. Barocchi (Florence, 1966–71).

earlier as a binding agent for painting;[91] but only protein can be found in the two panel paintings from Bruges (*The Shrine of St Ursula* and *The Calvary of the Tanners*) that precede Jan van Eyck's first recorded visit to the city. Van Eyck's phenomenal improvement and mastery of the medium are undeniably evident when his works are compared to any older oil painting. The improvement lay in selecting linseed and walnut oil, and using them (sometimes body-heated) in mixtures with pigments. Moreover, Van Eyck found the right siccatives to speed up the extremely slow polymerization of oil paint. This he applied mainly in thin, translucent layers of glazes one on top of another, resulting in optically mixed colours that are bright, translucent and jewel-like. By these means an unlimited number of illusionistic effects could be created through which any material could be imitated. This turned painting in oil into such a workable practice that Van Eyck's use of it is indeed close to an 'invention'.[92] Bruges was thenceforward considered as the cradle of oil painting, a technique that determined the art of painting in the Western world until the twentieth century. Even during Van Eyck's lifetime, the technique successfully spread across Europe, though few painters could imitate Van Eyck's skill in execution.[93] So magisterial was his mastery, that Van Eyck was able to translate every specific detail of his close observation of nature into an accurate rendering. Every material he painted, whether it were skin, hair, metal, gems, vegetation, or even water, was represented with the greatest attention to its physical properties, specific texture and reflection of light. The breathtaking accuracy with which he achieved a convincing realism was also based on a thorough understanding of structure and visual perception. Moreover, he must have been a learned man, well informed in many areas of contemporary knowledge: physics, and especially optics, botany, anatomy, alchemy (as attested by his technique), the nature of mankind, and theology. These qualities were much appreciated by Duke Philip the Good, who from 1425 employed Van Eyck as a valet de chambre: when his financial administration hesitated to pay out the

[91] P. Brinkman, *Het geheim van Van Eyck: Aantekeningen bij de uitvinding van het olieverven* (Zwolle, 1993); Gotthold E. Lessing, 'Vom Alter der Ölmalerey aus dem Theophilus Presbyter', in H. Göpfert, K. Eibl, H. Gobel et al. (eds.), *Gotthold Ephraim Lessing: Werke*, 8 vols. (Munich, 1974), vol. VI, pp. 509–51.

[92] Karel van Mander, *Lives of the Illustrious Netherlandish and German Painters by Karel Van Mander*, ed. H. Miedema (Doornspijk, 1994–9). The original text can be consulted online at www.dbnl.org/tekst/mand001schi01_01 (fo. 199^{r}).

[93] T.-H. Borchert (ed.), *The Age of Van Eyck, 1430–1530: The Mediterranean World and Early Netherlandish Painting* [exh. cat.] (Ghent andAmsterdam, 2002); T.-H. Borchert (ed.), *Van Eyck to Dürer: Early Netherlandish Painting and Central Europe 1430–1530* [exh. cat.] (Tielt, 2010).

painter's salary, the duke feared that 'he would never be able to find someone who pleased him as much, as excellent in his art and his science.'

Van Eyck died in 1441, but the dominant artists who came after him in the city continued to contribute to Bruges' reputation as one of the most prominent centres of painting in Europe: 'Brugensis' would become an epithet synonymous with artistic quality. Petrus Christus (act. Bruges, 1444–76) is usually considered to be Van Eyck's only direct follower.[94] Originating from the Brabantine village of Baerle, he acquired Bruges citizenship in 1444. His doll-like figures, soft schematized drapery style and abbreviated painting technique deviate from the Eyckian model. His main achievement is the introduction of the Italian geometrical method of linear perspective, which he applied for the first time in 1457 (as far as is known) in his *Madonna Enthroned with Saints Jerome and Francis*.[95] A scene of a goldsmith in his workshop, long considered to be St Eloi, has been identified as a *Portrait of the Goldsmith Willem van Vleuten*, and can therefore be considered as an early precursor of the later genre of the 'portrait historié'.[96] Hans Memling (act. Bruges, 1465–94) originated from Seligenstadt in Hessen. His style and many of his compositions were adapted from the work of Rogier van der Weyden, in whose Brussels studio he most probably stayed shortly before settling in Bruges.[97] His portraits, with frail, elegant and almost emotionless sacred figures, often set in a dream-like summer landscape, strongly appealed to a broad clientele, to foreign merchants residing in Bruges, as well as to the local burgher elites, guild officials, and even charitable institutions like St John's hospital. For this hospital he painted several

[94] M. J. Friedländer, *Die altniederländische Malerei*, 14 vols. (Berlin, 1924–1937), vol. I, pp. 142–60; eng. trans. as *Early Netherlandish Painting* (Leiden, 1967); P. Schabacker, *Petrus Christus* (Utrecht, 1974); U. Panhans-Bühler, *Eklektizismus und Originalität im Werk des Petrus Christus* (Vienna, 1978); J. Upton, *Petrus Christus: His Place in Fifteenth-Century Flemish Painting* (Penn State University Park, 1990); M. P. J. Martens, 'New Information on Petrus Christus. Biography and the Patronage of the Brussels Lamentation', *Simiolus*, 20 (1990/91), 5–23; M. Ainsworth and M. P. J. Martens, *Petrus Christus, Renaissance Master of Bruges* (New York, 1994); Ainsworth (ed.), *Petrus Christus*; D. Martens, 'La "Madone à l'arcade" de Petrus Christus et ses doubles', *Revue Belge d'archéologie et d'histoire de l'art*, 64 (1995), 25–31; H. van der Velden, 'Petrus Christus's Our Lady of the Dry Tree', *Journal of the Warburg and Courtauld Institute*, 60 (1997), 89–110; H. van der Velden, 'Defrocking St Eloi: Petrus Christus' Vocational Portrait of a Goldsmith', *Simiolus: Netherlands Quarterly for the History of Art*, 26 (1998), 243–76.

[95] Ainsworth and Martens, *Petrus Christus*, pp. 136–9.

[96] Van der Velden, 'Defrocking'.

[97] The bibliography on Memling is vast: see for instance D. De Vos, *Hans Memling: The Complete Works* (New York, 1994); T.-H. Borchert (ed.), *Memling's Portraits* [exh. cat.] (New York, 2005); B. Lane, *Hans Memling: Master Painter in Fifteenth-Century Bruges* (Turnhout, 2009); T.-H. Borchert (ed.), *Memling: Rinascimento fiammingo* (Rome, 2014).

works, of which the most famous is the *Triptych of the Two Saint Johns*.[98] Artists during Memling's time simplified the Eyckian oil technique mainly by reducing the number of transparent glazes; and the work of some, such as the Master of the Lucy Legend, the Master of the Ursula Legend or the Master of the Baroncelli Portraits,[99] became almost caricature-like in their attempt to imitate the naturalism of their predecessors. Abundant references appear in their work to buildings in Bruges, rendered with relative topographical accuracy.[100] Gerard David (act. Bruges, 1484–1523), who had emigrated from Oudewater in Holland,[101] elaborated upon Memling's style through study of Van Eyck's works. This knowledge is visible in such works as the *Salviati Altarpiece*;[102] while in his famous *Judgment of Cambyses* (see Figure 9.6) he reworked the design of his Louvain predecessor Dirk Bouts.

Most patrons of these artists belonged to the city's commercial elites; and the majority of the artists were of a social status comparable to that of other skilled artisans.[103] But artistic production in fifteenth-century Bruges was not restricted to the work of a few celebrated painters or paintings; and it was underpinned by a large number of journeymen, working in workshops, most of whom never became master craftsmen. During the fifteenth century, about 29 per cent of the members of the corporation of image makers were immigrants from Burgundian territories and beyond, and many foreigners established their workshops in Bruges.[104] The French painters Jan Fabiaen, Didier de la Rivière, Pierre Coustain, and Jan de Hervy settled in Bruges, where they received commissions from the magistracy and other local institutions. Production was shaped by the conditions of the workshop and craft regulation (from which only court painters were exempted).

98 M. P. J. Martens, 'Patronage and Politics: Hans Memling's St. John Altarpiece and "the Process of Burgundization"', in H. Verougstraete and R. Van Schoute (eds.), *Le dessin sous-jacent dans le processus de création* (Louvain-la-Neuve, 1995), pp. 169–75.

99 A. Janssens de Bisthoven, D. De Vos, M. Baes-Dondeyne et al. (eds.), *Primitifs flamands anonymes: Maîtres aux noms d'emprunts des Pays-Bas Méridionaux du XVe et du début du XVIe siècle* [exh. cat.] (Tielt, 1969). A recent attempt to identify the Master of the Lucy Legend as Fransois van de Pitte and the Master of the Ursula Legend as Pieter Casenbroot – A. Janssens, 'De Meesters van de Lucia- en Ursulalegende: Een poging tot identificatie', *HGG*, 141 (2004), 278–331 – is not uncontested.

100 C. Harbison, 'Fact, Symbol, Ideal: Roles for Realism in Early Netherlandish Painting', in Ainsworth (ed.), *Petrus Christus*, pp. 21–34.

101 On Gerard David, see H. J. Van Miegroet, *Gerard David* (Antwerp, 1989); and M. W. Ainsworth, *Gerard David: Purity of Vision in an Age of Transition* (New York, 1998).

102 L. Campbell, *The Fifteenth-Century Netherlandish Paintings* (London, 2000), pp. 122–33.

103 M. P. J. Martens, 'Artistic Patronage in Bruges Institutions, c.1440–1482', unpublished PhD thesis, University of California (Santa Barbara, CA, 1992), pp. 27–30 and passim.

104 Schouteet, *De Vlaamse Primitieven*, p. 9; Martens, 'Artistic Patronage', p. 29. On immigration to Bruges during this period see above, Chapter 6.

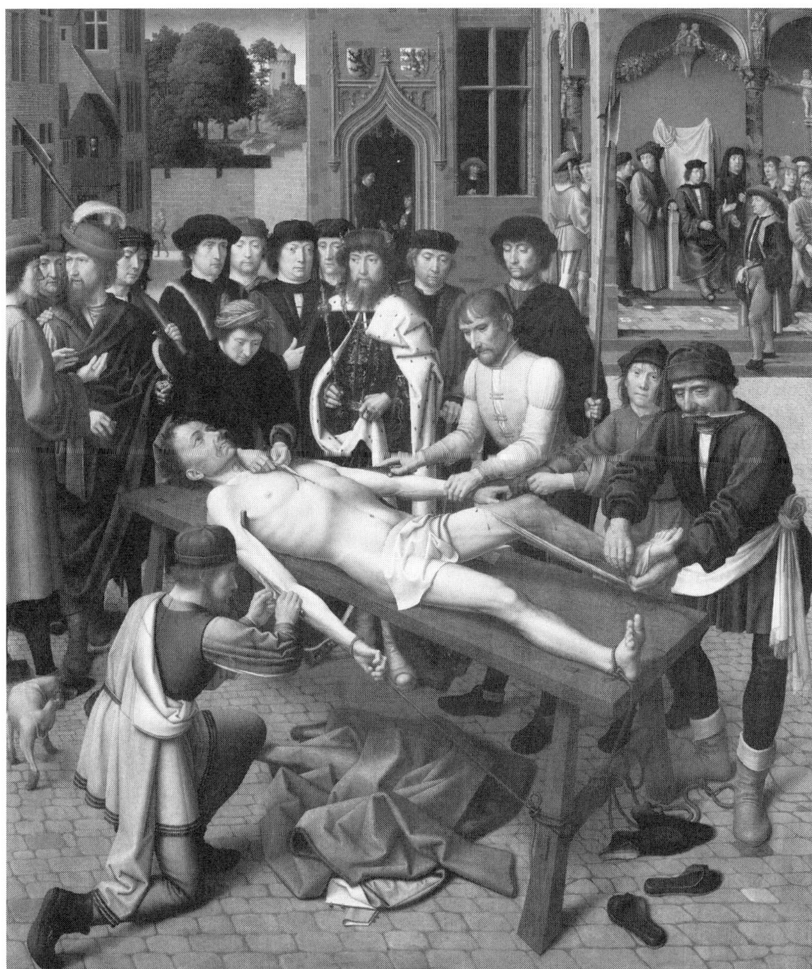

Figure 9.6 Gerard David, *The Judgment of Cambyses*, right panel (Bruges, Groeningemuseum)

Artists were allowed to have one shop and to exhibit part of their work at counters. The customer was protected by the corporation's control over the quality of the work and the materials used. When a work was commissioned from an artist, a contract was drawn up, listing the patron's wishes.[105] Few contracts from Bruges survive, though contracts from elsewhere reveal something about the relationship between artist and patron, and the control

[105] L. Campbell, 'The Art Market in the Southern Netherlands in the Fifteenth Century', *Burlington Magazine*, 118 (1976), 188–97 (at 192–4); and J. Dijkstra, 'Origineel en kopie: Een onderzoek naar de navolging van de Meester van Flemalle en Rogier van der Weyden', unpublished PhD thesis, University of Amsterdam (Amsterdam, 1990), pp. 7–10.

a client might exercise over the finished product.[106] They stipulated the nature of the work, its destination, and sometimes dimensions and iconographic details; occasionally, a model was submitted to be copied, or an existing work was mentioned as a standard of quality. Often the need to use materials of high quality was stressed. Each contract specified the price of the work and the terms of payment as well as the deadline for delivery and possible fines if the artist did not fulfil his obligation.

The significance of craft regulation to artistic production is particularly evident in book illumination. During the first half of the fifteenth century, the city continued to produce large quantities of books of hours, illuminated by artists such as those grouped under the name 'Gold Scrolls', both for the local market and export.[107] Of all the centres in the Netherlands, Bruges produced the greatest number of illuminated codices during the fifteenth century.[108] The intense and competitive activity of illuminators and other painters is highlighted by the long-running conflicts between different groups of them. The guild of librarians (those involved in the production of books, and a guild unique to Bruges),[109] quarrelled with the image makers over whether illuminators belonged to their respective trades.[110] Judicial decisions taken in 1402 and 1427 decided that miniaturists were free to work in the city, but also that illuminated books could be freely imported. This led again to a dispute about the illegal importing of single illuminated leaves, many of which came from Utrecht, upon which miniaturists were required to deposit a house mark.[111] Similar conflicts occurred repeatedly

106 These sources include payment records and court disputes. The dearth of contracts is related to procedures of the administrative organization of the municipal government. In Bruges, the task of legally confirming private contracts was delegated to the clerks of the municipal courtroom, and preservation of their archives did not begin until 1484: see A. Schouteet, *De klerken van de vierschaar te Brugge met inventaris van hun protocollen, bewaard op het Brugse Stadsarchief* (Bruges, 1973); and A. Vandewalle, *Beknopte inventaris van het Stadsarchief van Brugge*, vol. I: *Oud Archief* (Bruges, 1979), p. 93. The few contracts that do survive are clients' copies.

107 Smeyers et al. (eds.), *Naer natueren ghelike*, pp. 80–120; Smeyers, *Vlaamse miniaturen*, pp. 194–214, 234–54, 257–68.

108 Smeyers, *Vlaamse miniaturen*, pp. 99–134.

109 The guild's records begin in 1454: W. H. J. Weale, 'Documents inédits sur les enlumineurs de Bruges', *Le Beffroi*, 2 (1864–5), 298–319, and 4 (1872–3), 111–19, 238–337; and A. Vandewalle, 'Het librariërsgilde te Brugge in zijn vroege periode', in W. Le Loup (ed.), *Vlaamse kunst op perkament: Handschriften en miniaturen te Brugge van de 12de tot de 16de eeuw* [exh. cat.] (Bruges, 1981), pp. 39–43.

110 Smeyers et al. (eds.), *Naer natueren ghelike*, pp. 93–96; Vandewalle, 'Het librariërsgilde'.

111 B. Brinkmann, *Flämische Buchmalerei am Ende des Burgunderreiches: Der Meister des Dresdner Gebetbuchs und die Miniaturisten seiner Zeit* (Turnhout, 1997); T. Kren and S. McKendrick (eds.), *Illuminating the Renaissance: The Triumph of Flemish Manuscript Painting in Europe* [exh. cat.] (Los Angeles, CA, 2003).

among panel and canvas makers, in which the former always tried to control the trade and their market.[112] Panel painters maintained the monopoly on working in oils, while canvas painters bound their pigments with animal glue (tempera, *waterverve*). Bruges was evidently a place of opportunity for those involved in the book trade: in 1454, the miniaturist Willem Vrelant moved his workshop from Utrecht to Bruges;[113] and his example was followed in 1467 by Philippe de Mazerolles and in 1469 by Loyset Liédet, who were famous book illuminators from northern France. The first printers in Bruges, Colard Mansion and Jan Bartoen, were also immigrant scribes and illuminators. A significant number of illuminators working in Bruges during the second half of the fifteenth century remain anonymous, such as the Master of Margaret of York and the Master of the Dresden Prayer book.[114] Books of hours in particular were geared not only towards affluent residents of the city, but also towards many clients beyond Flanders, and are found throughout the Netherlands, in Italy, Spain, England and elsewhere. Their content, decoration and codicological features show standardization and highly rationalized production methods, for instance, tucked-in full-page miniatures, probably made on spec. The more lavish ones were commissioned and bore coats of arms or sometimes a kneeling donor accompanied by his or her patron saint in front of a religious scene. Of particular importance to the production of illuminated manuscripts in Bruges was the Burgundian court. Philip the Good actively began collecting from around 1445, and his patronage stimulated an unprecedented flowering of manuscript production in Bruges (as well as in Brussels, Ghent, Oudenaarde, Mons, Valenciennes, Hesdin and Lille).[115] The contribution of Bruges artists to the production of ducal manuscripts was substantial. The bibliophile

[112] Wolfthal, *Beginning of Netherlandish Canvas Painting*.

[113] B. Bousmanne, *"Item a Guillaume Wyelant aussi enlumineur": Willem Vrelant un aspect de l'enluminure dans les Pays-bas méridionaux sous le mécenat des ducs de Bourgogne Philippe le Bon et Charles le Téméraire* (Brussels, 1997).

[114] See G. Dogaer, *Flemish Miniature Painting in the Fifteenth and Sixteenth Centuries*, trans. A. E. C. Simoni et al. (Amsterdam, 1987). This reference work complements F. Winkler, *Die Flämische Buchmalerei des XV. und XVI. jahrhunderts: Künstler und Werke von den Briidern van Eyck bis zu Simon Bening* (Leipzig, 1925).

[115] On the Burgundian ducal library, see L. M. J. Delaissé, *Miniatures Médiévales de la librairie de Bourgogne au cabinet de mss de la Bibliothèque Royale de Belgique* (Geneva, 1959), pp. 1–20, 44–6; G. Dogaer and M. Debae (eds.), *La Librairie de Philippe le Bon: Exposition organisée a l'occasion du 500e anniversaire de la mort du duc* [exh. cat.] (Brussels, 1967), pp. 1–7; P. Cockshaw, C. Lemaire and A. Rouzet (eds.), *Charles le Téméraire: Exposition organisée a l'occasion du cinquième centenaire de sa mort* [exh. cat.] (Brussels, 1977), pp. 3–19; T. Kren and R. S. Wieck, *The Visions of Tondal from the Library of Margaret of York* (Malibu, 1990), pp. 8–18; and H. Wijsman, *Luxury Bound: Illustrated Manuscript Production and Noble and Princely Book Ownership in the Burgundian Netherlands (1400–1550)* (Turnhout, 2010).

interests of the dukes were emulated by other members of the court. Duchess Margaret of York, for instance, played a prominent role in the evolution of the production of de luxe manuscripts in Flanders during the last quarter of the century.[116] Other courtiers followed this example. After the dukes, Lodewijk van Gruuthuse was undoubtedly the greatest bibliophile in Flanders: 145 codices from his collection have been preserved.[117] Miniaturists who are commonly designated as the Ghent-Bruges school illuminated some of these.[118]

The close connections between different forms of visual art need to be emphasized. As discussed, the guild of image makers included a variety of different skills. The city's artists painted large altarpieces, objects for individual devotion, and portraits, but they also designed models for tapestries and goldsmiths' work.[119] Tapestries were woven (though not on the scale produced in Arras or Brussels) and retables and free-standing sculptures were carved.[120] Although most of this work is lost, a rare surviving work – the *Two Angels* by Tydeman Maes – attests to its unusually high quality.[121] The production of figurative brass tomb plates (serving the commemorative needs of burgher patrons) remained another traditional activity of local artists.[122] But most members of the image makers were not involved in the creation of 'high art'. The majority produced 'decorative work', often in the service of local institutions. Throughout the city, artists decorated public buildings, polychromed and gilded statues and fountains, and embellished them with the city's coats of arms and other heraldic motifs. Banners, flags and pennons – and in times of war, tents and artillery – all featured the Bruges lion (barry of eight gules and silver, a lion rampant azure). The court

116 On the duchess as a collector of manuscripts, see T. Kren (ed.), *Margaret of York, Simon Marmion and The Visions of Tondal* (Malibu, 1992).

117 M. P. J. Martens, 'De librije van Lodewijk van Gruuthuse', Martens (ed.), *Lodewijk van Gruuthuse*, pp. 113–47.

118 Kren and McKendrick (eds.), *Illuminating the Renaissance*, passim.

119 On Bruges tapestries, see Versyp, *De geschiedenis van de tapijtkunst*; and Delmarcel and Duverger, *Brugge en de tapijtkunst*. On goldsmiths' work, see D. Marechal (ed.), *Meesterwerken van de Brugse edelsmeedkunst* [exh. cat.] (Bruges, 1993).

120 On Bruges sculpture and decorative arts, see S. Vandenberghe, 'De Brugse beeldhouwkunst en sierkunst in Europa', in Vermeersch (ed.), *Brugge en Europa*, pp. 299–317; and S. Vandenberghe et al., *Vlaamse kunst in de 15de eeuw: Tentoonstelling van sculptuur, meubilair en kunstnijverheid uit de tijd van Lodewijk van Gruuthuse (ca. 1427–1492)* [exh. cat.] (Bruges, 1992).

121 Steyaert and Tahon-Vanroose (eds.), *Late Gothic Sculpture*, pp. 194–7; S. Kemperdick and F. Lammertse (eds.), *De Weg naar Van Eyck* [exh. cat.] (Rotterdam, 2012), pp. 212–13.

122 Vermeersch, *Grafmonumenten*; R. Van Belle, *Vlakke grafmonumenten en memorietaferelen met persoonsafbeeldingen in West-Vlaanderen: Een inventaris, funeraire symboliek en overzicht van het kostuum* (Bruges, 2006).

as well as the municipal authorities spent vast sums on the decorations for festivities and official ceremonies, entries of the duke, funerals of courtiers and high officials, chapter meetings of the Order of the Golden Fleece (held in Bruges in 1432, 1468 and 1478) and processions, jousts and banquets offered by the magistracy to visiting dignitaries and diplomatic emissaries.

Although many works of all kinds were still commissioned, the role of patrons in the Netherlands gradually became less important during the later fifteenth century. Many artists worked chiefly for the open market, producing a stock from which interested clients could choose, rather than taking prior commissions from individual patrons.[123] Works of art were exhibited in artists' shops or at counters on the street near the workshop. The exhibition of artworks at fairs is better known for Antwerp (by at least 1438 when Pero Tafur visited the local Franciscan friary to find 'todo lo de pintura' available for purchase). Direct documentary evidence of this increasing commercialization in contemporary Bruges is lacking, but statistical analysis of the available sources seems to indicate that the art market was undergoing transformation, especially during the last quarter of the century.[124] A turning point was perhaps reached about 1475. As we have already seen, certainly by 1482 the city council was collecting rents from stalls in the Pand, a gallery to display luxury products during fairs, held at the Franciscan church.[125] Towards the end of the fifteenth century and the beginning of the sixteenth, artists developed all sorts of price-cutting workshop practices. The size of an object, its utilitarian function, and the medium in which it was made played an important role in its possibilities for commercialization. Painters started to use uniform, repetitive background patterns and pricked drawings to duplicate compositions.[126]

[123] J.-P. Sosson, 'Une approche des structures économiques d'un métier d'art: La corporation des peintres et selliers de Bruges (Xve–XVIe siècles)', *Revue des archéologues et historiens d'art de Louvain*, 3 (1970), 91–100; Campbell, 'Art Market'; J. C. Wilson, 'Marketing Paintings in Late Medieval Flanders and Brabant', in X. Barral Altet (ed.), *Artistes, artisans et production artistique au Moyen Âge*, 3 vols. (Paris, 1986–90), vol. III, pp. 621–7; L. F. Jacobs, 'The Marketing and Standardization of South Netherlandish Carved Altarpieces: Limits on the Role of the Patron', *Art Bulletin*, 71 (1989), 208–29; D. Ewing, 'Marketing Art in Antwerp, 1460–1560: Our Lady's Pand', *Art Bulletin*, 72 (1990), 558–84; and J. M. Montias, 'Socio-Economic Aspects of Netherlandish Art from the Fifteenth to the Seventeenth Century: A Survey', *Art Bulletin*, 72 (1990), 358–73.

[124] For an evaluation of the situation in Bruges in light of preserved archival evidence, see Martens, 'Artistic Patronage', pp. 38–49.

[125] SAB, 216, 1482/3, fo. 40^{v}; J. C. Wilson, *Painting in Bruges at the Close of the Middle Ages* (Penn State University Park, 1998), p. 174.

[126] S. Goddard, *The Master of Frankfurt and his Shop* (Brussels, 1984); and S. Goddard, 'Brocade Patterns in the Shop of the Master of Frankfurt: An Accessory to Stylistic Analysis', *Art Bulletin*, 67 (1985), 401–17.

Sculptors assembled retables from standardized elements.[127] This enhanced productivity eventually caused a decrease in prices – which also stimulated the demand for works of art among a wider clientele.

Music for Clergy and Laity

In March 1442, the body of Jan van Eyck – 'solemnissimus pictor' – was moved from the parvis into the church of St Donatian's, next to the font:[128] the canons were among many in Bruges who held the painting of Jan van Eyck in high regard. But as an ecclesiastical institution, St Donatian's was more significant culturally for its production of sacred polyphonic music. Throughout the fifteenth century, the church was the most important place in the city for composition and performance. Several of its chaplains and canons were famous musicians holding their prebends in absentia, like the ducal singer Gilles Binchois (canon from 1430–68) and the papal singer and chaplain Guillaume Dufay (1397–1474, and canon from 1438). However, not all clerical staff were skilled in singing in descant.[129] Most of the musicians were 'clerici installati' or lay clerks, as was the case in the other churches of the city. Musical talent often gave entry into a promising church career (as Gilles Joye found – see Chapter 8), though in these circumstances, singers would need special dispensation to become a priest and be eligible for a chaplaincy. The clerk-musicians of St Donatian's – generally twelve in number from c.1440 – performed under the direction of the succentor and were sometimes complemented by the choirboys or the organ.[130] Singers from St Donatian's were highly esteemed: such was the demand for them from other Bruges churches that conflicts arose as a result of their absences from their own church. As St Donatian's fabric accounts reveal, the amplification of polyphonic practice through the training of 'chorales' and 'refectionales' necessitated frequent purchase of new descant books. Few sources now exist for the Bruges liturgy,[131] but new masses were composed every year for the

127 Jacobs, 'Marketing and Standardization', pp. 208–29.

128 BAB, A51, fo. 80^{r}.

129 A note on terminology: 'cantare' generally denotes the singing of plainsong, led by the cantor; 'decantare' and its derivatives indicate polyphony, led by the succentor or singing master.

130 On musical personnel in St Donatian's, see Strohm, *Music*, pp. 18–27; H. Callewier, 'The Clergy of Bruges and the Musical Chapel of the Dukes of Burgundy' in Blockmans et al. (eds.), *Staging the Court of Burgundy*, pp. 215–20.

131 For the exceptional *processionale* of the *Wijngaard* beguines (early sixteenth century), see in Brussels, Koninklijke Bibliotheek, Ms. IV 210, and Bruges, Archives of the Confraternity of the Holy Blood, Register 15; see B. Haggh, 'The Beguines of Bruges and the Procession of

collective celebrations of St Donatian's clergy by their succentor, from 1475/6 at the latest – for the Feast of the Cripples ('festum claudorum'), which included a procession to Aardenburg – and from 1489 for the Feast of the Ass-Bishop.[132] Endowments by benefactors, both clerical and lay, were crucial for the expansion of polyphonic practice, particularly for the elaboration in use of motets.[133] Individual canons funded the foundation of masses (Simon de Coene funded a suite of four masses in honour of St Donatian during the octave of his feast day in 1439[134] – shortly after the canon Van De Paele had commissioned his altarpiece, showing the same saint, from Jan van Eyck). Wealthy citizens commissioned music just as they commissioned paintings, for their commemorative needs. At first, mainly single motets and separate parts of the mass ordinary were endowed, but starting from 1460, cyclic mass settings (a unified polyphonic setting of all five parts of the mass ordinary), as well as other liturgical texts such as the Magnificat and Te Deum, were frequently required in St Donatian's. Within fewer than thirty years, from 1463 to 1491, ninety-one complete masses and thirty-six Magnificat settings were copied, besides many other works, though hardly a fragment of these manuscripts has survived.

Some of the most famous Bruges votive masses were composed by Jacob Obrecht, succentor at St Donatian's between 1485 and 1491 and again from 1498 till 1500.[135] His *Missa de Sancto Martino* was probably composed in 1486 for the endowment by Obrecht's colleague Pierre Basin.[136] Obrecht's *Missa de Sancto Donatiano* and *Missa graecorum*, however, have been traced to other churches, respectively St James' and the Jerusalem chapel of the Adornes family.[137] A particularly detailed example of an obit service with a polyphonic mass setting, demonstrating the experimentation invested

the Holy Blood', in P. Mannaerts (ed.), *Beghinae in cantu instructae – Music Patrimony from Flemish Beguinages (Middle Ages – Late 18th C.)* (Turnhout, 2010), pp. 27–50. For an overview of existing liturgical sources, see J. Bloxam, 'A Survey of Late Medieval Service Books from the Low Countries: Implications for Sacred Polyphony, 1460–1520', unpublished PhD thesis, Yale University (New Haven, CT, 1987), pp. 10–21.

132 See Chapter 8.

133 On foundations, feasts and polyphony, see Strohm, *Music*, pp. 29–31, 33–6. On memorials and motets, see Nosow, *Ritual Meanings*, pp. 105–34.

134 BAB, A51, fos. 13^{v}, 96^{r}.

135 On Obrecht, see amongst others R. Wegman, *Born for the Muses: The Life and Masses of Jacob Obrecht* (Oxford, 1994); and R. Wegman, 'Obrecht and Erasmus', *Journal of the Alamire Foundation*, 3 (2011), 9–126.

136 Strohm, *Music*, pp. 40–1; Wegman, *Born for the Muses*, pp. 165ff.

137 Strohm, *Music*, pp. 146–7; D. Bouzianis, 'Jacob Obrecht's Mysterious *Missa graecorum*', in J. Daverio and J. Ogasapian (eds.), *The Varieties of Musicology: Essays in Honor of Murray Lefkowitz* (Warren, MI, 2000), pp. 47–64.

in sacred music, is the foundation of the furrier and politician Donaas de Moor (d.1483), possibly first observed in 1487 on 14 October, the Feast day of St Donatian himself.[138] At seven o'clock in the morning, six singers were to celebrate de Moor's anniversary with the priest, deacon and subdeacon as well as the great organ, amidst the continuous tolling of bells. The service was based on the liturgy for Confessor Bishops and included the sequence *Dies nobis reparatur* recalling the saint's death and miracles. The final adornment, a polyphonic setting of the ordinary texts, was probably composed by Obrecht: the *Missa de Sancto Donatiano*.[139] Obrecht's polyphonic work punctuated the plainsong rendition of the texts of the mass proper. The composition is – like most masses at the time – a *cantus firmus* mass (a mass with at least one pre-existing melody in one or more voices). Obrecht based his composition on several chant melodies in honour of St Donatian: the suffrage antiphon *O beate pater Donatiane*, a plea for intercession befittingly combined with the *Kyrie* text but also employed in the *Sanctus* and its *Osanna*, and in the *Agnus Dei*; the responsory *Confessor Domini Donatianus* in the *Gloria*; another responsory and plea for intercession, *O sanctissime presul*, and the O-antiphon *O clavis David* in the *Credo*. Chant and polyphony thus interacted and together presented a complete narrative of St Donatian's life on a musical basis. Most remarkably, Obrecht combined the otherwise unknown Dutch song *Gefft den armen gefangen umb Got* (Give to the poor prisoners for God's sake) with *O beate pater Donatiane* in the second *Kyrie*, seemingly a reminder for the community to give alms to the poor of the *donkercamer* or prison. Obrecht further included musical references to the famous Johannes Ockeghem's *Missa Ecce ancilla Domini*, and the Virgin's role in the incarnation of Christ. The full meaning of the mass foundation, and in particular the role of the Virgin, was also clarified by a small triptych, painted by the Master of the Lucy Legend, that also adorned the chapel: its depiction of the Lamentation, flanked by portraits of Donaas de Moor and his wife and their patron saints, allowed the deceased de Moor a vicarious presence at the service.

Citizens contributed individually but also collectively to the expansion of liturgical music. Their guilds and fraternities were often required to oversee the foundations set up by their members (the furriers among others in the case of de Moor's); and they also endowed services themselves, especially on their patrons' or other major feast days. The earliest mention of polyphony

[138] RAB, Sint-Jacobs, 447.

[139] For the following, see J. Bloxam, 'Text and Context: Obrecht's *Missa de Sancto Donatiano* in its Social and Ritual Landscape', *Journal of the Alamire Foundation*, 3 (2011), 11–36; based on Strohm, *Music*, pp. 146–7.

in St James' church, for example, is in the barbers' endowment of 1432 that included a motet sung by the children at the altar of Sts Cosmas and Damian ('according to old custom') and a polyphonic high mass with six or seven singers and organ on 26 September.[140] The foundations requiring vocal music that accumulated in St James' during the fifteenth century outstripped the vocal resources of the church, and the succentor frequently hired singers from elsewhere, no fewer than eighteen for the procession on Corpus Christi day in 1467.[141] The absence of most fraternity accounts prevents detailed assessment of their musical needs. One fraternity better documented is that of Our Lady of the Dry Tree which had its chapel in the Franciscan friary: from 1396 it paid the friars to celebrate daily mass, a Sunday mass sung in descant in honour of Our Lady, and Marian feasts with polyphony.[142] While the confraternity had several friar-singers among its members, it also hired singers from other churches.

Foreign merchants were patrons of music as well as paintings. The fragmentary Lucca choirbook, once a magnificent parchment manuscript, as large as contemporary account books of the city treasury, was commissioned in Bruges around 1463, intended as a gift from the banker Giovanni Arnolfini to the cathedral of Lucca.[143] It reflects the breadth of religious repertory that was used at institutions in Bruges: this included a strong representation of English music, with masses by Walter Frye among others, and it also features chansons by Gillis Joye. English influences appear in other compositions connected to Bruges, like the anonymous three-voice motet *O sanctissime presul Christi Donatiane* (Trent, codex 92). A similar mass repertoire as that in the Lucca choirbook forms the oldest layer of manuscript Brussels, Royal Library MS 5557, which was probably copied in Bruges or Damme on the occasion of the 1468 wedding of Charles the Bold to Margaret of York and remained in use at the Bruges Prinsenhof chapel.[144]

The needs of the ducal household in Bruges made a significant impact on the musical landscape. The court chapel frequently used singers from St Donatian's, whose clergy sung at requiem masses in their church for dukes, their family and household. Other churches in Bruges were the recipients

140 RAB, Charters with blue numbers, 8128; SAB, 450, St Jacob: *Registrum sepulturarum novum*, fo. 3^{r-v}. See also Nosow, *Ritual Meanings*, pp. 127–8; and above, Chapter 8.

141 RAB, Sint-Jacobs, 24 (Rekeningen 1443–67), fo. 85^{r}.

142 R. Strohm, 'Muzikaal en artistiek beschermheerschap in het Brugse Ghilde vanden Droghen Boome,' *Biekorf*, 83 (1983), 5–18.

143 See R. Strohm (ed.), *The Lucca Choirbook* (Chicago, IL, 2009).

144 R. Wegman, 'New Data Concerning the Origins and Chronology of Brussels, Koninklijke Bibliotheek, Manuscript 5557', *Tijdschrift van de Vereniging voor Nederlandse Muziekgeschiedenis*, 36 (1986), 5–25.

of large polyphonic endowments, such as Our Lady's in 1451 from Philip the Good for the day following the Assumption, which specified that bell-ringing for the service be 'grande et notable'. This began a tradition of courtly endowment of Our Lady's church, culminating in the massive annuity fixed by Archduke Maximilian in 1496 for Mary of Burgundy's foundation, which established two daily polyphonic masses. Sound, vocal and instrumental, was also needed for more secular occasions: the wedding feast of Charles the Bold in 1468 was only one of many events that drafted musicians into princely celebration.[145]

The civic magistracy also demanded musical accompaniment for official occasions in Bruges, even more regularly than princes. Watchmen had once been employed for the double duty of signalling alarm and music making, but their functions became more specialized. From 1457 the city began to employ permanently a designated minstrel group of four to five players (a tradition that continued until 1761).[146] They formed an 'alta capella' or loud ensemble, consisting of several shawms and a sackbut. The ensemble performed at the many official occasions, whether stationary (from balconies on the Belfry and the city hall, on the Market Square, or in banquet halls), or in ad hoc processions (such as those made with the visiting relic of St Godelieve of Gistel on 6 and 30 July 1489).[147] From 1483 the ensemble also performed in St Donatian's after the *Lof* or *Salve* on the free-market days, a polyphonic service that the city government subsidized for the benefit of 'every citizen'.[148] Throughout the fifteenth century, regular subsidy continued for trumpeters on Holy Blood day. But municipal employment of minstrels was dependent on other well-established structures within the city. Learning the art of instrumental performance was based on oral culture and generally passed from father to son or through an apprentice living in the house of his master (like the two children whom Antheunis Pavillon taught to play the flute).[149] This stands in stark contrast to the training of

145 AGR, Trésor de Flandre, 1er série, 1698; and see Nosow, *Ritual Meanings*, pp. 106–18. For an overview, see Strohm, *Music*, pp. 92–101 and Callewier, 'The Clergy of Bruges'.

146 SAB, 96, 11, fo. 325r (referenced in Gilliodts-Van Severen, *Ménestrels*, pp. 44, 161).

147 Carton (ed.), *Het boeck*, pp. 286–7, 295; SAB, 216, 1488–89, fo. 161v; see N. Gabriëls, 'Bourgeois Music Collecting in Mid Sixteenth-Century Bruges: The Creation of the Zeghere van Male Partbooks (Cambrai, Médiathèque Municipale, MSS 125–128)', unpublished PhD thesis, Catholic University of Leuven (Leuven, 2010), pp. 188–9.

148 See Chapter 8. The payment for the market performance was higher than that for the *Salve* service (2 pounds 10s groten as opposed to 25s groten), indicating the higher importance of the former. St Donatian's singers (for instance the succentor Jeronimus de Clibano in 1496) also received payment for singing the *Lof*, 'daer in begrepen tluden, oorghelen ende luminaris' (SAB, 216, 1495–96, fo. 226v). See also Strohm, *Music*, pp. 39, 85–6.

149 The city subsidized various children to be educated in instrumental performance.

singing skills, which was more closely connected to written culture and increasingly went hand in hand with instruction in the theory of musical language (solmization, interval and modal theory). The minstrel schools were an important musical resource: their purpose was to exchange repertoire, while also providing excellent opportunities for training and for trading musical instruments, and they therefore made a major impact on musical practice.[150]

As municipal patronage shows, not all needs for music were sacred in character, and other groups in the city generated music for more secular occasions. Craft guilds, the shooting guilds and the jousters required trumpeters and other instrumentalists for their festivities: the St George crossbowmen sang mass in their chapel on their papagay day, but bell-ringers and trumpeters announced their progress from guildhouse to their competition venue.[151] May festivities are recorded in more detail in the fifteenth century, and involved burghers, courtiers and clergy. On the eve of 1 May, young men from all echelons of society presented girls with 'mayflowers', often accompanying the gift with a song.[152] Thomas Fabri, succentor at St Donatian's 1412–15, composed a courtly three-voice rondeaux-refrain *Die may so lieflic wol ghebloyt* (exceptional for its unusual disposition of three low voices, perhaps for performance by a small male group, and with instruments as depicted in later miniatures).[153] The Bruges courtly household picked up the May song tradition and may well have been the cradle for the French polyphonic May song represented by works, for instance, of Guillaume Dufay.[154]

Urban Cultural Networks

The many forms of cultural media in Bruges varied in their genres or patrons, but there were ways in which they were connected. Mass services (such as the performance of Obrecht's *Missa de Sancto Donatiano* before the de Moor altarpiece) involved an organic combination of more than one

[150] R. Wegman, 'The Minstrel School in the Late Middle Ages', *Historic Brass Society Journal*, 14 (2002), 11–30.

[151] The 'old' guild of St George owned two trumpets, and the 'young' guild, unusually, a 'claroen' (SAB, 385, Register, fo. 77^{v} (undated entry); SAB 385, II/11, 1459–1579, fo. 3^{r}.

[152] According to the Italian translator (see below) of the Chronicle of Flanders in 1452: see Oosterman, 'Ik bring u de mei', p. 173.

[153] Strohm, *Music*, p. 109.

[154] Ibid., p. 100.

medium; Holy Blood processions, like the marriage festivities in 1468, were visual as well as auditory experiences, drawing on artists and dramatists as well as musicians. The uses of text, image and sound were often interlinked within the urban context: supply and demand of many artistic products share features in common, as do the networks of cultural exchange that influenced their nature or facilitated their diffusion.

The wider influences on culture in the city reflected the many networks of exchange in which Bruges had long been situated. Parisian styles and north Italian techniques were known to Bruges artists; French poetic forms were familiar to its rhetoricians. Conversely, the works of Flemish masters influenced the Quattrocento;[155] the music of Flemish composers was well known in Italian courts.[156] Some of these exchanges were the result of commercial connections: certain artistic products of Bruges (the Lucca choirbook) were exported along with other commodities, finding their way to the distant homelands of Bruges' foreign merchants. Paintings could also follow well-travelled mercantile routes. Two of Hans Memling's known commissions, a *Madonna and Child* and *The Last Judgment*, came from Medici bankers in Bruges, and were both dispatched to Florence, though the latter, captured by pirates off Gravelines, never reached its destination.[157] Similar foreign connections perhaps allowed Bruges to serve as a conduit of early humanism, even if the city was not a centre of humanist study: two Venetian humanists, the Franciscan Antonio Gratia Dei and Hermolaus Barbarus, delivered classical orations in 1486. Other influences on culture in Bruges reflect the city's position within a more localized but intense urban network of cultural and commercial exchange in the Low Countries and northern France. The repeated prohibition of detached illuminations from Utrecht indicates the significance of regular commercial links with Dutch towns. The cycle of festive competitions organized by the rhetoricians in the fifteenth century was foreshadowed by inter-town jousting and shooting competitions; the continuing influence of French poetry, and attraction of Bruges to French poets, reflect a long tradition of cosmopolitanism even in vernacular literary culture.

Other important links with the outside world were created by the dynastic interests of its rulers, and by their burgeoning courts. Comital and noble patronage had earlier brought French romances to burgher attention. The temporary eclipse of the French Valois court in Paris from 1418 made it less

155 Borchert (ed.), *Age of Van Eyck*.

156 R. Strohm, *The Rise of European Music, 1380–1500* (Cambridge, 1993), pp. 153–81, 561–2, 597–607.

157 De Vos, *Hans Memling*, pp. 82–9.

attractive for artists in search of work, and many (among them Van Eyck) turned to other princely patrons further north. The Burgundian ducal household increasingly resided in the towns of Flanders and Brabant from the 1430s, and in Bruges within a revamped Prinsenhof; but they remained peripatetic, and their dynastic interests opened up other pathways of exchange. The diplomatic needs of Philip the Good sent Van Eyck to the court of the king of Portugal in 1428 and to the peace negotiations at Arras in 1435, resulting in the portraits of Isabella of Portugal and perhaps Cardinal Albergati. The growing magnificence of the Burgundian dukes' own court and household attracted the admiration of ambassadors from Italy, while their diplomatic and marriage ties with the Lancastrian and Yorkist monarchies brought English musicians to cities in which the dukes resided, Bruges among them.

While artistic exchange was facilitated by secular rulers, it was significantly increased also by the continuing importance of ecclesiastical networks within a universal church. The mendicant orders carried a spirituality that found its way into the early illuminated manuscripts produced in Bruges. The presence and cosmopolitan character of St Donatian's canons meant links to the highest ecclesiastical circles, such as those of Jean Gerson. Even the Papal Schism after 1378, which Gerson laboured to heal, did not necessarily fragment spiritual movements and cultural ties within Europe. The many church councils that met in the wake of the Schism brought clergy from different regions together: a trend to universality in fifteenth-century polyphony, albeit with local dialects, reflects the mobility between churches, councils and curia that was possible for musicians, such as Thomas Fabri, Gilles Binchois or Guillaume Dufay.[158] Artists and musicians also travelled along the traditional spiritual highways of Christendom: Van Eyck made pilgrimages to Santiago de Compostela, and (possibly) to Rome and Jerusalem. His landscapes are often thought to reflect visits to exotic locations, and his now lost *Mappa mundi* was reputedly so precise that distances between the places shown on it could even be measured.[159]

The many networks of cultural exchange in which Bruges was situated helped stimulate creativity, but the scale of cultural production in Bruges was dependent on the city's capacity to support such production.

[158] Strohm, *Rise of European Music*, pp. 3, 17, 145, 153–81.

[159] According to the Italian Bartolomeo Fazio: M. Baxandall, 'Bartolomaeus Facius on Painting', *Journal of the Warburg and Courtauld Institute* 27 (1964), 90–107 (at 102–3); J. Paviot, 'La Mappemonde attribuée à Jan van Eyck par Facio: Une pièce à retirer de son oeuvre', *Revue des Archéologues et Historiens d 'Art de Louvain*, 24 (1991), 57–62.

As explained above, infrastructures underpinning the manufacture of luxury goods were already in place by the mid fourteenth century: Bruges had become an international centre of commerce, attracting foreign merchants whose credit needs were met by local brokers and hostellers. Expertise in finance available in Bruges perhaps allowed specialist craftsmen, like painters, to invest in workshops; but the emergence of the image makers' guild was part of a shift in the local economy of the late fourteenth century from textile production to manufacture and trade in consumable and luxury goods (see Chapter 6). Books, illuminations and paintings depended on multiple workshops and craftsmen, and a degree of flexibility in guild structure.[160] The composite skills brought together under the guild of image makers were perhaps conducive to the development of new techniques. The ability of so many non-local journeymen to buy 'citizenship' and enter craft guilds in Bruges was important in boosting supply of reserve and specialist labour; and their attraction to Bruges was strengthened by the city's prosperity. Craft workshops would also facilitate the growth of an art market, making it possible for a wider clientele to purchase paintings more cheaply as finished products. The multimedia events of the Burgundian dynasty were entirely dependent on access to the widest possible array of artistic production, which in the mid fifteenth century was best available in Bruges. They also leant on the structures and resources of ecclesiastical centres: the production of sacred polyphonic music, requiring rood loft, organ and trained singers as well as scriptoria producing books of polyphony, was best supplied by large collegiate churches such as St Donatian's.

Supply of products was generated by demand. Part of the international demand for Bruges paintings was stimulated indirectly by ducal patronage. Duke Philip commissioned few panel paintings from Jan van Eyck, but his admiration of the painter conferred on Eyckian art the imprimatur of prestige. Such was the trend-setting magnificence of the Burgundian court that other rulers sought to acquire its trappings, sometimes doing so through commercial networks: in 1444/5 the king of Aragon's agent instructed a merchant from Valencia, residing in Bruges, to purchase at auction a painting (now lost) of St George by Van Eyck – 'lo gran pintor del illustre duch de Burgunya'.[161] Yet paintings such as this were also made to meet spiritual needs, and these too were widespread. Mendicant spirituality from

[160] P. Stabel, 'Selling Paintings in Late Medieval Bruges: Marketing Customs and Guild Regulation Compared', in N. De Marchi and H. J. Van Miegroet (eds.), *Mapping Markets for Paintings in Europe, 1450–1750* (Turnhout, 2006), pp. 89–103.

[161] Campbell, 'Art Market,' p. 197.

northern Italy had travelled well, continuing to be influential in many parts of fifteenth-century Europe; and new currents of devotion from the northern Low Countries and Rhineland (the *Devotio moderna*) spread south. The appeal of 'realistic' paintings of devotional subjects by Bruges artists to a clientele well beyond the city and the county of Flanders was partly that they spoke to meditative tastes which were similar in many regions.[162] As altarpieces, panel paintings also served commemorative needs that were ubiquitous in late medieval Christendom. So too did polyphonic masses. One of the earliest preserved foundation texts for such a mass was installed by the banker and merchant Dino Rapondi from Lucca in 1417, for the Feast of St John at the Latin Gate (6 May) and following the custom of polyphony on the Feast of St Machut and St Leonard.[163] Books of hours made for foreign clientele were adapted for the liturgical usages of the dioceses to which they were exported. Less transferable (at least beyond the Low German and Dutch-speaking world) were works written in the Middle Dutch vernacular – although part of the Chronicle of Flanders (containing the oldest known map of Flanders) was translated by an Italian who languished for a time in the city prison as a debtor.[164]

Foreign demand, and the many networks of exchange that linked Bruges to a wider world, help to explain the city's cultural vitality, but of greater importance in creating demand were the presence and needs of a variety of patrons and clientele within the city itself. Bruges catered to the requirements of its rulers when they were present. The Dampierre counts, whose visits and residence in Bruges became more prolonged in the second half of the fourteenth century, were hearty consumers of builders, painters and musicians.[165] The voracious appetite of the Burgundian dukes for singers, artists and writers was of particular importance from the 1440s when Bruges (after Brussels) became the duke's most favoured residence. Yet the direct impact of ducal patronage was perhaps more limited than might first

[162] For the admiration of Alessandra Strozzi in 1460 for the 'beauty' of a Holy Face painted in Bruges in 1460, see C. E. Gilbert, *Italian Art 1400–1500: Sources and Documents* (Englewood Cliffs, NJ, 1980), pp. 117–18.

[163] M. Monteyne, 'Foundations and their Impact on the Flourishing of Polyphony: Case-study of a Foundation at the Collegiate Church of Saint Donatian in Bruges by Dyno Rappondi, Merchant of Lucca', *Yearbook of the Alamire Foundation* 3 (1999), 121–33. Whether the music was specially composed for this foundation remains unclear.

[164] Bruges, OBB, Ms. 685, 'Cronache de singniori di Fiandra e de loro advenimenti' (c.1452); S. Corbellini, 'Cronache de singniori di Fiandra: Een Italiaanse kroniek van Vlaanderen', *HGG*, 134 (1997), 102–11. This text (one copy), though, was probably made for private use.

[165] M. Vale, *The Princely Court: Medieval Courts and Culture in North-West Europe 1270–1380* (Oxford, 2001), esp. pp. 155–9, 271–3, 292.

appear.[166] Burgundian patronage was spread over several towns in Flanders and Brabant; and it did not benefit all crafts equally, for some served their princely requirements better than others. As a cheaper medium, panel painting did not communicate magnificence as eloquently as tapestries, goldwork or illuminated manuscripts. The impact of ducal patronage in stimulating demand was more significant for its indirect effects. The presence of the comital household in earlier periods had no doubt encouraged the production of 'luxuries' as well as an early taste among burghers for chivalric romances; the presence of the Burgundian court sharpened a desire to 'live nobly' ('vivre noblement').[167] The prestige conferred on Van Eyck's art by ducal patronage stimulated commissions from 'court functionaries', often with iconography and details that reflected their social standing as well as religious needs; and their patronage in turn was emulated by their social inferiors. Indirectly, Duke Philip may have contributed to the influx of fresh talent by lowering the fees for citizenship in the 1440s (from which Petrus Christus benefited).

The importance of the Burgundian presence to cultural life in Bruges can be overstated. What distinguished the city from others in the region was the greater variety and number of other potential patrons: foreign merchants, local and regional nobility, wealthy clergymen, and in particular a finely gradated range of native burghers from the commercial elite to masters of crafts (see Chapter 6). In addition to this, were the various institutions, associations and locations – nodes in cultural networks – that brought these groups into close and productive contact with each other: the Bourse square, the houses of hostellers and 'lodges' of nations, as well as the collegiate, parish, hospital and mendicant churches, in which craft guilds and devotional fraternities maintained their altars. A hotspot of cultural creativity, in the middle years of the fifteenth century, was the parish and neighbourhood of St James', a short step from the Prinsenhof. The church was being rebuilt and endowed with new chapels and services, generating altar paintings and polyphony, by ducal bankers, Italian merchants, native burghers (de Moor among them) and craftsmen (furriers, butchers, coopers, masons and barbers).[168] The Franciscan friary accommodated the confraternity of Our Lady of the Dry Tree which paid for regular polyphonic masses. Its

166 Stabel, 'For Mutual Benefit'.

167 Wilson, *Painting in Bruges*, pp. 13–86.

168 Strohm, *Music*, pp. 56–8; A. Dewitte, 'Zangmeesters, organisten en schoolmeesters aan de Sint-Jacobparochie te Brugge 1419–1591: Bronnen en literatuur', *Biekorf*, 72 (1971), 332–49. See also Chapter 8.

members from the 1460s onwards included men and women, nobles, burghers, foreign merchants, clergy and many artists and musicians, such as the painters Petrus Christus and Gerard David, the ducal singers Adriaen Basin and Jean Cordier, and the organists Claeys Grape and Jacob Honin.[169] The importance of confraternities for stimulating cultural synergies can be exaggerated: their members did not meet often (since attendance at feast days or banquets was not a requirement). There were also other venues in which burghers gathered more regularly and intimately, for whose activities there are now only traces. The Poorters Loge, built in the early fifteenth century (see Chapter 4), was evidently a lively place of entertainment, drinking and conviviality among a burgher elite. Not insignificant were smaller, household groups, whose meetings may have offered social and spiritual refreshment. The intimate group responsible for the poems and songs of the Gruuthuse manuscript was perhaps one of several for which evidence is scarce. Another might have been the household of Anselmus Adornes: the pilgrimages he made with his son Jan to Rome and Jerusalem in 1470–1 were written up in a book that served as a practical guide as well as a text for spiritual meditation. He also owned a prayer book that was evidently shared by others; in fact the family's Jerusalem chapel seems to have operated as a kind of public library, and included texts with humanist interests.[170] Amateur musical groups may not have been uncommon: the set of partbooks copied out by the textile merchant Zeghere van Male in the sixteenth century (see Chapter 10) suggests a strong knowledge of polyphony among burgher circles that was perhaps long ingrained.

The decorative work on which so many artists were engaged also points to demands of a different kind.[171] Although an open art market was expanding in the later fifteenth century, the importance of institutional patronage, serving a public function, should not be underestimated. The court, but also the city magistracy, had representational needs. Pierre Coustain, a court painter who worked on decorations for the 1468 wedding festivities, was paid by the city for decorating public buildings and props in entry

[169] For various lists and guild names, see SAB, 505; A. Dewitte, 'De 173 ghildebroeders van Onser Vrauwe vanden Droghebome 1498', *Biekorf*, 99 (1999), 149–59.

[170] For the pilgrimage book, see Bruges, Archives of the OCMW, Register 1 (Handschrift, 1491–2). See www.historischebronnenbrugge.be for literature on this text. Adornes also owned a panel, bequeathed to his daughter in 1470, on which a St Francis was depicted 'by the hand of Jan van Eyck'. On the Jerusalem chapel library, see N. Geirnaert, 'De bibliotheek van de Jeruzalemkapel te Brugge, tot ca. 1465', *Biekorf*, 89 (1989), 313–21; A. Derolez, 'Vroeg humanisme en middeleeuwse bibliotheken: De bibliotheek van de Adornes en van de Jeruzalemkapel te Brugge', *TG*, 85 (1972), 161–70.

[171] Martens, 'Artistic Patronage', pp. 86–110.

ceremonies.[172] Fransoys van de Pitte, who was in regular service to the city in the 1470s and 1480s, was paid in 1479–80 for a 'tabellau' featuring the coats of arms of former foresters of the White Bear jousters which was to hang in the Poorters Loge, and in 1486 for gilding the St Michael's dragon placed on top of the newly completed tower of the Belfry.[173] In many of these contexts, artistic media served authority, as well as the corporate values that were thought to justify it: they were expressed in the architectural work on craft and municipal buildings, or in the display of civic hierarchy and sacred drama that unfolded annually during the Holy Blood procession.[174] Municipal authority was made to be heard as well as seen, and often loudly. In the late fifteenth century, the magistracy's *alta capella* group of minstrels performed regularly in secular and sacred contexts. The spoken word, especially through use of rhetoricians, was pressed into corporate service: Anthonis de Roovere was paid by the city for his work in entry ceremonies, and his poems commissioned on the occasion of general processions found their way into his Chronicle of Flanders. His positioning of Bruges in the Chronicle at the centre of contemporary events expresses a sense of civic pride that is also intimated visually in the many panel paintings from the late fifteenth century that place landmarks of Bruges architecture as backdrops to sacred scenes.[175]

De Roovere's Chronicle comes closest to what in other towns would be called a 'town chronicle' – expressing the views and outlook of the city council, and articulating a sense of 'urban self-consciousness'.[176] But even de Roovere was not apparently employed officially to write his Chronicle; nor were his writings always supportive of secular hierarchy. The city environment generated texts that were 'urban' in a wider sense,[177] reflecting a complex variety of lay and clerical authors, audiences, networks and even divisions of power within the city. The chronicle of events between 1477

172 SAB, 216, 1476/7, fo. 129^{v}.

173 SAB, 216, 1479/80, fo. 164^{v}; 1480/1, fo. 158^{r}; 1486/7, fo. 153^{r}.

174 See above, Chapters 3, 4, 7.

175 On depictions of the Bruges landscape, see J. De Rock, 'Beeld van de stad: Picturale voorstellingen van stedelijkheid in de laatmiddeleeuwse Nederlanden', unpublished PhD thesis, Ghent University (Ghent, 2011).

176 R. Schmid, 'Town Chronicles', in G. Dunphy (ed.), *Encyclopedia of the Medieval Chronicle*, 2 vols. (Leiden, 2010), vol. II, p. 1432; P. Trio, 'The Chronicle Attributed to "Olivier van Dixmude": A Misunderstood Town Chronicle of Ypres from Late Medieval Flanders', in E. Kooper (ed.), *The Medieval Chronicle V* (Amsterdam, 2008), pp. 211–25 (at 212).

177 For debate on the 'urban chronicle', see Trio, 'The Chronicle Attributed to "Olivier van Dixmude"'; A.-L. Van Bruaene, 'L'écriture de la mémoire urbaine en Flandre et en Brabant (XIVe–XVIe siècles)', in Crouzet-Pavan and Lecuppre-Desjardin (eds.) *Villes de Flandre et d'Italie*, pp. 149–64.

and 1491, which took a particular interest in the criminal cases prosecuted by the city government, was probably the work of a city clerk.[178] But other chronicles, like de Doppere's, to a degree reflect clerical concerns, and still others mirror divisions within the municipal elite: one version of the Chronicle of Flanders, composed between 1484 and 1490 by Jacob van Malen (a rhetorician, burgher and mercer, who served on quality-control commissions for the city council), appears to project the complaints of factional opposition to Maximilian onto its account of the county's early history.[179]

Corporate values in late medieval Bruges were underpinned by a delicate balance of power that was difficult to sustain, as aldermen were well aware. Some paintings (like the *Judgment of Cambyses* hung in the *scepenhuis* – see Figure 9.6) were a warning for those serving in civic office to rule justly. Criticism of social mores and secular power, as already noted, had a long literary and clerical history within the city, to which de Roovere contributed. De Roovere's chronicle also gives notice of textual activity that was more deliberately subversive. The urban environment of Bruges generated 'high culture' but also political unrest. In November 1475 de Roovere records that posters were put up on the walls near the Franciscan friary denouncing the city magistrates as 'whoresons', 'thieves' and 'liver-eaters' for imposing harsh taxation.[180] Such denunciation was by no means unique: it formed a pattern of subversion that was evidently well tried, frequently copied and with its own lexicon of stock phrases. For instance, in March 1476 an artisan was charged for placing 'brieven' on the church doors of St Donatian's, the Eekhout abbey and others, in which all city office-holders were described as 'liver-eaters';[181] Corneille vande Poorten in 1494 put up 'seditious and defamatory' letters and bills in public places in Bruges, particularly the Bourse, which defamed the three households that had employed him, and the city as a whole as a place where 'great sodomy reigned secretly and in public'.[182]

178 Carton (ed.), *Het boeck*.

179 L. Demets and J. Dumolyn, 'Urban Chronicle Writing in Late Medieval Flanders: The Case of Bruges during the Flemish Revolt of 1482–1490', *Urban History*, 43 (2015), 28–45; J. Oosterman, 'Jacob van Malen. Man langs de zijlijn van Brugges Gouden Eeuw', in H. Brinkman, J. Jansen and M. Mathijsen (eds.), *Helden bestaan! Opstellen voor Herman Pleij bij zijn afscheid als hoogleraar Historische Nederlandse Letterkunde aan de Universiteit van Amsterdam* (Amsterdam, 2008), pp. 200–6.

180 OBB, Ms. 437, fo. 365^{v}. De Roovere also echoed the insult 'liver-eaters' in one of his poems: see de Roovere, *De gedichten*, p. 327.

181 RAB, Proosdij, 1510, fo. 108^{r}.

182 SAB, 192, fo. 10^{r}–12^{r}.

Some writings give intimation of a culture of subversion that was oral as well as textual. In the fifteenth century 'tumult' and 'clamour' were as much part of the city soundscape as they had been in Galbert's day. Drama was also a potentially dangerous medium. On 6 March 1482, St Donatian's canons gave leave for their succentor Alianus de Groote and his 'associates' to take to the streets to perform a Passion Play, a 'ludum moralisantem', on a wagon, but on condition that their words were scrutinized beforehand to ensure that no 'scandal' or 'commotion' resulted. Censorship proved to be in vain: the canons later learned that certain players, full of wine, had conducted a more scurrilous (and surely politically motivated) play before the house of Jan van Nieuwenhove.[183] Music could be just as subversive, heightening the impact of words by setting them to memorable or popular tunes. When performed in public places, songs could be politically dangerous: in 1491 Thuene de Budt from Oudenburg was punished for singing 'regrettable songs' in 'The Mint', a respectable tavern in Bruges, about the recent revolt against Maximilian. Some street singers accompanied themselves on an instrument, as in the case of the blind man who sang a song 'against the prince and the prosperity of the land'.[184] Such fragments of artistic dissent are far outweighed by evidence for a more elite kind of cultural activity that has inevitably dominated this chapter; but they point to the widespread nature of texts and sounds that circulated in social groups and audiences beyond those reached by rhetoricians and composers.

While culture in Bruges appears at its most vibrant in the fifteenth century, its distinctive characteristics were products of a longer history. The texts, images and music produced in the city were the result of a creative mix of influences and networks that had encouraged both cosmopolitanism and local patriotism, multilingualism and vernacularity. They were also the result of a stimulating variety of patrons whose needs generated investment in cultural capital: the concerns of courtly, commercial and municipal elites, as well as middling groups, were reflected in a wide range of cultural media. Yet while these concerns promoted their social standing, political authority or aspirations, they could also reflect frictions and fissures in urban society, as well as articulate spiritual qualms and social complaints that questioned wealth and power. Traditions of craft guild and artisan rebellion were also given cultural expression, and these were as characteristic of Bruges society as the pomp of municipal processions and courtly ceremony. The prosperity of the city attracted talent and provided capital, but this in itself does

183 BAB, A55, fos. 158^{r}, 161^{r}.

184 SAB, 157, fos. 2^{v}, 45^{v}–6^{v}; see Dumolyn and Haemers, 'Bad Chicken', pp. 60–4.

not explain the demands for such investment: the diversity of needs among a host of different patrons marked out Bruges culturally from most other cities.

These needs to some extent persisted even when the fortunes of the city began to turn. The political and economic troubles that occurred in the late fifteenth century, particularly after the death of Charles the Bold in 1477, may seem to herald the end of Bruges as a 'creative environment'. The increasing withdrawal of the Burgundian and Habsburg court from residence in Bruges removed one significant source of patronage of art and music.[185] The flight of foreign nations from Bruges from the 1480s severed significant commercial and cultural links with a wider world, which were only partially restored when peace returned. Crisis depopulated the city and made it a less attractive environment for musicians and artists. The singer Jan de Vos threatened to leave Bruges in August 1482, claiming he could barely live on his salary.[186] The unexpected death of Anthonis de Roovere in May 1482, two months after that of Mary of Burgundy, seemed to bring a period of particular literary creativity to a close: later rhetoricians continued de Roovere's Chronicle of Flanders, but their canonization of his work appears as an attempt to preserve a golden era that was by then considered past. In this context, the shift to greater 'mass production' for an art market can easily be viewed as symptomatic of declining creativity and innovation in visual arts. Yet as the following chapter will show, the waning importance of Bruges as an economic centre of production and exchange did not lead immediately to cultural stagnation.

[185] Strohm, *Music*, pp. 36 (for the 'squandering' of the city's wealth on art and music in these years), 149–50.

[186] BAB, A55, fo. 224^{r}.

10 | Bruges in the Sixteenth Century: A 'Return to Normalcy'

LUDO VANDAMME, PETER STABEL, JAN DUMOLYN, ANDREW BROWN, MAXIMILIAAN P. J. MARTENS, NELE GABRIËLS AND JOHAN OOSTERMAN

In 1561, the rhetorician Eduard de Dene (1505–78) wrote his *Testament Rhetoricael*, a burlesque farewell to his fellow burghers, to the city government, and to various confraternities and religious houses, taking his reader on a virtual tour through the urban literary landscape.[1] In 1562, Eduard's friend, the painter Marcus Gerards (c.1521–c.1590), finished his masterly map of Bruges commissioned by the city government: Bruges appears with broad streets and internal waterways, surrounded by wide canals linked to its ports and to the sea, as though a city still brimming with commercial possibility.[2] In 1564, the Bruges jurist, town clerk and criminal registrar Joost de Damhouder (1507–81) praised the same town council in his treatise *De magnificentia politae amplissimae civitatis Brugarum*, which included a drawing of Gerards' map, and applauded the city's monuments, government and its accessible port.[3] In all these portrayals, the city still appears as a lively metropolis and a leading market-place in northern Europe. There were indeed signs of continuing prosperity. As late as 1569 Bruges was still a hotspot of economic life in the Habsburg Netherlands. In the midst of political and religious turmoil, the level of taxation generated from the 100th penny tax on movable and immovable goods initiated by the duke of Alva suggests the city was still wealthy. In terms of movable wealth, the city was second only to Antwerp, and it remained a significant commercial centre in northern Europe, despite the decreasing value of real estate in the city. Within Flanders, although second to Ghent in population size and industries, Bruges was by far the leading city economically.[4] However, little more

[1] Eduard de Dene, *Testament Rhetoricael*, ed. D. Coigneau and W. Waterschoot (Ghent, 1976–80); S. Mareel, 'In the Book of Life: Manuscript, *Memoria*, and Community in Eduard de Dene's *Testament Rhetoricael* (Bruges, 1562)', *Sixteenth Century Journal*, 43 (2012), 1013–35.

[2] A. Schouteet, *Marcus Gerards: The 16th-Century Painter and Engraver* (Bruges, 1985); E. Hodnett, *Marcus Gheeraerts the Elder of Bruges, London and Antwerp* (Utrecht, 1971).

[3] Also known as *De magnificentia politae amplissimae civitatis Brugensis* (Antwerp, 1564). On De Damhouder, see E. I. Strubbe, 'Joos de Damhouder als criminalist', in E. I. Strubbe, *De luister van ons oude recht: Verzamelde rechtshistorische studies* (Brussels, 1973), pp. 470–520.

[4] Stabel, *Dwarfs among Giants*, pp. 48–58; and P. Stabel and F. Vermeylen, *Het fiscale vermogen in Vlaanderen, Brabant en in de heerlijkheid Mechelen in 1569: De Honderdste Penning van de*

than two decades later, in the 1590s, quite a different impression emerges from a text called the *Deerlicke lamentatie ende beclagh vanden destructie vande stede van Brugghe* (The pitiful lamentation and complaint about the destruction of the city of Bruges). Its author, Zeghere van Male, a leading burgher and merchant, could only bemoan the economic ruin and religious and political uncertainties that by then characterized his hometown.[5]

By the late sixteenth century onwards, it was clear that Bruges had lost its leading European role for good; but around 1500, with stability tentatively returning after the crises of the late fifteenth century, the city's future seemed brighter. Vigorous attempts were being made to restore commerce and artisanal production. Textile manufacture was again at the heart of these attempts, as it had been before the mid fourteenth century. There were undeniable signs of difficulty. although Bruges still ranked just behind cities like Brussels and Ghent in size, the city's population was now smaller and less cosmopolitan, and because of the staggering growth of Antwerp (which by 1560 would contain over 100,000 inhabitants) it was becoming more peripheral to the centres of economic and political power.[6] The commercial elite pragmatically sought to connect itself to new international trade flows and to Antwerp, the new commercial capital of the North. By 1500 it was evident to most merchants, even to many burghers of Bruges, that Antwerp would eclipse Bruges as an international market. There had been complementarity between the two cities in the fifteenth century. Bruges had always been successful in attracting maritime commerce; Italian merchants and Hanseatic traders had been the real network makers on the banks of the Zwin. Antwerp had been oriented, more than its Flemish rival, towards transcontinental trade and the link with west and south German markets along the Rhine corridor and in Swabia and Bavaria. However, at the turn of the sixteenth century, when the English Merchant Adventurers, whose woollens had long been banned from Flemish markets, joined these transcontinental links in the Brabantine fairs of Antwerp and Bergen-op-Zoom, and when a second spice connection with the Portuguese colonial trade developed, the fate of maritime Bruges was sealed. The traditional trading communities at the Bruges market lost ground as they became marginalized in Europe. The German Hanse experienced increasing competition from the nascent Dutch maritime expansion, centred around Amsterdam

hertog van Alva, 1569–1572 (Brussels, 1997); Van Uytven, 'Stages of Economic Decline', esp. p. 261.

5 Zegher van Male, *De Lamentatie*.

6 On urban hierarchy in Flanders and in the southern Low Countries in the sixteenth century, see Stabel, *Dwarfs among Giants*, pp. 17–39; Stabel, 'Composition et recompositions des réseaux

(and for the moment also Antwerp), while the Italian merchant communities reoriented their activities, making more use of local agents (increasingly Antwerp-based and coming from the Low Countries themselves) and joining the transcontinental routes that were by then cheaper.[7]

The response of the Bruges commercial elites to the shift of international commerce to Antwerp is often described as short-sighted and reactionary: they defended their staple rights with too much conviction (in particular the ban on English cloth and the monopolies of locally manufactured textiles), hung on too long to their traditional markets and products, and allowed too much interference by rent-seeking corporatist organizations involved in the revolt against the new Habsburg rulers. All this, it is assumed, undermined Bruges' competitiveness.[8] Civil war in the 1480s and early 1490s doubtless undermined the city's attractiveness to foreign merchants; Maximilian of Austria used economic warfare against his rebellious cities, and Antwerp sided enthusiastically with Habsburg power.[9] On all other accounts, however, Bruges merchants and financial elites reacted proactively to changing commercial circumstance. They adopted new business techniques, became involved in active trade again, and invested heavily in the Brabantine fairs in order to coordinate the two market systems.[10] With similar pragmatism, the city's leading political families tried to maintain what was left of the city's autonomy against the encroachments of the early modern princely state. Even so, they were generally far more loyal to their princes than many of their medieval predecessors had been: never again would the city become the scene of large-scale revolts against princely power, even if it did sporadically experience social conflicts, strikes and hunger riots.[11]

urbains'; Deneweth, 'Een demografische knoop ontward'; J. Dambruyne, *Mensen en centen: Het 16de-eeuwse Gent in demografisch en economisch perspectief* (Ghent, 2001), pp. 167–79.

7 The debate about the transition from Bruges to Antwerp is lively. The traditional arguments are expressed in H. Van der Wee, *The Growth of the Antwerp Market and the European Economy, Fourteenth – Sixteenth Centuries*, 3 vols. (The Hague, 1963); and have been nuanced by Brulez, 'Bruges and Antwerp'. A more recent state of the art can be found in B. Blondé, O. Gelderblom and P. Stabel, 'Foreign Merchant Communities in Bruges, Antwerp and Amsterdam', in Calabi and Christensen (eds.), *Cultural Exchange*, vol. II, pp. 154–74. The rise of Antwerp merchants is discussed in Puttevils, *Merchants*.

8 The traditional point of view is discussed in Van Houtte, 'Bruges et Anvers'; Van Houtte, 'Rise and Decline'; Van der Wee, *Growth of the Antwerp Market*; and Brulez, 'Bruges and Antwerp'.

9 Haemers, *For the Common Good*; Haemers, *De strijd*; Haemers et al. (eds.), *Entre la ville.*

10 Mus, 'De Brugse compagnie Despars'; A. Harthoorn and P. Stabel, 'Handel en stedelijke ruimte: De buurt van de Antwerpse Grote Markt op het einde van de vijftiende eeuw', in I. Baatsen, T. Bisschops, J. De Groot et al. (eds.), *De stad als sociale ruimte: Antwerpen aan de vooravond van de Gouden Eeuw* (forthcoming); Asaert, 'Gasten uit Brugge'; and Verbist, 'Traditie'.

11 J. Vermaut, 'De wolkammers te Brugge: Hun aandeel in de sociale beroeringen tijdens de 17de en de l8de eeuw', *HGG*, 98 (1961), 5–47.

None of this, however, could prevent Bruges from becoming an entirely different type of city by the second half of the sixteenth century at the latest. By then, its population had fallen by at least 25 per cent compared to average fifteenth-century levels, its industrial functions had dwindled, and its central role in international commerce had become but a memory of the oldest burghers. Bruges would remain a sizeable provincial centre during the early modern period, with important regional market functions and artisanal industries that produced high-quality products. The city's religious and clerical character would be reinforced as Bruges became the seat of a bishopric and several new ecclesiastical institutions settled within its walls, but it would no longer be a real cultural hub, and its artists would be considered mediocre compared with their predecessors. Late sixteenth-century Bruges was no longer a 'metropolis'. In effect, under Habsburg rule it returned to being a 'normal town', a typical middle-sized city of the pre-industrial period. During the nineteenth century, the city would miss out on Belgium's precocious role in the Industrial Revolution and would even become one of the poorest towns in the country, until from the early twentieth century it gradually developed into a major site for tourism. The population levels of the Middle Ages were only reached again after 1900. It was precisely its diminishing importance that helped Bruges – certainly in the nineteenth century when it mostly escaped the changes visited upon the morphology of so many European towns – to maintain its 'medieval' appearance (though with the heavy assistance of neo-gothic interventions), and to preserve it as a sort of Sleeping Beauty, in ways that today satisfy the promoters of commercial tourism and medievalist fantasy. Only in the twentieth century, with the port of Zeebrugge, would Bruges regain its international importance.

Commercial Infrastructure, Urban Landscape and Population

After the imposition of peace following the final defeat of the Flemish Revolt against Maximilian in 1492, the restoration of the city's port infrastructure became a major priority. The problem of maintaining Bruges' link with the sea was not the prime cause of the city's commercial decay, as is often presumed in older scholarship, but it was a pressing problem.[12] By

[12] This viewpoint was formulated last by M. K. E. Gottschalk, 'Het verval van Brugge als wereldmarkt', *TG*, 56 (1953), 1–26, who argues with reason that the importance of the silting of the Zwin is also not to be underestimated.

1500, the sandbanks before the Zwin had become so large that only small ships could still enter the estuary. A masterplan to deal with silting was set up, drawing upon the experiences of the previous century. It was hoped – in vain – that scouring the Zwin would improve its accessibility for larger vessels. No more effective was the project of the Canal of Oostburg (the Nieuw Gedelf) between Sluis and the Western Scheldt. Begun in 1500 and finished in 1516, it was meant to reduce silting by intensifying the erosion caused by tidal movement. Another canal, the Verse Vaart, was dug between 1548 and 1566 between Sluis and Bruges, and improved with an impressive lock complex at Sluis between the canal and the Zwin in 1564. But in the long run, it failed to solve the problem of diminishing commerce.[13] The showpiece of these efforts was the city's purchase of Sluis in 1566; but Sluis had lost most of its fifteenth-century glory as a medium-sized town. Meanwhile, in Bruges itself, between 1519 and 1522 the so-called 'Three Doors', a new lock complex at the Minnewater, was constructed to funnel water from the city's hinterland into the centre.[14]

In the city, modest improvements were made to the infrastructure to encourage more traffic: the canals and arms of the Reie were deepened, quaysides repaired, and streets freed of porches and cellar stairs.[15] During the first half of the sixteenth century, streets continued to be repaired and restored to their full width to assist the flow of traffic and economic revival.[16] The urban ordinances, preserved from 1492, show that the economic use of public space was among the aldermen's major concerns. Storing goods on the street was discouraged or forbidden, display windows were limited, benches were removed and the parking of carts along the street was regulated. Owners were obliged to clean up and fence their vacant lots, which was a growing concern in a depopulating city. Private housing, and alleys that opened up passageways to houses, were increasingly incorporated into adjacent parcels, and many existing houses effectively became outbuildings of larger ones.[17]

13 Degryse, 'Brugge en de organisatie'; Gottschalk, *Stormvloeden*, vol. II, pp. 74, 100; Coornaert, *Knokke en het Zwin*, pp. 55–87; Verhulst, *Landschap*, pp. 57–63; Ryckaert and Vandewalle, 'De strijd'.

14 L. Vandamme, 'De drie deuren: De verbouwing van de sluis aan het Minnewater in Brugge (1519–1522)', *Biekorf*, 109 (2009), 214–30.

15 H. Deneweth, 'The Economic Situation and its Influence on Building and Renovating in Bruges, 16th–18th centuries', in J.-F. Chauvard and L. Mocarelli (eds.), *L'économie de la construction dans l'Italie Moderne*, special issue of *Mélanges de l'Ecole Française de Rome: Italie et Méditerrannée*, 119 (2007), 537–50 (at 540).

16 Ibid., p. 535.

17 H. Deneweth, 'De wisselwerking tussen bouwtechnische veranderingen en evoluerende samenlevingsvormen in drie Brugse buurten, late middeleeuwen tot negentiende eeuw', in

Marcus Gerards' map depicts about 8,000 individual buildings, but also large open spaces in the city, especially at its edges. Interpreting this feature is not easy as no earlier town plans exist for comparison, apart from the early sixteenth-century 'Oldest Painted Map of Bruges', which is more schematic.[18] The open spaces might have resulted from recent depopulation, but they may have been there when the 1297–1300 ramparts were built: most pre-industrial towns needed such spaces for urban gardening and industrial activities (for instance land for tenter frames and bleaching meadows). Then again, sixteenth-century Bruges counted far fewer workers, and in the industrial heyday of the thirteenth century workers had principally lived in peripheral areas, just inside the ramparts. The city's population had dropped to 30,000 around 1500. On the other hand, increasing house rents until 1520 suggests that population levels were not crumbling completely, and higher rents might reflect more elaborate housing in some areas, where plots were merged. Standards of living were not falling dramatically; wages were still higher than in most cities of the Low Countries. Population in the region even increased slightly in the second quarter of the sixteenth century and Bruges climbed to about 35,000 inhabitants. Nevertheless, this number would never be surpassed again, except in unusual circumstances such as during the Calvinist Republic (1578–84) when the city gave shelter to refugees.[19]

The restructuring of housing probably made life in Bruges cheaper and more comfortable than it was in the expanding cities of Antwerp and Brussels. There was still work in construction; entrepreneurs, master carpenters and masons speculatively invested in renovations. Even so, whereas in 1500 the city contained about 8,600 houses, in 1583 there were only 7,979. As many as 7,700 paupers in the crisis year of 1544 constituted 20 per cent of the population.[20] They usually lived in wooden cabins with straw roofs or in attics or cellars in the poorer neighbourhoods close to the Smedenpoort (Blacksmiths' Gate), the Meersen (the Marches), the Carmersstraat and the Langestraat, often with different families together. When standards of living collapsed because of inflation from the mid sixteenth century, even

J. D'hondt (ed.), *Huizenonderzoek en stadsgeschiedenis* (Bruges, 2009), pp. 41–56; H. Deneweth, 'Brugge zoekt en vindt alternatieven', in Vermeersch (ed.), *Brugge en Europa*, pp. 89–90.

18 M. Ryckaert, 'Plan van Brugge', in M. P. J. Martens (ed.), *Brugge en de Renaissance: Van Memling tot Pourbus*, 2 vols. (Bruges, 1998), vol. II, pp. 173–4.

19 Deneweth, 'Een demografische knoop ontward'; Van Uytven, 'Stages of Economic Decline', pp. 263–5.

20 L. Gilliodts-Van Severen, 'Quel était le nombre des pauvres en 1544?', *La Flandre: Revue des Monuments d'Histoire et d'Antiquités*, 6 (1874–5), 161–6.

middling social groups were forced to rent rather than buy a house. In 1583, only 34 per cent of people lived in a house they owned, considerably less than in Ghent. The city's built environment was only changing slowly. New ideas on education, lifestyle, arts and politics were assimilated but lacked the momentum to alter the urban landscape substantially. Changes in style and taste were only introduced hesitantly and there seems to have been some resistance to innovation. In architecture, the medieval tradition of craftsmanship remained dominant. More stone houses were built for elite groups, and for the poor in the form of small *cameren*; and contractors seem to have invested on a large scale. But the houses of middle-class artisans mostly retained their wooden façades; and falling standards of living slowed down their replacement with brick. In the later sixteenth century more than half of middle-class houses still had a wooden front. The process of rebuilding and improvement of building stock was further hindered when a new demographic crisis in the last decades of the sixteenth century reduced the city's population to 27,000.[21] It was only from the seventeenth century that the city government would enforce a policy of replacing houses. Compared with Antwerp, Brussels or Ghent, Bruges would thus have presented a somewhat old-fashioned appearance in the sixteenth century.[22] Gothic forms were still dominant, and even renovations were mostly executed in the traditional 'gothic' Bruges construction style.

Some innovations were introduced. The city government did offer incentives for a Renaissance style of building. New 'modern' buildings were built on the Burg square between 1533 and 1537. The building activities of the Liberty of Bruges, its administrative seat still in the city, were particularly trend-setting. A complex of several rooms for the administration of justice was erected in 1520–4 by Jan van de Poele on the square, though they were built in the late Gothic style. Between 1528 and 1531, a magnificent new chimney piece was added, designed by Lancelot Blondeel. It was a tribute to the emperor Charles V, and in effect the first major example in the city of the new Renaissance style. The same style was adopted next-door in the new building of the Bruges civil chancery between 1534 and 1537.[23] The nation house of the Basque merchants, built in the second quarter of the sixteenth century with municipal support, also had Renaissance features.

21 Deneweth, 'Economic Situation'; Deneweth, 'Brugge zoekt en vindt alternatieven', p. 91; W. Blockmans, '"Fondans en melencolie de povreté": Leven en werken in Brugge, 1482–1584', in Martens (ed.), *Brugge en de Renaissance*, vol. I, pp. 26–32 (at 30–1).

22 Deneweth, 'Economic Situation'; B. Beernaert, 'Renaissancewoonhuizen in Brugge: Zeldzame eenden in de bijt!', *BO*, 43 (2003), 247–60; Ryckaert, *Historische stedenatlas*, pp. 107–10.

23 Devliegher, *De Keizer Karel-schouw*, pp. 15–27.

The new nation house of the Castilians in the Spanjaardstraat, offered them by the city in 1494, was built in late gothic style but had a Renaissance entry gate added to it in 1573. The nearby Houtrei canal gradually became the Spaanse Loskaai, the quay where Spanish wool was unloaded: this quarter of town would continue to be dominated by a Castilian presence, the last remnant of the cosmopolitan commercial character of late medieval Bruges.[24] On the private housing market, rather later, a number of building entrepreneurs had houses built in the new fashion. In 1571 master carpenter Gillis vanden Coornhuse constructed a house called 'De Clyncke' (Oude Burg 33) with medallions of Mercury and Ceres in its Renaissance façade.[25] Renaissance architecture appealed primarily to the urban nobility, who converted their medieval 'courts' with turrets and an inner courtyard into new palaces, the Court of Cuba (Garenmarkt), Watervliet (Oude Burg) and Pittem (Heilige-Geeststraat) indicating their bids for social distinction.[26] As elsewhere in the Low Countries, the Bruges elites also invested in residences outside the city. Pleasure houses with large gardens at the edge of or just outside town became popular.[27] However, none of these initiatives transformed Bruges architecturally into a genuine Renaissance town.

The historical landscape of Bruges is still marked today by large religious houses; and these are mostly the relics of the early modern period rather than the medieval. During the sixteenth century, although some older smaller convents, especially those of the Third Order, disappeared (for example the Third Order female Franciscans of Magerzo in the Ganzestraat in 1535 and their male counterparts of the Staelyzerbroeders in 1588), many other religious orders settled within or just beyond the city walls. Several of them (the Annunciates outside the Ezelpoort and the Carthusians in the Holy Cross parish) were demolished in 1578, the city government fearing they would be used as strongholds by the Calvinist troops. As a result these religious communities settled inside the city walls. Protestant military threats from 1566 also caused other clerics to seek refuge *intra muros*,

[24] Ryckaert, *Historische stedenatlas*, p. 107.

[25] Beernaert, 'Renaissancewoonhuizen'; K. Wittenvrongel, 'De bouwgeschiedenis van de Burgerlijke Griffie te Brugge', *HGG*, 110 (1973), 186–97; A. Viaene, 'Het natiehuis van Biscaaie te Brugge', *Biekorf*, 39 (1933), 1–8.

[26] J. D'hondt, *Het vroegere huis Het Ei op het Beursplein, nu Adriaan Willaertstraat 9* (Bruges, 2005); B. Beernaert, J. Braet, J. Demulder et al., *Binnen en buiten: Winter- en zomerverblijven van de Brugse elite vanaf de late middeleeuwen* (Bruges, 2007); L. Vandamme, 'Huizenonderzoek en materiële cultuur in het zestiende-eeuwse Brugge', in D'hondt (ed.), *Huizenonderzoek*, p. 90.

[27] A.-M. Delepiere and M. Huys, 'Heesters of huyzekens van plaisance te Brugge', *Monumenten en Landschappen*, 9 (1990), 55–62.

as would some Catholic communities from England. The concentration of religious houses in the city continued throughout the seventeenth century.[28] After the Catholic Reformation in the late sixteenth and seventeenth centuries, Bruges gradually developed a more 'clerical look'. The Jesuits, for instance, settled in a large building at the Sint-Maartensplaats in 1595. The Capuchins founded a convent in the Sint-Clarastraat in 1592, later moving to another location at the Friday market (Vrijdagmarkt) in 1620.[29]

Artisanal Production and Social Conditions

If wages in Bruges were still relatively high until around 1520, they were soon surpassed by those in Antwerp. Demand in Bruges particularly for skilled labour must have dropped as immigration of new burghers faltered. Between 1500 and 1580 only 2,617 new burghers were matriculated, a mere 1.7 per 1,000 inhabitants each year: most other towns maintained an influx of about 3 per 1,000. This lack of interest in acquiring burgher status, a condition of entering the craft system, shows that burghership had become less necessary for engaging in economic activity. In 1492–4, after a decade of war and trade disruption, the Bruges city council had already launched a 'new drapery'. In order to participate in the manufacture of these woollens, it was no longer a requirement to become a burgher or guild member. This initiative failed dramatically, but later measures to stimulate textile manufacture had more success. In 1544, the inscription fee for masters in the textile crafts was reduced to 5 shillings Flemish groten, less than a tenth of what had been usual before.[30] The city government also tried to protect its burghers from the growing fiscal pressures of the Habsburg state by lobbying for exemptions, placing fiscal burdens on the countryside, protecting its outburghers from rural taxes, and more or less sabotaging the collection of

[28] Ryckaert, *Historische stedenatlas*, pp. 113–14.

[29] Van Houtte, *De geschiedenis van Brugge*, pp. 366–72; F. Bonneure, *De kapucijnen vierhonderd jaar in Brugge, 1592–1992* (Bruges, 1992); F. De Bouck, 'Sporen van de aanwezigheid van de kapucijnen in Brugge uit 1592', *Biekorf*, 112 (2012), 304–6.

[30] Deneweth, 'Een demografische knoop ontward'; H. Deneweth, 'Migratiebeleid, armenzorg en arbeidsmarktregulering: Brugge in de zestiende eeuw', in M. De Koster, B. De Munck, H. Greefs et al. (eds.), *Werken aan de stad: Stedelijke actoren en structuren in de Zuidelijke Nederlanden 1500–1900: Liber amicorum Catharina Lis en Hugo Soly* (Brussels, 2011), pp. 103–18; E. Thoen, 'Verhuizen naar Brugge in de late middeleeuwen: De rol van de immigratie van de poorters in de aanpassing van de stad Brugge aan de wijzigende economische omstandigheden (14e–16e eeuw)', in H. Soly and R. Vermeir (eds.), *Beleid en bestuur in de oude Nederlanden: Liber amicorum prof. dr. M. Baelde* (Ghent, 1993), pp. 329–49.

newly imposed central taxes such as a 'tenth penny' on real estate and commercial profits in 1544–8.[31]

The interventions of the city authorities, however, did not lead to a strong revival of artisanal activities. Prospects remained bleak. At the beginning of the sixteenth century, the Bruges textile industry suffered heavily from competition in Brabant, Tuscany, England and Holland.[32] Like most foreign merchants, many skilled craftsmen left Bruges for Antwerp, attracted by higher wages. Bruges elites were acutely aware of this. Zeghere van Male was to mention it in his *Lamentation*. Among those who left were comb makers, pinners, painters and satin weavers, in total some twenty specialized crafts. The once famous rosary makers of Bruges were also suffering. Other trades linked to international commerce, so Zeghere tells us, like folding linen and producing bales and other packaging such as tons, were now carried out by the men of Antwerp: 'farewell to our loss', he laments. The city had created two schools for orphans to provide cheap labour for artisanal workshops: the Bogard school for boys (1510) and the Elisabeth school for girls (1518). By 1550 more than 300 boys and 150 girls had been trained to work as apprentices or maid servants. Van Male himself became involved in these municipal initiatives.[33]

Bruges' economic activities were still quite diversified: the complaint in 1563 of the Spanish wool merchants that their ships were waiting in vain for a return cargo was slightly exaggerated. But clearly most export-oriented sectors were now sending out their products via the port of Antwerp. Textiles and clothing, and the processing of wool, silk, cotton and flax yarn, remained the principal industrial activities in the city, providing labour opportunities for about half the population, men and women. The manufacture of woollen cloth partially revived: 300 looms were operational again in 1508. But the sector went rapidly downhill, and only 50 looms were left by the mid sixteenth century. The city government tried to diversify manufacture by offering incentives – fiscal exemptions, advantageous loans, free housing and guaranteed markets – to lure textile entrepreneurs from elsewhere, particularly from the remaining successful Flemish textile-producing regions, such as the Leie valley (especially the town of Armentières in Walloon Flanders) and Hondschoote with its

31 N. Maddens, 'De invoering van de "nieuwe middelen" in het graafschap Vlaanderen tijdens de regering van keizer Karel V', *BTFG*, 57 (1979), 861–98 (at 895); and N. Maddens, *De beden in het graafschap Vlaanderen tijdens de regering van keizer Karel V (1515–1550)* (Kortrijk and Heule, 1978), pp. 284–8.

32 Deneweth, 'Economic Situation', p. 534.

33 Deneweth, 'Economic Situation', p. 535. Zegher Van Male, *De Lamentatie*, p. 52.

growing production of say (worsteds and semi-worsteds). The aim was clear. If markets for the traditional *draperie ointe*, the more expensive greased woollen cloth, were contracting, cloth manufacturers producing lighter types of woollens were doing well. Other traditional manufacturing centres, like Dendermonde and Menen, had similar goals and met with success. The Bruges authorities clearly wanted to develop the manufacture of cheaper fabrics. Other successful textile niches, like tapestry weaving in Oudenaarde, silks in Antwerp and luxury linen in Kortrijk, triggered similar responses. The Bruges cloth industry, even in the thirteenth century, had always been more geared towards the manufacture of cheaper fabrics, and Bruges entrepreneurs and aldermen were now trying to do the same.[34] In 1503 they also tried to produce cheaper woollens in the style of Leyden, the most important manufacturing centre in Holland. A Leyden clothier was even invited to Bruges to manufacture this type of cloth, but the experiment proved unprofitable, as were many other attempts.[35] What is important is that these new cloth industries were usually set up outside the traditional guild framework. As in the pre-guild period, quality-control commissions of authentication were run by merchants and entrepreneurs, often recruited from the same families who had themselves established the economic policies of the city council.

The long-term results of these initiatives were disappointing. At its peak Bruges say manufacture was a mere 8 per cent of the output in Hondschoote. Conversion to the manufacture of cheaper fabrics was not the long-term solution to the economic problems of a larger city like Bruges, where guild control had been characteristic and where wages were on average higher than those in the countryside. Hondschoote provided cheaper labour, its business structures were organized and controlled by businessmen from Antwerp (and even from Bruges) and its systems of putting out were more flexible and less prone to higher transaction costs.[36] Bruges entrepreneurs and politicians had gambled on the wrong kind of products. The only cities able to hang on to their cloth industries with some success (Mechelen, Ypres, Menen, Kortrijk) continued to specialize in the most expensive fabrics: heavy woollen cloth for which demand patterns were less elastic, skill was more important and the labour cost of manufacture was marginal relative to the cost of the expensive raw materials. But even these cities suffered from increased competition as some of the rural and urban textile

[34] Stabel, 'Les draperies urbaines'; Munro, 'Medieval Woollens: Textiles'.

[35] Vermaut, 'Structural Transformation'.

[36] Coornaert, *Un centre industriel d'autrefois*; Van der Wee, 'Industrial Dynamics'.

manufacturers in Western and Walloon Flanders started to specialize in mid-range woollens.[37]

One of the newly introduced industries, however, met with some success: the weaving of fustian, a light type of fabric mixing wool and flax or cotton. The technique had arrived from southern Germany (the region of Ulm and Augsburg) and northern Italy. It was initiated in Bruges in 1513. Fustians were among the most popular goods that south German merchants brought to the Brabantine fairs of Antwerp and Bergen-op-Zoom. In the middle of the century the yearly growth rate of the Bruges fustian industry was no less than about 20 per cent. Bruges manufacturers produced 42,000 pieces in 1522 and 45,000 at their peak in 1579. The fustian industry was a sign of changing times in the sense that it combined traditional industrial patterns with new approaches: it used colonial raw materials (cotton); it was produced outside the guild system and did not require the same levels of skill and division of labour, therefore allowing lower wages; some of the end products were also exported to the New World, but it continued to integrate rural labour (spinning, bleaching) and urban skill.[38] In the sixteenth century the number of bleach fields in and around the city rose from twenty-seven to forty-two. Eighteen were situated on land owned by ecclesiastical and charitable institutions, four were owned by the city and the remainder by private individuals from noble families to the mercantile elites. Most of the fields were situated near the Wijngaard beguinage, between the Westmeers and the Boeveriestraat and in the north periphery of town, often in spaces formerly used as tenter fields for the traditional woollen industry.[39]

Despite their temporary success, Bruges-manufactured fustians would only constitute a niche market. In the end, this kind of import substitution failed to trigger the dramatic change in the manufacturing structure which the city so desperately needed. If anything the relative success of light woollens and mixed fabrics shifted the character of urban society from one that was predominantly skilled, guild-organized and middle-class to one predominantly unskilled, unorganized and proletarianized. As a consequence

[37] Coornaert, 'Draperies rurales'; T. Soens, P. Stabel and T. Van de Walle, 'An Urbanized Countryside? A Regional Perspective on Rural Textile Production in the Flemish West-Quarter (1400–1600)', in R. W. M. van Schaik (ed.), *Economies, Public Finances and the Impact of Institutional Change in Interregional Perspective: The Low Countries and Neighbouring German Territories (14th–17th Centuries)* (Turnhout, 2015), pp. 35–60.

[38] Vermaut, 'Structural Transformation'; J. A. Van Houtte, 'De draperie van Leidse lakens in Brugge, 1503–1516: Een vroege poging tot inplanting van nieuwe nijverheden', in J. A. Van Houtte, *Essays on Medieval and Early Modern Economy and Society* (Leuven, 1977), pp. 291–302.

[39] Vermaut, 'De textielnijverheid', vol. I, pp. 199–200.

it reinforced the structural trend towards the declining living standards of industrial labourers. The shift away from highly skilled and better paid industrial labour, which had characterized the late medieval city, towards low-status and less well-paid jobs for a significant part of the labour market, represented a return almost to pre-1250 labour relations. There was, however, one difference: Bruges-based industries no longer dovetailed with the development of international export markets. The manufacture of Bruges fustians was a mere footnote to the commercial success of south German fustians, while Bruges says were far less successful than Hondschoote says and English worsteds. Bruges had lost its international connection, which had provided the backbone for industrial change in an earlier period. Although conversion enjoyed some success, its results were limited and the attempts to rebuild textile manufacture proved futile.

Attempts to Revive International Commerce

When Bruges emerged from the deep commercial and political crisis of the 1480s, the world was rapidly changing around it.[40] Transatlantic expansion had opened new commercial routes and was giving rise to new trading hubs. More importantly, the renewed success of European transcontinental trade, caused by lower transaction costs, to a large extent bypassed the city which had thrived for almost two centuries on its maritime connections. After the crisis of the 1480s and Maximilian's resumption of power in Flanders by 1492, the foreign nations and trading firms chose to return to Bruges in 1493. The city government, realizing the gravity of the situation and the danger of structural decay, offered them benefits to stay. The repair works at the port that were then undertaken, and the attempts to diversify industrial manufacture, suggest an optimism about the ability of the Bruges market to recover as fully as it had from previous crises. However, it soon became apparent that new global commercial players, like the Portuguese with their spice trade, the south Germans with their metals and textiles, the English with their wool and cloth and even the Venetians who increasingly opted for transcontinental trade, were starting to ignore the Bruges market, preferring to conduct business at the Brabantine fairs. The advantages to them of relocating to Antwerp quickly became obvious. In 1511, the Portuguese

[40] For what follows, see Blockmans, 'Fondans'; N. Geirnaert and L. Vandamme, 'Cultuur en mentaliteit', in Martens (ed.), *Brugge en de Renaissance*, vol. I, pp. 33–42; Deneweth, 'Brugge zoekt en vindt alternatieven'; H. Deneweth, 'Brugge, een veilige enclave in het krijgsgewoel', in Vermeersch (ed.), *Brugge en Europa*, pp. 100–7; Blockmans, *Metropolen*, pp. 532–648.

consulate, previously of modest importance in Bruges but whose commercial activities were rapidly increasing because of Portugal's colonial expansion, was the first to settle officially in the Scheldt city. Genoa, Florence and Lucca followed in 1516 and many banking activities and monetary transactions departed with them, although (typically for financial markets, which tend to be characterized by some inertia) Bruges would remain an important financial centre. Its market was still used to clear international credit transfers and its traders, both foreign and domestic, were involved in financial operations. The city also became a financial hub for the surrounding countryside where leasing and larger rural holdings led to a more prosperous and capital-intensive economy.[41] The Hanseatic merchants had in practice already been operating from Antwerp for decades when in 1563 the Kontor, their Low Countries headquarters, by then only a shadow of its fifteenth-century self, was formally moved there.[42] In addition, the flow of international exports was significantly diverted away from Bruges as the majority of merchants from the Low Countries were now operating from Antwerp. From 1540 onwards, for instance, this was the case for the export of fine textiles to Italy.[43]

Far-reaching transformations of international flows of trade and its commercial nodes were preventing Bruges from recovering its earlier economic glory. The attractiveness of Antwerp on the Scheldt, which had offered easier access to the sea since the early fifteenth century, had strengthened during the revolt against Maximilian, when most foreign nations had relocated to the city and had come to appreciate its potential as a permanent market. During the sixteenth century, the expanding regions such as the Iberian countries with their new colonies and the southern German cities who took advantage of new overland trade routes became major players on the Antwerp market. The Italian and the Hanseatic cities became less involved in commercial exchange in the North Sea ports. The new metropolis had usurped Bruges' former function as a gateway for industrial goods from the Low Countries and for all types of commodities imported from elsewhere and as the financial sorting house of northwest Europe. Antwerp's leading

41 Marechal, *Europese aanwezigheid*. See more general observations in Spufford, *Power and Profit*.

42 P. Stabel, 'Bruges, plaque tournante du commerce hanséatique avec la France (14e-15e siècles)', in I. Richefort and B. Schmidt (eds.), *Les relations entre la France et les villes hanséatiques de Hambourg, Brême et Lübeck: Moyen Âge–19e siècle / Die Beziehungen zwischen Frankreich und den Hansestädten Hamburg, Bremen und Lübeck: Mittelalter–19. Jahrhundert* (Paris, 2006), pp. 97–111.

43 J. Puttevils, 'Klein gewin brengt rijkdom in: De Zuid-Nederlandse handelaars in de export naar Italië in de jaren 1540', *Tijdschrift voor Sociale en Economische Geschiedenis*, 6 (2009), 26–52.

position was reinforced during a phase of accelerated growth between 1520 and 1550.[44]

The efforts in Bruges to improve access to the sea and to renovate its maritime infrastructure did not restore the city to its former commercial splendour, but they did have some effect. They were rewarded by the arrival of commercial fleets supplying the Bruges staple with Spanish wool and also with English wool (after the loss of Calais to the French) between 1558 and 1586. The 'new' port could deal with the increased capacity of naval transport in this period: the average cargo that vessels were capable of carrying rose from 120 barrels between 1505 and 1514 to 212 barrels between 1545 and 1554, the peak years of Bruges' commerce in the sixteenth century. Between 1500 and 1559, 1,791 freight ships (excluding English shipping) with a total volume of 165,234 barrels still reached Sluis.[45] Even at the end of the century, after the Dutch Revolt had caused further neglect of the port infrastructure, this connection to the sea proved resilient, and Bruges ports continued to receive international maritime transport.[46] New ways of 'city marketing' were used. In the later sixteenth century, the city government was actively promoting its port function by distributing copies of Marcus Gerards' city map, which exaggerated the width of its streets and canals to demonstrate its commercial viability. Of course, these efforts betrayed concerns that Bruges in reality was failing to recover. The port infrastructure remained limited and, as a result, from 1540 onwards larger Spanish wool ships increasingly used the facilities of nearby Zeeland ports like Middelburg and Arnemuiden. This Zeeland transport system did prove effective to a certain extent. Flemish and Zeeland barges were able to ship commodities to Bruges via inland canals. In 1570, no fewer than 574 of the 3,065 boats leaving Arnemuiden claimed Bruges as their hometown.[47]

Nevertheless, fewer ships were reaching Bruges; and this was the result not so much of problems of access to the sea, as of structural changes in international commerce. The great Venetian galleys no longer came to Bruges, principally because Venice was itself in commercial decline and

[44] P. Stabel and J. Haemers, 'From Bruges to Antwerp: International Commercial Firms in the Late 15th and Early 16th Century', in C. Sanz Ayán and B. J. García García (eds.), *Banca, crédito y capital: La Monarquía Hispánica y los antiguos Países Bajos (1505–1700)* (Madrid, 2006), pp. 21–38.

[45] R. Degryse, 'Brugge en de pilotage van de Spaanse vloot in het Zwin in de XVIde eeuw', *HGG*, 117 (1980), 105–78, 227–88.

[46] L. Vandamme, 'Sluis en Brugge (1587–1604): De handelsvaart op het Zwin herleeft', in A. R. Bauwens (ed.), *Niemandsland in Staats verband: West-Zeeuws-Vlaanderen ten tijde van de Republiek en daarna* (Aardenburg, 2004), pp. 17–32.

[47] Brulez, 'Brugge en Antwerpen', p. 20 n. 6.

because Venetians left active trade in northern Europe to intermediaries in Germany and Antwerp. The Hanseatic merchants, traditionally among the leading buyers of woollens in Bruges, stayed away because of internal problems and competition with Dutch trade.[48] Special circumstances explain the continued presence of some foreign merchants in Bruges. The Spanish presence was mostly the artificial result of the staple for merino wool, which attracted up to 50,000 bales in peak years. Around 1552 Bruges still accounted for about a quarter of all Iberian imports in the Low Countries (although the monopoly on wool at Bruges partly explains this figure; and Antwerp meanwhile took a much larger 68 per cent share of Iberian imports). Bruges' share was at least enough to convince the Basque traders, mostly shippers, and the merchants from Navarre to hang on to their nation houses in Bruges until 1585 and 1586 respectively. Of greater importance was the merchant nation of Castile, which still counted sixty-two members in 1562. Their prestigious consulate would only be abandoned in 1704. The most prominent Spanish merchant families were settled quasi-permanently in Bruges – although this did not prevent them from also having representatives in Antwerp and elsewhere. Typical examples were the Pardo family from Burgos and the Nagere family (de Nájera) from Logroño. Because of their permanent presence, Castilian wool merchants integrated better into Bruges elite society than the Iberian shippers who were typically from the Basque country. Many Castilians married into Bruges mercantile families and political elites, and even stimulated the local art market with their patronage.[49]

After the fall of Calais in 1558, the English wool staple was transferred to Bruges. Although this must have stimulated an international presence, the economic effects were disappointing. Only 54 ships arrived in 1558, carrying 530 barrels of English wool and 165,000 fleeces. In 1568, however, the number of ships had fallen to twenty-five. The English staple was never able to compete with the volumes of its Castilian counterpart. The great days of the high-quality heavy cloths, with Flanders as the primary destination of the finest English wool, had passed. Instead, unfinished English

[48] Degryse, 'Brugge en de pilotage', p. 260.

[49] L. De Wolf, 'De familie Pardo in de XVIde eeuw: Een bijdrage tot de studie van Spaanse kooplieden en hun ondernemingen in West-Europa', unpublished MA thesis, Catholic University of Leuven (Leuven, 1979); R. Fagel, *De Hispano-Vlaamse wereld: De contacten tussen Spanjaarden en Nederlanders, 1496–1555* (Brussels and Nijmegen, 1996), pp. 38–42; W. D. Phillips, Jr, 'Local Integration and Long-Distance Ties: The Castilian Community in Sixteenth-Century Bruges', *Sixteenth Century Journal*, 17 (1986), 33–49; W. D. Phillips, Jr, 'Merchants of the Fleece: Castillians in Bruges and the Wool Trade', in Stabel et al. (eds.), *International Trade*, pp. 75–86.

broadcloth was exported to Antwerp by the Merchant Adventurers for finishing and international distribution. Despite the importance of its finishing industries in the fifteenth century, Bruges was never able to attract this market. The century-long ban on English woollens had taken care of that. But despite the failure of the English staple, the Spanish wool staple was still supplying Flemish cloth entrepreneurs in the smaller towns and the rural textile regions of western and Walloon Flanders (Armentières, Nieuwkerke, Hondschoote). Around 1500 even some Florentine firms like the Frescobaldi, Altoviti and Gualterotti were still involved in the wool trade with both England and Castile, while supplying Flemish cloth entrepreneurs in Menen and Kortrijk. The Bruges hosteller and broker Wouter Ameyde played a major role in mediating raw materials like wool and dyestuffs and finished woollens. Bruges entrepreneurial families like the Sayon family were also active in the manufacture of cheaper semi-worsteds in Hondschoote. In the 1550s and 1560s they traded large volumes of says in Bruges but their company was, typically, also present in Antwerp.[50]

We can safely conclude, however, that although some dynamic developments occurred throughout the sixteenth century, international trade in Bruges shrank considerably in capital intensity, in diversity and in volume. Several Bruges commercial firms and individual merchants retained a significant presence on international markets, but many did so with strong links to their core business in Antwerp. In the early fifteenth century, Bruges merchants had already bought commercial buildings in Antwerp and they had been freighting ships in Middelburg, Arnemuiden and other outports in the Scheldt estuary. Because of the growing success of the Brabant fairs, Bruges was more or less devoid of merchants during the fair period. As Antwerp became a permanent market, by the mid sixteenth century commercial families like the Van Eyewerve and the Kethele started to settle there almost permanently. Other Bruges merchant families, the de Boodt, Lommelin, Rans, Van den Heede and Winckelman, engaged there in international trade as well.[51]

In a city suffering decline, the economic elites looked for alternative investment possibilities. Wealthy burghers became more active on the

[50] Stabel, 'Entre commerce'; L. Vandamme, 'Antoon Saijon, Brugge en de export van Hondschootse saaien omstreeks 1560', *Westhoek*, 26 (2010), 67–80; Puttevils, 'Klein gewin', p. 49.

[51] Few of these firms have been studied in detail. See K. Degryse, *Pieter Seghers: Een koopmansleven in troebele tijden* (Antwerp and Baarn, 1989), pp. 17–18; Brulez, *De firma Della Faille*; E. Wijnroks, *Handel tussen Rusland en de Nederlanden, 1560–1640: Een netwerkanalyse van de Antwerpse en Amsterdamse kooplieden handelend op Rusland* (Hilversum, 2003).

property market in the surrounding countryside and on the growing markets for annuities, which had been underused until well into the fifteenth century.[52] The city had already used annuities to finance its expenses from the late thirteenth century and the share of long-term public debt increased during the fifteenth.[53] The private market for annuities is less well documented. It seems that Bruges citizens before the mid fifteenth century had a preference for letters obligatory, rather than annuities (life or hereditary). Yet the popularity of this financial instrument increased during the later fifteenth century, and by the sixteenth, the capital markets aligned with the situation in other cities of the Low Countries, where annuities, with real estate as surety, had become one of the leading instruments of credit relations. Because indirect taxes on consumption (the economic basis for urban income) declined, the city also had to finance its large infrastructural projects in the port of Bruges by selling more and more annuities, to a point where it became caught in a negative financial cycle that eventually could no longer be controlled.[54]

Reduced Political Autonomy and Guild Power

Bruges' diminishing economic importance was also reflected in its declining place in political affairs. Bruges and Flanders had become part of the Habsburg empire, a much larger polity than the one assembled by the Burgundian dukes, and on which, it was said, 'the sun never set'. On 18 April 1515 the people of Bruges celebrated the arrival of their new count of Flanders, the young Charles V, with an entry ceremony, which ended with the count's customary oath to uphold the city's privileges before the people and the canons of St Donatian's. As on previous occasions, the entry provided an opportunity for the city to represent its position in relation to comital authority. Bruges made clear its high expectations of the

[52] Soens, *De spade in de dijk*, pp. 77–99, 272: between c.1390 and 1550, the number of landowners in the Flemish coastal plain was more than halved.

[53] Derycke, 'Public Annuity Market'.

[54] J. D. Tracy, *A Financial Revolution in the Habsburg Netherlands: Renten and Renteniers in the County of Holland, 1515–1565* (Berkeley, CA, 1985), pp. 110–122; SAB, 219; P. Delcelle, 'De Gentse rentenverkopen in de zestiende eeuw: Een studie van de motieven voor het gebruik van dit financiële instrument', *HMG*, 64 (2010), 327–40; L. Vandamme, 'De geldnood van keizer Karel, de Brugse kapitaalmarkt en renteniers (1554)', *Biekorf*, 110 (2010), 395–426; M. van der Heijden, *Geldschieters van de stad: Financiële relaties tussen stad, burgers en overheden 1550–1650* (Amsterdam, 2006). For the market for public credit, see Derycke, 'Public Annuity Market'.

prince's commitment to the city's economic welfare.[55] The report of this entry was among the most disseminated of all accounts of Bruges civic ceremonies: evidently the city's splendour was still able to impress the outside world. Yet contrary to tradition, the young Charles V waited a few days between his arrival in the city and the swearing of the accustomed oath.[56] It was a strong symbolic statement that showed that the centre of gravity in the relationship between the prince and his urban subjects had shifted significantly in favour of the central state. The role of Bruges as a princely residence also came to an end. The larger size of the Habsburg state meant that the ruling dynasty was less often physically present in the cities of the Low Countries, and its princes tended to rule more from residential cities that also hosted many of their councils and courtiers. In the sixteenth-century Low Countries this function was taken up first by Mechelen (which also hosted the Great Council, the highest court of law in the Low Countries) and then by Brussels. The palace of the Prinsenhof in Bruges, so often the setting for princely splendour under the Burgundian dukes, lost its residential function, and in 1576 King Philip II even sold off parts of the complex.[57] There were no other central or even provincial institutions in Bruges, although as we shall see the city did become an episcopal seat and it remained the capital of the surrounding rural district of the Liberty.

Along with their economic importance and autonomy, the political role of craft guilds contracted everywhere in Habsburg lands. In Bruges, guilds hung on to a good deal of their economic power, social capital and cultural prestige, but because of the change to urban industries, their importance was in no way comparable to that of their proud predecessors who between 1280 and 1490 had been at the heart of the political struggle for broader participation in urban government. The craft guilds and the Great Council did not formally lose all power, but they would never achieve the same political momentum in the sixteenth century as they had in earlier periods. Guilds did remain fundamental to the city's social and economic organization and to its corporate identity. The 'General Assembly', the institutional successor of the Great Council, included representatives of the guilds and former magistrates. It claimed to represent the urban community as a whole, but its meetings, strictly orchestrated by the aldermen, were only convoked when

55 Blockmans, 'Fondans', p. 26. See on entry ceremonies, Lecuppre-Desjardin, *La ville des cérémonies*; and Brown, *Civic Ceremony*.

56 Brown, *Civic Ceremony*, pp. 294–5; H. Soly, 'Plechtige intochten in de steden van de Zuidelijke Nederlanden tijdens de overgang van Middeleeuwen naar Nieuwe Tijd: Communicatie, propaganda, spektakel', *TG*, 97 (1984), 341–61 (at 351).

57 Hillewaert and Van Besien (eds.), *Het Prinsenhof*.

important financial matters were on the agenda. Masters representing the guilds were usually also very close to the magistracy.[58]

In general, the Bruges city government was loyal, even somewhat subservient, towards the central government, and complained little. But it still looked for pragmatic ways to serve the city's interests when negotiating with the prince. The burgomasters, aldermen and councillors were recruited annually from the ranks of the urban nobility, the mercantile and entrepreneurial elites, jurists and some of the influential guild masters. The two burgomasters were usually noblemen, often only indirectly linked to the city.[59] The prince and his councillors saw to it that only loyal subjects occupied the urban offices and that power was not monopolized by opposing family clans. Between 1501 and 1560 only nine 'families' (or at least people with the same surname) counted more than five representatives: de Baenst (6), Breydel (7), Van de Velde (7), Despars (8), Van den Heede (8), de Witte (10), Van den Berghe (10), de Boodt (12) and Van Vyve (16).[60] These were the same leading families who had dominated political life in the late medieval period, but their hold on city government became more permanent and less contested. Pensionaries like De Damhouder still played a key role in mediating between urban and central governments but they increasingly found their way into more prestigious princely offices and institutions.

A Continuing Importance of Luxury Industries and Fine Arts

Until about 1550, the late medieval tradition of luxury industries and artistic production in Bruges remained strong, particularly in jewellery, painting and illuminated manuscripts. These were mainly export-oriented sectors, now targeting Antwerp as their international outlet market. In a changing economic environment, they introduced technological and organizational innovations and dealt creatively with strict guild rules. The most expensive of these industries was tapestry production, which was soon influenced by the new forms and motifs of Renaissance art. Although much less important than the development of tapestry manufacture in the workshops of

58 Blockmans, 'Fondans', pp. 31–2. Studies of early modern craft guilds in Bruges include S. Gilté, 'Het bakkersambacht te Brugge: Samenstelling en werking', *HGG*, 137 (2000), 126–151; and K. van Quathem, 'Sociale mobiliteit en machtsverdeling in het Brugse schoenmakersambacht (1570–1790)', in C. Lis and H. Soly (eds.), *Werken volgens de regels: Ambachten in Brabant en Vlaanderen, 1500–1800* (Brussels, 1994), pp. 107–34.

59 Buylaert, 'Edelen in de Vlaamse stedelijke samenleving', p. 50.

60 The lists can be found in SAB, 114; and AGR, Staat en Audiëntie, 809/7.

Brussels or the mass production in and around Oudenaarde, the Bruges workshops produced not only for local and regional elite consumers, but also for international demand. Spanish customers were particularly interested in Bruges-manufactured tapestries, but there were others, such as the Polish King Sigismund I who commissioned an important series of Bruges tapestries in 1533. In the later sixteenth century, however, tapestry weaving lost momentum and a number of Bruges weavers left the city for other manufacturing centres inside the Low Countries and beyond (such as Florence and Orléans).[61]

Painting also remained important in the first half of the sixteenth century: although less capital-intensive than tapestry production, it was probably more significant because of the higher number of artisans involved. Late medieval traditions prevailed for a time. When Hans Memling died in 1494, Jan Provoost (Mons, c.1463–5 – Bruges, 1529) settled in Bruges, having worked with Simon Marmion in Valenciennes.[62] His artistic rival, Gerard David (active in Bruges between 1484 and 1523) had migrated from Oudewater in Holland ten years previously.[63] While Petrus Christus and Hans Memling in the fifteenth century must have worked mainly on commission, new masters tried to create new markets. Provoost and David both enrolled in the Antwerp painters' guild in 1493 and 1515 respectively. Provoost's works, such as the *Miser and Death*,[64] show the influence of Antwerp innovations, while David conformed more to the Bruges artistic canon. He had an influence on his direct followers the Master of the Bruges Passion Scenes, the Master of the Holy Blood, Adriaen Isenbrant (active in Bruges 1510–51 – see Figure 10.1), Albert Cornelis (1475–1532) and Ambrosius Benson (active in Bruges 1518–50).[65] The artistic traditions

[61] E. Duverger, 'Tapijtwevers, tapijthandel en tapijtwerk in Brugge van de late middeleeuwen tot in het begin van de achttiende eeuw', in Delmarcel and Duverger (eds.), *Brugge en de tapijtkunst*, pp. 16–99; F. Checa, *Vlaamse wandtapijten voor de Bourgondische hertogen, keizer Karel V en koning Filips II* [exh. cat.] (Brussels, 2008). On the complex organisation of tapestry manufacture in the Low Countries, see G. Delmarcel, *Flemish Tapestry, 15th to 18th Century* (London and New York, 1999); M. Vanwelden, *Productie van wandtapijten in de regio Oudenaarde: Een symbiose tussen stad en platteland (15de tot 17de eeuw)* (Leuven, 2006); Stabel, *De kleine stad*, pp. 190–6.

[62] R. Spronk, 'Jan Provoost', in Martens (ed.), *Brugge en de Renaissance*, vol. I, pp. 94–106; R. Spronk, 'The Reconstruction of a Triptych by Jan Provoost for the Jerusalem Chapel in Bruges', *Burlington Magazine*, 147 (2005), 109–11.

[63] Van Miegroet, *Gerard David*; Ainsworth, *Gerard David*.

[64] Bruges, Groeningemuseum, inventory number 0000.GRO0216.I-0218.I.

[65] For the Master of the Holy Blood, see L. Hendrikman, 'De Meester van het Heilig Bloed', in Martens (ed.), *Brugge en de Renaissance*, vol. I, pp. 109–19; for Isenbrant, see T.-H. Borchert, 'Adriaan Isenbrant', in Martens (ed.), *Brugge en de Renaissance*, vol. I, pp. 120–39; on Albrecht

Figure 10.1 Adriaen Isenbrant, *The Virgin of the Seven Sorrows* (Bruges, Church of Our Lady's)

of the fifteenth-century masters continued to be important in many workshops. Yet some experimented with the new Italianate 'Renaissance' formal idioms, for instance Jan Provoost and Lancelot Blondeel (Poperinge, 1498 – Bruges, 1561); while others like Ambrosius Benson adhered more to tradition. Lancelot Blondeel and his step-son, Pieter Pourbus (Gouda, c.1523 – Bruges, 1584) became the main representatives of the Bruges Renaissance. The latter was popular as a portrait painter,[66] and his work

Cornelis, see D. Tamis, 'Albracht Cornelis', in Martens (ed.), *Brugge en de Renaissance*, vol. I, pp. 140–1; on Benson, see D. Marechal, 'Ambrosius Benson', in Martens (ed.), *Brugge en de Renaissance*, vol. I, pp. 142–57.

[66] For Blondeel, see L. Jansen, 'Lanceloot Blondeel', in Martens (ed.), *Brugge en de Renaissance*, vol. I, pp. 173–88; for Pourbus, see P. Huvenne, 'Pieter Pourbus', in Martens (ed.), *Brugge en de Renaissance*, vol. I, pp. 189–215.

helped to integrate the innovations of Renaissance painting more fully into the Bruges tradition.[67]

The medieval guild system was able to adapt to the changing world market for art. It offered opportunities to maximize the effects of the division of labour, the application of advanced reproduction techniques, and working for more anonymous markets. To this effect, high-quality series of smaller-size paintings on panels with accessible themes were produced. Also aimed at foreign markets were the cheaper paintings on canvas produced by the canvas painters (*cleerscrivers*). Between 1500 and 1520 more new masters joined the St Luke guild than had been the case during the artistic heyday of the 1460s and 1470s. How exactly these workshops functioned and how production was managed is unclear, but it appears that masters recruited far fewer apprentices. In the later fifteenth century 15 per cent of masters trained only one apprentice and over 42 per cent were never engaged in training, but during the period 1500–30 these figures increased to 25 and 65 per cent respectively: compared with the earlier period only a tiny minority of master painters was still involved in training. The use of journeymen, allowing masters to deal with commissions in a flexible way, probably compensated partly for the falling number of apprentices.[68] But despite this upsurge of painting in the early sixteenth century, the tide was turning. In 1511, the city had to take direct control of more than 150 stalls in the Pand, the commercial infrastructure for arts and luxuries near the Franciscan friary, in order to support shrinking art markets. Bruges painters like Provoost, Isenbrant and David started working for the Antwerp market, using specialized art dealers as intermediaries. In 1532, Provoost finally moved to Antwerp, as did other less reputed masters. Antwerp had also become the centre for the import and treatment of colouring agents and other raw materials for painting.[69] Around 1530, the Bruges Pand lost its commercial importance for good. Products were now being sold in the workshops themselves and the artists reacted to the recession by exploiting their economic networks. Export was mainly directed towards Spain, where interest in Flemish art had become traditional, and artistic taste was more conservative. The Spanish merchants of Bruges mediated in the commercial outlet.[70] Local consumption of art and other luxury items in Bruges may

[67] M. Martens, 'De dialoog tussen artistieke traditie en vernieuwing', in Martens (ed.), *Brugge en de Renaissance*, vol. I, pp. 43–63.

[68] Stabel, 'Organisation corporative'.

[69] Wilson, *Painting in Bruges*; F. Vermeylen, *Painting for the Market: Commercialization of Art in Antwerp's Golden Age* (Turnhout, 2003).

[70] A case study in C. Perier-D'Ieteren, 'Production d'atelier et exportation: Cinq versions de Sainte Famille de l'entourage de Gerard David', *Belgisch Tijdschrift voor Oudheidkunde*

have suffered from decreasing commercial and entrepreneurial profit rates as well. An average Antwerp household inventory (1532–67) counted twice as many paintings as its equivalent in Bruges (1531–1620). Yet it seems that wider social groups were now investing in art to adorn private houses, and this trend partially benefited painting in Bruges. In a sample of about eighty Bruges inventories from 1438 to 1440, not one included a painting; so the private market that developed after the mid fifteenth century must have become an important outlet for Bruges painters. This market can probably explain the resilience of Bruges painting (especially of cheaper paintings) at the start of the sixteenth century. It is striking, in this respect, that Bruges households mostly possessed paintings of religious scenes that were presented on a cupboard in an almost devotional manner, while in Antwerp there was a larger appetite for new themes such as portraits and mythological scenes.[71]

Like panel painting, manuscript illumination retained its importance as a luxury craft product in the early sixteenth century. From about 1470 onwards Flemish illuminators started using new forms and motifs, among them 'three-dimensional' painted margins (the so-called Ghent-Bruges style), and their luxury manuscripts remained popular at European courts. Simon Bening (Ghent, c.1483 – Bruges, 1561), is generally considered to be the last great Flemish illuminator. He worked for many south European and German courts, contributing to the art of landscape painting, one of the key features of Low Countries painting in this period.[72] Bruges craftsmen also still manufactured high-quality parchment, which was sought after on foreign markets.[73] But this interest in manuscript production halted abruptly. After 1550 the production of illuminated manuscripts came to a standstill and the industry was unable to adapt to changing market circumstances, brought about by the printing press and its massifying effects. Within Bruges, the production of printed books had made a promising start with the printing of incunabula, but the output of printers like Colard Mansion

en Kunstgeschiedenis, 77 (2008), 27–44; B. Dewilde, 'On Noble Artists and Poor Craftsmen: Networking Painters in Renaissance Bruges', in K. Brosens, L. Kelchtermans and K. Van der Stighelen (eds.), *Art Production and Kinship Patterns in the Early Modern Low Countries* (Turnhout, 2012), pp. 85–101.

[71] B. Dewilde, 'Portretten en de markt: Het familiebedrijf Claeissens in zestiende-eeuws Brugge', unpublished MA thesis, Catholic University of Leuven (Leuven, 2007), pp. 8–24; M. P. J. Martens and N. Peeters, 'Paintings in Antwerp Houses (1532–1567)', in De Marchi and Van Miegroet (eds.), *Mapping Markets*, pp. 35–53.

[72] Kren and McKendrick (eds.), *Illuminating the Renaissance*.

[73] L. Vandamme, 'Perkament maken en verkopen in Brugge op het einde van de 16[de] eeuw', *HGG*, 144 (2007), 401–13.

remained firmly rooted in the city's tradition of luxury manuscripts.[74] Mansion unsuccessfully tried to adjust new techniques to the demands of his clientele. So in the sixteenth century, when the scope of printing changed, Bruges missed the opportunity to profit from it. Antwerp became the typographical capital of the Low Countries. Bruges authors aiming to distribute their works internationally, like the Valencia-born humanist Juan Luis Vives (1493–1540) and the historian Jacob de Meyere (Meyerus) who rewrote Flemish history in a style influenced by classical authors, expressed dissatisfaction with the limitations of printing shops in their own city. The printing trade became the most capital-intensive industry in the sixteenth century; so it is significant that the only Bruges workshop that produced books for the European market was privately financed by the rich patron Marcus Laurinus, Jr, who subsidized the Antwerp printer Hubert Goltzius to come to Bruges. When the financial arrangement stopped, the experiment ended in failure.[75]

Despite the declining international importance of Bruges as a cultural centre, certain forms of cultural activity within the city remained vibrant. Festive musicality among guilds and fraternities continued, and not always quietly. In 1533 the Sisters of the Syon convent accused the 'kolveniers' (arquebusiers) of 'committing great incivilities, piping, trumpeting, playing and screaming in their court, both during the day and by night'.[76] Guilds remained important consumers of music. When the crossbowmen from Lille visited in 1549, the New Court of St George hired four trumpet players for day-time heralding, as well as 'Gillis the minstrel' who joined the other guild musicians.[77] Many members of the middle and upper classes sponsored private music entertainment, either within their own households or as members of cultural networks. Language-learning conversation books testify to amateur polyphonic practices: music books were shared during a dinner party for host and guests to sing together around the table.[78] The music was not necessarily known to the guests, suggesting their sight-reading

[74] See above, Chapter 9.

[75] H. de la Fontaine Verwey, 'The First Private Press in the Low Countries: Marcus Laurinus and the Officina Goltziana', *Quaerendo*, 2 (1972), 294–310; W. Le Loup (ed.), *Hubertus Goltzius en Brugge, 1583–1983* [exh. cat.] (Bruges, 1983); L. Vandamme, 'Boeken', in Martens (ed.), *Brugge en de Renaissance*, vol. I, pp. 280–3.

[76] SAB, 387, St Barbara Guild, Folder 436, 'Copie vande acte anghaende eeneghe zaken vande colveureniers'.

[77] SAB, 385, II/11, 1549–1579, fo. 32.

[78] For instance H. Vanhulst, 'La musique dans les manuels de conversation bilingues de la Renaissance: Les 'Seer gemeiyne Tsamencoutingen / Collocutions bien familieres' de Jean Berthout', *Belgisch Tijdschrift voor Muziekwetenschap*, 59 (2005), 93–124.

Figure 10.2 Songbook of Zeghere van Male, Superius fo. 58r: Gheerkin de Hondt, *Missa Panis quem ego dabo*, Kyrie II

skills were advanced. Zeghere van Male, author of the *Lamentation*, possessed a set of partbooks (a music notation format, whereby each voice of the polyphonic music is notated in a separate volume), with sacred, secular and instrumental music, which must have served such entertainment (see Figure 10.2).[79] The Van Male partbooks also show that musical literacy was not limited to professional musicians or even to the nobility (among whom private music tuition is well attested).[80] Van Male was a middle-class textile merchant (*bocraenvercooper*) who hand-copied the entire collection in a practised hand – a total of c.1,200 pages – indicating good musical schooling. Many children developed basic musical skills. By the sixteenth century, reading instruction was based on well-known chant melodies and texts, and music served as a mnemonic aid to remember key texts like the Ten Commandments.[81] Mimicking was common practice, not only to

[79] Cambrai, Médiathèque Municipale, MSS 125–8. On the Van Male partbooks, see Gabriëls, 'Bourgeois Music Collecting'; G. K. Diehl, 'The Partbooks of a Renaissance Merchant, Cambrai: Bibliothèque Municipale, MSS 125–128', unpublished PhD thesis, University of Pennsylvania (Philadelphia, 1974).

[80] For an account of tuition of noble women in Antwerp, see K. Forney, 'A Proper Musical Education for Antwerp's Women', in R. E. Murray, S. Forscher Weiss and C. J. Cyrus (eds.), *Music Education in the Middle Ages and the Renaissance* (Bloomington, 2010), pp. 84–125.

[81] On the employment of music in general education, see K. van Orden, 'Children's Voices: Singing and Literacy in Sixteenth-Century France', *Early Music History*, 25 (2006), 209–56.

internalize chant melodies but also to learn simple polyphonic compositions. This was probably how pupils from the Bogaerden school, for Holy Blood day, learned a three-voice composition: the text for it was written by a rhetorician and the music by one of the city church's choirmasters.[82] Van Male probably learned music in this way as a child, perhaps having attended St James' choir school under Benedictus Appenzeller (succentor 1518–19) as the repertoire in his partbooks suggests.[83] Like many other pupils, Van Male took his musical proficiency into the amateur realm rather than joining the clergy. Membership of guilds like that of the crossbowmen (St George) and librarians (St Luke and St John) offered a fertile context where professional musicians met interested amateurs. Van Male probably belonged to one of the rhetorician circles that continued to contribute significantly to cultural life (as we shall see below).[84] The Bruges rhetorician guilds and their individual members were well connected outside the city. The rhetoric competitions created chances to connect on a structural basis. The lively popular song culture in Bruges is also reflected by a song contest within the 1517 rhetoricians' festival, the first festival in the Low Countries in which awards were given for monodic songs.[85] Another view on song culture in Bruges is offered by a diverse collection of early sixteenth-century songs from several rhetoricians, luckily incorporated into a printed songbook and published in Antwerp in 1539. It gives us a glimpse of minor poets, one of whom is only known thus: 'Bi him scrijft Borse sonder ghelt / Was dese leysen ghestelt' (By him who calls himself 'Wallet without money', this song was made).[86]

The collegiate churches of Bruges also continued to be important producers of polyphonic music – though the number of foundations that supported them severely declined from the end of the fifteenth century, as did their links with a wider world. Even so, some famous composers like Antonius Busnois ended up at St Saviour's (c.1490), and Jean Richafort at

[82] A. Dewitte, 'Scholen en onderwijs te Brugge gedurende de Middeleeuwen', *HGG*, 109 (1972), 145–217 (at 168).

[83] Gabriëls, 'Bourgeois Music Collecting', pp. 147–8.

[84] Van Male's membership is discussed in N. Gabriëls, 'Private Musical Culture Represented in Three Manuscripts from Bruges c.1525–1560: A Context for Amateur Composition', unpublished paper delivered at the Medieval and Renaissance Music Conference (Certaldo, 2013).

[85] J. Oosterman, 'Oogkleppen en grote lijnen: Een pleidooi voor onderzoek naar de dynamiek van literaire veranderingen', *Queeste*, 11 (2004), 152–62 (at 156).

[86] K. Vellekoop, 'Een liedboekje in het "Devoot ende profitelijck boecxken": De werkwijze van een verzamelaar', in F. Willaert (ed.), *Veelderhande liedekens: Studies over het Nederlandse lied tot 1600. Symposium Antwerpen 28 februari 1996* (Leuven, 1997), pp. 103–17.

St Giles' (1543–4 and 1548–50). Adriaen Willaert, chapel master of San Marco in Venice, travelled to Bruges in 1542 and visited his brother Anthonius, a chaplain at St Donatian's. Around the same time, Willaert composed the motet *Laus tibi sacra rubens* for the Holy Blood chapel, bringing Venetian musical fashion to the city.[87] The first appearance in the Low Countries of the newly fashioned Italian madrigal occurs in Van Male's 1542 partbooks, and may be connected to Willaert's travels.

The city government too continued to fund music for civic occasions. In 1528, Bruges followed a trend elsewhere in the Low Countries and commissioned eleven bells for the city's carillon (*voorslag)* in the Belfry.[88] In 1552, the singer and trombone player Jan Lenis received money for a new *versteekboek*, a pattern book for positioning the carillon pins.[89] By that time, the pins on the drum must have been movable, allowing for different tunes, religious and secular, to be played on the carillon during different seasons of the liturgical year. Besides the drum, a keyboard could set the bells in motion by 1532, when the priest Adriaen van der Sluus received 25 shillings from the city 'van alle mesavende te spelene upt voorslach deser stede' (to play the carillon of this city).[90]

Religious Life, Humanism and Reformation

Despite the disruptions of the 1480s and early 1490s, many of the practices that had characterized the city's religious life re-emerged with little change. A dense network of churches and chapels continued to cover the city: Eduard de Dene in his *Testament* mentions no fewer than eleven churches, twenty chapels, eight cloisters, eight religious guilds or fraternities, five 'houses of God' and nine houses of 'sisters', a list that was far from exhaustive.[91] In some churches, rebuilding programmes were continued: the expansion of the ambulatory of St Saviour's in the early sixteenth century was the culmination of a long tradition of ecclesiastical rebuilding in the city, and included two new chapels used by the stocking makers (1515) and wheelwrights (1516).[92] St Saviour's was also elevated to collegiate status in

87 K. Schiltz, 'Polyphony and Word-Sound in Adrian Willaert's *Laus tibi sacra rubens*', *Yearbook of the Alamire Foundation*, 6 (2008), 61–75.

88 SAB, 216, 1528–9, fo. 102^{r}; Andriessen, *Die van muziken gheerne horen*, pp. 38–9.

89 L. Gilliodts-Van Severen, *Le carillon de Bruges: Recueil de textes et analyses de documents inédits ou peu connus* (Bruges, 1912), p. 106.

90 SAB, 216, 1532–3, fo. 109^{r}.

91 De Dene, *Testament Rhetoricael*, passim.

92 Devliegher, *De Sint-Salvatorskathedraal te Brugge*, pp. 85–91, 160–1, 162–203.

1501 and, like St Donatian's and Our Lady's, it had a Latin school.[93] There was, however, a sharp reduction in the number of foundations in the early sixteenth century compared with the peak years between the 1460s and 1480s. In St Donatian's, the larger foundations of the dean Jan Bonivicini in 1514, the Genoese Andrea de la Costa in 1525, and of Jehan de Carondolet, archbishop of Palermo, after 1540, were exceptional for their size.[94]

Some of the older ecclesiastical traditions remained strong. St Donatian's continued to assert its pre-eminence over other churches in Bruges. The body of its patron saint was still a focus of city-wide devotion, and its arrival in Bruges was recalled in one of the dumbshows put on for Charles V's entry in 1515. As before, the traditional links between the ruling dynasty and the church served the interests of both. St Donatian's had not always appreciated its subservient position relative to the bishop of Tournai. The Burgundian dukes had attempted to have episcopal boundaries redrawn in order to reduce the bishop's control over prelates in their own territories. These ambitions were pursued by their Habsburg successors, during the schism that divided the bishopric of Tournai between 1483 and 1506;[95] and were finally realized on 12 May 1559. As part of a major ecclesiastical reform in the Low Countries, three new archbishoprics and fourteen new bishoprics were created. St Donatian's was a beneficiary: it was elevated from a collegiate church to a cathedral, the seat of a new bishop of Bruges.[96]

The interest taken by the city magistrates in religious life and public ceremony during the later Middle Ages was further pursued. City magistrates ordered respect for religious holidays: in 1527, following the bishop of Tournai's prescriptions, a city ordinance named twenty-nine festive days, besides Apostle days and Sundays, on which work was usually forbidden.[97] They continued to finance the Holy Blood procession. In 1517 the procession was the scene for a grand-scale competition among rhetoricians. The event was sponsored by a lottery organized by the city council.[98] Joost de Damhouder stated in 1564 that the procession benefited

93 A. Dewitte, 'Scolastri en rectores scolarum aan de O. L. Vrouw-kapittelschool te Brugge (ca. 1480–1553)', *HGG*, 99 (1962), 265–74; A. Dewitte, 'De kapittelschool van de collegiale Sint-Salvator te Brugge, 1516–1594', *HGG*, 104 (1967), 5–65.

94 BAB, A141, fos. 125^{v}–9^{v}, 137^{r}–41^{v}; Brown, *Civic Ceremony*, pp. 104, 311.

95 H. Callewier, '"Quis esset episcopus tornacensis ignorabatur": Le schisme tournaisien (1483–1506)', *Revue d'histoire ecclésiastique*, 107 (2012), 131–68.

96 E. Van Mingroot, 'Oprichting en omschrijving van het bisdom', in M. Cloet, R. Boudens and B. Janssens de Bisthoven (eds.), *Het bisdom Brugge (1559–1984): Bisschoppen, priesters, gelovigen* (Bruges, 1984), pp. 17–21. It was only in the nineteenth century that the present-day cathedral of St Saviour's would become the seat of the bishopric.

97 SAB, 120, III (1513–30), fos. 518^{v}–19^{r}.

98 SAB, 216, 1516–17, fos. 137^{r}–8^{r}.

the 'stadts assijsen', the city's taxes on consumption. General processions carrying relics and increasingly the Holy Sacrament, usually in collaboration with St Donatian's, continued to form part of the spiritual arsenal deployed by city governments to defend the city in times of crisis, or to celebrate a return to peace. In 1509, a new kind of event to offer relief from the plague was instituted, in which one person from every household was ordered to attend the weekly processions in their own parish churches. They were also to pray 'for the prosperity of the prince'. General processions continued to serve the needs of the ruling dynasty. Habsburg rulers demanded that city governments organize processions in support of their dynastic concerns, even more systematically than their Burgundian predecessors.[99] The Holy Blood relic continued to be processed at royal demand against the French and other enemies of the monarchy.[100] Deference to princely interests was reflected in the Holy Blood procession itself: the appearance from 1517 in the procession plays of the legendary horse 'Ros Beiaard', ridden by the four sons of Aymon, the vassal of Charlemagne, was a passing nod to Habsburg imperial ambitions.[101]

The claim that city governments had long asserted over the management of poor relief, as guardians or supervisors of hospitals, almshouses, orphans and parish poor-tables, was renewed with vigour. Measures dealing with poverty and vagrancy, sometimes decreed in line with Habsburg policy and at the request of the Council of Flanders, were already harsher at the end of the fifteenth century. They were followed by more comprehensive, but also more controversial attempts to reform and rationalize poor relief in the city, at a time (from the 1520s) when foundations for distributions to the parish poor had begun to decline. A blueprint for reform was produced by the humanist Juan Luis Vives on behalf of the city council, and placed emphasis on the need to ban begging and to put the unemployed to work. Vives' *De subventione pauperum* (1526) enjoyed fame throughout Europe, and between 1522 and 1545 the policies proposed led to practical results in many parts of the continent, including in fourteen cities of the Low Countries. But ironically in Bruges itself, the city council did not succeed

[99] Brown, *Civic Ceremony*, pp. 291–5; W. N. M. Hüsken, 'Kroniek van het toneel in Brugge, 1468–1556', *Verslagen en mededelingen van de Koninklijke Academie voor Nederlandse Taal- en Letterkunde* (1992), 219–52; E. Gailliard, 'De "processiën generael" en de "hallegeboden" te Brugge', *Verslagen en mededeelingen der Koninklijke Vlaamsche Academie voor Taal- en Letterkunde* (1912), 1061–229.

[100] See Holy Blood processions in 1545, 1553 and 1558: de Dene, *Testament*, pp. 31, 35. A list of these processions (for the years 1505, 1529, 1534, 1536, 1538, 1541, 1568 and 1576) is given in Bruges, BAB, C445.

[101] SAB, 216, 1516–17, fo. 139^{r}.

in implementing the final part of the proposed reform, setting up a central urban organization for the poor. Traditional church authorities, supported by the mendicant orders, successfully opposed these policies in the 1520s and in the 1560s.[102]

In many ways the festive and literary culture of late medieval Bruges continued unabated. The festivities of the shooting guilds (joined by the new guild of arquebusiers) flourished after peace was restored in 1492.[103] Rhetorician activity thrived, although in a cultural environment that inclined more strongly than before to consensus rather than opposition.[104] In 1494 an agreement was reached to sort out conflicts between the older Holy Spirit chamber and the newer chamber of the 'Three Female Saints' (*Drie Santinnen*): precedence was given to the older chamber in decisions over poetry and play writing for competitions, but in consultation with the newer one, and under the supervision of the city magistrates. The rhetoricians retained an important role in representations of identity and power.[105] Both chambers were apparently involved in reporting in verse on the entry of the new count Charles in 1515: 'Tstellen rethorijckelic te Brugghe binnen dede / Tgheselscip shelichs gheests en de drie sanctinnen mede' (Writing this down in a rhetorical way in Bruges was done by the Holy Ghost and the Three Female Saints in collaboration) – though in fact this long poem was the work of the poet Jan de Scheerere.[106] The entry ceremony was also described in French: the richly illustrated manuscript and the printed version of this text reveal the continuing bilingual nature of Bruges' elite culture.[107] The rhetoricians dominated literary life in sixteenth-century Bruges (or at any rate, their outputs have survived better than those of others because of their institutionalized status). The city bylaws (*hallegeboden*), the city accounts and the beautiful cartulary of the rhetoricians' chamber of the 'Three Female Saints' (*Drie Santinnen*), testify to their various activities.[108] Rhetoricians remained tightly linked with city government.

[102] C. Lis and H. Soly, *Armoede en kapitalisme in pre-industrieel Europa* (Antwerp and Weesp, 1986), pp. 100–17; A. Dewitte, 'Brugse armenzorg in de 16[de] eeuw', *Spieghel Historiael*, 4 (1969), 19–24.

[103] G. Philips, 'Brugge in de 16[de] eeuw: Een cultuurhistorisch essay', *Biekorf*, 92 (1992), 291–305.

[104] Van Bruaene, *Om beters wille*, pp. 89–112.

[105] Van Bruaene, *Om beters wille*, pp. 71–3; A.-L. Van Bruaene, *Repertorium van rederijkerskamers in de Zuidelijke Nederlanden en Luik 1400* (2004) (retrieved from www.dbnl.org/tekst/brua002repe01_01 on 17 July 2015).

[106] 'Jan de Scheereres *Triumphe*', ed. Mareel.

[107] S. Mareel, *Voor vorst en stad: Rederijkersliteratuur en vorstenfeest in Vlaanderen en Brabant (1432–1561)* (Amsterdam, 2010), pp. 130–1.

[108] M. Vandecasteele, 'Een rederijkersfeest te Brugge in 1517', *Jaarboek De Fonteine*, 17 (1967), 27–46.

Cornelis Everaert (c.1480–1556),[109] who was a dyer and fuller by trade and a member of both the Holy Spirit and Three Female Saints chambers, won a competition for plays put on following a general procession of the Holy Blood to celebrate Charles V's victory at Pavia in 1525.[110] In October 1545, following Charles V's victory over King Francis I, the Holy Blood was carried to St Saviour's church, and Eduard de Dene (as Anthonis de Roovere had done in 1471) composed a poem (*carnacion*) in honour of the relic.[111] But although rhetoricians generally served their municipal and princely masters, they could still cast a critical eye on social problems within the city, as their fifteenth-century predecessors had done, and occasionally their activities tended towards subversion: Everaert's *Tspel van dOnghleycke Munte* (Play of the Debased Coin), written in 1530, was banned by the city authorities for being too polemical.[112]

Some rhetoricians lamented a lost golden age of literary activity, recalling the heyday of de Roovere. Eduard de Dene had a large collection of de Roovere's poems printed in 1562 under the title *Rhetoricale Wercken*, and many other works of de Roovere were issued in print.[113] Yet for all their laments, sixteenth-century rhetoricians could be as innovative with poetical forms as their predecessors. Everaert's homage to de Roovere is part of a subtler game played with his predecessor, allowing Everaert to inscribe his own memory within earlier literary tradition. De Dene's publication of de Roovere's poems, as well as his own *Testament Rhetoricael*, represent an innovative approach to self-presentation, and an active attempt to construct a Bruges tradition of rhetorical work. The 1562 edition of de Roovere's poetry, printed in Antwerp, contains a preface in which de Dene honours de Roovere; but it is also above all an apology for poetry in the Flemish language. De Dene ranks Flemish poetry alongside French works by Molinet,

[109] W. N. M. Hüsken, 'De gelegenheidsdichter Cornelis Everaert en zijn tafelspelen in enge en ruimere zin', *Verslagen en mededelingen van de Koninklijke Academie voor Nederlandse taal- en letterkunde*, new series (1992), 62–78; S. Mareel, '"You Serve me Well": Representations of Gossip, Newsmongering and Public Opinion in the Plays of Cornelis Everaert', in J. Bloemendal, A. van Dixhoorn and E. Strietman (eds.), *Literary Cultures and Public Opinion in the Low Countries, 1450–1650* (Leiden, 2011), pp. 37–53.

[110] SAB, 120, III, 1513–30, fos. 417^r–20^r; 216 (1524/5), fo. 120^r; S. Mareel, 'Urban Literary Propaganda on the Battle of Pavia: Cornelis Everaert's "Tspel van den Hooghen Wynt ende Zoeten Reyn"', *Queeste*, 13 (2006), 97–108.

[111] De Dene, *Testament*, pp. 24–5.

[112] W. N. M. Hüsken (ed.), *De spelen van Cornelis Everaert: Opnieuw uitgegeven, van inleiding, annotaties en woordverklaringen voorzien* (Hilversum, 2005); S. Mareel, 'Entre ciel et terre: Le théâtre sociopolitique de Cornelis Everaert', *European Medieval Drama*, 12 (2008), 93–108.

[113] On the printed editions of de Roovere's works, see Oosterman, 'Anthonis de Roovere: Het werk'.

Villon and Marot. His *Testament Rhetoricael*, a well-composed and impressive compilation of older and new poems of his own, was probably inspired by François Villon's *Grand Testament* and shows the influence of Rabelais.[114] In nearly 20,000 verses, it is constructed as a testament in which de Dene recalls important places and events, bequeaths poems and memories to his friends, and gives a broad though tentative overview of the social, religious and literary infrastructure of Bruges. It reveals de Dene's individual talents as a poet and shows that French cultural influences were still at work in Bruges. Although preserved only as an autograph text, the work was widely followed in the Netherlands and beyond. It references near contemporary poets in Bruges, such as de Scheerere and Everaert, but also others about whom little is otherwise known (such as the authors of a text composed for the 1517 competition, and one Steven van der Gheenst who had corresponded with the fiercely anti-Lutheran Anna Bijns from Antwerp).[115] As an individual poet, de Dene was an innovator (and another of his works, *De warachtighe fabulen der dieren*, is the first Dutch emblem fable-book); but his work exemplifies the cultural links between Bruges and a wider world, as well as a thriving textual culture within the city, which had established for itself a literary tradition.[116]

The rhetoricians were also influenced by the renewed intellectual interest in antiquity, and by the Italian Renaissance, which had been developing from the later fifteenth century. Erasmus visited Bruges on several occasions between 1517 and 1521, once in 1520 to meet Juan Luis Vives and Thomas More.[117] Humanist influence was also felt in city government, whose officials often had academic training abroad and knowledge of Roman law. Erasmus' visits to Bruges can be explained by the circle of friends around Marc Laurin, the learned dean of St Donatian's, which included city officials like Frans van Cranevelt, Robert Hellin and Leonard Casembroot. They

114 D. Coigneau, 'Een Brugse Villon of Rabelais: Eduard de Dene en zijn *Testament Rhetoricael* (1561)', in B. A. M. Ramakers (ed.), *Conformisten en rebellen: Rederijkerscultuur in de Nederlanden (1400–1650)* (Amsterdam, 2003), pp. 199–211; S. Mareel, 'Performing the Dutch *Rederijker* Lyric: Eduard de Dene and his *Testament Rhetoricael* (1562)', *Modern Language Review*, 108 (2013), 1199–220; Mareel, 'In the Book of Life'.

115 J. Keßler, *Princesse der rederijkers: Het oeuvre van Anna Bijns: argumentatieanalyse – structuuranalyse – beeldvorming* (Hilversum, 2013), pp. 238–42.

116 D. Geirnaert and P. J. Smith, 'The Sources of the Emblematic Fable Book "De warachtighe fabulen der dieren" (1567)', in J. Manning, K. Porteman and M. van Vaeck (eds.), *The Emblem Tradition and the Low Countries: Selected Papers of the Leuven International Emblem conference, 18–23 August, 1996* (Turnhout, 1999), pp. 23–38.

117 A. Dewitte, 'Erasmus en Brugge, 1515–1536', *HGG*, 94 (1957), 5–21.

argued for tolerant government in religious affairs and for social policies that were encapsulated in Vives' tract on the poor.[118]

The commitment of government circles to humanist thinking is demonstrated by their patronage of educational institutions. Around 1518, the prestigious Collegium Trilingue for the study of classical languages and the ancient world, inspired and financed by the Mechelen councillor Hiëronymus Busleyden (c.1470–1517), another humanist friend of Erasmus, was set up in Leuven. But the university town of Brabant did not initially welcome the Collegium, and only accepted the new foundation when Bruges showed interest in hosting it. Bruges had to wait until 1540 before a humanistic establishment opened its doors, albeit in the modest form of the Collegium Bilingue or 'Cuba Foundation'. It relied heavily on the patronage of individuals, particularly of the merchant's son Jan de Witte (1470–1540), bishop of Cuba, but its chair was appointed by the city council. The 'Cuba Foundation' was modestly resourced and tightly run, but it provided impetus to intellectual activity in the city. At its opening, the first chair, Joris Cassander (1513–66), delivered an oration in praise of Bruges which compared the city to the ancient republic of Athens. Moreover, the study of Greek was nurtured in the school of St Donatian's from 1518–20, later also in the school of Our Lady's church and in four other schools, where the study of Lucian, Homer, Plato and Aristophanes formed part of the curriculum. This love of Greek led to successful careers for certain Bruges scholars who moved on to larger *studia*: Jan Strazeele to Paris, and at the end of the sixteenth century Bonaventura Vulcanius to Leyden. Bruges did not become a cultural backwater. Intellectual renewal and humanist ways of thinking thrived among political, clerical and economic elites. New schools, private initiatives and an expanded system of grants allowed students and teachers from Bruges to enter the major European centres of study, even if Bruges did not develop into one of them. Well-stocked bookstores, as well as private libraries and collections, allowed other inhabitants of Bruges access to the 'new study'. The Bruges bookseller Jacob Plante (Plantius) bought a thousand books from the famous print shop of Plantijn in Antwerp in the 1560s alone, suggesting a considerable market for these in Bruges.[119] Charles Saint-Omer (d.1568) left a collection of more than 1,400 watercolours of plants, inspired by his botanical gardens in Bruges

[118] A. De Smet, 'Iets over de geleerdenkring van en in verband met het "Hof van Watervliet" te Brugge in de 16e eeuw: Belangstelling te Brugge voor geografie en cartografie', in *Liber Amicorum René De Keyser*, pp. 101–4.

[119] Antwerp, Museum Plantin-Moretus, Archief, nos. 17, 39, 40, 110.

and Moerkerke.[120] The frequent visits by Erasmus and his intense correspondence with like-minded humanists in the city indicate that Bruges in the early 1500s remained part of the mainstream of European cultural life.

Links with the outside world also brought the Reformation to Bruges.[121] In 1519, the city council, at the command of the Council of Flanders, was already warning citizens against the teachings of Martin Luther, and in the two decades that followed, official decrees against the spread of new heresies were stepped up.[122] Such reactions indicate a perception in government circles that citizens were potentially receptive to reforming movements. The declining number of foundations (made by both the clergy and the laity) for religious holidays and for poor-table distributions from the 1520s, as well as the virtual cessation of church-building activity in the city, may be explained by the economic downturn;[123] but they also suggest that support for traditional Catholic practices was wavering. Some of the critical attitudes towards the church expressed by early reformers may have found a sympathetic audience in Bruges. The rhetoricians, traditionally the spokesmen of the educated urban laity, had never quite conformed to the preferred ecclesiastical model of lay passivity in sacred matters; and while they continued to support the public ceremonies that formed part of the ritual life of the church (after all, even the unruly Eduard de Dene remained steadfastly loyal to the Habsburg and Catholic cause), their meditative approach to the sacraments and personal study of the Bible distanced them from clerical emphasis on the clergy as sole mediators between God and mankind. Whether rhetoricians fomented Protestant reform in Bruges is not clear, but in Ghent chambers of rhetoric openly declared for reformist ideas in 1539.[124] Among a wider urban public, the high level of literacy did not in itself facilitate openness to Protestant thinking, but the transmission of heresy through books was a danger that the city authorities felt the need to counter: in 1530 they banned the works of Luther, Zwingli, Melanchthon

120 H. Wille, 'The Discovery of the Scientific Heritage of Karel van Sint-Omaars (1533–1569): The *Libri picturati* A16–30 in the Jagiellon Library in Krakow', *Scientiarum Historia*, 22 (1996), 67–80.

121 For an overview, see A. Dewitte, 'Chronologie van de reformatie te Brugge en in het Brugse Vrije (1485–1593)', in D. van der Bauwhede and M. Goetinck (eds.), *Brugge in de Geuzentijd* (Bruges, 1982), pp. 34–41.

122 SAB, 120, III, 1513–30, fos. 134^{v}–5^{r}, 176^{v}–9^{r} (1519), 189^{v} (1519), 193^{r} (1520), 335^{r} (1522), 474^{r}–8^{r} (1526) – when the books of Martin Luther were particularly condemned.

123 See Trio, *Volksreligie*, pp. 191–9.

124 Van Bruaene, *Om beters wille*, pp. 205–15; G. Waite, *Reformers on Stage: Popular Drama and Religious Propaganda in the Low Countries of Charles V, 1515–1556* (Toronto, 2000), pp. 134–64.

and many other heretics, including earlier ones such as John Wyclif and Jan Hus.[125] The clergy too had encouraged certain kinds of reform that would be applauded by early Protestants: the Tournai schism had provoked harsh criticisms of priests and their mores. These had been voiced most strongly by members of the clergy (among them Romboudt de Doppere); while the canons of St Donatian had openly demanded stricter standards of their clergy, for instance by replacing the riotous Feast of the Ass-Bishop after 1510 with a more anodyne Feast of the Boy-Bishop. In this they were encouraged by the city aldermen, who had become more proactive in promoting stricter standards of morality among clergy and laity.[126]

Concern for morality in government circles did not necessarily include sympathy for Protestant reformers. Instead, repressive measures were taken against them. In 1527, one of the earliest known Protestants or Sacramentarians in Bruges, Hector Dommele, a hat maker, was burnt at the stake. His group was dismantled by the city government between 1527 and 1531. During the sixteenth century, Bruges was to witness the death of more than seventy Protestant martyrs. Many of these came from radical Anabaptist or Mennonite sects, who began to appear in the city from 1530. Their social profile may have given the city authorities additional cause for alarm. The Anabaptists recruited largely from the lower social strata of Bruges society and among immigrants who found shelter at the city outskirts. Repression of perceived subversion also began to take another form, in the persecution of witches. Fear of the devil-worshipping Sabbath had long gripped clerical intellectuals, but had little influenced Bruges in the fifteenth century. The new threat posed by Protestant sects doubtless sharpened a fear of subversion of all kinds: witch-hunting became particularly acute in the years 1532–8 and 1543–7 (and later between 1589 and 1596).[127]

Anxiety that the social order was being undermined had a damaging effect on intellectual life. Humanistic learning, particularly that associated with Erasmus, was more likely to meet with suspicion. Leading and 'liberal-minded' scholars such as Joris Cassander, the influential lecturer at the Collegium Bilingue, felt impelled to leave Bruges. The study of the scholarly

[125] SAB, 120, III, 1513–30, fo. 630^{v}–5^{r}.

[126] Callewier, '*Quis esset episcopus*'; Callewier, 'De omgekeerde wereld'; Brown, *Civic Ceremony*, pp. 302–5.

[127] See also H. T. M. Roosenboom, 'Fray Lorenzo de Villavicencio: Een geheim rapporteur in de Nederlanden en zijn invloed op Filips II, 1563–1565', *Archief voor de Geschiedenis van de Katholieke Kerk in Nederland*, 21 (1979), 146–74. Sixty-six convictions for witchcraft were made in Bruges between 1468 and 1687.

canons at the collegiate churches turned increasingly towards Catholic apology and defence against Protestant reform.[128] Not that humanistic learning had necessarily encouraged toleration: knowledge of learned law and a university education made city aldermen familiar with the demonological theories of witchcraft. These are present in the *Praxis rerum criminalium* (first edition 1554) by Joost de Damhouder, and later in the library of Jan de Wree, both clerks influential in the city council.[129] Moderate humanist influences are still apparent among city councillors in the later sixteenth century; but humanist voices raised in favour of religious toleration became fainter, and by the mid sixteenth century the hardening of confessional lines and concern for social order caused humanistic learning to wither.

Repression does not entirely explain why early Protestant reformers met with limited success in Bruges. Perhaps the presence of a broad middle group of 'protestantized Catholics', sympathetic to some reforms, dampened early support for radical change. Municipal responses to Protestants were not uniformly negative or repressive. The pragmatism with which Bruges aldermen negotiated the new political order under the Habsburgs was to some extent replicated in its qualified implementation of religious policies demanded by the central government. The harsher reprisals taken against Protestants resulted in some civil disobedience even within municipal circles: city officials hesitated to put their own citizens on trial.[130] Later reforming movements profited from the experiences of earlier ones. Calvinism was more tightly organized and integrated into urban social structures. From 1560, it found increasing support particularly among international trade circles connected with the English wool staple, and among middling groups of craftsmen working for export markets. The Bruges Calvinist congregation soon had over 200 members and it collaborated closely with Protestants in Antwerp and with Flemish refugee churches in England and Germany. In the 'Wonder Year' of 1566, when iconoclasm spread in the Low Countries, Bruges citizens travelled to listen to public sermons preached

128 A. Dewitte, 'De geestelijkheid van de Brugse Lieve Vrouwekerk in de 16de eeuw', *HGG*, 107 (1970), 100–35; Dewitte, 'De kapittelschool'; A. Dewitte, 'De Brugse Salvatorkerk 1483–1516', *Biekorf*, 100 (2000), 262–6; Dewitte, 'Gegevens betreffende het muziekleven'.

129 D. Vanysacker, 'The Impact of Humanists on Witchcraft Prosecution in 16th- and 17th-Century Bruges', *Humanistica Lovaniensia*, 50 (2001), 393–434; J. Monballyu, 'De invloed van de Brugse strafrechtspraktijk op de *Praxis rerum criminalium* van Joost de Damhouder (1507–1581)', *HGG*, 144 (2007), 293–318; P. Vandermeersch, 'Bruggelingen aan de Leuvense universiteit in de 16de eeuw: Sociale universiteitsgeschiedenis op basis van een prosopografisch onderzoek', *HKZM*, 40 (1986), 159–73 (at 171–2).

130 J. Decavele, 'Protestantse invloeden in Brugge in het midden van de 16de eeuw: Een internationaal netwerk', *Tijdschrift voor Nederlandse Kerkgeschiedenis*, 16 (2013), 6–23.

outside the city limits. Temporary religious freedom broadened opportunities for Protestant recruitment.[131]

However, in Bruges no more than 10 per cent of the population ever aligned itself with Calvinism. Continuing support for a reforming kind of Catholicism may partly explain this reluctance. Some groups were more conservative than others: the Catholic allegiance of local guild masters and of inhabitants in the surrounding countryside was barely affected. This contrasts with the situation in industrial towns and industrialized rural settlements in Western Flanders (Hondschoote, Nieuwkerke), in cities facing steep economic recession (Ypres) and in the metropolis of Antwerp, where the impact of the 1566 uprising was far-reaching and iconoclasm fierce. But repression did prevent the further spread of Calvinism in Bruges: the harsh campaign conducted by the duke of Alva from 1566 forced Protestants into hiding or to find shelter among foreign refugee communities. Marcus Gerards, whose cartographical skills had been so valued by the city council, was the most famous of Bruges Calvinist refugees. From 1567 he was forced to build a new life for himself in London.[132] Even when the uprising gained ground in the late 1570s and Calvinist republics flourished in the southern Low Countries, Bruges did not prove to be among the most radical cities, unlike Ghent for example. When Bruges was conquered by Farnese in 1584, social and political peace was reimposed through repression and the Calvinist movement in the city lost its fervour for good.

The history of Bruges in the sixteenth century, the city's Indian summer, is not a straightforward tale. Even the burghers themselves were confused about it. They recognized and lamented the loss of their former economic and cultural splendour, as well as their political power and degree of autonomy, but they still hoped in the early sixteenth century that recovery was possible. The foreign merchants returned after 1492. The luxury and fashion industries, the pride of industrial Bruges, were starting to reconquer their lost markets. It might have seemed to many that the city's golden age would return. Indeed, for a long time economic indicators appeared positive. Even as late as 1569, when the duke of Alva began the repression

131 L. Vandamme, 'De socio-professionele recrutering van de reformatie in Brugge, 1566–1567', unpublished MA thesis, Catholic University of Leuven (Leuven, 1982).

132 L. Vandamme, 'Het Calvinisme te Brugge in beweging (1560–1566)', in Van der Bauwhede and Goetinck (eds.), *Brugge in de Geuzentijd*, pp. 102–22; J. Decavele, *De dageraad van de reformatie in Vlaanderen (1520–1565)*, 2 vols. (Brussels, 1975); L. Vandamme, 'Doopsgezinden in Brugge, 1555–1575', *Doopsgezinde Bijdragen*, 24 (1998), 9–24; J. Decavele, *De eerste protestanten in de Lage Landen: Geloof en heldenmoed* (Leuven, 2004), pp. 21–39; Decavele, 'Protestantse invloeden'.

of dissidence, the city still seemed to be a going concern. It was the second commercial centre in the Low Countries, even if it lagged a long way behind Antwerp. But the favourable signs were deceptive. Bruges' gradual and irreversible loss of commercial pre-eminence to Antwerp had begun in the fifteenth century, long before the difficult 1480s. The luxury industries inevitably followed this commercial trend, literally relocating to Antwerp, where many of Bruges' skilled artisans found jobs or investment opportunities. These economic sectors depended on close contacts with the world of taste and fashion, set at a gathering pace by princes, noblemen and wealthy townsmen, who would also increasingly place their orders in Antwerp. So Bruges gradually lost its distinctive and exceptional economic infrastructure. The merchants were the first to leave, followed by the highly skilled craftsmen. Yet the process was neither sudden nor total. Some merchants, like the wool-trading Castilians, stayed, although they probably did most of their business in Antwerp. Some specialized economic activities remained for quite some time. Painting and other luxury trades were still prominent in the early sixteenth century, although they all lost ground from the late 1520s.

The Bruges authorities and entrepreneurial elites did not look passively on while this downturn took place. They were deeply involved in Antwerp trade, as they had been in the fifteenth century. They made prolonged efforts to counter difficulties with surprising enterprise, tackling the problems of accessibility to the Bruges port infrastructure, and trying to lure specialist economic activities to the city. These attempts failed, however, despite some short-term successes. Conversion to more tapestry weaving seemed a good option initially, but Bruges entrepreneurs were not able to out-compete their more experienced rivals in Brussels or Oudenaarde. Not surprisingly, the only sectors that did well were those in which Bruges could still boast some comparative advantage. Hence the 'new draperies' and the manufacture of mixed fabrics met with some success. The supply lines for wool were very short in Bruges thanks to the important wool market in the city, while labour became relatively cheap, as guild organization in low-skill industries did not need to be very elaborate. Hence social relations in Bruges ironically came to mirror those of the early thirteenth century: once again, more proletarianized and non-guild-organized workers dominated textile output, rather than guild-organized small-commodity producers.

In the later sixteenth century circumstances worsened considerably, however. Political instability, inflation and growing competition with other Flemish textile manufacturers compounded the city's difficulties. Political and religious radicalization and the ensuing crisis of the century's last quarter caused a watershed. Changing political and religious loyalties, chronic warfare and the end of nearby Antwerp as a commercial centre in 1585 proved fatal for the last remnants of the old medieval infrastructure. The new direction that Bruges had begun to take during the sixteenth century became more apparent by the century's end. Instead of being a metropolitan city with international ambitions, Bruges would now become a regional administrative capital, still living in close harmony with regional and wealthy rural elites but with considerably fewer economic, cultural and political ties with Europe in general. The city's cultural, political and economic infrastructure took on more modest proportions. It no longer set trends for other places to follow; instead it followed those set elsewhere. Around 1590, the ageing Bruges merchant Zeghere van Male, who had lived through most of the sixteenth century, described the city simply as a *pennewaerde*, a small retail shop servicing the local and regional economy.[133] The former metropolis of the North Sea was no longer an international hub. Bruges, in other words, had become a normal city.

[133] Zegher Van Male, *De Lamentatie*, pp. 55, 67.

Conclusion: Bruges within the Medieval Urban Landscape

ANDREW BROWN AND JAN DUMOLYN

The importance of late medieval Bruges, certainly in terms of its central economic and cultural position within Europe, is reason enough to study its history. The approach of this book has not been to focus on any one aspect of the city that made it famous, for instance its prominence as a world market or as a centre of innovation in panel painting. Nor has it developed a single 'grand thesis' as to why Bruges was either an exceptional or typical medieval commercial city.[1] Instead, the authors have explored a wide range of the city's features to produce an 'urban biography', but in an integrated way to explain the many changes in Bruges' development between the Dark Ages and the beginning of the early modern period.[2] If the city in general is a 'total phenomenon',[3] then the study of particular cities, especially major ones like Bruges, has much to contribute to an understanding of social life in all its forms. Even so, important though Bruges was, there are wider historiographical issues in which the study of any one city needs to be set.

Bruges within Medieval Urban History

Interdisciplinary and long-term perspectives on urban history became more prominent during the 1960s and 1970s;[4] by viewing an entire urban society over seven centuries, this study follows in this vein. But the expanding fields of different disciplines have pushed the 'total' study of one city beyond the capacity of a single author. Accordingly, this book has been a collaboration of specialists with particular areas of expertise, as well as with knowledge of Bruges itself. One potential hazard (especially for editors who

1 As in the approaches of Murray, *Bruges*; or Gelderblom, *Cities of Commerce*.

2 Classic works include, for instance, D. Herlihy, *Medieval and Renaissance Pistoia: The Social History of an Italian Town, 1200–1430* (New Haven, CT, 1967); and G. Brucker, *The Civic World of Early Renaissance Florence* (Princeton, NJ, 1977).

3 See Introduction above.

4 For instance, the wide range covered by the contributions in H. J. Dyos (ed.), *The Study of Urban History* (London, 1968); and a collection of essays fundamental to urban history in P. Abrams and E. A. Wrigley (eds.), *Towns in Societies: Essays in Economic History and Historical Sociology* (Cambridge, 1978).

have been studying aspects of Bruges for more than twenty years) is of taking a too 'biographical' and 'localist' approach that puts aside comparative discussion and over-emphasizes the specificity of the city. Almost half of the authors of this book either were born in Bruges or work and live there and thus risk the accusation that they might be writing antiquarian and patriotic history; and indeed the people of this beautiful historic city and worldwide tourist attraction generally share a sense of civic pride. Medieval Bruges does deserve extensive treatment from the local or national point of view, not least because the city played a key role in Henri Pirenne's powerful if now outdated narrative of Belgian history.[5] But the city's importance on a European scale must inevitably make any history of it open to more comparative approaches.

Medieval urban history has a long-standing tradition; and historiographical attention to medieval Flemish cities is exceeded only by interest in their Italian counterparts. During the first half and middle of the twentieth century, German as well as Belgian scholars came to dominate the historical study of European towns. Pioneers such as Hans Planitz, Edith Ennen, Henri Pirenne, Hans van Werveke and Jan Dhondt were above all concerned with the origins of the ideal-typical medieval city, with its socio-economic and political character, and with its specific place in the medieval world or within 'feudal society'.[6] In this discussion, Flemish cities loomed large. Many works on medieval urban history during the early twentieth century focused on political events and institutions, but the broader generalizations of historians like Pirenne, and also of his contemporary the great sociologist Max Weber,[7] remain influential, even if more recent syntheses are more prudent and less visionary in their approach.

In this age of global history, the medieval town is primarily situated within a broader chronological and geographical framework.[8] Historiographical narratives on the medieval city have often been constructed as stories of

5 H. Pirenne, *Histoire de Belgique*, 7 vols. (Brussels, 1900–32).

6 For instance, Pirenne, *Les villes*; H. Pirenne, *Les anciennes démocraties des Pays-Bas* (Paris, 1910); F.-L. Ganshof, *Étude sur le développement des villes entre Loire et Rhin au Moyen Âge* (Paris and Brussels, 1943); H. Van Werveke, *Gand: Esquisse d'histoire sociale* (Brussels, 1946); Ennen, *Frühgeschichte der Europäischen Stadt*; J. Dhondt, *Das frühe Mittelalter* (Frankfurt am Main, 1968); E. Ennen, *Die europäische Stadt des Mittelalters*, 4th edn (Göttingen, 1987), trans. N. Fryde as *The Medieval Town* (New York, 1979); Planitz, *Die deutsche Stadt*.

7 M. Weber, *Economy and Society: An Outline of Interpretative Sociology*, 2 vols., ed. G. Roth and C. Wittich (Berkeley, CA, 2003).

8 Clark (ed.), *Oxford Handbook of Cities*, is a necessary first step in this direction but it is not a real global and comparative history of the city with the same range and ambitions as Weber, or a work like Sjoberg, *Pre-Industrial City*, or L. Mumford, *The City in History, its Origins, its Transformations and its Prospects* (San Diego, CA, 1961).

the development of markets, capital accumulation, democracy, community, creativity, innovation and modernity but also of inequality, social tensions, crime, social disintegration and moral depravity. To contribute to an international comparative approach, comparisons between medieval Bruges and other European towns need to be made. The preceding chapters have implicitly considered the wider comparative perspective; here in the conclusion the lens is widened more explicitly in both a geographically comparative and a historiographical sense. The publication of a number of overviews of medieval cities and of the world history of towns since the 1970s and especially in recent years, makes this necessary and opportune.[9]

Surface and Population

The simplest way to indicate Bruges' central role in the European urban landscape is to make quantitative comparisons. In terms of surface area, it was only by the twelfth century that Bruges became comparable with other strongly developing European towns. The city in 1127 covered 76 ha, like twelfth-century Florence (75 ha), more than Genoa in 1200 (52 ha) but substantially less than Cologne in 1180 (403 ha), though the latter was and remained less densely populated. By the end of the twelfth century Bruges had a greater surface area than in 1127 (perhaps over 100 ha, and it would reach 430 ha by 1300), but London in 1200 (at 134 ha), Paris around

[9] Without explicitly referring to these works in what follows, we have been guided by the general approaches of Clark, *European Cities*; Boucheron and Menjot, *Histoire de l'Europe urbaine*; M. Boone, 'Medieval Europe', in Clark (ed.), *Oxford Handbook of Cities*, pp. 221–39; and in a more 'national' framework, S. Reynolds, *An Introduction to the History of English Medieval Towns* (Oxford, 1977); C. Platt, *The English Medieval Town* (London, 1976); H. Swanson, *Medieval British Towns* (Basingstoke, 1999); Chédeville et al., *Histoire de la France urbaine*, vol. II: La ville médiévale, des Carolingiens à la Renaissance; B. Chevalier, *Les bonnes villes de France du XIVe au XVIe siècle* (Paris, 1982); Blockmans, *Metropolen*; E. Isenmann, *Die deutsche Stadt im Mittelalter 1150–1550: Stadtgestalt, Recht, Verfassung, Stadtregiment, Kirche, Gesellschaft, Wirtschaft* (Vienna, 2012); D. M. Palisser, P. Clark and M. Daunton (eds.), *The Cambridge Urban History of Britain*, 3 vols. (Cambridge, 2000); E. Crouzet-Pavan, *Les villes vivantes: Italie, XIIIe–XVe siècle* (Paris, 2009); Hyde, *Society and Politics*; R. Bordone, *La società urbana nell' Italia comunale (secoli XI–XIV)* (Turin, 1984); R. Bordone, *La società cittadina del regno d'Italia: Formazione e svillupe delle caratteristiche urbane nei secoli XI e XII* (Turin, 1987). For useful overviews covering a range of topics in medieval urban history, see Nicholas, *Growth of the Medieval City*; D. Nicholas, *The Later Medieval City, 1300–1500* (London and New York, 1997); for the early modern period, A. Cowan, *Urban Europe, 1500–1700* (London, 1998); C. R. Friedrichs, *The Early Modern City, 1450–1750* (London, 1995); and with a specific focus on medieval 'city states': L. Martines, *Power and Imagination: City-States in Renaissance Italy*, 2nd edn (Baltimore, MD, 1988); P. Jones, *The Italian City-State: From Commune to Signoria* (Oxford, 2004); T. Scott, *The City-State in Europe, 1000–1600* (Oxford, 2012).

1190–1208 (273 ha) and twelfth-century Milan (200 ha) were larger cities than Bruges and would continue to be so.[10]

Hard though it is to calculate population numbers before the later Middle Ages, there is no doubt that Italian cities – as well as the larger towns of Muslim Iberia and of course Constantinople – overshadowed all others before 1300. While we have estimated the population of Bruges at its peak around 1300 to have numbered well over 50,000 (a larger number than currently appears in most history textbooks), Paris counted perhaps up to 200,000 inhabitants, Florence, Genoa, Milan, Naples, Palermo and Venice had 100,000 or only slightly fewer before the Black Death, and London probably had up to 80,000 inhabitants. Rouen, Lyon and Cologne numbered between 20,000 and 40,000, while Lübeck, Danzig, Nuremberg, Vienna and Prague each had fewer than 20,000.[11] Together with Ghent, Bruges thus found itself immediately below this top level, and was larger than other towns in the Low Countries like Arras, Saint-Omer, Lille, Douai and Ypres, which all had between 20,000 and 30,000 people during the later Middle Ages. Around 1500, when the population was still recovering from successive epidemics, only twenty-seven European cities numbered more than 40,000 inhabitants. Bruges was by then probably no longer among them, and during the sixteenth century its population would further decline as the city lost its metropolitan position.[12] But during the later Middle Ages, Bruges' size and population certainly placed it on a tier of urban centres within Christendom below only the leviathans such as Paris.

Functions and Structures

Surface areas and population numbers, however, are tools too blunt to reflect on the specificity (or 'normalcy') of Bruges within the wider urban world: cities can also be classified and ranked in terms of their 'functions'. During the 1980s and 1990s, the dominant approach in medieval urban history was to situate towns within wider hierarchical urban networks and in relation to their hinterlands, emphasizing their 'central-place functions', for instance market, industrial, political, judicial, military but also educational

10 Keene, 'Towns and the Growth of Trade', pp. 51–2.

11 J.-P. Leguay, 'Urban Life', in M. Jones (ed.), *The New Cambridge Medieval History*, vol. VI (Cambridge, 2000), pp. 102–23 (at 104).

12 B. Dobson, 'Urban Europe', in C. Allmand (ed.), *The New Cambridge Medieval History*, vol. VII (Cambridge, 1998), pp. 121–44 (at 125); W. Blockmans and M. 't Hart, 'Power', in Clark (ed.), *Oxford Handbook of Cities*, pp. 421–37 (at 423–4).

or medical functions.[13] The number and diversity of functions that a city possesses correlate to some degree with its geographical and demographic size. Throughout this book, Bruges has been considered in relation to these functions, and from this viewpoint the city was central both within the dense Flemish urban network and within a broader European network of exchange of commodities, people and ideas. Its mainly commercial function was linked to the demand and production of both networks. Bruges has been described as forming a 'gateway city' for the commodities produced in the polycentric network of industrial cities in the Low Countries, a 'node within a network' of international commerce, or the port network linking Mediterranean and North Sea commerce (see Map 5), and as a result of these connections, also as a 'creative environment' for cutting-edge cultural production.

In terms of structure and function, Bruges was a typical medieval city of the southern Low Countries in the sense that its development was structurally determined by its artisan industries. However, even if Bruges was a major centre of artisanal production, its textile sector did not dominate the city's character to the degree that it did in other cloth towns of the Netherlands such as Ghent, Ypres, Douai or the smaller town of Leyden. Between the eleventh and the late thirteenth centuries, cloth production was the motor of the urban economy, but from the fourteenth century onwards, the economic structure of Bruges became more diverse than in any of these rival towns. By the fifteenth century, Bruges also surpassed Arras as the centre for the luxury industries in the region. Within north-western Europe, Bruges' wide range of products and available services, and its degree of capital accumulation, diversity, specialization and division of labour in artisanal production, was probably only exceeded by Paris. London was somewhat larger than Bruges, and so was the more industrial city of Ghent; Cologne and Lübeck were prosperous commercial cities; but at the end of the Middle Ages none of these urban centres equalled Bruges in terms of the variety of its specialized functions and cosmopolitan character. Bruges' real commercial and artistic rivals have to be sought in the more urbanized Mediterranean world, in cites such as Venice, Genoa, Florence and Milan, but probably also Valencia and Barcelona.[14]

13 Based on the older geographical model by Christaller (in *Die zentralen Orte*), the fundamental references are Hohenberg and Hollen Lees, *Making of Urban Europe*; and J. De Vries, *European Urbanization, 1500–1800* (London, 1984).

14 R. Cazelles, *Nouvelle histoire de Paris: De la fin du regne de Philippe Auguste a la mort de Charles V 1223–1380* (Paris, 1972); J. Favier, *Paris au XVe siècle, 1380–1500* (Paris, 1974); C. Brooke and G. Keir, *London, 800–1216: The Shaping of a City* (London, 1975); C. M. Barron, *London in the Later Middle Ages: Government and People, 1200–1500* (Oxford, 2004); F. Lane,

Urban Space

Besides considering central-place functions, other approaches to urban history have also been applied. The *Annales* school, although strongly associated with research on rural and regional history, has retained an appeal within urban history, particularly with reference to its distinctions between structures, conjunctures and events and to its emphasis on environmental and geographical determinism. Apart from the work of the French *Annalistes*, another brand of urban history that developed after the Second World War, inspired mainly by M. R. G. Conzen – a German scholar who had emigrated to Britain – and his students, focused attention on the morphological development of medieval towns as a built environment.[15] But recent historiography on the built environment has been particularly influenced by the work of Henri Lefebvre, which treated space itself not as an inert reflection of social pressures but as a productive force within society.[16] In the preceding chapters, we have studied the internal evolution of the Bruges landscape both from the structural perspective of its central-place functions, and from the perspective of the various socio-economic groups and political and clerical institutions that developed within the town.

Structures and functions in Bruges shaped the built landscape of the city into its distinctive forms. Bruges' growth in the thirteenth century into an industrial centre, as in other textile towns, created new areas for specialized economic activity, as well as suburban housing for a 'proletarian' workforce. It also stimulated the need (as it did in Ghent and other large urban centres) for new charitable institutions and religious houses, those of the friars in particular which were often strategically placed close to these areas. But other parts of the city, in contrast to the experience of other textile towns, reflect Bruges' commercial expansion, notably the agglomeration of buildings surrounding the Bourse square geared to the business of foreign merchants. These occupied different kinds of space than foreign merchants in

Venice: A Maritime Republic (Baltimore, MD, 1973); J. Najemy, *A History of Florence, 1200–1575* (Oxford, 2006); E. Crouzet-Pavan, *Venise: Une invention de la ville (XIIIe–XVe siècle)* (Paris, 1997); S. P. Bensch, *Barcelona and its Rulers, 1096–1291* (Cambridge, 1995).

15 J. W. R. Whitehand (ed.), *The Urban Landscape: Historical Development and Management: Papers by M. G. R. Conzen* (London, 1981); T. R. Slater (ed.), *The Built Form of Western Cities: Essays for M. R. G. Conzen on the Occasion of his Eightieth Birthday* (London, 1990); M. Aston and J. Bond, *The Landscape of Towns* (London, 1976). Also with a strong emphasis on the urban landscape: J. Heers, *La ville au Moyen Âge en Occident: Paysages, pouvoir et conflits* (Paris, 1990); Platt, *English Medieval Town*; archaeological: J. Schofield and A. Vince, *Medieval Towns* (London, 1994).

16 Lefebvre, *La production de l'espace*. For his influence, see Chapter 2.

some other cities (the German Hanse in Bruges not acquiring as they did in London their own enclave).[17] The same commercial expansion imprinted itself on the network of canals, quaysides and commercial buildings built to bring commerce to Bruges and link the city with a wider world.

Continuity and Change

The dynamic nature of the city's functions, structures and spaces has also to be placed within a chronology. An inherent danger in the urban-biographical approach, though, is to assume a classic (almost biological) logic of 'origins, growth, maturity and decay'. Historians have sometimes focused on a limited period of growth in which a particular socio-economic and political dynamic is discussed.[18] Or in other cases they have taken the physical and architectural development of a city as the starting point for a discussion of its development.[19] When we thus consider the structural evolution of medieval Bruges, a comparative approach must be set in a diachronic as well as a geographical framework. Over the longue durée, Bruges' location close to the sea, its access to markets, products and lines of communication over land and water, did indeed shape its development thoughout the medieval period. But the place perhaps called *Brugjo* or *Brygghia*, crouched at the foot of the Carolingian stronghold in the ninth century, was entirely different in nature from the vibrant and international city in which Jan van Eyck and Hans Memling would settle in the fifteenth century.

Bruges had no continuity with a Roman past, as was the case for many major cities in the Mediterranean and the Rhineland, but began more abruptly (as Venice had done earlier) as an urban centre during the high Middle Ages. Its location explains the first phase of its development. It was situated at two main junctions: between the coastal plain and the maritime world of the North Sea, and between the older centres of the more populated region of inland Flanders and the delta of the great rivers of the Low Countries. Bruges' development was also reinforced by the political

[17] D. J. Keene, 'Du seuil de la Cité à la formation d'une économie morale: L'environment hanséatique à Londres entre XIIe et XVIIe siècles', in J. Bottin and D. Calabi (eds.), *Les étrangers dans la ville: Minorités et espace urbain du bas Moyen Âge a l'époque moderne* (Paris, 1999), pp. 409–24.

[18] A classic example is D. Herlihy, *Pisa in the Early Renaissance: A Study of Urban Growth* (New Haven, CT, 1958); and more recently for instance, Saint-Denis, *Apogée d'une cité*.

[19] R. A. Goldthwaite, *The Building of Renaissance Florence: An Economic and Social History* (Baltimore, MD, 1980); P. Boucheron, *Le pouvoir de bâtir: Urbanisme et politique édilitaire à Milan (XIVe–Xve siècles)* (Rome, 1998).

aspirations of the new regional strongmen, the counts of Flanders. On these foundations, Bruges slowly developed into a major port within the North Sea area after the period which had been dominated by *wiks* such as Dorestad or Haithabu, but it was a market-place of a different type, one not only based upon international trade of a few valuable commodities for elite groups but directly connected to the development of princely power and the rise of agricultural productivity that created the conditions for larger towns to grow and for demand to rise.

The military, political and religious functions of the Bruges stronghold stimulated the development of proto-urban nuclei around it; the availability of pastures for sheep-breeding prompted the expansion of a textile industry, which in turn was an impetus for its commercial development in combination with its access to the sea. In a second phase, the town became a central player within a general Flemish economic development during the high Middle Ages, and its intensive demographic and industrial growth as well as the expansion of its built environment are comparable to other major medieval cities like Paris, London, Ghent, Milan or Florence. In the final stage of its medieval development, as the economy entered into periods of crisis and conversion from the 1280s, Bruges became a city with numerous and diversified industrial, financial and cultural functions, all of which showed a remarkable degree of flexibility and adaptability but also formed a battleground for intense social and political struggles. Both the textile industry and the international market functions of Bruges were subject to conjunctural economic movements and changes of a structural nature within Europe and beyond.

From the mid fourteenth century onwards, the key position of the textile industry was replaced by a more diverse artisanal production in which woollen cloth continued to be of importance, but alongside sectors like confection and innovative luxury objects, including pieces now considered among the finest of late medieval artworks. In the meantime, there had been a functional shift from 'active' towards 'passive' trade and the city developed some of the most progressive and efficient types of infrastructure and service for foreign merchants, features which secured its role as an international market until the late fifteenth century. During this period Bruges played a significant role in the development of medieval commercial capitalism and financial techniques. Political factors, new maritime and land commercial routes, and the development of the Atlantic economy finally put an end to its 'golden age'. But the trajectory we have traced in Bruges' history is not a straightforward one of growth, maturity and decline. The transition from its 'golden age' was a shift from exceptionality to normalcy, from a city exceptionally geared to benefit from certain conditions, to one unable to adapt when conditions changed.

Power and Politics

Changes in space, structures and functions did not occur without agency: analysis of them has been considered in relation to power and politics within urban society. Urban historiography in this regard has been fundamentally influenced by the sociology of Weber and Marx. For almost a century, Max Weber's conception of the self-governing urban commune as a privileged space for the development of rationality and modernity has been omnipresent (certainly implicitly) in histories of medieval towns.[20] Similarily, the Marxist model with its emphasis on socio-economic structures, class and political struggles has also influenced narratives of medieval urban politics.[21] Several classic works on medieval urban history have focused on politics and society,[22] but the history of Bruges in this respect has not hitherto been fully explored. As Chapters 4 and 7 have shown, Bruges' political history provides an illuminating example of the development of an incipient urban society into a fully fledged urban commune with liberties granted by a princely dynasty with which it cooperated but at times opposed. Bruges was also marked by internal conflicts of extraordinary frequency – comparable only to the intensive strife found in Ghent, Florence and perhaps a few other Italian and Rhineland cities – between strong corporate groups and an equally powerful commercial elite. Study of these groups has further shown how complex they were. Political conflicts could sometimes take on the lineaments of a class struggle (as they did perhaps in the later thirteenth century); but they often reflected more intricate alignments between opposing craft guilds, factions or elite families, as well as tensions between these urban groups on the one hand and princely power on the other.

20 On the reception of Weber's model of the occidental city, see B. Scheller, 'Das herrschaftsfremde Charisma der Coniuratio und seine Veralltäglichungen: Idealtypische Entwicklungspfade der mittelalterlichen Stadtverfassung in Max Webers "Stadt"', *Historische Zeitschrift*, 281 (2005), 307–36. But see the recent unashamed defence of the medieval city's importance in the development of modernity: M. Boone, *À la recherche d'une modernité civique: La société urbaine des anciens Pays-Bas au bas Moyen Âge* (Brussels, 2010).

21 For instance R. H. Hilton, *English and French Towns in Feudal Society: A Comparative Study* (Cambridge, 1992).

22 For instance, see Brucker, *Civic World*; W. M. Bowsky, *A Medieval Italian Commune: Siena under the Nine, 1287–1355* (Berkeley, CA, 1981); J. Najemy, *Corporatism and Consensus in Florentine Electoral Politics, 1280–1400* (Chapel Hill, NC, 1982); D. Queller, *The Venetian Patriciate: Reality versus Myth* (Urbana, IL, 1986).

The political development of Bruges formed part of a more general communal movement in northern France and at the western edge of the Holy Roman Empire at the end of the eleventh century and the first half of the twelfth. After the rise of a more oligarchic rule of a merchant class which maintained good relations with the prince, internal social and political polarization led to a polity of a permanently conflictual nature. Successive waves of strikes and revolts, especially during the last quarter of the thirteenth century, were typical of other cities in the Low Countries and northern France, but after the victorious 'revolution' of 1302 Bruges politics were characterized by an exceptionally strong development of a corporatist principle. During the fourteenth and fifteenth centuries, the political importance of the middling groups in urban society and their 'political guilds' was counterbalanced by an equally strong commercial elite. Thus, from a socio-political point of view, Bruges is comparable with other major towns, like Florence, Bologna, Siena, Cologne, Ghent or Liège, where the logic of corporatism and an involvement of broader layers of the urban population determined the struggles for power in the later Middle Ages. The power of guilds was generally more dominant in these towns than in smaller or middle-sized ones with more regional market functions and less developed artisanal industries; but it was also more pronounced than in great cities like Paris, London, Genoa, Venice or Lübeck which shared many of Bruges' socio-economic features but were primarily marked politically by the dominating presence either of royal power or oligarchic rule.

The political history of Bruges suggests that political constellations in sizeable medieval cities were not simply determined by their economic 'base': they also possessed a degree of autonomy or 'path dependency' of their own. Indeed, during the decades after 1302, Bruges became one of the most politically 'progressive' or 'democratic' towns of medieval Europe, in the less anachronistic sense that relatively larger parts of the population participated in the decision-making process. The self-assured commercial elite of Bruges derived its social and political power from the central commercial function of the city, but the middle classes of petty commodity producers drew upon their skilled labour and the relatively high standards of living to mobilize time and again in order to gain or defend their right to political participation. These aspirations and struggles also shaped the built environment, producing buildings like the elitist Poorters Loge and a proliferation of craft guildhouses in several parts of the city. It was only during the sixteenth century that the balance of power tilted to the advantage of the commercial classes, though this was a pyrrhic victory as the latter by then were no longer comparable in strength to their medieval forerunners.

The relations of these two main politically active groups with central power were by no means easy. Like the other major Flemish cities, Bruges had a large degree of autonomy from its prince, especially during the fourteenth century. It therefore differed from the more subservient English towns or the French *bonnes villes*, but it never became a city-state similar to Florence, Milan and other Italian towns, or to German free imperial cities (*Reichsstädte*) like Nuremberg or Augsburg. Historiographically, the advance of the princely state has often been treated as inexorable (and in the Low Countries, for Pirenne, as a welcome process after 1477 on the road to national unity); and the cities or at least their urban elites have been considered complicit in the process. But the political history of Bruges, while ultimately conforming to this pattern, suggests that the process was hardly a linear one. Neither middling groups nor even the commercial elite could be relied upon to fall into line behind the ruling dynasty; and the upheavals between 1477 and 1492 were a serious check to monarchical power.[23]

Culture and Religion in Urban Space

Discussion of culture and religion in this book has been set within the context of functions, stuctures and power within Bruges, but it is also informed by recent urban historiography influenced by new approaches to cultural life. Culture once tended to refer to a 'high' culture of artistic and intellectual achievement; and north Italian cities once reigned unchallenged as the sites of a 'Renaissance' spirit, those of northern Europe languishing in their shade.[24] This was a view that Johan Huizinga in effect endorsed, famously casting northern French and Flemish cities, Bruges among them, under a pall of autumnal and courtly decadence.[25] Yet the work particularly of Weber and Pirenne, both in different ways emphasizing the dynamic nature of communal aspirations within European cities, prepared the way

[23] The classic reference for the political history of the Burgundian Netherlands remains Blockmans and Prevenier, *Promised Lands*.

[24] J. Burckhardt, *Die Kultur der Renaissance in Italien* (Basel, 1860), trans. S. G. C. Middlemore and ed. L. Goldschedier as *The Civilization of the Renaissance in Italy: An Essay* (London, 1951). For a historiographical summary, see Belozerskaya, *Rethinking the Renaissance*, pp. 7–43.

[25] J. Huizinga, *Herfsttij der middeleeuwen: Studies over levens- en gedachtenvormen der veertiende en vijftiende eeuw in Frankrijk en de Nederlanden* (1919; Amsterdam, 1997) trans. R. J. Payton and U. Mammitzsch as *The Autumn of the Middle Ages*. Huizinga identified his attendance in Bruges at the exhibition of Flemish Primitives in 1902 as a defining moment for the development of his thesis; see E. Peters and W. Simons, 'The New Huizinga and the Old Middle Ages', *Speculum*, 74 (1999), 587–620. For continuing discussion of a 'Northern'

for more positive interpretations of medieval urban culture, northern and southern, by setting it within a framework of social practices. Emphasis on the interconnected nature of cultural artefact and social setting, and on a broader view of 'culture', has since increased. Artistic achievement also can no longer be viewed as the emanation of a 'Renaissance' spirit, or as the inert product of social forces. Set in the context of urban productivity and market networks, late medieval Bruges has emerged from the shadow of 'decline' as a European trend-setter of urban culture, most obviously in the visual arts.[26]

New approaches in sociology, cultural anthropology and critical theory have led historians to understand the city not just as a legal entity or economic centre but also as a 'state of mind',[27] a distinctive space of lived and living interaction,[28] a public sphere for social representation,[29] or an imagined community with the power to generate new discourses that themselves shaped the urban environment.[30] The role of civic governments, in embodying or claiming a sense of community, has been regarded as particularly important to these processes. The expansion of municipal control over urban territory, hinterland, landscape and population took on cultural forms that in turn transformed urban society. These processes may have been pronounced in the cities of northern Italy, but they are evident elsewhere.[31] In Bruges, the urban government's growing efforts, especially

Renaissance, see H. Wijsman, 'Northern Renaissance? Burgundy and Netherlandish Art in Fifteenth-Century Europe', in A. Lee, P. Péporté and H. Schnitker (eds.), *Renaissance? Perceptions of Continuity and Discontinuity in Europe, c.1300–c.1500* (Leiden, 2010), pp. 269–88.

26 Borchert (ed.), *Age of Van Eyck*.

27 R. Park, E. Burgess and R. D. McKenzie (eds.), *The City: Suggestions for the Study of Human Nature in the Urban Environment* (Chicago, IL, 1925). See also Ennen, *Die europäische Stadt*.

28 See again Lefebvre, *La production de l'espace*. See also P. Bourdieu, *Le sens pratique* (Paris, 1980), trans. R. Nice as *The Logic of Practice* (Stanford, CA, 1990); and M. de Certeau, *Arts de faire* (Paris, 1980), trans. S. Rendall as *The Practice of Every Day* (Berkeley, CA, 1984). For further references, see Introduction.

29 J. Habermas, *Strukturwandel der Öffentlichkeit: Untersuchungen zu einer Kategorie der bürgerlichen Gesellschaft* (1962), trans. T. Burger and F. Lawrence as *The Structural Transformation of the Public Sphere: An Inquiry into a Category of Bourgeois Society* (Cambridge, MA, 1989); P. Burke, 'Culture: Representations', in Clark (ed.), *Oxford Handbook of Cities*, pp. 438–54.

30 C. Frugoni, *A Distant City: Images of Urban Experience in the Medieval World*, trans. W. McCuaig (Princeton, NJ, 1991); D. Lord Smail, *Imaginary Cartographies: Possession and Identity in Late Medieval Marseille* (Ithaca, NY, 1999); C. Keen and D. Midgely (eds.), *Imagining the City: The Politics of Urban Space*, 2 vols. (Oxford, 2006).

31 See (for Venice) E. Crouzet-Pavan, *'Sopra le acque salse': Espaces, pouvoir et société à Venise à la fin du Moyen Âge*, 2 vols. (Rome and Paris, 1992); and contributions in Boone and Stabel (eds.), *Shaping Urban Identity*.

from the late thirteenth century, to master the city's infrastructures and waterways, as well as the lower orders, were expressed spatially and temporally: in the public squares, markets, communal buildings, prison, and gates deemed to enshrine communal virtues; in the archives, charters and chronicles that preserved and shaped communal memory; in ceremonies, dramas and processions that repeatedly reiterated preferred values by their performance; or in paintings that idealized the city as a Jerusalem.

Urban historiography on political and social divisions, however, has placed a very different complexion on cultural visions of civic unity. The rhetoric of community that appears in so many late medieval cities jarred with the obvious signs of hierarchy and disunity: the oligarchical and factional tendencies of city councils, the exclusive nature of 'citizenship' and the acute disparities of wealth. In this context, the aggrandizement of the Bruges town-council house (*scepenhuus*), would seem to legitimize the power of ruling groups rather than express communal values, just as the Poorters Loge promoted the pretensions of its exclusive clientele. Texts or plays written for social elites (by rhetoricians and their literary predecessors) could celebrate urban unity and virtues, but also uphold social hierarchy and disparage attempts by social inferiors to level it. A perception that irrational crowds of artisans threatened the social order was as characteristic among elites in Bruges as a fear was to be among early modern burghers of the urban 'mob'. As in many other large medieval towns, texts that reflect social grievances also echo a thriving oral and literate culture among the lower orders which was sometimes subversive of authority. Yet the case of Bruges also shows that extremes of division within urban cultural life were tempered by the importance of middling groups, represented chiefly by craft guildsmen, who sought power but were subject to conflicting agendas, and whose ideals of corporatism were therefore more than the self-serving ploys of a narrow social group. The dominant rhetoric of civic brotherhood, peace and charity was more than a collective urge towards self-government: the rhetoric also reflected an awareness in Bruges of the tensions threatening to fragment urban society, and the need felt among all social groups, whether aspiring to gain power or to overturn regimes, to frame their agendas within it.

The ideals of corporatism, as well as concerns with social conflict, were almost invariably expressed in the language of religion. The medieval perception of the ideal city was as a kind of sacred body or sworn association (*universitas*); and in modern historiography this perception has been reformulated in sociological terms, to reflect the rise and dynamic nature of urban communes. Max Weber's ideal type of the self-governing commune was a fraternal body bound by an oath, a 'Kulturverband' that expressed itself through devotion to civic saints, patronage of a civic church and participation in church celebrations.[32] Since the 1980s, historiography, notably of German towns, has focused on these and other religious phenomena (such as commemorative practices) to characterize the nature of authority and identity in urban society.[33] Historiography of north Italian cities, particularly by North American and Francophone scholars, has tended to recast the same kinds of phenomena as 'civic religion' or 'religion civique', focusing on cults, devotions and institutions in which municipal authorities played a determining role.[34] Arguably this role was most developed in the autonomous city-states of northern Italy, and perhaps in certain German cities, but it is apparent too in the cities of the Low Countries, despite their subjection to princely rule. Bruges after all was never dominated by an ecclesiastical landlord, and unlike Liège, Utrecht and many north Italian cities it was not the seat of a bishopric (until 1556). By 1127 its leading burghers were collectively swearing oaths over relics, and by 1304 were affirming corporate ideals in the Holy Blood procession. During the late medieval period, city magistrates exercised a strengthening grip over charity, relic processions and other religious practices; while individual citizens, families, guilds, as well as municipal governments, made commemorative foundations that significantly increased lay involvement in the cycle of liturgical life and could even contribute to local patriotism. At the same time, however, religious expressions of unity were often more aspirational than real or effective; while ceremonies like the Holy Blood could not entirely serve to legitimate the power of the magistracy or commercial elite.[35]

There are problems too with applying the models of 'civic religion' to Bruges, and to other towns. The often-implied association of medieval 'civic'

32 M. Weber, *The City*, trans. D. Martindale and G. Neuwirth (New York, 1958), pp. 102–3, 105, 109–10.

33 See for instance H. Schmidt, 'Bürgerliches Selbsverständnis und städtische Geschichtsschreibung im deutschen Spätmittelalter: Eine Erinnerung', in P. Johanek (ed.), *Städtische Geschictsschreibung im Spätmittelalter und in der Frühen Neuzeit* (Cologne, 2000), pp. 1–17; Signori, 'Religion civique'.

34 For 'civic religion', see for instance Herlihy, *Medieval and Renaissance Pistoia*, pp. 241–58; N. Terpstra, 'Civic Religion', in J. Arnold (ed.), *The Oxford Handbook of Medieval Christianity* (Oxford, 2014), pp. 148–65. For 'religion civique', see for instance Vauchez (ed.), *La religion civique*.

35 The ideas of the anthropologist Clifford Geertz, which accord a certain distance between rituals and their initiators, have been particularly productive for work on urban ceremonies since the 1980s: C. Geertz, *Negara: The Theatre-State in Nineteenth-Century Bali* (Princeton, NJ, 1981), esp. pp. 13–14, 102–5; C. Geertz, *The Interpretation of Cultures: Selected Essays* (London, 1973), esp. pp. 10, 87–125, 448). See Löther, *Prozessionen*, pp. 10–14.

religion with post-medieval 'civil' religion, and of Weber's communalism with a process of modern rationalization and secularization, are problematic.[36] In Bruges, as in so many other cities, celebration of the communal body in sacred oaths, fraternal structures, commemorative and liturgical ceremony necessarily involved the services of the clergy, and the deployment of saintly relics usually under clerical guardianship. 'Clerical' and 'urban' time[37] also remained blurred – or as synchronized as the chimes of the city's Belfry bells with those of St Donatian's church. The relatively high number of clergy in Bruges, and the wide range of ecclesiastical institutions and spiritual forms were as characteristic of the city as any lay or municipal involvement in religious practices. 'Civic religion' also implies a mode of religion that was specific to towns. Yet the distinctiveness of religion in towns arguably lay not in the dominance of any one mode, but in the multiplicity of its forms. The variety and contrasts of religious life – from comfortable benefice to voluntary poverty, elaborate ceremony to contemplative devotion, conformity to dissent – were the defining features of the urban religious environment in the later Middle Ages, and were notably so in a vibrant city such as Bruges.

Debate on the specific nature of urban religion informs a wider debate on the distinctive nature of urban culture. The greater assertion among communes from the twelfth century onwards of political autonomy from 'feudal' and ecclesiastical lordship, may imply that urban cultural forms increasingly diverged from those associated with the traditional orders of medieval society. A specifically 'bourgeois' culture though is hard to identify. Civic processions followed liturgical rites; the residences and habits of merchants aspired to resemble those of nobles and courtiers. But such urban borrowings of ceremonies, buildings or customs are best seen not as slavish adoptions of more elite cultural forms, but as creative adaptations, shaped to serve the priorities of communal life and of town-dwellers. 'Self-fashioning' (another cultural feature considered characteristic of the 'Renaissance')[38] may aptly describe the behaviour of fifteenth-century burghers in Bruges who read chivalric romances or commissioned realistic portraits of themselves in their altarpieces. At the same time, nobles and courtiers, as well

[36] For instance, see P. Boucheron, 'Religion civique, religion civile, religion séculière: L'ombre d'un doute', *Revue de Synthèse*, 134 (2013), 161–83; P. Monnet, 'Pour en finir avec la religion civique?', *Histoire urbaine*, 27 (2010), 107–20; A. Brown, 'Civic Religion in Late Medieval Europe', *JMH*, 42 (2016), 338–56.

[37] See the classic article J. Le Goff, 'Au Moyen Âge: Temps de l'église, temps de marchand', *Annales: Économies, Sociétés, Civilisations*, 15 (1960), 417–33.

[38] S. Greenblatt, *Renaissance Self-Fashioning: From More to Shakespeare* (Chicago, IL, 1980).

as high-ranking clergy who resided in town, did not live in cultural isolation from burghers. One of the distinctive features at an early date of urban life in the Low Countries and Bruges in particular was the close connections between noble and burgher elites, not least because nobles (like the Gruuthuse family) established residences within urban territory. 'Courtly' and 'noble' culture took on 'urban' forms, certainly from the fourteenth century: the so-called Gruuthuse manuscript reworked courtly love and spiritual traditions to the tastes of burgher elites or even middling groups; the Bruges jousts of the White Bear in which Burgundian dukes (and the Gruuthuse) participated were as much the products of urban networks of competition as they were of chivalric traditions. The *ars nova* patronized by canons and court functionaries, or the May songs enjoyed in Burgundian households, emerged less from courtly patronage than from a rich tradition of urban productivity. Clerical personnel, ceremonies and literacy were also absorbed into urban society. Clerics were drawn into expanding municipal bureaucracies that generated their own modes and uses of literacy.[39] St Donatian's canons and clerics moved in lay circles, too freely according to some; they permitted their patron saints to be carried in general processions called by the town council. The mendicants accommodated the chapels of guilds and nations in their churches, and preached sermons at the request of town governments.

As in other medieval towns, cultural forms in Bruges were hybrid and multivalent,[40] but more so than most: the density and variety of its social networks within the city walls and with the world outside made Bruges a particularly favourable environment for cultural exchange and renewal.[41] Some cultural forms were more dominant than others; but some also reflected tensions. Within the poems of the lay rhetorician Anthonis de Roovere, anticlericalism and clericalism – a disgust at clergymen's failings and a high regard for the ecclesiastical office – are both encountered; subservience to the court and sympathy for artisan grievances are found together. Contradictions were at the heart of urban life in Bruges, an environment where cosmopolitanism and local patriotism were nurtured; foreigners (merchants or productive immigrants) embraced, and natives (the socially undesirable) expelled; fellowship among burghers encouraged and undermined by social competition. Cities were troubled 'states of mind': while the

[39] Mostert and Adamska (eds.), *Writing and the Administration of Medieval Towns*; and M. Mostert and A. Adamska (eds.), *Uses of the Written Word in Medieval Towns: Medieval Urban Literacy II* (Turnhout, 2014).

[40] For 'multivalency' in generally smaller English towns, see Rosser, 'Urban Culture'.

[41] Calabi and Turk Christensen (eds.), *Cultural Exchange*, vol. II, esp. pp. xxvi–xxvii, 3–5.

ideal city was modelled on Jerusalem, there were other biblical cities that offered less salubrious comparisons, feeding a venerable monastic topos of distrust towards city living. Inhabitants of Bruges throughout the medieval period were acutely aware that their city fell short of spiritual and communal ideals: the cleric Galbert of Bruges in 1128 pondered whether Bruges in his day had not deserved the evils that befell it; the youth in a poem from the Gruuthuse manuscript (c.1400) could admit, to an admonishing hermit, that he had enjoyed the blandishments of town life a little too well; Anthonis de Roovere in the 1470s and 1480s knew his city to be full of corrupt officials, fraudulent merchants and simoniac priests; the merchant Zeghere van Male in the 1590s recalled the words of the prophet Jeremiah, and the fate of Sodom and Gomorrah, to explain divine punishment of the town.[42] Visions of urban dystopia were as much part of urban culture as communal idealism, as were the tensions between corporate aspirations and social fragmentation. These tensions, as well as the diversity of social networks, made the absorption of wider medieval cultures within the city a creative process, and one truly characteristic of a metropolis.

[42] Rider (ed.), *Galbertus Brugensis*, chap. 116; C. Carton (ed.), *Oudvlaemsche liederen en andere gedichten der XIVde en XVde eeuwen* (Ghent, 1849), pp. 490–1; de Roovere, *De gedichten*, pp. 326–9, 335–8; Zegher van Male, *De Lamentatie*, pp. 73, 80–2, 84.

Select Bibliography

Primary Sources

Unpublished

The primary sources listed refer only to the main classes of archival document that appear in the text or those most frequently cited.

Antwerp, Archives of Museum Plantin-Moretus
17, 39, 40, 110

Bruges, OCMW (Archives of the Openbaar Centrum voor Maatschappelijk Welzijn)
Charter 150 (*Potterie*)
Register 178 (*Onze-Lieve-Vrouwe armendis*)
Register 1 (*Sint-Walburga*)

Bruges, Archives of the Confraternity of the Holy Blood
Registers 5, 15

Bruges, Archives of the Discalced Carmelites of Bruges (Archief Ongeschoeide karmelieten)
Liber Oblongus

Bruges, Archives of the head guild Saint-Sebastian (Archief van Hoofgilde Sint-Sebastiaan)
Charters

Bruges, BAB (Bischoppelijk archief – Episcopal Archives)
A 47, 48, 49, 50, 51, 52, 53, 54, 55, 56, 57, 130, 141 (*Sint-Donaas*)
C 445 (*Sint-Juliaansgasthuis*)
D 42 (*Sint-Donaas*)
G 1, 2, 3, 6 (*Sint-Donaas*)
I 12 (*Sint-Donaas*)
S 289, 718 (*Sint-Salvator*)

Bruges, RAB (Rijksarchief – State Archives)
1, 64, 386 (*Ambachten – Crafts*)
7721, 8098, 8127, 8128, 8185, 8205 (*Charters with blue numbers*)
250, 385, 735, 1017, 1062, 1271, 1273, 1350, 1531, 2003 (*Onze-Lieve-Vrouw, oudarchief*)
1508, 1509–1513, 1619 (*Proosdij*)
5, 308, 309 (*Sint-Anna*)

24, 26, 27, 273, 377, 447 (*Sint-Gillis*)
396 (*Sint-Walburga*)
Bruges, SAB (Stadsarchief – City Archives)
64, 96 (*Cartularia)* 2, 11, 13, 14, 20
99, 100 (*Politeke oorkonde*)
114 (*Wetsvernieuwingen*)
118
120 (*Hallegeboden* I, II, III)
157, 164, 165, 166 (*Civiele sententïen*)
192 (*Verluydboek*)
196 (*Doncker camer* 9, 11)
216 (*Stadsrekeningen*)
219
277 (*Presentwijnen*)
291
299 (*Makelaars*)
304, 333, 336, 337, 360, 361, 385 (II/11), 387 (*Ambachten*)
450
505, 509, 519, 524 (*Gilden*)
Bruges, OBB (Openbare Bibliotheek – City Library)
Ms. 437, 'Excellente Cronike van Vlaanderen'
Ms. 685, 'Cronache de signiori di Fiandra e de loro advenimenti'
3877
Brussels, AGR (Archives Générales du Royaume – General State Archives)
Chambers of Accounts: 13771, 13780, 17404, 17412
Staat en Audiëntie: 809/7
Trésor de Flandre, 1er série: 1698
Brussels, Koninklijke Bibliotheek,
Ms. IV 210
Lille, ADN (Archives départementales du Nord)
B 1616, 1705, 5392, 6094, 7662
Utrecht, University Library
Ms. 1846

Published

Allossery, P. 'De oudste giften en fondatiën ten bate der arme gevangenen te Brugge (ca. 1300–1475)', *HGG*, 79 (1936), 67–130, and 80 (1937), 155–73.

Brinkman, H. (ed.). *Het Gruuthuse-handschrift: Hs. Den Haag, Koninklijke Bibliotheek, 79 K 10* (Hilversum, 2015).

Campbell, A. (ed.). *Encomium Emmae reginae* (London, 1949).

Carton, C. (ed.). *Het boeck van al 't gene datter gheschiedt is binnen Brugghe sichtent jaer 1477, 14 februarii, tot 1491* (Ghent, 1859).

de Damhouder, J. *Van de grootdadigheyt der breedt-vermaerde regeringhe van de stadt Brugge* (Amsterdam, 1684).

de Dene, Eduard. *Testament Rhetoricael*, ed. D. Coigneau and W. Waterschoot (Ghent, 1976–80).

de Doppere, Romboudt. *Fragments inédits de Romboudt de Doppere ... chronique Brugeoise de 1491 à 1498*, ed. P. H. Dussart (Bruges, 1892).

de Hemptinne, T., Verhulst, A. and De Mey, L., *De oorkonden der graven van Vlaanderen (Juli 1128 – September 1191), II. Uitgave*, vol. I: *Regering van Diederik van de Elzas (Juli 1128 – 17 Januari 1168)* (Brussels, 1988).

De oorkonden der graven van Vlaanderen (Juli 1128 – September 1191), II. Uitgave, vol. III: *Regering van Filips van de Elzas (tweede deel: 1178–1191)* (Brussels, 2009).

de Limburg-Stirum, T. (ed.). *Cartulaire de Louis de Male, comte de Flandre*, 2 vols. (Bruges, 1898–1909).

(ed.). *Codex Diplomaticus Flandriae*, 2 vols. (Bruges, 1889).

de Roovere, Anthonis. *De gedichten van Anthonis de Roovere*, ed J. J. Mak (Zwolle, 1955).

Despars, Nicolas. *Cronijcke van den lande ende graefscepe van Vlaenderen*, 4 vols., ed. J. De Jonghe (Bruges and Rotterdam, 1839–42).

Espinas, G. and Buntinx, J. (eds.). *Privilèges et chartes de franchise de la Flandre*, 2 vols. (Brussels, 1959).

Espinas, G., and Pirenne, H. (eds.). *Recueil de documents relatifs à l'histoire de l'industrie drapière en Flandre*, 4 vols. (Brussels, 1906).

Gessler, J. (ed.). *Het Brugsche Livre des mestiers en zijn navolgingen* (Bruges, 1931).

Gilles Li Muisis, 'Chronica Aegidii li Muisis', in J.-J. De Smet (ed.), *Corpus Chronicorum Flandriae*, 4 vols. (Brussels, 1837–65), vol. II, pp. 93–448.

Gilliodts-Van Severen, L. *Le carillon de Bruges: Recueil de textes et analyses de documents inédits ou peu connus* (Bruges, 1912).

Inventaire diplomatique des archives de l'ancienne école Bogarde à Bruges (Bruges, 1899–1900).

(ed.). *Cartulaire de l'ancien grand tonlieu de Bruges faisant suite au cartulaire de l'ancienne Estaple*, 2 vols. (Bruges, 1908–9).

(ed.). *Cartulaire de l'ancienne estaple de Bruges*, 3 vols. (Bruges, 1904–6).

(ed.). *Coutume de la prévôté de Bruges*, 2 vols. (Brussels, 1887).

(ed.). *Coutume de la ville de Bruges* (Brussels, 1874–5).

(ed.). *Mémoriaux de Bruges*, 2 vols. (Bruges, 1913).

Huyghebaert, N. (ed.). *Une translation de reliques à Gand en 944: Le Sermo de Adventu Sanctorum Wandregisili, Ansberti et Vulframni in Blandinium* (Brussels, 1978).

Johnstone, H. (ed.). *Annals of Ghent: Translated from the Latin with Introduction and Notes* (London, 1951).

Lambert, V. (ed.). *De oorkonden van het Sint-Donatiaanskapittel te Brugge (9de eeuw – 1300)* (Brussels, 2008).

Lambin, J. (ed.). *Dits de cronike ende genealogie van den prinsen ende graven van den foreeste van buc, dat heet Vlaenderlant, van 863 tot 1436* (Ypres, 1839).

Oosterman, J. 'Anthonis de Roovere: Het werk: Overlevering, toeschrijving en plaatsbepaling, *Jaarboek De Fonteine* (1997–8), 9–88.

Pirenne, H. (ed.). *Chronique rimée des troubles de Flandre en 1379–1380* (Ghent, 1902).

Rider, J. (ed.). *Galbertus Brugensis: De multro, traditione, et occisione gloriosi Karoli comitis Flandriarum* (Turnhout, 1994).

Schouteet, A. *Stadsarchief van Brugge: Regesten op de oorkonden*, vol I: *1089–1300* (Bruges, 1973).

Tafur, Pero. *Travels and Adventures 1435–1439*, trans. and intro. M. Letts (London, 1926).

van Dixmude, Jan. *Chronicke van den prinsen ende graven van Vlaenderen en Brabant van 1377 tot 1443*, ed. J. Lambin (Ypres, 1835).

van Male, Zegher. *De Lamentatie van Zeghere van Male, Brugge na de opstand tegen Spanje 1590*, ed. A. Dewitte and A. Viaene (Bruges, 1977).

Vercauteren, F. *Actes des comtes de Flandre, 1071–1128* (Brussels, 1938).

Wyffels, C., De Smet, J. and Vandewalle, A. (eds.). *De rekeningen van de stad Brugge, 1280–1319* (Brussels, 1965–97).

Secondary Sources

Abulafia, D. (ed.). *The New Cambridge Medieval History*, vol. V (Cambridge, 1999).

Aerts, E. 'The Absence of Public Exchange Banks in Medieval and Early Modern Flanders and Brabant (1400–1800): A Historical Anomaly to be Explained', *Financial History Review*, 18 (2011), 91–117.

Aerts, E. et al. (eds.). *Studia Historica Oeconomica: Liber amicorum Herman Van der Wee* (Leuven, 1993).

Ainsworth, M. W. (ed.). *Petrus Christus in Renaissance Bruges: An Interdisciplinary Approach* (New York, 1995).

Ainsworth, M. and Martens, M. P. J. *Petrus Christus, Renaissance Master of Bruges* (New York, 1994).

Album Albert Schouteet (Bruges, 1973).

Allmand, C. (ed.). *The New Cambridge Medieval History*, vol. VII (Cambridge, 1998).

Andriessen, P. *Die van muziken gheerne horen: Muziek in Brugge 1200–1800* (Bruges, 2002).

Arnade, P., Howell, M. C. and Simons, W. 'Fertile Spaces: The Productivity of Urban Space in Northern Europe', *Journal of Interdisciplinary History*, 32 (2002), 515–48.

Baes, W. (ed.). *Van Rame tot Coupure: Geschiedenis van een Brugse wijk* (Bruges, 1997).

Baeteman, C. 'History of Research and State of the Art of the Holocene Depositionary History of the Belgian Coastal Plain', in Thoen et al. (eds.), *Landscapes or Seascapes*, pp. 11–29.

Bardoel, A. A. 'The Urban Uprising at Bruges, 1280–1: Some New Findings about the Rebels and the Partisans', *BTFG*, 72 (1994), 761–91.

Becuwe, M., Beernaert, B. and Cardinael, P. *De Vesten anders bekeken: Een groene wandeling rond Brugge* (Bruges, 2005).

Beernaert, B., Braet, J., Demulder, J. et al. *Binnen en buiten: Winter- en zomerverblijven van de Brugse elite vanaf de late middeleeuwen* (Bruges, 2007).

Beernaert, B., Deleu, F., Hemeryck, A. et al. *Het Belfort van Brugge* (Bruges, 2012).

Berings, G. 'Het oude land aan de rand van het vroegmiddeleeuws overstromingsgebied van de Noordzee: Landname en grondbezit tijdens de Middeleeuwen', *HMG*, 39 (1985), 37–84.

Blickle, P. *Kommunalismus: Skizzen einer gesellschaftlichen Organisationsform* (Oldenbourg, 2000).

Blockmans, F. 'De oudste privileges der grote Vlaamsche steden', *Nederlandsche Historiebladen*, 1 (1938), 421–46.

Blockmans, W. 'The Creative Environment: Incentives to and Functions of Bruges Art Production', in Ainsworth (ed.), *Petrus Christus in Renaissance Bruges*, pp. 11–20.

'Inclusiveness and Exclusion: Trust Networks as the Origins of European Cities', *Theory and Society*, 39 (2010), 315–26.

Metropolen aan de Noordzee: De geschiedenis van Nederland, 1100–1560 (Amsterdam, 2010).

'The Social and Economic Effects of Plague in the Low Countries, 1349–1500', *BTFG*, 58 (1980), 833–66.

De volksvertegenwoordiging in Vlaanderen in de overgang van middeleeuwen naar nieuwe tijden (1384–1506) (Brussels, 1978).

Blockmans, W., Boone, M. and de Hemptinne, T. (eds.). *Secretum scriptorum: Liber alumnorum Walter Prevenier* (Leuven, 1999).

Blockmans, W., and Prevenier, W., *The Promised Lands: The Low Countries under Burgundian Rule, 1369–1530*, trans. E. Fackelman (Philadelphia, 1999).

Blondé, B., Stabel, P., Stobart, J. et al. (eds.). *Buyers and Sellers: Retail Circuits and Practices in Medieval and Early Modern Europe* (Turnhout, 2008).

Bloxam, J. 'A Survey of Late Medieval Service Books from the Low Countries: Implications for Sacred Polyphony, 1460–1520', unpublished PhD thesis, Yale University (New Haven, CT, 1987).

'Text and Context: Obrecht's *Missa de Sancto Donatiano* in its Social and Ritual Landscape', *Journal of the Alamire Foundation*, 3 (2011), 11–36.

Bolton, J. L. and Guidi Bruscoli, F. 'When Did Antwerp Replace Bruges as the Commercial and Financial Centre of North-Western Europe? The Evidence of the Boromei Ledger for 1438', *Economic History Review*, 61 (2008), 360–79.

Boogaart, T. *An Ethnogeography of Medieval Bruges: Evolution of a Communal Milieu* (Madison, WI, 2000).

Boone, M. *À la recherche d'une modernité civique: La société urbaine des anciens Pays-Bas au bas Moyen Âge* (Brussels, 2010).

'Armes, coursses, assemblees et commocions: Les gens de métiers et l'usage de la violence dans la société urbaine flamande à la fin du Moyen Âge', *RN*, 359 (2005), 7–34.

'Le comté de Flandre dans le long XIVe siècle: Une société urbanisée face aux crises du bas Moyen Âge', in Bourin et al. (eds.), *Rivolte urbane*, pp. 17–47.

'La construction d'un républicanisme urbain: Enjeux de la politique municipale dans les villes flamandes au bas Moyen Âge', in Menjot and Pinol (eds.), *Enjeux*, pp. 41–60.

Gent en de Bourgondische hertogen ca. 1384 – ca. 1453: Een sociaal-politieke studie van een staatsvormingsproces (Brussels, 1990).

'State Power and Illicit Sexuality: The Persecution of Sodomy in Late Medieval Bruges', *JMH*, 22 (1996), 135–53.

Boone, M., Davids, K. and Janssens, P. (eds.). *Urban Public Debts: Urban Government and the Market for Annuities in Western Europe (14th–18th Centuries)* (Turnhout, 2003).

Boone, M. and Howell, M. C. (eds.). *The Power of Space in Late Medieval and Early Modern Europe: The Cities of Italy, Northern France and the Low Countries* (Turnhout, 2013)

Boone, M. and Stabel, P. (eds.). *Shaping Urban Identity in Late Medieval Europe* (Leuven and Apeldoorn, 2000).

Borchert, T.-H. (ed.). *The Age of Van Eyck, 1430–1530: The Mediterranean World and Early Netherlandish Painting* [exh. cat.] (Ghent and Amsterdam, 2002).

(ed.). *Memling: Rinascimento fiammingo* (Rome, 2014).

Boucheron, P. and Menjot, D. *Histoire de l'Europe urbaine*, vol. II: *La ville médiévale* (Paris, 2003).

Bourguignon, M.-A., Dauven, B.. and Rousseaux, X. (eds.). *Amender, sanctionner et punir: Histoire de la peine du Moyen Âge au XXe siècle: Actes des journées d'études de Louvain-la-Neuve, 19–20 octobre 2009* (Louvain-la-Neuve, 2012).

Bourin, M., Cherubini, G. and Pinto, G. (eds.). *Rivolte urbane e rivolte contadine nell' Europa del trecento: Un confronto* (Florence, 2008).

Braekevelt, J., Buylaert, F., Dumolyn, J. et al. 'The Politics of Factional Conflict in Late Medieval Flanders', *Historical Research*, 85 (2012), 1–31.

Brinkman, H. 'De Brugse pelgrims in het Gruuthuse handschrift', in Oosterman (ed.), *Stad van koopmanschap en vrede*, pp. 9–39.

Brinkmann, B. *Flämische Buchmalerei am Ende des Burgunderreiches: Der Meister des Dresdner Gebetbuchs und die Miniaturisten seiner Zeit* (Turnhout, 1997).

Brown, A. *Civic Ceremony and Religion in Medieval Bruges, c.1300–1520* (Cambridge, 2011).

'Civic Religion in Late Medieval Europe', *JMH*, 42 (2016), 338–56.

Brulez, W. 'Bruges and Antwerp in the 15th and 16th Centuries: An Antithesis?', *Acta historiae Neerlandica*, 6 (1973), 1–26.

Buntinx, J. *De Audiëntie van de graven van Vlaanderen: Studie over het centraal grafelijk gerecht (c.1330–c.1409)* (Brussels, 1949).

Buylaert, F. 'Edelen in de Vlaamse stedelijke samenleving: Een kwantitatieve benadering van de elite van het laatmiddeleeuwse en vroegmoderne Brugge', *Tijdschrift voor Sociale en Economische Geschiedenis*, 4 (2007), 29–56.

'The Late Medieval 'Crisis of the Nobility' Reconsidered: The Case of Flanders', *Journal of Social History*, 45 (2012), 1–18.

'La "noblesse urbaine" à Bruges (1363–1563): Naissance d'un nouveau groupe social?', in T. Dutour (ed.), *Les nobles et la ville dans l'espace francophone (XIIe–XVIe siècles)* (Paris, 2010), pp. 245–74.

Calabi, D. and Christensen, S. T. (eds.). *Cultural Exchange in Early Modern Europe*, 4 vols. (Cambridge, 2006).

Callewier, H. *De papen van Brugge: De seculiere clerus in een middeleeuwse wereldstad (1411–1477)* (Leuven, 2014).

Campbell, L. 'The Art Market in the Southern Netherlands in the Fifteenth Century', *Burlington Magazine*, 118 (1976), 188–97.

The Fifteenth-Century Netherlandish Paintings (London, 2000).

Carlier, M. *Kinderen van de minne? Bastaarden in het vijftiende-eeuwse Vlaanderen* (Brussels, 2001).

Carlvant, K. *Manuscript Painting in Thirteenth-Century Flanders: Bruges, Ghent and the Circle of the Counts* (Turnhout, 2012).

Casado Alonso, H. 'La nation et le quartier des Castillans de Bruges (XVe et XVIe siècles)', *HGG*, 133 (1996), 61–77.

Cavaciocchi, S. (ed.). *Le interazioni fra economia e ambiente biologico nell'Europa preindustriale* (Prato, 2010).

(ed.). *Le migrazioni in Europa: Secc. XIII–XVIII* (Florence, 1994).

Chauvard, J.-F. and Mocarelli, L. (eds.). *L'économie de la construction dans l'Italie Moderne*, special issue of *Mélanges de l'Ecole Française de Rome: Italie et Méditerrannée*, 119 (2007).

Chédeville, A., Le Goff, J. and Rossiaud, J. *Histoire de la France urbaine*, vol. II: *La ville en France au Moyen Âge, des Carolingiens à la Renaissance*, 2nd edn (Paris, 1998).

Chorley, P. 'The Cloth Exports of Flanders and Northern France during the Thirteenth Century: A Luxury Trade?', *Economic History Review*, 40 (1987), 349–79.

Clark, P. *European Cities and Towns, 400–2000* (Oxford, 2009).

(ed.). *The Oxford Handbook of Cities in World History* (Oxford, 2013).

Clarke, H. and Ambrosiani, B. *Towns in the Viking Age* (London and Leicester, 1991).

Clarke, H. and Simms, A. 'Towards a Comparative History of Urban Origins', in H. Clarke and A. Simms (eds.), *The Comparative History of Urban Origins in*

Non-Roman Europe: Ireland, Wales, Denmark, Germany, Poland and Russia from the 9th to the 13th Century (Oxford, 1985), pp. 669–714.

Coigneau, D. 'Een Brugse Villon of Rabelais: Eduard de Dene en zijn Testament Rhetoricael (1561)', in B. A. M. Ramakers (ed.), *Conformisten en rebellen: Rederijkerscultuur in de Nederlanden (1400–1650)* (Amsterdam, 2003), pp. 199–211.

Coornaert, E. 'Draperies rurales, draperies urbaines: L'évolution de l'industrie flamande au Moyen Âge et au XVI siècle', *BTFG*, 28 (1950), 60–96.

Coornaert, M. 'Over de hydrografie van Brugge', *Album Albert Schouteet*, pp. 23–35.

Cornilly, J. *Monumentaal West Vlaanderen: Beschermde monumenten en landschappen in de provincie West Vlaanderen*, vol. II: *De fusiegemeente Brugge* (Bruges, 2003).

Coupland, S. 'Trading Places: Quentovic and Dorestad Reassessed', *Early Medieval Europe*, 11 (2002), 209–32.

Cowan, A. *Urban Europe, 1500–1700* (London, 1998).

Crombie, L. 'Honour, Community and Hierarchy in the Feasts of the Archery and Crossbow Guilds of Bruges, 1445–81', *JMH*, 30 (2011), 102–13.

Crouzet-Pavan, E. '*Sopra le acque salse*': *Espaces, pouvoir et société à Venise à la fin du Moyen Âge*, 2 vols. (Rome and Paris, 1992).

Les villes vivantes: Italie, XIIIe–XVe siècle (Paris, 2009).

Crouzet-Pavan, E. and Lecuppre-Desjardin, E. (eds.). *Villes de Flandre et d'Italie: Relectures d'une comparaison traditionnelle* (Turnhout, 2007).

Daelemans, F. and Kelders, A. (eds.). *Miscellanea in memoriam Pierre Cockshaw (1938–2008): Aspects de la vie culturelle dans les Pays-Bas Méridionaux (XIVe–XVIIIe siècle)*, 2 vols. (Brussels, 2009).

Danneel, M. *Weduwen en wezen in het laatmiddeleeuwse Gent* (Leuven, 1996).

Dauven, B. and Rousseaux, X. (eds.). *Préférant miséricorde à rigueur de justice: Pratiques de la grâce (XIIIe–XVIIe siècles): Actes de la journée d'études de Louvain-la-Neuve, 15 Octobre 2007* (Louvain-la-Neuve, 2012).

De Bruyne, H. *De godshuizen in Brugge* (Roeselare, 1994).

Decavele, J. 'Protestantse invloeden in Brugge in het midden van de 16de eeuw: Een internationaal netwerk', *Tijdschrift voor Nederlandse Kerkgeschiedenis*, 16 (2013), 6–23.

Declercq, G. 'Bruggas, Bruciam, Brutgis: De oudste eigentijdse vermeldingen van Brugge', in Hillewaert et al. (eds.), *Op het raakvlak*, pp. 129–36.

'Galbert van Brugge en de verraderlijke moord op Karel de Goede: Beschouwingen over tekst en auteur naar aanleiding van een nieuwe uitgave', *HMG*, 49 (1995), 71–117.

'Oorsprong en vroegste ontwikkeling van de burcht van Brugge (9de–12de eeuw)', in De Witte (ed.), *De Brugse Burg*, pp. 15–45.

'Vlaanderen en de Vlaanderengouw in de vroege middeleeuwen', *Vlaanderen: Tweemaandelijks Tijdschrift voor Kunst en Letteren*, 44 (1995), 10–17.

'Wanneer ontstond het Sint-Donaaskapittel te Brugge', *HGG*, 122 (1985), 145–57.

De Clercq, W. 'Roman Rural Settlements in Flanders: Perspectives on a 'Non-Villa' Landscape in Extrema Galliarum', in N. Roymans and T. Derks (eds.), *Villa Landscapes in the Roman North: Economy, Culture and Lifestyles* (Amsterdam, 2011), pp. 235–58.

De Clercq, W., Dumolyn, J. and Haemers, J. 'Vivre Noblement: The Material and Immaterial Construction of Elite-Identity in Late Medieval Flanders: The Case of Pieter Bladelin and William Hugonet', *Journal of Interdisciplinary History*, 38 (2007), 1–31.

Degryse, R. 'De oudste houten kranen in de Vlaamse en andere havens (13de–16de eeuw)', *HGG*, 128 (1991), 5–46, 153–87.

De Hemptinne, T. and Parisse, M. 'Thierry d'Alsace, comte de Flandre: Biographie et actes', *Annales de l'Est*, 43 (1991), 83–113.

De Jonge, K. 'Bourgondische residenties in het graafschap Vlaanderen: Rijsel, Brugge en Gent ten tijde van Filips de Goede', *HMG*, 54 (2000), 93–134.

De Koster, M., De Munck, B., Greefs, H. et al. (eds.). *Werken aan de stad: Stedelijke actoren en structuren in de Zuidelijke Nederlanden 1500–1900: Liber amicorum Catharina Lis en Hugo Soly* (Brussels, 2011).

Delmarcel, G. *Flemish Tapestry, 15th to 18th Century* (London and New York, 1999).

De Marchi, N. and Van Miegroet, H. J. (eds.). *Mapping Markets for Paintings in Europe, 1450–1750* (Turnhout, 2006).

De Meester, T. 'De ontstaansgeschiedenis van de Brugse Poortersloge', *Brugs Ommeland*, 53 (2013), 32–54.

Demets, L. and Dumolyn, J. 'Urban Chronicle Writing in Late Medieval Flanders: The Case of Bruges during the Flemish Revolt of 1482–1490', *Urban History*, 43 (2015), 28–45.

De Meyer, I. 'De sociale strukturen te Brugge in de 14e eeuw', in W. Blockmans, I. De Meyer, J. Mertens et al. (eds.), *Studiën betreffende de sociale strukturen te Brugge, Kortrijk en Gent in de 14e en 15e eeuw*, vol. I: *Tekst* (Kortrijk, 1971), pp. 7–78.

De Meyer, I. and Vanderpijpen, W. *Studiën betreffende de sociale strukturen te Brugge, Kortrijk en Gent in de 14e en 15e eeuw*, vol. II: *Tabellen* (Heule, 1972).

De Munck, B. 'From Brotherhood Community to Civil Society? Apprentices between Guild, Household and the Freedom of Contract in Early Modern Antwerp', *Social History*, 35 (2010), 1–20.

De Munck, B., Kaplan, S. L. and Soly, H. (eds.). *Learning on the Shop Floor: Historical Perspectives on Apprenticeship* (New York, 2007).

Deneweth, H. 'Een demografische knoop ontward? Brugse bevolkingscijfers voor de vroegmoderne tijd', *HGG*, 147 (2010), 3–48.

'The Economic Situation and its Influence on Building and Renovating in Bruges, 16th–18th centuries', in Chauvard and Mocarelli (eds.), *L'économie de la construction*, pp. 537–50.

Deneweth, H., D'hondt, J. and Leenders, K. *Een huis in Brugge: Vademecum voor de historische studie van woningen, eigenaars en bewoners* (Bruges, 2001).

Denys, L. and Baeteman, C. 'Holocene Evolution of Relative Sea-Level and Local Mean High Water Spring Tides in Belgium: A First Assessment', *Marine Geology*, 124 (1995), 1–19

De Rock, J. 'Beeld van de stad: Picturale voorstellingen van stedelijkheid in de laatmiddeleeuwse Nederlanden', unpublished PhD thesis, Ghent University (Ghent, 2011).

de Roover, R. 'La communauté des marchands lucquois à Bruges de 1377 à 1404', *HGG*, 86 (1949), 28–89.

Money, Banking and Credit in Medieval Bruges (Cambridge, MA, 1948).

Derville, A. *Les villes de Flandre et d'Artois (900–1500)* (Lille, 2002).

Derycke, L. 'The Public Annuity Market in Bruges at the End of the 15th Century', in Boone et al. (eds.), *Urban Public Debts*, pp. 165–81.

Derycke, L. and Van Bruaene, A.-L. 'Sociale en literaire dynamiek in het vroeg vijftiende-eeuwse Brugge: De oprichting van de rederijkerskamer De Heilige Geest ca. 1428', in Oosterman (ed.), *Stad van koopmanschap en vrede*, pp. 59–96.

De Smaele, H., Flour, E., Heyndrickx, V. et al. (eds.). *De Onze-Lieve-Vrouwekerk te Brugge: Kunst & Geschiedenis* (Bruges, 1997).

De Smet, A. 'L'origine des ports du Zwin: Damme, Mude, Monikerede, Hoeke et Sluis', in *Études d'histoire dédiées à la mémoire de Henri Pirenne* (Brussels, 1937), pp. 125–41.

De Smet, J. 'De Brugse WIIC-namen', *HGG*, 85 (1948), 112–17.

'De inrichting van de Poorterlijke ruiterij te Brugge in 1292 en haar indeling in gezindheden in 1302', *Verslagen en Mededeelingen der Koninklijke Vlaamse Academie voor Taal- en Letterkunde* (1930), 487–505.

Devliegher, L. *De Sint-Salvatorskathedraal te Brugge: Geschiedenis en architectuur.* Kunstpatrimonium van West-Vlaanderen 7 (Tielt, 1981).

Van Waterhalle tot Provinciaal Hof (Bruges, 1994).

De Vos, D. *Hans Memling: The Complete Works* (New York, 1994).

Dewilde, B. 'On Noble Artists and Poor Craftsmen: Networking Painters in Renaissance Bruges', in K. Brosens, L. Kelchtermans and K. Van der Stighelen (eds.), *Art Production and Kinship Patterns in the Early Modern Low Countries* (Turnhout, 2012), pp. 85–101.

Dewitte, A. 'Gegevens betreffende het muziekleven in de voormalige Sint-Donaaskerk te Brugge', 1251–1660, *HGG*, 111 (1974), 129–74.

'Het humanisme te Brugge: Een overtrokken begrip?', *HKZM*, 27 (1973), 5–26.

De Witte, H. (ed.). *De Brugse Burg: Van grafelijke versterking tot moderne stadskern* (Bruges, 1991).

Dezutter, W. P. and Goetinck, M. (eds.). *Op en om de bouwwerf* [exh. cat.] (Bruges, 1975).

Dhondt, J. 'Développement urbain et initiative comtale en Flandre au XIe siècle', *RN*, 30 (1948), 133–56.

'Les origines des états de Flandre', *Standen en Landen*, 1 (1950), 3–52.

'De vroege topografie van Brugge', *HMG*, 11 (1957), 5–13.

D'Hooghe, C. *De huizen van het Zuidproosse te Brugge van ca. 1400 tot 1920* (Bruges, 1997).

D'Hooghe, C. and Balthau, E. 'Een bijdrage tot de studie van het stadspatriciaat in de late middeleeuwen: De Brugse familie De Vos in de 14de–15de eeuw', *Castellum*, 5 (1988), 4–81.

Dobson, B. 'Urban Europe', in Allmand (ed.), *New Cambridge Medieval History*, vol. VII, pp. 121–44.

Dogaer, G. *Flemish Miniature Painting in the Fifteenth and Sixteenth Centuries*, trans. A. E. C. Simoni et al. (Amsterdam, 1987).

Dollinger, P. *The German Hanse*, trans. and ed. D. S. Ault and S. H. Steinberg (London, 1970).

Duclos, A. *Bruges: Histoire et souvenirs* (Bruges, 1910).

Dumolyn, J. *De Brugse opstand van 1436–1438* (Kortrijk, 1997).

'Economic Development, Social Space and Political Power in Bruges, c. 1127 – 1302', in Skoda et al. (eds.), *Contact and Exchange*, pp. 33–58.

'Guild Politics and Political Guilds in Fourteenth-Century Flanders', in Dumolyn et al. (eds.), *Voices of the People*, pp. 15–48.

'Une idéologie urbaine "bricolée" en Flandre médiévale: Les "Sept Portes de Bruges" dans le manuscrit Gruuthuse (début du 15e siècle)', *BTFG*, 88 (2010), 1039–84.

'"Our Land is Only Founded on Trade and Industry": Economic Discourses in Fifteenth-Century Bruges', *JMH*, 36 (2010), 374–89.

'Population et structures professionnelles à Bruges aux XIVe et XVe siècles,' *RN*, 81 (1999), 43–64.

'The "Terrible Wednesday" of Pentecost: Confronting Urban and Princely Discourses in the Bruges Rebellion of 1436–1438', *History: Journal of the Historical Association*, 92 (2007), 3–20.

Dumolyn, J. and Haemers, J. 'A Bad Chicken Was Brooding: Subversive Speech in Late Medieval Flanders', *Past and Present*, 214 (2012), 45–86.

'Patterns of Urban Rebellion in Medieval Flanders', *JMH*, 31 (2005), 369–93.

'Reclaiming the Common Sphere of the City: The Revival of the Bruges Commune in the Late Thirteenth Century', in Genet (ed.), *La légitimité implicite*, vol. II, pp. 161–88.

Dumolyn, J., Haemers, J., Oliva Herrer, H. R. et al. (eds.). *The Voices of the People in Late Medieval Europe: Communication and Popular Politics* (Turnhout, 2014).

Dumolyn, J. and Lenoir, M. 'De sociaal-politieke verhoudingen binnen het Brugse stadsbestuur tijdens het midden van de veertiende eeuw (1329–1361)', *HGG*, 151 (2015), 323–76.

Dupont, G. *Maagdenverleidsters, hoeren en speculanten: Prostitutie in Brugge tijdens de Bourgondische periode (1385–1515)* (Bruges, 1996).

'Le temps des compositions: Pratiques judiciaires à Bruges et à Gand du XIVe au XVIe siècle (Partie I)', in Dauven and Rousseaux (eds.), *Préférant miséricorde*, pp. 53–95.

'Le temps des compositions: Pratiques judiciaires à Bruges et à Gand du XIVe au XVIe siècle (Partie II)', in Bourguignon et al. (eds.), *Amender*, pp. 15–47.

Duvosquel, J.-M. and Dierkens, A. (eds.). *Villes et campagnes au Moyen Âge: Mélanges Georges Despy* (Liège, 1991).

Duvosquel, J.-M. and Thoen, E. (eds.). *Peasants and Townsmen in Medieval Europe: Studia in honorem Adriaan Verhulst* (Ghent, 1995).

Dyer, C. *Standards of Living in the Later Middle Ages: Social Change in England c.1200–1520* (Cambridge, 1989).

Dyos, H. J. (ed.). *The Study of Urban History* (London, 1968).

Ehrich, S. and Oberste, J. (eds.). *Städtische Kulte im Mittelalter* (Regensburg, 2010).

Ennen, E. *Die europäische Stadt des Mittelalters*, 4th edn (Göttingen, 1987), trans. N. Fryde as *The Medieval Town* (New York, 1979).

Epstein, S. A. 'Urban Society', in Abulafia (ed.), *New Cambridge Medieval History*, vol. V, pp. 26–37.

Epstein, S. R. 'Craft Guilds, Apprenticeship and Technological Change in Pre-Industrial Europe', *Journal of Economic History*, 58 (1998), 684–713.

Epstein, S. R., and M. Prak (eds.). *Guilds, Innovation, and the European Economy, 1400–1800* (Cambridge, 2008).

Espinas, G. *La draperie dans la Flandre française au Moyen Âge* (Paris, 1923).

Les origines du droit d'association dans les villes de l'Artois et de la Flandre française jusqu'au début du XVIe siècle, 2 vols. (Lille, 1941–2).

Fagel, R. *De Hispano-Vlaamse wereld: De contacten tussen Spanjaarden en Nederlanders, 1496–1555* (Brussels and Nijmegen, 1996).

Finot, J. *Étude historique sur les relations commerciales entre la Flandre et l'Espagne au Moyen Âge* (Paris, 1899).

Gabriëls, N. 'Bourgeois Music Collecting in Mid Sixteenth-Century Bruges: The Creation of the Zeghere van Male Partbooks (Cambrai, Médiathèque Municipale, MSS 125–128)', unpublished PhD thesis, Catholic University of Leuven (Leuven, 2010).

Galvin, M. T. 'Credit and Parochial Charity in Fifteenth-Century Bruges', *JMH*, 28 (2002), 131–54.

'The Poor Tables of Bruges, 1270–1477', unpublished PhD thesis, Columbia University (New York, 1998).

Ganshof, F.-L. 'Le droit urbain en Flandre au début de la première phase de son histoire (1127)', *Revue d'histoire du droit*, 19 (1951), 387–416.

Étude sur le développement des villes entre Loire et Rhin au Moyen Âge (Paris and Brussels, 1943).

'L'origine des constitutions urbaines en Flandre: A propos d'un livre récent', *Le Moyen Âge*, 26 (1926), 349–68.

Geirnaert, N. 'De oudste sporen van het Heilig Bloed in Brugge (1255–1310)', *HGG*, 147 (2010), 247–55.

Geirnaert, N. and Vandamme, L. *Bruges: Two Thousand Years of History* (Bruges, 1996).

Geirnaert, N. and Vandewalle, A. (eds.). *Adornes en Jeruzalem: Internationaal leven in het 15de- en 16de-eeuws Brugge* [exh. cat.] (Bruges, 1983).

Gelderblom, O. *Cities of Commerce: The Institutional Foundations of International Trade in the Low Countries, 1250–1650* (Princeton, NJ, 2013).

'The Decline of Fairs and Merchant Guilds in the Low Countries, 1250–1650', *Jaarboek voor Middeleeuwse Geschiedenis*, 7 (2004), 199–238.

Gelichi, S. and Hodges, R. (eds.). *From One Sea to Another: Trading Places in the European and Mediterranean Early Middle Ages* (Turnhout, 2009).

Genet, J.-P. (ed.). *La légitimité implicite: Le pouvoir symbolique en Occident*, 2 vols. (Paris, 2015).

Gilté, S., Vanwalleghem, A. and Van Aerschot-Van Haeverbeeck, S. (eds.). *Bouwen door de eeuwen heen: Inventaris van het cultuurbezit in België: Architectuur, deel 18nb, stad Brugge, middeleeuwse stadsuitbreiding noord* (Turnhout, 2004).

Gläser, M. (ed.). *Lübecker Kolloquium zur Stadtarchäologie im Hanseraum*, vol. III: *Der Hausbau* (Lübeck, 2001).

Goldthwaite, R. A. *Wealth and the Demand for Art in Italy, 1300–1600* (Baltimore, MD, 1993).

Goodson, C., Lester, A. E. and Symes, C. (eds.). *Cities, Texts and Social Networks, 400–1500: Experiences and Perceptions of Medieval Urban Space* (Farnham, 2010).

Gottschalk, M. K. E. 'Het verval van Brugge als wereldmarkt', *TG*, 56 (1953), 1–26.

Greve, A. *Hansische Kaufleute, Hosteliers und Herbergen im Brügge des 14. und 15. Jahrhunderts* (Frankfurt am Main, 2012).

Grierson, P. 'The Translation of the Relics of St. Donatian to Bruges', *Revue Bénédictine*, 49 (1937), 170–90.

Guidi Bruscoli, F. 'Trade with Northern Europe', in G. Nigro (ed.), *Francesco di Marco Datini: The Man, the Merchant* (Florence, 2010), pp. 395–417.

Gysseling, M. 'Etymologie van Brugge', *Handelingen van de Koninklijke Commissie voor Toponymie en Dialectologie*, 18 (1944), 69–79.

'Een nieuwe etymologie van Brugge', *Naamkunde*, 3 (1971), 1–4.

Haemers, J. *For the Common Good: State Power and Urban Revolts in the Reign of Mary of Burgundy (1477–1482)* (Turnhout, 2009).

De strijd om het regentschap over Filips de Schone: Opstand, facties en geweld in Brugge, Gent en Ieper (1482–1488) (Ghent, 2014).

Haggh, B. 'The Beguines of Bruges and the Procession of the Holy Blood', in P. Mannaerts (ed.), *Beghinae in cantu instructae – Musical Patrimony from Flemish Beguinages (Middle Ages – Late 18th C.)* (Turnhout, 2010), pp. 27–50.

Hamerow, H. et al. 'Migration Period Settlements and "Anglo-Saxon" Pottery from Flanders', *Medieval Archaeology*, 38 (1994), 1–18.

Hansotte, G. and Coppejans, H. (eds.). *Album Carlos Wyffels* (Brussels, 1987).

Häpke, R. *Brügges Entwicklung zum mittelalterlichen Weltmarkt* (Berlin, 1908).
Harbison, C. *Jan van Eyck: The Play of Realism* (London, 1991).
Heers, J. *La ville au Moyen Âge en Occident: Paysages, pouvoir et conflits* (Paris, 1990).
Heidinga, H. A. *Frisia in the First Millennium: An Outline* (Utrecht, 1997).
Henn, V. 'Der dudesche kopman zu Brügge und seine Beziehungen zu den nationes der übrigen Fremden im späten Mittelalter', in N. Jörn, D. Kattinger and H. Wernicke (eds.), *'Kopet uns werk by tyden': Walter Stark zum 75. Geburtstag* (Schwerin, 1999), pp. 131–42.
Herlihy, D. *Medieval and Renaissance Pistoia: The Social History of an Italian Town, 1200–1430* (New Haven, CT, 1967).
Hibbert, A. B. 'The Origins of the Medieval Town Patriciate', *Past and Present*, 3 (1953), 15–27.
Hillewaert, B. *Oostkerke-bij Brugge*, Archeologische Inventaris Vlaanderen 2 (Ghent, 1984).
Hillewaert, B., Hollevoet, Y. and Ryckaert, M. (eds.). *Op het raakvlak van twee landschappen: De vroegste geschiedenis van Brugge* (Bruges, 2011).
Hillewaert, B. and Van Besien, E. (eds.). *Het Prinsenhof in Brugge* (Bruges, 2007).
Hilton, R. H. *English and French Towns in Feudal Society: A Comparative Study* (Cambridge, 1992).
Hodges, R. *Dark Age Economics: A New Audit* (London, 2012).
Towns and Trade in the Age of Charlemagne (London, 2000).
Hohenberg, P. M. and Hollen Lees, L. *The Making of Urban Europe, 1000–1950* (Cambridge, MA, 1985).
Holbach, R. 'Some Remarks on the Role of "Putting-out" in Flemish and Northwest European Cloth Production', in M. Boone and W. Prevenier (eds.), *Drapery Production in the Late Medieval Low Countries: Markets and Strategies for Survival (14th–16th Centuries)* (Leuven and Apeldoorn, 1993), pp. 207–50.
Hollevoet, Y. and Hillewaert, B. 'Het archeologisch onderzoek achter de voormalige vrouwengevangenis Refuge te Sint-Andries/Brugge', *Archeologie in Vlaanderen*, 6 (1997/8), 197–207.
Hoppenbrouwers, P. C. M. and Van Zanden, J. L. (eds.). *Peasants into Farmers? The Transformation of Rural Economy and Society in the Low Countries (Middle Ages – 19th Century) in Light of the Brenner Debate* (Turnhout, 2001).
Howell, M. C. 'From Land to Love: Commerce and Marriage in Northern Europe during the Late Middle Ages', *Jaarboek voor Middeleeuwse Geschiedenis*, 10 (2007), 216–53.
The Marriage Exchange: Property, Social Place, and Gender in Cities of the Low Countries, 1300–1550 (Chicago, IL, 1998).
Women, Production and Patriarchy in Late Medieval Cities (Chicago, IL, 1986).
Huizinga, J. *Herfsttij der middeleeuwen: Studies over levens- en gedachtenvormen der veertiende en vijftiende eeuw in Frankrijk en de Nederlanden* (1919;

Amsterdam, 1997), trans. R. J. Payton and U. Mammitzsch as *The Autumn of the Middle Ages* (Chicago, IL, 1996).

Hunt, E. S. and Murray, J. M. *A History of Business in Medieval Europe, 1200–1550* (Cambridge, 1999).

Hüsken, W. N. M. 'Kroniek van het toneel in Brugge, 1468–1556', *Verslagen en mededelingen van de Koninklijke Academie voor Nederlandse Taal- en Letterkunde* (1992), 219–52.

Huyghebaert, N. 'Iperius et la translation de la relique du Saint Sang à Bruges', *HGG*, 100 (1963), 110–87.

Huys, E. *Duizend jaar mutualiteit bij de Vlaamsche gilden* (Dendermonde, 1923).

Hyde, J. K. *Society and Politics in Medieval Italy: The Evolution of the Civil Life, 1000–1350* (London and Basingstoke, 1973).

Isenmann, E. *Die deutsche Stadt im Mittelalter 1150–1550: Stadtgestalt, Recht, Verfassung, Stadtregiment, Kirche, Gesellschaft, Wirtschaft* (Vienna, 2012).

Jamees, A. *Brugse poorters opgetekend uit de stadsrekeningen*, 3 vols. (Handzame, 1974–90).

Jankuhn, H., Schlesinger, W. and Steuer, H. (eds.). *Vor- und Frühformen der europäische Stadt im Mittelalter* (Göttingen, 1973).

Janssens, A. 'Het Brugse Belfort: Wisselend uitzicht omstreeks 1480 en 1503', *BO*, 44 (2004), 67–84.

Middeleeuws Brugge door de ogen van Hans Memling (1465–1494) (Leuven, 2012).

'Wijn in Brugge tijdens het laatste kwart van de 15de eeuw: Hoeveelheden, prijzen en consumptie', *HGG*, 146 (2009), 141–68.

Jones, M. (ed.). *The New Cambridge Medieval History*, vol. VI (Cambridge, 2000).

Jones, P. *The Italian City-State: From Commune to Signoria* (Oxford, 2004).

Jongepier, I., Soens, T., Thoen, E. et al. 'The Brown Gold: A Reappraisal of Medieval Peat Marshes in Northern Flanders (Belgium)', *Water History*, 3 (2011), 73–93.

Jorgensen, D. '"All Good Rule of the Citee": Sanitation and Civic Government in England, 1400–1600', *Journal of Urban History*, 36 (2010), 300–15.

Jörn, N., Paravicini, W. and Wernicke, H. (eds.). *Hansekaufleute in Brügge*, vol. IV: *Beiträge der Internationalen Tagung in Brügge April 1996* (Frankfurt am Main, 2000).

Keene, D. J. 'Towns and the Growth of Trade', in Luscombe and Riley-Smith (eds.), *New Cambridge Medieval History*, vol. IV, pp. 47–85.

Kipling, G. *Enter the King: Theatre, Liturgy, and Ritual in the Medieval Civic Triumph* (Oxford, 1998).

Knox, P. *Urban Social Geography: An Introduction* (Harlow, 1987).

Köbler, G. '"Civitas" und "Vicus", "Burg", "Stat", "Dorf" und "Wik"', in Jankuhn et al. (eds.), *Vor- und Frühformen*, pp. 61–76.

Koch, A. C. F, 'Brugge's topografische ontwikkeling tot in de 12e eeuw', *HGG*, 99 (1962), 5–67.

De rechterlijke organisatie van het graafschap Vlaanderen tot in de 13de eeuw (Antwerp and Amsterdam, 1951).

Koldeweij, J., Geysen, I. and Tahon, E. (eds.). *Liefde en devotie: Het Gruuthusehandschrift: Kunst en cultuur omstreeks 1400* [exhibition catalogue] (Bruges, 2013).

Kren, T. and McKendrick, S. (eds.). *Illuminating the Renaissance: The Triumph of Flemish Manuscript Painting in Europe* [exh. cat.] (Los Angeles, CA, 2003).

Krüger, K. and Paravicini, W. (eds.). *Hansekaufleute in Brügge*, vol. I: *Die Brügger Steuerlisten 1360–1390* (Frankfurt am Main, 1992).

Lambert, B. *The City, the Duke and their Banker: The Rapondi Family and the Formation of the Burgundian State (1384–1430)* (Turnhout, 2006).

'Merchants on the Margin: Fifteenth-Century Bruges and the Informal Market', *JMH*, 42 (2016), 226–53.

Lane, B. *Hans Memling: Master Painter in Fifteenth-Century Bruges* (Turnhout, 2009).

Lantschner, P. 'The Ciompi Revolution Constructed: Modern Historians and the Nineteenth-Century Paradigm of Revolution', *Annali di Storia di Firenze*, 4 (2009), 277–97.

Lazzareschi, E. (ed.). *Il libro della communitá dei mercanti Lucchesi in Bruges* (Milan, 1947).

Lebecq, S. *Marchands et navigateurs frisons du haut Moyen Âge*, 2 vols. (Lille, 1983).

'The New *Wiks* or *Emporia* and the Development of a Maritime Economy in the Northern Seas (7th–9th Centuries)', in Gelichi and Hodges (eds.), *From One Sea to Another*, pp. 11–21.

Lebecq, S., Bethouart, B. and Verslype, L. (eds.). *Quentovic: Environment, archéologie, histoire* (Lille, 2010).

Lecuppre-Desjardin, E. *La ville des cérémonies: Essai sur la communication politique dans les anciens Pays-Bas bourguignons* (Turnhout, 2004).

Lefebvre, H. *La production de l'espace* (Paris, 1974), trans. D. Nicholson-Smith as *The Production of Space* (Oxford, 1991).

Le Goff, J. 'Au Moyen Âge: Temps de l'église, temps de marchand', *Annales: Économies, sociétés, civilisations*, 15 (1960), 417–33.

Leguay, J.-P. 'Urban Life', in Jones (ed.), *New Cambridge Medieval History*, vol. VI, pp. 102–23.

Le Loup, W. (ed.). *Vlaamse kunst op perkament: Handschriften en miniaturen te Brugge van de 12de tot de 16de eeuw* [exh. cat.] (Bruges, 1981).

Liddy, C. and Haemers, J. 'Popular Politics in the Late Medieval City: York and Bruges', *English Historical Review*, 128 (2013), 771–805.

Lingier, M., Ryckaert, M., Beernaert, B. et al. *De Brugse Reien, aders van de stad* (Tielt, 2005).

Lis, C., and Soly, H. *Worthy Efforts: Attitudes to Work and Workers in Pre-Industrial Europe* (Boston, 2012).

(eds.). *Werelden van verschil: Ambachtsgilden in de Lage Landen* (Brussels, 1997).

Lopez, R. *The Commercial Revolution of the Middle Ages, 950–1350* (Cambridge, 1971).

Löther, A. *Prozessionen in Spätmittelalterliche Städten: Politische Partizipation, obrigkeitliche Inszenierung, städtische Eintracht* (Cologne, 1999).

Luscombe, D. and Riley-Smith, J. (eds.). *The New Cambridge Medieval History*, vol. IV (Cambridge, 2004).

Luykx, T. *Johanna van Constantinopel, gravin van Vlaanderen en Henegouwen: Haar leven (1199/1200–1244), haar regeering (1205–1244), vooral in Vlaanderen* (Brussels, 1946).

Lyon, B. and Verhulst, A. *Medieval Finance: A Comparison of Financial Institutions in Northwestern Europe* (Bruges, 1967).

Marechal, D. (ed.). *Meesterwerken van de Brugse edelsmeedkunst* [exh. cat.] (Bruges, 1993).

Maréchal, G. 'Het Sint-Janshospitaal in de eerste eeuwen van zijn bestaan', in *Sint-Janshospitaal Brugge 1188–1976* [exh. cat.] (Bruges, 1976), pp. 41–75.

De sociale en politieke gebondenheid van het Brugse hospitaalwezen in de Middeleeuwen (Kortrijk, 1978).

'De zwarte dood te Brugge (1349–1351)', *Biekorf*, 80 (1980), 377–92.

Marechal, J. 'La colonie espagnole de Bruges du XIVe au XVI siècles', *RN*, 35 (1953), 5–40.

Europese aanwezigheid te Brugge: De vreemde kolonies (XIVde–XIXde eeuw) (Bruges, 1985).

Mareel, S. 'Performing the Dutch Rederijker Lyric: Eduard de Dene and his *Testament Rhetoricael* (1562)', *Modern Language Review*, 108 (2013), 1199–220.

Voor vorst en stad: Rederijkersliteratuur en vorstenfeest in Vlaanderen en Brabant (1432–1561) (Amsterdam, 2010).

Martens, M. P. J. 'Artistic Patronage in Bruges Institutions, c.1440–1482', unpublished PhD thesis, University of California (Santa Barbara, CA, 1992).

'Some Aspects of the Origins of the Art Market in Fifteenth-Century Bruges', in North and Ormrod (eds.), *Art Markets*, pp. 19–28.

(ed.). *Lodewijk van Gruuthuse: Mecenas en Europees diplomaat (ca. 1427–1492)* (Bruges, 1992).

Mattheus, A. 'Prosopografie van het Brugse stadsbestuur 1467–1477', 2 vols., unpublished MA thesis, Ghent University (Ghent, 2011).

Meersseman, G. G. 'L'épistolaire de Jean van der Veren et le début de l'humanisme en Flandre', *Humanistica Lovaniensia*, 19 (1970), 119–200.

Meijns, B. *Aken of Jeruzalem? Het ontstaan en de hervorming van de kanonikale instellingen in Vlaanderen tot circa 1155*, 2 vols. (Leuven, 2000).

'Het ontstaan van de Brugse parochies tijdens de vroege middeleeuwen: Nieuwe inzichten bij een oud vraagstuk', *HGG*, 152 (2015), 3–82.

Menjot, D. and Pinol, J.-L. (eds.). *Enjeux et expressions de la politique municipale (XIIe–XXe siècles)* (Paris, 1997).

Mertens, J. 'Woelingen te Brugge tussen 1359 en 1361', in Hansotte and Coppejans (eds.), *Album Carlos Wyffels*, pp. 325–32.

Metcalf, D. M. 'Coinage and the Rise of the Flemish Towns', in N. J. Mayhew (ed.), *Coinage in the Low Countries (880–1500)* (Oxford, 1979), pp. 1–23.

Meulemeester, J.-L. (ed.). *Sint-Donaas en de voormalige Brugse kathedraal* (Bruges, 1978).

Moesgaard, J. C. 'Le monnayage d'Arras, Bruges et Tournai dans les années 920 et 930', in C. Lorren (ed.), *La Gaule, le monde insulaire et l'Europe du Nord au haut Moyen Âge* (Saint-Germain-en-Laye, 2013), pp. 349–53.

Mumford, L. *The City in History, its Origins, its Transformations and its Prospects* (San Diego, CA, 1961).

Munro, J. H. A. 'Bruges and the Abortive Staple of English Cloth', in J. H. A. Munro, *Textiles, Towns and Trade: Essays in the Economic History of Late Medieval England and the Low Countries* (Aldershot, 1994), pp. 1138–59.

'Deflation and the Petty Coinage Problem in the Late Medieval Economy: The Case of Flanders, 1334–1484', *Explorations in Economic History*, 25 (1988), 387–423.

'Medieval Woollens: Textiles, Textile Technology, and Industrial Organisation, c. 800 – 1500', in D. Jenkins (ed.), *The Cambridge History of Western Textiles*, 2 vols. (Cambridge, 2003), vol. I, pp. 181–227.

'Medieval Woollens: The Western European Woollen Industries and their Struggles for Markets, c. 1000–1500', in D. Jenkins (ed.), *The Cambridge History of Western Textiles*, 2 vols. (Cambridge, 2003), vol. I, pp. 228–324.

Wool, Cloth and Gold: The Struggle for Bullion in Anglo-Burgundian Trade, 1340–1478 (Brussels, 1973).

Murray, J. M. *Bruges, Cradle of Capitalism, 1280–1390* (Cambridge, 2005).

Mus, O. 'De Brugse compagnie Despars op het einde van de 15e eeuw', *HGG*, 101 (1964), 5–118.

Najemy, J. *A History of Florence, 1200–1575* (Oxford, 2006).

Nicholas, D. 'Child and Adolescent Labour in the Late Medieval City: A Flemish Model in Regional Perspective', *English Historical Review*, 110 (1995), 1103–31.

'The English Trade at Bruges in the Last Years of Edward III', *JMH*, 5 (1979), 23–61.

Medieval Flanders (London, 1992).

'Of Poverty and Primacy: Demand, Liquidity and the Flemish Economic Miracle, 1050–1200', *American Historical Review*, 96 (1991), 17–41.

Town and Countryside: Social, Economic, and Political Tensions in Fourteenth-Century Flanders (Bruges, 1971).

Nieus, J.-F. 'Montreuil et l'expansion du comté de Flandre au Xe siècle', in Lebecq et al. (eds.), *Quentovic*, pp. 493–505.

North, M. and Ormrod, D. (eds.). *Art Markets in Europe 1400–1800* (Aldershot, 1998).

Nosow, R. *Ritual Meanings in the Fifteenth-Century Motet* (Cambridge, 2012).

Nowé, H. *Les baillis comtaux de Flandre, des origines à la fin du XIVe siècle* (Brussels, 1929).

Oexle, O. G. 'Die Kultur der Rebellion: Schwureinung und Verschwörung im früh- und hochmittelalterlichen Okzident', in M. T. Fögen (ed.), *Ordnung und Aufruhr im Mittelalter: Historische und juristische Studien zur Rebellion* (Frankfurt am Main, 1995), pp. 119–37.

Oksanen, E. *Flanders and the Anglo-Norman World, 1066–1216* (Cambridge, 2012).

Oliva Herrer, H. R., Challet, V., Dumolyn, J. et al. (eds.). *La comunidad medieval como esfera publica* (Seville, 2014).

Oosterman, J. 'Anthonis de Roovere, Dichter aus Brügge: Die Präsenz des Autors und die Aufführung seiner Gedichte', *Zeitschrift für deutsche Philologie*, Sonderheft, 130 (2011), 301–14.

'De "Excellente cronike van Vlaenderen" en Anthonis de Roovere', *Tijdschrift voor Nederlandse Taal en Letterkunde*, 118 (2002), 22–37.

(ed.). *Stad van koopmanschap en vrede: Literatuur in Brugge tussen Middeleeuwen en Rederijkerstijd* (Leuven, 2005).

Park, R., Burgess, E. and McKenzie, R. D. (eds.). *The City: Suggestions for the Study of Human Nature in the Urban Environment* (Chicago, IL, 1925).

Parmentier, R. A. *Indices op de Brugsche poorterboeken*, 2 vols. (Bruges, 1938).

Paviot, J. 'Les Portugais à Bruges au XVe siècle', *Arquivos do Centro Cultural Calouste Gulbenkian*, 38 (1999), 1–122.

Petti Balbi, G. *Mercanti e nationes nelle Fiandre: I Genovesi in età bassomedievale* (Pisa, 1996).

Phillips, W. D., Jr. 'Local Integration and Long-Distance Ties: The Castilian Community in Sixteenth-Century Bruges', *Sixteenth Century Journal*, 17 (1986), 33–49.

Pifarré Torres, D. *El comerç internacional de Barcelona i el Mar del Nord (Bruges) al final del segle XIV* (Barcelona, 2002).

Pirenne, H. *Les anciennes démocraties des Pays-Bas* (Paris, 1910).

'Draps de Frise ou draps de Flandre? Un petit problème d'histoire économique à l'époque carolingienne', *Vierteljahrschrift für Sozial- und Wirtschaftsgeschichte*, 7 (1909), 308–16.

Histoire de Belgique, 7 vols. (Brussels, 1900–32).

Les villes et les institutions urbaines, 2 vols. (Paris and Brussels, 1939).

Planitz, H. *Die deutsche Stadt im Mittelalter: Von der Römerzeit bis zu den Zunftkämpfen* (Graz and Köln, 1954).

Platelle, H. 'La violence et ses remèdes en Flandre au XIe siècle', *Sacris Erudiri*, 20 (1971), 101–73.

Pleij, H. *Het gevleugelde woord: Geschiedenis van de Nederlandse literatuur, 1400–1560* (Amsterdam, 2007).

Prak, M. (ed.). *Craft Guilds in the Early Modern Low Countries: Work, Power, and Representation* (Aldershot, 2006).

Prevenier, W. 'Bevolkingscijfers en professionele structuren der bevolking van Gent en Brugge in de XIVe eeuw', in *Album Charles Verlinden* (Ghent, 1975), pp. 269–303.

'La bourgeoisie en Flandre au XIIIe siècle', *Revue de l'Université de Bruxelles*, 4 (1978), 407–28.

'La démographie des villes du comté de Flandre aux XIVe et XVe siècles: État de la question: Essai d'interprétation,' *RN*, 65 (1983), 255–75.

Prevenier, W. and Augustyn, B. (eds.). *De gewestelijke en lokale overheidsinstellingen in Vlaanderen tot 1795* (Brussels, 1997).

De Vlaamse instellingen tijdens het Ancien Régime: Recent onderzoek in nieuw perspectief (Brussels, 1999).

Prevenier, W. and Blockmans, W. *Prinsen en poorters: Beelden van de laat-middeleeuwse samenleving in de Bourgondische Nederlanden (1384–1530)* (Antwerp, 1998).

Prevenier, W., Sosson, J.-P. and Boone, M. 'Le réseau urbain en Flandre (XIIIe–XIXe siècle): Composantes et dynamique', in *Le réseau urbain en Belgique dans une perspective historique (1350–1850): Une approche statistique et dynamique* (Brussels, 1992), pp. 157–200.

Puttevils, J. *Merchants and Trading in the Sixteenth Century: The Golden Age of Antwerp*, Perspectives in Economic and Social History 38 (London, 2015).

Ramakers, B. A. M. 'Multifaceted and Ambiguous: The Tableaux Vivants in the Bruges Entry of 1440', in Suntrup et al. (eds.), *Medien der Symbolik*, pp. 163–94.

Rider, J. *God's Scribe: The Historiographical Art of Galbert of Bruges* (Washington, DC, 2001).

(ed.). *The Murder, Betrayal, and Slaughter of the Glorious Charles, Count of Flanders*, by Galbert of Bruges (New Haven, CT, 2013).

Rider, J. and Murray, A. *Galbert of Bruges and the Historiography of Medieval Flanders* (Washington, DC, 2009).

Ross, J. B. 'Rise and Fall of a Twelfth-Century Clan: The Erembalds and the Murder of Count Charles of Flanders, 1127–1128', *Speculum*, 34 (1959), 367–90.

Ross, J. B. (trans.). *The Murder of Charles the Good, Count of Flanders*, by Galbert of Bruges (New York, 1960).

Rosser, G. 'Urban Culture and the Church 1300–1540', in D. M. Palliser (ed.), *The Cambridge Urban History of Britain*, vol. I: *600–1540* (Cambridge, 2000), pp. 335–69.

Rössner, R. *Hansekaufleute in Brügge*, vol. V: *Hansische Memoria in Flandern* (Frankfurt am Main, 2001).

Ryckaert, M. 'Ambachtshuizen te Brugge: De huizen van de timmerlieden, de metselaars, de tegeldekkers en de kapel van de smeden', in Dezutter and Goetinck (eds.), *Op en om de bouwwerf*, pp. 37–57.

Historische stedenatlas van België, vol. II: *Brugge* (Brussels, 1991).

Ryckaert, M. and Murray, J. M. 'Bruges in 1127', in Rider (ed.), *The Murder*, pp. lvii–lxxv.

Ryckaert, M., Vandewalle, A., D'hondt, J. et al. (eds.). *Brugge: De geschiedenis van een Europese stad* (Tielt, 1999).

Sabbe, J. *Vlaanderen in opstand 1323–1328: Nikolaas Zannekin, Zeger Janszone en Willem de Deken* (Bruges, 1992).

Scholliers, E. 'Lonen te Brugge en in het Brugse Vrije (XVe-XVIIIe eeuw)', in C. Verlinden (ed.), *Dokumenten voor de geschiedenis van prijzen en lonen in Vlaanderen en Brabant*, 4 vols. (Bruges, 1965), vol. II, pp. 87–160.

Schouteet, A. *De straatnamen van Brugge: Oorsprong en betekenis* (Bruges, 1977).

Schulz, K. *"Denn sie lieben die Freiheit so sehr…": Kommunale Aufstände und Entstehung des europäischen Bürgertums im Hochmittelalter* (Darmstadt, 1992).

Scott, T. *The City-State in Europe, 1000–1600* (Oxford, 2012).

Simons, W. *Bedelordekloosters in het graafschap Vlaanderen: Chronologie en topografie van de bedelordenverspreiding vóór 1350* (Bruges, 1987).

Cities of Ladies: Beguine Communities in the Medieval Low Countries, 1200–1565 (Philadelphia, 2003).

Stad en apostolaat: De vestiging van de bedelorden in het graafschap Vlaanderen (ca. 1225 – ca. 1350) (Brussels, 1987).

Sjoberg, G. *The Pre-Industrial City: Past and Present* (Glencoe, 1960).

Skoda, H., Lantschner, P. and Shaw, R. (eds.). *Contact and Exchange in Later Medieval Europe: Essays in Honour of Malcolm Vale* (Woodbridge, 2012).

Slater, T. R. (ed.). *The Built Form of Western Cities: Essays for M. R. G. Conzen on the Occasion of his Eightieth Birthday* (London, 1990).

Smeyers, M. 'Lubert Hautscilt, abt van de Brugse Eekhoutabdij (1393–1417): Over handschriften, planeten en de toekomst van Vlaanderen', *Academia Analecta*, 55 (1995), 39–104.

Vlaamse miniaturen van de 8ste tot het midden van de 16de eeuw (Leuven, 1998).

Snauwaert, L. and Devliegher, L. *Gids voor architectuur in Brugge* (Tielt, 2002).

Soens, T. *De spade in de dijk? Waterbeheer en rurale samenleving in de Vlaamse kustvlakte (1280–1580)* (Ghent, 2009).

Soens, T. and Thoen, E. 'Vegetarians or Carnivores? Standards of Living and Diet in Late Medieval Flanders', in Cavaciocchi (ed.), *Le interazioni fra economia*, pp. 495–527.

Soly, H. 'The Political Economy of European Craft Guilds: Power Relations and Economic Strategies of Merchants and Master Artisans in the Medieval and Early Modern Textile Industries', *International Review of Social History*, 53 (2008), 45–71.

Sosson, J.-P. 'Une approche des structures économiques d'un métier d'art: La corporation des peintres et selliers de Bruges (XVe–XVIe siècles)', *Revue des archéologues et historiens d'art de Louvain*, 3 (1970), 91–100.

'Finances communales et dette publique: Le cas de Bruges à la fin du XIIIe siècle', in Duvosquel and Thoen (eds.), *Peasants and Townsmen*, pp. 239–57.

'La structure sociale de la corporation médiévale: L'exemple des tonneliers de Bruges de 1350 à 1500', *BTFG*, 44 (1966), 457–78.

Les travaux publics de la ville de Bruges, XIVe–XVe siècle (Brussels, 1977).

Speakman Sutch, S. and Van Bruaene, A.-L. 'The Seven Sorrows of the Virgin Mary: Devotional Communication and Politics in the Burgundian-Habsburg Low Countries, c. 1490–1520', *Journal of Ecclesiastical History*, 61 (2010), 252–78.

Spronk, R. 'The Reconstruction of a Triptych by Jan Provoost for the Jerusalem Chapel in Bruges', *Burlington Magazine*, 147 (2005), 109–11.

Spufford, P. *Power and Profit: The Merchant in Medieval Europe* (London, 2002).

Stabel, P. *Dwarfs among Giants: The Flemish Urban Network in the Late Middle Ages* (Leuven, 1997).

'De gewenste vreemdeling: Italiaanse kooplieden en stedelijke maatschappij in het laat-middeleeuwse Brugge', *Jaarboek voor Middeleeuwse Geschiedenis*, 4 (2001), 189–221.

'Guilds in Late Medieval Flanders: Myths and Realities of Guild Life in an Export-Oriented Environment', *JMH*, 30 (2004), 187–212.

'The Market-Place and Civic Identity in Late Medieval Flanders', in Boone and Stabel (eds.), *Shaping Urban Identity*, pp. 43–64.

'Militaire organisatie, bewapening en wapenbezit in het laatmiddeleeuwse Brugge', *BTFG*, 89 (2011), 1049–73.

'Organisation corporative et production d'œuvres d'art à Bruges à la fin du Moyen Âge et au début des Temps modernes', *Le Moyen Âge*, 113 (2007), 91–134.

'Selling Paintings in Late Medieval Bruges: Marketing Customs and Guild Regulation Compared', in De Marchi and Van Miegroet (eds.), *Mapping Markets*, pp. 89–103.

'Women at the Market: Gender and Retail in the Towns of Late Medieval Flanders', in Blockmans, Boone and de Hemptinne (eds.), *Secretum scriptorum*, pp. 259–76.

Strohm, R. *Music in Late Medieval Bruges*, 2nd edn (Oxford, 1990).

Strubbe, E. I. 'Van de eerste naar de tweede omwalling van Brugge', *HGG*, 100 (1963), 271–300.

Suntrup, R., Veenstra, J. R. and Bolleman, A. (eds.). *Medien der Symbolik in Spätmittelalter und Früher Neuzeit* (Frankfurt am Main, 2005).

TeBrake, W. *A Plague of Insurrection: Popular Politics and Peasant Revolt in Flanders, 1323–1328* (Philadelphia, 1993).

Thoen, E. 'A "Commercial Survival Economy" in Evolution: The Flemish Countryside and the Transition to Capitalism (Middle Ages – 19th Century)', in Hoppenbrouwers and Van Zanden (eds.), *Peasants into Farmers*, pp. 102–57.

'The Count, the Countryside and the Economic Development of the Towns in Flanders from the Eleventh to the Thirteenth Century: Some Provisional Remarks and Hypotheses', in Aerts et al. (eds.), *Studia Historica Oeconomica*, pp. 259–78.

'Immigration to Bruges during the Late Middle Ages', in Cavaciocchi (ed.), *Le migrazioni*, pp. 335–53.

Thoen, E. et al. (eds.). *Landscapes or Seascapes? The History of the Coastal Environment in the North Sea Area Reconsidered* (Turnhout, 2013).

Thoen, H. *De Belgische kustvlakte in de Romeinse tijd* (Brussels, 1978).

Toussaert, J. *Le sentiment religieux en Flandre à la fin du Moyen Âge* (Paris, 1963).

Trio, P. 'The Emergence of New Devotions in Late Medieval Urban Flanders (Thirteenth–Fifteenth Centuries): Struggle and Cooperation between Church/Clergy and Urban Government/Bourgeoisie', in Ehrich and Oberste (eds.), *Städtische Kulte*, pp. 327–37.

'L'enlumineur à Bruges, Gand et Ypres (1300–1450): Son milieu socio-économique et corporatif', in M. Smeyers and B. Cardon (eds.), *Flanders in European Perspective: Manuscript Illumination around 1400 in Flanders and Abroad* (Leuven, 1995), pp. 721–9.

Volksreligie als spiegel van een stedelijke samenleving: De broederschappen te Gent in de late middeleeuwen (Leuven, 1993).

Tys, D. 'The Medieval Embankment of Coastal Flanders in Context', in Thoen et al. (eds.), *Landscapes or Seascapes*, pp. 199–239.

Van Bavel, B. *Manors and Markets: Economy and Society in the Low Countries, 500–1600* (Oxford, 2010).

Van Belle, R. *Vlakke grafmonumenten en memorietaferelen met persoonsafbeeldingen in West-Vlaanderen: Een inventaris, funeraire symboliek en overzicht van het kostuum* (Bruges, 2006).

Van Bruaene, A.-L. *Om beters wille: Rederijkerskamers en de stedelijke cultuur in de zuidelijke Nederlanden 1400–1650* (Amsterdam, 2008).

Van Caenegem, R. C. *Geschiedenis van het strafprocesrecht in Vlaanderen van de XIe tot de XIVe eeuw* (Brussels, 1956).

Geschiedenis van het strafrecht in Vlaanderen van de XIe tot de XIVe eeuw (Brussels, 1954).

Law, History, the Low Countries and Europe (London, 1994).

(ed.). *1302: Feiten en mythen van de guldensporenslag* (Antwerp, 2002).

Van Caenegem, R. C., Demyttenaere, A. and Devliegher, L. (eds.). *De moord op Karel de Goede* (Leuven, 1999).

Vandamme, L. 'De socio-professionele recrutering van de reformatie in Brugge, 1566–1567', unpublished MA thesis, Catholic University of Leuven (Leuven, 1982).

Vandeburie, J. 'De Zwarte Dood te Brugge: Een status quaestionis en enkele nieuwe beschouwingen', *HGG*, 147 (2010), 269–308.

Van den Abeele, A. *Het ridderlijk gezelschap van de Witte Beer* (Bruges, 2000).

Van den Auweele, D. 'Schepenbank en schepenen te Brugge (1127–1384): Bijdrage tot de studie van een gewone stedelijke rechts- en bestuursinstelling', 4 vols., unpublished PhD thesis, Catholic University of Leuven (Leuven, 1977).

Vandenberghe, S. et al., *Vlaamse kunst in de 15de eeuw: Tentoonstelling van sculptuur, meubilair en kunstnijverheid uit de tijd van Lodewijk van Gruuthuse (ca. 1427–1492)* [exh. cat.] (Bruges, 1992).

Van der Bauwhede, D. and Goetinck, M. (eds.). *Brugge in de Geuzentijd* (Bruges, 1982).

Vandermaesen, M., Ryckaert, M. and Coornaert, M. 'De Witte Kaproenen: De Gentse opstand (1379–1385) en de geschiedenis van de Brugse Leie', *Kultureel Jaarboek voor de Provincie Oost-Vlaanderen*, 10 (1979), 9–17.

Van der Velden, H. 'Defrocking St Eloi: Petrus Christus' Vocational Portrait of a Goldsmith', *Simiolus: Netherlands Quarterly for the History of Art*, 26 (1998), 243–76.

'Petrus Christus's Our Lady of the Dry Tree', *Journal of the Warburg and Courtauld Institute*, 60 (1997), 89–110.

Van der Wee, H. *The Growth of the Antwerp Market and the European Economy, Fourteenth - Sixteenth Centuries*, 3 vols. (The Hague, 1963).

'Structural Changes and Specialization in the Industry of the Southern Netherlands, 1100–1600', *Economic History Review*, 28 (1975), 203–21.

(ed.). *The Rise and Decline of Urban Industries in Italy and in the Low Countries (Late Middle Ages - Early Modern Times)* (Leuven, 1988).

Vandevyvere, E. *Watervoorziening te Brugge van de 13de tot de 20ste eeuw* (Bruges, 1983).

Vandewalle, A. 'De Brugse stadsmagistraat en de deelname van de ambachten aan het bestuur, 14de-15e eeuw', in Prevenier and Augustyn (eds.), *De Vlaamse instellingen*, pp. 27–40.

'Het librariërsgilde te Brugge in zijn vroege periode', in Le Loup (ed.), *Vlaamse kunst op perkament*, pp. 39–43.

(ed.). *De Brugse schoenmakers en timmerlieden: De ambachten en hun huizen 14de–20ste eeuw* (Bruges, 1985).

Vandewalle, A., Michiels, G. and Michiels, A. (eds.). *600 jaar Brugs stadhuis, 1376–1976* (Brussels, 1976).

Van Eenhooge, D. 'The Archaeological Study of Buildings and Town History in Bruges: Domestic Architecture in the Period 1200–1350', in Gläser (ed.), *Lübecker Kolloquium*, vol. III, pp. 121–41.

Vanhaverbeke, K. 'Het stadsbestuur in Brugge in de periode 1375–1407: Een sociaal-institutionele studie aan de hand van de prosopografische methode', *HGG*, 135 (1998), 3–54.

Van Houtte, J. A. 'Ambernijverheid en paternostermakers gedurende de 14e en 15e eeuw', *HGG*, 82 (1939), 149–84.

'Bruges et Anvers, marchés "nationaux" ou "internationaux" du XIVe au XVIe siècles', *RN*, 34 (1952), 89–108.

De geschiedenis van Brugge (Tielt, 1982).

'Makelaars en waarden te Brugge van de 13e tot de 16e eeuw', *Bijdragen voor de geschiedenis der Nederlanden*, 5 (1950–1), 1–30, 177–97.

'The Rise and Decline of the Market of Bruges', *Economic History Review*, 19 (1966), 29–47.

Van Oostrom, F. *Stemmen op schrift: Geschiedenis van de Nederlandse literatuur vanaf het begin tot 1300* (Amsterdam, 2006).

Wereld in woorden: Geschiedenis van de Nederlandse literatuur, 1300–1400 (Amsterdam, 2013).

Van Rompaey, J. *Het grafelijk baljuwsambt in Vlaanderen tijdens de Boergondische periode* (Brussels, 1967).

Van Uytven, R. 'Flämische Belfriede und südniederländische städtische Bauwerke im Mittelalter: Symbol und Mythos', in A. Haverkamp and E. Müller-Luckner (eds.), *Information, Kommunikation und Selbstdarstellung in mittelalterlichen Gemeinden* (Munich, 1998), pp. 125–59.

'Les origines des villes dans les anciens Pays-Bas, jusque vers 1300', in G. Despy (ed.), *La fortune historiographique des theses d'Henri Pirenne* (Brussels, 1986), pp. 13–26.

'Splendour and Wealth? Art and Economy in the Burgundian Netherlands', *Transactions of the Cambridge Bibliographical Society*, 10 (1992), 101–24.

'Stages of Economic Decline: Late Medieval Bruges', in Duvosquel and Thoen (eds.), *Peasants and Townsmen*, pp. 259–70.

Van Werveke, H. *"Burgus": Versterking of nederzetting?* (Brussels, 1965).

'La famine de l'an 1316 en Flandre et dans les régions voisines', *RN*, 41 (1959), 5–14.

Vanysacker, D. 'The Impact of Humanists on Witchcraft Prosecution in 16th- and 17th-Century Bruges', *Humanistica Lovaniensia*, 50 (2001), 393–434.

Van Zeir, P. 'De armenzorg te Brugge', *Biekorf*, 61 (1960), 357–79.

'De inrichting van de armendissen van de oude Brugse stadsparochies vóór 1526', in *HGG*, 97 (1960), 104–53.

Verbruggen, J. F. *Vlaanderen na de Guldensporenslag: De vrijheidsstrijd van het graafschap Vlaanderen, 1303–1305* (Bruges, 1991).

Verbruggen, R. *Geweld in Vlaanderen: Macht en onderdrukking in de Vlaamse steden tijdens de veertiende eeuw* (Bruges, 2005).

Verhulst, A. 'An Aspect of the Question of Continuity between Antiquity and Middle Ages: The Origin of the Flemish Cities between the North Sea and the Scheldt', *JMH*, 3 (1977), 175–205.

The Carolingian Economy (Cambridge, 2002).

'Les origines et l'histoire ancienne de la ville de Bruges', *Le Moyen Âge*, 66 (1960), 37–63.

Landschap en landbouw in middeleeuws Vlaanderen (Brussels, 1995).

'The Origins of Towns in the Low Countries and the Pirenne Thesis', *Past and Present*, 122 (1989), 3–35.

The Rise of Cities in North-Western Europe (Cambridge, 1999).

Vermaut, J. 'Structural Transformation in a Textile Centre: Bruges from the Sixteenth to the Nineteenth Century', in Van der Wee (ed.), *The Rise and Decline of Urban Industries*, pp. 187–205.

'De textielnijverheid in Brugge en op het platteland, Westelijk Vlaanderen voor 1800: Konjunktuurverloop, organisatie en sociale verhoudingen', 4 vols., unpublished PhD thesis, Ghent University (Ghent, 1974).

Vermeesch, A. *Essai sur les origines et la signification de la commune dans le nord de la France* (Heule, 1966).

Vermeersch, V. *Brugges kunstbezit: Vijftig kunsthistorische opstellen*, 2 vols. (Bruges and Utrecht, 1969–73).

Grafmonumenten te Brugge vóór 1578, 3 vols. (Bruges, 1976).

(ed.). *Brugge en Europa* (Antwerp, 1992).

Warlop, E. *The Flemish Nobility before 1300*, 2 vols. (Kortrijk, 1975–6).

Warnkoenig, L. A. and Gheldolf, A. E. *Histoire de la Flandre et de ses institutions civiles et politiques, jusqu'à l'année 1305*, 4 vols. (Brussels, 1835–64).

Weber, M. *The City*, trans. D. Martindale and G. Neuwirth (New York, 1958).

Wellens, R. 'La révolte brugeoise de 1488', *HGG*, 102 (1965), 5–52.

Whitehand, J. W. R. (ed.). *The Urban Landscape: Historical Development and Management: Papers by M. G. R. Conzen* (London, 1981).

Wickham, C. *Framing the Early Middle Ages: Europe and the Mediterranean 400–800* (Oxford, 2005).

'Rethinking the Structure of the Early Medieval Economy', in J. R. Davis and M. McCormick (eds.), *The Long Morning of Medieval Europe: New Directions in Early Medieval Studies* (Aldershot, 2008), pp. 19–32.

Wightmann, E. M. *Gallia Belgica* (London, 1985).

Wijsman, H. *Luxury Bound: Illustrated Manuscript Production and Noble and Princely Book Ownership in the Burgundian Netherlands (1400–1550)* (Turnhout, 2010).

Willaert, F. (ed.). *Het Gruuthuse-handschrift in woord en klank: Nieuwe inzichten, nieuwe vragen* (Ghent, 2010).

Willemsen, A. and Kik, H. (eds.). *Dorestad in an International Framework: New Research on Centres of Trade and Coinage in Carolingian Times* (Turnhout, 2010).

Wilson, J. C. *Painting in Bruges at the Close of the Middle Ages* (Penn State University Park, 1998).

Wyffels, C. 'Nieuwe gegevens betreffende een XIIIde eeuwse "democratische" stedelijke opstand: De Brugse "Moerlemaye" (1280–81)', *Bulletin de la Commission Royale*, 132 (1966), 37–142.

De oorsprong der ambachten in Vlaanderen en Brabant (Brussels, 1951).

'Twee oude Vlaamse ambachtskeuren: De vleeshouwers van Brugge (2 december 1302) en de smeden van Damme (eerste helft 1303)', *HGG*, 87 (1950), 93–109.

'De Vlaamse Hanze van Londen op het einde van de XIIIe eeuw', *HGG*, 97 (1960), 5–30.

Yamada, M. 'Le mouvement de foires en Flandre avant 1200', in Duvosquel and Dierkens (eds.), *Villes et campagnes*, pp. 773–89.

Index